Readings in Planning Theory

Readings in Planning Theory

Fourth Edition

Edited by

Susan S. Fainstein and James DeFilippis

WILEY Blackwell

This fourth edition first published 2016

© 2016 John Wiley & Sons, Ltd

Edition history: Blackwell Publishers Ltd (1e, 1996); Blackwell Publishing Ltd (2e, 2002; 3e, 2012)

Registered Office

John Wiley & Sons, Ltd, The Atrium, Southern Gate, Chichester, West Sussex, PO19 8SQ, UK

Editorial Offices

350 Main Street, Malden, MA 02148-5020, USA

9600 Garsington Road, Oxford, OX4 2DQ, UK

The Atrium, Southern Gate, Chichester, West Sussex, PO19 8SQ, UK

For details of our global editorial offices, for customer services, and for information about how to apply for permission to reuse the copyright material in this book please see our website at www.wiley.com/wiley-blackwell.

The right of Susan S. Fainstein and James DeFilippis to be identified as the authors of the editorial material in this work has been asserted in accordance with the UK Copyright, Designs and Patents Act 1988.

Library of Congress Cataloging-in-Publication data is available for this title

Paperback 9781119045069

A catalogue record for this book is available from the British Library.

Cover image: By Nikada iStock 181070373

Set in 11/13pt Dante by SPi Global, Pondicherry, India

Printed in Singapore by C.O.S. Printers Pte Ltd

1   2016

Contents

Acknowledgments

Scott Campbell was co-editor of earlier editions of this reader. Some of the introductory material and choices of readings in the present edition continue to reflect his participation.

Introduction

The Structure and Debates of Planning Theory

Susan S. Fainstein and James DeFilippis

What Is Planning Theory?

What is planning theory? We start with this question because it is the central focus of this book; one that the various readings grapple with in different ways. But we also start with it because there is no clear or easy answer to this question; and this absence makes planning theory both more demanding, and more exciting, than it would otherwise be. The purpose of this reader is twofold: (1) to define the boundaries of planning theory and the works that constitute its central focus; and (2) to confront the principal issues that face planners as theorists and practitioners.

Defining planning theory is hard: the subject is slippery, and explanations are often frustratingly tautological or disappointingly pedestrian. While most scholars can agree on what constitutes the economy and the polity – and thus what is economic or political theory – they differ as to the content of planning theory. Several reasons account for the complexity of defining planning theory. First, many of the fundamental questions concerning planning belong to a much broader inquiry concerning the roles of the state, the market, and civil society in social and spatial transformation. As John Friedmann has put it, planning theory has been "cobbled together from elements that were originally intended for altogether different uses" (Friedmann 2011, p. 131). Consequently, planning theory overlaps with theory in all the social science and design disciplines, making it difficult to limit its scope or to stake out a turf specific to planning. Second, the field of planning is divided among those who define it according to its object (producing and regulating the relations of people and structures in space) and those who do so according to its method (the process of decision making as it relates to spatial development). These different approaches lead to two largely separate sets of

Readings in Planning Theory, Fourth Edition. Edited by Susan S. Fainstein and James DeFilippis.
Editorial material and organization © 2016 John Wiley & Sons, Ltd.
Published 2016 by John Wiley & Sons, Ltd.

theoretical questions and priorities that undermine a singular definition of planning. Whether to emphasize one or the other is a problematic issue within planning theory and constitutes, as will be discussed later in this introduction, one of the principal debates in the field.

Third, planning theory is further divided into those who understand planning through analyzing existing practices and those who theorize in an effort to transform planning practices. Thus, planning theory may be either explanatory or normative. And while all theorizing contains some sort of normative framework (even it is not acknowledged or recognized), these forms of theorization follow different paths and ask different questions rooted in politically and analytically different concerns. Moreover, the questions dealt with by planning theory reflect its somewhat ungainly straddling of both academic and professional matters.

Even if the focus is narrowed to understanding practice, planning practice itself evades a coherent theoretical framework. The boundary between planners and related professionals (such as real estate developers, architects, city council members, civil society leaders) is not sharp: planners do not just plan, and non-planners also plan. Is planning theory about what planning professionals do or how places develop, regardless of who is doing the planning? And although many fields (such as economics) are defined by a specific set of methodologies, planners commonly use diverse methodologies from many different fields. Consequently its theoretical base cannot be easily defined by its tools of analysis. It is determined more by a shared interest in space and place, a commitment to civic community, and a pragmatic orientation toward professional practice. Taken together, the debates about the proper role for planning theory, the very scope and function of planning, and the problems of distinguishing who is actually a planner make difficult the specification of an appropriate body of theory.

Despite the difficulties we do believe that we can specify a central question of planning theory. We see that central question as the following: *What role can planning play in developing the good city and region within the constraints of a capitalist political economy and varying political systems?* Thus we are explicit in our normative goal of thinking that theory should inform and improve practice in ways that meaningfully improve cities and regions and the lives of the people that live and work within them now and in the future. Addressing this question requires examining what planning currently accomplishes, the constraints upon it, and the potential for changing it. Thus, planning theory must be both explanatory and normative.

Why Do Planning Theory?

This question, and our framing of it, presumes a relationship between theory and practice in planning. That is, it presumes that planning theory should, and does, inform planning practice, and should in turn be informed by planning practice. But the relationship between theory and practice in planning is a problematic one. Most planning practitioners largely disregard planning theory and do not often think fondly of any planning theory course they had to take as a student.[1] Planning is an applied field, and most planning students become practitioners not academic researchers. A professional political scientist, economist, or geographer is expected to "do theory" and is rewarded for theoretical contributions, not applied engagements. But in planning this is reversed, causing problems for practitioners who avoid theoretical analysis. Planning must be predictive, and predicting the future impacts of planning interventions requires theoretical understanding of the processes that shape the making of spaces and places. Thus, planners need theory and, while they may be relying on theory that is internalized, implicit and unexamined, it is present nonetheless. This raises another problem, which is that the devaluing of planning theory by practitioners leaves too much of the decision-making in day-to-day planning practice to be based on intuition and instinct. Such intuition and instinct is implicit planning theory but its implicitness raises obstacles to challenging it, altering it, or evaluating it. We argue that theory can and should inform practice and should do so in explicit ways that are reflective and emerge from a dialogical relationship between theory and practice.

Enabling practitioners to achieve a deeper understanding of the processes in which they are engaged has motivated us to edit this book and select the particular readings within it. We hope that this will enable planners to achieve better results than acting based only on simple intuition and common sense. Although many in the field have decried the gap between theory and practice, we do not envision eliminating it completely. Planning practice can never simply enact academic reflection. We do not expect practicing land use planners to implement the unadulterated arguments of the German philosopher Jürgen Habermas (who provides the conceptual foundations for communicative planning) in their jobs, nor do we wish graduate students to accept existing land-use practice uncritically. True, if the gap is *too big*, then planning education is irrelevant, but if there is *no* gap, then planning education is redundant. The role of planning theory should be to generate a creative tension that is both critical and constructive, and that provokes reflection on both sides. In other words, its role is to create both the reflective practitioner and the practical scholar. These two need not think alike, but they should at least be able to talk to each other.

Beyond this intention, we aim to establish a theoretical foundation that provides the field not only with a common structure for scientific inquiry but also with a means for defining what planning is. Theory allows for both professional and intellectual self-reflection. It tries to make sense of the seemingly unrelated, contradictory aspects of urban development and to create a framework within which to compare and evaluate the merits of different planning ideas and strategies. It seeks the underlying conceptual elements that tie together the disparate planning areas, from housing and community development to transportation policy and urban design. Providing a common language is an important function of introductory theory and history courses for Master's students, who gain a shared identity as planners with other students during their first year before veering into their sub-specialties in the second year. It can be both comforting and encouraging, when encountering the challenges of contemporary urban poverty, shortages of public space, the profit orientation and shortsightedness of urban developers, as well as the enormous informal settlements within the developing world, to know the ways in which earlier reform movements have addressed similar problems. We not only know that we have been here before, but we also remind ourselves that in many ways urban life *has* improved, and planners can take some credit for this.

Our Approach to Planning Theory

We place planning theory at the intersection of political economy, history, and philosophy. This does not mean that we see cities and regions as simply structurally determined outcomes of larger historical political economic forces. To do so would erase the actors and agents that produce, shape, mitigate, and struggle against such forces. In short, it would make planning either a simple tool for ruling elites (part of the "committee for managing the common affairs of the whole bourgeoisie" as Marx famously put it), or it would make planning pointless and ineffectual by definition. That is most definitely not how we theorize planning. However, such macro-scale forces are central to producing the contexts in which planning occurs, and all planning theory, properly done, must therefore make such forces central in its explanations. The challenge for this professional – and sometimes activist – discipline is to find the leeway within the larger social structure to pursue the good city. This requires imagination, a historical understanding of the field, and, yes, active theoretical reflection on the best ways forward given the contexts in which planning occurs.

We also see planning theory as sitting at the intersection of the *city and region* as a phenomenon and *planning* as a human activity. Planning adapts to changes in the city and region, which in turn are transformed by planning and politics. Planners not only plan places; they also negotiate, forecast, research, survey, and organize financing. Nor do planners have an exclusive influence over territories; developers, business groups, politicians, and other actors also shape urban and regional development. This interaction is not a closed system, as exogenous forces act on regions and localities, causing changes in the spatial system and the rethinking of planning interventions.

Debates within Planning Theory

The teaching of planning theory requires that we should explicitly explore the roots and implications of long-standing disputes in the field. In fact, describing the differences among approaches provides a perspective on the subject that is lacking when a single narrative is used to define its scope. In this light, we can identify a set of issues that have bedeviled it for quite some time. These are: (1) How do we understand the history of planning? (2) Is planning about means or ends, processes or outcomes, and should it emphasize one or the other? (3) Why should we plan, and when? (4) What are the constraints on planning in capitalist political economies, and how do those vary in different contexts? (5) What are the values that inform, and should, inform planning? (6) Is there a singular, identifiable "public interest"?

How do we understand the history of planning?

The first question for theory is one of planning's identity, which in turn leads to history. The traditional story told of modern city planning is that it arose from several separate movements at the turn of the twentieth century: the Garden City, the City Beautiful, and public health reforms (Krueckeberg 1983; Hall 2002). Four basic eras characterized its history: (1) the formative years during which the pioneers (Ebenezer Howard, Patrick Geddes, Daniel Burnham, etc.) did not yet call themselves planners (late 1800s to World War I); (2) the period of institutionalization, professionalization, and self-recognition of planning, together with the rise of regional and national planning efforts (*ca.* 1920–45); (3) the postwar era of standardization, crisis, and diversification of planning (1945–75); and (4) the time up to the present of redefining planning in relation to the private sector, with emphasis on the planner as mediator, strategist, and advocate within public–private partnerships.

This narrative, often repeated in introductory courses and texts, serves our understanding in several ways. The multiplicity of technical, social, and aesthetic origins explains planning's eclectic blend of design, civil engineering, local politics, community organization, and social concern. Its development as a twentieth-century, public sector, bureaucratic profession, rather than as a late-nineteenth-century, private sector one like medicine underlies its status as either a quasi- or secondary profession (Hoffman 1989). At the most basic level, this framework gives the story of planning (at least modern professional planning) a starting point. Planning emerges as the twentieth-century response to the nineteenth-century industrial city (Hall 2002). It also provides several foundational texts: Howard and Osborn's *Garden Cities of Tomorrow: A Peaceful Path to Real Reform* (1945 [1898]), Charles Robinson's *The Improvement of Towns and Cities; or the Practical Basis of Civic*

Aesthetics (1901), and Daniel Burnham's plan for Chicago (Commercial Club of Chicago et al. 1909), as well as several defining events: Baron Georges-Eugène Haussmann's redevelopment of Paris during the 1850s and 1860s; the Columbia Exposition in Chicago (1893), which launched the City Beautiful Movement in the United States; the construction of Letchworth, the first English Garden City (1903); and the first national conference on city planning, held in Washington, DC in 1909.

Despite this utility, there are several ways in which the usual story is suspect. First, the story has been repeated so much, as we have socialized new cohorts of planners into the profession with it, that it has taken on the status of a disciplinary/professional mythology. Thus the complexity and contingency of the earlier periods get lost. Second, and relatedly, this mythology too often comes without critical examination of the past. Third, this "great men with great ideas" view of planning history leaves out a whole set of other actors and other kinds of planners. It is the story of plans that have been influential – either by having been built or having shaped what others have built – but not of opposition and radical alternatives.

Some scholars have told planning's history in ways that have gotten past this mythologized history. Those who have pursued a more negative examination of the past have presented planning's history as a form of critique. Richard Foglesong's *Planning the Capitalist City* (1986; Chapter 5 is an excerpt), Peter Marcuse's large body of work on planning history (Chapter 6 is a version of this), David Harvey's *Paris: Capital of Modernity* (2003), Robert Fishman's *Bourgeois Utopias: The Rise and Fall of Suburbia* (1987), and Robert Self's *American Babylon* (2003) are some of the better examples. The second way has been to open up that history to the other actors that have been planners, in the broad sense of having made plans to shape spaces and the actions of people in those spaces. This is a history that people like James Holston (2009), Leonie Sandercock (1998), and others have been telling. It is a history in which planning is not just what the state does, or what influential white men do. Instead, planning's histor*ies* are plural and indigenous; marginalized and oppressed actors have their histories of planning told. The exclusion of so much of this other planning from standard texts does not mean that these planning efforts failed to occur; it simply means such plans and their planners have been largely erased from history.

The challenge is to write a planning history that encourages not only an accurate but also a critical, subtle, and reflective understanding of contemporary planning practice and the forces acting upon it. An effective planning history helps the contemporary planner shape his or her professional identity.

Is planning about means or ends, and which should it emphasize?

In its early days planning concerned itself primarily with outcomes. Baron Haussmann in Paris, Daniel Burnham in Chicago, among those who saw their vision translated into reality, pictured modern cities with efficient transportation systems, attractive public spaces, and imposing buildings. Their methods consisted primarily of influencing private developers and/or government officials to achieve these ends. While they assumed technical expertise on the part of those doing the actual designing, their orientation was toward the results of their efforts, not the process by which they were achieved.

Throughout the twentieth century, however, planners increasingly focused on procedures. Rules for creating master plans and zoning maps, formulating standards (e.g., the amount of parking spaces needed per housing unit or open space per person), proposing regulations that would ensure adherence to plans, and creating methodologies for calculating transport impacts became more and more prominent. During the years after World War II, approaches pioneered by the military and the private sector gave rise to the use of the "rational model" and cost–benefit analysis for decision-making. These strategies relied on quantification and involved figuring out the least-cost alternative to achieving desired goals. The underlying assumption was that following proper procedures would ensure beneficial outcomes. The goals would be developed external to the planning function, and the job of planners was to figure out the means.

Criticisms of these approaches exposed the subjectivity disguised by numerical exactitude. Reaction to the depredations caused by top-down decision-making justified by an apparently scientific methodology led to the development of the communicative model. In this approach planners would no longer prescribe either ends or means, but instead would act as negotiators or mediators among the various stakeholders, working out a consensus on what to do. The resulting compromise would constitute a plus game in which all participants would receive some benefit. Although communicative rationality represented a sharp break from earlier methods-based approaches, it resembled them in focusing on process rather than outcomes.

The emphasis on method and process has led to several counter moves, most of which have tried to integrate a normative vision of desired outcomes with a democratic ethos delimiting the processes involved in reaching those ends. Davidoff's classic "advocacy planning" framework (Chapter 21) is an early effort, as he focused not just on the power differentials in planning processes but also on the object of planning. His target was the top-down decision-making of the postwar period, and his work greatly shaped that of those who later articulated frameworks for "equity planning" (Krumholz and Forester 1990) or "the progressive city" (Clavel 1986; 2010). In these, the emphasis is shared between process and desired outcomes.

More recently, the model of the "just city" arose in response to the emphasis on communication. The argument of just city theorists is that inequalities of resources and power lead to unjust planning decisions, and that reducing the planner's role simply to mediation does nothing to counter initial inequality (Marcuse et al. 2009; Fainstein 2010). Overcoming inequity requires pressing for a contrary vision. Although planners alone cannot stop injustice, they can avoid contributing to it by always calling for more just outcomes and spelling out policies that can improve the situation of the relatively disadvantaged. This becomes especially crucial as, under neo-liberal regimes, income distributions have become more unequal and public benefits reduced within many metropolitan areas (see the discussion in Campbell *et al.*, Chapter 10, this volume). Justice planning requires sensitivity to differences among social groups and to democratic expression but most importantly to economic structure. It also calls for a greater emphasis within planning theory on the object of planning – that is, the metropolis – instead of a focus on the activities of planners (Fainstein, Chapter 13, this volume).

Why and when should we plan?

Planning is an intervention with an intention to alter the existing course of events. The timing and legitimacy of planned intervention therefore become questions central to planning theory: Why and in what situations should planners intervene? Implicit here is an understanding of the alternative to planning by the public sector. Though it is most commonly assumed that the alternative is the free market, it could equally be chaos or domination by powerful private interests. Proponents of relying on the market regard planning as producing sub-optimal results and, at an extreme, consider that it is antithetical to freedom (Hayek 1944). Supporters of planning argue that it can replace the uncertainty and cruelties of the market with the logic of the plan and thereby produce a more rational arrangement of the environment.

The duality between planning and the market is a defining framework in planning theory and is the leitmotiv of classic readings in the field (such as Mannheim 1949; Meyerson and Banfield 1964; Dahrendorf 1968; Galbraith 1971). As usually framed, the debate assumes a neat and tidy division between the public and private worlds, each with its unique advantages. But this is inherently wrong. The state has always been in the market, and the structures of capitalist markets rely upon the state. For instance, zoning may be an intervention that regulates the potential uses of private properties, but private property is always, in the first instance, legally created by the state, and one of the functions of zoning is to protect property values. In contemporary theory and practice, Hernando DeSoto's (2003) argument for giving legal title to occupants of informal housing units illustrates the co-constitution of state and market.

Evaluations of planning reflect assumptions about the relationships between the private and public sectors – and how much the government should "intrude." The safe stance in planning has been to see its role as making up for the periodic shortcomings of the private market ("market failures") (Klosterman, Chapter 9). In this interpretation planning acts as the patient understudy, filling in when needed or even helping the market along (Frieden and Sagalyn 1989). Accordingly planning should never presume to replace the market permanently or change the script of economic efficiency. This way of legitimizing planning significantly limits creative or redistributive planning efforts, but it does make a scaled-down version of planning palatable to all but the most conservative economists. In contrast, for the aforementioned equity, progressive and just-city planners, planning ought to confront the private actors directly and focus on remedying disadvantage. In this view privileging the private sector reinforces unjust outcomes, while empowering planning has the potential for enhancing equity.

The inter-connections between the public and private have become increasingly evident. The rise of public–private partnerships in the wake of urban renewal efforts reflects this blurring of sectoral boundaries (Squires 1989). Public sector planners borrow tools developed in the private sector, such as strategic planning and place marketing (Levy 1990). The emergence of autonomous public authorities to manage marine ports, airports, and other infrastructures, and of urban development corporations to promote economic growth has created hybrid organizations that act like both a public agency and a private firm (Walsh 1978; Doig 1987). In addition, the growing non-profit or "third sector," embodied in community development corporations within the United States (see Wolf-Powers, Chapter 16) and housing associations in Europe, clearly demonstrates the inadequacies of viewing the world in a purely dichotomous framework of the government versus the market (Harloe 1995; Rubin 2000).

More troublesome than the inter-weaving of the public and private, according to some theorists, is the appropriation of the public domain by the logic of privatization. Privatization of traditionally public services raises the question of whether democratic citizenship – and all its rights and responsibilities – is being reduced to consumerism and consumer freedom. This critique in one formulation regards the public sector as wholly captured by capitalist interests, engaging in activities imitative of ruthless corporations, and generally incapable of planning for the benefit of the mass of people (Harvey 1985, 1989). More temperate viewpoints regard the outcome of the tug of war between capitalist and community interests as dependent on conflict, bargaining, and the mobilization of political resources, the results of which are not predetermined (Stone 1993; Purcell 2008; Clavel 2010).

The constraints on planning power – how can planning be effective within a mixed economy?

Even if we agree that planners should routinely shape the operations of the private market, we have no assurance that their intervention will be effective; in other words, that they will be able to achieve their ends. Unlike some other professionals, planners do not have a monopoly on power or expertise over their object of work. They operate within the constraints of the capitalist political economy, and their urban visions compete with those of developers, consumers, politicians, and other more powerful groups. When they call for a type of development to occur, they do not command the resources to make it happen. Instead, they must rely on either private investment or a commitment from political leaders. They also work within the constraints of democracy and bureaucratic procedures (Foglesong, Chapter 5, this volume). Moreover their concerns may have low priority within the overall political agenda. Thus, despite the planning ideal of a holistic, proactive vision, planners may find themselves playing frustratingly reactive, regulatory roles, especially in the United States.

The most powerful American planners are those who can marshal public and private resources to effect change and get projects built (Doig 1987; Ballon and Jackson 2007). They bend the role of the planner and alter the usual dynamic between the public and private sectors. The resulting public–private partnerships make the planner more activist (Squires 1989); yet, they also strain the traditional non-political identity of the public planner and make many idealistic planners squirm. How else can one explain the uncomfortable mixture of disgust and envy that a lot of planners felt towards Robert Moses, who, as the head of various New York City agencies, had far more projects built than did all the traditional city planners he disparaged (Caro 1974)? Even Moses, however, for all his reputed power, relied on the support of the extremely powerful Rockefeller family to build his roads, playgrounds, etc. (Fitch 1993). The proliferation of neo-liberal ideologies and practices in the past 30 years has conceptually and practically limited the space for planners to shape developments (Campbell *et al.*, Chapter 10, this volume), thereby further reducing the scope of imagined possibilities of planning theory and practice.

What values inform planning?

To be a certified planner in most countries you must abide by a professional code of ethics. But applying professional ethics in planning presents many problems. First, if planners work in the private or quasi-private sectors, as is increasingly the case, do they still owe loyalty to the public at large? Planners are torn regarding whom they should serve: clients, consulting or development firms for which they are staff, the general public, or specific groups within the population (e.g. community organizations, homeowners' associations) (Marcuse 1976, 2011). Flyvberg, *et al.*(2005) have argued that the demonstrable underestimation of costs and overestimation of benefits by planning consultants involved in mega-projects involves lapses from professional ethics. But why should a private planning entity serve any interest other than that of its owners? And why should we expect private entities to behave as public ones?

Second, planners must deal with uncertainty. Planning, as we have already argued, is future-oriented and predictive. But as Wachs (Chapter 23) points out, the future is marked by uncertainty and our inability to ever fully foresee the impacts of our actions. Values and expectations fill in the gaps when empirical information is limited (and, of course, shape how we interpret the empirical information we do have). But planners' values are not rooted only in planning schools or in planning certification processes; they spring also from the families, communities, and cultures in which planners have grown up and lived.

Third, planning decisions are further complicated because so much of planning extends beyond technical activities and into much larger social, economic, and environmental challenges. Within society at large the values of democracy, equality, diversity, and efficiency often clash (Fainstein 2010). These conflicts arise in the choices that planners must make as they try to reconcile the goals of economic development, social justice, and environmental protection. Despite the long-term desirability of sustainable development, this triad of goals has created deep-seated tensions not only between planners and the outside world but also within planning itself (Campbell, Chapter 11, this volume).

Finally, ethical questions inevitably emerge from the planner's role as "expert." Questions concerning the proper balance between expertise and citizen input arise in issues like the siting of highways and waste disposal facilities, when particular social groups must bear the costs of more widespread social benefits. Planners mostly adhere to a utilitarian system of ethics, but utilitarianism has long been critiqued for its downplaying of distributional issues (see, most notably, Rawls 1971). Thus planners' claim to expertise incorporates a set of (hotly contested) value judgments, while at the same time obscuring such values in a cloak of objectivity and rationality. The ethical issues of the expert role are perhaps most evident when planners quantify risk, often placing a monetary value on human life (Fischer 1991).

The enduring question of the public interest

The most enduring question in planning theory revolves around the definition of the public interest. The American Institute of Certified Planners (AICP) states clearly that "our primary obligation is to serve the public interest." But planning continues to face the central controversy of whether a single public interest exists and, if it does, whether planners can recognize and serve it. Incremental planners (beginning with Lindblom 1959) claim that complexity makes discovering the public interest unrealistic, while advocate planners argue that what is portrayed as the public interest in fact represents merely the interests of the privileged. More recently, postmodernists and poststructuralists have challenged the universal master narrative that gives voice to the public interest, seeing instead a heterogeneous public with many voices and interests. In sum, attacks on the concept of the public interest take two forms: first we cannot know what the public interest is; and second, and more fundamentally, there is no such thing as a unified public that can have an interest.

Nevertheless, planners have not abandoned the idea of serving the public interest, and rightly so. Postmodernists provided planning with a needed perspective on its preoccupation with a monolithic "public" (epitomized by Le Corbusier's and Robert Moses's love of the public but disdain for people); yet, a rejection of Enlightenment rationality, shared values, and generally applicable standards leaves the planner without adequate tools for serving a fragmented population. Some have touted strategic planning and other borrowed private sector approaches as the appropriate path for planning, but these approaches neglect the "public" in the public interest. A belief in the public interest is the foundation for a set of values that planners hold dear: equal protection and equal opportunity, public space, and a sense of civic community and social responsibility.

The challenge is to reconcile these elements of a common public interest with the diversity that comes from many communities living side by side. David Harvey looked to generally held ideas of social justice and rationality as a bridge to overcome this dilemma (Harvey 2001); similarly, Susan S. Fainstein (2010; Chapter 13, this volume) presents the model of the just city. The recent interest in communicative action – planners as communicators rather than as autonomous, systematic thinkers – also reflects an effort to renew the focus of planning theory on the public interest (Forester 1989; Innes 1998). Within this approach planners accept the multiplicity of interests, combined with an enduring common interest in finding viable, politically legitimate solutions. Planners serve the public interest by negotiating a kind of multicultural, technically informed pluralism. Sandercock, who has done as much as anyone to question the idea of a unitary public, is making such a claim when she argues for the transformative possibility of dialogue in allowing different groups to occupy and collectively govern shared space (Chapter 20).

In the end, the question of the public interest is the leitmotiv that holds together the defining debates of planning theory. The central task of planners is serving the public interest in cities, suburbs, and the countryside. Questions of when, why, and how planners should intervene – and the constraints they face in the process – all lead back to defining and serving the public interest, even while it is not static or fixed. The restructured urban economy, the shifting boundaries between the public and private sectors, the effects of telecommunications and information technology, and the changing tools and available resources constantly force planners to rethink the public interest. This constant rethinking is the task of planning theory.

The Continuing Evolution of Planning Theory

Planning theory is an evolving field, and this book, therefore, is just a moment in that evolution. In the 20 years since the first edition of this reader was published, the subject has undergone a set of shifts and refinements. Debates and issues that had seemed central have receded from prominence – either discarded or, conversely, have become incorporated into "accepted wisdom." Postmodernism has thus faded as a major focus, but its influence endures in an increased emphasis on discourse, on varied ways of knowing, and on pluralism of interpretation. Similarly, communicative planning has arguably also entered a new phase: it is simultaneously more accepted, differentiated, and criticized. And the debates surrounding New Urbanism have also shifted, as many of its goals have become squarely part of planning practices.

Over a generation, the most significant advances in planning theory are a changing understanding of power (Brindley et al. 1996; Flyvbjerg 1998), of communicative action and the planner's role in mediating interactions among stakeholders (Forester, Chapter 18, this volume; Booher and Innes 2010), of modernization/modernism (Scott, Chapter 3, this volume), of the complex links between diversity, equity, democracy, and community (Young, Chapter 19, this volume; Thomas, Chapter 22, this volume, and Sandercock, Chapter 20, this volume), and of the relations between processes and outcomes (Fainstein, Chapter 13, this volume). Significant efforts have also been made to understand the concepts of sustainability (Campbell, Chapter 11, this volume), resilience (Gleeson, Chapter 12, this volume), and complexity (de Roo and Silva, 2010).

If we assume that planning theory will continue to evolve in response to changes in planning practice, the development of cities, and the rise of social movements, then we can speculate on future directions for planning theory. Planners urgently need a larger conceptual world view to absorb the ramifications of the digital revolution of the Internet, massive data storage and retrieval, and geographic information systems (GIS). Planning methodologies need to be revised to deal with the coming flood of data. The real-time tracking of flows in time–space coordinates (e.g., microchips and bar codes creating a world of geo-coded products, resources, and even people) creates new opportunities for planners to understand dynamic spatial processes, such as time–space-based user fees, the "sharing economy" facilitated by smart phone applications, development impact fees, and GIS-based performance zoning. However, this data revolution will also thrust the field into the tricky ethical world of data privacy issues.

Increasing globalization will force planning theory to incorporate different types of cities into what had been Euro-American models of urbanization; Shanghai, Tokyo, Mexico City, Mumbai, and so forth will more and more provide the basis for concepts of planning's role and aims. Thus questions of informality (Roy, Chapter 26, this volume) become central to planning the world's most rapidly growing metropolises. We would expect questions of equity and economic development to continue to be central parts of planning theory as applied to both the developing world and developed world. As globalization continues to raise tensions between the preservation of local communities and the acceleration of global networks, maintaining local communities as meaningful spaces for collective endeavor will remain crucial (DeFilippis 2004). The impact of climate change on all parts of the globe requires traditional planning concerns with environmental protection to encompass much broader ecological threats than before (Gleeson, Chapter 12, this volume).

All these examples suggest that the interaction between theory, urban change, and planning practice is symbiotic and often asynchronous. Planning theory acts as a kind of intellectual vanguard, pushing the professional field to rethink outdated practices and the assumptions underlying them. Planning theory aims also to bring our thinking about planning up to date and in line with both urban phenomena (sprawl, globalization, etc.) and social theories from other fields (such as deliberative democracy or critical theory) (Friedmann 2011). In addition, the theory–practice time lag may run the other way round: the task of planning theory is often to catch up with planning practice itself, codifying and restating approaches to planning that practitioners have long since used (such as disjointed incrementalism or dispute mediation). Planning theory can therefore alternately be a running commentary, parallel and at arm's length to the profession: a prescriptive avant-garde or instead a response to planning practice.

If there is a persistent gap between grand theory and modest accomplishment, it may also be overly simplistic to attribute it to the distance between theory and practice. It may instead reflect the discrepancy between what the theorist rightfully envisions as the ideal social–spatial arrangement of the world (i.e., the good, just city) and the more modest contributions that planners can make toward this ideal (given the political-economic constraints posed on the profession). Planning scholars frequently conflate the two, imagining an ideal urban society and then making all its characteristics the goals of the planning agenda. However, should the discipline be faulted for its lofty (and overreaching) ambitions?

The Readings

Compiling a reader in planning theory presents a dilemma. One can reprint the early postwar classics – thereby duplicating several other anthologies and providing little space for contemporary debates – or else risk over-representing transient contemporary ideas.[2] We have chosen a somewhat different path. Rather than trying to cover the whole field, whether historically or at the present moment, we have selected a set of readings – both "classic" and recent – that effectively address the pressing and enduring questions in planning theory. In particular, they address the challenges and dilemmas of planning as defined at the beginning of this introduction: *What role can planning play in developing the good city and region within the constraints of a capitalist global economy and varying political systems?* We approach this question primarily through texts that address specific theoretical issues. However, we have also included several case studies that provide vivid and concrete illustrations of these questions.

Planning theory is a relatively young field, yet one can already speak of "classic readings." Our guide has been to choose readings – both old and new – that still speak directly to contemporary issues. Most have been written in the past 10 years, though some articles from the 1960s are still the best articulation of specific debates. Most draw upon experiences in North America and Europe, but this edition differs from earlier ones in including a section on the developing world. The selections compiled here represent a substantial revision of the third edition of *Readings in Planning Theory* (Fainstein and Campbell 2011). Roughly half the selections are new, reflecting more recent or more accessible statements of planning theories or newly emerging themes. We have retained those readings from earlier editions that students and teachers of planning theory reported finding particularly useful and exciting.

The readings are organized into five parts, each prefaced with a short introduction to the main themes. We begin with the foundations of modern planning, including both traditional and critical views of planning history. We then turn to two interrelated questions: *What are planners trying to do?* And *The justifications and critiques of planning*. Addressing the political and economic justifications for planning, the chapters place planners in the larger context of the relationship between the private market and government (both local and national). They thus address the fundamental questions of why we plan and what we are trying to do when we do plan.

The third part of the book uses practice examples to inform theory-building. Thus it is not theory informing practice, but the other way around. These are not case studies, per se, but the use of examples from practice to explicitly theorize planning. Racial, ethnic, and gender politics have emerged as powerful, transformative, and conflictual forces in urban planning. The readings in the fourth part explore the themes of difference, discrimination, and inequality. These theories challenge planning to be more inclusive, to accept the city as home to divergent populations with radically different experiences and needs, to see how the existing city fabric perpetuates antiquated social and gender relations, and to pursue social justice more aggressively. Finally the book concludes with a set of readings that examine issues for planners in developing countries. The principal question raised here is whether the theories that have arisen in the West are applicable in parts of the world with vastly different economic circumstances, political frameworks, and social divisions, and how we should transform our theoretical apparatuses to understand planning in the cities where the majority of the world's people live.

Notes

1. One of us had a student who, early in the semester in a planning theory course, quoted the humorously dismissive Yogi Berra line that: "In theory there is no difference between theory and practice. In practice there is."
2. Faludi (1973) contains a classic set of readings. Hillier and Healey's (2008) three-volume collection is inclusive of the major writings in planning theory until that date.

References

Ballon, Hilary, and Kenneth T. Jackson, eds. 2007. *Robert Moses and the Modern City: The Transformation of New York*. New York: W.W. Norton.

Booher, David E., and Judith E. Innes. 2010. Governance for Resilience: CALFED as a Complex Adaptive Network for Resource Management. *Ecology and Society*, 15 (3): 337.

Brindley, Tim, Yvonne Rydin, and Gerry Stoker. 1996. *Remaking Planning: The Politics of Urban Change*. 2nd edn. New York: Routledge.

Caro, Robert. 1974. *The Power Broker: Robert Moses and the Fall of New York*. New York: Alfred Knopf.

Clavel, Pierre. 1986. *The Progressive City*. New Brunswick, NJ: Rutgers University Press.

Clavel, Pierre. 2010. *Activists in City Hall*. Ithaca, NY: Cornell University Press.

Commercial Club of Chicago, David Hudson Burnham, Edward H. Bennett, and Charles Moore. 1909. *Plan of Chicago*. Chicago, IL: The Commercial Club.

Dahrendorf, Ralf. 1968. *Essays in the Theory of Society*. Stanford, CA: Stanford University Press.

DeFilippis, James. 2004. *Unmaking Goliath*. New York: Routledge.

de Roo, Gert and Elisabete Silva (eds). 2010. *A Planner's Encounter with Complexity*. Farnham: Ashgate.

DeSoto, Hernando. 2003. *The Mystery of Capital: Why Capitalism Triumphs in the West and Fails Everywhere Else*. New York: Basic Books

Doig, Jameson. 1987. Coalition Building by a Regional Agency: Austin Tobin and the Port of New York Authority. In Clarence Stone and Heywood Sanders, eds, *The Politics of Urban Development*. Lawrence, KN: University Press of Kansas, pp. 73–104.

Fainstein, Susan S. 2010. *The Just City*. Ithaca, NY: Cornell University Press.

Fainstein, Susan S., and Scott Campbell (eds). 2011. *Readings in Urban Theory*, 3rd edn. Malden, MA: Wiley-Blackwell.

Faludi, Andreas (ed.). 1973. *A Reader in Planning Theory*. New York: Pergamon Press.

Fischer, Frank. 1991. Risk Assessment and Environmental Crisis: Toward an Integration of Science and Participation. *Industrial Crisis Quarterly*, 5(2): 113–32.

Fishman, Robert. 1987. *Bourgeois Utopias: The Rise and Fall of Suburbia*. New York: Basic Books.

Fitch, Robert. 1993. *The Assassination of New York*. New York: Verso Press.

Flyvbjerg, Bent. 1998. *Rationality and Power: Democracy in Practice*. Chicago, IL: University of Chicago Press.

Flyvbjerg, Bent, Mette K. Skamris Holm, and Søren L. Buhl. 2005. How (In)accurate Are Demand Forecasts in Public Works Projects? The Case of Transportation. *Journal of the American Planning Association*. 71(2): 131–46.

Foglesong, Richard E. 1986. *Planning the Capitalist City*. Princeton, NJ: Princeton University Press.

Forester, John. 1989. *Planning in the Face of Power*. Berkeley, CA: University of California Press.

Frieden, Bernard, and Lynn Sagalyn. 1989. *Downtown Inc. How America Rebuilds Cities*. Cambridge, MA: MIT Press.

Friedmann, John. 2011. *Insurgencies: Essays in Planning Theory*. Routledge: New York

Galbraith, John K. 1971. *The New Industrial State*. New York: New American Library.

Hall, Peter. 2002. *Cities of Tomorrow: An Intellectual History of Urban Planning and Design in the Twentieth Century*, 3rd edn. Oxford: Blackwell.

Harloe, Michael. 1995. *The People's Home*. Oxford: Blackwell.

Harvey, David. 1985. On Planning the Ideology of Planning. In *The Urbanization of Capital*, Baltimore, MD: Johns Hopkins University Press, pp. 165–84.

Harvey, David. 1989. From Managerialism to Entrepreneurialism: The Transformation in Urban Governance in Late Capitalism. *Geografiska Annaler: Series B, Human Geography*, 71(1): 3–17.

Harvey, David. 2001. Social Justice, Postmodernism and the City. In S. S. Fainstein and S. Campbell, eds, *Readings in Urban Theory*, 2nd edn. Cambridge, MA: Blackwell.

Harvey, David. 2003. *Paris: Capital of Modernity*. New York: Routledge.

Hayek, Friedrich A. 1944. *The Road to Serfdom*. Chicago, IL: University of Chicago Press.

Hillier, Jean, and Patsy Healey. 2008. *Critical Essays in Planning Theory* (3 vols). Burlington, VT: Ashgate.

Hoffman, Lily. 1989. *The Politics of Knowledge: Activist Movements in Medicine and Planning*. Albany, NY: SUNY Press.

Holston, James. 2009. *Insurgent Citizenship: Disjunctions of Democracy and Modernity in Brazil*. Princeton, NJ: Princeton University Press.

Howard, Ebenezer, and Frederic James Osborn. 1945 [1898]. *Garden Cities of Tomorrow*. London: Faber & Faber.

Innes, Judith E. 1998. Information in Communicative Planning. *Journal of the American Planning Association*, 64(Winter): 52–63.

Krueckeberg, Donald A. (ed.). 1983. The Culture of Planning. In D. A. Krueckeberg, ed., *Introduction to Planning History in the United States*, New Brunswick, NJ: Center for Urban Policy Research, pp. 1–12.

Krumholz, Norman and John Forester. 1990. *Making Equity Planning Work*. Philadelphia, PA: Temple University Press.

Levy, John M. 1990. What Local Economic Developers Actually Do: Location Quotients Versus Press Releases. *Journal of the American Planning Association*, 56(2): 153–60.

Lindblom, Charles. 1959. The Science of "Muddling Through." *Public Administration Review*. 19(2): 79–88.

Mannheim, Karl. 1949. *Man and Society in an Age of Reconstruction*. New York: Harcourt, Brace.

Marcuse, Peter. 1976. Professional Ethics and Beyond: Values in Planning. *Journal of the American Institute of Planning*, 42(3): 264–74.

Marcuse, Peter. 2011. Social Justice and Power in Planning History and Theory. In Naomi Carmon and Susan S. Fainstein, eds, *Urban Planning as if People Mattered*. Philadelphia, PA: Penn Press.

Marcuse, Peter, James Connolly, Ingrid Olivo Magana, Johannes Novy, Cuz Potter, and Justin Steil (eds). 2009. *Searching for the Just City*. New York: Routledge.

Meyerson, Martin, and Edward C. Banfield. 1964. *Politics, Planning and the Public Interest*. New York: Free Press.

Purcell, Mark. 2008. *Recapturing Democracy*. New York: Routledge.

Rawls, John. 1971. *A Theory of Justice*. Cambridge, MA: Harvard University Press.

Robinson, Charles Mulford. 1901. *The Improvement of Towns and Cities; or the Practical Basis of Civic Aesthetics*. New York: G. P. Putnam.

Rubin, Herbert J. 2000. *Renewing Hope within Neighborhoods of Despair*. Albany, NY: SUNY Press.

Sandercock, Leonie. 1998. *Towards Cosmopolis: Planning for Multicultural Cities*. New York: Academy Press.

Self, Robert O. 2003. *American Babylon*. Princeton, NJ: Princeton University Press.

Squires, Gregory D. (ed.). 1989. *Unequal Partnerships: The Political Economy of Urban Redevelopment in Postwar America*. New Brunswick, NJ: Rutgers University Press.

Stone, Clarence N. 1993. Urban Regimes and the Capacity to Govern: A Political Economy Approach. *Journal of Urban Affairs*, 15(1): 1–28.

Walsh, Annmarie Hauck. 1978. *The Public's Business: The Politics and Practices of Government Corporations*. Cambridge, MA: MIT Press.

Part I

The Development of Planning Theory

Introduction

The readings in this first section examine influential visions of modern planning. They offer both established and critical views of planning history. We begin with Robert Fishman's examination of two foundational figures in planning's intellectual

Readings in Planning Theory, Fourth Edition. Edited by Susan S. Fainstein and James DeFilippis.
Editorial material and organization © 2016 John Wiley & Sons, Ltd.
Published 2016 by John Wiley & Sons, Ltd.

history: Ebenezer Howard and Le Corbusier. (Fishman's larger book on *Urban Utopias*, from which this chapter is excerpted, also looks at a third visionary of twentieth-century urbanism: Frank Lloyd Wright.) Fishman goes beyond the standard account of Howard and Le Corbusier to examine the social history behind their distinctive utopias. Although all were reacting to the grimy reality of industrial cities, each took a fundamentally different path toward planning their ideal urban society. Corbusier's Radiant City was mass-scaled, dense, vertical, hierarchical – the social extension of modern architecture. Wright went to the other extreme: his Broadacre City was a mixture of Jeffersonian agrarian individualism and prairie suburbanism, linked by superhighways. Howard's Garden Cities were scaled somewhere in between: self-contained, relatively dense villages of 35,000 residents held together by a cooperative spirit, private industrial employers, and a communal greenbelt. The three utopias symbolize fundamental choices in the scale of human settlements: Corbusier's mass *Gesellschaft*, Howard's village-like *Gemeinschaft*, or Wright's American individualism.

Although spatial planning originated within the design professions, after World War II it increasingly became based in social science. Chapter 2 by Van Assche et al. examines the co-evolutions of planning and design in order to demonstrate the contribution of good design to good planning. The authors begin by distinguishing design from planning perspectives. They demarcate the planning system by those actors and institutions that regulate and coordinate the uses of space. In contrast, while urban design overlaps with planning, it is especially concerned with manipulating spatial imagery at the micro-scale, and it introduces an emphasis on aesthetics. In particular, a design perspective captures the character of specific places and allows for their differentiation. The authors recognize the tension between planning and design caused by differing priorities but argue that every resolution requires trade-offs, that the balance will be affected by the culture in which planning and design are embedded, and that each perspective can inform the other.

The political scientist James Scott traces the roots of modernist planning's effort to impose order on the messiness of humans and their environment – particularly focusing on what he calls "authoritarian high modernism." In an excerpt from his book, *Seeing Like a State: How Certain Schemes to Improve the Human Condition Have Failed* (Chapter 3, this volume), Scott traces the link between modernism and the modern nation-state's efforts to simplify and standardize, while rejecting local context and initiative, to make the nation legible, measurable, and counted. This is how the modern state "sees." Scott identifies three elements common to disastrous abuses of modern state development: administrative ordering of nature and society through simplification and standardization ("high modernism"); the unrestrained use of the power of the modern state to implement these rational designs; and a civil society too weak to resist effectively. "Social engineering" becomes the consequence of high modernism and nation-state power, and the authoritarian tendencies of the single modernist voice of rationality displace all other forms of judgment.

Scott sees three effective strategies to counter authoritarian high modernism: belief in a private sphere of activity outside the interference of the state (the idea of the private realm); liberal political economy (as in the free-market ideas of Frederick Hayek); and, most importantly, civil society and democratic political institutions. What are the implications for planning? Plans should not be so ambitious and meticulous that they are closed systems. Smaller and reversible steps, flexibly open to both surprises and human inventiveness, will break with the hubris of modernist planning. In Scott's call for local initiative ("metis"), as an alternative to state-level technocratic planning, one hears echoes of arguments also made by Jane Jacobs, John Forester, and others.

Jane Jacobs considers the design approaches embodied in the American urban renewal programs of the 1950s as destructive of the urban fabric. She argues that the modernist theories from which they derived suffer from a dangerous misconception of how real cities actually operate. She summarily labels the classic planning prototypes described by Fishman as producing the "Radiant Garden City Beautiful." She sees in Daniel Burnham, who was a progenitor of the City Beautiful model, along with Ebenezer Howard and Le Corbusier, an uneasiness with actual cities. She condemns each of them for seeking to replace the rich complexity of a real metropolis with the abstract logic of an idealized planned city. We include here the introductory chapter to her landmark 1961 critique of postwar American urban renewal, *The Death and Life of Great American Cities* (Chapter 4, this volume). This book arguably oversimplifies the evils of planning, while both neglecting the destructive role of the private sector in urban renewal and romanticizing the capabilities of small, competitive, neighborhood businesses. Yet the book remains one of the most compelling and well-written arguments for encouraging diversity and innovation in big, dense, messy cities. (That said, Jacobs' "diversity" is primarily about creating a wide range of building types and land uses, rather than a more contemporary definition of "diversity" as including a multicultural array of racial and ethnic urban residents.) Jacobs' ideas also signal the long transition of planning theory from an early faith in science, rationality, and comprehensiveness to a more self-critical, incremental approach. It thereby anticipates a later interest in complexity and emergence. Jacobs demonstrates that the simple process of daily, intimate observation can lead to an understanding of the complexity of cities.

In a brief excerpt from his book, *Planning the Capitalist City*, Richard Foglesong provides a general critique of planning, based on a Marxist view of the role of the state in maintaining the built environment as a support system for private enterprise and mediator between capital and civil society (Chapter 5, this volume). The key dynamic to understanding the ambivalent role of planning in capitalist society is the "property contradiction": the contradiction between the social character of land and its private ownership and control. The private sector resists government intrusion into its affairs, yet at the same time it needs government to regulate the use of land. For example, home owners look to zoning to prevent adjacent undesirable uses from lowering their property values, and businesses require the public provision of infrastructure. As a result, resistance to planning is not a simple rejection of planning as unnecessary. For Foglesong, this property contradiction is related to another contradiction: that between capitalism and democracy. Development interests have a particular agenda that is often at variance with views held by members of the public, and it is the role of planning to reconcile the two. In other words, planners act to legitimate policies in the face of public opposition.

Also critical of the role played by traditional planning, Peter Marcuse, in his discussion of three historic currents of city planning (Chapter 6, this volume), differentiates among "deferential technicism," social reform, and social justice as types of planning. He then breaks down each of these categories into subcomponents. He indicates that in real life the three approaches are not usually present in pure form but argues that they nonetheless indicate clearly different ways in which planners operate. Technicist planners aim at efficiently realizing the goals that their clients set, employing tools that they acquired through professional training and experience. Planners who come to their jobs from civil engineering, economics, or architecture typically fall into this category. For these planners, tools like cost–benefit analysis, computer modeling, and application of architectural principles allow them to maximize goals set by their clients. In line with Foglesong's argument concerning the property contradiction, Marcuse regards technicist planners as functioning to make the existing economic, social, and political order work smoothly.

Marcuse names social reform planning as an approach whereby planners accept the existing social order but focus on the needs of disadvantaged groups and support greater democratization of the planning process. Probably most practitioners with degrees from social-science-based master's programs in planning at least start out with such ideals. Marcuse's third category, social justice planning, is more radical. He regards this approach as challenging the powerful elements in society. He includes within it a variety of aspirations ranging from the application of principles of justice to the development of utopias. He concludes his essay by commenting that "the interplay between what is wanted, and by whom, and what is possible, between what is just and what is realistic, creates a constant tension in city development." His sympathies clearly lie with the third approach, but he does not claim that such an orientation is necessarily feasible. Indeed one might ask whether planners are sufficiently influential to affect the shaping of cities except when representing the interests of a powerful sponsor, whether that be a political elite or a popular movement.

References

Fishman, Robert. 1982. *Urban Utopias in the Twentieth Century: Ebenezer Howard, Frank Lloyd Wright, Le Corbusier.* Cambridge, MA: MIT Press.

Foglesong, Richard E. 1986. *Planning the Capitalist City.* Princeton, NJ: Princeton University Press.

Jacobs, Jane. 1961. *The Death and Life of Great American Cities.* London: Jonathan Cape.

Scott, James C. 1998. *Seeing Like a State: How Certain Schemes to Improve the Human Condition Have Failed.* New Haven, CT: Yale University Press.

1

Urban Utopias in the Twentieth Century
Ebenezer Howard, Frank Lloyd Wright, and Le Corbusier

Robert Fishman

Introduction

What is the ideal city for the twentieth century, the city that best expresses the power and beauty of modern technology and the most enlightened ideas of social justice? Between 1890 and 1930 three planners, Ebenezer Howard, Frank Lloyd Wright, and Le Corbusier, tried to answer that question. Each began his work alone, devoting long hours to preparing literally hundreds of models and drawings specifying every aspect of the new city, from its general ground plan to the layout of the typical living room. There were detailed plans for factories, office buildings, schools, parks, transportation systems – all innovative designs in themselves and all integrated into a revolutionary restructuring of urban form. The economic and political organization of the city, which could not be easily shown in drawings, was worked out in the voluminous writings that each planner appended to his designs. Finally, each man devoted himself to passionate and unremitting efforts to make his ideal city a reality.

Many people dream of a better world; Howard, Wright, and Le Corbusier each went a step further and planned one. Their social consciences took this rare and remarkable step because they believed that, more than any other goal, their societies needed new kinds of cities. They were deeply fearful of the consequences

Original publication details: Fishman, Robert. 1982. *Urban Utopias in the Twentieth Century: Ebenezer Howard, Frank Lloyd Wright, Le Corbusier*. Cambridge, MA: The MIT Press. pp. 3–20, 23–6, 40–51, 226–34. © 1982 Massachusetts Institute of Technology. Reproduced with permission from MIT Press.

Readings in Planning Theory, Fourth Edition. Edited by Susan S. Fainstein and James DeFilippis.
Editorial material and organization © 2016 John Wiley & Sons, Ltd.
Published 2016 by John Wiley & Sons, Ltd.

for civilization if the old cities, with all the social conflicts and miseries they embodied, were allowed to persist. They were also inspired by the prospect that a radical reconstruction of the cities would solve not only the urban crisis of their time, but the social crisis as well. The very completeness of their ideal cities expressed their convictions that the moment had come for comprehensive programs, and for a total rethinking of the principles of urban planning. They rejected the possibility of gradual improvement. They did not seek the amelioration of the old cities, but a wholly transformed urban environment.

This transformation meant the extensive rebuilding and even partial abandonment of the cities of their time. Howard, Wright, and Le Corbusier did not shrink from this prospect; they welcomed it. As Howard put it, the old cities had "done their work." They were the best that the old economic and social order could have been expected to produce, but they had to be superseded if mankind were to attain a higher level of civilization. The three ideal cities were put forward to establish the basic theoretical framework for this radical reconstruction. They were the manifestoes for an urban revolution.

These ideal cities are perhaps the most ambitious and complex statements of the belief that reforming the physical environment can revolutionize the total life of a society. Howard, Wright, and Le Corbusier saw design as an active force, distributing the benefits of the Machine Age to all and directing the community onto the paths of social harmony. Yet they never subscribed to the narrow simplicities of the "doctrine of salvation by bricks alone" – the idea that physical facilities could *by themselves* solve social problems. To be sure, they believed – and who can doubt this? – that the values of family life could be better maintained in a house or apartment that gave each member the light and air and room he needed, rather than in the cramped and fetid slums that were still the fate of too many families. They thought that social solidarity would be better promoted in cities that brought people together, rather than in those whose layout segregated the inhabitants by race or class.

At the same time the three planners understood that these and other well-intended designs would be worse than useless if their benevolent humanitarianism merely covered up basic inequalities in the social system. The most magnificent and innovative housing project would fail if its inhabitants were too poor and oppressed to lead decent lives. There was little point in constructing new centers of community life if the economics of exploitation and class conflict kept the citizens as divided as they had been in their old environment. Good planning was indeed efficacious in creating social harmony, but only if it embodied a genuine rationality and justice in the structure of society. It was impossible in a society still immured in what Le Corbusier called "the Age of Greed." The three planners realized that they had to join their programs of urban reconstruction with programs of political and economic reconstruction. They concluded (to paraphrase one of Marx's famous *Theses on Feuerbach*) that designers had hitherto merely *ornamented* the world in various ways; the point was to *change* it.

The ideal cities were therefore accompanied by detailed programs for radical changes in the distribution of wealth and power, changes that Howard, Wright, and Le Corbusier regarded as the necessary complements to their revolutions in design. The planners also played prominent roles in the movements that shared their aims. Howard was an ardent cooperative socialist who utilized planning as part of his search for the cooperative commonwealth; Wright, a Jeffersonian democrat and an admirer of Henry George, was a spokesman for the American decentrist movement; and Le Corbusier had many of his most famous designs published for the first time in the pages of the revolutionary syndicalist journals he edited. All three brought a revolutionary fervor to the practice of urban design.

And, while the old order endured, Howard, Wright, and Le Corbusier refused to adapt themselves to what planning commissions, bankers, politicians, and all the other authorities of their time believed to be desirable and attainable. They consistently rejected the idea that a planner's imagination must work within the system. Instead, they regarded the physical structure of the cities in which they lived, and the economic structure of the society in which they worked, as temporary aberrations which mankind would soon overcome. The three planners looked beyond their own troubled time to a new age each believed was imminent, a new age each labored to define and to build.

Their concerns thus ranged widely over architecture, urbanism, economics, and politics, but their thinking found a focus and an adequate means of expression only in their plans for ideal cities. The cities were never conceived of as blueprints for any actual project. They were "ideal types" of cities for the future, elaborate models rigorously designed to illustrate the general principles that each man advocated. They were convenient and attractive intellectual tools that enabled each planner to bring together his many innovations in design, and to show them as part of a coherent whole, a total redefinition of the idea of the city. The setting of these ideal cities was never any actual location, but an empty, abstract plane where no contingencies existed. The time was the present, not any calendar day or year, but that revolutionary "here and now" when the hopes of the present are finally realized.

These hopes, moreover, were both architectural and social. In the three ideal cities, the transformation of the physical environment is the outward sign of an inner transformation in the social structure. Howard, Wright, and Le Corbusier used their ideal cities to depict a world in which their political and economic goals had already been achieved. Each planner wanted to show that the urban designs he advocated were not only rational and beautiful in themselves, but that they embodied the social goals he believed in. In the context of the ideal city, each proposal for new housing, new factories, and other structures could be seen to further the broader aims. And, in general, the ideal cities enabled the three planners to show modern design in what they believed was its true context – as an integral part of a culture from which poverty and exploitation had disappeared. These cities, therefore, were complete alternative societies, intended as a revolution in politics and economics as well as in architecture. They were utopian visions of a total environment in which man would live in peace with his fellow man and in harmony with nature. They were social thought in three dimensions.

As theorists of urbanism, Howard, Wright, and Le Corbusier attempted to define the ideal form of any industrial society. They shared a common assumption that this form could be both defined and attained, but each viewed the ideal through the perspective of his own social theory, his own national tradition, and his own personality. Their plans, when compared, disagree profoundly, and the divergences are often just as significant as the agreements. They offer us not a single blueprint for the future, but three sets of choices – the great metropolis, moderate decentralization, or extreme decentralization – each with its corresponding political and social implications. Like the classical political triad of monarchy–aristocracy–democracy, the three ideal cities represent a vocabulary of basic forms that can be used to define the whole range of choices available to the planner.

Seventeen years older than Wright and thirty-seven years older than Le Corbusier, Ebenezer Howard started first. His life resembles a story by Horatio Alger, except that Alger never conceived a hero at once so ambitious and so self-effacing. He began his career as a stenographer and ended as the elder statesman of a worldwide planning movement, yet he remained throughout his life the embodiment of the "little man." He was wholly without pretension, an earnest man with a round, bald head, spectacles, and a bushy mustache, unselfconscious in his baggy pants and worn jackets, beloved by neighbors and children.

Yet Howard, like the inventors, enlighteners, self-taught theorists, and self-proclaimed prophets of the "age of improvement" in which he lived, was one of those little men with munificent hopes. His contribution was "the Garden City," a plan for moderate decentralization and cooperative socialism. He wanted to build wholly new cities in the midst of unspoiled countryside on land that would remain the property of the community as a whole. Limited in size to 30,000 inhabitants and surrounded by a perpetual "green belt," the Garden City would be compact, efficient, healthful, and beautiful. It would lure people away from swollen cities like London and their dangerous concentrations of wealth and power; at the same time, the countryside would be dotted with hundreds of new communities where small-scale cooperation and direct democracy could flourish.

Howard never met either Frank Lloyd Wright or Le Corbusier. One suspects those two architects of genius and forceful personalities would have considered themselves worlds apart from the modest stenographer. Yet it is notable that Wright and Le Corbusier, like Howard, began their work in urban planning as outsiders, learning their profession not in architectural schools but through apprenticeships with older architects and through their own studies. This self-education was the source of their initiation into both urban design and social theory, and it continued even after Wright and Le Corbusier had become masters of their own profession. Their interests and readings flowed naturally from architecture and design to city planning, economics, politics, and the widest questions of social thought. No one ever told them they could not know everything.

Frank Lloyd Wright stands between Howard and Le Corbusier, at least in age. If Howard's dominant value was cooperation, Wright's was individualism. And no one can deny that he practiced what he preached. With the handsome profile and proud bearing of a frontier patriarch, carefully brushed long hair, well-tailored suits and flowing cape, Wright was his own special creation. His character was an inextricable mix of arrogance and honesty, vanity and genius. He was autocratic, impolitic, and spendthrift; yet he maintained a magnificent faith in his own ideal of "organic" architecture.

Wright wanted the whole United States to become a nation of individuals. His planned city, which he called "Broadacres," took decentralization beyond the small community (Howard's ideal) to the individual family home. In Broadacres all cities larger than a county seat have disappeared. The center of society has moved to the thousands of homesteads that cover the countryside. Everyone has the right to as much land as he can use, a minimum of an acre per person. Most people work part-time on their farms and part-time in the small factories, offices, or shops that are nestled among the farms. A network of superhighways joins together the scattered elements of society. Wright believed that individuality must be founded on individual ownership. Decentralization would make it possible for everyone to live his chosen lifestyle on his own land.

Le Corbusier, our third planner, could claim with perhaps even more justification than Wright to be his own creation. He was born Charles-Édouard Jeanneret and grew up in the Swiss city of La Chaux-de-Fonds, where he was apprenticed to be a watchcase engraver. He was saved from that dying trade by a sympathetic teacher and by his own determination. Settling in Paris in 1916, he won for himself a place at the head of the avant-garde, first with his painting, then with his brilliant architectural criticism, and most profoundly with his own contributions to architecture. The Swiss artisan Jeanneret no longer existed. He had recreated himself as "Le Corbusier," the Parisian leader of the revolution in modern architecture.

Like other "men from the provinces" who settled in Paris, Le Corbusier identified himself completely with the capital and its values. Wright had hoped that decentralization would preserve the social value he prized most highly – individuality. Le Corbusier placed a corresponding faith in organization, and he foresaw a very different fate for modern society. For him, industrialization meant great cities where large bureaucracies could coordinate production. Whereas Wright thought that existing cities were at least a hundred times too dense, Le Corbusier thought they were not dense enough. He proposed that large tracts in the center of Paris and other major cities be leveled. In place of the old buildings, geometrically arrayed skyscrapers of glass and steel would rise out of parks, gardens, and superhighways. These towers would be the command posts for their region. They would house a technocratic elite of planners, engineers, and intellectuals who would bring beauty and prosperity to the whole society. In his first version of the ideal city, Le Corbusier had the elite live in luxurious high-rise apartments close to the center; their subordinates were relegated to satellite cities at the outskirts. (In a later version everyone was to live in the high-rises.) Le Corbusier called his plan "'the Radiant City,' a city worthy of our time."

The plans of Howard, Wright, and Le Corbusier can be summarized briefly, but the energy and resources necessary to carry them out can hardly be conceived. One might expect that the three ideal cities were destined to remain on paper. Yet, as we shall see, their proposals have already reshaped many of the cities we now live in, and may prove to be even more influential in the future.

The plans were effective because they spoke directly to hopes and fears that were widely shared. In particular, they reflected (1) the pervasive fear of and revulsion from the nineteenth-century metropolis; (2) the sense that modern technology had made possible exciting new urban forms; and (3) the great expectation that a revolutionary age of brotherhood and freedom was at hand.

Caught in our own urban crisis, we tend to romanticize the teeming cities of the turn of the century. To many of their inhabitants, however, they were frightening and unnatural phenomena. Their unprecedented size and vast, uprooted populations seemed to suggest the uncontrollable forces unleashed by the Industrial Revolution, and the chaos that occupied the center of modern life. Joseph Conrad eloquently expressed this feeling when he confessed to being haunted by the vision of a "monstrous town more populous than some continents and in its man-made might as if indifferent to heaven's frowns and smiles; a cruel devourer of the world's light. There was room enough there to place any story, depth enough there for any passion, variety enough for any setting, darkness enough to bury five millions of lives."[1]

The monstrous proportions of the big city were relatively new, and thus all the more unsettling. In the first half of the nineteenth century the great European cities had overflowed their historic walls and fortifications. (The American cities, of course, never knew such limits.) Now boundless, the great cities expanded into the surrounding countryside with reckless speed, losing the coherent structure of a healthy organism. London grew in the nineteenth century from 900,000 to 4.5 million inhabitants; Paris in the same period quintupled its population, from 500,000 to 2.5 million residents. Berlin went from 190,000 to over 2 million, New York from 60,000 to 3.4 million. Chicago, a village in 1840, reached 1.7 million by the turn of the century.[2]

This explosive growth, which would have been difficult to accommodate under any circumstances, took place in an era of laissez-faire and feverish speculation. The cities lost the power to control their own growth. Instead, speculation – the blind force of chance and profit – determined urban structure. The cities were segregated by class, their traditional unifying centers first overwhelmed by the increase in population and then abandoned. Toward the end of the nineteenth century the residential balance between urban and rural areas began tipping, in an unprecedented degree, towards the great cities. When Howard, Wright, and Le Corbusier began their work, they saw around them stagnation in the countryside, the depopulation of rural villages, and a crisis in even the old regional centers. First trade and then the most skilled and ambitious young people moved to the metropolis.

Some of these newcomers found the good life they had been seeking in attractive new middle-class neighborhoods, but most were caught in the endless rows of tenements that stretched for miles, interrupted only by factories or railroad yards. Whole families were crowded into one or two airless rooms fronting on narrow streets or filthy courtyards where sunlight never penetrated. In Berlin in 1900, for example, almost 50 percent of all families lived in tenement dwellings with only one small room and an even smaller kitchen. Most of the rest lived in apartments with two tiny rooms and a kitchen, but to pay their rent, some of these had to take in boarders who slept in the corners.[3] "Look at the cities of the nineteenth century," wrote Le Corbusier, "at the vast stretches covered with the crust of houses without heart and furrowed with streets without soul. Look, judge. These are the signs of a tragic denaturalization of human labor."[4]

Howard, Wright, and Le Corbusier hated the cities of their time with an overwhelming passion. The metropolis was the counter-image of their ideal cities, the hell that inspired their heavens. They saw precious resources, material and human, squandered in the urban disorder. They were especially fearful that the metropolis would attract and then consume all the healthful forces in society. All three visualized the great city as a cancer, an uncontrolled, malignant growth that was poisoning the modern world. Wright remarked that the plan of a large city resembled "the cross-section of a fibrous tumor"; Howard compared it to an enlarged ulcer. Le Corbusier was fond of picturing Paris as a body in the last stages of a fatal disease – its circulation clogged, its tissues dying of their own noxious wastes.

The three planners, moreover, used their insight into technology to go beyond a merely negative critique of the nineteenth-century metropolis. They showed how modern techniques of construction had created a new mastery of space from which innovative urban forms could be built. The great city, they argued, was no longer modern. Its chaotic concentration was not only inefficient and inhumane, it was unnecessary as well.

Howard, Wright, and Le Corbusier based their ideas on the technological innovations that inspired their age: the express train, the automobile, the telephone and radio, and the skyscraper. Howard realized that the railroad system that had contributed to the growth of the great cities could serve the planned decentralization of society equally well. Wright understood that the personal automobile and an elaborate network of roads could create the conditions for an even more radical decentralization. Le Corbusier looked to technology to promote an opposite trend. He made use of the skyscraper as a kind of vertical street, a "street in the air" as he called it, which would permit intensive urban densities while eliminating the "soulless streets" of the old city.

The three planners' fascination with technology was deep but highly selective. They acknowledged only what served their own social values. Modern technology, they believed, had outstripped the antiquated social order, and the result was chaos and strife. In their ideal cities, however, technology would fulfill its proper role. Howard, Wright, and Le Corbusier believed that industrial society was inherently harmonious. It had an inherent structure, an ideal form, which, when achieved, would banish conflict and bring order and freedom, prosperity and beauty.

This belief went far beyond what could be deduced from the order and power of technology itself. It reflected instead the revolutionary hopes of the nineteenth century. For the three planners, as for so many of their contemporaries, the conflicts of the early Industrial Revolution were only a time of troubles which would lead inevitably to the new era of harmony. History for them was still the history of progress; indeed, as Howard put it, there was a "grand purpose behind nature." These great expectations, so difficult for us to comprehend, pervaded nineteenth-century radical and even liberal thought. There were many prophets of progress who contributed to creating the optimistic climate of opinion in which Howard, Wright, and Le Corbusier formed their own beliefs. Perhaps the most relevant for our purposes were the "utopian socialists" of the early nineteenth century.

These reformers, most notably Charles Fourier, Robert Owen, and Henri de Saint-Simon, drew upon the tradition of Thomas More's *Utopia* and Plato's *Republic* to create detailed depictions of communities untainted by the class struggles of the Industrial Revolution. Unlike More or Plato, however, the utopian socialists looked forward to the immediate realization of their ideal commonwealths. Owen and Fourier produced detailed plans for building utopian communities, plans for social and architectural revolution which anticipated some of the work of Howard, Wright, and Le Corbusier. Two themes dominated utopian socialist planning: first, a desire to overcome the distinction between city and country; and second, a desire to overcome the physical isolation of individuals and families by grouping the community into one large "family" structure. Most of the designs envisioned not ideal cities but ideal communes, small rural establishments for less than 2,000 people. Owen put forward a plan for brick quadrangles which he called "moral quadrilaterals." One side was a model factory, while the other three were taken up with a communal dining room, meeting rooms for recreation, and apartments.[5] His French rival Fourier advanced a far more elaborate design for a communal palace or "phalanstery" which boasted theaters, fashionable promenades, gardens, and gourmet cuisine for everyone.[6]

The utopian socialists were largely forgotten by the time Howard, Wright, and Le Corbusier began their own work, so there was little direct influence from them. As we shall see, however, the search of each planner for a city whose design expressed the ideals of cooperation and social justice led him to revive many of the themes of his utopian socialist (and even earlier) predecessors. But one crucial element sharply separates the three planners' designs from all previous efforts. Even the most fantastic inventions of an Owen or a Fourier could not anticipate the new forms that twentieth-century technology would bring to urban design. The utopian socialists' prophecies of the future had to be expressed in the traditional architectural vocabulary. Fourier, for example, housed his cooperative community in a "phalanstery" that looked like the château of Versailles. Howard, Wright, and Le Corbusier were able to incorporate the scale and pace of the modern world into their designs. They worked at the dawn of the twentieth-century industrial era, but before the coming of twentieth-century disillusionment. Their imaginations were wholly modern; yet the coming era of cooperation was as real to them as it had been for Robert Owen. Their ideal cities thus stand at the intersection of nineteenth-century hopes and twentieth-century technology.

The three ideal cities, therefore, possessed a unique scope and fervor, but this uniqueness had its dangers. It effectively isolated the three planners from almost all the social movements and institutions of their time. In particular, it separated them from the members of two groups who might have been their natural allies, the Marxian socialists and the professional planners. The three ideal cities were at once too technical for the Marxists and too revolutionary for the growing corps of professional planners. The latter was especially intent on discouraging any suggestion that urban planning might serve the cause of social change. These architect–administrators confined themselves to "technical" problems, which meant, in practice, serving the needs of society – as society's rulers defined them. Baron Haussmann, that model of an administrative planner, had ignored and sometimes worsened the plight of the poor in his massive reconstructions of Paris undertaken for Louis Napoleon. But the plight of the poor was not his administrative responsibility. He wanted to unite the isolated sectors of the city and thus quicken the pace of commerce. The wide avenues he cut through Paris were also designed to contribute to the prestige of the regime and, if necessary, to serve as efficient conduits for troops to put down urban disorders. Haussmann's physically impressive and socially reactionary plans inspired worldwide imitation and further increased the gap between urban design and social purpose.[7]

Even the middle-class reformers who specifically dedicated themselves to housing and urban improvement were unable to close this gap. Men like Sir Edwin Chadwick in London bravely faced official indifference and corruption to bring clean air, adequate sanitation, and minimal standards of housing to the industrial cities. Yet these philanthropists were also deeply conservative in their social beliefs. Their rare attempts at innovation almost always assumed the continued poverty of the poor and the privileges of the rich. The model tenements, "cheap cottages," and factory towns that were commissioned in the second half of the nineteenth century were filled with good intentions and sound planning, but they never failed to reflect the inequities of the society that built them. When, for example, the English housing reformer Octavia Hill built her model tenements, she kept accommodations to a minimum so that her indigent tenants could pay rents sufficient not only to cover the complete cost of construction, but also to yield her wealthy backers 5 percent annual interest on the money they had advanced her.[8] (This kind of charitable enterprise was known as "philanthropy at 5 percent.") Not surprisingly, designs put forward under these conditions were almost as bleak as the slums they replaced.

Howard, Wright, and Le Corbusier were not interested in making existing cities more profitable or in building "model" tenements to replace the old ones. These views might have been expected to have attracted the sympathetic attention of the Marxian socialists who then controlled the most powerful European movements for social change. Indeed, the *Communist Manifesto* had already recognized the necessity for radical structural change in the industrial cities by putting the "gradual abolition of the distinction between town and country" among its demands. Nevertheless, the socialist movement in the second half of the nineteenth century turned away from what its leaders regarded as unprofitable speculation. In an important series of articles collected under the title *The Housing Question* (1872), Friedrich Engels maintained that urban design was part of the "superstructure" of capitalist society and would necessarily reflect that society's inhumanities, at least until after the socialist revolution had succeeded in transforming the economic base. He concluded that any attempt to envision an ideal city without waiting for the revolution was futile and, indeed, that any attempt to improve the cities signif-icantly was doomed so long as capitalism endured. The working class must forget attractive visions of the future and concentrate on immediate revolution after which the dictatorship of the proletariat would redistribute housing in the old industrial cities according to need. Then and only then could planners begin to think about a better kind of city.[9]

Howard, Wright, and Le Corbusier could therefore look neither to the socialists nor to the professional planners for support. Initially, at least, they were forced back upon themselves. Instead of developing their ideas through collaboration with others and through practical experience, they worked in isolation on more and more elaborate models of their basic ideas. Their ideal cities thus acquired a wealth of brilliant detail and a single-minded theoretical rigor that made them unique. This isolation was no doubt the necessary precondition for the three plan-ners' highly individual styles of social thought. Certainly their mercurial and independent careers showed a very different pattern from the solid institutional connections of, for example, Ludwig Mies van der Rohe or Walter Gropius. Mies, Gropius, and the other Bauhaus architects were also deeply concerned with the question of design and society; yet none of them produced an ideal city. They had more practical but also more limited projects to occupy them.[10] The ideal city is the genre of the outsider who travels at one leap from complete powerlessness to imaginary omnipotence.

This isolation encouraged Howard, Wright, and Le Corbusier to extend their intellectual and imaginative capacities to their limits, but it also burdened their plans with almost insurmountable problems of both thought and action. They had cre-ated plans that were works of art, but the city, in Claude Lévi-Strauss' phrase, is a "*social* work of art." Its densely interwoven structure is the product of thousands of minds and thousands of individual decisions. Its variety derives from the unexpected juxtapositions and the unpredictable interactions. How can a single individual, even a man of genius, hope to comprehend this structure? And how can he devise a new plan with the same satisfying complexities? For his design, whatever its logic and merits, is necessarily his alone. In imposing a single point of view, he inevitably simplifies the parts which make up the whole. Howard, Wright, and Le Corbusier each filled his ideal city with *his* buildings; *his* sense of proportion and color; and, most profoundly, with *his* social values. Would there ever be room for anyone else? The three ideal cities raise what is perhaps the most perplexing question for any planner: in attempting to create a new urban order, must he repress precisely that complexity, diversity, and individuality which are the city's highest achievements?

The problem of action was equally obvious and pressing. Deprived of outside support, the three planners came to believe that their ideas were inherently powerful. As technical solutions to urban problems and embodiments of justice and beauty, the three ideal cities could properly claim everyone's support. By holding up a ready-made plan for a new order, Howard, Wright, and Le Corbusier hoped to create their own movements. This strategy, however, led directly to the classic utopian dilemma. To appeal to everyone on the basis of universal principles is to appeal to no one in particular. The more glorious the plans are in theory, the more remote they are from the concrete issues that actually motivate action. With each elaboration and clarification, the ideal cities move closer to pure fantasy. Can imagination alone change the world? Or, as Friedrich Engels phrased the question: how can the isolated individual hope to *impose his idea* on history?

These two related problems of thought and action confronted Howard, Wright, and Le Corbusier throughout their careers; yet they never doubted that ultimately they could solve both. Each believed that if a planner based his work on the structure inherent in industrial society and on the deepest values of his culture, there could be no real conflict between his plan and individual liberty. Patiently, each searched for that harmonious balance between control and freedom: the order that does not repress but liberates the individual.

With equal determination, they sought a valid strategy for action. Their ideal cities, they knew, could never be constructed all at once. But at least a "working model" could be begun, even in the midst of the old society. This model would demonstrate both the superiority of their architectural principles and also serve as a symbol of the new society about to be born. Its success would inspire emulation. A movement of reconstruction would take on momentum and become a revolutionary force in itself. Rebuilding the cities could thus become, in a metaphor all three favored, the "Master Key" that would unlock the way to a just society.

The three planners, therefore, looked to the new century with confidence and hope. Against the overwhelming power of the great cities and the old order that built them, Howard, Wright, and Le Corbusier advanced their designs for planned growth, for the reassertion of the common interest and higher values, for a healthy balance between man's creation and the natural environment. It would seem to be an uneven contest. Nevertheless, the three planners still believed that an individual and his imagination could change history. The revolution they were seeking was precisely an assertion of human rationality over vast impersonal forces. They resolved that in the coming era of reconciliation and construction, the man of imagination must play a crucial role. He would embody the values of his society in a workable plan, and thus direct social change with his prophetic leadership. For Howard, Wright, and Le Corbusier, this next revolution would finally bring imagination to power. "What gives our dreams their daring," Le Corbusier proclaimed, "is that they can be achieved."[11]

Ebenezer Howard: The Ideal City Made Practicable

Town and country *must be married*, and out of this joyous union will spring a new hope, a new life, a new civilization. (Ebenezer Howard 1898)

Of the three planners discussed here, Ebenezer Howard is the least known and the most influential. His *To-morrow: A Peaceful Path to Real Reform* (1898, now known under the title of the 1902 edition, *Garden Cities of To-Morrow*) has, as Lewis Mumford acknowledged, "done more than any other single book to guide the modern town planning movement and to alter its objectives."[12] And Howard was more than a theoretician. He and his supporters founded two English cities, Letchworth (1903) and Welwyn (1920), which still serve as models for his ideas. More important, he was able to organize a city planning movement which continues to keep his theories alive. The postwar program of New Towns in Great Britain, perhaps the most ambitious of all attempts at national planning, was inspired by his works and planned by his followers.

In the United States the "Greenbelt Cities" undertaken by the Resettlement Administration in the 1930s owed their form to the example of the Garden City. The best recent example of an American New Town is Columbia, Maryland, built in the 1960s as a wholly independent community with houses and industry. In 1969 the National Committee on Urban Growth Policy urged that the United States undertake to build 110 New Towns to accommodate 20 million citizens.[13] The following year, Congress created a New Town Corporation in the Department of Housing and Urban Development to begin this vast task.[14] [At the time of writing], sixteen American New Towns have either been planned or are under construction. The most fruitful period of Ebenezer Howard's influence is perhaps only beginning.

If Howard's achievements continue to grow in importance, Howard the man remains virtually unknown. The present-day New Town planners are perhaps a little embarrassed by him. They are highly skilled professional bureaucrats or architects; Howard's formal education ended at fourteen, and he had no special training in architecture or urban design. The modern planners are self-proclaimed "technicians" who have attempted to adapt the New Town concept to any established social order. Howard was, in his quiet way, a revolutionary who originally conceived the Garden City as a means of superseding capitalism and creating a civilization based on cooperation. Howard's successors have neglected this aspect of his thought, and without it the founder of the Garden City movement becomes an elusive figure indeed. He shrank from the personal publicity which Frank Lloyd Wright and Le Corbusier so eagerly and so skillfully sought. Throughout his life he maintained the habits and the appearance of a minor clerk. He once said that he enjoyed his chosen profession, stenography, because it enabled him to be an almost invisible observer at the notable events he recorded. Even at the meetings of the association he headed, he preferred to sit in an inconspicuous position behind the podium, where he could take down the exact words of the other speakers. Frederic J. Osborn, one of his closest associates, remembered him as "the sort of man who could easily pass unnoticed in a crowd."[15] He was, Osborn added, "the mildest and most unassuming of men … universally liked, and notably by children."[16]

Nonetheless, Howard succeeded where more charismatic figures failed. In 1898 he had to borrow £50 to print *To-morrow* at his own expense. Five years later his supporters were advancing more than £100,000 to begin the construction of the first Garden City. The rapidity of this turn of events surprised Howard and is still difficult to explain. The root of the mystery is Howard himself. He had reached middle age before beginning his work on city planning and had never given any indication that he was capable of originality or leadership. His book, however, was a remarkable intellectual achievement. He concisely and rigorously outlined a new direction for the development of cities and advanced practical solutions that covered the whole range of city planning problems: land use, design, transportation, housing, and finance. At the same time, he incorporated these ideas into a large synthesis: a plan for a complete alternative society and a program for attaining it.

Howard, moreover, proved to be a surprisingly effective organizer. He was an indefatigable worker who bent with slavelike devotion to the task of promoting his own ideas. At cooperative societies, Labour Churches, settlement houses, temperance unions, debating clubs – at any group that would pay his railroad fares and provide a night's hospitality – he preached the "Gospel of the Garden City" under the title "The Ideal City Made Practicable, A Lecture Illustrated with Lantern Slides." He possessed a powerful speaking voice, and, more important, he was able to communicate an overwhelming sense of earnestness, an absolute conviction that he had discovered "the peaceful path to real reform." Mankind, he proclaimed, was moving inevitably toward a new era of brotherhood, and the Garden City would be the only fitting environment for the humanity of the future. His original supporters were not planners or architects but social reformers whose own dreams he promised would be realized in the Garden City. Patiently, he assembled a broad coalition of backers that ranged from "Back to the Land" agrarians to George Bernard Shaw. Working constantly himself, he felt free to draw upon the resources and talents of others. He thus made his ideas the basis of a movement which, fifty years after his death, continues to grow. As one of Shaw's characters in *Major Barbara* observes, absolute unselfishness is capable of anything.

[…]

Ebenezer Howard: Design for Cooperation

Between 1889 and 1892 Howard created the basic plan for his ideal community. He envisaged his Garden City as a tightly organized urban center for 30,000 inhabitants, surrounded by a perpetual "green belt" of farms and parks. Within the city there would be both quiet residential neighborhoods and facilities for a full range of commercial, industrial, and cultural activities. For Howard did not conceive the Garden City as a specialized "satellite town" or "bedroom town" perpetually serving some great metropolis. Rather, he foresaw the great cities of his time shrinking to insignificance as their people desert them for a new way of life in a decentralized society. No longer would a single metropolis dominate a whole region or even a whole nation. Nor would the palatial edifices and giant organizations of the big city continue to rule modern society. Instead, the urban population would be distributed among hundreds of Garden Cities whose small scale and diversity of functions embody a world in which the little person has finally won out.

Howard does not seem to have been familiar with the designs for geometric cities that utopian socialists had put forward earlier in the nineteenth century. Nonetheless the perfectly circular, perfectly symmetrical plan he devised for the Garden City bears a distinct resemblance to some of these, notably James Silk Buckingham's cast-iron Victoria (1849).[17] The explanation, however, lies not in direct influence but in shared values. For Howard had inherited that tradition in English utopian thought in which it was assumed that society could be improved just as a machine could – through the appropriate adjustments. A properly functioning society would thus take on the precise and well-calculated look of a good machine.

For Howard, therefore, there was nothing merely "mechanical" in the relentless symmetry of the Garden City. He wanted to make the design the physical embodiment of his ideal of cooperation, and he believed that his perfectly circular plan would best meet the needs of the citizens. He promised that every building would be "so placed to secure maximum utility and convenience."[18] This "unity of design and purpose" had been impossible in old cities formed, in Howard's view, by "an infinite number of small, narrow, and selfish decisions."[19] In the Garden City, however, an active common interest would make possible a uniform, comprehensive plan. With selfish obstructions removed, the city could assume that geometric form which Howard believed was the most efficient and the most beautiful. The symmetry of the Garden City would be the symbol and product of cooperation, the sign of a harmonious society.

The only relevant book he remembered reading was written by a physician, Dr Benjamin Richardson, and entitled *Hygeia, A City of Health*.[20] It was an imaginative presentation of the principles of public sanitation in which Dr Richardson depicted a city whose design would be the healthiest for its inhabitants. He prescribed a population density of twenty-five people per acre, a series of wide, tree-shaded avenues, and homes and public gardens surrounded by greenery. "Instead of the gutter the poorest child has the garden; for the foul sight and smell of unwholesome garbage, he has flowers and green sward."[21] Howard was happy to follow this prescription. The public health movement, of which Dr Richardson was a prominent representative, was a vital force for civic action; it had persuaded the public that there was a strong correlation between the health of a community and its political and moral soundness. Howard maintained that the Garden Cities would be the healthiest in the nation. He incorporated the low population density, the wide avenues, and other features of *Hygeia* into the geometry of his own city.

The problem of health was especially important because Howard planned the Garden City to be a manufacturing center in which the factories would necessarily be close to the homes. In order to separate the residential areas and also to ensure that everyone would be within walking distance of his place of work, Howard put the factories at the periphery of the city, adjacent to the circular railroad that surrounds the town and connects it to the main line. Here one can find the enterprises appropriate to a decentralized society: the small machine shop, or the cooperative printing works, or the jam factory where the rural cooperative processes its members' fruits. As usual in the plan, physical location has a symbolic aspect. Industry has its place and its function, but these are at the outskirts of the community. Howard had little faith in the role of work – even if cooperatively organized – to provide the unifying force in society. This he left to leisure and civic enterprise.

There are two kinds of centers in the Garden City: the neighborhood centers and the (one) civic center. The neighborhoods, or "wards" as Howard called them, are slices in the circular pie. Each ward comprises one-sixth of the town, 5,000 people or about 1,000 families. Each, said Howard, "should in some sense be a complete town by itself" (he imagined the Garden City being built ward by ward).[22] The basic unit in the neighborhood is the family living in its own home surrounded by a garden. Howard hoped to be able to provide houses with gardens to all classes. Most residents would be able to afford a lot 20 by 130 feet; the most substantial homes would be arranged in crescents bordering Grand Avenue, a park and promenade that forms the center of the ward. In the middle of Grand Avenue is the most important neighborhood institution, the school. This, Howard commented, should be the first building constructed in each ward and will serve as a library, a meeting hall, and even as a site for religious worship. Churches, when they are built, also occupy sites in Grand Avenue.[23]

There are two cohesive forces that bring the residents out of their neighborhoods and unite the city. The first is leisure. The center of the town is a Central Park, which provides "ample recreation grounds within very easy access of all the people."[24] Surrounding the park is a glassed-in arcade, which Howard calls the "Crystal Palace": "Here manufactured goods are exposed for sale, and here most of that class of shopping which requires the joy of deliberation and selection is done."[25]

The Crystal Palace, in addition to providing an attractive setting for consumption, also permits the town, by granting or withholding leases, to exercise some control over distribution. Howard, as always, recommended a balance between individualism and central organization. He rejected the idea of one great cooperative department store run by the community, like the one in *Looking Backward*. Instead, he advocated that there be many small shops, but only one for each category of goods. If customers complain that a merchant is abusing his monopoly, the town rents space in the Crystal Palace to another shopkeeper in the same field, whose competition then restores adequate service. Whatever the merits of this solution, it aptly reflects the Radical ambivalence toward the trades that supported so many of them, the desire for economic independence without the self-destructive competition that accompanied it.

Important as consumption and leisure were in his system, Howard nonetheless reserved the very center of the Central Park to the second cohesive force, "civil spirit." He wanted an impressive and meaningful setting for the "large public buildings": town hall, library, museum, concert and lecture hall, and the hospital. Here the highest values of the community are brought together – culture, philanthropy, health, and mutual cooperation.

We might wonder what kind of cultural life a Garden City of 30,000 could enjoy, but this question did not bother Howard. He never felt the need of that intensification of experience – the extremes of diversity and excellence – that only a metropolis can offer. We must also remember, however, that Howard lived in a milieu that did not look to others to provide entertainment or enlightenment. The English middle class and a sizable part of the working class created its own culture in thousands of voluntary groups: lecture societies, choral groups, drama guilds, chamber symphonies. Here, as elsewhere, Howard disdained the kind of centralization that focused the life of a nation on a few powerful metropolitan institutions. He looked to small-scale voluntary cooperation not only for the economic base of the community but also for its highest cultural attainments.

The Garden City occupies 1,000 acres in the middle of a tract of 5,000 acres reserved for farms and forests.[26] This "Agricultural Belt" plays an integral role in the economy of the Garden City; the 2,000 farmers who live there supply the town with the bulk of its food. Because transportation costs are almost nonexistent, the farmer receives a good price for his produce, and the consumer gets fresh vegetables and dairy products at a reduced price. The Agricultural Belt, moreover, prevents the town from sprawling out into the countryside and ensures that the citizens enjoy both a compact urban center and ample open countryside. "One of the first essential needs of Society and of the individual," wrote Howard, "is that every man, every woman, every child should have ample space in which to live, to move, and to develop."[27] He added a new element to the rights of man – the right to space.

The Garden City in all its aspects expressed Howard's ideal of a cooperative commonwealth. It was the Zion in which he and his fellow Radicals could be at ease, the environment in which all the Radical hopes could be realized. Yet the Garden City was more than an image of felicity for Howard had carefully wedded his vision of the ideal city to a concrete plan for action. Indeed, he devoted relatively little attention to the details of the new city and a great deal to the means of achieving it. He wanted to show that there was no need to wait for a revolution to build the Garden City: it could be undertaken immediately by a coalition of Radical groups working within the capitalist system. The first successful Garden City would be a working model of a better society, and those that succeeded it would decisively alter English society. Building the Garden City was itself the revolution. The planned transformation of the environment was the nonviolent but effective strategy that the Radical movement had been seeking. The Garden City was, as Howard put it, "the peaceful path to real reform."

Howard wanted the building of the first Garden City to be an example of voluntary cooperation, and he devoted most of his book to outlining and defending his method. The key to Howard's strategy was his contention that building a new city could be *practical*, i.e., that money advanced for its construction could be paid back with interest. Funds could thus be solicited from high-minded and thrifty Radicals with the assurance that they would be both helping the cause and earning a modest return for themselves. The germ of Howard's scheme could be found in an article written in 1884 by the distinguished economist Alfred Marshall.[28] Marshall had pointed out that the rail networks that covered Great Britain rendered the concentration of so many businesses in London economically irrational. Many businesses could be carried out far more cheaply, efficiently, and pleasantly where land was inexpensive and abundant. Marshall proposed that committees be established to buy up suitable land outside London and coordinate the movement of factories and working people. The value of the land in these new industrial parks would rise sharply, and the committees that owned them would reap a handsome profit.

Howard, who knew both the proposal and its author,[29] took up this suggestion and transformed it to suit his own ends. He began by asking the reader to assume that a group of his supporters – "gentlemen of responsible position and undoubted probity and honor," as he hopefully described them – had banded together to form a nonprofit company. They would raise money by issuing bonds yielding a fixed rate (4 or 5 percent), purchase 6,000 acres of agricultural land, and lay out a city according to Howard's plans. They would build roads, power and water plants, and all other necessities, and then seek to attract industry and residents. The company would continue to own all the land; as the population rose, the rents too would rise from the low rate per acre for agricultural land to the more substantial rate of a city with 30,000 residents. All rent would go to the company and would be used to repay the original investors. Any surplus that remained after the financial obligations had been discharged would provide additional services to the community.[30]

Howard proposed, in other words, that the Garden City be founded and financed by philanthropic land speculation. The scheme was speculative because it was a gamble on the rise in values that would result from attracting 30,000 people to a plot of empty farmland, and philanthropic because the speculators agreed in advance to forgo all but a fixed portion of the expected profits. The concept was not original with Howard. "Philanthropy at 5 percent" was a familiar feature in

English reform circles, and activists from the Owenites to the Christian Socialists made use of fixed-dividend corporations to raise money for cooperative stores and workshops. The Reverend Charles Kingsley, a Christian Socialist, aptly illustrated the spirit of this reconciliation of God and Mammon when he exhorted his followers to "seek first the Kingdom of God and his Righteousness with this money of yours and see if all things – profits and suchlike – are not added unto you."[31]

Howard did add a new emphasis to this method. He stipulated that part of the rental income each year be placed in a sinking fund and used to purchase the bonds of the original investors. As the number of bondholders decreased, the amount that the company had to pay each year to the ones remaining would also decrease. Meanwhile, income from rents would be constantly growing as the town grew; the surplus, as we have seen, was earmarked for community services. Eventually the Garden City would buy out all the original investors, and the entire income from rents could be used to benefit the citizens. Taxes would be unnecessary; rents alone would generously support schools, hospitals, cultural institutions, and charities.[32]

The residents of the Garden City would thus continue to pay rent, but landlords would be eliminated. The private ownership of land for the benefit of individuals would be replaced by collective ownership for the benefit of the community. Howard placed tremendous emphasis on this change. He, like almost every other Radical, believed that the "land question" – the concentration of the ownership of land in Great Britain in the hands of a few – was, as he put it, the "root of all our problems."[33] As late as 1873 an official survey had shown that 80 percent of the land in the United Kingdom was owned by less than 7,000 persons.[34] The spread of Garden Cities would transfer land ownership on a large scale from individuals to the community, thus inaugurating an economic and social revolution.

Howard's analysis of the crucial importance of the "land question" derived from the writings of the American reformer Henry George, a hero of English Radicals in the 1880s. George was probably the most influential man of one idea in nineteenth-century Anglo-American history. His panacea, the Single Tax (the appropriation of all rent by taxation) was based on his view that there was no real conflict between capital and labor. The "antagonism of interests," he argued, "is in reality between labor and capital on the one side and land ownership on the other."[35] The great landowners used their natural monopoly to demand exorbitant rents and thus appropriate without compensation the lion's share of the increased wealth from material progress that ought to go to the workmen and entrepreneurs who actually produced it. This perversion of the economic order impoverished the proletariat, imperiled the manufacturer, and upset the natural balance of supply and demand. It was the real cause of depression, class conflict, and the spreading poverty that seemed an inevitable companion to progress.

Characteristically, Howard accepted everything in George's theory that pointed toward reconciliation and rejected everything that promised conflict. He rejected the Single Tax because he saw that it meant the expropriation of a whole class. He accepted, however, George's view that the solution to the land question would restore the economy to a healthy balance and create the conditions for a reconciliation of capital and labor. He believed he had found the solution to the land question himself. The Garden City, he wrote, "will, by a purely natural process, make it gradually impossible for any landlord class to exist at all." Private landholding "will die a natural but not too sudden death."[36] Building Garden Cities would accomplish all of George's aims "in a manner which need cause no ill-will, strife or bitterness; is constitutional; requires no revolutionary legislation; and involves no direct attack on vested interest."[37] The Garden City company would, in fact, enjoy all the privileges of a profit-making concern. The legal forms that landlords had designed to protect their own interests would now foster the creation of a higher form of society.

The powers extended to the Garden City company as sole landlord would be greater than the legal authority possessed by any nineteenth-century English municipality. Through its control of all leases it could effectively enforce the ground plan and zone the community without special legal authority. Howard was a firm believer in "gas and water socialism," and he stipulated that the town's board of management should provide all utilities on a nonprofit basis. He also thought the town might well establish municipal bakeries and laundries.[38]

Although the Garden City company would have the legal right to own and operate all the industry in the Garden City, Howard favored a balance of public and private control. The large factories on the periphery were clearly to be established by private industry, though Howard hoped that through profit sharing they would eventually take on a cooperative character. They still would be subject to the authority that the town as sole landlord could impose: No polluters or employers of "sweated" labor would be allowed.[39] The board of management would also share responsibility for public services with private citizens. Howard hoped that individuals would establish a large group of what he called "pro-municipal enterprises." These were public services whose necessity was not yet recognized by the majority of the citizens, but "those who have the welfare of society at heart [would], in the free air of the city, be always able to experiment on their own responsibility, … and enlarge the public understanding."[40] In addition to the more conventional charitable and philanthropic activities, "pro-municipal enterprises" included cooperative building and pension societies.

As income from rents grew, the municipality would gradually take over the services that voluntary cooperation had initiated. In industry, too, Howard believed the evolutionary trend was toward greater public ownership and control. The most important principle, however, was that no one have the right to impose a degree of socialism for which the citizens were not ready. The elimination of landlord's rents would remove, in Howard's view, any immediate conflict of capital with labor and permit the peaceful coexistence of capitalist and socialist industry. The balance between the public and private sectors must shift slowly with the increasing capacity of the citizens for cooperation.

Howard had the patience to begin with imperfect forms because he had the capacity to see his ideal society evolving in time. He realized that a single Garden

City of 30,000 was too small to provide the full measure of diversity that a genuine city must have. A Garden City could not, however, increase its size or density; that would spoil its plan. He proposed that it grow by establishing a new sister city beyond the Agricultural Belt. Howard believed that the cities should eventually organize themselves into "town clusters, each town in the cluster being of different design from the others, yet the whole forming one large and well-thought-out plan."[41] A diagram that appeared in *To-morrow* showed six Garden Cities arranged in a circle around a larger Center City. The plan had the cities connected by a circular canal which provided power, water, and transportation. In the 1902 edition the canal was replaced by a more sober rapid-transit system.[42]

The Social City, as Howard called each cluster of towns, represented his most advanced conception of the marriage of town and country; here "each inhabitant of the whole group, though in one sense living in a town of small size, would be in reality living in, and would enjoy all the advantages of, a great and most beautiful city; and yet all the fresh delights of the country … would be within a very few minutes' ride or walk."[43] With small communities already established as the basic units in society, these units could be arranged in planned federations to secure the benefits of larger size as well. Rapid communications between the towns meant greater convenience for trade, and, "because the people, in their collective capacity own the land on which this beautiful group of cities is built, the public buildings, the churches, the schools and universities, the libraries, picture galleries, theatres, would be on a scale of magnificence which no city in the world whose land is in pawn to private individuals can afford."[44] Once established, the Social City would become the base for still higher stages of evolution that Howard never ventured to describe.

Howard's reluctance to prescribe every detail or to foresee every contingency is one of the most important aspects of his method. The visionary planner can easily become a despot of the imagination. Working alone, deprived of the checks and balances of other minds, he is tempted to become the *roi soleil* of his realm and to order every detail of life of his ideal society. If Howard's geometric plans resemble a Baroque *Residenzstadt*, Howard himself was singularly free of the pretensions of a Baroque monarch. His plans, as he pointed out, were merely diagrams to be modified when put into practice.

The same may be said for his plans for social organization. In Howard's time the advocates of Socialism and Individualism (both usually capitalized) confronted each other like Matthew Arnold's ignorant armies. Bellamy, as we have seen, believed that the entire economy of the United States could be centrally directed by a few men of "fair ability." Herbert Spencer in his individualist phase held that the use of tax money to support public libraries was a step toward collectivist slavery.[45] Howard did not presume to judge this momentous debate. He made the spatial reorganization of society his fundamental demand because he believed that a new environment would open possibilities for the reconciliation of freedom and order that neither Bellamy nor Spencer could imagine. Howard sought to discover the minimum of organization that would secure the benefits of planning while leaving to individuals the greatest possible control over their own lives. He was a collectivist who hated bureaucratic paternalism and an apostle of organization who realized that planning must stay within self-imposed limits.

[…]

Le Corbusier: The Radiant City

The Radiant City retained the most important principle of the Contemporary City: the juxtaposition of a collective realm of order and administration with an individualistic realm of family life and participation. This juxtaposition became the key to Le Corbusier's attempt to resolve the syndicalist dilemma of authority and participation. Both elements of the doctrine receive intense expression in their respective spheres. Harmony is in the structure of the whole city and in the complete life of its citizens.

The Radiant City was a more daring and difficult synthesis than the Contemporary City. In his effort to realize the contradictory elements of syndicalism, Le Corbusier made the Radiant City at once more authoritarian and more libertarian than its predecessor. Within the sphere of collective life, authority has become absolute. The Contemporary City had lacked any single power to regulate all the separate private corporations that accomplished the essential work of society; Le Corbusier had then believed that the invisible hand of free competition would create the most efficient coordination. The Great Depression robbed him of his faith. He now held that organization must extend beyond the large corporations. They had rationalized their own organizations, but the economy as a whole remained wasteful, anarchic, irrational. The planned allocation of manpower and resources which had taken place within each corporation must now be accomplished for society. In the Radiant City every aspect of productive life is administered from above according to one plan. This plan replaces the marketplace with total administration; experts match society's needs to its productive capacities.

The preordained harmony which Le Corbusier had called for in urban reconstruction would now be imposed on all productive life. The great works of construction would become only one element in the plan. This was a crucial extension of the concept of planning. Ebenezer Howard and Frank Lloyd Wright had believed that once the environment had been designed, the sources of disorder in society would be minimized and individuals could be left to pursue their own initiatives. This belief rested on a faith in a "natural economic order," a faith which Le Corbusier no longer shared. He confronted a world threatened by chaos and collapse. It seemed that only discipline could create the order he sought so ardently. Coordination must become conscious and total. Above all, society needed authority and a plan.

Syndicalism, Le Corbusier believed, would provide a "pyramid of natural hierarchies" on which order and planning could be based. The bottom of this pyramid is the *syndicat*, the group of workers, white-collar employees, and engineers who run their own factory. The workers have the responsibility of choosing their most able colleague to be their manager and to represent them at the regional trade council. Le Corbusier believed that although citizens would usually find it impossible to identify the most able man among a host of politicians, each worker is normally able to choose his natural leader. "Every man is capable of judging the facts of his trade," he observed.[46]

The regional council of plant managers represents the first step in the hierarchy. Each level corresponds to a level of administrative responsibility. The manager runs his factory; the regional leaders administer the plants in their region. The regional council sends its most able members to a national council, which is responsible for the overall control of the trade. The leader of this council meets with his fellow leaders to administer the national plan. This highest group is responsible for coordinating the entire production of the country. If, for example, the national plan calls for mass housing, they allot the capital needed for each region and set the goals for production. The order is passed down to the regional council, which assigns tasks to individual factories and contractors. The elected representatives of the *syndicat* return from the regional council with instructions that determine his factory's role in the national productive effort.

This hierarchy of administration has replaced the state. As Saint-Simon had urged, a man's power corresponds exactly to his responsibilities in the structure of production. He issues the orders necessary for fulfilling his quotas, and these orders provide the direction that society needs. The divisive issues of parliamentary politics cannot arise, for everyone shares a common concern that the resources of society be administered as efficiently as possible. Even the tasks of the national council are administrative rather than political. The members do not apportion wealth and power among competing interests groups. Their task, like that of all the other functionaries, is a "technical" one: they carry out the plan.

"Plans are not political," Le Corbusier wrote.[47] The plan's complex provisions, covering every aspect of production, distribution, and construction, represent a necessary and objective ordering of society. The plan is necessary because the Machine Age requires conscious control. It is objective because the Machine Age imposes essentially the same discipline on all societies. Planning involves the rational mastery of industrial process and the application of that mastery to the specific conditions of each nation. The plan is a "rational and lyric monument" to man's capacity to organize.

The plan is formulated by an elite of experts detached from all social pressure. They work "outside the fevers of mayors' and prefects' offices," away from the "cries of electors and the cries of victims." Their plans are "established serenely, lucidly. They take account only of human truths."[48] In the planner's formulations, "the motive forces of a civilization pass from the subjective realm of consciousness to the objective realm of facts." Plans are "just, long-term, established on the realities of the century, imagined by a creative passion."[49]

This plan for Le Corbusier was more than a collection of statistics and instructions; it was a social work of art. It brought to consciousness the complex yet satisfying harmonies of an orderly productive world. It was the score for the great industrial orchestra. The plan summed up the unity that underlay the division of labor in society; it expressed the full range of exchange and cooperation that is necessary to an advanced economy.

Le Corbusier used the vocabulary and structures of syndicalism to advance his own vision of a beautifully organized world. His "pyramid of natural hierarchies" was intended to give the human structure of organization the same clarity and order as the great skyscrapers of the business center. The beauty of the organization was the product of the perfect cooperation of everyone in the hierarchy. It was the expression of human solidarity in creating a civilization in the midst of the hostile forces of nature. The natural hierarchy was one means of attaining the sublime.

Man at work creates a world that is truly human. But that world, once created, is a realm of freedom where man lives in accord with nature, not in opposition to it. Like the Contemporary City, the Radiant City identifies the realm of freedom with the residential district. As if in recognition of the need to counterbalance the industrial realm's increased emphasis on organization, Le Corbusier has displaced the towers of administration from the central position they occupied in the earlier plan. The residential district stands in the place of honor in the Radiant City.

It is, moreover, a transformed residential district. Le Corbusier had lost the enthusiasm for capitalism which had led him originally to segregate housing in the Contemporary City according to class – elite in the center, proletariat at the outskirts. Now he was a revolutionary syndicalist, with a new appreciation of workers' rights. When he visited the United States in 1935, he found much to admire in the luxury apartment houses that lined Central Park and Lake Shore Drive, but he added, "My own thinking is directed towards the crowds in the subway who come home at night to dismal dwellings. The millions of beings sacrificed to a life without hope, without rest – without sky, sun, greenery."[50] Housing in the Radiant City is designed for them. The residential district embodies Le Corbusier's new conviction that the world of freedom must be egalitarian. "If the city were to become a human city," he proclaimed, "it would be a city without classes."[51]

No longer does the residential district simply mirror the inequalities in the realm of production. Instead, the relation between the two is more complex, reflecting Le Corbusier's resolve to make the Radiant City a city of organization *and* freedom. The realm of production in the Radiant City is even more tightly organized, its hierarchies of command and subordination even stricter than in the Contemporary City. At the same time, the residential district – the realm of leisure and self-fulfillment – is radically libertarian, its principles of equality and cooperation standing in stark opposition to the hierarchy of the industrial world. The citizen in Le Corbusier's syndicalist society thus experiences both organization and freedom as part of his daily life.

The centers of life in the Radiant City are the great high-rise apartment blocks, which Le Corbusier calls "Unités." These structures, each of which is a neighborhood with 2,700 residents, mark the culmination of the principles of housing that he had been expounding since the Dom-Inos of 1914. Like the Dom-Ino house, the Unité represents the application of mass-production techniques; but where the Dom-Ino represents the principle in its most basic form, the Unité is a masterful expression of scale, complexity, and sophistication. The disappointments of the 1920s and the upheavals of the 1930s had only strengthened Le Corbusier in his faith that a great new age of the machine was about to dawn. In the plans for the Unité he realized that promise of a *collective* beauty that had been his aim in the Dom-Ino design; he achieved a collective grandeur, which the Dom-Ino houses had only hinted at; and finally, he foresaw for all the residents of the Unité a freedom and abundance beyond even that which he had planned for the elite of the Contemporary City. The apartments in the Unité are not assigned on the basis of a worker's position in the industrial hierarchy but according to the size of his family and their needs. In designing these apartments, Le Corbusier remarked that he "thought neither of rich nor of poor but of man."[52] He wanted to get away both from the concept of luxury housing, in which the wasteful consumption of space becomes a sign of status, and from the concept of *Existenzminimum*, the design of workers' housing based on the absolute hygienic minimums. He believed that housing could be made to the "human scale," right in its proportions for everyone, neither cramped nor wasteful. No one would want anything larger nor get anything smaller.

The emphasis in the Unité, however, is not on the individual apartment but on the collective services provided to all the residents. As in the Villa-Apartment Blocks of the Contemporary City, Le Corbusier followed the principle that the cooperative sharing of leisure facilities could give to each family a far more varied and beautiful environment than even the richest individual could afford in a single-family house. These facilities, moreover, take on a clear social function as the reward and recompense for the eight hours of disciplined labor in a factory or office that are required of all citizens in a syndicalist society. The Unité, for example, has a full range of workshops for traditional handicrafts whose techniques can no longer be practiced in industries devoted to mass production. Here are meeting rooms of all sizes for participatory activities that have no place in the hierarchical sphere of production. There are cafes, restaurants, and shops where sociability can be cultivated for its own sake. Most important, in Le Corbusier's own estimation, the Unité provides the opportunity for a full range of physical activities that are severely curtailed during working hours in an industrial society. Within each Unité there is a full-scale gymnasium; on the roof are tennis courts, swimming pools, and even sand beaches. Once again, the high-rise buildings cover only 15 percent of the land, and the open space around them is elaborately landscaped into playing fields, gardens, and parkland.

The most basic services which the Unité provides are those that make possible a new concept of the family. Le Corbusier envisioned a society in which men and women would work full-time as equals. He therefore presumed the end of the family as an economic unit in which women were responsible for domestic services while men worked for wages. In the Unité, cooking, cleaning, and child raising are services provided by society. Each building has its day-care center, nursery and primary school, cooperative laundry, cleaning service, and food store. In the Radiant City the family no longer has an economic function to perform. It exists as an end in itself.

Le Corbusier and Frank Lloyd Wright were both intensely concerned with the preservation of the family in an industrial society, but here as elsewhere they adopted diametrically opposite strategies. Wright wished to revive and strengthen the traditional economic role of the family, to ensure its survival by making it the center both of the society's work and of its leisure. Wright believed in a life in which labor and leisure would be one, whereas Le Corbusier subjected even the family to the stark division between work and play that marks the Radiant City. The family belongs to the realm of play. Indeed, it virtually ceases to exist during the working day. When mother and father leave their apartment in the morning for their jobs, their children accompany them down on the elevator. The parents drop them off at the floor where the school or day-care center is located and pick them up after work. The family reassembles in the afternoon, perhaps around the pool or at the gym, and when the family members return to their apartment they find it already cleaned, the laundry done and returned, the food ordered in the morning already delivered and prepared for serving. Individual families might still choose to cook their own food, do their own laundry, raise vegetables on their balconies, or even raise their own children. In the Radiant City, however, these activities have become leisure-time hobbies like woodworking or weaving, quaint relics of the pre-mechanical age.

The Unité is thus high-rise architecture for a new civilization, and Le Corbusier was careful to emphasize that its design could only be truly realized after society had been revolutionized. He therefore never concerned himself with such problems as muggings in the parks or vandalism in the elevators. In the Radiant City, crime and poverty no longer exist.

But if the Unité looks to the future, its roots are in the nineteenth-century utopian hopes for a perfect cooperative society, the same hopes that inspired Ebenezer Howard's cooperative quadrangles. Peter Serenyi has aptly compared the Unité to that French utopian palace of communal pleasures, the phalanstery of Charles Fourier.[53] An early nineteenth-century rival of Saint-Simon, Fourier envisioned a structure resembling the château of Versailles to house the 1,600 members of his "phalanx" or rural utopian community. "We have no conception of the compound or collective forms of luxury," Fourier complained, and the phalanstery was designed to make up that lack.[54] He believed that in a properly run society all man's desires could find their appropriate gratification. The phalanstery, therefore, contains an elaborate series of lavish public rooms: theaters, libraries, ballrooms, and Fourier's special pride, the dining rooms where "exquisite food and a piquant selection of dining companions" can always be found.

The phalanstery can be seen as the nineteenth-century anticipation and the Unité as the twentieth-century realization of architecture in the service of collective pleasure. Both designs represent what Le Corbusier termed "the architecture of happiness," architecture created to deliver what he was fond of calling "the essential joys." Fourier, however, could only express his vision in the anachronistic image of the baroque palace. Le Corbusier finds the forms of collective pleasure in the most advanced techniques of mass production. For him, the architecture of happiness is also the architecture for the industrial era.

The comparison of the phalanstery and the Unité suggests, finally, the complexity of Le Corbusier's ideal city. For Fourier was the bitter antagonist of Saint-Simon, whose philosophy is so central to Le Corbusier's social thought. The rivalry of the two nineteenth-century prophets was more than personal. Since their time, French utopian thought has been divided into two distinct traditions. The Saint-Simonian tradition is the dream of society as the perfect industrial hierarchy. Its setting is urban, its thought technological, its goal production, and its highest value organization. Fourier and his followers have envisioned society as the perfect community: rural, small-scaled, egalitarian, dedicated to pleasure and self-fulfillment. In the Radiant City, Le Corbusier combines these two traditions into an original synthesis. He places a Fourierist phalanstery in the center of a Saint-Simonian industrial society. Community and organization thus find intense and appropriate expression: both are integral parts of Le Corbusier's ideal city for the Machine Age.

Notes

1. Joseph Conrad, *The Secret Agent* (New York, 1953), p. 11. The quotation is drawn from the Preface, first published in 1921.
2. For statistics of urban growth, see Adna Ferrin Weber, *The Growth of Cities in the Nineteenth Century* (Ithaca, NY, 1899).
3. Hsi-Huey Liang, "Lower-class Immigrants in Wilhelmine Berlin," in *The Urbanization of European Society in the Nineteenth Century*, eds. Andrew Lees and Lynn Lees (Lexington, Mass. 1976), p. 223.
4. Le Corbusier, *La Ville radieuse* (Boulogne-Seine, 1935), p. 181.
5. For Owen, see J. F. C. Harrison, *Quest for the New Moral World* (New York, 1969).
6. For Fourier, see Jonathan Beecher and Richard Bienvenu, eds., *The Utopian Vision of Charles Fourier* (Boston, 1971).
7. For Haussmann and his influence see David H. Pinkney, *Napoleon III and the Rebuilding of Paris* (Princeton, NJ, 1958); Howard Saalman, *Haussmann: Paris Transformed* (New York, 1971); and Anthony Sutcliffe, *The Autumn of Central Paris* (London, 1970).

8. Peter H. Mann, "Octavia Hill: An Appraisal," *Town Planning Review* 23, no. 3 (Oct. 1953): 223–37.

9. Friedrich Engels, *Zur Wohnungsfrage*, 2d edn. (Leipzig, 1887).

10. See Barbara Miller Lane, *Architecture and Politics in Germany, 1918–1945* (Cambridge, Mass., 1968).

11. Le Corbusier, *Urbanisme* (Paris, 1925), p. 135.

12. Lewis Mumford, "The Garden City Idea and Modern Planning," introductory essay to F. J. Osborn's edition of *Garden Cities of To-morrow* (Cambridge, Mass., 1965), p. 29. Although Osborn's edition bears the title of the 1902 edition, his text restores portions of the 1898 text that were cut in 1902. Osborn's is therefore a "definitive" text and I follow his usage in always referring to Howard's book as *Garden Cities of To-morrow*. All further references will come from Osborn's edition, abbreviated *GCT*.

13. See Donald Canty, ed., *The New City* (New York, 1969) for the details of this recommendation.

14. The New Towns, however, have had their problems. See "'New Towns' Face Growing Pains," *New York Times*, June 13, 1976, p. 26.

15. F. J. Osborn, Preface to *GCT*, p. 22.

16. Ibid., pp. 22–3.

17. James Silk Buckingham, *National Evils and Practical Remedies, with the Plan of a Model Town* (London, 1849). Although Howard mentions the utopian city of Buckingham in the text of *GCT* as one of the proposals he combined into the Garden City, he states in a footnote that in fact he had not seen Buckingham's plan until he had "got far on" with his project.

18. E. Howard, Papers, Early draft of *GCT*, Folio 3.

19. Ibid.

20. E. Howard, "Spiritual Influences Toward Social Progress," *Light*, April 30, 1910, p. 196. *Hygeia* was published in London in 1876.

21. Benjamin Ward Richardson, *Hygeia, A City of Health* (London, 1876), p. 21.

22. *GCT*, p. 76.

23. Ibid., pp. 50–6 and 71. Placing the churches along Grand Avenue means that no single church occupies the center of town. Howard's religious upbringing was Non-conformist.

24. *GCT*, p. 53.

25. Ibid., p. 54.

26. *GCT*, diagram #2. The diagram also shows such institutions as "convalescent homes" and the "asylums for blind and deaf" in the green belt. In an earlier version of his plan, Howard wanted the Agricultural Belt to cover 8,000 acres. See his "Summary of E. Howard's proposals for a Home Colony," *The Nationalisation News* 3, no. 29 (Feb. 1893): 20.

27. Howard Papers, Common Sense Socialism, Folio 10.

28. Alfred Marshall, "The Housing of the London Poor," *Contemporary Review* 45, no. 2 (Feb. 1884): 224–31.

29. Howard Papers, Folio 10. Howard recalled meeting Marshall in connection with stenography work he did for parliamentary commissions and discussing the Garden City idea with him. In a note added to *GCT* he claimed that he had not seen Marshall's article when he first formulated his ideas: *GCT*, p. 119.

30. *GCT*, pp. 58–88.

31. Howard Papers, quoted by Howard in an early draft of *GCT*, Folio 3.
32. *GCT*, pp. 89–111.
33. Ibid., p. 136.
34. "Return of Owners of Land Survey," analyzed in F. M. L. Thompson, *English Landed Society in the Nineteenth Century* (London, 1963), pp. 317–19.
35. Henry George, *Progress and Poverty* (New York, 1911), p. 201.
36. Howard, quoted in W. H. Brown's interview with him, "Ebenezer Howard, A Modern Influence," *Garden Cities and Town Planning* 7, no. 30 (Sept. 1908): 116.
37. *GCT*, p. 131.
38. Ibid., pp. 96–111.
39. Howard Papers, Lecture to a Fabian Society, January 11, 1901, Folio 3.
40. *GCT*, p. 104.
41. Ibid., p. 139.
42. I suspect the population of the Central City was put at 58,000 so that the whole complex would attain a population of exactly 250,000.
43. *GCT*, p. 142.
44. Ibid.
45. Ibid. Spencer held that public libraries in themselves were only "mildly communistic." See his "The New Toryism," *Contemporary Review*, 45, no. 2 (Feb. 1884): 153–67. These of course were Spencer's later views. A younger Spencer in *Social Statics* had called for the nationalization of the land. This permitted Howard to refer to Spencer as one of his influences: *GCT*, pp. 123–5.
46. Le Corbusier, *La ville radieuse* (Boulogne Seine, 1935), p. 192.
47. Ibid., title page.
48. Ibid., p. 154.
49. Ibid., p. 153.
50. Le Corbusier, *Quand les cathédrales étaient blanches* (Paris, 1937), pp. 280–1.
51. Le Corbusier, *La ville radieuse*, p. 167.
52. Ibid., p. 146.
53. Peter Serenyi, "Le Corbusier, Fourier, and the Monastery at Ema," cited footnote 15, chapter 21.
54. Charles Fourier, "An Architectural Innovation: The Street Gallery," in Jonathan Beecher and Richard Bienvenu, eds. and trans., *The Utopian Vision of Charles Fourier* (Boston, 1971), p. 243.

2

Co-evolutions of Planning and Design

Risks and Benefits of Design Perspectives in Planning Systems

Kristof Van Assche, Raoul Beunen,
Martijn Duineveld, and Harro de Jong

Introduction

Carl Steinitz observed in 1968: "Neither form nor activity should dominate city design. Form does not always follow function, and functions are not always adaptable to forms" (p. 147). The same applies to planning, we would say. Steinitz's insight can guide us in exploring the dialectics of planning and design in the organization of space.

Planning exists in many variations, in shapes and forms that differ with respect to many distinctions (Allmendinger, 2009; Mandelbaum et al., 1996). It can be more or less associated with government, with local governance, with scientific expertise, with planners and plans. It can be procedural or content-driven and dominated by political, economic, or legal actors in various combinations. In addition, it can codify a future spatial organization to different degrees and by different means. Various authors have elaborated on the relationship between planning and design and the specific position of different disciplines such as landscape architecture, architecture, and urban design in relation to each other (Banerjee, 2011; Childs, 2010; Gunder, 2011; Madanipour, 2006; Steiner, 2011). One can see design as an aspect of planning (e.g. Gunder, 2011), and one can emphasize the professional and disciplinary boundaries of the design disciplines, stressing their difference, possibly

Original publication details: Van Assche, Kristof. 2012. "Co-evolutions of planning and design: Risks and benefits of design perspectives in planning systems". In *Planning Theory*, 12(2) 177–198. Reprinted by Permission of SAGE Publications, Inc.

Readings in Planning Theory, Fourth Edition. Edited by Susan S. Fainstein and James DeFilippis. Editorial material and organization © 2016 John Wiley & Sons, Ltd. Published 2016 by John Wiley & Sons, Ltd.

looking for essences of the disciplines and professions. All, however, agree that planning and design share a common ground in shaping and governing (urban and rural) spaces; that it is important to take into account normative goals of achieving economic, social, and environmental public good; and that design should go beyond merely esthetic issues (Gunder, 2011; Madanipour, 2006). We would argue that it is fruitful to understand their historical entanglement in order to see the potential contribution the different perspectives can make to each other.

We would further argue, and this locates us in poststructuralist methodologies, that essences of disciplines and professions do not exist. Practices and the scientific reflection on them are the product of series of power/knowledge transformations, contingent results of histories marked by (identity) politics, competition, adaptation, routines of repetition, and habits of innovation (Fuchs, 2001; Seabright, 2010). *Naming practices* are part and parcel of this evolution: they cannot be extricated from this environment of competing and evolving identities (Bal, 2002). Names of disciplines and professions can therefore not be linked to presumably essential pursuits, and each application of a disciplinary name, in a situation ("This is true urban design") or to an organization ("Department of urban design"), should be analyzed against prevailing power/knowledge configurations. In terms of Fuchs (2001), it requires second-order observation, the observation of actors, or groups, making distinctions and defining themselves, using semantics, procedures, and images of relevant environments at their disposal. For that reason, we *start* from a basic distinction between naming practice (first-order observation) and observation of naming practice (second-order observation). *Second*, we deploy the already introduced distinction between profession and discipline, that is, the group active in planning and/or design under those labels, and the scientific community reflecting on, and possibly furthering, these practices. *Third*, we distinguish between disciplines and perspectives. Perspectives are theoretical constructs, our theoretical constructs, the result of second-order observation of the evolution of practices and reflections bearing various labels (architecture, landscape architecture, urban design, rural design, planning, etc.). We distinguish planning perspectives from design perspectives, with the aim to elucidate their dialectics later. Design perspectives, in this framing, can potentially not only be found with design practitioners and academics (bearing the name) but also in other disciplines and professions. We will gradually refine these definitions.

Our main goal in this article is to investigate the potential contribution of design perspectives to the functioning of a planning system, as the network of organizations that embodies the coordinated organization of space in a given community (Van Assche and Verschraegen, 2008). We take an evolutionary approach and draw upon a review of planning and design literature to reconstruct the historical development of the disciplines (and professions) in different places. We argue that such endeavor can be worthwhile and novel when deploying a perspective that is abstract enough to grasp the wide variety of empirical roles of planning, without defining a priori superior role distributions. We analyze key aspects of the dialectics between planning and design perspectives in the evolution of planning systems.

It is demonstrated that the incorporation of design perspectives offers advantages to planning systems, as well as risks, and that evaluating the potential for new inclusions of design hinges on an understanding of key aspects of the planning/ design dialectics. Each community will be marked by different dialectics and will represent an imperfect planning system, as perfect adaptation to changing internal and external environments is impossible and because simultaneous optimization for all values targeted is equally impossible.

Planning

Spatial planning is concerned with the ways in which people shape and govern spaces and takes into account social, economic, and environmental issues. Planning is both a set of practices as well as a scientific discipline reflecting upon those practices. At a more abstract level, we define spatial planning as the coordination of policy and practice affecting spatial organization (Van Assche and Verschraegen, 2008). Planning as such can focus on procedures, and on content, on a perfect way of organizing the process of planning, and on certain aspects of the result that are desirable (Allmendinger, 2009). Focus on content tends to blind people for procedural problems and vice versa. The web of organizations that is involved in this effort is called the planning system. Planning, thus, does not uniquely pertain to the domain of people labeled "planners," and of state organizations called "planning departments." Within a planning system, planning perspectives, as perspectives on the coordination of space, are unevenly distributed. More planning in this view is more coordination, not more planners and planning departments. Spatial planning can have many rationales, practical and ideological, legal, scientific, and economic, but we argue that the benefits of coordination in spatial organization can be defined as the possibility to envision and work on several problems at the same time and create new qualities or assets. (A traditional illustration is the twofold motivation to formalize planning in the United States of the early twentieth century: reducing health and safety problems *and* protecting property rights (cf. Platt 2003)). This is possible, we argue, because planning can bring together in one perspective the various users of a space with an image of the space itself. Both diversity of players and space itself generate insights in the combinatory possibilities of interests, conflicts, and assets.

Each community has its own planning system, and the development of large, centralized, and bureaucratic states since the renaissance in Europe brought at least part of the planning system under supervision of the state (Hillier, 2002; Scott, 1998). When those states became more democratic, the planning system followed, to various degrees and at various speeds (Flyvbjerg, 1998). As communities and their institutions evolve, governance evolves and so does planning. The planning system changes over time, and this means that different players will crystallize that in turn shape the future interactions in and of the planning system

(Van Assche et al., 2010). Thus, the planning system and its pattern of organizations, rules, and actors are marked by strong path dependencies, but these never entirely halt the evolution of the system (Chettiparamb, 2006; Van Assche et al., 2011). Once certain actors or a certain perspective are in place, such configuration tends to reproduce itself (Seidl, 2005; cf. Luhmann, 1995).

This is not a trivial observation. Planning as coordination necessarily involves a number of players that ought to remain committed and rules that ought to maintain their credibility (Van Assche et al., 2012b). The cost of establishing coordination is high. It takes time, trust, and social capital. It involves trial and error, and a reigning set of institutions can thus not easily be replaced (Greif, 2006; Ostrom, 2005). Furthermore, a change of institutions could lead to a breakdown, and the costs of altering the arrangement are unpredictable and therefore to be avoided. Coordination of spatial organization is coordination of land use, carrying high political risks. One is tinkering with the everyday environment of voters. One should add economic risks (large investments) and legal risks (planning is often at the limit of what is constitutionally possible). For all these reasons, once an arrangement is found, it tends to remain in place.

There are certainly counter-forces. Within the planning system, positions of actors and perspectives *can* shift. We analyze underlying mechanisms when discussing the dialectics of planning and design. The shifts are reflected in (and sometimes influenced by) the academic debates about planning and design, where certain forms of planning and design are criticized and alternative role distributions are promoted (Anselin et al., 2011; Gunder, 2011; Madanipour, 2006). These debates focus on the tension between regulation and flexibility, about desired and undesired social and environmental effects of planning and design interventions, and on the relation between science and practice.

Design

The search for sense and attractiveness of place has been the subject of theory formation in architecture, landscape architecture, urban design, and philosophy (e.g. Braunfels, 1990; Child, 2010; Duany and Plater-Zyberk, 1991; Lynch, 1981; Rossi, 1982). We will not engage deeply here with debates on the perfect architectural language or the precise importance of beauty, consistency, practicality, and sustainability in design (cf. Alberti, 1988; Vitruvius, 20BC). We are more interested in the dynamic position of design in the planning system. Different design ideologies do play a role in this positioning (Gunder, 2011).

When talking about design, we do not limit ourselves to the pursuit of beauty, nor to the individuals, organizations, and disciplines labeled as design-related (architecture, urban design, and landscape architecture). A spatial design perspective, we argue in line with Kevin Lynch (1981), is "the playful creation and strict evaluation of the possible forms of something, including how it is to be made" (p. 290). While a planning perspective, in our definition, entails an image of the place, and the presence of that image in decision making makes it easier to recombine interests, assets, and problems, a design perspective is marked by continuously entertaining the possibility to manipulate these images of place (and physical space further down the line). According to Sternberg (2000), urban design is the "manipulation of the concrete elements of distance, material, scale, view, vegetation, land area, water features, road alignment, building style" (p. 266).

Planning and design perspectives thus overlap. Manipulation of place images can be experimentation, followed by evaluation (cf. Lynch, 1981), in terms of the goals of players, perceived community interests, and problems and qualities. We argue (cf. infra) that the give-and-take that is necessarily a part of planning can generate more solutions and assets *when the design perspective is never left*, that is, when it accompanies spatial decision making, instead of finishing it, as part of "implementation." Montgomery (1965), reflecting on Urban Renewal experiences, considers the best examples as the ones where, indeed, design is part of each step of the process. Chapman (2011) argues that urban design is the logical form of spatial planning at the smaller scale, not restricted to the implementation phase, and more in general, the best way to "localize" planning.

Planning-as-design, then, envisions the spatial referent from the beginning, reflects on its malleability, and generates design options every step of the process. The more complex the image of the place, the more variety in design options, and the better the implications of planning decisions can be envisioned (e.g. by operating on an image of landscape as a web of ecological and hydrological feedback loops). Bacon (1963) states,

> The first step is to orient one's mind to the fullest extent possible to the concept of space as the dominating element. One must be able to respond to space as the basic element in itself and to conceive abstractly in space. (p. 6)

Reflexive versions of spatial design can incorporate thinking on the selection of malleable and less-changeable features of the space under consideration. If, for example, for an environmental planning problem, the water system is not to be altered, design can still use hydrological knowledge to produce design options as variations of location within the water framework. In other cases, the manipulation of space can start earlier in the reasoning, and include more landscape features.

Planning focusing on procedures cannot be spatial design but planning focusing on content could be. Design can leave the domain of planning, entering decision spaces where few actors are involved in spatial interventions or when manipulation of the space hardens early in the planning process or dramatically reinterprets planning outcomes at the end. One can think of a garden design, with one person taking decisions on what comes where, and one can even imagine the design of the larger areas where just one designer and a willing patron are deciding.

The Dialectics: A Very Brief History

Planning and design, as disciplines and (self-conscious and self-labeled) professions, have different histories. Planning in this sense is a product of the 20th century (Allmendinger, 2002; Platt, 2003), while design (first architecture) is self-identified at least since ancient Greek times. Planning and design perspectives, as defined above, are bound to be much older, as their emergence can plausibly be linked to Neolithic city formation, or the Neolithic revolution itself. Villages, agricultural land use, trade, and cities required specialization, role formation, diversification of land use, and much higher levels of spatial coordination (Luhmann, 1995; Seabright, 2010). The lineages of spatial planning and spatial design perspectives are quite different though. Although the complexity of coordination in spatial planning increased with the centralization of the state and later its democratization (involving more actors), the history of spatial design is also tied to state development, but more indirectly, through the increase of patronage. Complex cities produced rich citizens and proud city governments that could engage in private and public works that were the product of a design philosophy, with the sum of city space given higher consideration than the separate parts (Braunfels, 1990; Krieger, 2000; Mumford, 1961; Rios, 2008).

Architectural design and the reflection on it, architectural theory, were quickly accompanied by the practice and theory of urban design (Braunfels, 1990; Rossi, 1982; Vitruvius, 20BC), although a separate profession developed only much later. Landscape architecture came later, as its emergence required the removal of more conceptual obstacles (Waldheim, 2006). One can say that only during the renaissance, the concepts of landscape, the perception of human power, and the traditions of garden architecture and city design were developed far enough, and the political structures were centralized enough, to bring forth what we would call landscape architecture (Van Assche, 2004). It took an understanding of our surroundings as somehow unified, somehow structured, and an idea that people were allowed and capable of grasping and improving that structure (Hunt, 2000, 1992). The beauty of forests and meadows had been sung long before, but in the Middle Ages, it was inconceivable to design a picturesque rural landscape (Glacken, 1967; Hunt, 1992). Once landscape architecture became thinkable and practically possible, the tradition started to develop, accompanied by modes of reflection that brought styles, fashions, and disputes with them (Swaffield, 2002; Wimmer, 1989). At different points in time, architecture, poetry, philosophy, and painting infused the young discipline with new ideas (Hunt, 1992; Le Dantec and Le Dantec, 1993). Sternberg (2000), writing after a few centuries of capitalism, considers the essence of urban design (but the argument applies to landscape architecture as well) as the *re-integration* of the (concept of) human living environments, whose unity was fragmented by commodification and the ensuing spatial, economic, legal, and conceptual parceling.

The fashion of reflection on design that emerged in the renaissance spurred the practice of design (Luhmann, 2000), while the intellectual ambitions of rulers became more and more visible in large-scale design interventions. It obviously required money, manpower, and expertise, and with economic growth and political consolidation in postrenaissance Europe, similar evolutions could be observed everywhere. The new nation states France and Spain developed city-design schemes that were not thinkable before the centralization of power and the intensification of reflection (Braunfels, 1990; Van Assche, 2004). In France, in the 18th century, engineering became an integral part of city planning, and city planning became the blend of design, science, and politics, which many still recognize as its essence (Gutkind, 1970; Van de Vijver, 2003). In the Europe of the baroque period, good design was seen as the application of universal rules and the judicious deviation from those (Hall, 1997; Choay, 1969). The rules were seen as rules of form, and application of the rules was expected to lead to a certain appearance.

City design became a part of both the scientific and artistic canons in the 17th century, the century of absolutism and centralized monarchies (Braunfels, 1990). There was little reflection on the coordination of actors and on planning as we defined it, but the practice of planning was emerging, as even in absolutist Europe, larger projects (with the exception of parks and palaces) did involve a variety of actors that did more than just following orders. The forms of civil governance and local democracy that rose to prominence in the city development of the 11th and 12th centuries survived the Middle Ages, and new designs were rarely unilaterally imposed on cities (Waterhouse, 1993). Cities had an independence, and their internal political ecology was still very much alive and very complex in the age of nationalism and centralization (Mumford, 1961).

Thus, one can speak of actors that had to look for some form of coordination and one can speak of planning. The strong family-likeness of baroque and neoclassical designs tend to veil the case- and site-specific negotiations that are behind them. Architects, with a technical and artistic background, were responsible, and the same architects were schooled in the arts of politics and diplomacy since the Middle Ages (Benevolo, 1980), when the chief architect of large churches had to be a skilled politician amid a wealth of civil and religious organizations that all wanted something different.

While the practice of landscape architecture was born in 18th-century England, once the design of large areas – transcending the size of private grounds and the language of geometry – was established, it took a hold on the European imagination very quickly (Hunt, 1992; Swaffield, 2002). The landscape architect as a role emerged, a tradition of reflection took off, and the practice of landscape architecture was transferred in the late 18th century to urban areas. First, the landscape architect was restricted to parks that were made to look more "natural," but in the course of the 19th century, the whole city fabric became observable as a landscape that could be manipulated and improved. The difference with the older city design traditions was not only the possibility of more natural forms, a different design language (cf. Spirn, 1984), but the possibility to make visions that included old and new elements, natural and artificial elements, and the possibility to combine different languages of form in the same urban fabric (Madanipour, 1997; Rossi, 1982; Van Assche, 2004). Certainly older cities did have these features in reality, but they were not part of the imagination of the city designer.

In that same 19th century, nation states became fully consolidated and centralized, but these new strong containers of power were permeated by a new ideology, a combination of democratic empowerment and technoscientific control (Scott, 1998). Both citizens and the territory could be reshaped by scientific means, and the optimal functioning of the state and the elevation of the community required such combination of social and physical engineering (Gunder, 2010). In the United States, with its rapidly growing urban areas, park and parkway systems were widely applied, examples of large-scale landscape architecture under the auspices of the planning state (Mumford, 1961). In Europe, around the turn of the 20th century, many countries had developed various policies, plans, and departments that contributed to spatial planning (Hall, 2002; Sutcliffe, 1981). City planning transformed easily into rural planning, regional planning, and transportation planning, as design became less and less a consideration, and as scientific evidence and bureaucratic/procedural approaches took the upper hand. The scientific reflection on "planning" started to distinguish itself from early sociology, and from the more architecturally driven traditions of city design and landscape architecture (Hall, 2002; Handlin and Burchard, 1966).

What became called "urban design" in the second half of the 20th century (Cuthbert, 2010), practiced by architects, landscape architects, city planners, artists, and also by professionals opting for the new label, drew on a myriad of older traditions, including town planning (in its design orientation), landscape architecture, architecture, and art. Initially, the label referred mostly to esthetic approaches of small-scale city spaces (squares and street-scaping), but later, its semantics expanded, to include larger scale designs, environmental, social, and economic considerations—although Cuthbert (2007) observes that different professions and schools return to their own preferred definition, entailing that some versions still restrict the phenomenon to large-scale architecture. With the more inclusive definitions, the overlap with planning grew, as well as with landscape architecture and architecture (e.g. in the *architecture urbaine* tradition).

Even if these broad developments can be traced in European and American history, an understanding of the current roles of planning and design in a specific place, as well as transformation options, requires first of all a mapping of the evolutionary paths in the governance of a community. In other words, the actors, rules, and organizations developed differently in different communities, and the history of their interactions is what mostly shaped the current set of institutions (cf. Greif, 2006; Luhmann, 1995; North, 2005; Van Assche et al., 2011). It is in the broader history sketched that ideas, political structures, and scientific tools became available to shape the spatial environment. Which tools where used when, and by whom, is a product of political games and institutional evolutions at a smaller scale (cf. Cuthbert, 2006; Nielsen and Simonsen, 2003). In areas with very strong local governments (as in the United States), the deepest understanding can be gained by looking at local evolutions, while in Europe, where the nation state was clearly the essential container of power, the evolution of national administrations and policies has to be included more explicitly as a context for local games. In the words of Kunzmann (1999), "An Italian planner trained in Milan would not find herself comfortable in the Ruhr convincing traditional Labour governments that protecting the environment is more important than the development of industrial areas on virgin lands" (p. 512). The pathway of governance shapes the evolution of a planning arena (cf. Geddes, 1968[1915]; Harvey, 1989). In evolving governance, different actors vie for a position of power, for impact on spatial organization: different governmental organizations, scientific disciplines, professional roles, and an array of economic actors (Flyvbjerg, 1998; Hillier, 2002).

Mapping of actors, rules, policies, and documents is not enough to understand the dialectics of planning and design. It is essential to discern what the roles of these actors and documents are and which effects they have on spatial decision making. In addition, each actor creates its own perspective and interprets the history of the planning system and of society differently (Luhmann, 1995; Van Assche and Verschraegen, 2008). Talen (2009: 146) traces form-based coding back to the codex of Hammurabi, about 4,000 years ago, a reconstruction of history that is not untrue but certainly framed by the contemporary design approach of new urbanism, and the associated identity politics. Consequently, actors tend to have a different image of their own present and future roles than what would be ascribed to them by other players (Gunder and Hillier, 2009). Cuthbert (2010), in an insightful overview of readers on urban design, duly notes that some consider the field to be born at Harvard circa 1950, tied to (small-scale) "project design" and carried out by architects, while others find "staking the claim for urban design on the basis of *naming* a phenomenon that has existed since Catal Huyuk, let us say 10,000 years, seems far-fetched to say the least" (p. 446).

In order to understand the evolution of specific roles of planning and design perspectives, we believe that the following six key aspects of the dialectics of planning and design require analysis: (1) institutionalization, (2) flexible policy integration, (3) professional and disciplinary traditions, (4) the role of esthetics, (5) overlap between planning and design, and (6) transformation capacity. Once again, we intend to delineate the dialectics between these two perspectives, not between the actors that bear their names.

Key Aspects of a Planning/Design Dialectics

Institutionalization

In the processes of institutionalization, planning is both enabled and delimited. A certain institutionalization influences which roles and which forms of planning are possible and to what extent spatial design can occur. It also determines which design discourse has access to the planning system. Vigier, writing in 1965, deplores the influence in planning of

> the responses of a small group of aesthetically inclined individuals (architects, urban designers, planners, artists) who have tended to institutionalize their perhaps atypical reactions into intuitive formulae. The Greek and Renaissance fascination with the application of mathematics to architecture and, more recently, Le Corbusier's *Modulor* are examples of these intuitive rationalizations. (p. 22)

If planning is not institutionalized in a community, spatial design is unlikely to be institutionalized. If spatial design has a strong impact on the organization of space, that is usually because there is a strong planning system (often in a social democracy) in which actors with a design perspective acquired a strong position (Carmona, 2009; Davis, 1999; Kostof, 1991). These actors can be labeled planners or designers; they can work directly for the government or for firms and others advising or subcontracting for governments. Planning becomes significantly easier in communities with a planning tradition (Van Assche and Djanibekov, 2012; Van Assche and Verschraegen, 2008), and in such traditions, spatial design can also emerge as a significant perspective. The Town and Country Planning Association, identifying with a spatial design perspective, was aware of it and lobbied intensely for the legislation that institutionalized planning, for example, the Town Planning Act of 1946.

If, in the pathway of institutionalization of planning, property rights are the primary rules shaping spatial coordination, planning is likely to be reduced to the enforcement of property rights and the minimizing of risk in a society made up of players, each asserting rights that are sometimes contradictory (Jacobs, 1991; cf. North, 2005) or, in the words of Moore (1978), to minimize market imperfections. It might still be possible to impose rules and zones that restrict the use of private property in the name of public safety, environmental quality, health, or other more easily agreed upon common goods (Platt, 2003), but since each restriction will have to be linked to these arguments, chances are slim that in such regime comprehensive visions are possible. The restricted possibilities to intervene in property rights makes planning with plans and planning-as-design unlikely (Van Assche and Leinfelder, 2008).

In such regimes, spatial design is usually restricted to places that are under a different form of governance, for example, a university or hospital campus, a state park, or a place that is under control of one private party, such as a new urbanism development (Falconer-Al Hindi and Staddon, 1997; Talen, 2011). If property rights are strong, and a large property is in the hands of one player, then, paradoxically, such a place can become the subject of design more easily than similar places under a strong planning regime. F.L. Olmsted was freer in the design of the Stanford University campus under Mr Stanford than he would have been under a city council assisted by a city planning department.

Flexible policy integration

We argue that design perspectives in planning systems tend to emerge in places with a tradition of spatial integration of policies. Indeed, spatial planning can be regarded as a privileged site of policy integration, and the requirements of spatial policy scream for policy integration (Van Assche and Djanibekov, 2012). Often, planning as a governmental activity emerged after the recognition of a need for policy integration (Platt, 2003). Everything takes place in space, and many policies have spatial effects, and so at a certain point, it became clear to governments that it would make sense to distinguish a task (and often create a department) especially for it, a planning department. Strong (1962) noted, "The necessities of our time have turned us to planning and to the establishment of planning agencies" (p. 99). Policy integration in a planning system is not necessarily flexible, as all sorts of planning, and also forms of design, that hinder planning as coordination can be codified and ossified into spatial policies. Kunzmann (1999) explicitly argues that a return to more design-oriented planning education in Europe would be disastrous, under the assumption that design dominance has traditionally caused too many blind spots in planning.

Policy integration in planning can take place in different ways and at different scales. It seems clear that communities that found ways to pursue spatial policy integration without relying exclusively on formal institutions (laws, procedures, or plans with legal status) can respond in more different ways to changing necessities (cf. North, 2005). Combinations of formal and informal institutions allow more flexibility in policy integration, and they also allow for more different policy options and more different design options to emerge (Roy, 2009). In the Soviet system, rural areas were organized by means of three parallel steering systems, each claiming comprehensiveness and authority in the organization of space. This apparent contradiction de facto created space for more flexible adaptation by means of informal institutions governing the selection of formal rules to be applied in particular cases (Eichholz et al., 2013)

Spatial design, we argue, can only work and can only remain design, when it is not *reduced* to the application of rules and procedures (in line with Talen 2009; Madanipour, 2006). There are bound to be a variety of restrictions imposed by law, resources, and sensitivities, but if there is flexible policy integration, design can play a role.

Professional and disciplinary traditions

The design disciplines tend to exist semi-independent of the planning system in a given community. Self-images and aspirations of architects, landscape architects, and urban designers will differ everywhere, and these differences cannot be fully ascribed to differences between planning systems. In other words, how designers see themselves hinges on what is practically possible for them in the governance context (cf. Cuthbert, 2001; Forester, 1999; Gunder, 2011), but not entirely. Professions and disciplines can long and pine and reminisce for generations, weeping for a better past and hoping for a brighter future, with the past and future seen as places where they have a different role in society. Architects have been drawing perfect cities for centuries, often in times and places where implementation was out of the question (Rossi, 1982; Van Assche et al., 2009). One can think of the extensive collections of "paper architecture" now in Soviet archives, but just as well of contemporary architectural competitions, where planners, urban designers, landscape architects, as well as democratic and economic controls are often forgotten in a release of the architectural imagination that presents the city as an abstract composition (in the tradition of Le Corbusier).

The self-descriptions of the disciplines are partly shaped by the history of encounters with the other disciplines and professions. Only part of these encounters took place within the planning system (cf. Soja, 1996). Where there is a strong planning system with a long tradition, the self-definitions of the planning and design profession tend to be shaped largely by the games and encounters in the frame of the planning system. If certain functions were created for the planning system, competition opens within the system to fill new niches. The European Malta treaty obliged the signing countries to assign a place to archaeology in the planning system, and the result was an intense competition over that new spot, between archaeologists entering the system and older actors retooling and refashioning themselves as more attentive to cultural heritage (Duineveld, 2006). If functions were relinquished, the associated actors compete to take over other niches in the planning ecology. In the Netherlands, several years into the current economic crisis, and after a wave of liberalization that shrunk the planning system, real estate developers under pressure are redefining themselves as socially and ecologically sensitive comprehensive planners and designers.

As with any other group playing a role in governance, the self-definition will do the following:

- partly emerge out of a simple differentiation (we are different from a and b);
- partly emerge out of a delineation of core values (we are x because we believe in, know y);
- partly emerge as result of a history of strategizing and opposing (the political game);
- partly emerge as a result of reflection in and on the profession (e.g. by the associated discipline).

Ladner Birch (2001) illustrates beautifully how the American planning profession originally shaped the academic planning discipline, but states that, in recent decades, a reverse movement can also be observed. She also shows that such academic influence can both harm and help the adaptation of the profession, and its status in the planning system. Depending on the context, a design perspective might be an asset or a liability. In systems where such perspective was already seen as an asset, but the actors most closely associated with such perspective abandon it, usually because of internal ideological struggles, this will create a niche (as in the Netherlands, where an entrepreneurial landscape architecture profession took over, since the 1980s, the practice of urban design from town planners – *stedenbouwers* – who had moved in the direction of socioeconomic programming (cf. Van Assche, 2004)). The expectation of the perspective by other actors will create an implicit demand, a pressure for others, either existing or new actors, to take over that role. If planners or urban designers abandon a design perspective where it previously existed, it might be taken over by landscape architects or urban designers.

Once a design perspective has conquered a place in the planning system, the actors representing it can change. Not only can actors shape, shift, and change perspectives, it can also happen that a particular approach to design loses support. This can apply to the procedure of designing, which can be considered outdated after a semantic shift (Luhmann, 2000), and to the result, the dominant geometries, or its functioning. Urban renewal in the American tradition was tied to a social democratic vision of society, an important role of spatial planning, and planning as design in a modernist esthetic. All three lost support after the results of urban renewal were found wanting (e.g. Jacobs, 1961).

The role of esthetics

Of particular importance, we believe, is the role of esthetics in the self-description of the actors professing a design perspective. Camillo Sitte's (1965[1889]) seminal book speaks of city planning according to *artistic principles*, and Raymond Unwin's 1909 treatise morphed the garden city idea into a vocabulary of esthetically pleasing form (later emulated by the New Urbanists). If the pursuit of beauty becomes the primary goal of these actors, this has a series of consequences that are likely to dominate the relation between planning and design perspectives.

First, if design is mostly esthetics, then it is more likely that other considerations are not given much weight. When dealing with larger spaces, especially when those have to accommodate many different uses and users, design-as-esthetics is bound to create problems with use and maintenance, to negatively affect daily life (cf. De Certeau, 1984). This, in turn, will provoke resistance with users and soon after with other players within the planning system (Duany et al., 2008). Such esthetic emphasis also makes spatial design more susceptible to fashions and infatuations within the art world (compare Cuthbert, 2010). It increases the chance that designs and designers communicate implicitly with other designers and with art critics and architectural magazines, instead of with the end users and the other players that could enrich the resulting plan (Van Assche, 2004). Steiner (2011) understands why planners are wary of "an emphasis on the new and on personalities results in the elevation of 'starchitects' and on objects" (p. 213). If this ends up to be the case, then the intended meaning of the designed space will remain muted for most users, not schooled in the latest fashions in art and architecture (Madanipour, 1996; Van Assche et al., 2012a). Many new projects applauded in architecture magazines are therefore barely appreciated by residents, while many older celebrated projects survived neither changing professional tastes nor residents' critiques. Punter (2007) states that "the tensions between professional and lay taste have to be constructively managed, and need to be explored through a variety of collaborative, consultative, educational and cultural programmes" (p. 188). However, the gap between "managing" and "exploring" the difference is a real one. It is also the site of politics.

The claim on the part of designers to be the only ones capable of understanding and using the language of space (cf. Gunder, 2011), to distinguish objectively good from objectively bad spatial structure, is de facto a claim to a monopoly position in the planning system. If such rhetoric is allowed to be persuasive, the results are problematic. If such claim of unique access to the language of space (e.g. Alexander, 1979; Cullen, 1961; Duany and Plater-Zyberk, 1991; Unwin, 1909) is honored, spatial design will still evolve, but this will be a matter of changing styles, not a matter of adaptation to changing environments and necessities (cf. Luhmann, 2000). In that sense, it makes the planning system rigid by rendering it immune to input from many players, by dismissing their arguments as irrelevant. In such a situation, spatial design stops being spatial planning (Gunder, 2011). Coordination of interests and perspectives does not happen anymore, or it happens in a fashion that is opaque, removed from democratic controls.

The imposition of esthetics in the design process reduces not only the democratic legitimacy but also the capacity to enhance the planning process by looking for site-specific synergies. (Madanipour, 1996, 2004, 2006; Steiner, 2011). Earlier versions of New Urbanism suffered from this. They started from a repertoire of design elements and combinatory rules (e.g. Duany and Plater-Zyberk, 1991), but this proved too inflexible, and more recent versions of form-based coding (Talen, 2009) reduce rigidity by allowing the imposition of form on use schemes at varying times in the process and in more variations.

Overlap between planning and design

A further feature of the dialectics of planning and design that ought to be grasped is the pattern and intensity of their overlap as visible in the planning system. The rarity or abundance of these perspectives, and their position in a community, with certain actors holding certain powers, makes a substantial difference for the dialectics and the relative impact of planning and design.

Names of departments, actors, or documents do not necessarily coincide with what they do, nor do they coincide with the perspective dominant in their discourse and actions. If powerful players embrace a design perspective, a planning perspective, or a planning-as-design perspective, this will have an impact. If a number of major US real estate developers would adopt New Urbanism, this would likely trigger changes in local politics and planning and in architecture and planning schools. It is also possible that certain approaches are favored because they are embedded in rules and organizational structures inherited from the past (Booth, 1996; Schurch, 1999). If the chief planner is traditionally an architect (as in the former Soviet Union), this is likely to have an influence (Van Assche et al., 2010). If planning is de facto development planning and developers copy their designs from catalogs, this is likely to have a very different impact.

We argue that not only the location of these perspectives is relevant for understanding their interactions but also their overlaps. Overlap has two meanings here:

1. Overlaps between planning and design perspectives with the same actors.
2. Overlaps between the perspectives of several actors within the planning system.

This distinction can help in understanding discursive migration from actor to actor, the pattern of transformation of actors, and the system as a whole. It also opens the doors to an understanding of transformation capacity and the options and limits for institutional (re)design.

Overlap creates cognitive openness and this enables discursive migration (Luhmann, 1990). Discursive migration then produces similar understandings of similar situations (cf. Bal, 2002) and makes it easier to compromise and coordinate. Yet, even in a system with a high degree of overlap between planning and design perspectives, each actor can embody different internal dialectics between planning and design (including a different version of a design discourse), and this will shape the overall dialectics within the planning system. In a Swedish planning process, architects, urban designers, landscape architects, and design-oriented environmental specialists can be around the table, all embracing the general idea of planning-as-design, but cherishing a different variation of the planning/design dialectics, inherited from their disciplines, from competition in the planning system, and derived from the basic need to identify and legitimize their presence.

Transformation capacity

We consider planning as necessarily adaptive (cf. Geddes, 1968 [1915]; Montgomery, 1998). For the planning system to be adaptive to external changes, it requires the capacity to harvest its internal complexity: the diversity in perspectives, skills, and resources (cf. Luhmann, 1995; Seidl, 2005; Van Assche et al., 2011). It will also need the skills to reshuffle internal positions. Otherwise, political and economic pressures go unheeded and are likely to trigger less-manageable change later in time. The adaptive capacity can thus be described as a combination of learning capacity and transformative capacity (Forester, 1999; Forsyth, 2007; Vigier, 1965). These qualities are desirable for the individual actors and for the system as a whole. If the system can respond to change, for example, a different desire in society with regard to its spatial environment and with regard to heritage or pollution, this does not entail that each actor can adapt. In the internal competition, actors will disappear, be marginalized, or become more prominent. Adaptivity will be an asset in such internal competition (Harvey, 1989).

A very different competitive asset can be the claim to exclusive knowledge. Exclusive knowledge, especially knowledge that is deemed absolutely true, can bring dominance in planning games, and it is bound to introduce rigidity and problematic adaptation. This has been diagnosed as a problem in procedural planning and science-based planning (Gunder and Hillier, 2009; Van Assche, 2004), and it is a problem with certain versions of esthetic design (Duany and Plater-Zyberk, 1991; Gunder, 2011). Strong (1962), discussing "utopian surgeons" in city design, notes,

> Following in the footsteps of Plato, he discovers to us the perfect form, the archetype, to which each actual city should conform, either by breaking the new ground of a Brasilia or Canberra or by transformation of San Francisco, Los Angeles, or other metropolis. (p. 100)

Rigidities in planning perspectives, like an ideology of planning as esthetic design, tend to undermine the learning capacity of the whole planning system. If planning is seen as the application of a timeless or otherwise superior language of form, with other actors and institutions merely facilitating this (e.g. Alexander, 1979; Lynch, 1981), then the dominant design actors and the system as a whole are unlikely to learn and transform. A more subtle form of monopolizing design (and hence planning) discourse and hindering genuine self-transformation is the "educating" of supposedly ignorant citizens in a supposedly objective design syntax. According to Greene (1992) "community design involves many different voices speaking in seemingly different languages. The taxonomy presented here attempts to resolve the confusion" (p. 186). Not only does this represent a major democratic deficit, it also means that the system will be inefficient, that it will create unobserved problems and will not observe problems acknowledged elsewhere in society. This represents a major risk of breakdown of coordination, after which players will pursue their interests at the expense of the common good (North, 2005; Verdery, 2003).

Dilemmas

The perfect planning system does not exist. We would go further, and say that it cannot exist. A number of reasons have been treated extensively in the planning literature already: planning always creates losers, it cannot be fully inclusive; it is driven by volatile political and economic games and unpredictable citizen preferences (Harvey, 1985; Hillier, 2002; Gunder, 2010; Madanipour et al., 2001). Citizens can be charmed, or blinded, by a certain approach that is then institutionalized without thoroughly discussing the drawbacks or without putting in place the structures and incentives to generate debate and adaptation – rules to change the rules (Garde, 2004). Such is a recipe for rigidity, and in time, for disaster. Based on the line of reasoning in this article, we would add a few other reasons why perfect planning is impossible.

First, from the perspective of planning as coordination, it transpires right away that coordination can never be perfect. Not all interests can be met at the same distance, not each common good can be approached to the same extent, and not every common good can be agreed upon or even articulated in the political and planning arenas. The same is true for design as spatial coordination. Moreover, planning-as-design has to struggle to balance different interests, and the often diverging goals of sustainability, attractiveness, practicality, and affordability (Breheny, 1992; Garde, 2004; Greene, 1992). A strong spatial structure that can accommodate many uses, users, and desires and stay within a series of constraints can never be optimized for all these factors at the same time. (Congrès International d'Architecture Moderne (CIAM), the lobby for modernist planning *après* Le Corbusier, collapsed for that reason, but that lesson is not remembered well.)

The form of coordination in planning can never be perfect, while the same is true for coordination in design. Furthermore, there is no perfect balance between planning and design perspectives in a planning system. The way the planning system is institutionalized represents a choice regarding that balance, but that configuration can never be perfectly adapted to any specific problem at hand. Moreover, optimization for perfect adaptability, stability, and predictability cannot be combined (Scott, 1998). In the Netherlands, once environmental design was established in the 1990s, cultural heritage specialists deplored the erasure of history, and when heritage design became more prominent after 2000, its lack of comprehensive environmental vision was criticized. Both approaches were selectively used and criticized by the real estate industry, optimizing according to different criteria. Finally, there is the fit between the planning system and society, where society changes at a different speed when compared with the planning system – usually faster, sometimes slower (Van Assche, 2004; Throgmorton, 1996). Expert groups within the planning system might finally have agreed on a balance between nature and culture, but that consensus might be rendered irrelevant if society at large has made a turn to the right (as in many European countries).

One can say that in the structure of the system, its institutionalization, the optimization for this or that is always an imperfection when dealing with a specific situation (cf. Luhmann, 1990, 1995). In the functioning of the system, where prudence has to complement institutions, the balancing between perspectives is a shifting between selections of blind spots. It is impossible to see everything at the same time, and an emphasis on planning as coordination of interests or content will yield different observations than an emphasis on planning-as-design. Within a design perspective, the emphasis can imperceptibly move to one of the embedded criteria (beauty, practicality, etc.), thus undermining the comprehensive character of the design, its synergetic and context-sensitive qualities (Carmona et al., 2002; Julier, 2005). If the emphasis of design comes to lay on esthetics, it quickly ceases to be planning. As Albrechts (2005) observes, creativity – and the preconditions of flexibility and openness for redefinition – is needed in all aspects of adaptive planning, from selection of actors over design of procedures to the production of visions.

The flexibility of the system, its ability to recombine perspectives according to the situation at hand, is essential. An inherent tension exists with the need for internal checks and balances. It might look like only formalization, only formal institutions, and thus a dominance of procedural planning, make checks and balances, and hence democratic planning, possible. Design reviews in such line of reasoning represent the answer to the instabilities introduced by design (cf. Dawson and Higgins, 2009; Donovan and Larkham, 1996; Nasar and Grannis, 1999; Punter, 2007). One can counter (in the line of Machiavelli) that democracies always combine formal and informal institutions, that the working of checks and balances always involves prudent leadership, active citizenship and habits, and traditions upholding them and making their enforcement possible (Mansfield, 1996). One cannot avoid responsibility and risk by full reliance on formalization. Planning, in its positioning of design, needs both formalized checks and balances and informal coordination mechanisms.

Checks and balances will be embodied in legal constraints and formalized procedures and documents. According to Punter (2007),

> Arguably, design ambitions are best imbedded in a statutory plan such as a comprehensive, municipal structure or local development plan. Then they can become mainstream strategic planning objectives, can shape development in a more profound and constructive way, and be regularly monitored and updated. (p. 173)

Yet, informal institutions create space for leadership (Childs, 2010; Forester, 1999; Ladner Birch, 2001) and for creativity (Albrechts, 2005; Madanipour, 2006), and give a place to shifting combinations of perspectives (cf. Massey, 2005; Punter and Carmona, 1997). Embedding of design perspectives in a planning system is a starting point for the balancing of formal and informal coordination. Gaffikin et al (2010) observe that "carefully considered urban design, within the context of a strategic planning framework, can have a beneficial influence in a contested situation" (p. 508).

Conclusion

The relations between planning and design perspectives in a planning system are multifaceted, as they are usually spread over many different actors, and as the different forms of coordination represented by planning and design are internally varied. Planning-as-design can be regarded as a highly valuable perspective for a planning system, allowing it to capture the qualities of a specific place, to accommodate many different needs and inspire specific solutions. Planning-as-design can increase the efficiency of planning and improve the quality of its product, the resulting space. Planning can slide into blind procedure, and design can deteriorate into blind esthetics, but in each community, the search for a workable and unique balance between planning and design perspectives is an economic, political, and we would add, ecological, necessity.

A thorough familiarity with the structure and workings of the planning system, and, more broadly, of governance, evolution, of the dialectics between formal and informal institutions and between planning and design perspectives, is a prerequisite when considering a modification of the planning system. If planning theorists or other scientific observers want to have an impact on planning practice, their analyses should at least start from the complexity of the current system. In many cases, the scientific observer will discern a need for a planning or design perspective to solve problems identified in and by the community. Introducing it at the very minimum requires seeing through the rhetoric and the self-descriptions of the current actors, and the rhetoric on the rules governing their interactions. In all likelihood, the help of the political system will be required to craft and implement a strategy that might remedy the absence of planning and/or design, and reintroduce those perspectives without increasing the rigidity of the planning system. Luckily, the history of the planning and design disciplines, as well as the history of wildly varying institutionalizations of planning and design perspectives, offer plenty of materials to craft such strategies.

References

Alberti LB (1988 [ca. 1452]) *On the Art of Building in Ten Books*. Cambridge, MA:MIT Press.

Albrechts L (2005) Creativity as a drive for change. *Planning Theory* 4(3): 247–63.

Alexander C (1979) *The Timeless Way of Building*. New York: Oxford University Press.

Allmendinger P (2002) *Planning Theory*. Basingstoke: Palgrave.

Allmendinger P (2009) *Planning Theory*. Basingstoke: Palgrave Macmillan.

Anselin L, Nasar JL and Talen E (2011) Where do planners belong? Assessing the relationship between planning and design in American Universities. *Journal of Planning Education and Research* 31(2): 196–207.

Bacon E (1963) Urban design as a force in comprehensive planning. *Journal of the American Institute of Planners* 29(1): 2–8.

Bal M (2002) *Travelling Concepts*. New Haven, CT: Yale University Press.

Banerjee T (2011) Response to "Commentary: Is Urban Design Still Urban Planning?": Whither urban design? Inside or outside planning? *Journal of Planning Education and Research* 31(2): 208–10.

Benevolo L (1980) *The History of the City*. Cambridge, MA: MIT Press.

Booth P (1996) *Controlling Development: Certainty and Discretion in Europe, the USA and Hong Kong*. London: UCL Press.

Braunfels W (1990) *Urban Design in Western Europe: Regime and Architecture, 900–1900* (KJ Northcott, Trans.) Chicago, IL: University of Chicago Press.

Breheny M (ed.) (1992) *Sustainable Development and Urban Form*. London: Pion.

Carmona M (2009) Design coding and the creative, market and regulatory tyrannies of practice. *Urban Studies* 46(12): 264–7.

Carmona M, De Magalhaes C and Edwards M (2002) Stakeholder views on value and urban design. *Journal of Urban Design* 7(2): 145–69.

Chapman D (2011) Engaging places: Localizing urban design and development planning. *Journal of Urban Design* 16(4): 511–30.

Chettiparamb A (2006) Metaphors in complexity theory and planning. *Planning Theory* 5(1): 71–91.

Childs MC (2010) A spectrum of urban design roles. *Journal of Urban Design* 15(1): 1–19.

Choay F (1969) *The Modern City: Planning in 19th Century*. London: Studio Vista.

Cullen G (1961) *Townscape*. London: Architectural Press.

Cuthbert A (2001) Going global: Reflexivity and contextualism in urban design education. *Journal of Urban Design* 6(3): 297–316.

Cuthbert A (2006) *The Form of Cities: Political Economy and Urban Design*. Oxford: Blackwell.

Cuthbert A (2007) Urban design: Requiem for an era – review and critique of the last 50 years. *Urban Design International* 12(4): 177–226.

Cuthbert A (2010) Whose urban design? *Journal of Urban Design* 15(3): 443–8.

Davis H (1999) *The Culture of Building*. New York: Oxford University Press.

Dawson E and Higgins M (2009) How planning authorities can improve quality through the design review process: Lessons from Edinburgh. *Journal of Urban Design* 14(1): 101–14.

De Certeau M (1984) *The Practice of Everyday Life*. Berkeley, CA: University of California Press.

Donovan J and Larkham P (1996) Rethinking design guidance. *Planning Practice & Research* 11(3): 303–18.

Duany A and Plater-Zyberk E (1991) *Towns and Town-Making Principles*. New York: Rizzoli.

Duany A, Sorlien S and Wright W (2008) *SmartCode Version 9*. Ithaca, NY: New Urban News Publications, Inc.

Duineveld M (2006) *Van Oude Dingen, De Mensen, Die Voorbij Gaan. Over De Voorwaarden Meer Recht Te Kunnen Doen Aan De Door Burgers Gewaardeerde Cultuurhistories*. Delft: Eburon.

Eichholz M, Van Assche K, Oberkircher L, et al. (2013) Trading capitals?—Bourdieu, land and water in rural Uzbekistan. *Journal of Environmental Planning and Management*. 56(6), 868–92.

Falconer Al-Hindi K and Staddon C (1997) The hidden histories and geographies of neotraditional town planning: The case of Seaside, Florida. *Environment and Planning D: Society and Space* 15(3): 349–72.

Flyvbjerg B (1998) *Rationality and Power*. Chicago, IL: Chicago University Press.

Forester J (1999) *The Deliberative Practitioner*. Cambridge, MA: MIT Press.

Forsyth A (2007) Innovation in urban design: Does research help? *Journal of Urban Design* 12(3): 461–73.

Fuchs S (2001) *Against Essentialism*. Cambridge, MA: Harvard University Press.

Gaffikin F, Mceldowney M and Sterrett K (2010) Creating shared public space in the contested city: The role of urban design. *Journal of Urban Design* 15(4): 493–513.

Garde A (2004) New urbanism as sustainable growth? A supply side story and its implications for public policy. *Journal of Planning Education and Research* 24(2): 154–70.

Geddes P (1968 [1915]) *Cities in Evolution*. London: Ernest Benn.

Glacken C (1967) *Traces on the Rhodian Shore. Nature and Culture in Western Thought from Ancient Times to the End of the Eighteenth Century*. Berkeley, CA: University of California Press.

Greene S (1992) Cityshape: Communicating and evaluating community design. *Journal of the American Planning Association* 58(2): 177–89.

Greif A (2006) *The Path to the Modern Economy. Lessons from Medieval Trade*. Cambridge: Cambridge University Press.

Gunder M (2010) Planning as the ideology of (neo-liberal) space. *Planning Theory* 9(4): 298–314.

Gunder M (2011) Commentary: Is urban design still urban planning? An exploration and response. *Journal of Planning Education and Research* 31(2): 184–95.

Gunder M and Hillier J (2009) *Planning in ten words or less. A Lacanian Entanglement with Spatial Planning*. Farnham: Ashgate.

Gutkind EA (1970) *Urban Development in Western Europe: France and Belgium*. London: The Free Press.

Hall P (2002) *Cities of Tomorrow*. Oxford: Blackwell.

Hall T (1997) *Planning Europe's Capital Cities: Aspects of Nineteenth-Century Urban Development*. London: Spon Press.

Handlin O and Burchard J (1966) *The Historian and the City*. Cambridge, MA: MIT Press.

Harvey D (1985) *The Urbanization of Capital*. Oxford: Blackwell.

Harvey D (1989) From managerialism to entrepreneurialism: The transformation in urban governance in late capitalism. *Geografiska Annaler Series B Human Geography* 1(71): 3–17.

Hillier J (2002) *Shadows of Power*. London: Routledge.

Hunt JD (1992) *Gardens and the Picturesque: Studies in the History of Landscape Architecture*. Cambridge, MA: MIT Press.

Hunt JD (2000) *Greater Perfections. The Practice of Garden Theory*. Philadelphia, PA: University of Philadelphia Press.

Jacobs H (1991) *The Politics of Property Rights*. Madison, WI: University of Wisconsin Press.

Jacobs J (1961) *The Death and Life of Great American Cities*. New York: Random House.

Julier G (2005) Urban designscapes and the production of aesthetic consent. *Urban Studies* 42(5/6): 869–887.

Kostof S (1991) *The City Shaped. Urban Patterns and Meanings through History*. London: Thames & Hudson.

Krieger M (2000) Planning and design as the manufacture of transcendence. *Journal of Planning Education and Research* 19(3): 257–64.

Kunzmann K (1999) Planning education in a globalized world. *European Planning Studies* 7(5): 549–55.

Ladner Birch E (2001) Practitioners and the art of planning. *Journal of Planning Education and Research* 20(4): 407–21.

Le Dantec D and Le Dantec JP (1993) *Reading the French Garden. Story and History.* Cambridge, MA: MIT Press.

Luhmann N (1990) *Political Theory in the Welfare State.* New York: De Gruyter.

Luhmann N (1995) *Social Systems.* Stanford, CA: Stanford University Press.

Luhmann N (2000) *Art as a Social System.* Stanford, CA: Stanford University Press.

Lynch K (1981) *Good City Form.* Cambridge, MA: MIT Press.

Madanipour A (1996) *Design of Urban Space: An Inquiry into a Socio-Spatial Process.* Chichester: John Wiley.

Madanipour A (1997) Ambiguities in urban design. *Town Planning Review* 68(3): 363–83.

Madanipour A (2004) Viewpoint: Why urban design? *Town Planning Review* 75(2): i–iv.

Madanipour A (2006) Roles and challenges of urban design. *Journal of Urban Design* 11(2): 173–93.

Madanipour A, Hull A and Healey P (eds) (2001) *The Governance of Place: Space and Planning Processes.* Aldershot: Ashgate.

Mandelbaum SJ, Mazza L and Burchell RW (eds) (1996) *Explorations in Planning Theory.* New Brunswick, NJ: Center for Urban Policy Research.

Mansfield H (1996) *Machiavelli's Virtue.* Chicago, IL: University of Chicago Press.

Massey D (2005) *For Space.* London: SAGE.

Montgomery J (1998) Making a city: Urbanity, vitality and urban design. *Journal of Urban Design* 3(1): 93–116.

Montgomery R (1965) Improving the Design Process in Urban Renewal. *Journal of the American Institute of Planners* 31(1): 7–20.

Moore T (1978) Why allow planners to do what they do? A justification from economic theory. *Journal of the American Institute of Planners* 44: 387–98.

Mumford L (1961) *The City in History: Its Origins, Its Transformations, and Its Prospects.* New York: Harcourt Brace & World.

Nasar JL and Grannis P (1999) Design review reviewed: Administrative versus discretionary methods. *Journal of the American Planning Association* 65(4): 424–33.

Nielsen E and Simonsen K (2003) Scaling from 'below': Practices, strategies and urban spaces. *European Planning Studies* 11(8): 911–27.

North DC (2005) *Understanding the Process of Economic Change.* Princeton, NJ: Princeton University Press.

Ostrom E (2005) *Understanding Institutional Diversity.* Cambridge: Cambridge University Press.

Platt D (2003) *Land Use and Society.* Washington, DC: Island Press.

Punter J (2007) Developing urban design as public policy: Best practice principles for design review and development management. *Journal of Urban Design* 12(2): 167–202.

Punter JV and Carmona M (1997) *The Design Dimension of Planning: Theory, Policy and Best Practice.* London: Spon Press.

Rios M (2008) Envisioning citizenship: Toward a polity approach in urban design. *Journal of Urban Design* 13(2): 213–29.

Rossi A (1982) *The Architecture of the City.* Cambridge, MA: MIT Press.

Roy A (2009) Why India cannot plan its cities: Informality, insurgence and the idiom of urbanization. *Planning Theory* 8(1): 76–87.

Schurch T (1999) Reconsidering urban design: Thoughts on its definition and status as a field or profession. *Journal of Urban Design* 4(1): 5–28.

Scott J (1998) *Seeing Like a State*. New Haven, CT: Yale University Press.

Seabright P (2010) *The Company of Strangers. A Natural History of Economic Life*. Princeton, NJ: Princeton University Press.

Seidl D (2005) *Organizational Identity and Self-Transformation*. Aldershot: Ashgate.

Sitte C (1965 [1889]) City planning according to artistic principles (GR Collins and CC Collins, Trans.). New York: Random House.

Soja E (1996) *Thirdspace. Journeys to Los Angeles and Other Real-and-Imagined Places*. Oxford: Blackwell.

Spirn A (1984) *The Granite Garden*. New York: Basic Books.

Steiner F (2011) Commentary: Planning and design – oil and water or bacon and eggs? *Journal of Planning Education and Research* 31(2): 213–16.

Steinitz C (1968) Meaning and the congruence of urban form and activity. *Journal of the American Institute of Planners* 34(4): 233–48.

Sternberg E (2000) An integrative theory of urban design. *Journal of the American Planning Association* 66(3): 265–78.

Strong E (1962) The amplitude of design. *Journal of the American Institute of Planners* 28(2): 98–102.

Sutcliffe A (1981) *Towards the Planned City: Germany, Britain, the United States and France 1780–1914*. Oxford: Blackwell.

Swaffield SR (ed.) (2002) *Theory in Landscape Architecture. A Reader*. Philadelphia, PA: University of Pennsylvania Press.

Talen E (2009) Design by the rules: The historical underpinnings of form-based codes. *Journal of the American Planning Association* 75(2): 144–60.

Talen E (2011) Response to "commentary": Is urban design still urban planning? *Journal of Planning Education and Research* 31(2): 211–12.

Throgmorton J (1996) *Planning as Persuasive Storytelling*. Chicago, IL: Chicago University Press.

Unwin R (1909) *Town Planning in Practice: An Introduction to the Art of Designing Cities and Suburbs*. London: T. Fisher Unwin.

Van Assche K (2004) *Signs in Time. An Interpretive Account of Urban Planning and Design, the People and their Histories*. Wageningen: Wageningen University.

Van Assche K, Beunen R, Jacobs J, et al. (2011) Crossing trails in the marshes. Flexibility and rigidity in the governance of the Danube delta. *Journal of Environmental Planning and Management* 54(8): 997–1018.

Van Assche K and Djanibekov N (2012) Spatial planning as policy integration: The need for an evolutionary perspective. Lessons from Uzbekistan. *Land Use Policy* 29(1): 179–86.

Van Assche K, Duineveld M, De Jong H, et al. (2012a) What place is this time? Semiotics and the analysis of historical reference in landscape architecture. *Journal of Urban Design* 17(2): 233–54.

Van Assche K, Duineveld M and Salukvadze J (2012b) Under pressure: Speed, vitality and innovation in the reinvention of Georgian planning. *European Planning Studies* 20(6): 999–1015.

Van Assche K and Leinfelder H (2008) Nut en noodzaak van een kritische planologie. Suggesties vanuit Nederland en Amerika op basis van Niklas Luhmann's systeemtheorie. *Ruimte en planning* 28: 28–38.

Van Assche K, Salukvadze J and Shavishvilli N (2009) *City Culture and City Planning in Tbilisi. Where Europe and Asia Meet.* Lewiston: Mellen Press.

Van Assche K, Verschraegen G and Salukvadze J (2010) Changing frames. Expert and citizen participation in Georgian planning. *Planning Practice and Research* 25(3): 377–95.

Van Assche K and Verschraegen K (2008) The Limits of Planning: Niklas Luhmann's systems theory and the analysis of planning and planning ambitions. *Planning Theory* 7(3): 263–83.

Van de Vijver D (2003) *Ingenieurs en architecten op de drempel van een nieuwe tijd (1750-1830)* [Engineers and architects on the threshold of a new era (1750–1830)]. Leuven: Leuven University Press.

Verdery K (2003) *The Vanishing Hectare.* New Haven, CT: Yale University Press.

Vigier F (1965) An experimental approach to urban design. *Journal of the American Institute of Planners* 31(1): 21–31.

Vitruvius P (20BC) The Ten Books on Architecture (HM Morgan Trans.). Available at: http://www.gutenberg.org/etext/20239 (accessed 30 May 2012).

Waldheim C (ed.) (2006) *The Landscape Urbanism Reader.* New York: Princeton Architectural Press.

Waterhouse A (1993) *Boundaries of the City: The Architecture of Western Urbanism.* Toronto, ON, Canada: University of Toronto Press.

Wimmer CA (1989) *Geschichte der Gartentheory.* Darmstadt: Wissenschaflichte Buckgeschelshaft.

3

Authoritarian High Modernism

James C. Scott

Then, as this morning on the dock, again I saw, as if for the first time in my life, the impeccably straight streets, the glistening glass of the pavement, the divine parallelepipeds of the transparent dwellings, the square harmony of the grayish blue rows of Numbers. And it seemed to me that not past generations, but I myself, had won a victory over the old god and the old life.

Eugene Zamiatin, We

Modern science, which displaced and replaced God, removed that obstacle [limits on freedom]. It also created a vacancy: the office of the supreme legislator-cum-manager, of the designer and administrator of the world order, was now horrifyingly empty. It had to be filled or else.... The emptiness of the throne was throughout the modern era a standing and tempting invitation to visionaries and adventurers. The dream of an all-embracing order and harmony remained as vivid as ever, and it seemed now closer than ever, more than ever within human reach. It was now up to mortal earthlings to bring it about and to secure its ascendancy.

Zygmunt Bauman, Modernity and the Holocaust

… [S]tate simplifications … have the character of maps. That is, they are designed to summarize precisely those aspects of a complex world that are of immediate interest to the mapmaker and to ignore the rest. To complain that a map lacks nuance and detail makes no sense unless it omits information necessary to its function. A city map that aspired to represent every traffic light, every pothole, every building, and every bush and tree in every park would threaten to become as

Original publication details: Scott, James C. 1998. *Seeing Like a State: How Certain Schemes to Improve the Human Condition Have Failed*. New Haven, CT: Yale University Press, pp. 87–102, 376–81. Reproduced with permission from Yale University Press.

Readings in Planning Theory, Fourth Edition. Edited by Susan S. Fainstein and James DeFilippis. Editorial material and organization © 2016 John Wiley & Sons, Ltd. Published 2016 by John Wiley & Sons, Ltd.

large and as complex as the city that it depicted.[1] And it certainly would defeat the purpose of mapping, which is to abstract and summarize. A map is an instrument designed for a purpose. We may judge that purpose noble or morally offensive, but the map itself either serves or fails to serve its intended use.

In case after case, however, we ... [see] the apparent power of maps to transform as well as merely to summarize the facts that they portray. This transformative power resides not in the map, of course, but rather in the power possessed by those who deploy the perspective of that particular map.[2] A private corporation aiming to maximize sustainable timber yields, profit, or production will map its world according to this logic and will use what power it has to ensure that the logic of its map prevails. The state has no monopoly on utilitarian simplifications. What the state does at least aspire to, though, is a monopoly on the legitimate use of force. That is surely why, from the seventeenth century until now, the most transformative maps have been those invented and applied by the most powerful institution in society: the state.

Until recently, the ability of the state to impose its schemes on society was limited by the state's modest ambitions and its limited capacity. Although utopian aspirations to a finely tuned social control can be traced back to Enlightenment thought and to monastic and military practices, the eighteenth-century European state was still largely a machine for extraction. It is true that state officials, particularly under absolutism, had mapped much more of their kingdoms' populations, land tenures, production, and trade than their predecessors had and that they had become increasingly efficient in pumping revenue, grain, and conscripts from the countryside. But there was more than a little irony in their claim to absolute rule. They lacked the consistent coercive power, the fine-grained administrative grid, or the detailed knowledge that would have permitted them to undertake more intrusive experiments in social engineering. To give their growing ambitions full rein, they required a far greater hubris, a state machinery that was equal to the task, and a society they could master. By the mid-nineteenth century in the West and by the early twentieth century elsewhere, these conditions were being met.

I believe that many of the most tragic episodes of state development in the late nineteenth and twentieth centuries originate in a particularly pernicious combination of three elements. The first is the aspiration to the administrative ordering of nature and society, an aspiration ... at work in scientific forestry, but one raised to a far more comprehensive and ambitious level. "High modernism" seems an appropriate term for this aspiration.[3] As a faith, it was shared by many across a wide spectrum of political ideologies. Its main carriers and exponents were the avant-garde among engineers, planners, technocrats, high-level administrators, architects, scientists, and visionaries. If one were to imagine a pantheon or Hall of Fame of high-modernist figures, it would almost certainly include such names as Henri Comte de Saint-Simon, Le Corbusier, Walther Rathenau, Robert McNamara, Robert Moses, Jean Monnet, the Shah of Iran, David Lilienthal, Vladimir I. Lenin, Leon Trotsky, and Julius Nyerere.[4] They envisioned a sweeping, rational engineering of all aspects of social life in order to improve the human condition. As a conviction, high modernism was not the exclusive property of any political tendency; it had both right- and left-wing variants, as we shall see. The second element is the unrestrained use of the power of the modern state as an instrument for achieving these designs. The third element is a weakened or prostrate civil society that lacks the capacity to resist these plans. The ideology of high modernism provides, as it were, the desire; the modern state provides the means of acting on that desire; and the incapacitated civil society provides the leveled terrain on which to build (dis)utopias.

We shall return shortly to the premises of high modernism. But here it is important to note that many of the great state-sponsored calamities of the twentieth century have been the work of rulers with grandiose and utopian plans for their society. One can identify a high-modernist utopianism of the right, of which Nazism is surely the diagnostic example.[5] The massive social engineering under apartheid in South Africa, the modernization plans of the Shah of Iran, villagization in Vietnam, and huge late-colonial development schemes (for example, the Gezira scheme in the Sudan) could be considered under this rubric.[6] And yet there is no denying that much of the massive, state-enforced social engineering of the twentieth century has been the work of progressive, often revolutionary elites. Why?

The answer, I believe, lies in the fact that it is typically progressives who have come to power with a comprehensive critique of existing society and a popular mandate (at least initially) to transform it. These progressives have wanted to use that power to bring about enormous changes in people's habits, work, living patterns, moral conduct, and world view.[7] They have deployed what Václav Havel has called "the armory of holistic social engineering."[8] Utopian aspirations per se are not dangerous. As Oscar Wilde remarked, "A map of the world which does not include Utopia is not worth even glancing at, for it leaves out the one country at which Humanity is always landing."[9] Where the utopian vision goes wrong is when it is held by ruling elites with no commitment to democracy or civil rights and who are therefore likely to use unbridled state power for its achievement. Where it goes brutally wrong is when the society subjected to such utopian experiments lacks the capacity to mount a determined resistance.

What is high modernism, then? It is best conceived as a strong (one might even say muscle-bound) version of the beliefs in scientific and technical progress that were associated with industrialization in Western Europe and in North America from roughly 1830 until World War I. At its center was a supreme self-confidence about continued linear progress, the development of scientific and technical knowledge, the expansion of production, the rational design of social order, the growing satisfaction of human needs, and, not least, an increasing control over nature (including human nature) commensurate with scientific understanding of natural laws.[10] *High modernism* is thus a particularly sweeping vision of how the benefits of technical and scientific progress might be applied – usually through the state – in every field of human activity.[11] If, as we have seen, the simplified, utilitarian *descriptions* of state officials had a tendency, through the exercise of state power, to bring the facts into line with their representations, then one might say that the high-modern state began with extensive *prescriptions* for a new society, and it intended to impose them.

It would have been hard not to have been a modernist of some stripe at the end of the nineteenth century in the West. How could one fail to be impressed – even awed – by the vast transformation wrought by science and industry?[12] Anyone who was, say, sixty years old in Manchester, England, would have witnessed in his or her lifetime a revolution in the manufacturing of cotton and wool textiles, the growth of the factory system, the application of steam power and other astounding new mechanical devices to production, remarkable breakthroughs in metallurgy and transportation (especially railroads), and the appearance of cheap mass-produced commodities. Given the stunning advances in chemistry, physics, medicine, math, and engineering, anyone even slightly attentive to the world of science would have almost come to expect a continuing stream of new marvels (such as the internal combustion engine and electricity). The unprecedented transformations of the nineteenth century may have impoverished and marginalized many, but even the victims recognized that something revolutionary was afoot. All this sounds rather naive today, when we are far more sober about the limits and costs of technological progress and have acquired a postmodern skepticism about any totalizing discourse. Still, this new sensibility ignores both the degree to which modernist assumptions prevail in our lives and, especially, the great enthusiasm and revolutionary hubris that were part and parcel of high modernism.

The Discovery of Society

The path from description to prescription was not so much an inadvertent result of a deep psychological tendency as a deliberate move. The point of the Enlightenment view of legal codes was less to mirror the distinctive customs and practices of a people than to create a cultural community by codifying and generalizing the most rational of those customs and suppressing the more obscure and barbaric ones.[13] Establishing uniform standards of weight and measurement across a kingdom had a greater purpose than just making trade easier; the new standards were intended both to express and to promote a new cultural unity. Well before the tools existed to make good on this cultural revolution, Enlightenment thinkers such as Condorcet were looking ahead to the day when the tools would be in place. He wrote in 1782: "Those sciences, created almost in our own days, the object of which is man himself, the direct goal of which is the happiness of man, will enjoy a progress no less sure than that of the physical sciences, and this idea so sweet, that our descendants will surpass us in wisdom as in enlightenment, is no longer an illusion. In meditating on the nature of the moral sciences, one cannot help seeing that, as they are based like physical sciences on the observation of fact, they must follow the same method, acquire a language equally exact and precise, attaining the same degree of certainty."[14] The gleam in Condorcet's eye became, by the mid-nineteenth century, an active utopian project. Simplification and ratio-nalization previously applied to forests, weights and measures, taxation, and fac-tories were now applied to the design of society as a whole.[15] Industrial-strength social engineering was born. While factories and forests might be planned by private entrepreneurs, the ambition of engineering whole societies was almost exclusively a project of the nation-state.

This new conception of the state's role represented a fundamental transfor-mation. Before then, the state's activities had been largely confined to those that contributed to the wealth and power of the sovereign, as the example of scientific forestry and cameral science illustrated. The idea that one of the central purposes of the state was the improvement of all the members of society – their health, skills and education, longevity, productivity, morals, and family life – was quite novel.[16] There was, of course, a direct connection bet-ween the old conception of the state and this new one. A state that improved its population's skills, vigor, civic morals, and work habits would increase its tax base and field better armies; it was a policy that any enlightened sovereign might pursue. And yet, in the nineteenth century, the welfare of the population came increasingly to be seen, not merely as a means to national strength, but as an end in itself.

One essential precondition of this transformation was the discovery of society as a reified object that was separate from the state and that could be sci-entifically described. In this respect, the production of statistical knowledge about the population – its age profiles, occupations, fertility, literacy, property ownership, law-abidingness (as demonstrated by crime statistics) – allowed state officials to characterize the population in elaborate new ways, much as scientific forestry permitted the forester to carefully describe the forest. Ian Hacking explains how a suicide or homicide rate, for example, came to be seen as a characteristic of a people, so that one could speak of a "budget" of homicides that would be "spent" each year, like routine debits from an account, although the particular murderers and their victims were unknown.[17] Statistical facts were elaborated into social laws. It was but a small step from a simplified description of society to a design and manipulation of society, with its improve-ment in mind. If one could reshape nature to design a more suitable forest, why not reshape society to create a more suitable population?

The scope of intervention was potentially endless. Society became an object that the state might manage and transform with a view toward perfecting it. A progressive nation-state would set about engineering its society according to the most advanced technical standards of the new moral sciences. The existing social order, which had been more or less taken by earlier states as a given, reproducing itself under the watchful eye of the state, was for the first time the subject of active management. It was possible to conceive of an artificial, engineered society designed, not by custom and historical accident, but according to conscious, rational, scientific criteria. Every nook and cranny of the social order might be improved upon: personal hygiene, diet, child rearing, housing, posture, recreation, family structure, and, most infamously, the genetic inheritance of the population.[18] The working poor were often the first subjects of scientific social planning.[19] Schemes for improving their daily lives were promulgated by progressive urban and public-health policies and instituted in model factory towns and newly founded welfare agencies. Subpopulations found wanting in ways that were potentially threatening – such as indigents, vagabonds, the mentally ill, and criminals – might be made the objects of the most intensive social engineering.[20]

The metaphor of gardening, Zygmunt Bauman suggests, captures much of this new spirit. The gardener – perhaps a landscape architect specializing in formal gardens is the most appropriate parallel – takes a natural site and creates an entirely designed space of botanical order. Although the organic character of the flora limits what can be achieved, the gardener has enormous discretion in the overall arrangement and in training, pruning, planting, and weeding out selected plants. As an untended forest is to a long-managed scientific forest, so untended nature is to the garden. The garden is one of man's attempts to impose his own principles of order, utility, and beauty on nature.[21] What grows in the garden is always a small, consciously selected sample of what *might* be grown there. Similarly, social engineers consciously set out to design and maintain a more perfect social order. An Enlightenment belief in the self-improvement of man became, by degrees, a belief in the perfectibility of social order.

One of the great paradoxes of social engineering is that it seems at odds with the experience of modernity generally. Trying to jell a social world, the most striking characteristic of which appears to be flux, seems rather like trying to manage a whirlwind. Marx was hardly alone in claiming that the "constant revolutionizing of production, uninterrupted disturbance of all social relations, everlasting uncertainty and agitation, distinguish the bourgeois epoch from all earlier times."[22] The experience of modernity (in literature, art, industry, transportation, and popular culture) was, above all, the experience of disorienting speed, movement, and change, which self-proclaimed modernists found exhilarating and liberating.[23] Perhaps the most charitable way of resolving this paradox is to imagine that what these designers of society had in mind was roughly what designers of locomotives had in mind with "streamlining." Rather than arresting social change, they hoped to design a shape to social life that would minimize the friction of progress. The difficulty with this resolution is that state social engineering was inherently authoritarian. In place of multiple sources of invention and change, there was a single planning authority; in place of the plasticity and autonomy of existing social life, there was a fixed social order in which positions were designated. The tendency toward various forms of "social taxidermy" was unavoidable.

The Radical Authority of High Modernism

The real thing is that this time we're going to get science applied to social problems and backed by the whole force of the state, just as war has been backed by the whole force of the state in the past. (C. S. Lewis, *That Hideous Strength*)

The troubling features of high modernism derive, for the most part, from its claim to speak about the improvement of the human condition with the authority of scientific knowledge and its tendency to disallow other competing sources of judgment.

First and foremost, high modernism implies a truly radical break with history and tradition. Insofar as rational thought and scientific laws could provide a single answer to every empirical question, nothing ought to be taken for granted. All human habits and practices that were inherited and hence not based on scientific reasoning – from the structure of the family and patterns of residence to moral values and forms of production – would have to be reexamined and redesigned. The structures of the past were typically the products of myth, superstition, and religious prejudice. It followed that scientifically designed schemes for production and social life would be superior to received tradition.

The sources of this view are deeply authoritarian. If a planned social order is better than the accidental, irrational deposit of historical practice, two conclusions follow. Only those who have the scientific knowledge to discern and create this superior social order are fit to rule in the new age. Further, those who through retrograde ignorance refuse to yield to the scientific plan need to be educated to its benefits or else swept aside. Strong versions of high modernism, such as those held by Lenin and Le Corbusier, cultivated an Olympian ruthlessness toward the subjects of their interventions. At its most radical, high modernism imagined wiping the slate utterly clean and beginning from zero.[24]

High-modernist ideology thus tends to devalue or banish politics. Political interests can only frustrate the social solutions devised by specialists with scientific tools adequate to their analysis. As individuals, high modernists might well hold democratic views about popular sovereignty or classical liberal views about the inviolability of a private sphere that restrained them, but such convictions are external to, and often at war with, their high-modernist convictions.

Although high modernists came to imagine the refashioning of social habits and of human nature itself, they began with a nearly limitless ambition to transform nature to suit man's purposes – an ambition that remained central to their faith. How completely the utopian possibilities gripped intellectuals of almost every political persuasion is captured in the paean to technical progress of the *Communist Manifesto*, where Marx and Engels write of the "subjection of nature's forces to man, machinery, and the application of chemistry to agriculture and industry, steam navigation, railways, electric telegraphs, clearing of whole continents for cultivation, canalization of rivers, whole populations conjured out of the ground."[25] In fact, this promise, made plausible by capitalist development, was for Marx the point of departure for socialism, which would place the fruits of capitalism at the service of the working class for the first time. The intellectual air in the late nineteenth century was filled with proposals for such vast engineering projects as the Suez Canal, which was completed in 1869 with enormous consequences for trade between Asia and Europe. The pages of *Le Globe*, the organ of utopian socialists of Saint-Simon's persuasion, featured an endless stream of discussions about massive projects: the construction of the Panama Canal, the development of the United States, far-reaching schemes for energy and transportation. This belief that it was man's destiny to tame nature to suit his interests and preserve his safety is perhaps the keystone of high modernism, partly because the success of so many grand ventures was already manifest.[26]

Once again the authoritarian and statist implications of this vision are clear. The very scale of such projects meant that, with few exceptions (such as the early canals), they demanded large infusions of monies raised through taxes or credit. Even if one could imagine them being financed privately in a capitalist economy, they typically required a vast public authority empowered to condemn private property, relocate people against their will, guarantee the loans or bonds required, and coordinate the work of the many state agencies involved. In a statist society, be it Louis Napoleon's France or Lenin's Soviet Union, such power was already built into the political system. In a nonstatist society, such tasks have required new public authorities or "super-agencies" having quasi-governmental powers for sending men to the moon or for constructing dams, irrigation works, highways, and public transportation systems.

The temporal emphasis of high modernism is almost exclusively on the future. Although any ideology with a large altar dedicated to progress is bound to privilege the future, high modernism carries this to great lengths. The past is an impediment, a history that must be transcended; the present is the platform for launching plans for a better future. A key characteristic of discourses of high modernism and of the public pronouncements of those states that have embraced it is a heavy reliance on visual images of heroic progress toward a totally transformed future.[27] The strategic choice of the future is freighted with consequences. To the degree that the future is known and achievable – a belief that the faith in progress encourages – the less future benefits are discounted for uncertainty. The practical effect is to convince most high modernists that the certainty of a better future justifies the many short-term sacrifices required to get there.[28] The ubiquity of five-year plans in socialist states is an example of that conviction. Progress is objectified by a series of preconceived goals – largely material and quantifiable – which are to be achieved through savings, labor, and investments in the interim. There may, of course, be no alternative to planning, especially when the urgency of a single goal, such as winning a war, seems to require the subordination of every other goal. The immanent logic of such an exercise, however, implies a degree of certainty about the future, about means–ends calculations, and about the meaning of human welfare that is truly heroic. That such plans have often had to be adjusted or abandoned is an indication of just how heroic are the assumptions behind them.

In this reading, high modernism ought to appeal greatly to the classes and strata who have most to gain – in status, power, and wealth – from its world view. And indeed it is the ideology par excellence of the bureaucratic intelligentsia, technicians, planners, and engineers.[29] The position accorded to them is not just one of rule and privilege but also one of responsibility for the great works of nation building and social transformation. Where this intelligentsia conceives of its mission as the dragging of a technically backward, unschooled, subsistence-oriented population into the twentieth century, its self-assigned cultural role as educator of its people becomes doubly grandiose. Having a historic mission of such breadth may provide a ruling intelligentsia with high morale, solidarity, and the willingness to make (and impose) sacrifices. This vision of a great future is often in sharp contrast to the disorder, misery, and unseemly scramble for petty advantage that the elites very likely see in their daily foreground. One might in fact speculate that the more intractable and resistant the real world faced by the planner, the greater the need for utopian plans to fill, as it were, the void that would otherwise invite despair. The elites who elaborate such plans implicitly represent themselves as exemplars of the learning and progressive views to which their compatriots might aspire. Given the ideological advantages of high modernism as a discourse, it is hardly surprising that so many postcolonial elites have marched under its banner.[30]

Aided by hindsight as it is, this unsympathetic account of high-modernist audacity is, in one important respect, grossly unfair. If we put the development of high-modernist beliefs in their historical context, if we ask who the enemies of high modernism actually were, a far more sympathetic picture emerges. Doctors and public-health engineers who did possess new knowledge that could save millions of lives were often thwarted by popular prejudices and entrenched political interests. Urban planners who could in fact redesign urban housing to be cheaper, more healthful, and more convenient were blocked by real-estate interests and existing tastes. Inventors and engineers who had devised revolutionary new modes of power and transportation faced opposition from industrialists and laborers whose profits and jobs the new technology would almost certainly displace.

For nineteenth-century high modernists, the scientific domination of nature (including human nature) was emancipatory. It "promised freedom from scarcity, want and the arbitrariness of natural calamity," David Harvey observes. "The development of rational forms of social organization and rational modes of thought promised liberation from the irrationalities of myth, religion, superstition, release from the arbitrary use of power as well as from the dark side of our human natures."[31] Before we turn to later versions of high modernism, we should recall two important facts about their nineteenth-century forebears: first, that virtually every high-modernist intervention was undertaken in the name of and with the support of citizens seeking help and protection, and, second, that we are all beneficiaries, in countless ways, of these various high-modernist schemes.

Twentieth-Century High Modernism

The idea of a root-and-branch, rational engineering of entire social orders in creating realizable utopias is a largely twentieth-century phenomenon. And a range of historical soils have seemed particularly favorable for the flourishing of high-modernist ideology. Those soils include crises of state power, such as wars and economic depressions, and circumstances in which a state's capacity for relatively unimpeded planning is greatly enhanced, such as the revolutionary conquest of power and colonial rule.

The industrial warfare of the twentieth century has required unprecedented steps toward the total mobilization of the society and the economy.[32] Even quite liberal societies like the United States and Britain became, in the context of war mobilization, directly administered societies. The worldwide depression of the 1930s similarly propelled liberal states into extensive experiments in social and economic planning in an effort to relieve economic distress and to retain popular legitimacy. In the cases of war and depression, the rush toward an administered society has an aspect of *force majeure* to it. The postwar rebuilding of a war-torn nation may well fall in the same category.

Revolution and colonialism, however, are hospitable to high modernism for different reasons. A revolutionary regime and a colonial regime each disposes of an unusual degree of power. The revolutionary state has defeated the *ancien régime*, often has its partisans' mandate to remake the society after its image, *and* faces a prostrate civil society whose capacity for active resistance is limited.[33] The millennial expectations commonly associated with revolutionary movements give further impetus to high-modernist ambitions. Colonial regimes, particularly late colonial regimes, have often been sites of extensive experiments in social engineering.[34] An ideology of "welfare colonialism" combined with the authoritarian power inherent in colonial rule have encouraged ambitious schemes to remake native societies.

If one were required to pinpoint the "birth" of twentieth-century high modernism, specifying a particular time, place, and individual – in what is admittedly a rather arbitrary exercise, given high modernism's many intellectual wellsprings – a strong case can be made for German mobilization during World War I and the figure most closely associated with it, Walther Rathenau. German economic mobilization was the technocratic wonder of the war. That Germany kept its armies in the field and adequately supplied long after most observers had predicted its collapse was largely due to Rathenau's planning.[35] An industrial engineer and head of the great electrical firm A.E.G. (Allgemeine Elektricitäts-Gesellschaft), which had been founded by his father, Rathenau was placed in charge of the Office of War Raw Materials (Kriegsrohstoffabteilung).[36] He realized that the planned rationing of raw materials and transport was the key to sustaining the war effort. Inventing a planned economy step by step, as it were, Germany achieved feats – in industrial production, munitions and armament supply, transportation and traffic control, price controls, and civilian rationing – that had never before been attempted. The scope of planning and coordination necessitated an unprecedented mobilization of conscripts, soldiers, and war-related industrial labor. Such mobilization fostered the idea of creating "administered mass organizations" that would encompass the entire society.[37]

Rathenau's faith in pervasive planning and in rationalizing production had deep roots in the intellectual connection being forged between the physical laws of thermodynamics on one hand and the new applied sciences of work on the other. For many specialists, a narrow and materialist "productivism" treated human labor as a mechanical system which could be decomposed into energy transfers, motion, and the physics of work. The simplification of labor into isolated problems of mechanical efficiencies led directly to the aspiration for a scientific control of the entire labor process. Late nineteenth-century materialism, as Anson Rabinbach emphasizes, had an equivalence between technology and physiology at its metaphysical core.[38]

This productivism had at least two distinct lineages, one of them North American and the other European. An American contribution came from the influential work of Frederick Taylor, whose minute decomposition of factory labor into isolable, precise, repetitive motions had begun to revolutionize the organization of factory work.[39] For the factory manager or engineer, the newly invented assembly lines permitted the use of unskilled labor and control over not only the pace of production but the whole labor process. The European tradition of "energetics," which focused on questions of motion, fatigue, measured rest, rational hygiene, and nutrition, also treated the worker notionally as a machine, albeit a machine that must be well fed and kept in good working order. In place of workers, there was an abstract, standardized worker with uniform physical capacities and needs. Seen initially as a way of increasing wartime efficiency at the front and in industry, the Kaiser Wilhelm Institut für Arbeitsphysiologie, like Taylorism, was based on a scheme to rationalize the body.[40]

What is most remarkable about both traditions is, once again, how widely they were believed by educated elites who were otherwise poles apart politically. "Taylorism and technocracy were the watchwords of a three-pronged idealism: the elimination of economic and social crisis, the expansion of productivity through science, and the reenchantment of technology. The vision of society in which social conflict was eliminated in favor of technological and scientific imperatives could embrace liberal, socialist, authoritarian, and even communist and fascist solutions. Productivism, in short, was politically promiscuous."[41]

The appeal of one or another form of productivism across much of the right and center of the political spectrum was largely due to its promise as a technological "fix" for class struggle. If, as its advocates claimed, it could vastly increase worker output, then the politics of redistribution could be replaced by class collaboration, in which both profits and wages could grow at once. For much of the left, productivism promised the replacement of the capitalist by the engineer or by the state expert or official. It also proposed a single optimum solution, or "best practice," for any problem in the organization of work. The logical outcome was some form of slide-rule authoritarianism in the interest, presumably, of all.[42]

A combination of Rathenau's broad training in philosophy and economics, his wartime experience with planning, and the social conclusions that he thought were inherent in the precision, reach, and transforming potential of electric power allowed him to draw the broadest lessons for social organization. In the war, private industry had given way to a kind of state socialism; "gigantic industrial enterprises had transcended their ostensibly private owners and all the laws of property."[43] The decisions required had nothing to do with ideology; they were driven by purely technical and economic necessities. The rule of specialists and the new technological possibilities, particularly huge electric power grids, made possible a new social-industrial order that was both centralized and locally autonomous. During the time when war made necessary a coalition among industrial firms, technocrats, and the state, Rathenau discerned the shape of a progressive peacetime society. Inasmuch as the technical and economic requirements for reconstruction were obvious and required the same sort of collaboration in all countries, Rathenau's rationalist faith in planning had an internationalist flavor. He characterized the modern era as a "new machine order … [and] a consolidation of the world into an unconscious association of constraint, into an uninterrupted community of production and harmony."[44]

The world war was the high-water mark for the political influence of engineers and planners. Having seen what could be accomplished in extremis, they imagined what they could achieve if the identical energy and planning were devoted to popular welfare rather than mass destruction. Together with many political leaders, industrialists, labor leaders, and prominent intellectuals (such as Philip Gibbs in England, Ernst Jünger in Germany, and Gustave Le Bon in France), they concluded that only a renewed and comprehensive dedication to technical innovation and the planning it made possible could rebuild the European economies and bring social peace.[45]

Lenin himself was deeply impressed by the achievements of German industrial mobilization and believed that it had shown how production might be socialized. Just as Lenin believed that Marx had discovered immutable social laws akin to Darwin's laws of evolution, so he believed that the new technologies of mass production were scientific laws and not social constructions. Barely a month before the October 1917 revolution, he wrote that the war had "accelerated the development of capitalism to such a tremendous degree, converting monopoly capitalism into *state*-monopoly capitalism, that *neither* the proletariat *nor* the revolutionary petty-bourgeois democrats *can* keep within the limits of capitalism."[46] He and his economic advisers drew directly on the work of Rathenau and Mollendorf in their plans for the Soviet economy. The German war economy was for Lenin "the ultimate in modern, large-scale capitalist techniques, planning and organization"; he took it to be the prototype of a socialized economy.[47] Presumably, if the state in question were in the hands of representatives of the working class, the basis of a socialist system would exist. Lenin's vision of the future looked much like Rathenau's, providing, of course, we ignore the not so small matter of a revolutionary seizure of power.

Lenin was not slow to appreciate how Taylorism on the factory floor offered advantages for the socialist control of production. Although he had earlier denounced such techniques, calling them the "scientific extortion of sweat," by the time of the revolution he had become an enthusiastic advocate of systematic control as practiced in Germany. He extolled "the principle of discipline, organization, and harmonious cooperation based upon the most modern, mechanized industry, the most rigid system of accountability and control."[48]

> The Taylor system, the last word of capitalism in this respect, like all capitalist progress, is a combination of the subtle brutality of bourgeois exploitation and a number of its great scientific achievements in the fields of analysing mechanical motions during work, the elimination of superfluous and awkward motions, the working out of correct methods of work, the introduction of the best system of accounting and control, etc. The Soviet Republic must at all costs adopt all that is valuable in the achievements of science and technology in this field. ... We must organize in Russia the study and teaching of the Taylor system and systematically try it out and adapt it to our purposes.[49]

By 1918, with production falling, he was calling for rigid work norms and, if necessary, the reintroduction of hated piecework. The first All-Russian Congress for Initiatives in Scientific Management was convened in 1921 and featured disputes between advocates of Taylorism and those of energetics (also called ergonomics). At least twenty institutes and as many journals were by then devoted to scientific management in the Soviet Union. A command economy at the macrolevel and Taylorist principles of central coordination at the microlevel of the factory floor provided an attractive and symbiotic package for an authoritarian, high-modernist revolutionary like Lenin.

Despite the authoritarian temptations of twentieth-century high modernism, they have often been resisted. The reasons are not only complex; they are different from case to case. While it is not my intention to examine in detail all the potential obstacles to high-modernist planning, the particular barrier posed by liberal democratic ideas and institutions deserves emphasis. Three factors seem decisive. The first is the existence and belief in a private sphere of activity in which the state and its agencies may not legitimately interfere. To be sure, this zone of autonomy has had a beleaguered existence as, following Mannheim, more heretofore private spheres have been made the object of official intervention. Much of the work of Michel Foucault was an attempt to map these incursions into health, sexuality, mental illness, vagrancy, or sanitation and the strategies behind them. Nevertheless, the idea of a private realm has served to limit the ambitions of many high modernists, through either their own political values or their healthy respect for the political storm that such incursions would provoke.

The second, closely related factor is the private sector in liberal political economy. As Foucault put it: unlike absolutism and mercantilism, "political economy announces the unknowability for the sovereign of the totality of economic processes and, as a consequence, the *impossibility of an economic sovereignty.*"[50] The point of liberal political economy was not only that a free market protected property and created wealth but also that the economy was far too complex for it ever to be managed in detail by a hierarchical administration.[51]

The third and by far most important barrier to thoroughgoing high-modernist schemes has been the existence of working, representative institutions through which a resistant society could make its influence felt. Such institutions have thwarted the most draconian features of high-modernist schemes in roughly the same way that publicity and mobilized opposition in open societies, as Amartya Sen has argued, have prevented famines. Rulers, he notes, do not go hungry, and they are unlikely to learn about and respond readily to curb famine unless their institutional position provides strong incentives. The freedoms of speech, of assembly, and of the press ensure that widespread hunger will be publicized, while the freedoms of assembly and elections in representative institutions ensure that it is in the interest of elected officials' self-preservation to prevent famine when they can. In the same fashion, high-modernist schemes in liberal democratic settings must accommodate themselves sufficiently to local opinion in order to avoid being undone at the polls.

Notes

1. My colleague Paul Landau recalls the story by Borges in which a king, unhappy at maps that do not do justice to his kingdom, finally insists on a map with a scale of one-to-one. When complete, the new map exactly covers the existing kingdom, submerging the real one beneath its representation.

2. A commonplace example may help. One of the ordinary frustrations of the modern citizen, even in liberal democracies, is the difficulty of representing his unique case to a powerful agent of a bureaucratic institution. But the functionary operates with a simplified grid designed to cover all the cases that she confronts. Once a decision has been made as to which "bin" or "pigeonhole" the case falls into, the action to be taken or the protocol to be followed is largely cut-and-dried. The functionary endeavors to sort the case into the appropriate category, while the citizen resists being treated as an instance of a category and tries to insist, often unsuccessfully, that his unique case be examined on its singular merits.

3. I have borrowed the term "high modernism" from David Harvey, *The Condition of Post-Modernity: An Enquiry into the Origins of Social Change* (Oxford: Basil Blackwell, 1989). Harvey locates the high-water mark of this sort of modernism in the post–World War II period, and his concern is particularly with capitalism and the organization of production. But his description of high modernism also works well here: "The belief 'in linear progress, absolute truths, and rational planning of ideal social orders' under standardized conditions of knowledge and production was particularly strong. The modernism

that resulted was, as a result, 'positivistic, technocratic, and rationalistic' at the same time as it was imposed as the work of an elite avant-garde of planners, artists, architects, critics, and other guardians of high taste. The 'modernization' of European economies proceeded apace, while the whole thrust of international politics and trade was justified as bringing a benevolent and progressive 'modernization process' to a backward Third World" (p. 35).

4. For case studies of "public entrepreneurs" in the United States, see Eugene Lewis's study of Hyman Rickover, J. Edgar Hoover, and Robert Moses, *Public Entrepreneurs: Toward a Theory of Bureaucratic Political Power: The Organizational Lives of Hyman Rickover, J. Edgar Hoover, and Robert Moses* (Bloomington: Indiana University Press, 1980). Monnet, like Rathenau, had experience in economic mobilization during World War I, when he helped organize the transatlantic supply of war material for Britain and France, a role that he resumed during World War II. By the time he helped plan the postwar integration of French and German coal and steel production, he had already had several decades of experience in supranational management. See François Duchene, *Jean Monnet: The First Statesman of Interdependence* (New York: Norton, 1995).

5. I will not pursue the argument here, but I think Nazism is best understood as a reactionary form of modernism. Like the progressive left, the Nazi elites had grandiose visions of state-enforced social engineering, which included, of course, extermination, expulsion, forced sterilization, and selective breeding and which aimed at "improving" genetically on human nature. The case for Nazism as a virulent form of modernism is made brilliantly and convincingly by Zygmunt Bauman in *Modernity and the Holocaust* (Oxford: Oxford University Press, 1989). See also, along the same lines, Jeffery Herf, *Reactionary Modernism: Technology, Culture, and Politics in Weimar and the Third Reich* (Cambridge: Cambridge University Press, 1984), and Norbert Frei, *National Socialist Rule in Germany: The Führer State, 1933–1945*, trans. Simon B. Steyne (Oxford: Oxford University Press, 1993).

6. I am grateful to James Ferguson for reminding me that reactionary high-modernist schemes are about as ubiquitous as progressive variants.

7. This is not by any means meant to be a brief for conservatism. Conservatives of many stripes may care little for civil liberties and may resort to whatever brutalities seem necessary to remain in power. But their ambitions and hubris are much more limited; their plans (in contrast to those of reactionary modernists) do not necessitate turning society upside down to create new collectivities, new family and group loyalties, and new people.

8. Václav Havel, address given at Victoria University, Wellington, New Zealand, on March 31, 1995, reprinted in the *New York Review of Books* 42, no. 11 (June 22, 1995): 36.

9. Quoted in Zygmunt Bauman, *Socialism: The Active Utopia* (New York: Holmes and Meier, 1976), p. 11.

10. For an enlightening discussion of the intellectual lineage of authoritarian environmentalism, see Douglas R. Weiner, "Demythologizing Environmentalism," *Journal of the History of Biology* 25, no. 3 (Fall 1992): 385–411.

11. See Michael Adas's *Machines as the Measure of Men: Science, Technology, and Ideologies of Western Dominance* (Ithaca: Cornell University Press, 1989) and Marshall Berman's *All That Is Solid Melts into Air: The Experience of Modernity* (New York: Penguin, 1988). What is new in high modernism, I believe, is not so much the aspiration for comprehensive

planning. Many imperial and absolutist states have had similar aspirations. What are new are the administrative technology and social knowledge that make it plausible to imagine organizing an entire society in ways that only the barracks or the monastery had been organized before. In this respect, Michel Foucault's argument, in *Discipline and Punish: The Birth of the Prison*, trans. Alan Sheridan (New York: Vintage Books, 1977), is persuasive.

12. Here I want to distinguish between advances in scientific knowledge and inventions (many of which occurred in the eighteenth century or earlier) and the massive transformations that scientific inventions wrought in daily material life (which came generally in the nineteenth century).

13. Witold Kula, *Measures and Men*, trans. R. Szreter (Princeton: Princeton University Press, 1986), p. 211.

14. Quoted in Ian Hacking, *The Taming of Chance* (Cambridge: Cambridge University Press, 1990), p. 38. A few years later, the Jacobins were, one could argue, the first to attempt to actually engineer happiness by transforming the social order. As Saint-Just wrote, "The idea of happiness is new in Europe." See Albert O. Hirschman, "Rival Interpretations of Market Society: Civilizing, Destructive, or Feeble," *Journal of Economic Literature* 20 (December 1982): 1463–84.

15. I am greatly indebted to James Ferguson, whose perceptive comments on an early draft of the book pointed me in this direction.

16. See, for example, Graham Buschell, Colin Gordon, and Peter Miller, eds., *The Foucault Effect: Studies in Governmentality* (London: Harvester Wheatsheaf, 1991), chap. 4.

17. Hacking, *The Taming of Chance*, p. 105. Hacking shows brilliantly how a statistical "average" metamorphosed into the category "normal," and "normal," in turn, into a "normative" standard to be achieved by social engineering.

18. By now, a great deal of historical research has made crystal clear how widespread throughout the West was the support for eugenic engineering. The belief that the state must intervene to protect the races' physical and mental characteristics was common among progressives and animated a well-nigh international social movement. By 1926, twenty-three of the forty-eight US states had laws permitting sterilization.

19. See Gareth Stedman-Jones, *Languages of Class: Studies in English Working-Class History, 1832–1982* (Cambridge: Cambridge University Press, 1983). It is important to recognize that, among Western powers, virtually all the initiatives associated with the "civilizing missions" of colonialism were preceded by comparable programs to assimilate and civilize their own lower-class populations, both rural and urban. The difference, perhaps, is that in the colonial setting officials had greater coercive power over an objectified and alien population, thus allowing for greater feats of social engineering.

20. For a science-fiction account of the attempt to create a "technocratic and objective man" who would be free of "nature," see C. S. Lewis, *That Hideous Strength: A Modern Fairy Tale for Grown-Ups* (New York: Macmillan, 1946).

21. There is the interesting and problematic case of the "wild" garden, in which the precise shape of "disorder" is minutely planned. Here it is a matter of an aesthetic plan, designed to have a certain effect on the eye – an attempt to copy untended nature. The paradox is just as intractable as that of a zoo designed to mimic nature – intractable, that is, until one realizes that the design does not extend to allowing the critters to eat one another!

22. Karl Marx, from the *Communist Manifesto*, quoted in Berman, *All That Is Solid Melts into Air*, p. 95.

23. The airplane, having replaced the locomotive, was in many respects the defining image of modernity in the early twentieth century. In 1913, the futurist artist and playwright Kazimir Malevich created the sets for an opera entitled *Victory over the Sun*. In the last scene, the audience heard from offstage a propeller's roar and shouts announcing that gravity had been overcome in futurist countries. Le Corbusier, Malevich's near contemporary, thought the airplane was the reigning symbol of the new age. For the influence of flight, see Robert Wohl, *A Passion for Wings: Aviation and the Western Imagination, 1908–1918* (New Haven: Yale University Press, 1996).

24. The Jacobins intended just such a fresh start, starting the calendar again at "year one" and renaming the days and months according to a new, secular system. To signal its intention to create a wholly new Cambodian nation, the Pol Pot regime began with "year zero."

25. Quoted in Harvey, *The Condition of Post-Modernity*, p. 99.

26. In this section, the masculine personal pronoun is less a convention than a choice made with some deliberation. See Carolyn Merchant, *The Death of Nature: Women, Ecology, and the Scientific Revolution* (San Francisco: Harper, 1980).

27. See, for example, Margaret M. Bullitt, "Toward a Marxist Theory of Aesthetics: The Development of Socialist Realism in the Soviet Union," *Russian Review* 35, no. 1 (January 1976): 53–76.

28. Baruch Knei-Paz, "Can Historical Consequences Falsify Ideas? Or, Karl Marx after the Collapse of the Soviet Union," paper presented to Political Theory Workshop, Department of Political Science, Yale University, New Haven, November 1994.

29. Raymond Aron's prophetic dissent, *The Opium of the Intellectual*, trans. Terence Kilmartin (London: Secker & Warburg, 1957), is a key document in this context.

30. The larger, the more capital-intensive, and the more centralized the schemes, the greater their appeal in terms of power and patronage. For a critique of flood-control projects and World Bank projects in this context, see James K. Boyce, "Birth of a Megaproject: Political Economy of Flood Control in Bangladesh," *Environmental Management* 14, no. 4 (1990): 419–28.

31. Harvey, *The Condition of Post-Modernity*, p. 12.

32. See Charles Tilly's important theoretical contribution in *Coercion, Capital, and European States, a.d. 990–1992* (Oxford: Blackwell, 1990).

33. A civil war, as in the Bolshevik case, may be the price of consolidating the revolutionaries' power.

34. White-settler colonies (e.g., South Africa, Algeria) and anti-insurgency campaigns (e.g., Vietnam, Algeria, Afghanistan) have carried out huge population removals and forced resettlements. In most such cases, however, even the pretense that the comprehensive social planning was for the welfare of the affected populations has been paper-thin.

35. Here I am particularly indebted to the discussion of George Yaney, *The Urge to Mobilize: Agrarian Reform in Russia* (Urbana: University of Illinois Press, 1982), pp. 448–62.

36. Anson Rabinbach, *The Human Motor: Energy, Fatigue, and the Origins of Modernity* (Berkeley: University of California Press, 1992), pp. 260–71. In 1907, long before the war,

Rathenau and a number of architects and political leaders had founded Deutsche Werkbund, which was devoted to fostering technical innovation in industry and the arts.

37. See Gregory J. Kasza, *The Conscription Society: Administered Mass Organizations* (New Haven: Yale University Press, 1995), especially chap. 1, pp. 7–25.

38. Rabinbach, *The Human Motor*, p. 290.

39. For recent assessments of the evolution of technology and production in the United States, see Nathan Rosenberg, *Perspectives on Technology* (Cambridge: Cambridge University Press, 1976); Rosenberg, *Inside the Black Box: Technology and Economics* (New York: Cambridge University Press, 1982); and Philip Scranton, *Figured Tapestry: Production, Markets, and Power in Philadelphia, 1885–1942* (New York: Cambridge University Press, 1989).

40. See the inventive article by Ernest J. Yanorella and Herbert Reid, "From 'Trained Gorilla' to 'Humanware': Repoliticizing the Body-Machine Complex between Fordism and Post-Fordism," in Theodore R. Schatzki and Wolfgang Natter, eds., *The Social and Political Body* (New York: Guildford Press, 1996), pp. 181–219.

41. Rabinbach, *The Human Motor*, p. 272. Rabinbach is here paraphrasing the conclusions of a seminal article by Charles S. Maier, "Between Taylorism and Technocracy: European Ideologies and the Vision of Industrial Productivity in the 1920s," *Journal of Contemporary History* 5, no. 2 (1970): 27–63.

42. Thorstein Veblen was the best-known social scientist expounding this view in the United States. Literary versions of this ideology are apparent in Sinclair Lewis's *Arrowsmith* and Ayn Rand's *Fountainhead*, works from very different quadrants of the political spectrum.

43. Rabinbach, *The Human Motor*, p. 452. For Rathenau's writings, see, for example, *Von kommenden Dingen* (Things to come) and *Die Neue Wirtschaft* (The new economy), the latter written after the war.

44. Walther Rathenau, *Von kommenden Dingen* (1916), quoted in Maier, "Between Taylorism and Technocracy," p. 47. Maier notes that the apparent harmony of capital and labor in wartime Germany was achieved at the cost of an eventually ruinous policy of inflation (p. 46).

45. Michael Adas, *Machines as the Measure of Men: Science, Technology, and Ideologies of Western Dominance* (Ithaca: Cornell University Press, 1989), p. 380. Sheldon Wolin, in *Politics and Vision: Continuity and Innovation in Western Political Thought* (Boston: Little, Brown, 1960), provides an extensive list of like-minded thinkers spanning the political spectrum, from fascists and nationalists at one end to liberals, social democrats, and communists at the other, and hailing from France, Germany, Austria-Prussia (the Prussian Richard von Moellendorf, a close associate of Rathenau and a publicist for a managed postwar economy), Italy (Antonio Gramsci on the left and fascists Masimo Rocca and Benito Mussolini on the right), and Russia (Alexej Kapitonovik Gastev, the "Soviet Taylor").

46. V. I. Lenin, *The Agrarian Programme of Social-Democracy in the First Russian Revolution, 1905–1907*, 2nd rev. ed. (Moscow: Progress Publishers, 1954), p. 195, written September 28, 1917 (first emphasis only added).

47. Leon Smolinski, "Lenin and Economic Planning," *Studies in Comparative Communism* 2, no. 1 (January 1969): 99. Lenin and Trotsky were explicit, Smolinski claims, about how electric centrals would create a farm population dependent on the center and thus make state control of agricultural production possible (pp. 106–7).

48. Lenin, *Works* (Moscow, 1972), 27: 163, quoted in Ranier Traub, "Lenin and Taylor: The Fate of 'Scientific Management' in the (Early) Soviet Union," trans. Judy Joseph, *Telos* 34 (Fall 1978): 82–92 (originally published in *Kursbuch* 43 (1976). The "bard" of Taylorism in the Soviet Union was Alexej Kapitonovik Gastev, whose poetry and essays waxed lyrical about the possibilities of a "union" between man and machine: "Many find it repugnant that we want to deal with human beings as a screw, a nut, a machine. But we must undertake this as fearlessly as we accept the growth of trees and the expansion of the railway network" (quoted in ibid., p. 88). Most of the labor institutes were closed and their experts deported or shot in the Stalinist purges of the 1930s.

49. Lenin, "The Immediate Tasks of the Soviet Government," *Izvestia*, April 28, 1918, cited in Maier, "Between Taylorism and Technocracy," p. 51 n. 58.

50. Graham Burchell, Colin Gordon, and Peter Miller, *The Foucault Effect: Studies in Governmentality*, with two lectures by and an interview with Michel Foucault (London: Wheatsheaf, 1991), p. 106.

51. This point has been made forcefully and polemically in the twentieth century by Friedrich Hayek, the darling of those opposed to postwar planning and the welfare state. See, especially, *The Road to Serfdom* (Chicago: University of Chicago Press, 1976).

4

The Death and Life of Great American Cities

Jane Jacobs

This chapter is an attack on current city planning and rebuilding. It is also, and mostly, an attempt to introduce new principles of city planning and rebuilding, different and even opposite from those now taught in everything from schools of architecture and planning to the Sunday supplements and women's magazines. My attack is not based on quibbles about rebuilding methods or hairsplitting about fashions in design. It is an attack, rather, on the principles and aims that have shaped modern, orthodox city planning and rebuilding.

In setting forth different principles, I shall mainly be writing about common, ordinary things: for instance, what kinds of city streets are safe and what kinds are not; why some city parks are marvelous and others are vice traps and death traps; why some slums stay slums and other slums regenerate themselves even against financial and official opposition; what makes downtowns shift their centers; what, if anything, is a city neighborhood, and what jobs, if any, neighborhoods in great cities do. In short, I shall be writing about how cities work in real life, because this is the only way to learn what principles of planning and what practices in rebuilding can promote social and economic vitality in cities, and what practices and principles will deaden these attributes.

There is a wistful myth that if only we had enough money to spend – the figure is usually put at $100 billion – we could wipe out all our slums in ten years, reverse decay in the great, dull, gray belts that were yesterday's and day-before-yesterday's suburbs, anchor the wandering middle class and its wandering tax money, and perhaps even solve the traffic problem.

Original publication details: Jacobs, Jane. 1961. *The Death and Life of Great American Cities*. London: Jonathan Cape. © 1961, 1989 by Jane Jacobs. Used in the UK and Commonwealth (excl. Canada) with permission from The Random House Group Limited and in the rest of the world and in electronic formats worldwide with permission from Random House, an imprint and division of Penguin Random House LLC.

Readings in Planning Theory, Fourth Edition. Edited by Susan S. Fainstein and James DeFilippis. Editorial material and organization © 2016 John Wiley & Sons, Ltd. Published 2016 by John Wiley & Sons, Ltd.

But look what we have built with the first several billions: low-income projects that become worse centers of delinquency, vandalism, and general social hopelessness than the slums they were supposed to replace. Middle-income housing projects that are truly marvels of dullness and regimentation, sealed against any buoyancy or vitality of city life. Luxury housing projects that mitigate their inanity, or try to, with a vapid vulgarity. Cultural centers that are unable to support a good bookstore. Civic centers that are avoided by everyone but bums, who have fewer choices of loitering place than others. Commercial centers that are lackluster imitations of standardized suburban chain-store shopping. Promenades that go from no place to nowhere and have no promenaders. Expressways that eviscerate great cities. This is not the rebuilding of cities. This is the sacking of cities.

Under the surface, these accomplishments prove even poorer than their poor pretenses. They seldom aid the city areas around them, as in theory they are supposed to. These amputated areas typically develop galloping gangrene. To house people in this planned fashion, price tags are fastened on the population, and each sorted-out chunk of price-tagged populace lives in growing suspicion and tension against the surrounding city. When two or more such hostile islands are juxtaposed the result is called "a balanced neighborhood." Monopolistic shopping centers and monumental cultural centers cloak, under the public relations hoo-ha, the subtraction of commerce, and of culture too, from the intimate and casual life of cities.

That such wonders may be accomplished, people who get marked with the planners' hex signs are pushed about, expropriated, and uprooted much as if they were the subjects of a conquering power. Thousands upon thousands of small businesses are destroyed, and their proprietors ruined, with hardly a gesture at compensation. Whole communities are torn apart and sown to the winds, with a reaping of cynicism, resentment, and despair that must be heard and seen to be believed. A group of clergymen in Chicago, appalled at the fruits of planned city rebuilding there, asked,

> Could Job have been thinking of Chicago when he wrote:
> Here are men that alter their neighbor's landmark ...
> shoulder the poor aside, conspire to oppress the friendless.
> Reap they the field that is none of theirs, strip they the vine-yard wrongfully seized
>   from its owner ...
> A cry goes up from the city streets, where wounded men lie groaning ...

If so, he was thinking of New York, Philadelphia, Boston, Washington, St Louis, San Francisco, and a number of other places. The economic rationale of current city rebuilding is a hoax. The economics of city rebuilding do not rest soundly on reasoned investment of public tax subsidies, as urban renewal theory proclaims, but also on vast, involuntary subsidies wrung out of helpless site victims. And the increased tax returns from such sites, accruing to the cities as a result of this "investment," are a mirage, a pitiful gesture against the ever-increasing sums of public money needed to combat disintegration and instability that flow from the cruelly shaken-up city. The means to planned city rebuilding are as deplorable as the ends.

Meantime, all the art and science of city planning are helpless to stem decay – and the spiritlessness that precedes decay – in ever more massive swatches of cities. Nor can this decay be laid, reassuringly, to lack of opportunity to apply the arts of planning. It seems to matter little whether they are applied or not. Consider the Morningside Heights area in New York City. According to planning theory it should not be in trouble at all, for it enjoys a great abundance of parkland, campus, playground, and other open spaces. It has plenty of grass. It occupies high and pleasant ground with magnificent river views. It is a famous educational center with splendid institutions – Columbia University, Union Theological Seminary, the Juilliard School of Music, and half a dozen others of eminent respectability. It is the beneficiary of good hospitals and churches. It has no industries. Its streets are zoned in the main against "incompatible uses" intruding into the preserves for solidly constructed, roomy, middle-and upper-class apartments. Yet by the early 1950s Morningside Heights was becoming a slum so swiftly, the surly kind of slum in which people fear to walk the streets, that the situation posed a crisis for the institutions. They and the planning arms of the city government got together, applied more planning theory, wiped out the most run-down part of the area and built in its stead a middle-income cooperative project complete with shopping center and a public housing project – all interspersed with air, light, sunshine, and landscaping. This was hailed as a great demonstration in city saving.

After that Morningside Heights went downhill even faster.

Nor is this an unfair or irrelevant example. In city after city, precisely the wrong areas, in the light of planning theory, are decaying. Less noticed, but equally significant, in city after city the wrong areas, in the light of planning theory, are refusing to decay.

Cities are an immense laboratory of trial and error, failure and success, in city building and city design. This is the laboratory in which city planning should have been learning and forming and testing its theories. Instead the practitioners and teachers of this discipline (if such it can be called) have ignored the study of success and failure in real life, have been incurious about the reasons for unexpected success, and are guided instead by principles derived from the behavior and appearance of towns, suburbs, tuberculosis sanatoria, fairs, and imaginary dream cities – from anything but cities themselves.

If it appears that the rebuilt portions of cities and the endless new developments spreading beyond the cities are reducing city and countryside alike to a monotonous, unnourishing gruel, this is not strange. It all comes, first-, second-, third-, or fourth-hand, out of the same intellectual dish of mush, a mush in which the qualities, necessities, advantages, and behavior of great cities have been utterly confused with the qualities, necessities, advantages, and behavior of other and more inert types of settlements.

There is nothing economically or socially inevitable about either the decay of old cities or the fresh-minted decadence of the new unurban urbanization. On the contrary, no other aspect of our economy and society has been more purposefully manipulated for a full quarter of a century to achieve precisely what we are getting. Extraordinary governmental financial incentives have been required to achieve this degree of monotony, sterility, and vulgarity. Decades of preaching, writing, and exhorting by experts have gone into convincing us and our legislators that mush like this must be good for us, as long as it comes bedded with grass.

Automobiles are often conveniently tagged as the villains responsible for the ills of cities and the disappointments and futilities of city planning. But the destructive effects of automobiles are much less a cause than a symptom of our incompetence at city building. Of course planners, including the highwaymen with fabulous sums of money and enormous powers at their disposal, are at a loss to make automobiles and cities compatible with one another. They do not know what to do with automobiles in cities because they do not know how to plan for workable and vital cities anyhow – with or without automobiles.

The simple needs of automobiles are more easily understood and satisfied than the complex needs of cities, and a growing number of planners and designers have come to believe that if they can only solve the problems of traffic, they will thereby have solved the major problem of cities. Cities have much more intricate economic and social concerns than automobile traffic. How can you know what to try with traffic until you know how the city itself works and what else it needs to do with its streets? You can't.

It may be that we have become so feckless as a people that we no longer care how things do work but only what kind of quick, easy outer impression they give. If so, there is little hope for our cities or probably for much else in our society. But I do not think this is so.

Specifically, in the case of planning for cities, it is clear that a large number of good and earnest people do care deeply about building and renewing. Despite some corruption, and considerable greed for the other man's vineyard, the intentions going into the messes we make are, on the whole, exemplary. Planners, architects of city design, and those they have led along with them in their beliefs are not consciously disdainful of the importance of knowing how things work. On the contrary, they have gone to great pains to learn what the saints and sages of modern orthodox planning have said about how cities *ought* to work and what *ought* to be good for people and businesses in them. They take this with such devotion that when contradictory reality intrudes, threatening to shatter their dearly won learning, they must shrug reality aside.

Consider, for example, the orthodox planning reaction to a district called the North End in Boston. This is an old, low-rent area merging into the heavy industry of the waterfront, and it is officially considered Boston's worst slum and civic shame. It embodies attributes that all enlightened people know are evil, because so many wise men have said they are evil. Not only is the North End bumped right up against industry, but worse still it has all kinds of working places and commerce mingled in the greatest complexity with its residences. It has the highest concentration of dwelling units, on the land that is used for dwelling units, of any part of Boston, and indeed one of the highest concentrations to be found in any American city. It has little parkland. Children play in the streets. Instead of superblocks, or even decently large blocks, it has very small blocks; in planning parlance it is "badly cut up with wasteful streets." Its buildings are old. Everything conceivable is presumably wrong with the North End. In orthodox planning terms, it is a three-dimensional textbook of "megalopolis" in the last stages of depravity. The North End is thus a recurring assignment for MIT and Harvard planning and architectural students, who now and again pursue, under the guidance of their teachers, the paper exercise of converting it into superblocks and park prome-nades, wiping away its nonconforming uses, transforming it to an ideal of order and gentility so simple it could be engraved on the head of a pin.

Twenty years ago, when I first happened to see the North End, its buildings – town houses of different kinds and sizes converted to flats, and four- or five-storey tenements built to house the flood of immigrants first from Ireland, then from Eastern Europe, and finally from Sicily – were badly overcrowded, and the general effect was of a dis-trict taking a terrible physical beating and certainly desperately poor.

When I saw the North End again in 1959, I was amazed at the change. Dozens and dozens of buildings had been rehabilitated. Instead of mattresses against the windows, there were Venetian blinds and glimpses of fresh paint. Many of the small, converted houses now had only one or two families in them instead of the old crowded three or four. Some of the families in the tenements (as I learned later, visiting inside) had uncrowded themselves by throwing two older apart-ments together, and had equipped these with bathrooms, new kitchens, and the like. I looked down a narrow alley, thinking to find at least here the old, squalid North End, but no: more neatly repointed brickwork, new blinds, and a burst of music as a door opened. Indeed, this was the only city district I have ever seen – or have seen to this day – in which the sides of buildings around parking lots had not been left raw and amputated, but repaired and painted as neatly as if they were intended to be seen. Mingled all among the buildings for living were an incredible number of splendid food stores, as well as such enterprises as upholstery making, metalworking, carpentry, food processing. The streets were alive with children playing, people shopping, people strolling, people talking. Had it not been a cold January day, there would surely have been people sitting.

The general street atmosphere of buoyancy, friendliness, and good health was so infectious that I began asking directions of people just for the fun of getting in on some talk. I had seen a lot of Boston in the past couple of days, most of it sorely distressing, and this struck me, with relief, as the healthiest place in the city. But I could not imagine where the money had come from for the rehabilitation, because it is almost impossible today to get any appreciable mortgage money in districts of American cities that are not either high-rent, or else imitations of suburbs. To find out, I went into a bar and restaurant (where an animated conversation about fishing was in progress) and called a Boston planner I know.

"Why in the world are you down in the North End?" he said. "Money? Why, no money or work has gone into the North End. Nothing's going on down there. Eventually, yes, but not yet. That's a slum!"

"It doesn't seem like a slum to me," I said.

"Why, that's the worst slum in the city. It has 275 dwelling units to the net acre! I hate to admit we have anything like that in Boston, but it's a fact."

"Do you have any other figures on it?" I asked.

"Yes, funny thing. It has among the lowest delinquency, disease, and infant mortality rates in the city. It also has the lowest ratio of rent to income in the city. Boy, are those people getting bargains. Let's see ... the child population is just above average for the city, on the nose. The death rate is low, 8.8 per thousand, against the average city rate of 11.2. The TB death rate is very low, less than 1 per ten thousand, can't understand it, it's lower even than Brookline's. In the old days the North End used to be the city's worst spot for tuberculosis, but all that has changed. Well, they must be strong people. Of course it's a terrible slum."

"You should have more slums like this," I said. "Don't tell me there are plans to wipe this out. You ought to be down here learning as much as you can from it."

"I know how you feel," he said. "I often go down there myself just to walk around the streets and feel that wonderful, cheerful street life. Say, what you ought to do, you ought to come back and go down in the summer if you think it's fun now. You'd be crazy about it in summer. But of course we have to rebuild it eventually. We've got to get those people off the streets."

Here was a curious thing. My friend's instincts told him the North End was a good place, and his social statistics confirmed it. But everything he had learned as a physical planner about what is good for people and good for city neighborhoods, everything that made him an expert, told him the North End had to be a bad place.

The leading Boston savings banker, "a man way up there in the power structure," to whom my friend referred me for my inquiry about the money, confirmed what I learned, in the meantime, from people in the North End. The money had not come through the grace of the great American banking system, which now knows enough about planning to know a slum as well as the planners do. "No sense in lending money into the North End," the banker said. "It's a slum! It's still getting some immigrants! Furthermore, back in the Depression it had a very large number of foreclosures; bad record." (I had heard about this too, in the meantime, and how families had worked and pooled their resources to buy back some of those foreclosed buildings.)

The largest mortgage loans that had been fed into this district of some 15,000 people in the quarter-century since the Great Depression were for $3,000, the banker told me, "and very, very few of those." There had been some others for $1,000 and for $2,000. The rehabilitation work had been almost entirely financed by business and housing earnings within the district, plowed back in, and by skilled work bartered among residents and relatives of residents.

By this time I knew that this inability to borrow for improvement was a galling worry to North Enders, and that furthermore some North Enders were worried because it seemed impossible to get new building in the area except at a price of seeing themselves and their community wiped out in the fashion of the students' dreams of a city Eden, a fate that they knew was not academic because it had already smashed completely a socially similar – although physically more spacious – nearby district called the West End. They were worried because they were aware also that patch and fix with nothing else could not do forever. "Any chance of loans for new construction in the North End?" I asked the banker.

"No, absolutely not!" he said, sounding impatient at my denseness. "That's a slum!"

Bankers, like planners, have theories about cities on which they act. They have gotten their theories from the same intellectual sources as the planners. Bankers and government administrative officials who guarantee mortgages do not invent planning theories nor, surprisingly, even economic doctrine about cities. They are enlightened nowadays, and they pick up their ideas from idealists, a generation later. Since theoretical city planning has embraced no major new ideas for considerably more than a generation, theoretical planners, financiers, and bureaucrats are all just about even today.

And to put it bluntly, they are all in the same stage of elaborately learned superstition as medical science was early in the last century, when physicians put their faith in bloodletting, to draw out the evil humors that were believed to cause disease. With bloodletting, it took years of learning to know precisely which veins, by what rituals, were to be opened for what symptoms. A superstructure of technical complication was erected in such deadpan detail that the literature still sounds almost plausible. However, because people, even when they are thoroughly enmeshed in descriptions of reality that are at variance with reality, are still seldom devoid of the powers of observation and independent thought, the science of bloodletting, over most of its long sway, appears usually to have been tempered with a certain amount of common sense. Or it was tempered until it reached its highest peaks of technique in, of all places, the young United States. Bloodletting went wild here. It had an enormously influential proponent in Dr Benjamin Rush, still revered as the greatest statesman-physician of our revolutionary and federal periods, and a genius of medical administration. Dr Rush Got Things Done. Among the things he got done, some of them good and useful, were to develop, practice, teach, and spread the custom of bloodletting in cases where prudence or mercy had heretofore restrained its use. He and his students drained the blood of very young children, of consumptives, of the greatly aged, of almost anyone unfortunate enough to be sick in his realms of influence. His extreme practices aroused the alarm and horror of European bloodletting physicians. And yet as late as 1851, a committee appointed by the State Legislature of New York solemnly defended the thoroughgoing use of bloodletting. It scathingly ridiculed and censured a physician, William Turner, who had the temerity to write a pamphlet criticizing Dr Rush's doctrines and calling "the practice of taking blood in diseases contrary to common sense, to general experience, to enlightened reason, and to the manifest laws of the divine Providence." Sick people needed fortifying, not draining, said Dr Turner, and he was squelched.

Medical analogies, applied to social organisms, are apt to be farfetched, and there is no point in mistaking mammalian chemistry for what occurs in a city. But analogies as to what goes on in the brains of earnest and learned men, dealing with complex phenomena they do not understand at all and trying to make do with a pseudoscience, do have a point. As in the pseudoscience of bloodletting, just so in the pseudoscience of city rebuilding and planning, years of learning and a plethora of subtle and complicated dogma have arisen on a foundation of nonsense. The tools of technique have steadily been perfected. Naturally, in time, forceful and able men, admired administrators, having swallowed the initial fallacies and having been provisioned with tools and with public confidence, go on logically to the greatest destructive excesses, which prudence or mercy might previously have forbade. Bloodletting could heal only by accident or insofar as it broke the rules, until the time when it was abandoned in favor of the hard, complex business of assembling, using, and testing, bit by bit, true descriptions of reality drawn not from how it ought to be but from how it is. The pseudoscience of city planning and its companion, the art of city design, have not yet broken with the specious comfort of wishes, familiar superstitions, oversimplifications, and symbols – and have not yet embarked upon the adventure of probing the real world.

So in this chapter we shall start, if only in a small way, adventuring in the real world, ourselves. The way to get at what goes on in the seemingly mysterious and perverse behavior of cities is, I think, to look closely, and with as little previous expectation as is possible, at the most ordinary scenes and events and attempt to see what they mean and whether any threads of principle emerge among them ....

One principle emerges so ubiquitously, and in so many and such complex different forms, ... [that it] becomes the heart of my argument. This ubiquitous principle is the need of cities for a most intricate and close-grained diversity of uses that give each other constant mutual support, both economically and socially. The components of this diversity can differ enormously, but they must supplement each other in certain concrete ways.

I think that unsuccessful city areas are areas that lack this kind of intricate mutual support, and that the science of city planning and the art of city design, in real life for real cities, must become the science and art of catalyzing and nourishing these close-grained working relationships. I think, from the evidence I can find, that there are four primary conditions required for generating useful great city diversity, and that by deliberately inducing these four conditions, planning can induce city vitality (something that the plans of planners alone, and the designs of designers alone, can never achieve). ...

Cities are fantastically dynamic places, and this is strikingly true of their successful parts, which offer a fertile ground for the plans of thousands of people. ...

The look of things and the way they work are inextricably bound together, and in no place more so than cities. But people who are interested only in how a city "ought" to look and uninterested in how it works will be disappointed. … It is futile to plan a city's appearance, or speculate on how to endow it with a pleasing appearance of order, without knowing what sort of innate, functioning order it has. To seek for the look of things as a primary purpose or as the main drama is apt to make nothing but trouble.

In New York's East Harlem, there is a housing project with a conspicuous rectangular lawn that became an object of hatred to the project tenants. A social worker frequently at the project was astonished by how often the subject of the lawn came up, usually gratuitously as far as she could see, and how much the tenants despised it and urged that it be done away with. When she asked why, the usual answer was, "What good is it?" or "Who wants it?" Finally one day, a tenant more articulate than the others made this pronouncement: "Nobody cared what we wanted when they built this place. They threw our houses down and pushed us here and pushed our friends somewhere else. We don't have a place around here to get a cup of coffee or a newspaper even, or borrow fifty cents. Nobody cared what we need. But the big men come and look at that grass and say, 'Isn't it wonderful! Now the poor have everything!'"

This tenant was saying what moralists have said for thousands of years: Handsome is as handsome does. All that glitters is not gold.

She was saying more: There is a quality even meaner than outright ugliness or disorder, and this meaner quality is the dishonest mask of pretended order, achieved by ignoring or suppressing the real order that is struggling to exist and to be served.

In trying to explain the underlying order of cities, I use a preponderance of examples from New York because that is where I live. But most of my basic ideas come from things I first noticed or was told in other cities. For example, my first inkling about the powerful effects of certain kinds of functional mixtures in the city came from Pittsburgh, my first speculations about street safety from Philadelphia and Baltimore, my first notions about the meanderings of downtown from Boston, my first clues to the unmaking of slums from Chicago. Most of the material for these musings was at my own front door, but perhaps it is easiest to see things first where you don't take them for granted. The basic idea, to try to begin understanding the intricate social and economic order under the seeming disorder of cities, was not my idea at all, but that of William Kirk, head worker of Union Settlement in East Harlem, New York, who, by showing me East Harlem, showed me a way of seeing other neighborhoods, and downtowns too. In every case, I have tried to test out what I saw or heard in one city or neighborhood against others, to find how relevant each city's or each place's lessons might be outside its own special case.

I have concentrated on great cities, and on their inner areas, because this is the problem that has been most consistently evaded in planning theory. I think this may also have somewhat wider usefulness as time passes, because many of the parts of today's cities in the worst, and apparently most baffling, trouble were suburbs or dignified, quiet residential areas not too long ago; eventually many of today's brand-new suburbs or semisuburbs are going to be engulfed in cities and will succeed or fail in that condition depending on whether they can adapt to functioning successfully as city districts. Also, to be frank, I like dense cities best and care about them most.

But I hope no reader will try to transfer my observations into guides as to what goes on in towns, or little cities, or in suburbs that still are suburban. Towns, suburbs, and even little cities are totally different organisms from great cities. We are in enough trouble already from trying to understand big cities in terms of the behavior, and the imagined behavior, of towns. To try to understand towns in terms of big cities will only compound confusion.

I hope any reader will constantly and skeptically test what I say against his or her own knowledge of cities and their behavior. If I have been inaccurate in observations or mistaken in inferences and conclusions, I hope these faults will be quickly corrected. The point is, we need desperately to learn and to apply as much knowledge that is true and useful about cities as fast as possible.

I have been making unkind remarks about orthodox city planning theory, and shall make more as occasion arises to do so. By now, these orthodox ideas are part of our folklore. They harm us because we take them for granted. To show how we got them, and how little they are to the point, I shall give a quick outline here of the most influential ideas that have contributed to the verities of orthodox modern city planning and city architectural design.[1]

The most important thread of influence starts, more or less, with Ebenezer Howard, an English court reporter for whom planning was an avocation. Howard looked at the living conditions of the poor in late-nineteenth-century London and justifiably did not like what he smelled or saw or heard. He not only hated the wrongs and mistakes of the city, he hated the city and thought it an outright evil and an affront to nature that so many people should get themselves into an agglomeration. His prescription for saving the people was to do the city in.

The program he proposed, in 1898, was to halt the growth of London and also repopulate the countryside, where villages were declining, by building a new kind of town – the Garden City, where the city poor might again live close to nature. So that they might earn their livings, industry was to be set up in the Garden City; for while Howard was not planning cities, he was not planning dormitory suburbs either. His aim was the creation of self-sufficient small towns, really very nice towns if you were docile and had no plans of your own and did not mind spending your life among others with no plans of their own. As in all utopias, the right to have plans of any significance belonged only to the planners in charge. The Garden City was to be encircled with a belt of agriculture. Industry was to be in its planned preserves; schools, housing, and greens in planned living preserves; and in the center were to be commercial, club, and cultural places, held in common. The town and green belt, in their totality, were to be permanently controlled by the public authority under which the town was developed, to prevent speculation or supposedly irrational changes in land use and also to do away with temptations to increase its density – in brief, to prevent it from ever becoming a city. The maximum population was to be held to thirty thousand people.

Nathan Glazer has summed up the vision well in *Architectural Forum*: "The image was the English country town – with the manor house and its park replaced by a community center, and with some factories hidden behind a screen of trees, to supply work."

The closest American equivalent would probably be the model company town, with profit sharing, and with the parent–teacher associations in charge of the routine, custodial political life. For Howard was envisioning not simply a new physical environment and social life but a paternalistic political and economic society.

Nevertheless, as Glazer has pointed out, the Garden City was "conceived as an alternative to the city, and as a solution to city problems; this was, and is still, the foundation of its immense power as a planning idea." Howard managed to get two garden cities built, Letchworth and Welwyn, and of course Great Britain and Sweden have, since World War II, built a number of satellite towns based on Garden City principles. In the United States, the suburb of Radburn, New Jersey, and the depression-built, government-sponsored green belt towns (actually suburbs) were all incomplete modifications of the idea. But Howard's influence in the literal, or reasonably literal, acceptance of his program was as nothing compared to his influence on conceptions underlying all American city planning today. City planners and designers with no interest in the Garden City as such are still thoroughly governed intellectually by its underlying principles.

Howard set spinning powerful and city-destroying ideas: He conceived that the way to deal with the city's functions was to sort and sift out of the whole certain simple uses, and to arrange each of these in relative self-containment. He focused on the provision of wholesome housing as the central problem, to which everything else was subsidiary; furthermore he defined wholesome housing in terms only of suburban physical qualities and small-town social qualities. He conceived of commerce in terms of routine, standardized supply of goods, and as serving a self-limited market. He conceived of good planning as a series of static acts; in each case the plan must anticipate all that is needed and be protected, after it is built, against any but the most minor subsequent changes. He conceived of planning also as essentially paternalistic, if not authoritarian. He was uninterested in the aspects of the city that could not be abstracted to serve his utopia. In particular, he simply wrote off the intricate, many faceted, cultural life of the metropolis. He was uninterested in such problems as the way the great cities police themselves, or exchange ideas, or operate politically, or invent new economic arrangements, and he was oblivious to devising ways to strengthen these functions because, after all, he was not designing for this kind of life in any case.

Both in his preoccupations and in his omissions, Howard made sense in his own terms but none in terms of city planning. Yet virtually all modern city planning has been adapted from, and embroidered on, this silly substance.

Howard's influence on American city planning converged on the city from two directions: from town and regional planners on the one hand, and from architects on the other. Along the avenue of planning, Sir Patrick Geddes, a Scots biologist and philosopher, saw the Garden City idea not as a fortuitous way to absorb population growth otherwise destined for a great city but as the starting point of a much grander and more encompassing pattern. He thought of the planning of cities in terms of the planning of whole regions. Under regional planning, garden cities would be rationally distributed throughout large territories, dovetailing into natural resources, balanced against agriculture and woodland, forming one far-flung logical whole.

Howard's and Geddes's ideas were enthusiastically adopted in America during the 1920s, and developed further by a group of extraordinarily effective and dedicated people – among them Lewis Mumford, Clarence Stein, the late Henry Wright, and Catherine Bauer. While they thought of themselves as regional planners, Catherine Bauer has more recently called this group the "Decentrists," and this name is more apt, for the primary result of regional planning, as they saw it, would be to decentralize great cities, thin them out, and disperse their enterprises and populations into smaller, separated cities or, better yet, towns. At the time, it appeared that the American population was both aging and leveling off in numbers, and the problem appeared to be not one of accommodating a rapidly growing population but simply of redistributing a static population.

As with Howard himself, this group's influence was less in getting literal acceptance of its program – that got nowhere – than in influencing city planning and legislation affecting housing and housing finance. Model housing schemes by Stein and Wright, built mainly in suburban settings or at the fringes of cities, together with the writings and the diagrams, sketches, and photographs presented by Mumford and Bauer, demonstrated and popularized ideas such as these, which are now taken for granted in orthodox planning: The street is bad as an environment for humans; houses should be turned away from it and faced inward, toward sheltered greens. Frequent streets are wasteful, of advantage only to real estate speculators who measure value by the front foot. The basic unit of city design is not the street but the block and, more particularly, the superblock. Commerce should be segregated from residences and greens. A neighborhood's demand for goods should be calculated "scientifically," and this much and no more commercial space allocated. The presence of many other people is, at best, a necessary evil, and good city planning must aim for at least an illusion of isolation and suburbany privacy. The Decentrists also pounded in Howard's premises that the planned community must be islanded off as a self-contained unit, that it must resist future change, and that every significant detail must be controlled by the planners from the start and then stuck to. In short, good planning was project planning.

To reinforce and dramatize the necessity for the new order of things, the Decentrists hammered away at the bad old city. They were incurious about successes in great cities. They were interested only in failures. All was failure. A book like Mumford's *The Culture of Cities* was largely a morbid and biased catalog of ills. The great city was Megalopolis, Tyrannopolis, Nekropolis, a monstrosity, a tyranny, a living death. It must go. New York's midtown was "solidified chaos" (Mumford). The shape and appearance of cities were nothing but "a chaotic accident ... the summation of the haphazard, antagonistic whims of many self-centered, ill-advised individuals" (Stein). The centers of cities amounted to "a foreground of noise, dirt, beggars, souvenirs, and shrill competitive advertising" (Bauer).

How could anything so bad be worth the attempt to understand it? The Decentrists' analyses, the architectural and housing designs that were companions and offshoots of these analyses, the national housing and home financing legislation so directly influenced by the new vision – none of these had anything to do with understanding cities or fostering successful large cities, nor were they intended to. They were reasons and means for jettisoning cities, and the Decentrists were frank about this.

But in the schools of planning and architecture – and in Congress, state legislatures, and city halls too – the Decentrists' ideas were gradually accepted as basic guides for dealing constructively with big cities themselves. This is the most amazing event in the whole sorry tale: that finally people who sincerely wanted to strengthen great cities should adopt recipes frankly devised for undermining their economies and killing them.

The man with the most dramatic idea of how to get all this anticity planning right into the citadels of iniquity themselves was the European architect Le Corbusier. He devised in the 1920s a dream city, which he called the Radiant City, composed not of the low buildings beloved of the Decentrists but instead mainly of skyscrapers within a park. "Suppose we are entering the city by way of the Great Park," Le Corbusier wrote. "Our fast car takes the special elevated motor track between the majestic skyscrapers: as we approach nearer, there is seen the repetition against the sky of the twenty-four skyscrapers; to our left and right on the outskirts of each particular area are the municipal and administrative buildings; and enclosing the space are the museums and university buildings. The whole city is a Park." In Le Corbusier's vertical city the common run of mankind was to be housed at 1,200 inhabitants to the acre, a fantastically high city density indeed, but because of building up so high, 95 percent of the ground could remain open. The skyscrapers would occupy only 5 percent of the ground. The high-income people would be in lower, luxury housing around courts, with 85 percent of their ground left open. Here and there would be restaurants and theaters.

Le Corbusier was planning not only a physical environment. He was planning for a social utopia too. Le Corbusier's utopia was a condition of what he called maximum individual liberty, by which he seems to have meant not liberty to do anything much, but liberty from ordinary responsibility. In his Radiant City nobody, presumably, was going to have to be his brother's keeper any more.

Nobody was going to have to struggle with plans of his own. Nobody was going to be tied down.

The Decentrists and other loyal advocates of the Garden City were aghast at Le Corbusier's city of towers in the park, and still are. Their reaction to it was, and remains, much like that of progressive nursery school teachers confronting an utterly institutional orphanage. And yet, ironically, the Radiant City comes directly out of the Garden City. Le Corbusier accepted the Garden City's fundamental image, superficially at least, and worked to make it practical for high densities. He described his creation as the Garden City made attainable. "The garden city is a will-o'-the-wisp," he wrote. "Nature melts under the invasion of roads and houses and the promised seclusion becomes a crowded settlement. ... The solution will be found in the 'vertical garden city.'"

In another sense too, in its relatively easy public reception, Le Corbusier's Radiant City depended upon the Garden City. The Garden City planners and their ever-increasing following among housing reformers, students, and architects were indefatigably popularizing the ideas of the superblock; the project neighborhood; the unchangeable plan; and grass, grass, grass. What is more, they were successfully establishing such attributes as the hallmarks of humane, socially responsible, functional, high-minded planning. Le Corbusier really did not have to justify his vision in either humane or city-functional terms. If the great object of city planning was that Christopher Robin might go hoppety-hoppety on the grass, what was wrong with Le Corbusier? The Decentrists' cries of institutionalization, mechanization, depersonalization seemed to others foolishly sectarian.

Le Corbusier's dream city has had an immense impact on our cities. It was hailed deliriously by architects and has gradually been embodied in scores of projects, ranging from low-income public housing to office-building projects. Aside from making at least the superficial Garden City principles superficially practical in a dense city, Le Corbusier's dream contained other marvels. He attempted to make planning for the automobile an integral part of his scheme, and this was, in the 1920s and early 1930s, a new, exciting idea. He included great arterial roads for express one-way traffic. He cut the number of streets because "cross-roads are an enemy to traffic." He proposed underground streets for heavy vehicles and deliveries, and of course like the Garden City planners he kept the pedestrians off the streets and in the parks. His city was like a wonderful mechanical toy. Furthermore, his conception, as an architectural work, had a dazzling clarity, simplicity, and harmony. It was so orderly, so visible, so easy to understand. It said everything in a flash, like a good advertisement. This vision and its bold symbolism have been all but irresistible to planners, housers, designers – and to developers, lenders, and mayors too. It exerts a great pull on "progressive" zoners, who write rules calculated to encourage nonproject builders to reflect, if only a little, the dream. No matter how vulgarized or clumsy the design, how dreary and useless the open space, how dull the close-up view, an imitation of Le Corbusier shouts, "Look what I made!" Like a great, visible ego it tells of someone's achievement. But as to how the city works, it tells, like the Garden City, nothing but lies.

Although the Decentrists, with their devotion to the ideal of a cozy town life, have never made peace with the Le Corbusier vision, most of their disciples have. Virtually all sophisticated city designers today combine the two conceptions in various permutations. The rebuilding technique variously known as "selective removal" or "spot renewal" or "renewal planning" or "planned conservation" – meaning that total clearance of a run-down area is avoided – is largely the trick of seeing how many old buildings can be left standing and the area still converted into a passable version of Radiant Garden City. Zoners, highway planners, legislators, land-use planners, and parks and playground planners – none of whom live in an ideological vacuum – constantly use, as fixed points of reference, these two powerful visions and the more sophisticated merged vision. They may wander from the visions, they may compromise, they may vulgarize, but these are the points of departure.

We shall look briefly at one other, less important, line of ancestry in orthodox planning. This one begins more or less with the great Columbian Exposition in Chicago in 1893, just about the same time that Howard was formulating his Garden City ideas. The Chicago fair snubbed the exciting modern architecture that had begun to emerge in Chicago and instead dramatized a retrogressive imitation Renaissance style. One heavy, grandiose monument after another was arrayed in the exposition park, like frosted pastries on a tray, in a sort of squat, decorated forecast of Le Corbusier's later repetitive ranks of towers in a park. This orgiastic assemblage of the rich and monumental captured the imagination of both planners and public. It gave impetus to a movement called the City Beautiful, and indeed the planning of the exposition was dominated by the man who became the leading City Beautiful planner, Daniel Burnham of Chicago.

The aim of the City Beautiful was the City Monumental. Great schemes were drawn up for systems of baroque boulevards, which mainly came to nothing. What did come out of the movement was the Center Monumental, modeled on the fair. City after city built its civic center or its cultural center. These buildings were arranged along a boulevard as at Benjamin Franklin Parkway in Philadelphia, or along a mall like the Government Center in Cleveland, or were bordered by park, like the Civic Center at St Louis, or were interspersed with park, like the Civic Center at San Francisco. However they were arranged, the important point was that the monuments had been sorted out from the rest of the city and assembled into the grandest effect thought possible, the whole being treated as a complete unit, in a separate and well-defined way.

People were proud of them, but the centers were not a success. For one thing, invariably the ordinary city around them ran down instead of being uplifted, and they always acquired an incongruous rim of ratty tattoo parlors and secondhand-clothing stores, or else just nondescript, dispirited decay. For another, people stayed away from them to a remarkable degree. Somehow, when the fair became part of the city, it did not work like the fair.

The architecture of the City Beautiful centers went out of style. But the idea behind the centers was not questioned, and it has never had more force than it does today. The idea of sorting out certain cultural or public functions and decontaminating their relationship with the workaday city dovetailed nicely with the Garden City teachings. The conceptions have harmoniously merged, much as the Garden City and the Radiant City merged, into a sort of Radiant Garden City Beautiful, such as the immense Lincoln Square project for New York, in which a monumental City Beautiful cultural center is one among a series of adjoining Radiant City and Radiant Garden City housing, shopping, and campus centers.

And by analogy, the principles of sorting out – and of bringing order by repression of all plans but the planners' – have been easily extended to all manner of city functions, until today a land-use master plan for a big city is largely a matter of proposed placement, often in relation to transportation, of many series of decontaminated sortings.

From beginning to end, from Howard and Burnham to the latest amendment on urban renewal law, the entire concoction is irrelevant to the workings of cities. Unstudied, unrespected, cities have served as sacrificial victims.

Note

1. Readers who would like a fuller account, and a sympathetic account, which mine is not, should go to the sources, which are very interesting, especially *Garden Cities of To-morrow*, by Ebenezer Howard; *The Culture of Cities*, by Lewis Mumford; *Cities in Evolution*, by Sir Patrick Geddes; *Modern Housing*, by Catherine Bauer; *Toward New Towns for America*, by Clarence Stein; *Nothing Gained by Overcrowding*, by Sir Raymond Unwin; and *The City of Tomorrow and Its Planning*, by Le Corbusier. The best short survey I know of is the group of excerpts under the title "Assumptions and Goals of City Planning," contained in *Land-Use Planning, A Casebook on the Use, Misuse and Re-use of Urban Land*, by Charles M. Haar.

5

Planning the Capitalist City

Richard E. Foglesong

Capitalism and Urban Planning

David Harvey, a Marxist social geographer, has conceptualized urban conflict as a conflict over the "production, management and use of the urban built environment."[1] Harvey uses the term "built environment" to refer to physical entities such as roads, sewerage networks, parks, railroads, and even private housing – facilities that are collectively owned and consumed or, as in the case of private housing, whose character and location the state somehow regulates. These facilities have become politicized because of conflict arising out of their being collectively owned and controlled, or because of the "externality effects" of private decisions concerning their use. At issue is how these facilities should be produced – whether by the market or by the state, how they should be managed and by whom; and how they should be used – for what purposes and by what groups, races, classes, and neighborhoods. Following Harvey, the development of American urban planning is seen as the result of conflict over the production, management, and use of the urban built environment.

The development of this analysis depends on the recognition that capitalism both engenders and constrains demands for state intervention in the sphere of the built environment. First, let us consider some of the theories about how capitalism engenders demands for state intervention.

Original publication details: Fogelsong, Richard E. 1986. *Planning the Capitalist City: The Colonial Era to the 1920s*. Princeton, NJ: Princeton University Press. Reproduced with permission from Princeton.

Readings in Planning Theory, Fourth Edition. Edited by Susan S. Fainstein and James DeFilippis.
Editorial material and organization © 2016 John Wiley & Sons, Ltd.
Published 2016 by John Wiley & Sons, Ltd.

Sources of urban planning

Within the developing Marxist urban literature, there have been a variety of attempts to link urban conflict and demands for state intervention to the reproduction processes of capitalist society. Manuel Castells, one of the leading contributors to this literature, emphasizes the connection between state intervention in the urban development process and the reproduction of labor power.[2]

The Problem of Planning

The market system cannot meet the consumption needs of the working class in a manner capable of maintaining capitalism; this, according to Castells, is the reason for the growth of urban planning and state intervention. To the extent that the state picks up the slack and assumes this responsibility, there occurs a transformation of the process of consumption, from individualized consumption through the market to collective consumption organized through the state. This transformation entails not only an expansion of the role of the state, which is seen in the growth of urban planning, but also a politicization of the process of consumption, which Castells sees as the underlying dynamic of urban political conflict.

By contrast, David Harvey and Edmond Preteceille, writing separately, have related state intervention in the urban development process to the inability of the market system to provide for the maintenance and reproduction of the immobilized fixed capital investments (for example, bridges, streets, sewerage networks) used by capital as *means of production*.[3] The task of the state is not only to maintain this system of what Preteceille calls "urban use values" but also to provide for the coordination of these use values in space (for example, the coordination of streets and sewer lines), creating what he terms "new, complex use values."[4] François Lamarche, on the other hand, relates the whole question of urban planning and state intervention to the *sphere of circulation* and the need to produce a "spatial organization which facilitates the circulation of capital, commodities, information, etc."[5] In his view capitalism has spawned a particular fraction of capital, termed "property capital," which is responsible for organizing the system of land use and transportation; and urban planning is a complement and extension of the aims and activities of this group. In addition, and somewhat distinct from these attempts to relate urban planning to the reproduction processes of capitalist society, David Harvey has linked urban planning to the problems arising from the *uniqueness of land as a commodity*, namely the fact that land is not transportable, which makes it inherently subject to externality effects.[6]

The theories discussed above demonstrate that there are a variety of problems arising from relying upon the market system to guide urban development. At various times, urban planning in the United States has been a response to each of these problems. Yet these problems have different histories. They have not had equal importance throughout the development of planning. Moreover, not one of these problems is sufficient in itself to explain the logic of development of planning.

Constraints on urban planning

If the problems noted above arise from the workings of the market system, so that capitalism can be said to engender demands for state intervention in response to these problems, the capitalist system also constrains the realization of these demands. The operative constraint in this connection is the institution of private property. It is here that we confront what might be termed the central contradiction of capitalist urbanization: the contradiction between the social character of land and its private ownership and control. Government intervention in the ordering of the urban built environment – that is, urban planning – can be seen as a response to the social character of land, to the fact that land is not only a commodity but also a collective good, a social resource as well as a private right. Indeed, as the Marxist urban literature has sought to demonstrate, the treatment of land as a commodity fails to satisfy the social needs of either capital or labor. Capital has an objective interest in socializing the control of land in order to (1) cope with the externality problems that arise from treating land as a commodity; (2) create the housing and other environmental amenities needed for the reproduction of labor power; (3) provide for the building and maintenance of the bridges, harbors, streets, and transit systems used by capital as means of production; and (4) ensure the spatial coordination of these infrastructural facilities for purposes of efficient circulation. Yet the institution of private property stands as an impediment to attempts to socialize the control of land in order to meet these collective needs. Thus, if urban planning is necessary for the reproduction of the capitalist system on the one hand, it threatens and is restrained by the capitalist system on the other; and it is in terms of this Janus-faced reality that the development of urban planning is to be understood. Moreover, this contradiction is intrinsic to capitalist urbanization, for the impulse to socialize the control of urban space is as much a part of capitalism as is the institution of private property. Each serves to limit the extension of the other; thus, they are in "contradiction."[7] This contradiction, which will be termed the "property contradiction," is one of two that have structured the development of planning.[8]

The "property contradiction"
To state that capitalist urbanization has an inherent contradiction is *not* to predict the inevitable downfall of capitalism (although it does indicate a weakness in the capitalist structure of society that oppositional forces could conceivably exploit). Rather, it is assumed that capitalism is capable of coping with this contradiction, within limits, but that it is a continuing source of tension and

a breeding ground of political conflict. Thus, our analytical interest is in the institutional means that have been devised to keep this contradiction from exploding into a system-threatening crisis. In recognizing this contradiction, we therefore gain a better appreciation of the importance, both politically and theoretically, of the institutional forms that urban planning has adopted over the course of its development, and of how (and how well) those institutional forms have responded to the contradiction between the social character of land and its private ownership and control.

In addition, recognizing this contradiction helps us to understand the patterns of alliance formation around planning issues, as well as the role of planners in mediating between different groups and group interests. For if the effort to socialize the control of urban land is potentially a threat to the whole concept of property rights, it is directly and immediately a threat to only one particular group of capitalists, those whom Lamarche terms "property capital." Included are persons who, in his words, "plan and equip space" – real estate developers, construction contractors, and directors of mortgage lending institutions.[9] It is this fraction of capital, in particular, that can be expected to oppose efforts to displace or diminish private control of urban development. Other capitalists, in contrast, may seek an expanded government role in the planning and equipping of space. For example, manufacturing capital may want government to provide worker housing and to coordinate the development of public and private infrastructure (such as utilities and railroads), and commercial capitalists may desire government restrictions on the location of manufacturing establishments. Likewise, nonowner groups have an interest in state intervention that will provide for or regulate the quality of worker housing, build parks, and improve worker transportation, for example. It is possible, therefore, for certain fractions of capital to align with nonowner groups in support of planning interventions that restrict the "rights" of urban landholders. The property contradiction thus manifests itself in the pattern of alliances around planning issues by creating, in intracapitalist class conflict, the possibility of alliances between property-owning and nonproperty-owning groups and allowing planners to function as mediators in organizing these compromises. Inasmuch as the property contradiction is inherent in the capitalist structure of society, existing independent of consciousness and will, recognition of this contradiction enables us to link the politics of planning to the structural ordering of capitalist society.

The "capitalist–democracy contradiction"

The other contradiction affecting the development of urban planning is the "capitalist–democracy contradiction." If the property contradiction is internal to capitalism in that it arises out of the logic of capitalist development, the capitalist–democracy contradiction is an external one, originating between the political and economic structures of a democratic–capitalist society. More specifically, it is a contradiction between the need to socialize the control of urban space to create the conditions for the maintenance of capitalism on the one hand and the danger to capital of truly socializing, that is, democratizing, the control of urban land on the other. For if the market system cannot produce a built environment that is capable of maintaining capitalism, reliance on the institutions of the state, especially a formally democratic state, creates a whole new set of problems, not the least of which is that the more populous body of nonowners will gain too much control over landed property. This latter contradiction is conditioned on the existence of the property contradiction, in that it arises from efforts to use government action to balance or hold in check the property contradiction. Once government intervention is accepted, questions about how to organize that intervention arise: What goals should be pursued? How should they be formulated and by whom? This pattern of the capitalist–democracy contradiction following on the heels of the property contradiction is apparent in the actual history of planning, for while both contradictions have been in evidence throughout the history of planning in America, the property contradiction was a more salient generator of conflict in the earlier, pre-1940 period. The capitalist–democracy contradiction – manifested in the controversy over how to organize the planning process – has been a more potent source of conflict in the history of planning after World War II. It should also be emphasized that the capitalist–democracy contradiction is conditioned on the formally democratic character of the state, out of which the danger of government control of urban development arises. Were it not for the majority-rule criterion and formal equality promised by the state, turning to government to control urban development would not pose such a problem for capital.

Consideration of the capitalist–democracy contradiction leads us back to Offe's analysis of the internal structure of the state. Following Offe's analysis, it can be postulated that capitalism is caught in a search for a decision process, a method of policy making that can produce decisions corresponding with capital's political and economic interests. Politically, this decision process must be capable of insulating state decision making from the claims and considerations of the numerically larger class of noncapitalists, a task made difficult by the formally democratic character of the state. Economically, this decision process must be capable of producing decisions that facilitate the accumulation and circulation of capital (for example, promoting the reproduction of labor power and coordinating the building up of local infrastructure), a function that the market fails to perform and that capitalists do not (necessarily) know how to perform. Both of these problems are captured in the concept of the capitalist–democracy contradiction. The question we are led to ask, then, is: In what ways has the development of urban planning – viewed here as a method of policy formulation – served to suppress or hold in balance the capitalist–democracy contradiction in a manner conducive to the reproduction of capitalism?

Notes

1. "Labor, Capital, and Class Struggle around the Built Environment in Advanced Capitalist Societies," p. 265.
2. *Urban Question*, pp. 460–1. Castells modifies his view in his recent book, *The City and the Grass Roots*, which appeared after the manuscript of *Planning the Capitalist City* was essentially written. In this new book, Castells seeks to avoid the "excesses of theoretical formalism" that marked some of his earlier work (p. xvii). He also asserts that "although class relationships and class struggle are fundamental in understanding the process of urban conflict, they are by no means the only or even the primary source of urban social change" (p. xviii). My critical evaluation of Castells's earlier work is still valid and useful, however, since it lends emphasis and historical reference to some of Castells's own criticisms. Furthermore, my criticisms apply to a literature and a theoretical orientation that encompasses, as I point out, more than Castells's work.
3. Harvey, "The Political Economy of Urbanization in Advanced Capitalist Societies: The Case of the United States," p. 120; Preteceille, "Urban Planning: The Contradictions of Capitalist Urbanization," pp. 69–76. For Harvey, the need for a built environment usable as a collective means of production is only one of the connections between urban planning and capitalist development; he also recognizes the need for facilities for collective consumption to aid in reproducing labor power. See, e.g., his "Labor, Capital, and Class Struggle around the Built Environment."
4. Preteceille, "Urban Planning," p. 70.
5. "Property Development and the Economic Foundations of the Urban Question," p. 86.
6. *Social Justice*, chapter 5.
7. For a discussion of this use of *contradiction*, see Godelier, "Structure and Contradiction in *Capital*," pp. 334–68.
8. Cf. Michael Dear and Allen Scott's assertion that the "urban question" (a reference to the work of Castells) is "structured around the particular and indissoluble geographical and land-contingent phenomena that come into existence as capitalist social and property relations are mediated through the dimension of urban space." They also write that planning is "a historically-specific and socially-necessary response to the self-disorganizing tendencies of *privatized* capitalist social and property relations as these appear in urban space" ("Towards a Framework for Analysis," pp. 6, 13). Cf. also, in the same volume, Shoukry Roweis's statement that "[u]rban planning in capitalism, both in theory and in practice, and whether intentionally or unknowingly, attempts to grapple with a basic question: how can *collective action* (pertinent to decisions concerning the social utilization of urban land) be made possible under capitalism?" ("Urban Planning in Early and Late Capitalist Societies," p. 170). These two theoretical analyses relate urban planning under capitalism to the problem of "collective control" – how to organize socially necessary forms of collective consumption and control in a society based upon private ownership – but they do not take note of the contradiction between capital's need for collective control in its own interest and the limits imposed by the internal structure of the *state*. This is the issue raised by Offe and which I capture in my concept of the "capitalist–democracy contradiction".
9. "Property Development," pp. 90–3.

Further Reading

Castells, Manuel. *The Urban Question*. Cambridge: MIT Press, 1977.

Dear, Michael, and Scott, Allen J., "Towards a Framework for Analysis." In *Urbanization and Urban Planning in Capitalist Society*, edited by Michael Dear and Allen J. Scott, pp. 3–18. London: Methuen, 1981.

Godelier, Maurice. "Structure and Contradiction in *Capital*." In *Ideology and Social Science*, edited by Robin Blackburn, pp. 334–68. New York: Vintage Books, 1973.

Harvey, David. "Labor, Capital, and Class Struggle around the Built Environment in Advanced Capitalist Societies," *Politics & Society* 6 (1976): 265–95.

Harvey, David. "The Political Economy of Urbanization in Advanced Capitalist Societies: The Case of the United States." In *The Social Economy of Cities*, Urban Affairs Annual, edited by Gary Grappert and Harold M. Rose, no. 9, pp. 119–63. Beverly Hills: Russell Sage, 1975.

Harvey, David. *Social Justice and the City*. Baltimore: Johns Hopkins University Press, 1973.

Lamarche, François. "Property Development and the Economic Foundations of the Urban Question." In *Urban Sociology: Critical Essays*, edited by Chris Pickvance, pp. 85–118. London: Tavistock Press, 1976.

Offe, Claus. "The Abolition of Market Control and the Problem of Legitimacy (I)." *Kapitalistate*, no. 1 (1973): 109–16.

Preteceille, Edmond. "Urban Planning: The Contradictions of Capitalist Urbanization." *Antipode* 8 (March 1976): 69–76.

Roweis, Shoukry. "Urban Planning in Early and Late Capitalist Societies." In *Urbanization and Urban Planning in Capitalist Society*, edited by Michael Dear and Allen J. Scott, pp. 159–78. London: Methuen, 1981.

6

The Three Historic Currents of City Planning

Peter Marcuse

Introduction

Three quite different approaches characterize the mainstream of modern planning: a technical one, a social reform one, and a social justice one. Each is prominent at a particular time and place, forming three identifiable approaches in planning history, in most but not all cases with the simultaneous presence of the others. The three approaches thus often mix, sometimes conflict, are rarely pure, but differ significantly in their methods and goals.

The deferential technicist approach, going back millennia, builds on the urban work of engineers, and is necessarily responsive to those in power that have the authority and resources to commission the work. In modern history it developed out of a concern with the inefficiencies, initially mainly the physical, in the organization of the new industrial economy, inefficiencies which inhibited economic growth and prosperity. It did not question, but rather deferred to, the maintenance of existing institutional relationships, and focused on the value of efficiency, taking the continuance of those relationships for granted. It thus had primary support from established political, economic, and social groups. Technicist planning is inherently, in this definition, subservient to the power structures of the status quo.

Original publication details: Marcuse, Peter. 2011. "The Three Historic Currents of City Planning". In *The New Blackwell Companion to the City*, edited by Gary Bridge and Sophie Watson. Oxford: Blackwell Publishing Ltd, pp. 643–55. Reproduced with permission from John Wiley & Sons.

Readings in Planning Theory, Fourth Edition. Edited by Susan S. Fainstein and James DeFilippis.

The social reform approach similarly developed out of a concern with the externalities of industrialization, but with their social welfare aspects: health, crime, unsanitary housing, social unrest, pollution, not with their economic processes. It approached those issues in the spirit of reform, expecting to, and often succeeding in, remedying social problems within the existing structures of power. Its view of social problems was generally from outside and above, from how they might affect the health and wellbeing of those benefiting from existing established economic and political relationships, not from those suffering from them. It prioritized evaluating results in terms of the extent to which needs were satisfied rather than the cost efficiency of the methods, although the latter also continued to play a role. Its definition of social was a narrow one, focusing on the disadvantaged, the weak, the poor, the minority, the excluded, rather than seeing the problems of such groups as aspects of the broad social system in which they occur, which includes dealing with those that take advantage as well as the disadvantaged, with the majority as well as the minority, the excluders as well as the excluded – in other words, seeing the social as the entire set of interpersonal and inter-group relations that constitute a society.[1]

The social justice approach arose out of concern with the human costs to those adversely affected by rapid urbanization and industrialization, visible in the burgeoning cities and slums with their impoverished populations. It was broadly critical of existing urban social and institutional relationships, proposing sweeping alternatives, and seeing the physical as ancillary to broader social change. It saw social issues from the point of view of those suffering from them, from below, and had broad but varying levels of support from the poor and oppressed.

This essay attempts to define the separate approaches in broad terms, and for each to give selected examples from their history and evolution. Attention will be drawn to two aspects in each, as they appear: (1) critical vs. deferential attitudes towards existing relations of power and (2) social vs. efficiency concerns. It concludes with the suggestion that the main approaches are in tension today, a tension visible in both planning theory and planning practice, and contends that a recent partial resolution of the tension, undertaken without widespread and explicit discussion, was a missed opportunity to advance the cause of planning generally.

The discussion relies on and is in counterpoint to, three classic treatments of planning's history: Leonardo Benevolo's *The Origins of Modern Town Planning*,[2] Peter Hall's *Cities of Tomorrow*,[3] and Mel Scott's *American City Planning*.[4] As will be clear, it draws heavily on their research but attempts to extend their discussion to paint a broader picture of key underlying trends and tensions in that history.

Deferential Planning ("Technicist Planning")

Deferential or technicist is the term used here for planning devoted to maximizing the efficiency of whatever system or place is being planned. Efficiency is of course a goal of virtually any form of planning; certainly no plan is so framed as to be inefficient, just as no plan is framed so as to be unsustainable. Thus planning in the critical social justice approach is expected to be efficient in the service of its purposes also. But deferential technicist planning, as used here, elevates the use of the technical tools of planning, those aspects devoted to efficiency, to be its characteristic and driving force. It sees the planner as a professional, an expert, a technician with a special training and knowledge, capable of using a bag of tools in which he or she has had specific technical training. It is formulated thus in the Green Book, often taken as the leading manual for professional planners:

> The central aim [of planning] is to muster the best knowledge, skill, and imagination in solving complex problems and in making the solutions work. The active client sets the priorities among problems, judges whether the best effort has been used, and in addition judges whether the solution is effective, whether its cost is too high, and whether the solution gets in the way of other good things.[5]

Karl Polanyi said it well: the role of planning has been to embed the market in society. The market militates against the production of equity or justice; indeed, it does not claim otherwise. Even its strongest defenders, such as Hayek, concede that the market should not be looked to for social ends, and will not do what it does best if it is interfered with by the state (or planners working for the state) in the interests of social objectives. Thus, one of the three streams of planning action that I want to identify, the technicist, is inherently conservative: it is to serve an economic and social and political order in which its role is to make that order function smoothly. The social component of planning enters in only to the extent necessary to permit the market to function efficiently. Thus planning needs to provide infrastructure, needs to avoid clashing land uses that interfere with economic efficiency, and needs to regulate social abuses to the extent they may interfere with order. The City Scientific is the clearest historical expression of that stream of planning activity, and it is in practice mainstream. Planning's function in this view is akin to engineering: not to ask why something is built, but to build it well. So this is the first stream of planning: efficient functioning. It is a technical view of planning – or, since all planning is by its very nature technical, it is "technicist," making planning *only* the technical, ignoring all other considerations.[6]

In terms of the interests supporting such a technicist planning approach, Mel Scott's history is replete with narratives of the extent to which established groups in positions of power played a decisive role: business groups, chambers of commerce, and real-estate interests were prime movers, from the White City Exposition in Chicago to the adoption of zoning in New York City to the urban redevelopment and urban renewal programs of the post-World War II years. Indeed, one line of analysis argues that it was precisely the role of planning to smooth out the contradictions of economic growth and urban development under advancing capitalism that required the development of planning and a planning profession.[7]

Within deferential technicist planning three variations may be differentiated: "scientific" planning, designer planning, contractual planning, and process planning.

Efficiency is the central concern. But where planning is defined simply as problem-solving, leaving the statement of the problem and the goals to be sought to others, efficiency becomes not merely a criterion to judge the quality of planning in the pursuit of its goals, but the goal itself. Planning theory offers a variety of models suggesting principles for professionals to use in efficient planning practice.

"Scientific" planning

"Scientific" planning views the function of planning as producing the scientifically most efficient machine through which to perform the activities of the current city, whatever they happen to be. It is concerned with efficiency, but it makes efficiency the master, not the servant, itself the goal, not one criterion of measures to reach a goal generated elsewhere. The city, working efficiently like a machine or a natural organism, becomes the norm, and planning is dedicated to ensuring that it does in fact work efficiently. Problems are technical, physical, primarily civil engineering, planning as urban engineering. There is no critical edge to the approach, and the social is, if mentioned at all, one subcategory analogous to transportation or sewage disposal, not an overriding goal. The process goal of planning is to garner support for that vision, and the planner should try to convince his or her client of the validity and feasibility of that vision.[8] Mel Scott speaks of it alternately as "the City Efficient or the City Functional."[9]

We find this view at the very beginnings of planning as a profession in the United States. Nelson Lewis, author of the ground-breaking *The Planning of the Modern City*, put it this way in 1912: "The creation of a city plan is ... essentially the work of the engineer, or rather of the regular engineering staff of the city."[10]

Frederick Law Olmsted, Jr, in 1910, compared the city to "one great social organism,"[11] a vision of a city without conflicts of interest, in which planners could act to the benefit of all its residents – implicitly affirming the continuance of existing and established relations of power.

The engineering approach to city planning evident in the origins of the profession in the United States has been broadened over the ensuing years to become a fuller technicist view, which goes beyond the physical focus of the earlier approach to apply technical solutions to social matters also, in a deferential manner that avoids criticism but attempts to ameliorate the undesired social consequences of existing arrangements without questioning their source. Technicist social planning thus becomes very similar to the reform element in social justice planning. The difference lies in the extent to which criticism is explicit, the extent to which the support for the initiatives comes from established groups concerned to protect the status quo, and the extent to which technical expertise is seen as a central element in addressing social concerns. Thus recommendations such as those of Castells and Borja for a management approach to city planning[12] strike some critics as technicist,[13] although social issues are certainly important among their concerns.[14]

Designer planning

Designer planning elevates the role of the planner to one which, because of outstanding technical competence and/or perhaps imaginative genius, enables the planner to develop a unique vision of the most desirable design for what should be built. It is typically unconcerned with process, and sees physical designs as resulting in, rather than stemming from, the social and individual characteristics of its users. It shares with much of reform planning an appreciation of the need for change, an implicit criticism of particular aspect of the current situation, but sees the imaginative solutions of the designer planner as providing the answer.

Le Corbusier is perhaps the primary example of such an approach, although more socially oriented planners, such as Ernst May or Bruno Taut, were not dissimilar in their view of the importance of their own expertise in formulating plans, and similarly were rarely concerned with the participation of their intended beneficiaries in the planning of their new developments. Today, the term "designer planner," with all its overtones, may well be applied to "star" architects such as Frank Gehry, Rem Koolhas, or Lord Norman Foster, who take the position that the solution to social problems is not their concern. As one journalist has it:

> Lord Foster is not a social critic; his job, as he sees it, is to create an eloquent expression of his client's values. What he has designed is a perfect monument for the emerging city of the enlightened megarich: environmentally aware, sensitive to history, confident of its place in the new world order, resistant to sacrifice.[15]

While designer planners tend overwhelmingly to be architects, this is not a criticism of architecture as such, but does have to do with the disciplinary boundaries among the professions, and the priority given to imaginative design for its own sake in some of professional education in architecture, with only secondary attention devoted to social concerns. The scale of the urban design they are often empowered to practice may not be called "planning," although it often is,[16] but what it does is in the mainstream of deferential technicist planning.[17]

Contractual planning

In contractual planning, deferential technicist planners see themselves simply as obedient servants of their employer, bringing to the job the special skills, training, and experience of professional planners, with a kit of tools that experience and training have provided, to accomplish those purposes for which they are hired. There is of course a difference between a planner who is an independent contractor and one who is an employee, but both are subject to contractual terms that require loyalty, subjection to the interests of the client or employer, confidentiality of the work, etc. For purposes of this account, the key question relates to the independence of the planner on matters having to do with the objectives of the plan. Good planning of any sort requires clarity as to its objectives, and a deferential technicist planner will indeed press a client or an employer to clarify their stated goals, often in the process needing to question the beginning statement provided him or her. But the questioning is only to clarify, not to question the ethics, the morality, the ultimate vision, towards which the employer desires. Thus in narrowly contracted planning, alternate visions of the purpose of planning are irrelevant, excluded. In the various Codes of Ethics of planners and civil servants, the point is sometimes acknowledged, but issues of contractual obedience are stated as formal and enforceable requirements of the profession, whereas adherence to substance goals, principles, values, visions may be included but as aspirational rather than enforceable.[18]

Contractual planning is not only relevant in the private sector; it is also a pervasive aspect of public planning, although the client is a public employer. Case study and practitioner accounts one after another reveal the tensions that arise when planners ignore the restrictions on what they are expected to do, and show how they succeed when they act within those expectations.[19]

Process planning

Much, perhaps most, of planning theory is theory as to how deferential planning really works or how it should work. It is not concerned with what the goals of planning should be, except in process terms. It suggests that planning should make certain that the client, who establishes its goals, has thought through what is desired and clarified what goals should be pursued. It sees planning as a method of problem-solving, and concerns itself with how that process, as a method of work, can most efficiently function. It is critical only to the extent that it may highlight the gap between what it claims it is doing and what is actually done.[20] Primarily, however, it analyzes the procedures used in deferential planning, and does it in the context of established planning practices and for the benefit of their established clients.

Social Reform Planning

Social reform planning constitutes by far the largest channel into which concern with social issues in planning has flowed, although it is indebted to utopian forerunners, where, it will be argued below, social criticism of urban conditions first developed. Urban reform in its modern sense began well before there was such a concept as urban planning, or a profession called "planning." Concern with hygiene and the avoidance of epidemics was an early central part of this movement for public regulation of urban development.

Reform planning of one kind or another has played a role in much of modern planning. Even when its focus has been purely on the physical aspect of urban space, on harmony or beauty or order, it has seen those characteristics as requiring changes in the urban environment contributing to general human welfare, and as requiring changes in conditions as they are with that purpose in mind. As with utopian planning, there is a grounding in social ideas and values, but, as opposed to utopian planning, the changes viewed as needed are not fundamental but are capable of being accomplished within the framework of the existing social, political, and economic order, even if they may lead to or be dependent on changes in that order at the margins. Thus the scope, the depth, of reform is limited, both in nature and in scale, in most reform endeavors.

Some, indeed, have aspirations that are large in scale and, if carried to their logical conclusions, might be fully utopian. The City Beautiful movement in the United States, for instance, set its sights on characteristics of the city over its entire expanse, but it saw its goals in terms of physical improvements, avoiding the social, political, and economic issues that a broad adoption of aesthetics as a criterion of urban development might entail. And its implicit critique of the day-to-day ugliness of the industrial city was one that emerged for a predominantly upper-class milieu, of which social reform was not a part. The parks movement, of which Frederick Law Olmsted Sr's Central Park in New York City was a model, had a similar social base, and its social justice and reformist concerns did not extend to those displaced by its construction.[21]

Concern for environmental sustainability, often if not always linked to environmental justice, is a growing component of the reform approach in planning today. Green planning is reformist, and shares social values with much of traditional reform planning, simply giving greater emphasis to respect for nature and ecological balance as values in themselves, sometimes, as in hard ecology, raising such values to foundational levels, akin to the values and orientation for fundamental change of utopian planning. "Sustainable" planning, if it means anything other than ecologically sensitive planning, is a misnomer. No planning is intended to be unsustainable; every plan, except perhaps those to deal with temporary emergencies, is intended to be sustainable in pursuit of its own objectives.[22]

In the United States, the Society for Decongestion of the Population and the movement for reform of the tenement house laws and the National City Planning Conference were originally substantially joint affairs; they separated out only in 1910[23] in a series of events that signaled the separation of the reform from the deferential technicist approaches of planning. Zoning had its origins in a concern with the negative impact of nuisances; it may appropriately be considered deferential technicist planning, interested in the efficient use of land and the correction of inefficiencies, and closely related to issues of traffic and congestion, avoiding undesired social mix that interfered with the efficient rationalization of land values. Housing planning separated from this stream and moved to social reform concerns.

Public participation in planning, its democratization, became a main ingredient of almost all reform planning in the mid-1960s, largely in the context of the civil rights movement, and became embodied in law in the War on Poverty and Model Cities programs, and is continued in the Empowerment Zone legislation in effect today. Sherry Arnstein laid out the spectrum of participation in a leading article in 1969.[24] The distinction between participation and democratic decision-making has been highlighted since.[25] Participation is not power; its reform is not radical. Virtually no significant planning project today can be undertaken without some form of participation, although democratic processes of decision-making lagged behind. Participation is a reform that, at least in name, seems firmly embedded as a commitment of the profession today. In the new revision of the AICP Code of Ethics the first rule reads:

> 1. We shall not deliberately or with reckless indifference fail to provide adequate, timely, clear and accurate information on planning issues.[26]

Equity planning, a term associated with the work of Norman Krumholz in Cleveland between 1969 and 1979,[27] is perhaps as comprehensive a formulation of the goals of reform efforts in the profession as we have seen to date. Krumholz was elected President of both the American Planning Association and the American Institute of Certified Planners, and thus played a role significantly different from those of most of the otherwise ideologically related planners of the social justice approach next taken up here; in content it was very closely allied to that more critical view of existing realities.

Social Justice Planning

Most social reform planning is professional planning, advocates' planning, experts' planning, planning within established bureaucratic/legal structures. Paralleling such planning is social justice planning based on grass-roots groups, which at their strongest become social movements. Such groups have been major actors in obtaining planning decisions reflecting social justice concerns. Sometimes they have worked within and/or used existing structures, as those described by Leonie Sandercock and Tom Angotti;[28] sometimes they have been deliberately outside of and disruptive of such structures, as those Frances Piven and Richard Cloward describe in *Poor People's Movements*.[29] Their planning, and that of their supporters, differs from social reform planning in its direct confrontation with issues of power, putting the interests of social justice ahead of competing claims on planning oriented towards efficiency as the primary goal.

I mean by social justice the complex of goals and values, changing over time, that center about human development, the expansion of capabilities, values such as equity, equality, diversity, caring.[30] Historically, social justice approaches are supported by a different array of groups, interests, and advocates than the deferential technicist approaches.[31] More than deferential technicist planning and most social reform planning, it calls, not merely for participation, but for decision-making from below on issues of planning.

Ethical/cultural principles planning

The most recent approach to planning, and one as yet lodged primarily in planning theory discussions, might be called principles planning. It is planning that would put ahead of any immediate target of planning action the fundamental principle or principles that should be applied in the situation, and require any proposed action towards the immediate target to meet the requirements imposed by that principle. Its origins lie in a variety of socially oriented criticisms of conventional planning, which argue that particular approaches are undemocratic, opaque, unfair or unjust, productive of inequality, disrespectful of individual differences, directed at growth without regard to human consequences, unsustainable. In response, proposals are made for alternate approaches, under names such as trans-active planning,[32] just city planning,[33] communicative planning,[34] planning for sustainability, planning for diversity, multi-cultural planning,[35] planning for the full development of human capabilities, and others.

The extent to which these various forms of principles planning have made their way into the actual practice of the profession is variable. Thus far, most remain either in the realm of planning theory, where they are recognized, for instance in the American Institute of Certified Planners (AICP) qualifying exam for certification,[36] or they are dedicated to the procedures and methods of planning, rather than posing substantive issues going beyond a single objective, e.g., ecological sustainability, as their subject-matter. They are thus far virtually ignored in the newly adopted Code of Ethics of the AICP, where words such as "justice," "diversity," and "culture" do not appear.

Community-based planning

Another channel towards the radical side of the social justice stream of planning combines elements of the utopian (below) and the reform. It shares with the utopian the concern with the ideal, but it moves towards the reform and shares with the reform the concern with the practically possible. Its most visible manifestation today is probably in community-based planning, a movement given substantial impetus in the United States by the anti-poverty and model cities legislation of the 1960s, which in turn received their impetus from the civil rights movement and political unrest of the 1960s,[37] in opposing discrimination and supporting integration, supporting public housing and its expansion, staffing community design centers under the War on Poverty program, espousing advocacy planning both in theory and in practice,[38] and most recently, if still largely at the level of theory, in the growing discussions around planning for empowerment,[39] insurgent planning,[40] indigenous planning, feminist planning, and critical planning.[41]

Radical or critical planning

Radical or critical planning adopts the core principles of social justice planning, but differs from ethical or community-based planning in its insistence on pressing its underlying analysis to confront the functioning of the social, economic, and/or political system that gives rise to the particular issues a planning effort confronts. In so doing it sees power not as something to be dealt with tactically, to successfully implement immediate gains, but as something that must be confronted in most cases more fundamentally and long-range. In examining what needs to be done in dealing with the impact of Hurricane Katrina on the residents of New Orleans, for instance, technicist planning focuses on the most efficient way of determining how and whether low-lying areas should continue to be occupied and how and where dykes should be fortified; social reform planning focuses on how most fairly to distribute the available federal aid and how to give priority assistance to the poor and minority occupants of flooded areas and aid them to return to better planned neighborhoods (stressing the involvement of their residents in the planning process). Critical planning, however, would also examine the structure of the planning process itself in New Orleans and highlight the unjust distribution of power underlying the decision-making process in the city, while pointing out the responsibility of the real-estate industry, tourist businesses, and shipping concerns for the ecological damage that permitted the flooding in the first place.[42]

Utopian planning

Utopian thinking is concerned with ideal end states or proposals leading to ideal states, and places them in critical contrast to existing realities.[43] It addresses issues of power only by implication; by pressing proposals that amount to a complete overhaul, and indeed rejection, of existing arrangements, it by implication rejects the systems of power on which such arrangements rest, although how explicitly it raises the issue of power varies. But there are variations within utopian thinking that have to do with the extent of the focus on the built environment, the forms and shapes of utopias, and the aspects as to which they stand in critical contrast.

There are three main variations of utopian thinking. The first, design utopias, address directly ideals of a perfect society but are little concerned with its physical form. The second, symbolic utopias, use the forms of the built environment simply to illustrate broad social concepts of such a society. The third, physical utopias, see defining forms of the built environment as in fact decisively incorporating the desired ideal. While abstract utopias have a long history, as concrete planning proposals aimed at the improvement of the built environment they are of relatively recent vintage.

Design utopias are oldest, going back millennia. They focus at the societal scale, are sharply critical of existing forms, and share with other utopias a lack of concern with implementation, developing instead ideal models, not so much concerned with physical arrangements, urban or rural, as with the social, with relationships of government, or among individuals, or between individuals and society. Plato might be an early contributor, Thomas More's *Utopia*, Thomas Campanella's *City of the Sun*, St. Augustine's *City of God*, are among others.

Symbolic utopias, deceptively related to the structuring of the built environment, used physically shaped proposals to illustrate graphically, or symbolize, desired social arrangements. Butler's *Erewhon*, H. G. Wells's *A Modern Utopia*, Edward Bellamy's *Looking Backward*, Jack London's *Iron Heel*, and George Orwell's *1984*, are examples. Both of these types are what David Harvey would call utopias of process.[44] The third type of utopian planning is what Harvey would call utopias of product: planning whose primary focus is affecting spatial and physical relationships.

Applied utopias are those often seen as being in a direct line from the early utopias, although their social justice edge is often implicit rather than explicit – the proposals for the design of city forms and social relationships, such as Ebenezer Howard's Garden Cities proposals. They are physical utopias and share the heart of utopianism, the grounding in ideals involving fundamentally different new social, economic, or institutional arrangements, derived from a critical view of the existing society. But they make serious physical proposals as the way to those changes, rather than seeing physical changes as the result or simply accompaniment of broader social changes. It may well be that such proposals entered the imagination only at the point when physical changes in the organization of urban life began to appear as something subject to public control.

Garden Cities ideas have had wide popularity, and have been implemented to varying degrees. The ideas of the Regional Planning Association of America in the United States, the new towns developments in the United Kingdom and in the Scandinavian countries, the housing developments of the between-wars periods in Germany, all owe much to analogous thinking. None has produced developments operating at the scale of the large city or the megalopolis, although they were centrally concerned with issues of regionalism, and all have been severely limited by the dependence on national political and economic structures that have curtailed the resources available to their full development. The abortive New Towns initiative in the United States in the 1970s is a classic example of the limitations within a broader national context little focused on social justice ideals.

What is important about all of these evolutions that social justice planning took from its roots in the early utopian schemes is their central concern with the social and their critical view of the existing conditions, both aspects of which vary from one to the other in their scale, their depth, and their concern with implementation, but not in their willingness to challenge the conventional and the established in their efforts.

Conclusion

So there have been three different approaches in the history of planning, each with multiple differing aspects. They range from the technicist to the social, running sometimes parallel, almost always mixing to some degree, often in tension with each other. Their separate natures can be formulated in many different ways. Their difference is analogous to that between substantive rationality and instrumental rationality in Habermasian terms, between conventional planning and justice planning in the current discussions about the Just City.[45] Israel Stollman, the well-respected long-time leader of both the American Planning Association and the American Institute of Certified Planners, phrased it as the tension between planners following the precepts of their clients and planners asserting their own values.[46]

Thus this essay should not be taken as suggesting a moral judgment on the actions of individual planners, but rather as an attempt to highlight the divergent roles that planning has been asked to play historically in the shaping of cities. The interplay between what is wanted, and by whom, and what is possible, between what is just and what is realistic, creates a constant tension in city development. Clarity on the causes of that tension and attention to the alternatives for its resolution ought to be an on-going mandate for those concerned about the future of cities.

Notes

1. The difference between the two definitions roughly corresponds to the uses of the word "social" in schools of social work and in departments of sociology. As planners use the term, it often corresponds to the "soft" concerns of planning, as opposed to the "hard" of physical concerns.

2. Leonardo Benevolo (1967) *The Origins of Modern Town Planning*. Trans. Judith Landry. London: Routledge and Kegan Paul.

3. Peter Hall (2001) *Cities of Tomorrow: An Intellectual History of Urban Planning and Design in the Twentieth Century*. 3rd edn. Oxford: Basil Blackwell.

4. Mel Scott (1969) *American City Planning*. Berkeley, CA: University of California Press.

5. Israel Stollman (1979) The values of the city planner. In *The Practice of Local Government Planning*, eds Frank So and Israel Stollman, American Planning Association, *et al*. Washington, DC: International City Management Association in cooperation with the American Planning Association (hereafter "The Green Book"), 7. Subsequently, Stollman talks explicitly about the values of "the planner," but of the planner as an individual, not of planning as a profession.

6. Both Coke in the first ICMA Green Book (James G. Coke (1968) Antecedents of local planning. In *Principles and Practice of Urban Planning*, eds William I. Goodman and Eric C. Freund. Washington, DC: International City Managers' Association, 5–28) and David Harvey (1978) On planning the ideology of planning. In *Planning for the '80s: Challenge and Response*, ed. J. Burchall. New Brunswick, NJ: Rutgers University Press, separate out that component of planning that is technical.

7. See for instance David Harvey (1976) Labor, capital, and class struggle around the built environment in advanced capitalist societies. *Politics and Society* 6: 265–95; Edmond Preteceille (1976) Urban planning: the contradictions of capitalist urbanization. *Antipode* March: 69–76; Richard E. Foglesong (1986) *Planning the Capitalist City: The Colonial Era to the 1920s*. Princeton, NJ: Princeton University Press; Christine Boyer (1983) Dreaming the Rational City. Cambridge, MA: MIT Press.

8. T. J. Schlereth (1981) Burnham's Plan and Moody's Manual: city planning as progressive reform. *Journal of the American Planning Association* 47 (1981): 70–82.

9. Scott, *American City Planning*, 123.

10. *Proceedings of the Engineers' Club of Philadephia* July 1912: 198–215 at p. 201.

11. In 1910 before the Second National Conference on City Planning and Congestion of Population, reprinted as F. L. Olmsted (1910) The basic principles of city planning. *American City* 3: 6772.

12. M. Castells and J. Borja, in collaboration with Belil Mireira and Benner Chris (1997) *Local and Global. The Management of Cities in the Information Age*. United Nations Centre for Human Settlements (Habitat). London: Earthscan Publications Ltd.

13. Peter Marcuse (2002) Depoliticizing globalization: from neo-Marxism to the network society of Manuel Castells. In *Understanding the City*, eds John Eade and Christopher Mele. Oxford: Blackwell, 131–58.

14. Castells and Borja, *Local and Global*.

15. Nicolai Ouroussoff (2006) Injecting a bold shot of the new on the Upper East Side. *New York Times* October 10. Available online at www.nytimes.com/2006/10/10/arts/design/10fost.html?scp=1&sq=ouroussoff%20Upper%20East%20Side%20October%2010%202006&st=cse (accessed October 21, 2010).

16. See, for instance, the columns of Nicolai Ouroussoff, architect critic of the *New York Times*. On Gehry in particular, see (with a symptomatic headline "What will be left of Gehry's vision for Brooklyn?") *New York Times* March 21, 2008: E25.

17. The most recent examples run from downtown Los Angeles to Atlantic Yards in Brooklyn, New York.

18. For a more detailed discussion of the multiple roles of planners in practice, see Peter Marcuse (1976) Professional ethics and beyond: values in planning. *Journal of the American Institute of Planners* 42 (3): 254–74. Reprinted in *Public Planning and Control of Urban and Land Development: Cases and Materials*, ed. Donald Hagman. 2nd edn. Minneapolis, MN: West Publishing Co. (1980), 393–400.

19. See, for instance, the accounts collected in Bruce W. McClendon and Anthony James Catanese (1996) *Planners on Planning: Leading Planners Offer Real-Life Lessons on What Works, What Doesn't, and Why*. Jossey-Bass Public Administration Series. San Francisco, CA: Jossey-Bass Publishers.

20. Bent Flyvbjerg (1998) *Rationality and Power: Democracy in Practice*. Chicago, IL: University of Chicago Press.

21. See Elizabeth Blackmar and Roy Rosenzweig (1992) *The People and the Park: A History of Central Park*. Ithaca, NY: Cornell University Press.

22. Peter Marcuse (1998) Sustainability is not enough. *Environment and Urbanization* 10 (2): 103–12. Also in *The Future of Sustainability*, ed. Marco Keiner. Heidelberg: Springer Verlag (2006), 55–68.

23. See Peter Marcuse (1980) Housing in early city planning. *Journal of Urban History* 6 (2): 153–76, reprinted in slightly different form as Peter Marcuse (1980) Housing policy and city planning: the puzzling split in the United States, 1893–1931. In *Shaping an Urban World*, ed. Gordon E. Cherry. London: Mansell.

24. S. Arnstein (1969) The ladder of citizen participation. *Journal of American Institute of Planners* 35 (4): 216–24.

25. Peter Marcuse (1970) *Tenant Participation – for What?* Washington, DC: The Urban Institute, Working Paper No. 112–20, July 30.

26. As adopted by the American Institute of Certified Planners, March 19, 2005. The full text, and its history, is available at www.planning.org/ethics/ethicscode.htm (accessed October 21, 2010).

27. Norman Krumholz and John Forester (1990) *Making Equity Planning Work. Leadership in the Public Sector*, foreword by Alan A. Altshuler. Philadelphia, PA: Temple University Press; Norman Krumholz and Pierre Clavel (1994) *Reinventing Cities: Equity Planners Tell Their Stories*. Philadelphia, PA: Temple University Press.

28. Leonie Sandercock (ed.) (1998) *Making the Invisible Visible*. Berkeley, CA: University of California Press; Thomas Angotti (2008) *New York for Sale: Community Planning Confronts Global Real Estate*. Cambridge, MA: MIT Press.

29. Frances Fox Piven and Richard A. Cloward (1977) *Poor People's Movements: Why They Succeed, How They Fail*. New York: Pantheon Books.

30. In Amartya Sen and Martha Nussbaum's sense of the term: Martha C. Nussbaum and Amartya Sen (1993) *The Quality of Life*. Oxford: Oxford University Press.

31. This characteristic needs to be spelled out in more detail. It is intuitively likely that working-class groups, immigrants, minority group members, women, non-conformists in lifestyle or ideology, are to be found active within or supportive of critical social justice planning, but the detailed evidence remains to be marshaled. It is one of the lacunae in existing research that this has not yet been done systematically.

32. John Friedmann (1987 [1973]) *Retracking America: A Theory of Transactive Planning*. Garden City, NY: Doubleday; John Friedmann (1987) The social mobilization tradition of planning. In *Planning in the Public Domain: From Knowledge to Action*. Princeton, NJ: Princeton University Press, 225–310.

33. Susan Fainstein (2009) Planning and the just city. In *Searching for the Just City*, eds Peter Marcuse, James Connolly, Johannes Novy, Ingrid Olivo, Cuz Potter, and Justin Steil. New York and London: Routledge, 19–39.

34. John Forester (1989) *Planning in the Face of Power*. Berkeley, CA: University of California Press.

35. Michael Burayidi (ed.) (2000) *Urban Planning in a Multicultural Society*. Westport, CT: Praeger, 225–34.

36. Clare G. Hurley (1999) Planning theory … approaching the millennium … *Study Manual for the Comprehensive AICP Exam of the American Institute of Certified Planners*. Chapter President's Council, the American Planning Association.

37. Angotti, *New York for Sale*, and James DeFilippis (2004) *Unmaking Goliath: Community Control in the Face of Global Capital*. New York: Routledge.

38. Paul Davidoff (1965) Advocacy and pluralism in planning. *Journal of the American Institute of Planners* 31: 331–8; Linda Davidoff and Nel Gold (1974) Suburban action: advocacy planning for an open society. *Journal of the American Institute of Planners* 40: 12–21.

39. June Thomas (1998) Racial inequality and empowerment: necessary theoretical constructs for understanding US planning history. In *Making the Invisible Visible*, ed. L. Sandercock, 198–208.

40. Sandercock, *Making the Invisible Visible*.

41. Peter Marcuse (2007) Social justice in New Orleans: planning after Katrina. *Progressive Planning* summer: 8–12.

42. The argument is developed in P. Marcuse (2005) Katrina disasters and social justice. *Progressive Planning, the Magazine of Planners Network* 165 (fall): 1, 30–5.

43. For background, I have found Malcolm Miles (2007) *Urban Utopias: The Built and Social Architectures of Alternative Settlements*. London: Routledge, exceptionally useful. There is a Society for Utopian Studies, whose website has links to a substantial bibliography.

44. David Harvey (2000) *Spaces of Hope*. Berkeley, CA: University of California Press.

45. See Peter Marcuse, James Connolly, Johannes Novy, Ingrid Olivo, Cuz Potter, and Justin Stein (eds) (2009) *Searching for the Just City: Debates in Urban Theory and Practice*. Oxford: Routledge.

46. Stollman, The values of the city planner, 8.

Part II

What Are Planners Trying to Do?
The Justifications and Critiques of Planning

Readings in Planning Theory, Fourth Edition. Edited by Susan S. Fainstein and James DeFilippis.
Editorial material and organization © 2016 John Wiley & Sons, Ltd.
Published 2016 by John Wiley & Sons, Ltd.

Introduction

This section addresses a perennial question of planning theory: What is the justification for planning intervention? Rather than offering an abstract, ideological answer, the readings examine planning's larger environment and the effects of different approaches to intervention. Underlying these questions is the boundary mapping of planning thought and action given the limits of human rationality, coordination, and authority. A further issue is who has claim to expertise – planners, elected officials, or affected communities? A core task of planning theory has long been to examine arguments for and against planning, alternately using neo-classical economic, institutional, and structuralist perspectives and placing the profession in the political-economic context of the relationship between the private market and government (both the local and national states). Overall the selections point to the contradictory aims of planning and the difficulties presented in trying to resolve the tensions among them.

We begin, in Chapter 7, with Patsy Healey's defense of the planning project. Healey, who is perhaps Britain's most influential contemporary planning theorist, is notable for attempts to bridge the gulf between academic theorizing and planning practice. She begins with three stories of planning conflicts and uses them to illustrate the kinds of divisions that arise in the planning process. These involve clashes among different community interests, between members of the community and politicians, and between planners and the public. How planning is institutionalized is key to the ways in which these oppositions are mediated. She points to what is now a widely accepted truth about planning – that it is an inherently political activity not simply a technical exercise, even in the case of scientists predicting the environmental consequences of development. In her account of planning dilemmas, she indicates the constant tension among goals, as is spelled out by Scott Campbell in his article on the planner's triangle ("Green Cities, Growing Cities, Just Cities," see Chapter 11, this volume). Healey emphasizes that planning "for the many" cannot assume the existence of a unified public interest but rather a plurality of interests, often conflicting. Planning, in her view, consists of explicitly formulated, intentional collective action. Her essay, however, does not explain what to do when consensus does not develop, as in the case she presents of Nazareth, where the two sides remained implacably opposed and where planning brought latent conflict to the surface.

Ash Amin, who respects Healey's vision of planning as mediation among differing social interests, nevertheless considers that this view does not adequately address risk (Chapter 8, this volume). First, he argues that deliberation does not sufficiently address aspects of urban life that are not controllable and that interact to create a whole transcending the sum of its parts. Second, he contends that skepticism toward expert judgment fails to deal with the need to devise substantive responses to the hazards of urban life. He critiques the theories of urban pragmatists who, while believing that planners should articulate visions of the good city, do not describe what could be the content of these visions. He sees potential trade-offs between expert judgment and deliberative democracy rather than assuming the latter will always produce the best outcome. Thus, while he does not defend a concept of planning as the rule of experts, neither does he doubt the need for technical expertise nor dismiss the efforts of planners to shape agendas.

The dichotomy between regulation and laissez-faire has been a staple of planning theory debates. More recently it has become subsumed within discussions of neo-liberalism. Although Americans usually define the term "liberalism" as supportive of leftist programs, neo-liberalism's roots are in nineteenth-century economic thought that would be considered conservative within contemporary debates. Neo-liberalism thus calls for free markets, individual autonomy, and businesses unhindered by government controls. Usually incorporating arguments for privatization, deregulation, and competitiveness, neo-liberal proponents argue that planning introduces inefficiencies, restricts freedom, stifles entrepreneurship, and limits economic growth. The argument for competitiveness extends beyond the economist's concern with competition among firms to the contest among cities and regions to retain, attract, and develop industries and facilities that contribute to economic growth. This focus leads governments to subsidize private entities, use their capital budgets to build sports venues, convention centers, and iconic public buildings, and give low priority to welfare and social services.

In a 1985 essay Richard Klosterman sums up the debate between advocates of free-market liberalism and defenders of planning. Even though this piece was written two decades ago, before the term neo-liberalism had gained currency, it identifies the ways in which the argument for privatization had already taken hold. This article had been included in the first two editions of this reader. We are returning it in this fourth edition because it still represents the best exposition we could find of the arguments for and against planning (Chapter 9, this volume). Essentially Klosterman shows how irreconcilable values underlie the two viewpoints and that no empirical test can validate the superiority of one over the other, since the criteria of evaluation differ.

Klosterman begins by outlining the standard market failure model, whereby planning steps in to address the periodic shortcomings of the free-market system. This is perhaps the safest ground for planning, since it justifies government intervention based on its ability to improve and assist the functioning of an efficient market. He comments, however, that arguments based wholly on efficiency ignore questions of distribution. He lists some additional defenses of planning: planners address the shortcoming of the political system, which militates against long-term thinking and lacks the capability to achieve collective goals; and planners possess unique professional expertise that allows them to reach reasoned judgments. In taking note of the Marxist critiques of planning as primarily serving the interests of capitalism, he agrees that they offer insights into the nature of planning in capitalist societies, but judges them to offer little practical guidance. He leaves open the potential of planning to attain its theoretical claims.

In Chapter 10, this volume, Heather Campbell, Malcolm Tait, and Craig Watkins respond to Klosterman's challenge. Writing 20 years later, they start by placing planning within the context of a world in which the precepts of neo-liberalism have become globally dominant but avoid pessimism. Rather than indulging in abstract arguments of justification or critique, they seek to develop a realistic argument for better planning in an imperfect world. They discuss a public sector where the arguments of "new public management," by which the public sector acts like a private entrepreneur, have been particularly influential. They develop their argument by analyzing a case of "ordinary" planning to discover what choices were available for planners. They conclude that the planners working on the case of central city redevelopment in Exeter had little understanding of real estate dynamics and failed to exploit the opportunity presented by public land ownership. According to their analysis, if the planners had held an overarching vision of the desired outcome, they would have produced a better redevelopment scheme even if not the best imaginable. While accepting the neo-liberal emphasis on growth and markets, the planners could have fostered competition and promoted several smaller-scale projects rather than acceding to the massive proposal of a single, conservative developer.

Campbell et al.'s discussion points to the centrality of the goal of economic growth in contemporary planning doctrine. Other professed aims include environmental preservation and social justice. In Scott Campbell's contribution (Chapter 11, this volume), he questions whether the idea of sustainability is a useful rallying cry for the urban planning profession. Its broad promises attract a wide and hopeful following but also undercut its strategic credibility. The remarkable consensus in favor of the idea is encouraging but also reason for skepticism, since sustainability can mean many things to many people without requiring commitment to any specific policies. The danger is that in the end, though all will endorse the principle of sustainability, few will actually practice it. The result would be simply superficial, feel-good solutions: by merely adding "sustainable" to existing planning documents (sustainable zoning, sustainable economic development, sustainable transportation planning, sustainable housing, and so on), this would create the illusion that we are actually doing sustainable planning. (This is reminiscent of the addition of the term "comprehensive" to planning 50 years ago, "strategic" planning in the 1980s, and resilience in the new millennium [see Gleeson, Chapter 12, this volume]).

Campbell argues for a broader definition of sustainability. He develops the idea of the "planner's triangle" to distinguish the field's three fundamental goals – economic development, environmental protection, and social justice – and more importantly, to articulate the resulting conflicts over property, resources, and development. At the theoretical center of this triangle lies the sustainable city but the path to this elusive center is neither direct nor simple; instead, as the struggle for sustainability becomes more advanced, it will also become more sharply contentious, since it will involve increasingly explicit and sobering trade-offs between interest groups in society.

Increasingly the term "resilience" has substituted for sustainability in the discourse of planning. Stimulated by the threat of climate change and recent disasters caused by earthquakes, forest fires, hurricanes, and typhoons, use of the term encompasses sustainability but also refers to dealing with risk. Like sustainability it is innocuous and subject to varied interpretations. The most prevalent interpretation involves responding to threat not simply through avoidance but through adaptation – for example, by letting forest fires burn themselves out, restoring wetlands, and constructing structures near shorelines on stilts to accommodate flooding. In Chapter 12, Gleeson takes issue with the seemingly benign emphasis on resilience, asserting that unlike sustainability, it is not an essentially progressive concept. Ash Amin (Chapter 8, this volume) considers risk as endemic to the urban world and requiring expert knowledge for responding to it. Gleeson, however, warns against a facile transfer of concepts from biological science and ecology to planning, seeing its potential to be used to mask the distribution of benefits from plans justified in terms of resilience. He worries that the analogies to natural processes in discussions of resilience disguise the agency exerted by the powerful. Although he accepts that resilience planning can be a progressive move, he worries that it may be used to justify adapting to global warning rather than trying to prevent it.

Gleeson's distinction between sustainability and resilience may be overdrawn. Often environmentalism, regardless of the labels placed on it, has been a refuge for propertied people seeking to preserve their privileges. Opposition to affordable housing has frequently been framed in terms of protecting natural environments. Even if residents are not consciously promoting ethnic exclusion, they often resist higher densities as threatening pollution from greater traffic or putting too much pressure on water systems and sewers. Just as cost–benefit analysis does not distinguish between winners and losers, the science mechanically incorporated into resilience planning may likewise ask the least advantaged to bear the costs of adaptation, for example, by demarcating areas of low-income population for displacement because they are environmentally sensitive.

In her article on spatial justice and planning Susan Fainstein directly addresses the question of how planning can produce a more just city (Chapter 13, this volume). She is particularly concerned with the trade-off between economic growth and justice that Scott Campbell depicts. She defines urban justice in terms of the three principles of material equality, diversity, and democracy, sees them as existing in tension with each other, and gives priority to equality. Although she regards the vision of a just city as utopian, she nevertheless sees it as a template against which to evaluate the policies of existing cities and compare them to each other. She thus looks at three cities – New York, London, and Amsterdam – to determine how they stack up against the criteria she establishes. She concludes by listing specific policies for planners that would increase social justice. She emphasizes the importance of substance – i.e. the content of policy – rather than process – i.e. the procedures by which a plan is developed. Critics of her approach, however, have contended that just outcomes will only occur as a consequence of fair and open processes (see the selections by Fischer and Forester, Chapters 17 and 18, this volume).

7

The Planning Project

Patsy Healey

Places in Our Lives

We care about the places where we live our lives. We get used to their pathways and pleasures, and learn to navigate their tensions and dark corners. We want freedom to find our own ways, but often agitate for collective action to define some rules, some general constraints to protect what we value and to reduce the tensions that arise as we co-exist with others in shared spaces. There are stories from across the world of people mobilising to improve and protect the qualities of the places they live in, work in and care about. Such struggles are especially intense where many different groups, often with different cultures, values and modes of living, share common resources or, as in urban areas, inhabit the same physical space. In these struggles, we form and re-form our ideas of ourselves and our social worlds, of identity and solidarity, of individual freedoms and social responsibilities.

Three cameos illustrate such stories and struggles. They range from routine conflicts over neighbourhood development in England to struggles over knowledge about environmental pollution in New York and well-meaning initiatives in Nazareth, Israel, which ended tragically.

The first case comes from affluent southern England.[1] Ditchling is a small village of around 2,000 people on the Sussex Downs, near the motorway from London to Brighton. Here people who have lived in the village for generations mingle with all kinds of people who have moved there, attracted by the image of village life and the reality of a beautiful downland landscape close to the amenities and social worlds of both London and Brighton. In this respect, it is like very many villages

Original publication details: Healey, Patsy. 2010. "The Planning Project". In *Making Better Places: The Planning Project in the Twenty-First Century*. London: Palgrave Macmillan. pp. 1–22. Reproduced with permission from Palgrave Macmillan.

Readings in Planning Theory, Fourth Edition. Edited by Susan S. Fainstein and James DeFilippis.

across South East England. All kinds of people co-exist here. There are farmers worried about the future of their activity, followers of hunting defending their sport, and a group of artists and craftspeople, linked to a co-operative craft guild set up by engraver Eric Gill in the early twentieth century. There are retired managers of multinational companies, retired actresses and singers, including Dame Vera Lynn,[2] and people who have refused promotions if this meant they had to leave their village. There are 44 societies of one kind or another, and a local museum that attracts people from all over the world. Local residents put on shows and get involved in fêtes, festivals and morris dancing. There is some overlapping of the networks of all these different people, but also some carefully maintained distances. Not everyone is happy about the hunting and there are considerable reservations about the lifestyle of the engraver, whose work still attracts so much attention.

Some villagers are prepared to mobilise to defend village qualities. The heart of the village has for many years been a formally declared 'conservation area' under English planning legislation. Until recently the village had four pubs. Each had its own clientele and ambience, though some people moved around from pub to pub. However, the owner of one of these, a rather ordinary building with a large garden, saw better prospects in developing the site for housing. Regular drinkers were naturally upset at the prospect of losing their pub, as were the football players, the darts team and the bell ringers, whose regular meeting place it was. Others in the village felt that the loss of one of the pubs meant that the overall assets of the village would be reduced. Some were ideologically troubled and disliked the idea that village assets could be 'stripped' so that private developers could make money. A few people thought that it might be better to have houses nearby rather than a noisy pub, but on balance, the village 'majority', orchestrated by an action group, was against the development. This view prevailed in the Parish Council.

However, Parish Councils in the English government structure have very limited powers. The key decision-making body is the District Council, which covers a much larger area. And District Councils have only limited powers too. In issues to do with planning they have to follow national guidelines, which have influenced the policies in the local plans that they are required to prepare. These are approved after complex inquiry processes. A planning authority in England has no powers to demand that an enterprise such as a pub be kept open. Its powers relate to whether proposed new development can go ahead. In this case, the Ditchling parish councillor was also the representative of the village on the District Council. The district councillors realised how much opposition there was in the village to the housing proposal, but were unsure how to respond to this, as the local plan had indicated that it would be appropriate to have a housing development on the site in question. And if the developer appealed against the council decision and won, costs would be awarded against the Council, so the Council did not have very much power either. The district planning officers negotiated a reduction in the scale of the scheme, but recommended to the councillors that they should approve it. Neither the local plan nor national planning policy gave them grounds for refusal, and refusal would not only potentially incur costs, but also could undermine the Council's reputation as a capable planning authority.

In this context, the application was approved and the housing development has now been completed. The residents enjoy their new homes. But many villagers remain deeply upset, not just about the loss of their pub but about their inability to make their voice heard. They were horrified that their parish councillor, who had supported the action group's position, actually supported the decision in favour of the housing development at the Planning Committee meeting. How, they asked, can a local council override what a village has voted for? Why are there no rights for villagers to appeal against a planning decision?[3] How can their local councillor be so two-faced? Doesn't this show that the national planning laws are just a 'developer's charter'? Through such everyday encounters with the English planning system, local residents and their equivalents across the country get a real and uncomfortable experience of what democracy means in England today.

The second case is about how local knowledge confronted government specialists. It takes us to New York and a neighbourhood in Brooklyn, opposite the downtown on Manhattan Island. The Greenpoint/Williamsburg neighbourhood, as described by Jason Coburn, 'is one of the most polluted communities in New York City' (Corburn 2005:12). Around 160,000 people, from a variety of backgrounds, live in an area that is less than 1,300 hectares (5 square miles) in extent. In 2000, it was calculated that over a third of the population lived in poverty.[4] It was also an area with a concentration of industrial plants and many polluting facilities. Studies in recent years showed that the area had a very high concentration of facilities dealing in hazardous substances. In addition, the area suffered pollution from heavy traffic crossing from Manhattan to Brooklyn. The US Environmental Protection Agency and the New York City Department of Environmental Protection had undertaken studies to identify the health consequences of these hazards. Under pressure from the US environmental justice movement, which campaigned for more attention to the environmental hazards suffered by poorer communities, these public agencies set out to study in more depth the relationship between the hazards and health experiences in the area.

However, local people were suspicious of this kind of approach. They felt that the 'scientific knowledge' with which such agencies worked might miss their own experience of life 'on the street'. They struggled to get their knowledge recognised by the environmental health scientists. In various ways, they organised community knowledge around different issues. Corburn explores their work in relation to water pollution and local fishing to supplement family diets, the high rates of asthma experienced in the area, the high incidence of lead poisoning among children, and the risks arising from local air pollution. He highlights the way in which local knowledge could indicate cultural practices and fine-grained variations from street to street, which scientists dealing in abstracted data sets could easily miss. Yet, although there were many struggles and suspicions between the trained environmental scientists and community members, in the end what was achieved was a way of joining 'local insights with professional techniques' (Corburn 2005:3). Corburn calls this 'street science' and shows how such a science can both inform decision making about improving health conditions in the area and focus scientific enquiry in new ways. He argues that communities are full of 'experts' in knowledge about the flow of daily life in their areas. What they often lack, especially in poor, ethnically mixed communities, is 'voice', the capacity to make their concerns heard in the wider world that controls the location and regulation of the activities and facilities that cause their problems. Corburn argues that, in the Greenpoint/ Williamsburg case, getting heard was the result of several factors: building coalitions among different groups within the neighbourhood who were worried about different aspects of the environment; linking community activism with the wider environmental justice movement; the presence of 'intermediaries' who acted as 'boundary spanners'; connecting community knowledge with professionals in various agencies; and attention to short-term actions that could really make a difference and that residents could recognise.

The third case, from the town of Nazareth in Israel, illustrates how a well-meaning planning initiative can generate disturbing conflicts. It is told by Yosef Jabareen (2006). At the end of the twentieth century around 70,000 people lived there, all of Palestinian background, of whom 67 per cent were Muslim Arabs and 33 per cent Christian Arabs. They had suffered in the mid-twentieth century as a result of the displacement and resettlement produced as the State of Israel was formed. Both groups lost land in this process. Since then, the town's conditions and development had been largely neglected by the Israeli national government. It was left to local initiatives to mobilise improvement activity, but in a situation of limited resources. Living conditions were difficult, but the different groups lived peaceably together and the town was a major international tourist destination.

In the early 1990s, the national government adopted a more positive attitude to the town's development needs. The Mayor of Nazareth was at this time a government member. The ambition of the government, and the Mayor, was to enhance the peace process generally between Israelis and Palestinians, then full of promise, and to improve conditions in the neglected city of Nazareth. This led to an initiative that became the Nazareth 2000 Plan. Nazareth was to be a key location for the 2000 millennium celebrations. The focus was on tourism as a generator of economic benefits – 'a unique cultural-tourist destination for international tourism' (Jabareen 2006:309). The plan included several valuable development projects across the city, with a significant budget allocation. One of these projects was for a new plaza, designed by an Israeli government architect, to create a good view of the town's main monument, the Church of the Annunciation. However, Muslim groups argued that the land had been dedicated to the nearby mosque. It therefore belonged to the Muslim religious community and could not be developed for other purposes.

On the eve of Easter Sunday, the night between 3 and 4 April 1999, unexpected clashes erupted ... between thousands of (the town's) Christian and Muslim residents. These clashes, which shocked the Palestinian minority in Israel, were the first in modern history between these religious groups who had lived together peacefully in the city for hundreds of years. (Jabareen 2006:305)

The source of the tension was the plan for the new plaza. The promoters of the plan had hoped to host a visit from the Pope as part of the millennium celebrations. But Muslims in the city wanted to build a mosque next to the Church of the Annunciation.

As a response to the city plan, hundreds of Muslims constructed a large tent at the site of the planned plaza, built the foundations for a new mosque, and initiated a sit-in protest that lasted for four years. Following intensive international interventions (by such leaders as President Bush, the Pope, and President Putin) asking for the destruction of the tent and the foundations of the mosque, the Government of Israel, deploying thousands of soldiers, destroyed the tent and the beginnings of the mosque in April 2003 ...This event, which began as a plaza plan for a small site in Nazareth, mushroomed beyond that, causing political, social, and cultural urban crises in the city. Above all, it triggered religious conflict in Nazareth ... Astonishingly, the Central Plaza Plan, which simply designates a small piece of land for public use ... succeeded in tearing [a] long-sustained social fabric and creating new social and political risks in Nazareth. (Jabareen 2006:305–6)

By January 2006 the plaza was complete, but was not opened until a few years later. There are many different views in Nazareth about who was responsible for this sad outcome, but all agree that the security of their place of dwelling is worse than it was and they feel divided and fearful in a way that was not present before. 'Today, Nazareth is a city of veils and crucifixes,' said an interviewee. 'Planning served as a conflict producer' (Jabareen 2006:317).

It is from cases such as these that the ideas and practices associated with planning activity get their justifications and meanings. The focus of this broad field of ideas and practices is on deliberate, collective attempts to improve place qualities, as a contribution to the management and development of places. In this respect, it is part of the governance infrastructure that contributes to the physical shaping of locales within an urban area. However, it is about much more than this physical shaping and ordering. Planning ideas and planning activity both express, and contribute to, the way people understand and feel about places. They may come to affect and express people's sense of identity as well as their material conditions.

The Politics of Place

Stories such as those recounted above, which can be repeated from across the globe, have often been treated as somehow 'local' phenomena, below the radar of the great themes of national and international politics and the power play of ideologies and political movements. Yet these apparently local experiences do not only have local effects, and small conflicts can grow into bigger struggles. Even small encounters with planning activity can provide important experiences of the governance institutions in a society, of their strengths and, especially, their failings. When a place-related issue confronts them – a proposed new building, or the expansion of a traffic-generating hospital or school, or a proposal for a new motorway route or airport expansion – people recall and revise their views of what they think about the political arrangements in their society as well as about the particular issue in hand. They learn about what they value, who has the same views as them and who seems to have a different view. They are reminded that they have to co-exist with others. They discover how all kinds of issues interrelate, clash and get tangled up when they come together in particular places. The institutional sites or arenas where 'planning' and local development issues are discussed and where conflicts are arbitrated may then become places where citizens learn about politics. People become aware of how their concerns inter-relate not only with those of their neighbours, but with those of people elsewhere whose concerns are raised in the discussion.

In Europe in the twentieth century, formal governments were not well equipped to deal with this place-centred politics. Some countries were very centralised, making it difficult to grasp citizens' concerns about their living environments. The dominant focus, as politics shifted into more democratic forms, was to provide for people's needs. But the way these needs were thought about was shaped by the class struggles of industrialisation, especially the demand for better conditions for the working classes. These important struggles set the masses in opposition to elites in the search for a more just distribution of resources and less exploitative working conditions. The aim of the welfare states that developed in Western Europe and North America in the second part of the twentieth century was to create welfare by an economic project of full employment through industrial expansion and a social project of better housing, health and education for all. As more and more people came to live in urban environments, the challenge of managing the collective daily life of both people and firms became ever more significant. It is in this context that the ideas and actions associated with the planning field commanded the attention of political leaders. During the twentieth century, the project of improving place qualities moved from the advocacy and experimentation of activists into a significant activity of formal governments. 'Planning systems' were created to regulate how land was used and developed, and how space and place qualities could be provided to serve economic and sociocultural purposes (Sutcliffe 1981, Ward 2002).

This planning project, as it developed in the first part of that century, was advocated both as a means of achieving wider access to economic opportunities and as a way of developing places in which work opportunities, housing provision and social welfare facilities for all could be situated. In the post-World War II period in Europe, planning as city building and rebuilding was a major element in the effort to revive social and economic conditions after the 1930s economic depression and the damage done by wartime bombing. In the US, the planning project was given a different emphasis, focusing on regional development and the promotion of more rational, scientifically informed public administration, both more democratic and more efficient than the patronage politics that grew up in a governance context in which local administrations had considerable autonomy (Friedmann 1973, 1987). However, in both contexts, experts and elite politicians articulated policies on behalf of citizens, who tended to be considered as largely undifferentiated masses with similar wants and needs. As the American sociologist Herbert Gans remarked, planners tended to plan for people like themselves (Gans 1969). Planning systems and development projects were thus rolled out across national territories with little attention to local variety. How such systems then worked out depended on the wider political and administrative context. In decentralised government systems, such as the US, the institutions and instruments made available by planning legislation might release local energies to pursue citizens' concerns about place qualities in inclusive ways, sensitive to different conditions and experiences. But equally, these same institutions and instruments could also be captured by particular interests. Commentators in the later twentieth century argued that governance elites dominated by business coalitions ruled most urban areas in the US (Fainstein and Fainstein 1986, Logan and Molotch 1987). In highly centralised systems, the development of local place management capacity might be ignored in the drive for wider goals such as economic growth. Or local management might be shaped to conform to national perceptions of what the planning project should achieve.

However, the general idea of planning as a welfare project articulated by technical experts faced other challenges when translated into government institutions and procedures. People increasingly questioned the capacity of elites and experts to articulate their concerns. Pressure groups, social movements and lobby groups demanded a greater say in policy-making processes. The diversity of people's experiences, aspirations and social worlds became increasingly evident, as civil rights movements in the 1960s and 1970s challenged systemic injustices, not only of class, but gender, race, ethnic and religious background, and physical ability. From the 1960s, the environmental costs of economic growth and resource exploitation became ever more obvious, leading to fundamental shifts in thinking about the relations and responsibilities of humans to the natural environment. While scientific knowledge was a key resource in this environmental movement, it also opened up such knowledge in ways that allowed people to see that science itself was full of contested concepts and uncertain conclusions, as residents in Greenpoint/Williamsburg argued. So neither scientific knowledge nor political representatives could be trusted to know enough, and especially to know enough about particular conditions in specific places. A wider approach to the intelligence needed to inform place-governance practices was needed.

In any case, the behaviour of those involved in politics and public administration, as reported in the media, seemed to suggest that politicians, their advisers and their officials were as likely to be corruptly pursuing their own interests or those of their favoured cronies as to be committed to the concerns of the citizens they were supposed to represent. Instead of responsible representatives of citizens' concerns, politicians were increasingly perceived as a discrete class, buttressed by self-interested officials and lobby groups, distanced from people's everyday lives. These shifts in thinking about government, politicians and governance capacity, now widely spread across the globe, have reduced citizens' interest in engaging with nation-state politics. Nevertheless, this does not mean that citizens and businesses are not interested in place qualities. Concerns about pollution and congestion, about rights to define which place qualities to promote, about the quality of streets and public spaces, and about access to physical and social facilities and infrastructures, become increasingly important once minimum basic needs for food and shelter are met. And people do not merely want a certain quantity of these place qualities. They want them arranged in such a way that they are accessible to them – physically, socially and in economic terms. Struggles over the quality of place management and development may lead to previously disenfranchised or disaffected citizens re-engaging with political life. In doing so, they may help to transform the qualities of the governance culture of their political community.

In such a context, the nature of planning institutions and practices, and their relation to all kinds of other arenas where place politics are acted out, become more than merely local matters. They begin to shape the overall way in which government and politics are done. They become institutional sites where national priorities, such as promoting economic development or providing more housing, bump up against other concerns about place qualities, such as infrastructure provision, environmental quality and sustainable development principles. They create arenas where international companies and global pressure groups may confront local residents in clashes over development proposals. As the weekly journal *The Economist* has remarked, 'Britain's inefficient planning rules ... [are] a subject that raises passions like few others' (*Economist*, 9 Dec 2006:36). This recognises the intensity of the conflicts that can arise among the many different people who have a stake in what happens in a place, the 'stakeholders' in place qualities. In such situations, the arenas and institutions created by governments to undertake 'planning' activity are judged both as a hope and a problem. If only we had good planning, some people think, conflicts would become less intense. If only we could get rid of 'planning constraints', these conflicts could be bypassed. Planning activity and those who do planning work are caught in the centre of this ambiguous attitude (see Figure 7.1).

I argue in this book that the politics of place cannot be bypassed. More than half of us now live in urban areas of one kind of another, and have a stake in working out how to combine our own opportunities for flourishing[5] with those of others with whom we co-exist. As thinking creatures always interacting with the rest of the natural world, and with pasts and futures, we also cannot avoid being concerned about how the way we live now may compromise future conditions for life, for

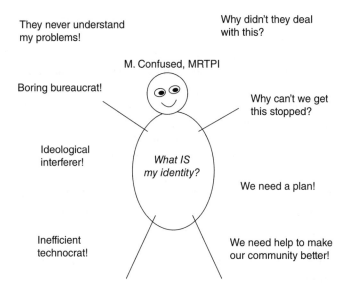

Figure 7.1   The ambiguous position of planners.

ourselves and for others. It therefore matters in the twenty-first century how we, as social beings in political communities, approach the challenges of place management and development.

The Evolving Planning Project

What does it mean to approach place-governance with a planning orientation? Answers to this question evolved significantly through the twentieth century. An enduring concept embedded in the idea of planning is the belief that it is worth acting now to try to bring into being some aspiration for the future. A planning way of approaching place-governance therefore emphasises some aspirations about future place qualities. But what qualities and whose aspirations get to count?

A century ago, as urbanisation proceeded apace in rapidly industrialising countries, the planning project was promoted for several reasons (UN-Habitat 2009). For some, the ambition was to display the power of leaders and their commitment to 'modernising' their cities. There are still leaders today whose ambitions have created the skyscraper displays of Pudong in Shanghai or Dubai in the Gulf States. Such 'grand projects' have been as much about display and beautification as about providing space for urban activities. Another motivation for taking up the planning project was to manage the process of urban expansion. In developed countries in the early to mid-twentieth century, and increasingly now in the urban megalopolises of the developing world, national and municipal governments have sought to control urban expansion by regulating how land is used and developed. Major concerns in attempts to regulate urban expansion centred throughout the twentieth century on relating land development to infrastructure provision, and protecting areas where people live from polluting industries. The mechanism of 'zoning' land for particular uses arose from these concerns. Such concerns remain an important idea in the planning project today, emphasising the value of the convenience and operating efficiency of urban areas. A third motivation for the planning project was to make a contribution to redressing the social inequalities that have been a persistent feature of urban life. While the emphasis on beautification seemed to pander to the aspirations of affluent elites, efficiency and convenience were valued by the expanding urban middle classes. But poorer citizens and marginalised minority groups have faced hard struggles to get a foothold from which to satisfy basic needs and access to urban opportunities. Many of those promoting the planning project a century ago were motivated by finding ways to improve housing and living conditions for the poorest. Concern for justice in the way in which urban opportunities are distributed remains an important idea within the planning project.

A century ago, the planning project was conceived primarily in terms of its role in improving the physical fabric of cities. It was closely linked to concepts of the progressive 'modernising' of cities, though there were struggles over whether this modernisation should reflect the ambitions of elites or the aspirations of ordinary city dwellers. However, as the century wore on, much more attention was given to the social and economic dimensions of the way in which places change and develop. Advocates of the planning project became concerned with how local economies developed and how places experiencing economic hardship could be helped by development initiatives. This in turn encouraged more attention to understanding social and economic dynamics, especially through systematic social scientific analysis. Understood in this way, the planning project could be associated with bringing knowledge to bear on public policy choices (Friedmann 1987). But this still left open the question of what and whose knowledge got to count, the issue that preoccupied the residents in Greenpoint/Williamsburg. For many, it seemed once again that it was the knowledge of elites that counted, a distant 'them', far from the worlds of 'us'. This perception came to exist even in states formally committed to promoting the welfare of their citizens, as that welfare often seemed to be articulated in paternalist, top-down ways.

In the second part of the twentieth century these critical voices grew in volume. As projects informed by planning ideas rolled out across city cores, neighbourhoods and peripheries, protest movements and lobby groups began to articulate some serious failings of the planning project. Some of these protests helped to build the positive planning experiences presented in this book. One critique charged the planning project with being little more than a creature of business elites driven by capitalist profit making rather than any concern for the wider collective interest. Others argued that the institutions and practices of formal government planning systems were being used systematically to oppress minorities or, in some post-colonial situations, to allow urban political elites to cream off the benefits of urban development for themselves. Manuel Castells showed in a study of a French city how the machinery of the planning system was used systematically to advance the interests of business and property owners, while limiting the possibilities of working-class residents (Castells 1977).[6] Oren Yiftachel (1994, 1998) later highlighted how planning mechanisms were used in ways that discriminated against Palestinians in Israeli towns. Sub-Saharan African countries provide several examples of political elites using planning systems to maximise personal or tribal benefits.[7] Such experiences and accounts encouraged a critical view of the planning project, as too close to the values of modernising elites and/or potentially corruptible by forms of politics with little concern for the collective interest of a political community.

These criticisms, however, were only in part about the planning project as such. They were just as much about the way in which the institutions and practices set up to advance deliberate place management and development could be subverted by powerful groups. How can governance practices and cultures develop with the capacity to prevent such subversion? How is it possible to undertake place-governance work that gives more attention to people's varied experiences and aspirations about living in urban areas? It is here that the planning project during the later part of the twentieth century came to draw on wider debates about the nature of political community and democratic life. It is not enough to leave the governance of places to elites and their advisers, nor to leave it merely to the mechanisms of formal representative democracy. Citizens and other stakeholders have knowledge to contribute and values to assert. This increases the conflict and argument over what place qualities to privilege and what the priorities for place management and development in any urban area should be. Yet conflict and argument reflect the real diversity of experiences, imaginations and aspirations. This diversity is not only about conflicts between the interests of different groups. Political communities may value, at a general level, the promotion of better living conditions for all, greater efficiency in relating development to infrastructure, better-quality design of the physical fabric of urban areas and more attention to the longer-term environmental consequences of the way we live today. But how do these values get prioritised and translated when specific place management and development actions are taken up? How can one value be balanced against another?

This became a particularly important issue by the end of the twentieth century. By this time, concern for the condition of the natural environment and the relation between humans and nature had become a major concern, as evidence of the damage that human action has caused to our planetary life was difficult to avoid. At the same time, economic activity had become more crisis prone and more globally inter-related, with some places being hubs of dynamic growth and others faced with economic collapse. Reviving business to make 'places' more competitive became a major preoccupation of many countries and cities in the 1980s and

1990s. These economic and environmental concerns co-existed with concerns about social justice, often transformed into an emphasis on how to make political communities more 'cohesive' and less prone to major inequalities and the resentment this generates. In this context, the search for a way of moving into the future in sustainable ways became an orienting goal for many governments, both national and local. Figure 7.2 presents an influential expression of this idea developed within a European context.

Thus, at the beginning of the twenty-first century, a number of concepts have become central to the planning project. The concept of sustainability gives an important slant to thinking about future possibilities. The concept of balancing and integrating diverse values recognises the reality of conflict, but also the necessity of moving beyond disagreement to enable action to be taken where this is considered necessary or appropriate for the political community as a whole. The concept of participation recognises that elites and experts cannot be trusted alone to deliver 'what is best' for communities. The planning project has thus become associated with promoting conceptions of urban life that recognise human diversity, acknowledging that humans need to give respect to the environmental conditions that sustain them and understanding that human flourishing depends on giving attention to multiple dimensions of human existence, as realised in particular places. Within this conception, the planning project partly centres on providing understanding and expertise and making a contribution to public debate about place management and development possibilities. But it also has a practical focus on what is required to realise programmes, policies and projects in specific conditions. It gives attention to practical action, to doing place-governance work. This book provides a journey through examples of such work inspired by a planning orientation.

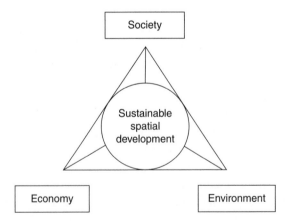

Figure 7.2 Balanced and sustainable development: A European perspective.[8]
Source: Committee for Spatial Development 1999:10. European Spatial Development Perspective, 1999.

A Focus for the Planning Project

The planning project is therefore an approach to deliberate place management and development that is infused with a specific orientation or philosophy. It carries with it conceptions of place qualities and of a way of doing governance work. What these conceptions and approaches are and should be is vigorously debated and contested among those interested in the planning field. In what follows, I draw out the debates associated with progressive traditions, in which a concern for the present and future living conditions of the many, and not only the privileged few, is given precedence.

Overall, the idea of planning as an enterprise of collective activity, of public policy, is linked to a belief that it is worth striving to improve the human condition as lived in particular situations in the context of interaction with others, human and non-human. As people we are a diverse lot, continually forming and re-forming our sense of ourselves and our relations with others. Governance activity provides a way of stabilising our collective concerns. Given our diversity, and the potential for some people and groups to dominate over others, the struggle for inclusively democratic forms of governance remains an important enterprise. But rather than the ideal of governance performed by the formally elected representatives of a consensus society, advised by technocratic experts and carried out by administrative bureaucrats, contemporary ideas about democracy stress the importance of multiple governance arenas and multiple ways of establishing legitimacy for collective action. They emphasise the significance of argumentation, discord, lively debate and conflict in generating a rich, inclusive governance culture, which is continually revising itself (see Cunningham 2002, Connolly 2005, Briggs 2008, Callon et al. 2009).

Not only are we diverse, with many different ideas about and needs for collective action, we are highly mobile, as we explore the material world and the worlds of ideas and imagination. We dwell in multiple dimensions of existence, in all kinds of relations with others. In our webs of relations, we are also socially and culturally 'placed', in relation to others and in places of dwelling and encounter. We value these places, as they give shape to our daily life flow, and as they collect meanings through the encounters of daily life and of special occasions and incidents, as the examples of Ditchling and Nazareth illustrate. Nevertheless, my meanings may not be the same as my neighbour's. My social networks are likely to be different, though transecting and interacting with those of my neighbours in various ways. It is the potentials and tensions within these transactions and interactions that arise as we co-exist in places that create the demand for collective action – to promote the opportunities and potentials of place qualities, but also to make the inevitable frictions and tensions more tolerable.

With these general points as a context, Box 7.1 lists five distinctive attributes that are central to a progressive interpretation of the planning project in the

> **Box 7.1**   Attributes of a twenty-first century 'planning project'
>
> • An orientation to the future and a belief that action now can shape future potentialities.
> • An emphasis on liveability and sustainability for the many, not the few.
> • An emphasis on interdependences and interconnectivities between one phenomenon and another, across time and space.
> • An emphasis on expanding the knowledgeability of public action, expanding the 'intelligence' of a polity.
> • A commitment to open, transparent government processes, to open processes of reasoning in and about the public realm.

contemporary period. First, the idea of planning emphasises that it is worth thinking forward into the future with some hope in the ability of collective action to produce better conditions and some belief that it is possible, by setting out on a collective trajectory, to resist pressures that might reduce potentialities and possibilities for some and all, and to open up opportunities that could enhance the future chances of human flourishing. This idea was expressed nicely by the philosopher William James a century ago:

> that which proposes to us, through an act of belief, an end which cannot be attained except by our own efforts, and that which carries us courageously into action in cases where success is not assured to us in advance. (James 1920:82, trans. from original French by author)

This implies a rich and sensitive understanding of the complex ways in which people live in, move around and care about particular places, but it also emphasises that the future does not just happen. It is also in part 'willed' into existence by collective effort.

Secondly, a major strand of thought within the planning field centres on promoting ways to advance the liveability and sustainability of daily life environments, not just for the few but for the many. What is different now from earlier, twentieth century conceptions is that the 'many' are conceived not as a mass with common values and concerns, but as a plurality of individuals and groups, with potentially diverse values and ways of living. In such a conception, economic issues are not neglected. Instead, they are subsumed into a broader conception of human flourishing in a sustainable planetary context.

Thirdly, the planning idea pays attention to the complex ways in which phenomena relate to one another, their 'connectivities'. It encourages people to look for chains of impact, which particular projects and activities create, and how these weave across time and space. It calls for consideration of relations between the various dimensions of our lives – home, work, leisure, etc. – and how we move around to reach them all. It cultivates attention not merely to our individual interests, but to the complex interdependences and obligations we have with other people, other places and other times, in the past and in the future.

Fourthly, the planning idea stresses the importance of knowing about the issues, experiences, potentialities and conflicting pressures that arise in any context of collective action. However, this 'knowing about' does not necessarily imply scientific or systematic knowledge, or technical expertise, though these may be very valuable resources to inform collective action. It also includes all kinds of experiential knowledge and cultural appreciations. Translated into the field of place-governance, this implies drawing on people's experiences of dwelling and moving around in time and space, but also on cultural expressions in all kinds of media, as well as the systematic sciences of urban and regional dynamics.

Fifthly, the planning idea values forms of government that do not hide their processes inside the procedures of bureaucracy or the cloaks and daggers of political gamesmanship. Instead, the ambition is to seek open and transparent ways of arriving at an understanding of what issues are at stake, how they could be addressed and what difference it might make, to what and to whom, if they were to be addressed in one way or another. The idea thus stresses carrying out policy argumentation in the open, in transparent ways. It is this element of the planning idea that has helped to create the paraphernalia of plans, policy statements, visions and strategies that, paradoxically, often then seem to clutter up the practice of planning in many situations. Nevertheless, it is not the idea of open argumentation that is at fault here. The clutter arises partly from a failure to think through carefully what it means to argue in the open, but also because the planning idea itself has been drowned by other ways of doing governance work.

The planning project, then, understood as an orienting and mobilising set of ideas, centres on deliberate collective action; that is, on governance activity, to improve place qualities, infused with a particular orientation. Such an orientation is not necessarily lodged in organisations and government systems that carry the name 'planning'. Because the idea of planning has often been subverted in the practices that invoke the name of planning, I refer to practices that are infused with the project's values by the longer phrase 'place-governance with a planning orientation'. Both as a set of ideas and as practices seeking to realise them, the planning project has arisen in the particular context of complex, urbanised societies. In such situations, we humans, with our diverse experiences and aspirations, are 'throwntogether' (Massey 2005), in political communities and in places, and then have to sort out how to live with each other and with non-humans. When institutionalised, the idea will always be challenged and struggled over. If a stable strategy is arrived at in one period, however inclusive its intentions and however much it has liberated potentialities among most members of the relevant political community, it will also be experienced as a constraining piece of government infrastructure. And the danger of capture by a narrow group of interests or a narrow definition of the project is ever present. The planning idea is always liable to lose its meanings if it settles unreflexively into an organisational niche, discarding elements that do not seem to fit. So practices of place-governance need to be subject to continual evaluation and critique to assess whether they still have any connection to a planning orientation. The general attributes of the planning idea that I have articulated here provide one way to evaluate place-governance practices, and to challenge the subversion of planning-oriented governance practices by narrower, regressive interests.

Notes

1. This story is taken from Luke Holland's television series for the BBC, *A Very English Village* (a ZEF production for BBC Storyville, zef@mistral.co.uk, 2006).
2. A British singer who made her reputation in World War II.
3. In UK planning legislation, only applicants for planning permission have a right to request a review of a planning decision. This lack of 'third-party rights' disturbs many, including environmental groups (see Ellis 2002).
4. That is, the formal definition of poverty used in the US.
5. I use the term 'human flourishing' rather than 'well-being' to emphasise that our lives are about more than just basic needs, although the latter are of great importance. The term flourishing is one translation of the Greek term *eudaimonia*, which also sometimes gets translated as 'happiness', which again seems too narrow a meaning (see Nussbaum 2001:31, fn 23).
6. This analysis was echoed in later accounts of urban politics in the US. See Fainstein and Fainstein 1986, Logan and Molotch 1987.
7. See www.UN-Habitat.org, *Regional Overview of the Status of Urban Planning and Planning Practice in Anglophone (Sub-Saharan) African Countries*, undertaken as background material for UN-Habitat 2009.
8. The ESDP is the product of the promotion of a spatial planning perspective by advocates in member states and the European Commission, and has had some effects on the subsequent development of planning ideas and practices in EU member states and elsewhere (see Faludi and Waterhout 2002, Faludi 2003).

References

Briggs, X.d. S. (2008) *Democracy as Problem-Solving*, MIT Press, Boston, MA.
Callon, M., Lascoumes, P. and Barthe, Y. (2009) *Acting in an Uncertain World: An Essay on Technical Democracy*, MIT Press, Cambridge, MA.
Castells, M. (1977) *The Urban Question*, Edward Arnold, London.
Connolly, W. E. (2005) *Pluralism*, Duke University Press, Durham, NC.
Corburn, J. (2005) *Street Science: Community Knowledge and Environmental Health Justice*, MIT Press, Cambridge, MA.
Cunningham, F. (2002) *Theories of Democracy: A Critical Introduction*, Routledge, London.
Fainstein, S. and Fainstein, N. (eds) (1986) *Restructuring the City: The Political Economy of Urban Redevelopment*, Longman, New York.

Friedmann, J. (1973) *Re-tracking America: A Theory of Transactive Planning*, Anchor Press, New York.

Friedmann, J. (1987) *Planning in the Public Domain*, Princeton University Press, Princeton.

Gans, H. (1969) Planning for people not buildings, *Environment and Planning A*, 1, 33–46.

Jabareen, Y. (2006) Spaces of risk: The contribution of planning policies to conflicts in cities: Lessons from Nazareth, *Planning Theory and Practice 7*, 305–23.

James, W. (1920) *Collected Essays and Reviews*, Longmans, Green, London.

Logan, J. and Molotch, H. (1987) *Urban Fortunes: The Political Economy of Place*, University of California Press, Berkeley, CA.

Massey, D. (2005) *For Space*, Sage, London.

Sutcliffe, A. (1981) *Towards the Planned City: Germany, Britain, the United States and France, 1780–1914*, Blackwell, Oxford.

UN-Habitat (2009) *Global Report on Human Settlements 2009: Revisiting Urban Planning*, London, Earthscan.

Ward, S. (2002) *Planning in the Twentieth Century: The Advanced Capitalist World*, Wiley, London.

Yiftachel, O. (1994) The dark side of modernism: Planning as control of an ethnic minority, in Watson, S. and Gibson, K. (eds) Postmodern Cities and Spaces, Blackwell, Oxford, pp. 216–42.

Yiftachel, O. (1998) Planning and social control: Exploring the dark side, *Journal of Planning Literature*, 12, 396–406.

Suggested Further Reading

Much of the literature on planning ideas and practices is based on experiences within particular countries. For wider reviews of the history of planning ideas with respect to improving conditions in towns, cities and urban regions, see:

Boyer, C. (1983) *Dreaming the Rational City*, MIT Press, Cambridge, MA.

Hall, P. (1988) *Cities of Tomorrow*, Blackwell, Oxford.

For a more recent account of urban design ideas within the field, see:

Madanipour, A. (2003) *Public and Private Spaces in the City*, Routledge, London.

For an accessible overview of 'planning theory' discussion of planning ideas, see:

Allmendinger, P. (2009) *Planning Theory* (2nd edn), Palgrave Macmillan, London.

For my own contribution to planning theory discussion, see:

Healey, P. (1997/2006) *Collaborative Planning: Shaping Places in Fragmented Societies*, Macmillan, London.

8

Urban Planning in an Uncertain World

Ash Amin

Introduction

How should city planners act in an urban environment that is daily shaped by distant forces and hidden interdependencies that generate unpredictable and unexpected outcomes? Cities have become sprawling entities and plural universes with complex relational dynamics that make them difficult to map, track, and coordinate. They are increasingly made and unmade through these relational dynamics, which include the returns of repetition, inertia, and legacy, and the unanticipated lurches produced by emergent combinations or perturbations transmitted across an entire network space. They are thoroughly enmeshed in global processes over which they have little control, exposed to transnational flows of one kind or another, world-level or distant developments, decisions taken at various spatial scales, and the circulations of virtual, symbolic, and material inputs.

As the sum of multiple geographies of formation, cities increasingly defy the staples of territorially based planning. City planners face the dual challenge of intervening effectively in an urban system geared for novelty and surprise, as well as finding grip in a meshwork of connections and flows with multiple nodes of authority and authorizing capacity (De Landa 2006). They confront the problem of acting without purchase, exactly at a time of high public expectation in face of mounting unpredictability and risk linked to rapidly spreading hazards such as pandemics, global warming, economic turbulence, large-scale human displacement, and transnational warfare. This problem is by no means unique to

Original publication details: Amin, Ash. 2011. "Urban Planning in an Uncertain World". In *The New Blackwell Companion to the City*, edited by Gary Bridge and Sophie Watson. Oxford: Blackwell Publishing Ltd, pp. 631–42. Reproduced with permission from John Wiley & Sons.

Readings in Planning Theory, Fourth Edition. Edited by Susan S. Fainstein and James DeFilippis.
Editorial material and organization © 2016 John Wiley & Sons, Ltd.
Published 2016 by John Wiley & Sons, Ltd.

urban planning. It is symptomatic of the general difficulty of finding expertise, authority, and grip in a multi-polar and interconnected world that is not only risk prone but also regulated by its own internal dynamics.

In *Acting in an Uncertain World*, for example, Callon *et al.* (2009) address the problem of responding to major science-led hazards that, on the one hand, require specialist knowledge and decisive action but, on the other hand, also possess a life of their own or are perceived differently by publics from experts and the authorities. They analyze the fraught and contested history of response in France to controversies such as nuclear waste disposal, bovine spongiform encephalopathy (BSE), and muscular dystrophy, which traditionally have been tackled in a closed and dirigiste manner by the state, based on assuming that experts and politicians know best. Callon *et al.* criticize this approach, arguing that publics must be seen as knowledgeable subjects and stakeholders, that expertise is only ever partial and circumstantial, that interests are never neutral or impartial, and that risks are compound, mutable, and non-programmable. They propose, instead, an approach based on a science and politics of concerns made public, active stakeholder involvement, distributed responsibility, and the enrolment of expert and lay knowledge, acting in an open, experimental, and democratic manner in an uncertain world and staying close to developments as they unfold.

In some senses, the globalization of risk and hazard itself is forcing a shift in state practice, but in contradictory directions. One the one hand, faced with the threat of, say, an unforeseen terrorist attack, a sudden health pandemic, a catastrophic climatic event, or a market shock with uninsurable losses, states have begun to scale back on promises of avoidance or universal protection, choosing instead to prepare publics to live in a crisis-prone environment, to mobilize all manner of knowledge, lay and expert, to build resistance and resilience, and to redefine their own role as crisis managers rather than crisis avoiders. A logic of preparedness and shared responsibility is replacing a logic of avoidance and centered authority (Dillon 2008). On the other hand, states have moved fast to introduce – and make permanent – emergency measures that allow them to intervene unilaterally with warlike authority and conviction (Ophir 2007; Graham 2009; Amoore and de Goede 2008). This change follows a logic of meeting uncertainty with unconstrained state power, free from democratic accountability, on permanent alert, ready to strike before being attacked, reliant on an elaborate infrastructure of surveillance, conformity, and counter-attack. The steps to stop, search, and lock up suspects, prop up ailing markets, build tidal defenses, close down borders, wage war with aberrant states, roll out mass vaccination programs are all acts of certitude and determinacy, reassertions of centered authority.

The kind of thinking advanced by Callon *et al.*, thus, is both reflected in, and contradicted by, current state practice. However, it resonates strongly in urban planning theory, which, though less concerned with the issues of risk and uncertainty, has long grappled with the problem of how best to intervene democratically in the variegated, open and multi-polar city. Planning theory has shifted away from a "knowing" towards a "deliberative" tradition in recent years. The former – epitomized by the projects of modernist planning – endeavored to observe the city from a privileged vantage point, know the pulse that beats through urban life, intervene through a central authority, and roll out a plan of the good life. So, for example, it acted to save cities from disaster, lift the masses out of want and poverty, and re-engineer the urban fabric to meet the goals of modernity. The latter, in contrast, pointing to the mutability and multiplexity of the city and to the arrogance and mistakes of the knowing tradition, has chosen to work through micro-practices, seeking to weave a way through multiple voices, conflicting demands, and contradictory developments. It sees knowledge as situated, problems as complex, outcomes as temporary, and interventions as catalysts rather than solutions, defining planning as the art of intermediation, working pragmatically through opposing interests and concerns, making things visible, and intervening in relational dynamics for communal local advantage.

The knowing tradition has by no means disappeared. It persists in the vanities of strategic urban plans, large architectural impositions, design-led urban regeneration, massive infrastructure projects, sweeping slum clearances, new megacity developments in countries such as China. It does not lack powerful protagonists – political, professional, and corporate – but conceptually the deliberative tradition seems to have come to the forefront due to the ideas developed over the last 20 years by an influential body of planning theorists such as John Friedmann, John Forester, Leonie Sandercock, Patsy Healey, Andreas Faludi, Luigi Mazza, Bent Flyvberg, Judy Innes, Alessandro Balducci, and Jean Hillier. These theorists have mounted compelling critiques of the knowing tradition, revealed the complexities of the contemporary city, elucidated an epistemology of relational and situated knowing, articulated the principles and practices of deliberative / pragmatic planning, and worked closely with communities, activities, and urban leaders on specific projects and urban plans. They have formed a school of thought with solid theoretical and philosophical foundations and clear principles and practices of intervention.

The deliberative tradition calls upon planners to: act as intermediaries who can harness lay knowledge, broker agreements, and speak for the disempowered; address issues of common concern, seek pragmatic solutions, and work with imperfections, incertitude, and constitutive disagreement; redefine strategic planning as the articulation of "motivating visions" (Healey 2007) and diagrams of possibility (Hillier 2007) rather than as a blueprint of action; accept that interventions are specific, partial, and experimental, and not total, systemic, or certain; and intervene with care and modesty in trajectories that are democratically and deliberatively constructed. In short, the approach to issues of immediate public concern as well as developments beyond the horizon is a blend of visionary sketching and democratic consultation.

Although I am sympathetic to the arguments and proposals of the deliberative tradition and also believe that the relationally constituted city requires a negotiated approach (Amin and Thrift 2002; Amin 2007), two aspects of its thinking strike me as problematic regarding the urgency to act decisively in an uncertain world that generates grave hazards and risks. The first concerns what counts as a stakeholder and intermediary in urban life. My claim is that the deliberative tradition makes light of non-human and non-cognitive inputs, an omission that not only overstates the potential of inter-human deliberation but also limits thinking on how the materiality of cities – brick, stone, metal, wires, software, and physical space – is implicated in the regulation of uncertainty. The second concerns the skepticism of the deliberative tradition towards expert judgment and programmatic intervention, which raises the important question of how to respond effectively to serious hazards and risks without recourse to the authoritarian excesses of the knowing tradition. Is it possible to act with authority in an uncertain urban environment without compromising stakeholder involvement and the mobilization of diverse knowledges? This chapter addresses these two issues in turn.

Material Culture

Thus far, the deliberative tradition has remained decidedly humanist. Its address to power is based on empowering communities, building social voice, intermediating between diverse interests, and organizing for agonistic engagement between stakeholders. The ambition is to rehumanize the city by returning authority and control to the citizens and residents of a city; to ensure that decision-makers are not allowed to fall into rule-based, depersonalized, or centralized governance of urban life. The full spectrum of urban affairs, from civil defense and waste or traffic management to economic planning, cultural management, and housing allocation, is expected to be subjected to democratic audit, measured for human consequence, and placed under the scrutiny of the city's many communities.

It is hard to disagree with much of this, not only because it makes democratic sense, but also because much damage – to those without rights, power, or means – has been done as a consequence of centralized planning. The unfortunate legacy of urban monoculture (consumption only, production only, spectacle only, gentrification) – sprawl, erosion of the commons, social and spatial marginalization of the poor or minorities, heavy policing of difference and dissent, ejection of migrants and itinerants – might have been avoided without such planning. The question I wish to pose, instead, is whether the humanism of deliberative thinking is able to deliver its ambition, whether the unspoken assumption that it is conscious/deliberating human actors – in and beyond the city – who make and unmake urban social life is valid. It is a question that goes to the heart of the determinants of social life – including human rationality, behavior, and culture – in a city. My argument is that urban material culture, that is, the entanglements of humans and non-humans that make up social practice and associational life, profoundly affects urban possibility. Conscious deliberations form a small part of an urban society supported by, and made through, a "pre-cognitive" and "trans-human" environment that brings into play many actants and structuring rhythms.

Nigel Thrift and I (2002) have argued that cities might be thought of as machinic entities; engines of order, repetition, and innovation (sparked by the clash of elements and bodies) that drive the urban experience, including what humans make of themselves, others, and their environment. The urban environment is a meshwork of steel, concrete, natural life, wires, wheels, digital codes, and humans placed in close proximity and it is the rhythms of the juxtapositions and associations – coming together in symbolic projections, cultural routines, institutional practices, regulatory norms, physical flows, technological regimes, experience of the landscape, software systems – that surge through the human experience. The machinic rhythms of the city, I would argue, blend together the human and the urban condition, making people subjects of a specific kind, with their demeanor and outlook (compared to that of humans in other time-spaces) formed by their inhabitation of the urban environment and, most importantly, its inhabitation in them, fixed through these rhythms. Such material ordering of urban being is by no means confined to local inputs, but includes others of various spatial composition and provenance that form part of the spatially dispersed meshwork in which cities exist as nodes regulated from many directions (e.g., government bureaucracies, internet traffic, weather systems, commodity chains).

The precise details of such ordering are far from fully understood. However, some of the behavioral pushes, in our times of experiencing the city of extreme urban global exposure and hybridization, might include an adaptability to multiple sensory, technological, and environmental inputs, an ability to inhabit many time-spaces of dwelling, meaning, and community, and to cohabit with significant others that include non-humans, and a requirement to negotiate a world fully revealed, with all its risks and opportunities, delights and disenchantments. Urban planners, including deliberative planners, can hardly be described as unaware of the city's material environment. If anything, a central professional imperative is to manage social life through interventions in the city's physical, technological, and natural environment (e.g., zoning regulations, infrastructure projects, land and building planning decisions, policies towards housing, public space, and the economy, urban landscape and architecture projects). My point, instead, is that the material environment tends to be treated as an exogenous factor serving or affecting human practice, rather than as an intrinsic component of human being in the city, threaded into the social conscious and unconscious (Amin and Thrift 2012).

This difference is vividly revealed in the treatment of the role of public space in urban civic culture. Humanist planning (deliberative or other) has long looked for ways of enhancing civic behavior by altering the terms of human interaction in public space. Typically, interventions have ranged from facilitating leisurely circulation and mingling in open spaces such as parks, squares, shopping malls, and marinas, to planning for social diversity and interaction in neighborhoods, housing estates, and schools. In recent times of urban social fracture and fragmentation, it has been hoped that schemes such as pedestrianized streets, well-managed parks, open-air events, community gardens, and mixed housing schemes can help to rebuild a sense of the shared commons, civic responsibility, and social recognition out of a combination of public appreciation of the shared spaces and enhanced contact between people from diverse backgrounds. The quality of play among strangers is considered to be the key to civic becoming. Outcomes on the ground, however, as a rich archive of research on public spaces confirms, have been mixed – social indifference or hostility towards the stranger in some instances, self-interest or resigned tolerance in others, or glimmers of recognition in yet others.

I am less interested here in explaining this variety than in asking whether the achievements (and disappointments) of urban public culture can be traced to *inter-human dynamics* in a city's public spaces. I have argued elsewhere that even when public spaces resonate with civic energy and mutual regard, for example, in the busy street, the noisy market, the multicultural festival, the well-used library, they do so because of largely pre-cognitive practices of human habitation of these spaces, experienced as negotiations of "situated surplus" rather than encounters between friendly / unfriendly strangers (Amin 2008). My claim is that the situation itself – characterized by many bodies and things placed in close juxtaposition, many temporalities, fixities and flows tangled together, many rhythms and repetitions of use, many visible and hidden patterns of ordering, many domestications of time, orientation, and flow, many framings of architecture, infrastructure, and landscape – profoundly shapes human conduct, including the balance between civic and non-civic behavior and belief. Accordingly, practices of recognition of the commons, curiosity for others, or civic responsibility may have more to do with the disciplines of presence and regulation in a plural space and with the everyday nego-tiation of ordered multiplicity (human and non-human) than has been hitherto rec-ognized. The rhythms themselves of "throwntogetherness" (Massey 2005) might be at work in producing social affects such as sensing the crowd as safe, diversity as unthreatening, the commons as provisioning, individual claim as provisional and partial, and public presence as being among rather than with others.

In this reading of civic culture, the ways in which humans are entangled in the material culture of public space, in the rhythms of a given landscape, come to the fore. If this thesis has some merit, what are its implications for deliberative / humanist planning? I think it shows up the limitations of, and possibilities beyond, a focus on human deliberation and recognition as the staple of urban citizenship. It forces us to consider, for example, how the aesthetic of public space, manifest on billboards, public art, symbolic projections (e.g., advertising slogans and political manifestos), architectural style, landscape design, and so on, works upon public culture. Many a lament – often exaggerated – is heard about the manipulations of public culture by the spectacles of capitalism, fomenting consumerism, materialist escape, flight from the present, selfishness, and greed. But why not consider the possibility of alternative projections that work on the side of civic regard and living with difference or for the commons? This might involve experiments with public art and drama to expose the excesses of commodity fetishism, or visualizations – on the sides of buildings, through public performances – of the everyday multicultural city, the public goods that everyone benefits from, the hidden infrastructures that support collective wellbeing.

The hidden infrastructures – the elaborate technologies that regulate public space, from traffic flow systems to surveillance technologies and network cables – are centrally implicated in the formation of urban public culture. Some of the connections are recognized, so for example, humanist planning is quick to condemn the excesses of urban surveillance and control and keen to rebalance the relationship between rule by technological or bureaucratic systems and urban governance through extensive public deliberation. It would be odd indeed to fault this concern in our times of excessive, unaccountable, and often unnecessary public surveillance, ritually targeting the vulnerable and defenseless. Yet, it is also interesting that humanist planning does not recognize how the "technological unconscious" (Thrift 2005) contributes to urban civic culture in positive ways, by keeping things on the move, ensuring rapid recovery from urban breakdown or disaster, making public spaces safe and intelligible, holding the complex urban system together, facilitating communication across time and space, supplying the basics of life and communal existence, and so on. This silent machinery of regulation is more than just that. It also shapes collective understanding of the well-functioning and livable city, everyday expectation in public life, the possibilities on offer in a given urban environment, and more. At most times, these social perceptions are latent and barely acknowledged, but in times of infrastructural collapse or threat, they can come to the fore as the consequences of urban malfunction become all too clear.

Deliberative planning can do much in building public awareness of the technological unconscious that supports social wellbeing, urban democracy, and civic culture. These are two examples of possibility beyond the canons of deliberative planning, and in just one sphere of urban life. No doubt there are other possibilities, but the point is clear. Liberated from an idea of the good city as the product of closer ties between strangers, new openings involving the material culture of the city become immediately available for practical consideration.

Programmatic Planning

To return, however, to the problem of acting in an uncertain world, awareness of the urban as an assemblage of human and non-human entanglements also forces recognition of the limits of managing uncertainty. If situated surplus, the city formed as a meshwork, and the collective urban unconscious possess an actancy of their own, the engineering of certainty – top-down or deliberative, through humans or non-humans – is rendered an imprecise art. The urban assemblage generates its own rhythms, rules, and surprises. Its machinery may, for example, slow down or dampen the impact of external shocks, perhaps even dissipate the impact of unforeseen or large shocks such as a pandemic or natural disaster. This machinery can "domesticate" change, absorb a shock, fold newness into the everyday. It can also affect the efficacy of emergency or disaster planning: a city's sanitation or sewage system will reveal its agency in responses to flood risk or global pandemics, as will the density of build and topography of streets in effective use of digital technologies to combat door-to-door urban warfare (Graham 2009). Similarly, the meshwork of nodes, lines, and flows in which a city and its parts find themselves located is a formative ecology in its own right, constantly producing both repetitions and surprises out of its multiple combinations and interactions, including unanticipated emergencies such as digital infestations or pollution fogs. The urban meshwork itself is a source of uncertainty in an uncertain world.

In these complex circumstances of trans-human formation, urban generative power, and heightened environmental uncertainty, does it suffice for urban planners to act as listening intermediaries? Do the circumstances not demand more, for example, an urgency and power that work the grain, strategic interventions that make the most of professional expertise, or alterations to material culture that enhance human wellbeing? Or is the urban machinery so strong and so independent that all that remains open to influence from planners are the micro-spaces in which squabbles between humans still count (e.g., in the schoolyard, town hall, housing estate, public amenity)? Could it be that inadvertently the epistemological shift from the knowing to the deliberative tradition has occurred because of some inadvertent recognition of the limits to planning?

Deliberative planners are by no means against strategic planning (see especially Healey 2007), but are wary of comprehensive, expert-driven, urban plans. Their emphasis, instead, falls on motivating visions, scenarios, and diagrams of possibility placed under democratic scrutiny. The strategic role of the planner is not to draw up a plan for implementation, but to offer a vision, to map alternatives. I wonder, however, if something has been lost of the knowing tradition in this otherwise laudable attentiveness to urban complexity and multiplicity; a certain programmatic clarity over the overall aims and priorities of urban living, made all the more necessary in a context of radical uncertainty. Is it not possible for planners to draw up an urban program without the pretensions of total vision, teleological fulfillment and systemic certitude, offering a clear diagnosis of the threats that cities face, the matters of collective concern that must be addressed, the goals that must be defended to improve urban living for the many and not the few? Has the attentiveness of deliberative planners to procedures of decision-making compromised the necessity to know about substantive matters of urban change and wellbeing?

It is an irony that US pragmatist thought of the early twentieth century that inspired deliberative planning theory during its formative years in the 1980s and which has been revisited for new inspiration more recently (Healey 2009; see also Bridge 2005) was pretty clear about the substantive goals of an emerging democracy that faced turbulent and uncertain times. The criticisms of James, Peirce, and Dewey of logical positivism, structuring totalities, and rational planning, their theorization of non-linearity, incertitude, and emergence in complex open systems, their commitment to radical pluralism, did not prevent them from outlining a new model for a just and democratic America. Their principled attachment to a politics of attention, that is, to addressing pressing issues of the day and making visible latent social concerns and harms, went hand in hand with a clear and coherent program of reform. The campaigns launched by the pragmatists on, say, anti-trust legislation, welfare reform, mass education, anti-poverty, legal and institutional protection of rights, regulated capitalism, participatory democracy, anti-corporatism, urban wellbeing, and ethical responsibility, were simultaneously issue-specific and threads of a particular model of future promise. This was a model of equity-enhancing, participatory, and regulated capitalism, posited as a distinctive alternative to socialism or corporatist capitalism (Amin and Thrift 2012). Awareness of the unexpected novelties of a plural order, of democracy as multiple becomings and belongings, of radical uncertainty in an America facing major changes (due to mass migration, urbanization, and capitalist transformation) did not get in the way of articulating a coherent vision and program of practical reforms, to be pursued with urgency through a variety of means (from legislation and government to popular mobilization and organized opposition).

In many respects, early twentieth-century America faced as uncertain a world as we do today, but while the pragmatists managed to draft manifestos out of their substantive, procedural, and methodological concerns, contemporary urban pragmatists seem to have lost clarity over the devils of urban living and the fundamentals of the good life in the equitable and just city. If Healey (2007) and Hillier (2007) are right in asking planners to articulate "motivating visions" and "scenarios of possibility," what should these look like, and with what order of priority or urgency placed on the proposals? Is it time to balance the progress made by deliberative planners on matters of procedure and practice with more of the substantive certitude that characterized the knowing tradition?

If so, a first step might be to critically evaluate the urban implications – substantive and political – of major social transformations said to be under way, such as the rise of liquid modernity (Bauman 2000), the end of craft culture (Sennett 2008), the clashes and entanglements of territorial and network power (Sassen 2006), the emergence of risk society (Beck 1992), the urbanization of war (Graham 2007), the associations between soft capitalism, heterarchical organization, and distributed power (Thrift 2005; Stark 2009; Lazzarato 2004), the financialization and digitalization of the economy (MacKenzie 2006; Knorr Cetina and Bruegger 2002), the extensions of biopolitics and related modes of human classification and control (Rose 2007; Diken and Laustsen 2005), the rise of hyper-individualism and new mobilizations of community based on ethnicity and religion (Connolly 2008; Žižek, 2008), the jostle between local, national, and new transnational modes of governance and interest (Slaughter 2004), the threats of ecological and environmental failure. These transformations, summarized only cursorily here, signal a profound alteration of the world and its orderings, and necessitate new analysis of the ways in which urban life is being recomposed and the challenges of social cohesion and equity associated with these transformations. This will help to identify the issues and interests to be championed, their urgency, and their place in a comprehensive vision of urban wellbeing.

This is a challenge for all urban actors, not just urban planners, let alone deliberative planners. But, given the explicit call of some deliberative planners for visionary designs and scenarios and given the uncertain implications of the above social transformations and also warnings of mounting global hazard and risk, an exercise that would focus attention is the imagination of an *emergency* urban plan. If Callon and others are right that contemporary uncertainty comes with potentially drastic outcomes, a "catastrophe audit" of cities would help to sharpen thinking on the urban fragilities – the threats to sustained collective wellbeing – that need to be tackled. Some are already well known, and they include the steady privatization and fragmentation of urban public culture, the intensification of social intolerance, poverty, and vulnerability, the rudimentary nature of risk assessment and catastrophe management procedures, muted response to climate change and environmental destruction, heightened vulnerability in the face of economic and financial globalization, growing infrastructural stress and militarization (after 9/11), continuing urban sprawl, spatial disconnection and social polarization, and the trend towards elite- or growth-driven governance of cities. The audit of these fragilities, grasped and contextualized with the help of appropriate theorizations of contemporary social transformation, would act as a call to attention, a solicitation for rapid response from those with the relevant powers, an opportunity to make things public and mobilize publics.

Such moves would return planning to the heart of programmatic urbanism, expecting planners not only to use the tools of their trade to find solutions to the fragilities and challenges identified, but also to use their substantive knowledge and insight to help outline the shape of the new house on the hill. Modernist planning – in the worst cases – went too far in trying to spell out every detail of the house, the journey up the hill, and the kinds of inhabitants expected. It laid itself open to the risk of disappointment and criticisms of vanity, false promise, and authoritarianism. The outline I have in mind here is different. It is one that offers clarity on the values and expectations of the city that works for the benefit of all its citizens (human and non-human), as it does on the ethical orientations of such an urbanism, explaining how the proposals address contemporary global hazard and risk (in all its varieties) and contemporary social transformation (in all its dimensions). The imperative, thus, is to trace the outline of the city that is able to build resilience against unfolding threat and instability (as far as is possible in a system of multi-nodal and distributed power), in ways that do not compromise the commons or collective wellbeing, explaining why this kind of city is to be valued or necessary.

Programmatic acting in an uncertain and, we can add, trans-human world, however, cannot mean returning to the logic of linear rationality and intentionality. Instead, it means openly accepting that the realization of strongly held values, aims, and visions is a journey freighted with contingency, constraint, and surprise, and therefore in need of continual audit, update, and adjustment. This requires cultivating expert judgment, anticipatory intelligence, contingency planning, and responsiveness to new and unexpected developments. It requires a particular kind of leadership; one that is steadfast about overall goals, but open-minded about methods and the debris thrown up by contingency and evolving developments, one that knows when expert judgment and deliberative democracy must be combined or traded off, and one that accepts that the relationship between urban legacy, policy intentionality, and meshwork agency is one of progression through durations, spirals, and jumps. Above all, it requires knowing what to make of the potency of matter, about how the urban environment and non-humans shape human behavior and intentionality, and about how to harness, for example, the technological unconscious, the object-world, the built and natural landscape, to make humans feel and act differently, to stop the urban process from drifting towards danger, division, and discord.

Conclusion

Arguing for a change in direction along these lines, to return to the question posed at the start of this chapter, is not to diminish the value of deliberative planning or multiple knowledges in an uncertain world. Instead, it is to ask for more in the context of heightened hazard and risk (e.g., programmatic expertise and clarity of purpose) and for less in the context of non-human agency (e.g., moderating the possibilities of human intentionality). Relational planners could helpfully take a lead in imagining an urbanism able to work its way through uncertainty, hazard, and risk without compromising collective wellbeing and security, and in mobilizing the unconscious, symbolic, aesthetic, material, and intentional to this end.

There is no shortage of emergency planning in the urban arena, but how far openness to the unknown and the emergent or unassimilated remains in efforts to deal with uncertainty almost always read as threat, is questionable. The risk posed by a governmentality based on elaborate forecasting intelligence, disaster simulation exercises, extensive and intrusive surveillance and control, a filigree of covert actions, and the cultivation of public suspicion in face of hazards such as pandemics, natural disasters, economic meltdowns, technological failures, or warfare and attack, is that exceptional forms of intervention that prey on fear and anxiety, compromise democracy, and legitimate authoritarian rule become the norm (Ophir 2007). Emergency planning, by dint or design, becomes reason to suspend civil liberties, the principle of the open society, and public accountability and trust.

It slides into a state of emergency, allowing the state and others in power to deal with uncertainty in ways that close down that which is unilaterally – and often vicariously – deemed alien or undesirable.

There are, of course, dangers in drawing parallels between the suspension of democratic procedure, on the one hand, in action against pandemics or natural and economic disasters that require quick and effective response, and, on the other hand, in action against threats of terror, war, or sedition, when direct or collateral damage is inflicted to citizens and strangers whose guilt has yet to be proven. The point of the comparison, however, is to note that once the emergency state becomes legitimated, a single mindset towards uncertainty can prevail, one that considers it reasonable – in the process of dealing with suspected threat – to stifle due process or criticism, justify harsh measures and consequences in the name of emergency planning, and apportion blame or claim victory with little regard for accuracy.

Might there be a role for urban planners in helping to develop an alternative approach that responds quickly and effectively to uncertainty without compromising the principles of universal obligation, public accountability, and measured response? This would require mobilizing independent expertise on impending threats and vulnerabilities, using it to expose the dangers of the solutions offered by the emergency state, harnessing it to an ethos of risk aversion based on prevention, precaution, and minimized harm, and building momentum around a response to uncertainty that draws on distributed resilience and fortitude rather than hysteria and suspicion.

Such an approach would stay close to the causes of danger and harm, doing everything possible to tackle them or, when this is not possible, building resistance without punitive overload. It would – through and beyond the urban – invest in universal welfare, multicultural understanding, an efficient and inclusive technological unconscious, hope in the open society, an active public culture and strong sense of shared commons, security for the weak, vulnerable, and exposed, extensive regulation of risk, modes of discipline harnessed to principles of just and fair retribution, robust risk monitoring and mitigation systems, and distributed resilience. It would understand that tackling risk and hazard requires mobilization across a broad spectrum, including in arenas yet to be seen as essential for urban security and wellbeing in an uncertain age. It would accept that acting in a turbulent environment to preserve the open and inclusive city is partly a matter of building human equivalence and solidarity, and partly a matter of enrolling the non-human infrastructure to that effect.

References

Amin, A. (2007) Rethinking the urban social. *City* 11 (1): 100–14.
Amin, A. (2008) Collective culture and urban public space. *City* 2 (1): 5–24.
Amin, A., and Thrift, N. (2002) *Cities: Re-imagining the Urban.* Cambridge: Polity Press.

Amin, A., and Thrift, N. (2012) *Political Openings: Recovering Left Political Will*. Durham, NC: Duke University Press.

Amoore, L., and de Goede, M. (2008) *Risk and the War on Terror*. London: Routledge.

Bauman, Z. (2000) *Liquid Modernity*. Cambridge: Polity Press.

Beck, U. (1992) *Risk Society: Towards a New Modernity*. London: Sage.

Bridge, G. (2005) *Reason in the City of Difference*. London: Routledge.

Callon, M., Lascoumes, P., and Barthe, Y. (2009) *Acting in an Uncertain World*. Cambridge, MA: MIT Press.

Connolly, W. (2008) *Capitalism and Christianity, American Style*. Durham, NC: Duke University Press.

De Landa, M. (2006) *A New Philosophy of Society*. London: Continuum.

Diken, B., and Laustsen, C. (2005) *The Culture of Exception: Sociology Facing the Camp*. London: Routledge.

Dillon, M. (2008) Underwriting security. *Security Dialogue* 39 (2–4): 309–32.

Graham, S. (2007) War and the city. *New Left Review* 44: 121–32.

Graham, S. (2009) *Cities Under Siege: The New Military Urbanism*. London: Verso.

Healey, P. (2007) *Urban Complexity and Spatial Strategies*. London: Routledge.

Healey, P. (2009) The pragmatic tradition in planning thought. *Journal of Planning Education and Research* 28 (3): 277–92.

Hillier, J. (2007) *Stretching Beyond the Horizon*. Aldershot: Ashgate.

Knorr Cetina, K., and Bruegger, U. (2002) Global microstructures: the virtual societies of financial markets. *American Journal of Sociology* 107 (4): 905–95.

Lazzarato, M. (2004) *Les révolutions de capitalisme*. Paris: Les Empêcheurs de Penser en Rond.

MacKenzie, D. (2006) *An Engine, not a Camera: How Financial Models Shape Markets*. Cambridge, MA: MIT Press.

Massey, D. (2005) *For Space*. London: Sage.

Ophir, A. (2007) The two-state solution: providence and catastrophe. *Journal of Homeland Security and Emergency Management* 4 (1): 1–44.

Rose, N. (2007) *The Politics of Life Itself*. Princeton, NJ: Princeton University Press.

Sassen, S. (2006) *Territory, Authority, Rights*. Princeton, NJ: Princeton University Press.

Sennett, R. (2008) *The Craftsman*. London: Allen Lane.

Slaughter, A.-M. (2004) *A New World Order*. Princeton, NJ: Princeton University Press.

Stark, D. (2009) *The Sense of Dissonance: Accounts of Worth in Economic Life*. Princeton, NJ: Princeton University Press.

Thrift, N. (2005) *Knowing Capitalism*. London: Sage.

Žižek, S. (2008) *Violence*. London: Profile Books.

9

Arguments For and Against Planning

Richard E. Klosterman

Formal governmental attempts to plan for and direct social change have always been controversial. However, public and academic attention to planning peaked in the 'great debate' of the 1930s and 1940s between proponents of government planning such as Karl Mannheim, Rexford Tugwell, and Barbara Wootton and defenders of 'free' markets and laissez faire such as Friedrich Hayek and Ludwig von Mises.[1] By the 1950s the debate had apparently been resolved; the grand issues of the desirability and feasibility of planning had been replaced by more concrete questions concerning particular planning techniques and alternative institutional structures for achieving society's objectives. Planning's status in modern society seemed secure; the only remaining questions appeared to be 'who shall plan, for what purposes, in what conditions, and by what devices?'[2]

Recent events in Great Britain, the United States, and other western societies indicate that planning's status is again being questioned and that the 'great debate' had never really ended. National planning efforts have been abandoned in Britain and the United States and the public agenda in both countries now focuses on deregulation, privatization, urban enterprise zones, and a host of other proposals for severely restricting government's role in economic affairs. Planning is increasingly attacked in the popular press, academic literature, and addresses to Parliament and Congress.[3] Graduate planning enrolments have declined dramatically and government retrenchment around the world has severely reduced job opportunities for professional planners at all levels.[4] At a more fundamental level, practitioners, students, and academics increasingly view planning as nothing more than a way to

Original publication details: Klosterman, Richard E. 1985. "Arguments for and against planning". In *Town Planning Review*, 56 (1), 5–20. Used with permission from Liverpool University Press.

Readings in Planning Theory, Fourth Edition. Edited by Susan S. Fainstein and James DeFilippis.
Editorial material and organization © 2016 John Wiley & Sons, Ltd.
Published 2016 by John Wiley & Sons, Ltd.

make a living, ignoring its potential to serve as a vocation, filling one's professional life with transcending purpose.[5]

In this environment it seems essential to return to fundamentals and examine carefully the case for and against planning in a modern industrial context. This article will critically examine four major types of argument which have been used as two-edged rhetorical swords both to criticise and defend government planning efforts and consider the implications which these arguments have for planning in the 1980s and beyond. The analysis will consider only formal governmental efforts at the local and regional level to achieve desired goals and solve novel problems in complex contexts or what in Britain is called 'town and country planning' and in America 'city and regional planning'.[6] As a result, the arguments considered below are not necessarily applicable to national economic planning or to the planning done by private individuals and organisations. Also not considered are the legal arguments for planning in particular constitutional or common law contexts or arguments such as Mannheim's[7] which have had little effect on the contemporary political debate.

Economic Arguments

Contemporary arguments for abandoning planning, reducing regulation, and restricting the size of government are generally accompanied by calls for increased reliance on private entrepreneurship and the competitive forces of the market. That is, it is often argued, government regulation and planning are unnecessary and often harmful because they stifle entrepreneurial initiative, impede innovation, and impose unnecessary financial and administrative burdens on the economy.

These arguments find their historical roots in the work of Adam Smith, John Stuart Mill, and others of the classical liberal tradition.[8] Emphasising individual freedom, reliance on the 'impersonal' forces of the market, and the rule of law, these authors called for minimal state interference in society's economic affairs to protect individual liberty and promote freedom of choice and action. On pragmatic grounds they argued that competitive markets could be relied upon to coordinate the actions of individuals, provide incentives to individual action, and supply those goods and services which society wants, in the quantities which it desires, at the prices it is willing to pay.[9]

Building on these foundations, contemporary 'neo-classical' economists have demonstrated mathematically that competitive markets are capable in theory of allocating society's resources in an 'efficient' manner. That is, given an initial distribution of resources, a market-generated allocation of these resources cannot be redistributed to make some individuals better off without simultaneously making other individuals worse off.[10] However, this Pareto efficient allocation will occur only in perfectly competitive markets which satisfy the following conditions: (i) a large number of buyers and sellers trade identical goods and services; (ii) buyers and sellers possess sufficient information for rational market choice; (iii) consumer selections are unaffected by the preferences of others; (iv) individuals pursue the solitary objective of maximising profits; and (v) perfect mobility exists for production, labour, and consumption.[11]

The numerous obvious divergences between markets in the real world and economists' competitive market ideal justify a range of government actions fully consistent with private property, individual liberty, and decentralised market choice.[12] The need to increase market competition and promote informed consumer choice in a world of huge multinational firms and mass advertising helps justify restrictions on combinations in restraint of trade and prohibitions on misleading advertising. Indicative planning efforts at a national level in France and elsewhere are likewise justified as providing the information required for rational market choice. The development of municipal information systems and the preparation of long-range economic forecasts are similarly justified as promoting informed market choice with respect to locational decisions for which the relevant information is difficult to obtain, experience is limited, and mistakes can be exceptionally costly.[13]

More importantly, both classical and neo-classical economists recognise that even perfectly competitive markets require government action to correct 'market failures' involving: (i) public or collective consumption goods; (ii) externalities or spill-over effects; (iii) prisoners' dilemma conditions; and (iv) distributional issues.[14]

Public goods

Public goods are defined by two technical characteristics: (i) 'jointed' or 'non-rivalrous' consumption such that, once produced, they can be enjoyed simultaneously by more than one person; and (ii) 'non-excludability' or 'non-appropriability' such that it is difficult (in some cases impossible) to assign well-defined property rights or restrict consumer access.[15] Private goods such as apples, bread, and most 'normal' consumer goods exhibit neither characteristic; once produced they can be consumed by only one individual at a time. It is thus easy to restrict access to these goods and charge a price for their enjoyment. On the other hand, public goods such as open-air concerts, television broadcasts, and a healthy and pleasant environment simultaneously benefit more than one individual because one person's enjoyment does not prohibit another's enjoyment (except for any congestion effects). As a result, controlling access to these goods is either difficult, e.g. scramblers must be installed to restrict access to television broadcasts, or impossible, e.g. clean air.

Competitive markets can effectively allocate private goods which can only be enjoyed if they are purchased; as a result, the prices individuals are willing to pay for alternative goods accurately reflect their preferences for these goods. For public goods the benefit individuals receive is dependent on the total supply of the good, not on their contribution toward its production. Thus, in making voluntary market contributions to pay for, say, environmental protection, individuals are free to understate their real preferences for environmental quality in the hope that others will continue to pay for its protection – enabling them to be 'free riders', enjoying a pleasant environment at no personal expense. Of course if everyone did this, the money required to protect the environment adequately would no longer be available. Individuals may also underestimate others' willingness to contribute and 'overpay', thereby ending up with more public goods and fewer private goods than they really desire. In either case, the aggregated market preferences of individuals do not accurately reflect individual or social preferences for alternative public and private goods – the 'invisible hand' fumbles.

Similar arguments can be made for public provision of 'quasi-public' goods such as education, public health programmes, transportation facilities, and police and fire protection which simultaneously benefit particular individuals and provide shared, non-rationable benefits to society as a whole. As a result, public goods can be used to justify over 96 per cent of public purchases of goods and services and an almost open-ended range of government activities.[16]

Externalities

Closely related to the concept of public goods are externalities or spill-over effects of production and consumption which are not taken into account in the process of voluntary market exchange.[17] The classical example is a polluting industrial plant which imposes aesthetic and health costs on neighbouring firms and individuals which are not included in its costs of production. Similar spill-over effects are revealed by land developers who can freely ignore the costs of congestion, noise, and loss of privacy which high-intensity development imposes on neighbouring landowners. Positive external economies include the increased land values associated with the construction of new transportation links and other large-scale improvements which adjoining landowners can enjoy without compensation.

As is true for public goods, the divergence between public and private costs and benefits associated with externalities causes even perfectly competitive markets to misallocate society's goods and services. Profit-maximising firms concerned only with maximising revenues and controlling costs are encourged to increase output even though the associated negative external costs vastly outweigh any increases in revenue because the external 'social' costs are not reflected in their production costs. Neighbourhood beautification projects and similar goods with positive external effects similarly tend to be under-produced because private entrepreneurs cannot appropriate the full economic benefits of their actions. In both situations the 'invisible hand' again fails to reflect accurately the needs and desires of society's members.

Prisoners' dilemma conditions

Similar difficulties are revealed in circumstances in which individuals' pursuit of their own self-interest does not lead to an optimal outcome for society or for the individual involved. Consider, for example, the situation faced by landlords in a declining neighbourhood who must decide whether to improve their rental property or invest their money elsewhere.[18] If a landlord improves his property and the others do not, the neighbourhood will continue to decline, making his investment financially inadvisable. On the other hand, if he does not improve his property and the others improve theirs, the general improvement of the neighbourhood will allow him to raise rents without investing any money. As a result, it is in each individual's self-interest to make no improvements; however, if they all refuse to do so, the neighbourhood will decline further, making things worse for everyone. An identical inevitable logic leads the competitive market to over-utilise 'common pool' resources with a limited supply and free access such as wilderness areas and a healthy environment.[19]

The fundamental problem here, as for public goods and externalities, lies in the interdependence between individual actions and the accompanying disjunction between individual benefits and costs and social benefits and costs. The only solution in all three cases is government action to deal with the public and external effects which are neglected in the pursuit of individual gain. Solutions for declining neighbourhoods include compulsory building codes, public acquisition and improvement of entire neighbourhoods, and 'enveloping' – public improvements to neighbourhood exteriors which will encourage private investments.

Distributional questions

As was pointed out above, economists have demonstrated that, given an initial distribution of resources, perfectly competitive markets will allocate those resources in such a way that no one can benefit without someone else being harmed. However, neither the initial nor the final distribution can be assumed to be in any way 'optimal.' Both are determined largely by inherited wealth, innate talent, and blind luck and can range from states of perfect equality to extremes of tremendous wealth and abject poverty. Economic efficiency alone provides no criterion for judging one state superior in any way to another. As a result, given a societal consensus on the proper allocation of resources, e.g. that all babies should receive adequate nutrition and that the elderly should be cared for, government tax collection and income transfer programmes are justified to achieve these objectives with minimal market interference.[20]

Implications of the economic arguments

The preceding discussion has identified a range of government functions fully consistent with consumer sovereignty, individual freedom in production and trade, and decentralised market choice. Each of these functions justifies a major area of contemporary planning practice: first, providing the information needed for informed market choice through indicative planning, the development of urban information systems, and the preparation of long-range population, economic, and land use projections; secondly, the provision of public goods through transportation, environmental, and economic development planning; thirdly, the control of externalities and resolution of prisoner dilemma conditions through urban renewal, community development and natural resources planning and the use of traditional land regulatory devices; and lastly, health, housing, and other forms of social planning to compensate for inequities in the distribution of basic social goods and services. Specific government actions to reduce conflicts between incompatible land uses, coordinate private development and public infrastructure, preserve open space and historic buildings, and examine the long-range impacts of current actions can similarly be justified as needed to correct market failures revealed in the physical development of the city.

It must be recognised, however, that while *necessary* to justify government planning in a market society, these arguments are not *sufficient* to do so. This is true, first, because those activities which are the proper responsibility of government in a market society need not be *planning* matters at all. Government decisions concerning the provision of public goods, the control of externalities, and so on can be made in a number of ways: by professional planners, by elected or appointed public officials, by the proclamations of a divine ruler, or by pure happenstance involving no deliberate decision process at all. If planning is justified by the economic arguments for government alone, it is impossible to differentiate between government planning and government non-planning – 'government' is reduced to an undifferentiated mass.

More fundamentally, the inability of existing markets to allocate society's resources adequately does not necessarily imply that government provision, regulation, or planning are necessary or even advisable. Suitably defined and administered performance standards, building codes, and development requirements may more effectively guide the land development process than traditional master planning and zoning techniques; effluent charges can often control pollution discharges more efficiently than the direct enforcement of effluent standards; and public facilities and services may be provided more equitably by leasing and voucher systems than directly by government. Thus, in these and other areas, the appropriate role for 'planning' may not be the preparation of formal end-state plans but the establishment and maintenance of an appropriate system of 'quasi-markets'.[21]

As a result, the case for planning in a market society cannot be based solely on the theoretical limitations of markets outlined above. Popular dissatisfaction with the free enterprise system is not based on an appreciation of the various theories of market failure, but on its inability to provide stable economic growth and an adequate standard of living for all of society's members. Conversely, the informed critiques of planning are not made in ignorance of the theoretical limitations of markets, but in the belief that, despite these limitations, markets are still more effective than attempts at centralised coordination by government.[22] As a result, the case for planning in a modern market society cannot be made in the abstract, but requires a careful evaluation of planning's effectiveness relative to alternative institutional mechanisms for achieving society's objectives.

Pluralist Arguments

Other arguments for and against planning emerged during the 1960s and 1970s to complement the economic arguments considered above. Accepting the economic arguments for government outlined above, Lindblom, Wildavsky, and other critics of planning suggest that government actions should not be guided by long-range planning or attempts at comprehensive coordination but by increased reliance on existing political bargaining processes.[23] Underlying these arguments is a political analogue to the economists' perfectly competitive market in which competition between formal and informal groups pursuing a range of divergent goals and interests is assumed to place all important issues on the public agenda, guarantee that no group dominates the public arena, maintain political stability, and improve individuals' intellectual and deliberative skills. In this model, government has no independent role other than establishing and enforcing the rules of the game and ratifying the political adjustments worked out among the competing groups. Thus, it is assumed, political competition, like market competition, eliminates the need for independent government action, planning, and coordination.[24]

Unfortunately, the pluralist model is subject to the same fundamental limitations which face the economic model of perfect market competition. Just as real-world markets are dominated by gigantic national and multinational conglomerates, the political arena is dominated by individuals and groups who use their access to government officials and other élites to protect their status, privilege, and wealth and ensure that government acts in their interest. Particularly privileged are corporate and business leaders whose cooperation is essential for government's efforts to maintain full employment and secure stable economic growth. As a result, government officials, particularly at the local level, cannot treat business as only another special interest, but must provide incentives to stimulate desired business activity such as tax rebates and low interest-loans to attract new industry and downtown improvement projects to encourage retail and commercial activity in the central business district. Further supporting business's unique position in the group bargaining process is an unrecognised acceptance of the needs and priorities of business which pervades our political and governmental processes, media, and cultural and educational institutions.[25]

Systematically excluded from the group bargaining process are minority and low-income individuals and groups residing in decaying urban centres and rural hinterlands. Lacking the time, training, resources, leadership, information, or experience required to participate effectively in the political process, these groups have no effective voice in determining the public policies which shape their world. By thus tying individuals' political voice to underlying disparities in political power and resources, existing political processes exacerbate existing inequalities in income and wealth and fail to provide adequate information for fully informed policy-making.[26]

Group bargaining also fails adequately to provide collective goods and services which provide small benefits to a large number of individuals. In small groups, each member receives a substantial proportion of the gain from a collective good; as a result, it is clearly in their interest to ensure that the good be provided. For large groups, individual benefits are so small and organisational costs are so large that it is in no one's immediate interest to provide for the common good. The result is an 'exploitation of the great by the small' in which small groups with narrow, well-defined interests such as doctors and lawyers can organise more effectively to achieve their objectives than larger groups such as consumers who share more broadly defined interests. By turning government power over to the most interested parties and excluding the public from the policy formulation and implementation process, pluralist bargaining systematically neglects the political spill-over effects of government actions and policies on unrepresented groups and individuals.[27]

The limitations of pluralist bargaining, like the limitations of market competition, provide the theoretical justification for a wide range of planning functions. Accepting the critiques of comprehensive planning by Lindblom and others, some authors propose that planning be limited to the 'adjunctive' functions of providing information, analysing alternative public policies, and identifying bases for improved group interaction. The objective here, as for indicative planning, is improving existing decentralised decision processes by providing the information needed for more informed decision-making.[28]

The pluralist model is incorporated directly in the advocacy planning approach which rejects the preparation of value-neutral 'unitary' plans representing the overall community interest for the explicit advocacy of 'plural plans' representing all of the interests involved in the physical development of the city.[29] Recognising the inequities of existing political processes, advocate planners have acted primarily as advocates for society's poor and minority members. Particularly noteworthy here are the efforts of the Cleveland Planning Commission to promote 'a wider range of choices for those Cleveland residents who have few, if any, choices'.[30]

Experience has demonstrated, however, that advocacy planning shares many of the limitations of the pluralist model on which it is based: (i) urban neighbourhoods are no more homogeneous and the neighbourhood interest no more easy to identify than is true at the community level; (ii) group leaders are not representative of the group's membership; (iii) it is easier to represent narrowly-defined interests and preserve the status quo than to advocate diffuse and widely-shared interests or propose new alternatives; and (iv) public officials still lack the information required for adequate decision-making.[31]

As a result, there remains a fundamental need for public sector planners who can represent the shared interests of the community, coordinate the actions of individuals and groups, and consider the long-range effects of current actions. This does not imply that the shared interests of the community are superior to the private interests of individuals and groups or that the external and long-term effects of action are more important than their direct and immediate impacts. It assumes only that these considerations are particularly important *politically* because only government can ensure that they will be considered at all.[32] It is on these foundations that the traditional arguments for town and country planning have been made.

Traditional Arguments

The planning profession originated at the turn of the century with the widespread dissatisfaction with the results of existing market and political processes reflected in the physical squalor and political corruption of the emerging industrial city. The profession's organisational roots in architecture and landscape architecture were reflected in early views of planning as 'do|ing| for the city what ... architecture does for the home' – improving the built environment to raise amenity levels, increase efficiency in the performance of necessary functions, and promote health, safety, and convenience. The profession's political roots in progressive reform were reflected in arguments for planning as an independent 'fourth power' of government promoting the general or public interest over the narrow conflicting interests of individuals and groups. Others viewed planning as a mechanism for coordinating the impacts of public and private land uses on adjoining property owners and considering the future consequences of present actions in isolation from day-to-day operating responsibilities. Underlying all of these arguments was the belief that the conscious application of professional expertise, instrumental rationality, and scientific methods could more effectively promote economic growth and political stability than the unplanned forces of market and political competition.[33]

Implicit in these traditional arguments for planning are many of the more formal justifications examined above. The arguments for planning as an independent function of government promoting the collective public interest obviously parallel the economic and pluralist arguments for government action to provide public or collective consumption goods. The calls for planning as comprehensive coordination similarly recognise the need for dealing with the external effects of individual and group action. And the arguments for planning which consider the long-range effects of current actions likewise acknowledge the need for more informed public policy-making. Noteworthy by its absence is any concern with the distributional effects of government and private actions which were largely ignored in planners' attempts to promote a collective public interest.[34]

By mid-century social scientists who had joined the ranks of academic planners began severely to question each of these arguments for public sector planning: planners' concern with the physical city was viewed as overly restrictive; their perceptions of the urban development process seen as politically naive; their technical solutions found to reflect their protestant middle-class views of city life; their attempts to promote a collective public interest revealed to serve primarily the needs of civic and business élites; and democratic comprehensive coordination of public and private development proven to be organisationally and politically impossible.[35]

Accompanying these critiques were new conceptions of planning as a value-neutral, rational process of problem identification, goal definition, analysis, implementation, and evaluation. In recent years the rational planning model has come under severe attack as well for failing to recognise the fundamental constraints on private and organisational decision-making, the inherently political and ethical nature of planning practice, and the organisational, social and psychological realities of planning practice. As a result, while the social need for providing collective goods, dealing with externalities, and so on remains, the planning profession currently lacks a widely accepted procedural model for defining planning problems or justifying planning solutions.[36]

Marxist Arguments

The recent emergence of Marxist theories of urban development has added a new dimension to the debate about the desirability and feasibility of planning.[37] From the Marxist perspective, the role of planning in contemporary society can only be understood by recognising the structure of modern capitalism as it relates to the physical environment. That is, it is argued, the fundamental social and economic institutions of capitalist society systematically promote the interests of those who control society's productive capital over those of the remainder of society. The formal organisation of the state is likewise assumed to serve the long-term interests of capital by creating and maintaining conditions conducive to the efficient accumulation of capital in the private sector, subordinating the conflicting short-run interests of the factions of capital to the long-run interests of the capitalist class, and containing civil strife which threaten the capitalist order. These actions are legitimised by a prevailing democratic ideology which portrays the state as a neutral instrument serving the interests of society as a whole.

Marxists argue that fundamental social improvements can result only from the revolutionary activity of labour and the replacement of existing social institutions benefiting capital by new ones which serve the interests of society at large. Essential reforms include public ownership of the means of production and centralised planning which would replace existing market and political decision processes by the comprehensive coordination of investment decisions and democratic procedures for formulating social priorities and restricting individual actions which conflict with the long-term interests of society.[38]

Applying this perspective to urban planning, Marxist scholars have been highly critical of traditional planning practice and planning theory. The arguments for and against planning examined above are dismissed as mere ideological rationalisations which fail to recognise the material conditions and historical and political forces which allowed planning to emerge and define its role in society. Accepting the limitations of market and political competition outlined above, Marxists interpret planners' actions in each sphere as primarily serving the interests of capital at the expense of the rest of society. Planners' attempts to provide collective goods and control externalities are assumed to serve the needs of capital by helping manage the inevitable contradictions of capitalism revealed in the physical and social development of the city. Planners' attempts to employ scientific techniques and professional expertise are seen as helping legitimise state action in the interest of capital by casting it in terms of the public interest, neutral professionalism, and scientific rationality. And planners' attempts to advance the interests of deprived groups are dismissed as merely coopting these groups, forestalling the structural reforms which are ultimately required for real improvement to their positions in society.[39]

While extremely valuable in helping reveal the underlying nature of contemporary planning, the Marxist perspective has obvious limitations as a guide to planning practice.[40] A strict Marxist analysis which sees all social relations and all government actions as serving the interests of capital identifies no mechanism for reform other than a radical transformation of society which is highly unlikely in the near future: If needed reforms can result only from the revolutionary action of labour and all attempts to help the needy merely delay necessary structural changes, there is no significant role for reform-minded planners who occupy an ambiguous class position between labour and capital. And rejection of planners' attempts to apply professional expertise and scientific methods to public policy-making as merely legitimising and maintaining existing social and economic relations deprives professional planners of their main political resource for dealing with other political actors – their claims to professional expertise.

As a result, as was true for the arguments for and against planning examined earlier, the Marxist arguments cannot be evaluated in the abstract but must be examined critically in the light of present economic and political realities. Thus while it may be desirable in the abstract to replace existing market and political decision processes, this is highly unlikely in most Western democracies. The lack of a revolutionary role for planners in traditional Marxist analysis does not mean that they cannot work effectively for short-term reforms with other progressive professionals and community-based organisations. And while contemporary planning may indeed serve the interests of capital, it need not serve these interests alone and is clearly preferable to exclusive reliance on the fundamentally flawed processes of market and political competition.

Conclusions and Implications

The preceding discussion has examined a variety of arguments for and against planning in a modern industrial context. Underlying this apparent diversity is an implicit consensus about the need for public sector planning to perform four vital social functions – promoting the common or collective interests of the community, considering the external effects of individual and group action, improving the information base for public and private decision-making, and considering the distributional effects of public and private action.

The first need is reflected in the economic arguments for government action to resolve prisoners' dilemma conditions and provide public or collective consumption goods such as a healthy and pleasant environment which cannot be provided adequately by even perfectly competitive markets. The second results from the inability of markets to deal with social costs and benefits of production and consumption which are not reflected in market prices or revenues. The third is reflected in the public and private need for improved information on the long-term effects of locational decisions necessary for making adequately informed market decisions. And the fourth results from the fact that market competition alone is incapable in principle of resolving distributional questions in a socially acceptable manner.

From the pluralist perspective, planning is required to represent broadly defined interests which are neglected in the competition between organised groups representing more narrow interests. And it is required to represent the external effects of political decisions on groups and individuals who are not directly involved in the political bargaining process. Improved information on the short- and long-term consequences of alternative public policies and actions is required to facilitate the group bargaining process. And planners are required to serve as advocates for society's most needy members who are systematically excluded from the group bargaining process.

The traditional arguments for planning reflect the need for representing the collective interests of the community in the calls for planning as an independent function of government charged with promoting the public interest. The need for considering the external effects of individual action is reflected in the conceptions of planning as comprehensive coordination. From this perspective, planning is required to provide information on the physical development of the city and the long-range implications of current actions. Distributional questions were regretfully largely ignored in traditional planning's efforts to promote an aggregate public interest.

While largely critical of contemporary planning practice, the Marxist perspective recognises each of the arguments for planning identified by the other perspectives. The need for representing the collective interests of the community is reflected in the Marxist prescriptions for replacing existing decentralised markets by centralised planning in the interests of society as a whole. The need for considering externalities is reflected in calls for the comprehensive coordination of investment decisions.

From the Marxist perspective, traditional forms of planning information primarily serve the interests of capital; thus to promote fundamental social change planners are called upon to inform the public of the underlying realities of capitalist society. And the need to correct the structural imbalances in power and wealth which shape contemporary society underlies the Marxist call for the radical reformation of society.

While all four perspectives propose that planning is required *in theory* to fulfil these fundamental social requirements, they each recognise in their own way that these theoretical arguments for planning are insufficient. Contemporary economists argue that market competition, properly structured and augmented, can be more efficient and equitable than traditional forms of public-sector planning and regulation. Critics such as Lindblom have revealed planners' traditional models of centralised coordination to be impossible in a decentralised democratic society. And the social critics of the 1960s and 1970s and Marxist critics of today have demonstrated convincingly that traditional planning practice, while couched in terms of neutral technical competence and the public interest, has primarily served the interests of society's most powerful and wealthy members.

An objective evaluation of sixty years' experience with town and country planning in Great Britain and the United States must recognise the tremendous gap between planning's potential and its performance. While there have been several remarkable successes, much of contemporary practice is still limited to the preparation of 'boiler plate' plans, the avoidance of political controversy, and the routine administration of overly rigid and conservative regulations.[41] It is thus an open question whether planning, as currently practised the world over, deserves high levels of public support or whether other professional groups and institutional arrangements can better perform the vital social functions identified above. As a result, the arguments for planning outlined above cannot be taken as a defence of the status quo in planning, but must serve as a challenge to the profession to learn from its mistakes and build on new and expanded conceptions of the public interest, information, and political action to realise its ultimate potential.[42]

Notes and References

1. See, for example, Mannheim, Karl, *Man and Society in an Age of Reconstruction: Studies in Modern Social Structure*, New York, Harcourt, Brace, and World, 1944, pp. 41–75; Tugwell, Rexford G., 'Implementing the General Interest', *Public Administration Review*, 1 (1) Autumn 1940, pp. 32–49; Wootton, Barbara, *Freedom Under Planning*, Chapel Hill, University of North Carolina Press, 1945; Hayek, Friedrich A., *The Road to Serfdom*, Chicago, University of Chicago Press, 1944; and von Mises, Ludwig, *Planning for Freedom and Other Essays*, South Holland, Illinois, Libertarian Press, 1952.
2. Examples here include Schonfield, Andrew, *Modern Capitalism*, New York, Oxford University Press, 1965; and Dahl, Robert A. and Lindblom, Charles E., *Politics, Economics, and Welfare*, New York, Harper and Row, 1953. The quotation is from Dahl and Lindblom, p. 5.

3. For recent critiques of planning see Friedman, Milton and Friedman, Rose, *Free to Choose*: A *Personal Statement*, New York, Harcourt, Brace and Jovanovich, 1979; Simon, William E., *A Time for Truth*, New York, Reader's Digest Press, 1978; and Wildavsky, Aaron, 'If Planning is Everything, Maybe It's Nothing,' *Policy Sciences*, 4 (3) June 1973, pp. 277–95.

4. The dramatically declining enrolments in American planning schools are documented and analysed by Krueckeberg. Donald A., 'Planning and the New Depression in the Social Sciences', *Journal of Planning Education and Research*, 3 (2) Winter 1984, pp. 78–86.

5. Friedmann, John, 'Planning as a Vocation', *Plan (Canada)*, 6 (2) April 1966, pp. 99–124 and 7 (3) July 1966, pp. 8–26.

6. A similar definition of planning is proposed by Alexander, Ernest R., 'If Planning Isn't Everything, Maybe It's Something', *Town Planning Review*, 52 (2) April 1981, pp. 131–42.

7. Mannheim, op. cit.

8. These writers are 'classical' liberals in that their views of government and liberty are fundamentally different from those associated with contemporary liberalism. Classical liberals define liberty in the negative sense in which freedom is determined by the extent to which individuals' actions are *externally* constrained by the actions of others; the wider the sphere of non-interference, the greater an individual's liberty. Thus to increase the (negative) liberty of individuals by decreasing the external interference of the state, classical liberals call for a sharply reduced role for government in the domestic and foreign economy. 'Contemporary' liberals, on the other hand, view liberty largely in the positive sense in which individuals are free when no *internal* constraints such as a lack of knowledge, resources, or opportunities restrain their actions. From this perspective, increasing the (positive) liberty of individuals, particularly the most deprived, requires deliberate government action to promote social welfare and reduce the internal constraints on individual action, even though this may restrain the actions (and negative liberty) of some individuals. Compare Friedman, Milton, *Capitalism and Freedom*, Chicago, University of Chicago Press, 1962, pp. 5–6; and Finer, Herman, *Road to Reaction*, Boston, Little Brown and Co., 1945, pp. 221–8. Contemporary examples of the classical liberal argument include Hayek, op. cit., Friedman and Friedman, op. cit., Friedman, op. cit. and Sorensen, Anthony D. and Day, Richard A., 'Libertarian Planning', *Town Planning Review*, 52 (4) October 1981, pp. 390–402.

9. Heilbroner, Robert L., *The Worldly Philosophers*, New York, Simon and Schuster, 1969 (3rd edn), pp. 48–61; Friedman and Friedman, op. cit., pp. 9–27.

10. See, for example, Bator, Francis M., 'The Simple Analytics of Welfare Maximization', *American Economic Review*, 47 (1) March 1957, pp. 22–59.

11. Seventeen more restrictive assumptions including perfectly divisible capital and consumer goods and an absence of risk and uncertainty are identified by De. V. Graaff, J., *Theoretical Welfare Economics*, London, Cambridge University Press, 1957.

12. For analyses of the many empirical limitations of real markets see Lindblom, Charles E., *Politics and Markets: The World's Politics-Economic Systems*, New York, Basic Books, 1977, pp. 76–89 and 144–57; and Heilbroner, Robert L. and Thurow, Lester C., *The Economic Problem*, Englewood Cliffs, Prentice Hall, 1978 (5th edn), pp. 201–19.

13. Cohen, Stephen, *Modern Capitalist Planning: The French Model*, Cambridge, Harvard University Press, 1969; Foster, Christopher, 'Planning and the Market', in Cowan, Peter (ed.), *The Future of Planning: A Study Sponsored by the Centre for Environmental Studies*, London, Heinemann, 1973, pp. 135–40; Meyerson, Martin, 'Building the Middle-range Bridge for Comprehensive Planning', *Journal of the American Institute of Planners*, 22 (1) 1956, pp. 58–64; and Skjei, Stephen S., 'Urban Problems and the Theoretical Justification of Urban Planning', *Urban Affairs Quarterly*, 11 (3) March 1976, pp. 323–44.

14. Thus, for example, Adam Smith recognised that government must be responsible for: (i) 'protecting the society from the violence and invasion of other independent societies'; (ii) 'establishing an exact administration of justice'; and (iii) 'erecting and maintaining those public institutions and those public works, which … are … of such a nature that the profit could never repay the expense of an individual or small number of individuals', Smith, Adam, *An Enquiry into the Nature and Causes of the Wealth of Nations* (edited by Edwin Cannon), New York, Modern Library, 1937, pp. 653, 669, and 681; his third category of justified state functions is discussed in pages 681–740. Other government functions recommended by the classical economists include: the regulation of public utilities, the establishment of social insurance systems, the enactment of protective labour legislation, and compensatory fiscal and monetary policy. See Robbins, Lionel, *The Theory of Economic Policy in English Classical Political Economy*, London, Macmillan, 1952, esp. pp. 55–61.

15. The literature on public goods is extensive. For excellent reviews see Burkhead, Jesse and Miner, Jerry, *Public Expenditure*, Chicago, Aldine, 1971; and Head, John G., *Public Goods and Public Welfare*, Durham, North Carolina, Duke University Press, 1974, pp. 68–92 and 164–83. In the planning literature see Moore, Terry. 'Why Allow Planners to do What They Do? A Justification from Economic Theory', *Journal of the American Institute of Planners*, 44 (4) October 1978, pp. 387–98. The discussion below generally follows that in Bator, Francis M., *The Question of Government Spending: Public Needs and Private Wants*, New York, Collier Books, 1960, pp. 80–102.

16. Bator, op. cit., p. 104; Friedman and Friedman, op. cit., pp. 27–37. Similar arguments can be used to justify government provision of highways, dams, and other 'decreasing cost' goods with large initial costs and decreasing marginal costs; see Bator, op. cit., pp. 93–5.

17. The relevant literature here is extensive as well. For excellent reviews: Mishan, E. J., 'The Postwar Literature on Externalities: An Interpretive Review', *Journal of Economic Literature*, 9 (1) March 1971, pp. 1–28, and Head, op. cit., pp. 184–213. In the planning literature see Lee, Douglas B. Jr, 'Land Use Planning as a Response to Market Failure' in de Neufville, Judith I., (ed.), *The Land Use Planning Debate in the United States*, New York, Pleneum Press, 1981, pp. 153–4.

18. This example is adapted from Davis, Otto A., and Whinston, Andrew B., 'The Economics of Urban Renewal', *Law and Contemporary Problems*, 26 (2) Winter 1961, pp. 106–17.

19. See the classic article by Garret Hardin, 'The Tragedy of the Commons', *Science*, 162, 13 December 1968, pp. 242–8. For more general discussions see Luce, Duncan and Raiffa, Howard, *Games and Decision: Introduction and Critical Survey*, New York, John Wiley, 1957, pp. 88–154. In the planning literature see Moore, op. cit.

20. Bator, op. cit., pp. 87–9; Musgrave, Richard S., *The Theory of Public Finance: A Study in Public Economy*, New York, McGraw Hill, pp. 17–22. These points do not, of course, exhaust the economic arguments for and against planning. Thus while Friedman, op. cit., pp. 7–21, and Hayek, op. cit., pp. 43–118, defend unrestricted markets as necessary to protect individual liberty, Barbara Wootton, op. cit., argues that government planning is fully compatible with the whole range of cultural, civil, political, and economic freedoms. For other economic arguments for planning see Webber, Melvin, 'Planning in an Environment of Change, Part Two: Permissive Planning', *Town Planning Review*, 39 (4) January 1969, pp. 282–4; Oxley, op. cit.; and Lee, op. cit. More fundamental 'Marxist' critiques of reliance on competitive markets are considered below.

21. See Webber, op. cit., pp. 284–95; Lee, op. cit., pp. 158–64; Friedman, op. cit., pp. 84–107; Moore, op. cit., pp. 393–6; and Foster, op. cit., pp. 153–65.

22. See, for example, Becker, Gary S., 'Competition and Democracy', *Journal of Law and Economics*, 1, October 1958, pp. 105–9 and Wolf, Charles Jr., 'A Theory of Nonmarket Failure: Framework for Implementation Analysis', *Journal of Law and Economics*. 22 (1) April 1979, pp. 107–40.

23. See, for example, Lindblom, Charles E., 'The Science of Muddling Through', *Public Administration Review*, 19 (1) January 1959, pp. 79–88 and Wildavsky, op. cit.

24. Conolly, William E. (ed.), *The Bias of Pluralism*, New York, Atherton, 1969, pp. 3–13.

25. Lindblom, op. cit., pp. 170–233; Elkin, Stephen L., 'Market and Politics in Liberal Democracy', *Ethics*, 92 (4) July 1982, pp. 720–32; Miliband, Ralph, *The State in Capitalist Society*, New York, Basic Books, 1969.

26. Gamson, William A., 'Stable Underrepresentation in American Society', *American Behavioral Scientist*, 12 (1) November/December 1968, pp. 15–21; Skjei, Stephen S., 'Urban Systems Advocacy', *Journal of the American Institute of Planners*, 38 (1) January 1972, pp. 11–24; also see Dye, Thomas R. and Zeigler, L. Harmon, *The Irony of Democracy: An Uncommon Introduction to American Politics*, North Scituate, Mass., Duxbury Press, 1975 (3rd edn), pp. 225–84.

27. Olson, Mancur, *The Logic of Collective Action: Public Goods and the Theory of Groups*, Cambridge, Harvard University Press, 1965; Lowi, Theodore J., 'The Public Philosophy: Interest-group Liberalism', *American Political Science Review*, 61 (1) March 1967, pp. 5–24. For an extensive discussion of other forms of 'non-market failure' see Wolf, op. cit.

28. See, for example, Rondinelli, Dennis A., 'Adjunctive Planning and Urban Policy Development', *Urban Affairs Quarterly*, 6 (1) September 1971, pp. 13–39; and Skjei, Stephen S., 'Urban Problems and the Theoretical Justification of Planning', *Urban Affairs Quarterly*, 11 (3) March 1976, pp. 323–44.

29. Davidoff, Paul, 'Advocacy and Pluralism in Planning', *Journal of the American Institute of Planners*, 31 (6) November 1965, pp. 331–8.

30. Krumholz, Norman, Cogger, Janice and Linner, John, 'The Cleveland Policy Planning Report', *Journal of the American Institute of Planners*, 41 (3) September 1975, pp. 298–304; Krumholz, Norman, 'A Retrospective View of Equity Planning: Cleveland, 1969–1979', *Journal of the American Planning Association*, 48 (2) Spring 1982, pp. 163–74.

31. Peattie, Lisa R., 'Reflections on Advocacy Planning', *Journal of the American Institute of Planners*, 34 (2) March 1968, pp. 80–8; Skjei, Stephen S., 'Urban Systems Advocacy',

Journal of the American Institute of Planners, 38 (1) January 1972, pp. 11–24; Mazziotti, Donald F., 'The Underlying Assumptions of Advocacy Planning: Pluralism and Reform', *Journal of the American Institute of Planners*, 40 (1) January 1974, pp. 38, 40–7.

32. Klosterman, Richard E., 'A Public Interest Criterion', *Journal of the American Planning Association*, 46 (3) July 1980, p. 330; Barry, Brian, *Political Argument*, New York, Humanities Press, 1965. pp. 234–5.

33. For examples of each argument see: (i) Robinson, Charles Mulford, *City Planning*, New York, G. P. Putnams, 1916, pp. 291–303 (the quotation is from p. 291); (ii) Howard, John T., 'In Defense of Planning Commissions', *Journal of the American Institute of Planners*, 17 (1) Spring 1951, pp. 89–93, and Tugwell, op. cit.; and (iii) Bettman, Alfred, *City and Regional Planning Papers* (edited by Arthur C. Comey), Cambridge, Mass, Harvard University Press, pp. 5–30, and Dunham, Allison, 'A Legal and Economic Basis for City Planning', *Columbia Law Review*, 58, 1958, pp. 650–71.

34. The earliest example of this concern in the planning literature known to the author is Webber, Melvin M., 'Comprehensive Planning and Social Responsibility: Toward an AIP Consensus on the Profession's Role and Purposes', *Journal of the American Institute of Planners*, 29 (4) November 1963, pp. 232–41.

35. For examples of these now-familiar critiques see Gans, Herbert J., 'City Planning in America: A Sociological Analysis' in Gans, Herbert J., *People and Plans: Essays on Urban Problems and Solutions*, New York, Basic Books, 1963; Altshuler, Alan A., 'The Goals of Comprehensive Planning', *Journal of the American Institute of Planners*, 31 (5) August 1965, pp. 186–95; Bolan, Richard S., 'Emerging Views of Planning', *Journal of the American Institute of Planners*, 33 (4) July 1967, pp. 233–46; and Kravitz, Alan S., 'Mandaranism: Planning as Handmaiden to Conservative Politics' in Beyle Thad L., and Lathrop George T. (eds), *Planning and Politics: Uneasy Partnership*, New York, Odyssey Press, 1970.

36. Critiques of the 'rational' planning model have dominated the planning theory literature for the last decade. For reviews of this literature and their implications for contemporary planning practice see DiMento, Joseph F., *The Consistency Doctrine and the Limits of Planning*, Cambridge, Mass., Oelgeschlager, Gunn, and Hain, 1980, pp. 44–117; and Alexander, Ernest R., 'After Rationality, What? A Review of Responses to Paradigm Breakdown', *Journal of the American Planning Association*, 50 (1) Winter 1984, pp. 62–9.

37. Examples here include Castells, Manuel, *The Urban Question: A Marxist Approach*, Cambridge, Mass., The MIT Press, 1977; Harvey, David, *Social Justice and the City*, Baltimore, Johns Hopkins University Press, 1973, pp. 195–238; Paris, Chris (ed.), *Critical Readings in Planning Theory*, Oxford, Pergamon, 1982; and the articles cited in footnote 39 below.

38. Harrington, Michael, *Socialism*, New York, Saturday Review Press, 1972, pp. 270–307; Baran, Paul A., *The Longer View: Essays Toward a Critique of Political Economy*, New York, Monthly Review Press, 1969, pp. 144–9; Huberman, Leo and Sweezy, Paul M., *Introduction to Socialism*, New York, Monthly Review Press, 1968, pp. 60–5.

39. See, for example, Fainstein, Norman I. and Fainstein, Susan S., 'New Debates in Urban Planning: The Impact of Marxist Theory Within the United States', *International Journal of Urban and Regional Research*, 3 (3) September 1979, pp. 381–403; Beauregard, Robert A., 'Planning in an Advanced Capitalist State' in Burchell, Robert W. and

Sternlieb, George (eds), *Planning Theory in the 1980s: A Search for New Directions*, New Brunswick, NJ, Center for Urban Policy Research, 1978; Harvey, David, 'On Planning the Ideology of Planning' in ibid.; Boyer, M. Christine, *Dreaming the Rational City: The Myth of City Planning*, Cambridge, Mass., The MIT Press, 1983.

40. The discussion here draws heavily on that in Fainstein and Fainstein, op. cit.

41. Also see Branch, Melville C., 'Delusions and Defusions of City Planning in the United States', *Management Science*, 16 (12) August 1970, pp. 714–32, and Branch, Melville C., 'Sins of City Planners', *Public Administration Review*, 42 (1) January/February 1982, pp. 1–5.

42. See Alexander, op. cit., pp. 138–40; Klosterman, op. cit.; Forester, John, 'Critical Theory and Planning Practice', *Journal of the American Planning Association*, 46 (3) July 1980, pp. 275–86; Clavel, Pierre, Forester, John and Goldsmith, William W. (eds), *Urban and Regional Planning in an Age of Austerity*, New York, Pergamon, 1980: and Dyckman, John W., 'Reflections on Planning Practice in an Age of Reaction', *Journal of Planning Education and Research*, 3 (1) Summer 1983, pp. 5–12.

10

Is There Space for *Better* Planning in a Neoliberal World?

Implications for Planning Practice and Theory

Heather Campbell, Malcolm Tait, and Craig Watkins

Introduction

> Pessimism has become something of a fashion, a kind of intellectual pose to demonstrate one's moral seriousness. The terrible experiences of [last] century have taught us that one never pays the price for being unduly gloomy, whereas naive optimists have been the object of ridicule. (Fukuyama 1993, cited in Tallis 1997, 358)

There seem few grounds for suggesting that Francis Fukuyama's observation about the intellectual climate of the 1990s is any less the case today. Rather, the global economic crisis, combined with the stark implications of climate change, and the seeming frequency of natural disasters reinforces a feeling of individual and collective insecurity and powerlessness. Such sentiments resound in popular and intellectual debates, whether the perspective is that of citizen, public official, politician, or academic. The confidence of the immediate postwar years in the capacity of public policy to affect positive change has dissipated. In its place is a neoliberal discourse, which disparages the effectiveness of public intervention and celebrates the efficiency and even morality of markets (Harvey 2005; Marquand 2004; Peck 2003). This line of argument has shown enormous resilience, even in the face of the terrible upheaval wrought by the recent banking crisis (Lovering 2009; Peck, Theodore, and Brenner 2010). But where does this leave planning (and planners)?

Original publication details: Campbell, Heather, Malcolm Tait, and Craig Watkins. 2014. "Is There Space for Better Planning in a Neoliberal World? Implications for Planning Practice and Theory". In *Journal of Planning Education and Research*, 34(1): 45–59. Reprinted with permission from SAGE.

Normatively, planning is premised on the inherently hopeful conviction that a better future is possible than would have occurred in the absence of "planned" intervention. If, as some argue, planning is the "organisation of hope,"[1] what capacity, or space – practical and conceptual – still remains for planning to change the world for the *better*? The purpose behind this article therefore is to explore how far planning can make a positive difference, in the face of economic pressures. Must planning surrender to free market agendas or might there be ways to resist this reductionist but totalizing position?

Planning, as concept and practice, is written about from the vantage points of grand narratives about public policy (e.g., neoliberalism or deliberative democracy) as well as the particularities of everyday practices (e.g., dull-minded bureaucrats or accomplished mediators). The former provide justification for (damming) critiques or (high-minded) aspiration, the latter for variously constructing planners as villains or heroes. Planning is about all these things. But in considering the space for better, the argument presented in this article is positioned at the interface of the connections between these narratives, more particularly the worlds of constraint and possibility.

Despite the hopefulness inherent to planning (as with other public policy domains), the intellectual and political backdrop on both the left and the right stresses the failings and inadequacies. Paradoxically, planning is criticized both for being too pro-growth and too anti-growth: for exclusionary practices that favor dominant interests, hence fostering injustice and inequality, and yet simultaneously for imposing undue constraints on the freedoms of businesses and communities. In light of such critiques, there has been an erosion of confidence in the very idea of planning to bring about positive change (Campbell 2012a). Planning scholars have often expressed their wish to avoid idealism and what may be deemed impractical. Critical appraisal of the inadequacies of policy initiatives is of course important, and perhaps a prerequisite for progressive change. However, there are intellectual and practical dangers if failure, immutable constraints, and a narrowing of aspiration become the assumed norm, as such perspectives prompt conservatism, erode confidence, and justify inaction (Sandel 2009; Squires 1993).

In everyday public policy debates across the globe, the capacity of public policy interventions, such as planning, to effect positive change has rarely appeared quite so constrained (see, e.g., recent studies in England, Sweden, Norway, Finland and Australia) (Gunn and Hillier 2012; Hrelja 2011; Mäntysalo and Saglie 2010; MacCullum and Hopkins 2011). Currently in the United Kingdom, more especially England,[2] planning faces stark challenges. During the last decade, there have been several reforms of planning legislation and procedures by central government, even by the same Government, all premised on the need to make Britain more economically competitive (see Cullingworth and Nadin 2014). These recent reforms follow a trajectory that goes back to the first Thatcher government of 1979. The then Secretary of State for the Environment, Michael Heseltine, referred to planners as keeping "jobs locked up in filing cabinets."[3] The most recent Labour Governments used similar language, with Gordon Brown (2005) for example stating, "planning, we all know has been inflexible for decades. … [O]ur reforms [will] make planning law and procedures simpler, more efficient and more responsive to business and the long-term needs of the economy." Notwithstanding these statements, the rhetoric of the current Coalition Government could not be more explicit. The Prime Minister, David Cameron, said when announcing the latest relaxation of planning controls in September 2012:

> We're determined to cut through the bureaucracy that holds us back. That starts with getting planners off our backs. Getting behind the businesses that have the ambition to expand, and meeting the aspirations of families that want to buy or improve a house.

Similarly, David Cameron said in his speech to the Conservative Party's Spring Conference in March 2011:

> I can announce today that we are taking on the enemies of enterprise. The bureaucrats in government departments who concoct those ridiculous rules and regulations that make life impossible for small firms. The town hall officials who take forever to make those planning decisions that can be make or break for a business and the investment and jobs that go with it. … enterprise is not just about markets – it's about morals too. We understand that enterprise is not just an economic good, it's a social good.

Those within the planning community may argue that such comments by politicians are merely polemical gestures. Rhetorical flourishes they may be, but the traction of such arguments is highly significant in itself, as well as for the dispiriting context they create. In other countries, the language may be slightly less stark, but it is clear that policy agendas are narrowing, and the value of public policy intervention, including planning, questioned and scrutinized. This is evident in debates even in countries with the strongest postwar welfare state traditions (Brenner and Theodore 2002; Sager 2013).

Given this context, the concern of this article is to address the extent to which planning can contribute to the realization of outcomes that are "better" than would have occurred in the absence of planned intervention. The term *better* is chosen to imply outcomes that seek to further the normative ideals of planning, which in the words of Paul Davidoff is "making an urban life more beautiful, exciting, and creative, and more just" (1965, 337). Better suggests a direction of travel without being specific about the exact destination. Recently, Catney and Henneberry (2012) have demonstrated how planners seem increasingly disinclined to exercise their scope for discretion, while Gunn and Hillier (2012) point to planners' reliance on policy prescription from central government over the most modest forms of invention and innovation. So, in the face of neoliberal policy agendas, which result in the narrowing of perspectives, this article probes further the extent of the choices open to planners. The presence of choices is crucial, as choice implies that there is space, whether practical, conceptual, or material, to do better.

The argument is constructed in four stages. The first identifies a framework of alternative policy frameworks. Given the current dominance of neoliberalism, the purpose is to suggest the possibility of a range of policy options. The second stage of the argument explores a reasonably typical case of a major development set in the context of the English planning system. Most academic analyses of such a case would point to the failings of planning in the face of a pro-growth (neoliberal style) policy agenda, and the way the interests of capital crowd out the possibility of realizing other public goods. We attempt to unpack this standard analytical approach in the third stage of the argument. Specifically, we seek to identify the alternative choices, which were available to policy makers. In so doing, we do not shy away from the power of economic structures, but neither do we take their immutability for granted. The final step is to indicate the argument's practical and theoretical implications.

Our approach is controversial and experimental. It is inherent to empirical analysis that an account describing what happened in a particular case is equivalent to saying what must happen. This is the basis for explanation. However, our concern is rather different. Our interest is not with the usual analytical task of explaining what did happen, of what went well or badly there in the past, but rather with the more synthetic capacity of learning about what might have happened, and hence could (or should) happen in such circumstances in the future (Campbell 2012b).[4] Consequently, while the argument is situated in relation to empirical evidence, this is not essentially a traditional "empirical" study. The argument probes the possibilities of how research can move beyond the analytical and, based on an understanding of contextual constraints, seek out the possibilities for different forms of action, more particularly for *better* planning.

The immutability of markets is often seen as the major constraint on planning possibilities. The experiment represented in this article does not side step the implications of structural constraints. Rather it takes this as the context in which to confront the possibilities of the space to do better.

Market actors are widely assumed to operate as simple profit maximizers, basing their decisions on a calculation. Yet such decisions (and calculations) involve doubt, uncertainty, and interpretation. Economics and more specifically property (or real estate) markets are social constructs (Hodgson 2000; Stanfield 1999).[5] This argument is therefore understood in terms of the fragility and uncertainties inherent to both the worlds of planning and real estate. This potential uncertainty leaves open the possibility that investment and development choices can be shaped by wider public policy priorities.

So to summarize, the purpose of the article is twofold: first, to explore the extent of the possible choices open to planners and hence the scope to realize better outcomes; and second, the potential for empirical research not just to provide analytical evidence, which explains past events, but as a source of conceptual and practical learning as to how events might have been different and therefore could be different in the future.

Background – Is There *Conceptually* Space for Better Public Policy?

"Planning" as concept and as practices is hugely amorphous and slippery. It is about individual development decisions and the making of plans, but set against trends in public policy and politics. The sensibilities and traditions of different countries provide quite different frameworks through which the theory and practice of planning is understood. Moreover, in many countries (including the United Kingdom), the work of planning, and the job title of "planner," is not limited to those who hold professional qualifications or membership of the professional body. At its most narrow, planning may be viewed as those statutory tasks undertaken by professional planners, at its widest, planning concerns any intervention or action associated with space and place, and is not restricted to the activities of "planners" but includes policy makers, politicians, as well as civil society.[6] Even those engaged in planning disagree as to its scope. But the position adopted has significant implications. A narrow perspective results in much being ruled as beyond the remit of planning (and planners), while a broader perspective suggests that little differentiates planning from public policy and politics. Linked to this is a continuum of aspiration, moving from a limited concern with the maintenance of existing procedures and practices, through to an ambition that planning can contribute to wider social transformation.

In this article, we take a broad view of planning. Our concern is with *planning* in the round: as an idea made up of concepts and sets of practices, which aspire to change the world for the better, not with specific planners and their actions. It therefore follows that options and possibilities for planning should be viewed against a backdrop of developments more generally in public policy.

Politics the world over is currently dominated by the language of neoliberalism (Brenner and Theodore 2005; Harvey 2005; Peck 2003). This in turn has established a policy context, across all sectors including planning, which suggests such policy solutions to be "the only show in town." This was not always the case. The immediate postwar period saw the ascendency of the "welfare state model" and a focus on state intervention as the means to deliver outcomes in the public interest. Both these public policy discourses should be regarded as umbrella terms for what individually are complex groupings of theoretical ideas and policy solutions. They act as shorthand phrases, indicating a general orientation rather than precise definitions. However, given that the purpose of this article is to probe the

Table 10.1 Dominant traditions in public policy.

Generalized models	Conception of interests	How interests are discovered	Emphasis of just urban policy
Welfare state: paternalistic city	Public interest – based on an undifferentiated public	Representative democracy plus technical professional expertise	Redistribution
Neoliberal state: entrepreneurial city	Individualistic wants (private utility) – based on interests of capital and consumers	Consumption through markets or quasi-markets	Competition/pluralism
Politics of difference: city of diversity	Communal interests based on shared identity	Deliberative democracy and inclusive	Recognition leading to redistribution
Equitable distribution: just city	Collective needs – individual as an end but within a context based on interdependency	Representative democracy, supported by deliberation, practical judgment, and equity-oriented expertise	Redistribution and recognition

Source: Campbell and Fainstein (2012).

possibility of alternatives to these dominant narratives, the first step required in such an argument is to identify, at least in theory, the existence of such positions. In planning, normative ideas over the last decade or so have focused on two areas of possibility: communicative or collaborative planning, and the "just city" or just planning (Fainstein and Campbell 2012). Both approaches are premised on the assumption that better planning outcomes are achievable. The main characteristics of these four generalizations about the nature of public policy making and planning (welfare state; neoliberal state; deliberative city or city of diversity; or just city) are summarized in Table 10.1.

There is much that could be said about each of the generalizations, and all should be regarded as groupings of policy ideas and solutions, rather than singular positions. They each incorporate complex bodies of theoretical justification, carefully considered analysis, and popular rhetoric. But as our purpose here is simply to demonstrate a range of possibilities and outline the types of rhetoric used in policy debates, it is sufficient to highlight a few key features.

Proponents of neoliberal ideas advocate the benefits of releasing entrepreneurial potential from undue regulation, of participation freeing markets and extending property rights. Local, national, and even transnational policy rhetoric assumes that not merely economic well-being, but social and even environmental well-being, are most effectively advanced through the facilitation of market interests (see, e.g., Commission of the European Community 1999; Communities and Local Government 2006; Her Majesty's Treasury 2007). Expectations of "trickle down" suggest economic growth to be a prerequisite for social, and even environmental, goods. This contrasts with the presumption of the immediate postwar years that state initiated, directed, managed, and financed interventions would ensure the welfare of citizens, be that in relation to housing, transport infrastructure, or employment opportunities. Hence, there have been attempts at all spatial scales to change the role of the state from that of paternalistic "provider" to "facilitator" or "enabler" (Osborne and Gaebler 1992). Policy and political rhetoric abound with analogies to the conditions assumed necessary to create a thriving market, leading to the appearance in the everyday language of public service provision, of the importance of "competition," "individual choice," and "consumer satisfaction" (Carrithers and Peterson 2006).[7] With this has come a focus on the merits of "partnership," "the entrepreneurial city," "responsible" citizens, deregulation, and performance management. At times, the language has a softer edge, but there is an underlying acceptance that the logic which (it is assumed) makes markets efficient will have similar benefits in relation to public services, including the shaping of cities and hence the distribution of spatial opportunities, that is to say planning. Efficient public services, it is argued, are effective services and, therefore, are also as equitable and just as present circumstances allow (Le Grand 1991; Propper 1993; Deakin and Michie 1997, and associated critiques [see McMaster 2002] and also discussions about the changing nature of the public sector: see du Gay 2000 and Marquand 2004).

The technologies of neoliberalism (Foucault 1991), inscribed in governmental structures and practices, most particularly various forms of performance management, when combined with the orthodoxy of the "entrepreneurial city," have had the powerful effect of constraining planners' perceptions of their room-for-maneuver (Catney and Henneberry 2012; Gunn and Hillier 2012). The rhetoric of "delivery" drives the need for visible signs of change, often with minimal focus on who benefits from the change and whether it is desirable. In such a culture where, quite literally, concrete signs of change are of highly symbolic political importance, the planning activity has inevitably come under close scrutiny. Local and national governments want to see (any) development. It is therefore, perhaps, inevitable that we find planners commenting, "we didn't have any choice … the developer would have gone somewhere else," or, "policy dictated that the development should go ahead," while also indicative of a lack of professional confidence (Campbell 2012a).

This might seem to suggest, as the Thatcherite mantra would have us believe, that "there is no alternative" to neoliberal policy choices. However, at least conceptually within planning, this is far from the case. More particularly, two key lines of normative argument have emerged, each suggesting ways to achieve better planning practices, both having antecedents in prior approaches such as advocacy and equity planning (Davidoff 1965; Krumholz and Forester 1990).[8] Communicative, or collaborative, planning starts from a position that acknowledges the diverse nature of contemporary societies. Recognition that knowledge is partial, transitory, and contested leads emphasis to be placed on the need to realize more inclusive forms of deliberation (see, e.g., Forester 1999; Healey 1997; Innes 1995).[9] More recently, there has been a (re-)emergence of interest in planning with substantive forms of justice, captured in a concern for the "just city" (see, e.g., Campbell 2006; Fainstein 2000, 2010; Marcuse et al. 2009). This body of work is most usually differentiated from the communicative turn for its emphasis on material redistribution and substantive outcomes, over deliberation and inclusive participation (Fraser and Honneth 2003). The interrelationships between just processes and just outcomes in both these theoretical positions are undoubtedly more complex and subtle than this relatively superficial distinction suggests. In relation to this article's argument, what is significant is what these groups of ideas have in common. More particularly, both sets of approaches share an underlying concern with the *normative* and a commitment to offering *alternatives*, set against a context of wider public policy discourses.

The critical challenge for the theory and practice of planning is that the conceptual development of alternative normative policy positions is of limited relevance in the absence of actual or, perhaps more importantly, perceived spaces in which to exercise choice.[10] This gets to the heart of the purpose behind our argument. We are not, in this article, concerned with the merits of collaborative planning over the "just city," but rather with the prior question of how far conceptual and practical space exists for planning practices to make a (progressive) difference in the current context.

In order to examine such possibilities, it is important to focus on the experience of "ordinary" planning practices, not of exceptional cases. An argument premised on the need for uncommonly gifted individuals or extraordinary circumstances can have little general purchase. The case through which the argument is interwoven has therefore been positively chosen for its typicality in planning and unremarkable qualities. It is therefore set in the context of local government, more particularly the case of a major redevelopment scheme for Exeter city center.[11] The resulting redevelopment, known as Princesshay, looks like many others across the United Kingdom, and probably worldwide, and included the displacement of many existing independent retailers and the ceding of control of formally public space to the developer. While it is a very major scheme in terms of its scale and the implications for Exeter, it did not attract major public disquiet. In Britain, and we suspect in many other contexts, much (perhaps most) of the development sanctioned by the state takes place in the face of some, but limited, public protest. Similarly, Exeter as the context for the development is not a city characterized by extremes. It is not a large city, having a population of 119,600 (Exeter City Council, 2006), but it does play a significant role in the largely rural South West region. Such an "unremarkable" setting is a highly appropriate context in which to explore the space of possibility in the entangled relationships between the market and the state.

The research from which the case is derived was undertaken as part of a British Academy grant, which enabled one of the authors to spend three months actually working as a development control officer[12] for Exeter City Council in 2007. Interviews and document analysis were undertaken prior to and following the period of work as a planner (Tait 2011).

The fieldwork consisted of two periods of active participant observation during 2007, with the researcher working as a planner, in the planning office of the local authority, totally three months. This involved observing meetings, attending forums, and conducting planning work as a means of understanding the dynamics of the planning office. During and following the periods of participant observation, thirty-five interviews were conducted between May 2007 and June 2008, with senior officers, all the planners, politicians, representatives of developers, and members of the public who had come into contact with the planning office. All interviews were recorded and transcribed. In addition, the researcher had access to the complete public files concerning Princesshay.

The remainder of the argument is woven through a case of a major redevelopment project and is presented in two halves. The first offers a conventional analysis outlining the story of the redevelopment scheme; the second adopts a more reflective and synthetic approach, examining how the framing of priorities affected perceptions of the development possibilities and hence what further choices existed.

The Redevelopment of Exeter City Center – Is There Space for Better Planning *in Practice*?

Exeter is best known as a historic city with a 12th-century cathedral and a university. Overall, Exeter is a relatively prosperous city, with unemployment at nearly half the national average, although there are pockets of deprivation, with the Wonford ward/area being ranked in the most deprived 10 percent nationally. The city is currently governed under a two-tier local government system, with Exeter City Council responsible for many local services, including city planning and the larger Devon County Council responsible for broader scale and more strategic services (such as education and highways). This case study principally involves Exeter City Council, which has the powers to control development, as well as owns large tracts of city center land. The City Council is divided politically and for the last decade and more no party has held overall control.

The policy context – entrepreneurial Exeter

The policy context for planning and hence for the redevelopment was shaped from the 1990s onwards by the City Council's promotion of Exeter as an entrepreneurial and business-friendly city, mirroring virtually word-for-word neoliberal rhetoric.

The realization of this policy agenda required senior politicians and officials, including planners, to define a problem, create new institutions and actors, and identify areas of action, which they did. During the 1990s, key interests within and outside the City Council came together in defining Exeter as in danger of becoming a "backwater", side-lined from economic growth opportunities while investment was going to Bristol, Plymouth and other cities in the South West. Furthermore the city was perceived as having weak business organizations, which in turn did not communicate effectively with the City Council. It therefore follows that new senior staff appointed in the late 1990s were amenable to, and charged with, altering the ways the Council related to the business community. To that end, Exeter Business Forum was set up to facilitate dialogue between the Council and businesspeople. It assumed significance, not only for its role as a forum for communication but also in the establishment of the "Vision Partnership" in 1998, which was composed of business people, senior officers and local politicians. The Partnership produced "Vision 2020", a document setting out an agenda for business growth in Exeter. As the Director of Economy and Development (essentially the Head of Planning) noted in an interview, Vision 2020 "had a strong proactive focus and basically said the city should move from being a sleepy county town to one that was an economic force to be reckoned with." Moreover, he characterized Exeter's current approach as: "We are very open to debate and discussion about where we are going in business and we are listening to business all the time and where they are going."

The policy was cemented rhetorically in the frequently used phrase "entrepreneurial Exeter", and operationalized by the positioning of the Vision Partnership as the leaders of this strategy. The Vision Partnership was quickly transformed into the Local Strategic Partnership[13] (LSP), placing it in the role of producing the City's Community Strategy. The Partnership drew heavily on ideals of "lean" organizations (a description used in interview by the Chair of the Partnership) and entrepreneurial energy. It was recognized that this small partnership of business leaders, local politicians and senior officers was not representative of all sectors and interests in Exeter, but was seen as necessary to develop consensus, and more than this, an unquestioning momentum around the need for virtually any form of economic development.

Central to the work of the Partnership was repositioning the policy dialogue, both generally and with respect to planning, to ensure explicit focus on the perceived needs of the "market". Whilst the nature of those markets was never precisely specified it is clear the Partnership was most concerned with two areas: firstly, the city center retail market, for which the subsequent efforts to regenerate are described below; and secondly, a market for high-tech knowledge products. The latter was evidenced by securing the relocation of the UK Meteorological Office (Met Office) to the city in the late 1990s. Many within the Partnership regarded this as proof that Exeter had turned a corner in becoming more entrepreneurial and market-oriented.

This overall policy framework captured in the shorthand of "entrepreneurial Exeter" was very influential, and whether or not it reflected the personal aspirations of individual planners, the planning team regarded it as largely beyond challenge or question. A policy planner explained, "If strategists don't look like they are pulling together and going in the same direction then … we look like fools." It is this policy context, which provides the backdrop for the Princesshay redevelopment.

Regenerating the city center – the Princesshay redevelopment

City centers are key to the identity of any place and hence in turn redevelopment of the core inevitably became central to debate over how Exeter should change. The focus for the redevelopment centered on an area known as Princesshay. This area had already undergone significant changes in the past century. Bombing in 1942 destroyed much of the existing Georgian architecture and the City Council commissioned the planner Thomas Sharp (then President of the Town Planning Institute) to produce a reconstruction plan not only for this area but for the city as a whole (see Sharp 1946). His plan recommended constructing a shopping area anchored by a new street – Princesshay. This street of shops, the first purpose-built pedestrianized shopping street in Britain, was finished in the early–mid 1950s and consisted of brick and concrete buildings constructed in "Festival of Britain" style. However, by the 1990s, Princesshay was perceived to be run down and poorly performing. Indeed, the Partnership's "Vision 2020" document described it as "the worst in mundane post-war architecture" (Exeter City Council 2008, 6–7).

The emergence of a redevelopment plan

The roots of the plans to redevelop Princesshay lay in the late 1980s, when Exeter received several applications for out-of-town shopping developments (Exeter City Council 2008). This stimulated reconsideration of the retail provision, and by 1993 national government guidance was emphasizing the need to prioritize retail development within town centers. As a result, and because the city center was viewed as "under-performing," the Planning Department on behalf of the City Council commissioned consultants Hillier Parker to assess the potential for new retail development within the city center. The report identified three sites (Mary Arches Street, the Coach Station, and Princesshay) and concluded: "the Princesshay area will be likely to provide the best opportunity to accommodate the needs of modern retailers for prime shop and store floorspace" (Hillier Parker 1993, quoted in Exeter City Council 2008, 6). Nevertheless, some planners recognized that the other sites had merits. One senior planning officer commented: "In terms of net gain, in terms of regeneration and in terms of 'can we raise a place from a lower benchmark?' the Coach Station and Mary Arches Street were more beneficial. So the business case won the argument at the end of the day." This reflects the emerging policy agenda of the late 1990s, but when no development took place the local authority considered additional work to be necessary to attract a developer. This priority was further emphasized by the need to compete against other shopping destinations. The City Centre Strategy states: "Cities which diversify and change remain prosperous and vibrant; without this most of them stagnate and, at worst, decay and contract. The twin threats are competition from the region's other principal shopping destinations, and the impact of the likely growth in 'e-commerce'" (Exeter City Council 1999, 1).

In the wake of broader trends in retail development, the provision of a "competitive" shopping center became rooted in the presumption of the need for a complete redevelopment of the city center. The view was actively articulated by the Vision Partnership and the chosen developer, as well as most senior officers, planners, and elected members. The arguments in favor of this position were widely accepted and supported, with the developer making the case that the costs of retaining the existing buildings would be prohibitively expensive, as they were incapable of providing "modern" retail space and were unsuitable for large "anchor" units. A planning officer noted that the developer wished to reduce the amount of public space: "Literally, the amount of space between buildings was more in the original Princesshay and Thomas Sharp scheme and the viability of this scheme depended on taking that space and making buildings higher." As the same planner went on to say: "There was never amongst anybody in positions of considerable responsibility, shall I put it that way, an aspiration business-wise that they would convert or retain Princesshay." Thus, the aim of regeneration became heavily aligned with providing a "modern" retail space, which was suitable for large stores. Contrary arguments, based on the quality of urban design, were expressed by a few planning officers and local citizens. The argument being that the existing layout of streets was a good example of postwar planning (see Miller 1998) and hence the 1950s architecture was worthy of retention (see Gould and Gould 1999). However, even proponents of such arguments regarded them as marginal and as a result they never gained much traction.

The initial proposal for redevelopment

Discussion of the future of Princesshay crystallized with the submission of a planning application by a large international developer, Land Securities,[14] in 1998 for a mixed-use (but retail-dominated) scheme. The scheme envisaged wholesale demolition of the 1950s buildings and replacement with retail units, including a large glazed arcade. The development would largely be on City Council-owned land, for which Land Securities would become the primary leaseholder. Some opposition emerged to this scheme from a small local campaign group named "Exeter People's

Choice." They argued that wholesale redevelopment was not necessary on a number of grounds, including scale, traffic generation, the impact on the viability of other parts of the city center, and that Exeter was not in competition with other retail centers (see Exeter People's Choice 1999). They were also concerned that the City Council as principal landowner in the area was intending to enter into agreement with Land Securities. However, other groups active in the fields of planning and regeneration, such as Exeter Civic Society, did not raise any significant opposition.

More formal opposition did come from Devon County Council, whose main objections were related to traffic generation and design, and English Heritage,[15] which objected to the scale of the development and its impact on archaeological remains. There was also some opposition from within Exeter City Council, particularly from one elected member and disquiet among a few planning officers. Nevertheless, the dominant position within the Council was overwhelmingly in favor of the proposal. The Council had been in discussion with Land Securities for some time prior to submission of the planning application and the scheme was in turn approved. As a planning officer recounted: "There was enormous political pressure to approve that … scheme and I must admit, in my role, I did say it was not acceptable. But that's where the business or economic development side won the day." This comment, which is mirrored in the observations of other planning officers, indicates a clear concern about the implications of the proposal but importantly little sense that an alternative course of action was really possible, and little willingness even to ask questions.

Despite the City Council's support for the proposal, national government decided that the scheme should be examined further at a public inquiry. The grounds for this were very specific and related to English Heritage's objections that the construction of a large underground car park would destroy archaeological remains, and, although seemingly more significant, the lesser argument of the potential impact on the wider economy of the city center. Regardless of this, Land Securities decided to withdraw the scheme before the public inquiry could commence. Interviews indicate that while the developer expressed some concerns that the scheme would not withstand scrutiny at what would prove an expensive public inquiry, more significant were changing trends in retailing, which meant that the quality of finish of the scheme would not be attractive to the "right sort" of high-rental-paying tenants.

The revised proposal for redevelopment

Land Securities subsequently decided not to retain the same architects and appointed three new architectural practices to redesign the Princesshay development. The new scheme still involved substantial demolition of the 1950s buildings, but proposed a new layout for the retail area with open-air streets (rather than a covered mall) and an increased number of apartments. Land Securities argued that retention of the 1950s architecture would "limit the area's capacity for effective mixed-use living" (Exeter City Council 2008, 8), a subtle shift in argument but one that reflected newer national government policy on city-center living. Overall, the scheme was viewed as a significant improvement by professional bodies and statutory agencies (the bodies invited to comment on planning applications), which had previously raised objections, as well as having strong support from the City Council. Nevertheless, opposition remained from Exeter People's Choice and a few planning officers continued to have misgivings, particularly regarding the scale and massing of the buildings; the loss of open, public space; and the encouragement of car use by the provision of on-site car parking. However these misgivings did not prevent the planners' recommending approval of the scheme, and the Planning Committee granted formal consent to develop in May 2003. The development of the area took another four years and the main part of Princesshay opened in September 2007.

The final Princesshay development is very similar to many other retail developments constructed across Britain by Land Securities. For the City Council, it is the visible representation of change, more particularly of Exeter as an entrepreneurial city. This is most obviously manifest in the demolition of the 1950s buildings and layout. However, the replacement buildings change not just the appearance of the area but also its socioeconomic character. The larger floorspaces of the new retail units make them attractive to a different type of retail user than previously. The scheme incorporates twelve units for "independent" retailers but even these are targeted at national-scale, high-end, niche retailers, rather than the local independent retailers, which were originally present in the area. Although in some ways a before and after comparison of retail rental levels is misleading, as the nature of the product changed, a retailer wishing to locate at the same address as previously would now incur far higher business occupancy costs. Similarly, the new residential property was priced at levels only affordable by the relatively wealthy.

The sense that the resulting development represented an opportunity lost is captured in the observations of an elected member, who compared the outcome of the Exeter scheme unfavorably with that completed by the same developer in another historic town, Canterbury. Such comparisons are always problematic and the elected member concerned was the only politician really to oppose the scheme, but they are suggestive of other possibilities. He said:

> I feel it [the development] is far too Land Securities led. ... I wanted to go to Canterbury because it gave the chance to see the Land Securities development there. The scale is better than ours. ... The detail and finish I couldn't fault it at all in Canterbury but I have a feeling – it's only a suspicion, but I think Canterbury Council watched the scheme differently than we have. I can't imagine the developer not wanting to have done something bigger in Canterbury and I'm sure they must have been told. That is the contrast between that one and this one because it is in a similar historic city site as well on a post war development.

A further, if more subtle, illustration of the development's implications is that control of open space in the area has largely been ceded to Land Securities. While Exeter City Council owned and managed public spaces, roads, and walkways before 2002, Land Securities entered a deal with the City Council to take a two-hundred-year lease of the publicly owned land in the area. This gives Land Securities control of these spaces, which they (rather than the City Council) maintain. Some routes through the area have been formally designated as "public highway" and the public enjoy the same rights as on any other streets (though maintenance of these streets is by Land Securities). However, other routes, including the main access through the shopping area, are not designated public highways and are effectively privately controlled. For these routes, the City Council entered into a "Walkways Agreement" with Land Securities, which states that they should be open twenty-four hours a day. But the Agreement also prevents the public from "carrying out retail activities, distributing newspapers or leaflets, playing musical instruments except when authorized, playing radios, roller skating, consuming alcoholic drinks or causing a nuisance or annoyance" (Byrne 2008, 9). Land Securities employs its own security personnel in the area to enforce these restrictions. Local newspapers even reported that members of the public were requested not to take pictures of the new development "for security reasons" (Byrne 2008).

Land Securities also exercise control in other arenas, notably in the management of the area and in the design of shop-fronts. As a result, regulatory control normally exercised through the planning process of approving the appearance of shop-fronts was largely ceded to Land Securities. The company employs their own retail design specialist to evaluate and determine retailers' proposals for shop-front design.

As in many cases of major development, Exeter City Council was both the primary landowner in the area and also responsible for determining the planning application. A planning officer involved in the negotiations over Princesshay considered that rather than these responsibilities being complementary they were incompatible. He commented that

> the other point about Princesshay is this detachment between the City Council as a corporate body and the City Council as a planning authority, and the ability of Planning Services to remain detached to an extent in the development process so that we can give clear planning advice and not have pressure or have the waters muddied by issues which are not to do with planning. I think the process was flawed in that regard because the ownership we set up did not allow essential debate on design and principles we normally have.

There is within this planning officer's observation a sense of the importance of separating planning decisions from the issue of land ownership, of not, as it is suggested, "muddying the waters." Presumptions of what is, or is not, within the ambit of planning, and therefore open to consideration and questioning is crucially important to the way arguments were constructed in this case.

The significance of Princesshay, not only to the City Council and in relation to its land holdings, but also to its perceived importance to the city as a whole, meant that the principle of development (*any* development) was viewed by many (but not all) planning officers, senior officials, and elected members in Exeter City Council as the overriding objective. The redevelopment was connected to the discourse of "entrepreneurial Exeter," and crucially even those that privately harbored concerns perceived that asking questions or presenting counterarguments was inappropriate or pointless.

Planning and the Development Industry – *Could* There Be Space for Better?

Thus far, the story of the Princesshay redevelopment mirrors many other studies of contemporary planning. A "modern retail" development became in many ways the embodiment of the neoliberal discourse of the "entrepreneurial city." The city's economic well-being was inextricably associated with a particular form of city center redevelopment. Alternative arguments, in terms of principle, although more especially matters of detail, were presented by policy officials including planners and some local groups, but were not accorded much significance.

However, it is at this point we want to step aside from standard analysis, to probe more deeply into the lessons that can be drawn from the case study, not about the dominance of neoliberal discourses but about the choices that were overlooked and the questions that were not asked or perceived would not be heard. There are many aspects of this development that could be explored. However, the main justification for not considering policy options inspired by more idealistic normative conceptions of planning is the needs of market actors. Hence, it is this, the most intractable constraint on the possibility for choice, that has been selected for further scrutiny. The purpose is to extend the existing planning literature, by getting beyond the empirical analysis of what happened, to consider what could have happened.

Perhaps the most striking aspect of the case is the silences. The sense of futility among the planners (and for that matter politicians and senior officials) that the trajectory of the development should be questioned. Even those who did venture to raise issues limited themselves to matters of detail. Exeter's interactions with the development sector largely became an end in itself, rather than a means to secure other collective goods. There are three arenas of interaction between the state and the market illustrated by this case. These concern the role of land ownership; the selection of the developer, and related to this, awareness of the diversity within the development industry; and the role of policy agendas in shaping the marketplace. The fundamental question therefore is how far the perceptions of Exeter's planners about the nature, and most tellingly limits, of planning, significantly constrained their room-for-maneuver. How far the needs of the market, as understood by politicians and senior officers, required planners to act in particular ways and how far their understandings and even misconceptions of the development industry led to a particular development outcome. Each of the areas of interaction between the state and the market are examined below.

It is striking how easily the City Council was prepared to cede control of their land to the developer. This course of action reflects a view that the public sector should be involved in land disposal, often at discounts, in order to promote commercial development. However, by agreeing to a (very) long lease, they ceded control of both the retail project and the surrounding public spaces. Yet, the Council's ownership of most of the land to be developed provided them with an excellent means of exercising control over the nature and direction of the project. This was recognized in part by the planner quoted above, but only in the sense that "planning" practices should not be distorted by the land ownership issue. This wish to detach planning judgments from issues of land ownership and property finance is ingrained within British professional planning traditions (Adams and Tiesdell 2010; Campbell and Henneberry 2005). Yet this position simultaneously handicaps planners, limiting their understanding of the economics of development and hence the scope of questions that can be asked, and of possible alternatives.

More significantly but less obviously, local policy makers (including planners), in their haste to be seen to be facilitating competition, failed to promote the kind of market competition, which would generate wider and collectively better outcomes. The conceptualization of property markets in one-dimensional terms is perhaps what advocates of neoliberal agendas desire. But for critics and state actors to take such a view is deeply disempowering, as it leaves the parameters for dialogue to be set by market actors. Planning as an activity, as with the planners in Exeter, may have traditionally placed property economics outside its remit, but without even a basic understanding of the workings of commercial real estate markets, the basis on which to generate alternative propositions is reduced (Adams and Tiesdell 2010). As the case study illustrates, very few of the arguments put forward by the planners were framed through an understanding of the property industry.

In the absence of a well-grounded understanding of the property industry, there is a tendency to underestimate its heterogeneity. There are numerous types of developers, which have quite different attitudes toward risk. Larger investor-developers such as Land Securities are now structured as Real Estate Investment Trusts and are very conservative. They engage in development activity with a view to holding the property as a financial asset for a relatively long time period or with a view to selling to an institutional investor. These developers are subject to considerable scrutiny from their equity investors and are risk averse. Their focus is generally on highly transparent, prime commercial property markets. This conservatism is reinforced by the behavior of property fund managers, the large developers' main "customers." These fund managers control a substantial proportion of investment capital in global commercial real estate markets and operate in an environment where their performance is assessed against an industry benchmark. This encourages asset managers to follow the rest of the market (Henneberry and Roberts 2008). Although investors seek to hold geographically diversified portfolios, they are concerned about being able to liquidate their assets quickly and this limits the types of schemes they are interested in financing in "thin" provincial markets such as Exeter. Developers by necessity bring forward schemes that exhibit the qualities sought after by these large financial institutions.

In contrast, many smaller developers seek to operate within particular localities. They actively capitalize on local knowledge and networks, and generally adopt more "entrepreneurial" business models (Charney 2007). These developers have a far better track record of developing schemes in areas most in need of urban regeneration (Adair et al. 1999), but there are limits to the scale of project they might tackle. It is private investors, rather than major financial institutions, that tend to provide the finance and funding for the more "entrepreneurial" commercial developments undertaken in disadvantaged areas and in provincial markets (Key and Law 2005). The divergent behaviors of different types of developers and investors are reflected in local variations in development activity, in the levels of development pressure and in the finance and funding models used for commercial schemes. Moreover, the financial returns on development by locally based developers are more likely to stay local.

A greater appreciation of the diverse working practices of developers would enable planners to achieve a wider variety of development outcomes. In the Exeter case, by breaking up the redevelopment into a number of smaller schemes the Council could have secured an outcome that would have been better for the local economy, with the attendant socioeconomic benefits, as well as being more environmentally and aesthetically sensitive. But this would have required a different understanding of the nature of planning and the role of planners than is exemplified, and as a consequence such options were never considered.

One of the most forceful messages from the Exeter case was the extent to which even detailed questioning of the merits of the scheme was ruled inappropriate by all concerned, in the face of the perceived needs of the market. The policy community, at local and national scales, tends to overlook how far the practices and values of the property industry can be altered. Yet markets are not immutable; they are "made" economic (Callon 1998; Smith, Munro, and Christie 2006). As a result, choices exist and development outcomes can be "made" better. There is considerable evidence at the meta-level that the property industry will respond to a changing political climate. For example, institutional investors in the United Kingdom have changed the nature of their retail developments to reflect Government policies, so as to contribute to the "vitality and vibrancy" of cities through mixed use developments. Real estate investors' objectives are now articulated in a language that is quite different from that used in the industry a decade ago, following the policy agendas of national and local governments (see Jackson and Watkins 2008). There is, of course, a financial rationale for this. But the financial motives have followed changes in governmental policies and the needs and preferences of real estate users. The economic has been "authored" by social and political processes. Property markets do respond to the "climate of opinion." Witness, for example, the rapid emergence of socially responsible investment strategies and the way this has subtly altered developer responses to the green agenda (Eicholtz, Kok, and Quigley 2009). Developers tend to respond relatively quickly to changes in investor preferences. The withdrawal of the original application by Land Securities demonstrates the combined influence the demands of potential tenants and the regulatory process can have on developers, as does the nature of their developments elsewhere.

Despite these general trends, the Princesshay scheme suggests there can be a lack of boldness in planning, particularly when it comes to interactions with developers at the level of individual projects. Institutional investors and developers are willing to invest significant resources in building informal relationships in the hope of maximizing the medium- and long-term returns to their assets. This is driven by an appreciation that they may receive preferential treatment in relation to future decisions and, in particular, in limiting the scope for competitors to enter certain markets. This presents planning with significant opportunities, but at present the benefits appear largely to flow in the direction of the developers. Politicians and planners all too rarely use these relationships toward the greater good. Moreover, they often also fail to harness the economic competitiveness rhetoric effectively. Despite the rhetorical claims of business interest groups, the real estate industry does not find competition attractive. Consequently, there are opportunities for the public sector to be more proactive in promoting competition between developers within local markets. In too many cases, including the Exeter redevelopment, there is fear of territorial competition, exacerbated by the widespread conviction of the spatial mobility of investment capital. These pressures in turn act to limit the willingness of many planners to ask questions within the institutional contexts in which they work, and hence press developers to produce schemes, which incorporate longer-term public benefits.

Conclusions – Making *Practical and Conceptual* Space for Better

At the outset of this article, it was suggested that the current policy debate is characterized by a sense of pessimism about the possibilities of securing better planning outcomes. However, while critical analysis of current practices is undoubtedly important, critique on its own is dispiriting and arguably also disempowering (Storper 2001; Tallis 1997). In this article we have attempted to go further than standard analyses, to explore not only what did happen in a particular case but what might have happened, what further choices and options were available, and hence the possibility for *better* outcomes. In doing this, the power of market forces has not been ignored; rather existing presumptions have been interrogated to explore how far they might have been understood differently and hence created the space – practical and conceptual – to make a difference.

The view of real estate markets in much critical analysis is very one-dimensional, assuming an inevitability about the nature of development outcomes. The findings of this article challenge this premise. One reading of the Exeter redevelopment scheme presents a conventional story of policy makers in the thrall of neoliberal rhetoric. Yet a simplistic model of the real estate industry limits possibilities. Within planning, uncertainty and complexity are often viewed as problematic and challenging (Christensen 1985) but understanding complexity, uncertainty, and diversity also opens up opportunities and the potential for agendas to be molded and something "better" to be delivered. However, this requires planning (both practitioners and researchers) to develop a much more sophisticated understanding of the pressures and priorities of developers and their investors. Development outcomes are not entirely immutable and inevitable: they are shaped by socio-political forces, which have the potential to be molded to achieve a variety of ends, admittedly, for better and worse. But understanding alone is not enough. It is the perception that the resulting questions such knowledge opens up are worth asking, and can be asked, which is crucial.

There are several dimensions to the implications of these findings. We start with the more specific and practical and move to the more general and conceptual.

The Exeter case study suggests that the "state" could have used its regulatory controls, land ownership, and even market competition to achieve more, if only policy makers and planners had had a greater sense of what was possible. The state has considerable economic assets at its disposal, which can be used to exert leverage. A greater capacity and willingness by such planners to capitalize on state ownership, and the resulting control of large quantities of valuable (in all senses of the term) development land, would produce different outcomes. It seems so obvious that the point should not need to be made, but if developers are to make money from new development they need land, and certainly in most contexts for major schemes, the permission of the state to develop that land. These mechanisms of leverage and influence need to be harnessed effectively and intelligently.

There can be no doubt that market forces impose major structural constraints, but the extent and nature of the constraint are open to influence and, yes, manipulation by astute planners and politicians. This requires creativity in networking with real estate investors and developers and in using policy levers to shape market behaviors. Responses to the following questions would assist in the process of framing appropriate strategies:

** Who are the key development actors?
** What are the motivations of these actors?

** What pressures are they responding to?
** What impact might additional competition have on behaviors?

One of the most telling aspects of the case study is the power that asking questions can exert, or in this case, how far questioning was circumscribed to a relatively limited set of issues. The availability of alternative choices is directly linked to a capacity to ask questions, including at the level of a particular scheme, the sorts of questions identified above. This in turn is underpinned by the need for a clear underlying vision of the sort of places that ought to be created and a sense of what form better and worse outcomes should take. In relation to the Exeter case, if there had been more of a sense of a broader (and different) vision and purpose, a different outcome was possible. However, silence and hence the absence of alternatives allowed a pretty typical neoliberal policy agenda to fill the void, making the furtherance of market interests an undefined end in itself, rather than a means to be exploited to achieve greater goods.

Our argument also has broader implications; firstly, in relation to the approach adopted for the examination of the empirical evidence and, secondly, for planning theory. It is inherent to empirical studies that they are analytical in nature and seek to provide explanation of why certain events or outcomes took place. This must inevitably be a retrospective process and tends to assume that what did take place, for whatever reasons, had to take place and that in similar contexts such outcomes might be expected in the future. The purpose of this article has been rather different, to explore whether empirical research could be used not as the basis for explanation but rather as the basis for conceiving of alternative possibilities and most importantly for learning. Much more detailed work needs to be done to develop further this synthetic approach, but the findings at least suggest it has potential to provide forward-looking practical, action-oriented, as well as critical analytical insights.

The importance of an underlying vision in shaping and creating the conceptual and practical capacity to do better raises challenges about the boundaries delimiting the construction of planning debates and the nature of the outcomes planning practices seek to realize. If boundaries are drawn tightly either by choice and conviction, or by understandings as to the nature of the system and expectations of one's seniors, then the scope of possibility will be highly circumscribed. It follows from this that the transformative potential of planning reflects and depends on the way boundaries are constructed.

Concern with the outcomes of planning inevitably leads to a focus on the normative. Engagement with matters of a normative nature can be problematic and discomforting. A concern with what "ought to be" involves making choices, which will be to the benefit of some but not all. However, not engaging with such matters does not make them disappear (O'Neill 2000; Squires 1993). Rather other discourses fill the vacuum, and one of neoliberalism's great successes is precisely this, while simultaneously espousing an antiideological and pragmatic position.

Arguably, given the premise underlying planning and much public policy, that intervention results in better outcomes than would otherwise have been the case, one of the great practical and intellectual challenges is to understand and articulate more clearly what state regulation is good for. The vast majority of political rhetoric and critical analysis highlights the failings of state intervention. While acknowledging that a return to welfare state-type policies would be neither desirable nor practical, greater understanding of the enabling capacity of the state and governments in a contemporary context is merited, perhaps fundamental to the development of space in which to ask genuinely constructive questions. Moreover, such an enabling capacity is also vital for the effective functioning of civil society and social movements.

There are, of course, dangers in asserting a normative position or providing a framework for a vision of the future. Visions must necessarily exclude, in that they suggest some things are more important than others. The challenge for planners lies in being able to move between abstract concepts, such as justice, equity, or beauty, and apply them to specific planning problems in particular places (Campbell 2006; Healey 2012). It is the iteration between the universal principles and local particularities, and local particularities and universal principles, which avoids decisions becoming piecemeal and random, or contextually insensitive.

A concern with the normative is not about the assertion of a rigid utopian ideal, but nor is it without a sense of purpose and direction (Levitas 2007). Amartya Sen (2009) suggests that the quest to find an ideal form of justice– if you like, "the best" – has tended to discourage and even obscure the ability to seek out better. This seems to have resonance for our approach to planning. Planning practices will always be flawed and produce imperfect results, but this should not dissuade the planning community from the search to do better. The "best," as the goal for planning practices, will not just fail to be realized but, because it is so problematic to conceptualize and challenging to achieve, has the tendency to foster inertia and discourage creativity. A focus on "better" in contrast opens up a space of possibilities – a range of *betters* – and crucially the potential for constructive achievement. In this messiness, Bish Sanyal (2002) encourages planners (both theorists and practitioners) to understand more about the nature of a *good* compromise.[16] What are the qualities of a wise compromise, and when does a compromise become a hollow shell in which what really matters has been lost? Most, perhaps all, planning decisions involve compromise, but good compromises are not unprincipled and therefore require an understanding of the nature of better, of ethical enquiry.

The findings of this article suggest that the planning community should be hopeful, that there is space for better. It is in the silences that planning (and planners) betray the limits of its (our) aspirations. In contrast, it is in the questions which are asked that willingness and commitment to push the boundaries of what seemed possible are demonstrated: a concern to achieve *better*.

Notes

1. John Forester has often used this term to describe planning. It was more recently adopted as a title of book by Howell Baum.
2. National government continues to have responsibility for planning in England, while in Scotland, Wales, and Northern Ireland, planning is the responsibility of the various devolved administrations.
3. This phrase, first used by Michael Heseltine in 1978, continues to be widely cited today (see Simmie 2004, 131)
4. See Campbell 2012b for discussion of the qualities of analysis and synthesis in relation to planning.
5. See Giddens's (1984) work on structuration and its implications for social theory and the recent revival of interest in the long-standing work on institutional economics (Stanfield 1999; Hodgson 2000).
6. Patsy Healey (1997) adopts this wider sense in her definition of planning as "spatial governance," and the Royal Town Planning Institute's Education Commission reflects this perception in defining planning as "critical thinking about space and place as the basis for action or intervention" (2003, para. 4.17).
7. Here is evidence of the power of mainstream economic analysis to offer a complete ethical system that links analysis to action and policy prescription (Carrithers and Peterson 2006).
8. The antecedents of these normative positions lie in much earlier bodies of work, including the advocacy planning approach of Paul Davidoff (1965) and the equity planning of Norman Krumholz in Cleveland, Ohio (Krumholz and Forester 1990).
9. However, it should be noted that this is not a singular set of ideas.
10. Elisabeth Howe's (1994) work exploring the ethical values of planners in the 1980s, particularly in the United States, highlights the variability in the ways planners construct their scope and capacity for action.
11. The redevelopment area totaled 565,000 square feet (Exeter City Council 2008) with a complete floorspace, including shops, apartments, cafes, restaurants, and the civic square) of 530,000 square feet (Land Securities 2008).
12. A development control officer in the United Kingdom, an activity now sometimes referred to as "development management," undertakes a similar range of activities to planners who process zoning permits or review proposals in other contexts.
13. A Local Strategic Partnership is a partnership between public, private, voluntary, and community sectors within a local authority area. Their key task (as defined under the Local Government Act 2000) is to produce a "Community Strategy" that sets priorities for change within the area. There is no statutory stipulation as to membership or leadership, though guidance strongly advocates the active role of local politicians.
14. Land Securities is one of the world's five largest investor-developers by asset value. Although it is based in London and its activities are UK-dominated, it holds substantial international investment portfolios. Land Securities concentrates on commercial property development and has extensive experience of undertaking city center retail redevelopment schemes, including recently in the United Kingdom in Bristol, Birmingham, and Portsmouth.

15. English Heritage is the national Government's statutory advisor on the historic environment.
16. See also Gutmann and Thompson's (2012) recent book, considering compromise more generally within politics and governing.

References

Adair, A., J. Berry, W. S. McGreal, W. Deddis, and S. Hirst. 1999. "Evaluation of Investor Behaviour in Urban Regeneration." *Urban Studies* 36 (12): 2031–45.

Adams, D., and S. Tiesdell. 2010. "Planners as Market Actors: Rethinking State-Market Relations and Land and Property." *Planning Theory and Practice* 11 (2): 187–207.

Brenner, N., and N. Theodore, eds. 2002. *Spaces of Neoliberalism: Urban Restructuring in North America and Western Europe*. Oxford: Blackwell.

Brenner, N., and N. Theodore. 2005. "Neoliberalism and the Urban Condition." *City* 9: 101–107.

Brown, G. 2005. Gordon Brown's Speech to the Confederation of British Industry Conference, 28 November 2005. http://www.theguardian.com/business/2005/nov/28/economicpolicy.budget2006 (accessed March 14, 2013).

Byrne, M. 2008. "Picture Puzzle Shows Princesshay Is Public – But Only up to a Point." *Express and Echo* (Exeter), January 30.

Callon, M. 1998. *The Laws of Markets*. Oxford: Blackwell.

Cameron, D. 2011. David Cameron's Speech to the Conservative Party Spring Conference, 6 March 2011. http://www.bbc.co.uk/news/uk-politics-12657524 (accessed March 14, 2013).

Cameron, D. 2012. David Cameron's Statement on the Announcement of the New Planning Reforms, 6 September 2012. http://www.bbc.co.uk/news/uk-politics-19496204 (accessed March 14, 2013).

Campbell, H. 2006. "Just Planning: The Art of Situated Ethical Judgment." *Journal of Planning Education and Research* 26 (1): 92–106.

Campbell, H. 2012a. "'Planning Ethics' and Rediscovering *the Idea of Planning*." *Planning Theory* 11 (4): 379–99.

Campbell, H. 2012b. "Planning to Change the World: Between Knowledge and Action Lies Synthesis." *Journal of Planning Education and Research* 32 (2): 135–46.

Campbell, H., and S. Fainstein. 2012. "Justice, Urban Politics and Policy." In *Oxford Handbook of Urban Politics*, edited by K. Mossberger, S. E. Clarke, and P. John, pp. 545–66. Oxford: Oxford University Press.

Campbell, H., and J. Henneberry. 2005. "Contradictions in the Operation of the Planning Obligations System." *Journal of Property Research* 22 (1): 37–59.

Catney, P., and J. Henneberry. 2012. "(Not) Exercising Discretion: Environmental Planning and the Politics of Blame-Avoidance." *Planning Theory and Practice* 13 (4): 549–68.

Carrithers, D. F., and D. Peterson. 2006. "Conflicting Views of Markets and Economic Justice." *Journal of Business Ethics* 69: 373–87.

Charney, I. 2007. "Intra-metropolitan Preferences of Property Developers in Greater Toronto's Office Market." *Geoforum* 38: 1179–89.

Christensen, K. 1985. "Coping with Uncertainty in Planning." *Journal of the American Planning Association* 51 (1): 63–73.

Commission of the European Community. 1999. *European Spatial Development Framework (ESDP) – Towards Balanced and Sustainable Development of the Territory of the EU.* Luxembourg: Office for Official Publications of the European Communities.

Communities and Local Government. 2006. *Barker Review of Land Use Planning: Final Report – Recommendations.* London: Stationery Office.

Cullingworth, B., and V. Nadin. 2014. *Town and Country Planning in the UK.* Abingdon: Routledge.

Davidoff, P. 1965. "Advocacy and Pluralism in Planning." *Journal of the American Planning Association* 31 (4): 331–38.

Deakin, S., and J. Michie. (eds). 1997. *Contracts, Co-operation and Competition: Studies in Economics, Management and Law.* Oxford: Oxford University Press.

du Gay, P. 2000. *In Praise of Bureaucracy.* London: Sage.

Eicholtz, P., K. Kok, and J. Quigley. 2009. *Doing Well by Doing Good? Green Office Buildings.* London: RICS Research Report.

Exeter City Council. 1999. *City Centre Strategy.* Exeter: Exeter City Council.

Exeter City Council. 2006. *2006 Mid-Year Population Estimate Briefing Paper.* Exeter: Exeter City Council.

Exeter City Council. 2008. *Princesshay: A Summary of the Redevelopment in Exeter's City Centre.* Exeter: Exeter City Council. http://www.exeter.gov.uk/media/pdf/0/g/Princesshay_ Summary.pdf (accessed September 18, 2008).

Exeter People's Choice. 1999. *The Case against Land Security's Princesshay Development.* http://www.eclipse.co.uk/exeter/epc/phay.htm (accessed September 18, 2008).

Fainstein, S. 2000. "New Directions in Planning Theory." *Urban Affairs Review* 35 (4): 451–78.

Fainstein, S. 2010. *The Just City.* Ithaca, NY: University of Cornell Press.

Fainstein, S., and S. Campbell. (eds.). 2012. *Readings in Planning Theory*, 3rd ed. Oxford: Wiley-Blackwell.

Forester, J. 1999. *The Deliberative Practitioner: Encouraging Participatory Planning Processes.* London: MIT Press.

Foucault, M. 1991. "Governmentality." In *The Foucault Effect: Studies in Governmentality*, edited by G. Burchell, C. Gordon, and P. Miller, pp. 87–104. London: Harvester Wheatsheaf.

Fraser, N., and A. Honneth. 2003. *Redistribution or Recognition?* (Trans. J. Golb, J. Ingram, J. and C. Wilke). London: Verso.

Fukuyama, F. 1993. "In the Zone of Peace." *Times Literary Supplement,* November 26.

Giddens, A. 1984. *The Constitution of Society.* Cambridge: Polity Press.

Gould, J., and C. Gould. 1999. *Phoenix Flying: The Buildings of Princesshay, Bedford Street and High Street, Exeter.* Report commissioned by English Heritage.

Gunn, S., and J. Hillier. 2012. "Processes of Innovation: Reformation of the English Strategic Spatial Planning System." *Planning Theory and Practice* 13 (3): 359–81.

Gutmann, A., and D. Thompson. 2012. *The Spirit of Compromise: Why Governing Demands It and Campaigning Undermines It.* London: Belknap.

Her Majesty's Treasury. 2007. *The Economics of Climate Change: The Stern Review.* Cambridge: Cambridge University Press.

Harvey, D. 2005. *A Brief History of Neoliberalism.* Oxford: Oxford University Press.

Healey, P. 1997. *Collaborative Planning: Shaping Places in Fragmented Societies.* Basingstoke: Palgrave.

Healey, P. 2012. "The Universal and the Contingent: Some Reflections on the Transnational Flow of Planning Ideas and Practices." *Planning Theory* 11 (2): 188–207.

Henneberry, J., and C. Roberts. 2008. "Calculated Inequality? Portfolio Benchmarking and Regional Office Property Investment in the UK." *Urban Studies* 45: 1217–41.

Hodgson, G. 2000. "What Is the Essence of Institutional Economics?" *Journal of Economic Issues* 34 (2): 317–29.

Howe, E. 1994. *Acting on Ethics in City Planning*. New Brunswick, NJ: Center for Urban Policy Research.

Hrelja, R. 2011. "The Tyranny of Small Decisions. Unsustainable Cities and Local Day-to-Day Transport Planning." *Planning Theory and Practice* 12 (4): 511–24.

Innes, J. 1995. "Planning Theory's Emerging Paradigm: Communicative Action and Interactive Practice." *Journal of Planning Education and Research* 14 (3): 183–91.

Jackson, C., and C. Watkins. 2008. *Retail Property Investment Behaviour and Planning Policy*. London: Investment Property Forum.

Key, T., and V. Law. 2005. *The Size and Structure of the UK Property Market*. London: Investment Property Databank.

Krumholz, N., and J. Forester. 1990. *Making Equity Planning Work: Leadership in the Public Sector*. Philadelphia, PA: Temple University Press.

Land Securities. 2008. *Princesshay – Key Facts*. London: Land Securities.

Le Grand, J. 1991. "Quasi-markets and Social Policy." *Economic Journal* 101 (4): 1256–67.

Levitas, R. 2007. "Looking for the Blue: The Necessity of Utopia." *Journal of Political Ideologies* 12 (3): 289–306.

Lovering, J. 2009. "The Recession and the End of Planning as We Have Known It." *International Planning Studies* 14 (1): 1–6.

MacCullum, D., and D. Hopkins. 2011. "The Changing Discourse of City Plans: Rationalities of Planning in Perth, 1955–2010." *Planning Theory and Practice* 12 (4): 485–510.

Mäntysalo, R., and I. Saglie. 2010. "Private Influence Preceding Public Involvement: Strategies for Legitimizing Preliminary Partnership Arrangements in Urban Housing Planning in Norway and Finland." *Planning Theory and Practice* 11 (3): 317–38.

Marcuse, P., J. Connolly, I. Olivo Magana, J. Novy, C. Potter, and J. Steil, eds. 2009. *Searching for the Just City*. New York: Routledge.

Marquand, D. 2004. *Decline of the Public: The Hollowing Out of Citizenship*. Cambridge: Polity Press.

McMaster, R. 2002. "The Analysis of Welfare State Reform: Why the 'Quasi-markets' Narrative Is Descriptively Inadequate and Misleading." *Journal of Economic Issues* 36 (2): 769–94.

Miller, M. 1998. *Princesshay Exeter: Concept, Development and Context*. Report commissioned by English Heritage.

O'Neill, O. 2000. *Bounds of Justice*. Cambridge: Cambridge University Press.

Osborne, D., and T. Gaebler. 1992. *Reinventing Government*. New York: Plume.

Peck, J. 2003. "Geography and Public Policy: Mapping the Penal State." *Progress in Human Geography* 27 (2): 222–32.

Peck, J., N. Theodore, and N. Brenner. 2010. "Postneoliberalism and Its Malcontents." *Antipode* 41 (1): 94–116.

Propper, C. 1993. "Quasi-Markets and Regulation." In *Quasi-markets and Social Policy*, edited by J. Le Grand and W. Bartlett, pp. 183–200. Basingstoke: Macmillan.

Royal Town Planning Institute. 2003. *RTPI Education Commission Report*. London: Royal Town Planning Institute.

Sager, T. 2013. *Reviving Critical Planning Theory: Dealing with Pressure, Neo-liberalism and Responsibility in Communicative Planning*. Abingdon: Routledge.

Sandel, M. 2009. *Justice: What's the Right Thing to Do?* London: Allen Lane.

Sanyal, B. 2002. "Globalization, Ethical Compromise and Planning Theory." *Planning Theory* 1 (2): 116–23.

Sen, A. 2009. *The Idea of Justice*. London: Allen Lane.

Sharp, T. 1946. *Exeter Phoenix: A Plan for Rebuilding*. London: Architectural Press.

Simmie, J. 2004. *Planning at the Crossroads*. Abingdon: Taylor and Francis e-Library.

Smith, S., M. Munro, and H. Christie. 2006. "Performing (Housing) Markets." *Urban Studies* 43: 81–98.

Squires, J. 1993. "Introduction." In *Principled Positions: Postmodernism and the Rediscovery of Value*, edited by J. Squires, pp. 1–13. London: Lawrence and Wishart.

Stanfield, J. R. 1999. "The Scope, Method and Significance of Original Institutional Economics." *Journal of Economic Issues* 33 (2): 230–55.

Storper, M. 2001. "The Poverty of Radical Theory Today: From False Promises of Marxism to the Mirage of the Cultural Turn." *International Journal of Urban and Regional Research* 25: 155–79.

Tait, M. 2011. "Trust and the Public Interest in the Micropolitics of Planning Practice." *Journal of Planning Education and Research* 31 (2): 157–71.

Tallis, R. 1997. *Enemies of Hope: A Critique of Contemporary Pessimism*. Basingstoke: Macmillan.

11

Green Cities, Growing Cities, Just Cities?

Urban Planning and the Contradictions of Sustainable Development

Scott Campbell

In the coming years planners face tough decisions about where they stand on protecting the green city, promoting the economically growing city, and advocating social justice. Conflicts among these goals are not superficial ones arising simply from personal preferences. Nor are they merely conceptual, among the abstract notions of ecological, economic, and political logic, nor a temporary problem caused by the untimely confluence of environmental awareness and economic recession. Rather, these conflicts go to the historic core of planning, and are a leitmotif in the contemporary battles in both our cities and rural areas, whether over solid waste incinerators or growth controls, the spotted owls or nuclear power. And though sustainable development aspires to offer an alluring, holistic way of evading these conflicts, they cannot be shaken off so easily.

This chapter uses a simple triangular model to understand the divergent priorities of planning. My argument is that although the differences are partly due to misunderstandings arising from the disparate languages of environmental, economic, and political thought, translating across disciplines alone is not enough to eliminate these genuine clashes of interest. The socially constructed view of nature put forward here challenges the view of these conflicts as a classic battle of "man versus nature" or its current variation, "jobs versus the environment." The triangular model is then used to question whether sustainable development, the current object of planning's fascination, is a useful model to guide planning practice. I argue that

Original publication details: Campbell, Scott. "Green Cities, Growing Cities, Just Cities? Urban Planning and the Contradictions of Sustainable Development". In *Journal of the American Planning Association*, 62 (3) (Summer 1996), pp. 296–312. Used with permission from Taylor & Francis Group.

Readings in Planning Theory, Fourth Edition. Edited by Susan S. Fainstein and James DeFilippis.
Editorial material and organization © 2016 John Wiley & Sons, Ltd.
Published 2016 by John Wiley & Sons, Ltd.

the current concept of sustainability, though a laudable holistic vision, is vulnerable to the same criticism of vague idealism made thirty years ago against comprehensive planning. In this case, the idealistic fascination often builds upon a romanticized view of preindustrial, indigenous, sustainable cultures – inspiring visions, but also of limited modern applicability. Nevertheless, sustainability, if redefined and incorporated into a broader understanding of political conflicts in industrial society, can become a powerful and useful organizing principle for planning. In fact, the idea will be particularly effective if, instead of merely evoking a misty-eyed vision of a peaceful ecotopia, it acts as a lightning rod to focus conflicting economic, environmental, and social interests. The more it stirs up conflict and sharpens the debate, the more effective the idea of sustainability will be in the long run.

The chapter concludes by considering the implications of this viewpoint for planning. The triangle shows not only the conflicts, but also the potential complementarity of interests. The former are unavoidable and require planners to act as mediators, but the latter area is where planners can be especially creative in building coalitions between once-separated interest groups, such as labor and environmentalists, or community groups and business. To this end, planners need to combine both their procedural and their substantive skills and thus become central players in the battle over growth, the environment, and social justice.

The Planner's Triangle: Three Priorities, Three Conflicts

The current environmental enthusiasm among planners and planning schools might suggest their innate predisposition to protect the natural environment. Unfortunately, the opposite is more likely to be true: our historic tendency has been to promote the development of cities at the cost of natural destruction: to build cities we have cleared forests, fouled rivers and the air, leveled mountains. That is not the complete picture, since planners also have often come to the defense of nature, through the work of conservationists, park planners, open space preservationists, the Regional Planning Association of America, greenbelt planners, and modern environmental planners. Yet along the economic–ecological spectrum, with Robert Moses and Dave Foreman (of *Earth First!*) standing at either pole, the planner has no natural home, but can slide from one end of the spectrum to the other; moreover, the midpoint has no special claims to legitimacy or fairness.

Similarly, though planners often see themselves as the defenders of the poor and of socio-economic equality, their actions over the profession's history have often belied that self-image (Harvey 1985). Planners' efforts with downtown redevelopment, freeway planning, public–private partnerships, enterprise zones, smokestack-chasing and other economic development strategies don't easily add up to equity planning. At best, the planner has taken an ambivalent stance between the goals of economic growth and economic justice.

In short, the planner must reconcile not two, but at least three conflicting interests: to "grow" the economy, distribute this growth fairly, and in the process not degrade the ecosystem. To classify contemporary battles over environmental racism, pollution-producing jobs, growth control, etc., as simply clashes between economic growth and environmental protection misses the third issue, of social justice. The "jobs versus environment" dichotomy (e.g., the spotted owl versus Pacific Northwest timber jobs) crudely collapses under the "economy" banner the often differing interests of workers, corporations, community members, and the national public. The intent of this chapter's title is to focus planning not only for "green cities and growing cities," but also for "just cities."

In an ideal world, planners would strive to achieve a balance of all three goals. In practice, however, professional and fiscal constraints drastically limit the leeway of most planners. Serving the broader public interest by holistically harmonizing growth, preservation, and equality remains the ideal; the reality of practice restricts planners to serving the narrower interests of their clients, that is, authorities and bureaucracies (Marcuse 1976), despite efforts to work outside those limitations (Hoffman 1989). In the end, planners usually represent one particular goal – planning perhaps for increased property tax revenues, or more open space preservation, or better housing for the poor – while neglecting the other two. Where each planner stands in the triangle depicted in Figure 11.1 defines such professional bias. One may see illustrated in the figure the gap between the call for integrative, sustainable development planning (the center of the triangle) and the current fragmentation of professional practice (the edges). This point is developed later.

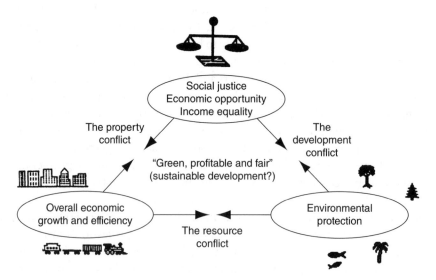

Figure 11.1 The triangle of conflicting goals for planning, and the three associated conflicts. Planners define themselves, implicitly, by where they stand on the triangle. The elusive ideal of sustainable development leads one to the center.

The points (corners) of the triangle:
The economy, the environment, and equity

The three types of priorities lead to three perspectives on the city: the economic development planner sees the city as a location where production, consumption, distribution, and innovation take place. The city is in competition with other cities for markets and for new industries. Space is the economic space of highways, market areas, and commuter zones.

The environmental planner sees the city as a consumer of resources and a producer of wastes. The city is in competition with nature for scarce resources and land, and always poses a threat to nature. Space is the ecological space of greenways, river basins, and ecological niches.

The equity planner sees the city as a location of conflict over the distribution of resources, of services, and of opportunities. The competition is within the city itself, among different social groups. Space is the social space of communities, neighborhood organizations, labor unions: the space of access and segregation.

Certainly there are other important views of the city, including the architectural, the psychological, and the circulatory (transportation); and one could conceivably construct a planner's rectangle, pentagon, or more complex polygon. The triangular shape itself is not propounded here as the underlying geometric structure of the planner's world. Rather, it is useful for its conceptual simplicity. More importantly, it emphasizes the point that a one-dimensional "man versus environment" spectrum misses the social conflicts in contemporary environmental disputes, such as loggers versus the Sierra Club, farmers versus suburban developers, or fishermen versus barge operators (Reisner 1987; Jacobs 1989; McPhee 1989; Tuason 1993).[1]

Triangle axis 1: The property conflict

The three points on the triangle represent divergent interests, and therefore lead to three fundamental conflicts. The first conflict – between economic growth and equity – arises from competing claims on and uses of property, such as between management and labor, landlords and tenants, or gentrifying professionals and long-time residents. This growth–equity conflict is further complicated because each side not only resists the other, but also needs the other for its own survival. The contradictory tendency for a capitalist, democratic society to define property (such as housing or land) as a private commodity, but at the same time to rely on government intervention (e.g., zoning, or public housing for the working class) to ensure the beneficial social aspects of the same property, is what Richard Foglesong (1986) calls the "property contradiction." This tension is generated as the private sector simultaneously resists and needs social intervention, given the intrinsically contradictory nature of property. Indeed, the essence of property in our society is the tense pulling between these two forces. The conflict defines the boundary between private interest and the public good.

Triangle axis 2: The resource conflict

Just as the private sector both resists regulation of property, yet needs it to keep the economy flowing, so too is society in conflict about its priorities for natural resources. Business resists the regulation of its exploitation of nature, but at the same time needs regulation to conserve those resources for present and future demands. This can be called the "resource conflict." The conceptual essence of natural resources is therefore the tension between their economic utility in industrial society and their ecological utility in the natural environment. This conflict defines the boundary between the developed city and the undeveloped wilderness, which is symbolized by the "city limits." The boundary is not fixed; it is a dynamic and contested boundary between mutually dependent forces.

Is there a single, universal economic–ecological conflict underlying all such disputes faced by planners? I searched for this essential, Platonic notion, but the diversity of examples – water politics in California, timber versus the spotted owl in the pacific Northwest, tropical deforestation in Brazil, park planning in the Adirondacks, greenbelt planning in Britain, to name a few – suggests otherwise. Perhaps there is an *Ur-Konflikt*, rooted in the fundamental struggle between human civilization and the threatening wilderness around us, and expressed variously over the centuries. However, the decision must be left to anthropologists as to whether the essence of the spotted owl controversy can be traced back to Neolithic times. A meta-theory tying all these multifarious conflicts to an essential battle of "human versus nature" (and, once tools and weapons were developed and nature was controlled, "human versus human") – that invites skepticism. In this discussion, the triangle is used simply as a template to recognize and organize the common themes; to examine actual conflicts, individual case studies are used.[2]

The economic–ecological conflict has several instructive parallels with the growth–equity conflict. In the property conflict, industrialists must curb their profit-increasing tendency to reduce wages, in order to provide labor with enough wages to feed, house, and otherwise "reproduce" itself – that is, the subsistence wage. In the resource conflict, the industrialists must curb their profit-increasing tendency to increase timber yields, so as to ensure that enough of the forest remains to "reproduce" itself (Clawson 1975; Beltzer and Kroll 1986; Lee, Field, and Burch 1990). This practice is called "sustained yield," though timber companies and environmentalists disagree about how far the forest can be exploited and still be "sustainable." (Of course, other factors also affect wages, such as supply and demand, skill level, and discrimination, just as lumber demand, labor prices, transportation costs, tariffs, and other factors affect how much timber is harvested.) In both cases, industry must leave enough of the exploited resource, be it human labor or nature, so that the resource will continue to deliver in the future. In both cases, how much is "enough" is also contested.

Triangle axis 3: The development conflict

The third axis on the triangle is the most elusive: the "development conflict," lying between the poles of social equity and environmental preservation. If the property conflict is characterized by the economy's ambivalent interest in providing at least a subsistence existence for working people, and the resource conflict by the economy's ambivalent interest in providing sustainable conditions for the natural environment, the development conflict stems from the difficulty of doing both at once. Environment–equity disputes are coming to the fore to join the older dispute about economic growth versus equity (Paehlke 1994, pp. 349–50). This may be the most challenging conundrum of sustainable develop-ment: how to increase social equity and protect the environment simultaneously, whether in a steady-state economy (Daly 1991) or not. How could those at the bottom of society find greater economic opportunity if environmental protection mandates diminished economic growth? On a global scale, efforts to protect the environment might lead to slowed economic growth in many countries, exacer-bating the inequalities between rich and poor nations. In effect, the developed nations would be asking the poorer nations to forgo rapid development to save the world from the greenhouse effect and other global emergencies.

This development conflict also happens at the local level, as in resource-dependent communities, which commonly find themselves at the bottom of the economy's hierarchy of labor. Miners, lumberjacks, and mill workers see a grim link between environmental preservation and poverty, and commonly mistrust environmentalists as elitists. Poor urban communities are often forced to make the no-win choice between economic survival and environmental quality, as when the only economic opportunities are offered by incinerators, toxic waste sites, landfills, and other noxious land uses that most neighborhoods can afford to oppose and do without (Bryant and Mohai 1992; Bullard 1990, 1993). If, as some argue, environmental protection is a luxury of the wealthy, then environmental racism lies at the heart of the development conflict. Economic segregation leads to environmental segregation: the former occurs in the transformation of natural resources into consumer products; the latter occurs as the spoils of production are returned to nature. Inequitable development takes place at all stages of the materials cycle.

Consider this conflict from the vantage of equity planning. Norman Krumholz, as the planning director in Cleveland, faced the choice of either building regional rail lines or improving local bus lines (Krumholz et al. 1982). Regional rail lines would encourage the suburban middle class to switch from cars to mass transit; better local bus service would help the inner-city poor by reducing their travel and waiting time. One implication of this choice was the tension between reducing pollution and making transportation access more equitable, an example of how bias toward social inequity may be embedded in seemingly objective transit proposals.

Implications of the Planner's Triangle Model

Conflict and complementarity in the triangle

Though I use the image of the triangle to emphasize the strong conflicts among economic growth, environmental protection, and social justice, no point can exist alone. The nature of the three axial conflicts is mutual dependence based not only on opposition, but also on collaboration.

Consider the argument that the best way to distribute wealth more fairly (i.e., to resolve the property conflict) is to increase the size of the economy, so that society will have more to redistribute. Similarly, we can argue that the best way to improve environmental quality (i.e., to resolve the resource conflict) is to expand the economy, thereby having more money with which to buy environmental protection. The former is trickle-down economics; can we call the latter "trickle-down environmentalism"? One sees this logic in the conclusion of the Brundtland Report: "If large parts of the developing world are to avert economic, social, and environmental catastrophes, it is essential that global economic growth be revitalized" (World Commission on Environment and Development 1987). However, only if such economic growth is more fairly distributed will the poor be able to restore and protect their environment, whose devastation so immediately degrades their quality of life. In other words, the development conflict can be resolved only if the property conflict is resolved as well. Therefore, the challenge for planners is to deal with the conflicts between competing interests by discovering and implementing complementary uses.

The triangle's origins in a social view of nature

One of the more fruitful aspects of recent interdisciplinary thought may be its linking the traditionally separate intellectual traditions of critical social theory and environmental science/policy (e.g., Smith 1990; Wilson 1992; Ross 1994). This is also the purpose of the triangle figure presented here: to integrate the environmentalist's and social theorist's world views. On one side, an essentialist view of environmental conflicts ("man versus nature") emphasizes the resource conflict. On another side, a historical materialist view of social conflicts (e.g., capital versus labor) emphasizes the property conflict. By simultaneously considering both perspectives, one can see more clearly the social dimension of environmental conflicts, that is, the development conflict. Such a synthesis is not easy: it requires accepting the social construction of nature but avoiding the materialistic pitfall of arrogantly denying any aspects of nature beyond the labor theory of value.

Environmental conflict should not, therefore, be seen as simply one group representing the interests of nature and another group attacking nature (though it often appears that way).[3] Who is to say that the lumberjack, who spends all his or her days among trees (and whose livelihood depends on those trees), is any less close to nature than the environmentalist taking a weekend walk through the woods? Is the lumberjack able to cut down trees only because s/he is "alienated" from the "true" spirit of nature – the spirit that the hiker enjoys? In the absence of a forest mythology, neither the tree cutter nor the tree hugger – nor the third party, the owner/lessee of the forest – can claim an innate kinship to a tree. This is not to be an apologist for clear-cutting, but rather to say that the merits of cutting versus preserving trees cannot be decided according to which persons or groups have the "truest" relationship to nature.

The crucial point is that all three groups have an interactive relationship with nature: the differences lie in their conflicting *conceptions* of nature, their conflicting *uses* of nature, and how they incorporate nature into their systems of values (be they community, economic, or spiritual values). This clash of human values reveals how much the ostensibly separate domains of community development and environmental protection overlap, and suggests that planners should do better in combining social and environmental models. One sees this clash of values in many environmental battles: between the interests of urban residents and those of subsidized irrigation farmers in California water politics; between beach homeowners and coastal managers trying to control erosion; between rich and poor neighborhoods, in the siting of incinerators; between farmers and environmentalists, in restrictions by open space zoning. Even then-President George Bush weighed into such disputes during his 1992 campaign when he commented to a group of loggers that finally people should be valued more than spotted owls (his own take on the interspecies equity issue). Inequity and the imbalance of political power are often issues at the heart of economic–environmental conflicts.

Recognition that the terrain of nature is contested need not, however, cast us adrift on a sea of socially constructed relativism where "nature" appears as an arbitrary idea of no substance (Bird 1987; Soja 1989). Rather, we are made to rethink the idea and to see the appreciation of nature as an historically evolved sensibility. I suspect that radical environmentalists would criticize this perspective as anthropocentric environmentalism, and argue instead for an ecocentric world view that puts the Earth first (Sessions 1992; Parton 1993). It is true that an anthropocentric view, if distorted, can lead to an arrogant optimism about civilization's ability to reprogram nature through technologies ranging from huge hydroelectric and nuclear plants down to genetic engineering. A rigid belief in the anthropocentric labor theory of value, Marxist or otherwise, can produce a modern-day Narcissus as a social-constructionist who sees nature as merely reflecting the beauty of the human aesthetic and the value of human labor. In this light, a tree is devoid of value until it either becomes part of a scenic area or is transformed into lumber. On the other hand, even as radical, ecocentric environmentalists claim to see "true nature" beyond the city limits, they are blind to how their own world view and their definition of nature itself are shaped by their socialization. The choice between an anthropocentric and an ecocentric world view is a false one. We are all unavoidably anthropocentric; the question is which anthropomorphic values and priorities we will apply to the natural and the social world around us.

Sustainable Development: Reaching the Elusive Center of the Triangle

If the three corners of the triangle represent key goals in planning, and the three axes represent the three resulting conflicts, then I will define the center of the triangle as representing sustainable development: the balance of these three goals. Getting to the center, however, will not be so easy. It is one thing to locate sustainability in the abstract, but quite another to reorganize society to get there.

At first glance, the widespread advocacy of sustainable development is astonishing, given its revolutionary implications for daily life (World Commission World Commission on Environment and Development, The Brundtland Commission, 1987; Daly and Cobb 1989; Rees 1989; World Bank 1989; Goodland 1990; Barrett and Bohlen 1991; Korten 1991; Van der Ryn and Calthorpe 1991). It is getting hard to refrain from sustainable development; arguments against it are inevitably attached to the strawman image of a greedy, myopic industrialist. Who would now dare to speak up in opposition? Two interpretations of the bandwagon for sustainable development suggest themselves. The pessimistic thought is that sustainable development has been stripped of its transformative power and reduced to its lowest common denominator. After all, if both the World Bank and radical ecologists now believe in sustainability, the concept can have no teeth: it is so malleable as to mean many things to many people without requiring commitment to any specific policies. Actions speak louder than words, and though all endorse sustainability, few will actually practice it. Furthermore, any concept fully endorsed by all parties must surely be bypassing the heart of the conflict. Set a goal far enough into the future, and even conflicting interests will seem to converge along parallel lines. The concept certainly appears to violate Karl Popper's requirement that propositions be falsifiable, for to reject sustainability is to embrace nonsustainability – and who dares to sketch that future? (Ironically, the nonsustainable scenario is the easiest to define: merely the extrapolation of our current way of life.)

Yet there is also an optimistic interpretation of the broad embrace given sustainability: the idea has become hegemonic, an accepted meta-narrative, a given. It has shifted from being a variable to being the parameter of the debate, almost certain to be integrated into any future scenario of development. We should therefore neither be surprised that no definition has been agreed upon, nor fear that this reveals a fundamental flaw in the concept. In the battle of big public ideas, sustainability has won: the task of the coming years is simply to work out the details, and to narrow the gap between its theory and practice.

Is sustainable development a useful concept?

Some environmentalists argue that if sustainable development is necessary, it therefore must be possible. Perhaps so, but if you are stranded at the bottom of a deep well, a ladder may be impossible even though necessary. The answer espoused may be as much an ideological as a scientific choice, depending on whether one's loyalty is to Malthus or Daly. The more practical question is whether sustainability is a useful concept for planners. The answer here is mixed. The goal may be too far away and holistic to be operational: that is, it may not easily break down into concrete, short-term steps. We also might be able to *define* sustainability yet be unable ever to actually measure it or even know, one day in the future, that we had achieved it. An old eastern proverb identifies the western confusion of believing that to name something is to know it. That may be the danger in automatically embracing sustainable development: a facile confidence that by adding the term "sustainable" to all our existing planning documents and tools (sustainable zoning, sustainable economic development, sustainable transportation planning), we are *doing* sustainable planning. Conversely, one can do much beneficial environmental work without ever devoting explicit attention to the concept of sustainability.

Yet sustainability can be a helpful concept in that it posits the long-term planning goal of a social–environmental system in balance. It is a unifying concept, enormously appealing to the imagination, that brings together many different environmental concerns under one overarching value. It defines a set of social priorities and articulates how society values the economy, the environment, and equity (Paehlke 1994, p. 360). In theory, it allows us not only to calculate whether we have attained sustainability, but also to determine how far away we are. (Actual measurement, though, is another, harder task.) Clearly, it can be argued that, though initially flawed and vague, the concept can be transformed and refined to be of use to planners.

History, equity, and sustainable development

One obstacle to an accurate, working definition of sustainability may well be the historical perspective that sees the practice as pre-existing, either in our past or as a Platonic concept. I believe instead that our sustainable future does not yet exist, either in reality or even in strategy. We do not yet know what it will look like; it is being socially constructed through a sustained period of conflict negotiation and resolution. This is a process of innovation, not of discovery and converting the nonbelievers.

This point brings us to the practice of looking for sustainable development in pre-industrial and nonwestern cultures (a common though not universal practice). Searching for our future in our indigenous past is instructive at both the philosophical and the practical level (Turner 1983; Duerr 1985). Yet it is also problematical, tapping into a myth that our salvation lies in the pre-industrial sustainable culture.

The international division of labor and trade, the movement of most people away from agriculture into cities, and exponential population growth lead us irrevocably down a unidirectional, not a circular path: the transformation of pre-industrial, indigenous settlements into mass urban society is irreversible. Our modern path to sustainability lies forward, not behind us.

The key difference between those indigenous, sustainable communities and ours is that they had no choice but to be sustainable. Bluntly stated, if they cut down too many trees or ruined the soil, they would die out. Modern society has the options presented by trade, long-term storage, and synthetic replacements; if we clear-cut a field, we have subsequent options that our ancestors didn't. In this situation, we must *voluntarily choose* sustainable practices, since there is no immediate survival or market imperative to do so. Although the long-term effects of a nonsustainable economy are certainly dangerous, the feedback mechanisms are too long-term to prod us in the right direction.

Why do we often romanticize the sustainable past? Some are attracted to the powerful spiritual link between humans and nature that has since been lost. Such romanticists tend, however, to overlook the more harsh and unforgiving aspects of being so dependent on the land. Two hundred years ago, Friedrich Schiller (1965, p. 28) noted the tendency of utopian thinkers to take their dream for the future and posit it as their past, thus giving it legitimacy as a cyclical return to the past.[4] This habit is not unique to ecotopians (Kumar 1991); some religious fundamentalists also justify their utopian urgency by drawing on the myth of a paradise lost. Though Marxists don't glorify the past in the same way, they, too, manage to anticipate a *static* system of balance and harmony, which nonetheless will require a cataclysmic, revolutionary social transformation to reach. All three ideologies posit some basic flaw in society – be it western materialism, original sin, or capitalism – whose identification and cure will free us from conflict. Each ideology sees a fundamental alienation as the danger to overcome: alienation from nature, from god, or from work. Each group is so critical of existing society that it would seem a wonder we have made it this far; but this persistence of human society despite the dire prognoses of utopians tells us something.

What is the fallout from such historical thinking? By neglecting the powerful momentum of modern industrial and postindustrial society, it both points us in the wrong direction and makes it easier to marginalize the proponents of sustainable development. It also carries an anti-urban sentiment that tends to neglect both the centrality and the plight of megacities. Modern humans are unique among species in their propensity to deal with nature's threats, not only through flight and burrowing and biological adaptation, nor simply through spiritual understanding, but also through massive population growth, complex social division of labor, and the fundamental, external transformation of their once-natural environment (the building of cities). Certainly the fixation on growth, industry, and competition has degraded the environment. Yet one cannot undo urban-industrial society. Rather, one must continue to innovate through to the other side of industrialization, to reach a more sustainable economy.

The cyclical historical view of some environmentalists also hinders a critical understanding of equity, since that view attributes to the environment a natural state of equality rudely upset by modern society. Yet nature is inherently neither equal nor unequal, and at times can be downright brutal. The human observer projects a sense of social equity onto nature, through a confusion, noted by Schiller, of the idealized future with myths about our natural past. To gain a sense of historical legitimacy, we project our socially constructed sense of equality onto the past, creating revisionist history in which nature is fair and compassionate. Society's path to equality is perceived not as an uncertain progress from barbarism to justice, but rather as a return to an original state of harmony as laid out in nature. In this thinking, belief in an ecological balance and a social balance, entwined in the pre-industrial world, conjures up an eco-Garden of Eden "lost" by modern society.[5]

It will be more useful to let go of this mythic belief in our involuntary diaspora from a pre-industrial, ecotopian Eden.[6] The conflation of ecological diasporas and utopias constrains our search for creative, urban solutions to social–environmental conflict. By relinquishing such mythic beliefs, we will understand that notions of equity were not lying patiently in wait in nature, to be first discovered by indigenous peoples, then lost by colonialists, and finally rediscovered by modern society in the late twentieth century. This is certainly not to say that nature can teach us nothing. The laws of nature are not the same thing, however, as natural law; nor does ecological equilibrium necessarily generate normative principles of equity. Though we turn to nature to understand the context, dynamics, and effects of the economic–environmental conflict, we must turn to social norms to decide what balance is fair and just.

How, then, do we define what is fair? I propose viewing social justice as the striving towards a more equal distribution of resources among social groups across the space of cities and of nations – a definition of "fair" distribution. It should be noted that societies view themselves as "fair" if the *procedures* of allocation treat people equally, even if the *substantive* outcome is unbalanced. (One would hope that equal treatment is but the first step towards narrowing material inequality.) The environmental movement expands the space for this "equity" in two ways: (1) intergenerationally (present versus future generations) and (2) across species (as in animal rights, deep ecology, and legal standing for trees). The two added dimensions of equity remain essentially abstractions, however, since no one from the future or from other species can speak up for their "fair share" of resources. Selfless advocates (or selfish ventriloquists) "speak for them."

This expansion of socio-spatial equity to include future generations and other species not only makes the concept more complex; it also creates the possibility for contradictions among the different calls for "fairness." Slowing worldwide industrial expansion may preserve more of the world's resources for the future (thereby increasing intergenerational equity), but it may also undermine the efforts of the underdeveloped world to approach the living standards of the west (thereby lowering international equity). Battles over Native American fishing practices, the spotted owl, and restrictive farmland preservation each thrust together several divergent notions of "fairness." It is through resolving the three sorts of conflicts on the planner's triangle that society iteratively forms its definition of what is fair.

The path towards sustainable development

There are two final aspects of the fuzzy definition of sustainability: its path and its outcome. The basic premise of sustainable development is one that, like the longterm goal of a balanced US budget, is hard not to like. As with eliminating the national debt, however, two troubling questions about sustainable development remain: How are you going to get there? Once you get there, what are the negative consequences? Planners don't yet have adequate answers to these two questions; that is, as yet they have no concrete strategies to achieve sustainable development, nor do they know how to counter the political resistance to it.

On the *path* towards a sustainable future, the steps are often too vague, as with sweeping calls for a "spiritual transformation" as the prerequisite for environmental transformation. Sometimes the call for sustainable development seems to serve as a vehicle for sermonizing about the moral and spiritual corruption of the industrial world (undeniable). Who would not want to believe in a holistic blending of economic and ecological values in each of our planners, who would then go out into the world and, on each project, internally and seamlessly merge the interests of jobs and nature, as well as of social justice? That is, the call to planners would be to stand at every moment at the center of the triangle.

But this aim is too reminiscent of our naive belief during the 1950s and 1960s in comprehensive planning for a single "public interest," before the incrementalists and advocacy planners pulled the rug out from under us (Lindblom 1959; Altshuler 1965; Davidoff 1965; Fainstein and Fainstein 1971). I suspect that planners' criticisms of the sustainable development movement in the coming years will parallel the critique of comprehensive planning thirty years ago: The incrementalists will argue that one cannot achieve a sustainable society in a single grand leap, for it requires too much social and ecological information and is too risky. The advocacy planners will argue that no common social interest in sustainable development exists, and that bureaucratic planners will invariably create a sustainable development scheme that neglects the interests both of the poor and of nature. To both groups of critics, the prospect of integrating economic, environmental and equity interests will seem forced and artificial. States will require communities to prepare "Sustainable Development Master Plans," which will prove to be glib wish lists of goals and suspiciously vague implementation steps. To achieve consensus for the plan, language will be reduced to the lowest common denominator, and the pleasing plans will gather dust.

An alternative is to let holistic sustainable development be a long-range goal; it is a worthy one, for planners do need a vision of a more sustainable urban society. But during the coming years, planners will confront deep-seated conflicts among economic, social and environmental interests that cannot be wished away through admittedly appealing images of a community in harmony with nature. One is no more likely to abolish the economic–environmental conflict completely by achieving sustainable bliss than one is to eliminate completely the boundaries between the city and the wilderness, between the public and private spheres, between the haves and have-nots. Nevertheless, one can diffuse the conflict, and find ways to avert its more destructive fall-out.

My concern about the *ramifications* of a sustainable future is one that is often expressed: steady-state, no-growth economics would be likely to relegate much of the developing world – and the poor within the industrialized world – to a state of persistent poverty. The advocates of sustainable development rightly reject as flawed the premise of conventional economics that only a growth economy can achieve social redistribution. And growth economics has, indeed, also exacerbated the environment's degradation. However, it is wishful thinking to assume that a sustainable economy will automatically ensure a socially just distribution of resources.[7] The vision of no-growth (commonly thought not universally assumed to characterize sustainable development) raises powerful fears, and planners should be savvy to such fears. Otherwise, they will understand neither the potential dangers of steady-state economics nor the nature of the opposition to sustainable development.

Rethinking/redefining sustainable development

Despite the shortcomings in the current formulation of sustainable development, the concept retains integrity and enormous potential. It simply needs to be redefined and made more precise. First, one should avoid a dichotomous, black-and-white view of sustainability. We should think of American society not as a corrupt, wholly unsustainable one that has to be made pure and wholly sustainable, but rather as a hybrid of both sorts of practices. Our purpose, then, should be to move further towards sustainable practices in an evolutionary progression.

Second, we should broaden the idea of "sustainability." If "crisis" is defined as the inability of a system to reproduce itself, then sustainability is the opposite: the long-term ability of a system to reproduce. This criterion applies not only to natural ecosystems, but to economic and political systems as well. By this definition, western society already does much to sustain itself: economic policy and corporate strategies (e.g., investment, training, monetary policy) strive to reproduce the macro- and micro-economies. Similarly, governments, parties, labor unions, and other political agents strive to reproduce their institutions and inter-ests. Society's shortcoming is that as it strives to sustain its political and economic systems, it often neglects to sustain the ecological system. The goal for planning is therefore a broader agenda: to sustain, simultaneously and in balance, these three sometimes competing, sometimes complementary systems.[8]

Third, it will be helpful to distinguish initially between two levels of sustainability: specific versus general (or local versus global). One might fairly easily imagine and achieve sustainability in a single sector and/or locality, for example, converting a Pacific Northwest community to sustained-yield timber practices. Recycling, solar power, cogeneration, and conservation can lower consumption of nonsustainable resources. To achieve complete sustainability across all sectors and/or all places, however, requires such complex restructuring and redistribution that the only feasible path to global sustainability is likely to be a long, incremental accumulation of local and industry-specific advances.

What this incremental, iterative approach means is that planners will find their vision of a sustainable city developed best at the conclusion of contested negotiations over land use, transportation, housing, and economic development policies, not as the premise for beginning the effort. To first spend years in the hermetic isolation of universities and environmental groups, perfecting the theory of sustainable development, before testing it in community development is backwards. That approach sees sustainable development as an ideal society outside the conflicts of the planner's triangle, or as the tranquil "eye of the hurricane" at the triangle's center. As with the ideal comprehensive plan, it is presumed that the objective, technocratic merits of a perfected sustainable development scheme will ensure society's acceptance. But one cannot reach the sustainable center of the planner's triangle in a single, holistic leap to a pre-ordained balance.

The Task Ahead for Planners: Seeking Sustainable Development within the Triangle of Planning Conflicts

The role of planners is therefore to engage the current challenge of sustainable development with a dual, interactive strategy: (1) to manage and resolve conflict; and (2) to promote creative technical, architectural, and institutional solutions. Planners must both negotiate the procedures of the conflict and promote a substantive vision of sustainable development.

Procedural paths to sustainable development: Conflict negotiation

In negotiation and conflict resolution (Bingham 1986; Susskind and Cruikshank 1987; Crowfoot and Wondolleck 1990), rather than pricing externalities, common ground is established at the negotiation table, where the conflicting economic, social, and environmental interests can be brought together. The potential rewards are numerous: not only an outcome that balances all parties, but avoidance of heavy legal costs and long-lasting animosity. Negotiated conflict resolution can also lead to a better understanding of one's opponent's interests and values, and even of one's own interests. The very process of lengthy negotiation can be a powerful tool to mobilize community involvement around social and environmental issues. The greatest promise, of course, is a win–win outcome: finding innovative solutions that would not have come out of traditional, adversarial confrontation. Through skillfully led, back-and-forth discussion, the parties can separate their initial, clashing substantive demands from their underlying interests, which may be more compatible. For example, environmentalists and the timber industry could solve their initial dispute over building a logging road through alternative road design and other mitigation measures (Crowfoot and Wondolleck 1990, pp. 32–52).

However, conflict resolution is no panacea. Sometimes conflicting demands express fundamental conflicts of interest. The either-or nature of the technology or ecology may preclude a win–win outcome, as in an all-or-nothing dispute over a proposed hydroelectric project (Reisner 1987) – you either build it or you don't. An overwhelming imbalance of power between the opposing groups also can thwart resolution (Crowfoot and Wondolleck 1990, p. 4). A powerful party can simply refuse to participate. It is also hard to negotiate a comprehensive resolution for a large number of parties.

Planners are likely to have the best success in using conflict resolution when there is a specific, concise dispute (rather than an amorphous ideological clash); all interested parties agree to participate (and don't bypass the process through the courts); each party feels on equal ground; there are a variety of possible compromises and innovative solutions; both parties prefer a solution to an impasse; and a skilled third-party negotiator facilitates. The best resolution strategies seem to include two areas of compromise and balance: the procedural (each party is represented and willing to compromise); and the substantive (the solution is a compromise, such as multiple land uses or a reduced development density).

Procedural paths to sustainable development: Redefining the language of the conflict

A second strategy is to bridge the chasms between the languages of economics, environmentalism, and social justice. Linguistic differences, which reflect separate value hierarchies, are a major obstacle to common solutions. All too often, the economists speak of incentives and marginal rates, the ecologists speak of carrying capacity and biodiversity, the advocate planners speak of housing rights, empowerment, and discrimination, and each side accuses the others of being "out of touch" (Campbell 1992).

The planner therefore needs to act as a translator, assisting each group to understand the priorities and reasoning of the others. Economic, ecological and social thought may at a certain level be incommensurable, yet a level may still be found where all three may be brought together. To offer an analogy, a Kenyan Gikuyu text cannot be fully converted into English without losing something in translation; a good translation, nevertheless, is the best possible way to bridge two systems of expression that will never be one, and it is preferable to incomprehension.

The danger of translation is that one language will dominate the debate and thus define the terms of the solution. It is essential to exert equal effort to translate in each direction, to prevent one linguistic culture from dominating the other (as English has done in neocolonial Africa). Another lesson from the neocolonial linguistic experience is that it is crucial for each social group to express itself in its own language before any translation. The challenge for planners is to write the best translations among the languages of the economic, the ecological, and the social views, and to avoid a quasi-colonial dominance by the economic *lingua franca*, by creating equal two-way translations.[9]

For example, planners need better tools to understand their cities and regions not just as economic systems, or static inventories of natural resources, but also as *environmental systems* that are part of regional and global networks trading goods, information, resources and pollution. At the conceptual level, translating the economic vocabulary of global cities, the spatial division of labor, regional restructuring, and technoburbs/edge cities into environmental language would be a worthy start; at the same time, of course, the vocabulary of biodiversity, landscape linkages, and carrying capacity should be translated to be understandable by economic interests.

This bilingual translation should extend to the empirical level. I envision extending the concept of the "trade balance" to include an "environmental balance," which covers not just commodities, but also natural resources and pollution. Planners should improve their data collection and integration to support the environmental trade balance. They should apply economic–ecological bilingualism not only to the content of data, but also to the spatial framework of the data, by rethinking the geographic boundaries of planning and analysis. Bioregionalists advocate having the spatial scale for planning reflect the scale of *natural* phenomena (e.g., the extent of a river basin, vegetation zones, or the dispersion range of metropolitan air pollution); economic planners call for a spatial scale to match the *social* phenomena (e.g., highway networks, municipal boundaries, labor market areas, new industrial districts). The solution is to integrate these two scales and overlay the economic and ecological geographies of planning. The current merging of environmental Raster (grid-based) and infrastructural vector-based data in Geographic Information Systems (GIS) recognizes the need for multiple layers of planning boundaries (Wiggins 1993).

Translation can thus be a powerful planner's skill, and interdisciplinary planning education already provides some multilingualism. Moreover, the idea of sustainability lends itself nicely to the meeting on common ground of competing value systems. Yet translation has its limits. Linguistic differences often represent real, intractable differences in values. An environmental dispute may arise not from a misunderstanding alone; both sides may clearly understand that their vested interests fundamentally clash, no matter how expressed. At this point, translation must give way to other strategies. The difficulties are exacerbated when one party has greater power, and so shapes the language of the debate as well as prevailing in its outcome. In short, translation, like conflict negotiation, reveals both the promises and the limitations of communication-based conflict resolution.

Other procedural paths

Two other, more traditional approaches deserve mention. One is political pluralism: let the political arena decide conflicts, either directly (e.g., a referendum on an open space bond act, or a California state proposition on nuclear power), or indirectly (e.g., elections decided on the basis of candidates' environmental records and promised legislation). The key elements here, political debate and ultimately the vote, allow much wider participation in the decision than negotiation does. However, a binary vote cannot as easily handle complex issues, address specific land-use conflicts, or develop subtle, creative solutions. Choosing the general political process as a strategy for deciding conflict also takes the process largely out of the hands of planners.

The other traditional strategy is to develop market mechanisms to link economic and environmental priorities. Prices are made the commonality that bridges the gap between the otherwise noncommensurables of trees and timber, open space and real estate. The marketplace is chosen as the arena where society balances its competing values. This economistic approach to the environment reduces pollution to what the economist Edwin Mills (1978, p. 15) called "a problem in resource allocation." This approach can decide conflicts along the economic–environmental axis (the resource conflict), but often neglects equity. However, the market does seem to be dealing better with environmental externalities than it did ten or twenty years ago. Internalizing externalities, at the least, raises the issues of social justice and equity: e.g., who will pay for cleaning up abandoned industrial sites or compensate for the loss of fishing revenues due to oil spills. The recent establishment of a pollution credit market in the South Coast Air Quality Management District, for example, is a step in the right direction – despite criticism that the pollution credits were initially given away for free (Robinson 1993).

The role of the planner in all four of these approaches is to arrange the procedures for making decisions, not to set the substance of the actual outcomes. In some cases, the overall structure for decision-making already exists (the market and the political system). In other cases, however, the planner must help shape that structure (a mediation forum; a common language), which, done successfully, gives the process credibility. The actual environmental outcomes nevertheless remain unknowable: you don't know in advance if the environment will actually be improved. For example, environmentalists and developers heralded the Coachella Valley Fringe-Toed Lizard Habitat Conservation Plan as a model process to balance the interests of development and conservation; yet the actual outcome may not adequately protect the endangered lizard (Beatley 1992, pp. 15–16). Similarly, although the New Jersey State Development Plan was praised for its innovative cross-acceptance procedure, the plan itself arguably has not altered the state's urban sprawl.

The final issue that arises is whether the planner should play the role of neutral moderator, or of advocate representing a single party; this has been a long-standing debate in the field. Each strategy has its virtues.

Substantive paths to sustainable development: Land use and design

Planners have substantive knowledge of how cities, economies, and ecologies interact, and they should put forth specific, farsighted designs that promote the sustainable city. The first area is traditional planning tools of land-use design and control. The potential for balance between economic and environmental interests exists in design itself, as in a greenbelt community (Elson 1986). Sometimes the land-use solution is simply to divide a contested parcel into two parcels: a developed and a preserved. This solution can take crude forms at times, such as the "no-net-loss" policy that endorses the dubious practice of creating wetlands. A different example, Howard's turn-of-the-century Garden City (1965), can be seen as a territorially symbolic design for balance between the economy and the environment, though its explicit language was that of town–country balance. It is a design's articulated balance between the built development and the unbuilt wilderness that promises the economic–environmental balance. Designs for clustered developments, higher densities, and live-work communities move toward such a balance (Rickaby 1987; Commission of the European Communities 1990; Hudson 1991; Van der Ryn and Calthorpe 1991). Some dispute the inherent benefits of the compact city (Breheny 1992). A further complication is that not all economic–environmental conflicts have their roots in spatial or architectural problems. As a result, ostensible solutions may be merely symbols of ecological–economic balance, without actually solving the conflict.

Nevertheless, land-use planning arguably remains the most powerful tool available to planners, who should not worry too much if it does not manage all problems. The trick in resolving environmental conflicts through land-use planning is to reconcile the conflicting territorial logics of human and of natural habitats. Standard real estate development reduces open space to fragmented, static, green islands – exactly what the landscape ecologists deplore as unable to preserve biodiversity. Wildlife roam and migrate, and require large expanses of connected landscape (Hudson 1991). So both the ecological and the economic systems require the interconnectivity of a critical mass of land to be sustainable. Though we live in a three-dimensional world, land is a limited resource with essentially two dimensions (always excepting air and burrowing/mining spaces). The requirement of land's spatial interconnectivity is thus hard to achieve for both systems in one region: the continuity of one system invariably fragments continuity of the other.[10] So the guiding challenge for land-use planning is to achieve simultaneously spatial/territorial integrity for both systems. Furthermore, a sustainable development that aspires to social justice must also find ways to avoid the land-use manifestations of uneven development: housing segregation, unequal property-tax funding of public schools, jobs–housing imbalance, the spatial imbalance of economic opportunity, and unequal access to open space and recreation.

Substantive paths to sustainable development: Bioregionalism

A comprehensive vision of sustainable land use is bioregionalism, both in its 1920s articulation by the Regional Planning Association of America (Sussman 1976) and its contemporary variation (Sale 1985; Andrus et al. 1990; Campbell 1992). The movement's essential belief is that rescaling communities and the economy according to the ecological boundaries of a physical region will encourage sustainability. The regional scale presumably stimulates greater environmental awareness: it is believed that residents of small-scale, self-sufficient regions will be aware of the causes and effects of their environmental actions, thereby reducing externalities. Regions will live within their means, and bypass the environmental problems caused by international trade and exporting pollution.

The bioregional vision certainly has its shortcomings, including the same fuzzy, utopian thinking found in other writing about sustainable development. Its ecological determinism also puts too much faith in the regional "spatial fix": no geographic scale can, in itself, eliminate all conflict, for not all conflict is geographic. Finally, the call for regional self-reliance – a common feature of sustainable development concepts (Korten 1991, p. 184) – might relegate the regional economy to underdevelopment in an otherwise nationally and internationally interdependent world. Yet it can be effective to visualize sustainable regions within an interdependent world full of trade, migration, information flows and capital flows, and to know the difference between *healthy interdependence* and *parasitic dependence*, that is, a dependence on other regions' resources that is equivalent to depletion. Interdependence does not always imply an imbalance of power; nor does self-sufficiency guarantee equality. Finally, the bioregional perspective can provide a foundation for understanding conflicts among a region's interconnected economic, social and ecological networks.

Other substantive paths

One other approach is technological improvement, such as alternative fuels, conservation mechanisms, recycling, alternative materials, and new mass transit design. Stimulated by competition, regulation, or government subsidies, such advances reduce the consumption of natural resources per unit of production and thereby promise to ameliorate conflict over their competing uses, creating a win–win solution. However, this method is not guaranteed to serve those purposes, for gains in conservation are often cancelled out by rising demand for the final products. The overall increase in demand for gasoline despite improvements in automobile fuel efficiency is one example of how market forces can undermine technologically achieved environmental improvements. Nor, importantly, do technological improvements guarantee fairer distribution.

The role of the planner in all these substantive strategies (land use, bioregionalism, technological improvement) is to design outcomes, with less emphasis on the means of achieving them. The environmental ramifications of the solutions are known or at least estimated, but the political means to achieve legitimacy are not. There also is a trade-off between comprehensiveness (bioregions) and short-term achievability (individual technological improvements).

Merging the substantive and procedural

The individual shortcomings of the approaches described above suggest that combining them can achieve both political and substantive progress in the environmental–economic crisis. The most successful solutions seem to undertake several different resolution strategies at once. For example, negotiation among developers, city planners, and land-use preservationists can produce an innovative, clustered design for a housing development, plus a per-unit fee for preserving open space. Substantive vision combined with negotiating skills thus allows planners to create win–win solutions, rather than either negotiating in a zero-sum game or preparing inert, ecotopian plans. This approach is not a distant ideal for planners: they already have, from their education and experience, both this substantive knowledge and this political savvy.

In the end, however, the planner must also deal with conflicts where one or more parties have no interest in resolution. One nonresolution tactic is the NIMBY, Not In My Back Yard, response: a crude marriage of local initiative and the age-old externalizing of pollution. This "take it elsewhere" strategy makes no overall claim to resolve conflict, though it can be a productive form of resistance rather than just irrational parochialism (Lake 1993). Nor does eco-terrorism consider balance. Instead, it replaces the defensive stance of NIMBY with offensive, confrontational, symbolic action. Resolution is also avoided out of cavalier confidence that one's own side can manage the opposition through victory, not compromise ("My side will win, so why compromise?"). Finally, an "I don't care" stance avoids the conflict altogether. Unfortunately, this ostensible escapism often masks a more pernicious NIMBY or "my side will win" hostility, just below the surface.

Planners: Leaders or Followers in Resolving Economic–Environmental Conflicts?

I turn finally to the question of whether planners are likely to be leaders or followers in resolving economic–environmental conflicts. One would think that it would be natural for planners, being interdisciplinary and familiar with the three goals of balancing social equity, jobs, and environmental protection, to take the lead in resolving such conflicts. Of the conflict resolution scenarios mentioned above, those most open to planners' contributions involve the built environment and local resources: land use, soil conservation, design issues, recycling, solid waste, water treatment. Even solutions using the other approaches – environmental economic incentives, political compromise, and environmental technology innovations – that are normally undertaken at the state and federal levels could also involve planners if moved to the local or regional level.

But the planners' position at the forefront of change is not assured, especially if the lead is taken up by other professions or at the federal, not the local, level. The lively debate on whether gasoline consumption can best be reduced through higher-density land uses (Newman and Kenworthy 1989) or through energy taxes (Gordon and Richardson 1990) not only reflected an ideological battle over interpreting research results and the merits of planning intervention, but also demonstrated how local planning can be made either central or marginal to resolving environmental–economic conflicts. To hold a central place in the debate about sustainable development, planners must exploit those areas of conflict where they have the greatest leverage and expertise.

Certainly planners already have experience with both the dispute over economic growth versus equity and that over economic growth versus environmental protection. Yet the development conflict is where the real action for planners will be: seeking to resolve both environmental and economic equity issues at once. Here is where the profession can best make its unique contribution. An obvious start would be for community development planners and environmental planners to collaborate more (an alliance that an internal Environmental Protection Agency memo found explosive enough for the agency to consider defusing it) (Higgins 1993, 1994). One possible joint task is to expand current public–private partnership efforts to improve environmental health in the inner city. This urban-based effort would help planners bypass the danger of environmental elitism that besets many suburban, white-oriented environmental organizations.

If planners move in this direction, they will join the growing environmental justice movement, which emerged in the early 1980s and combined minority community organizing with environmental concerns (Higgins 1993, 1994). The movement tries to reduce environmental hazards that directly affect poor residents, who are the least able to fight pollution, be it the direct result of discriminatory siting decisions or the indirect result of housing and employment discrimination. The poor, being the least able to move away, are especially tied to place and therefore to the assistance or neglect of local planners. Understandably, local civil rights leaders have been preoccupied for so long with seeking economic opportunity and social justice that they have paid less attention to inequities in the local environment. The challenge for poor communities is now to expand their work on the property conflict to address the development conflict as well, that is, to challenge the false choice of jobs over the environment. An urban vision of sustainable development, infused with a belief in social and environmental justice, can guide these efforts.

Yet even with the rising acceptance of sustainable development, planners will not always be able, on their own, to represent and balance social, economic, and environmental interests simultaneously. The professional allegiances, skills, and bureaucracies of the profession are too constraining to allow that. Pretending at all times to be at the center of the planner's triangle will only make sustainability a hollow term. Instead, the trick will be for individual planners to identify their specific loyalties and roles in these conflicts accurately: that is, to orient themselves in the triangle. Planners will have to decide whether they want to remain outside the conflict and act as mediators, or jump into the fray and promote their own visions of ecological-economic development, sustainable or otherwise. Both planning behaviors are needed.

Notes

1. A curious comparison to this equity–environment–economy triangle is the view of Arne Naess (1993), the radical environmentalist who gave Deep Ecology its name in the 1970s, that the three crucial postwar political movements were the social justice, radical environmental, and peace movements, whose goals might overlap but could not be made identical.
2. Perhaps one can explain the lack of a universal conflict in the following way: if our ideas of the economy, equity, and the environment are socially / culturally constructed, and if cultural society is local as well as global, then our ideas are locally distinct rather than universally uniform.
3. For planners, if one is simply "planning for place," then the dispute about suburban housing versus wetlands does indeed reflect a conflict between an economic and an environmental use of a specific piece of land. But if one sees this conflict in light of "planning for people," then the decision lies between differing social groups (e.g., environmentalists, fishermen, developers) and between their competing attempts

to incorporate the piece of land into their system and world view. (This classic planning distinction between planning for people or for place begs the question: Is there a third option, "planning for nonpeople, i.e., nature"?)

4. Schiller, using Kant's logic, recognized 200 years ago this human habit of positing the future on the past: "He thus artificially retraces his childhood in his maturity, forms for himself a *state of Nature* in idea, which is not indeed given him by experience but is the necessary result of his rationality, borrows in this ideal state an ultimate aim which he never knew in his actual state of Nature, and a choice of which he was capable, and proceeds now exactly as though he were starting afresh.... ."

5. Some radical ecologists take this lost world a step further and see it not as a garden, but as wilderness (e.g., Parton 1993).

6. I use the term diaspora to mean the involuntary dispersal of a people from their native home, driven out by a greater power (Hall 1992). The curious nature of the diaspora implied by the environmental world view is that it is ambiguously voluntary: western positivistic thinking is the villain that we developed, but that eventually enslaved us. Then, too, diasporas invariably combine dislocations across both time and space, but the mythic "homeland" of this environmental diaspora is only from an historical era, but from no specific place.

7. The reverse may also not be automatic. David Johns (1992, p. 63), in advocating a broad interspecies equity, reminds us that not all forms of equity go hand-in-hand: "The nature of the linkages between various forms of domination is certainly not settled, but deep ecology may be distinct in believing that the resolution of equity issues among humans will not automatically result in an end to human destruction of the biosphere. One can envision a society without class distinctions, without patriarchy, and with cultural autonomy, that still attempts to manage the rest of nature in utilitarian fashion with resulting deterioration of the biosphere.... . But the end of domination in human relations is not enough to protect the larger biotic community. Only behavior shaped by a biocentric view can do that."

8. The ambiguity of the term sustainable development is therefore not coincidental, given that reasonable people differ on which corner of the triangle is to be "sustained": a fixed level of natural resources? current environmental quality? current ecosystems? a hypothetical pre-industrial environmental state? the current material standards of living? long-term economic growth? political democracy?

9. These issues of language and translation were raised by Ngũgĩ wa Thiong-o and Stuart Hall in separate distinguished lectures at the Center for the Critical Analysis of Contemporary Cultures, Rutgers University (March 31 and April 15, 1993).

10. Conservationists have in fact installed underpasses and overpasses so that vulnerable migrating species can get around highways.

References

Altshuler, Alan. 1965. The Goals of Comprehensive Planning. *Journal of the American Institute of Planning* 31, 3: 186–94.

Andrus, Van, et al., eds. 1990. *Home: A Bioregional Reader*. Philadelphia, PA and Santa Cruz, CA: New Catalyst/New Society.

Barrett, Gary W., and Patrick J. Bohlen. 1991. Landscape Ecology. In *Landscape Linkages and Biodiversity*, edited by Wendy E. Hudson. Washington, DC and Covelo, CA: Island Press.

Beatley, Timothy. 1992. Balancing Urban Development and Endangered Species: The Coachella Valley Habitat Conservation Plan. *Environmental Management* 16, 1: 7–19.

Beltzer, Dena, and Cynthia Kroll. 1986. *New Jobs for the Timber Region: Economic Diversification for Northern California*. Berkeley, CA: Institute of Governmental Studies, University of California.

Bingham, Gail. 1986. *Resolving Environmental Disputes: A Decade of Experience*. Washington, DC: The Conservation Foundation.

Bird, Elizabeth Ann R. 1987. The Social Construction of Nature: Theoretical Approaches to the History of Environmental Problems. *Environmental Review* 11, 4: 255–64.

Breheny, M. J., ed. 1992. *Sustainable Development and Urban Form*. London: Pion.

Bryant, Bunyan, and Paul Mohai, eds. 1992. *Race and the Incidence of Environmental Hazards*. Boulder, CO: Westview Press.

Bullard, Robert D. 1990. *Dumping in Dixie: Race, Class, and Environmental Quality*. Boulder, CO: Westview Press.

Bullard, Robert D., ed. 1993. *Confronting Environmental Racism: Voices from the Grassroots*. Boston, MA: South End Press.

Campbell, Scott. 1992. *Integrating Economic and Environmental Planning: The Regional Perspective*. Working Paper No. 43, Center for Urban Policy Research, Rutgers University.

Clawson, Marion. 1975. *Forests: For Whom and For What?* Washington, DC: Resources for the Future.

Commission of the European Communities. 1990. *Green Paper on the Urban Environment*. Brussels: EEC.

Crowfoot, James E., and Julia M. Wondolleck. 1990. *Environmental Disputes: Community Involvement in Conflict Resolution*. Washington, DC and Covelo, CA: Island Press.

Daly, Herman E. 1991. *Steady State Economics*. 2nd edition, with new essays. Washington, DC and Covelo, CA: Island Press.

Daly, Herman E., and John B. Cobb, Jr. 1989. *For the Common Good: Redirecting the Economy toward Community, the Environment, and a Sustainable Future*. Boston, MA: Beacon Press.

Davidoff, Paul. 1965. Advocacy and Pluralism in Planning. *Journal of the American Institute of Planners* 31, 4: 544–55.

Duerr, Hans Peter. 1985. *Dreamtime: Concerning the Boundary between Wilderness and Civilization*. Oxford: Basil Blackwell.

Elson, Martin J. 1986. *Green Belts: Conflict Mediation in the Urban Fringe*. London: Heinemann.

Fainstein, Susan S., and Norman I. Fainstein. 1971. City Planning and Political Values. *Urban Affairs Quarterly* 6, 3: 341–62.

Foglesong, Richard E. 1986. *Planning the Capitalist City*. Princeton, NJ: Princeton University Press.

Goodland, Robert. 1990. Environmental Sustainability in Economic Development – with Emphasis on Amazonia. In *Race to Save the Tropics: Ecology and Economics for a Sustainable Future*, edited by Robert Goodland. Washington, DC and Covelo, CA: Island Press.

Gordon, Peter, and Harry Richardson. 1990. Gasoline Consumption and Cities – A Reply. *Journal of the American Planning Association*. 55, 3: 342–5.

Hall, Stuart. 1992. Cultural Identity and Diaspora. *Framework* 36.

Harvey, David. 1985. *The Urbanization of Capital*. Baltimore, MD: Johns Hopkins University Press.

Higgins, Robert R. 1993. Race and Environmental Equity: An Overview of the Environmental Justice Issue in the Policy Process. *Polity*, 26, 2 (Winter): 281–300.

Higgins, Robert R. 1994. Race, Pollution, and the Mastery of Nature. *Environmental Ethics*, 16, 3 (Fall): 251–64.

Hoffman, Lily. 1989. *The Politics of Knowledge: Activist Movements in Medicine and Planning*. Albany, NY: SUNY Press.

Howard, Ebenezer. 1965. *Garden Cities of To-Morrow (first published in 1898 as To-Morrow: A Peaceful Path to Real Reform)*. Cambridge, MA: MIT Press.

Hudson, Wendy E., ed. 1991. *Landscape Linkages and Biodiversity*. Washington, DC and Covelo, CA: Island Press.

Jacobs, Harvey. 1989. Social Equity in Agricultural Land Protection. *Landscape and Urban Planning* 17, 1: 21–33.

Johns, David. 1992. The Practical Relevance of Deep Ecology. *Wild Earth* 2, 2.

Korten, David C. 1991. Sustainable Development. *World Policy Journal* 9, 1: 157–90.

Krumholz, Norman, et al. 1982. A Retrospective View of Equity Planning: Cleveland, 1969– 1979, and Comments. *Journal of the American Planning Association* 48, 2: 163–83.

Kumar, Krishan. 1991. *Utopia and Anti-Utopia in Modern Times*. Oxford and Cambridge, MA: Basil Blackwell.

Lake, Robert. 1993. Rethinking NIMBY. *Journal of the American Planning Association* 59, 1: 87–93.

Lee, Robert G., Donald R. Field, and William R. Burch, Jr, eds. 1990. *Community and Forestry: Continuities in the Sociology of Natural Resources*. Boulder, CO: Westview Press.

Lindblom, C. E. 1959. The Science of Muddling Through. *Public Administration Review* 19 (Spring): 79–88.

Marcuse, Peter. 1976. Professional Ethics and Beyond: Values in Planning. *Journal of the American Institute of Planning* 42, 3: 264–74.

McPhee, John. 1989. *The Control of Nature*. New York: Farrar, Straus, Giroux.

Mills, Edwin S. 1978. *The Economics of Environmental Quality*. New York: Norton.

Naess, Arne. 1993. The Breadth and the Limits of the Deep Ecology Movement. *Wild Earth* 3, 1: 74–5.

Newman, Peter W. G., and Jeffrey R. Kenworthy. 1989. Gasoline Consumption and Cities – A Comparison of US Cities with a Global Survey. *Journal of the American Planning Association* 55, 1: 24–37.

Paehlke, Robert C. 1994. Environmental Values and Public Policy. In *Environmental Policy in the 1990s*, 2nd edition, edited by Norman J. Vig and Michael E. Kraft. Washington, DC: Congressional Quarterly Press.

Parton, Glenn. 1993. Why I am a Primitivist. *Wild Earth* 3, 1: 12–14.

Rees, William. 1989. *Planning for Sustainable Development*. Vancouver, BC: UBC Centre for Human Settlements.

Reisner, Marc. 1987. *Cadillac Desert: The American West and its Disappearing Water*. New York: Penguin Books.

Rickaby, P. A. 1987. Six Settlement Patterns Compared. *Environment and Planning B: Planning and Design* 14: 193–223.

Robinson, Kelly. 1993. *The Regional Economic Impacts of Marketable Permit Programs: The Case of Los Angeles*. In *Cost Effective Control of Urban Smog*, Federal Reserve Bank of Chicago (November): 166–88.

Ross, Andrew. 1994. *The Chicago Gangster Theory of Life: Ecology, Culture, and Society*. London and New York: Verso.

Sale, Kirkpatrick. 1985. *Dwellers in the Land: The Bioregional Vision*. San Francisco, CA: Sierra Club Books.

Schiller, Friedrich. 1965. *On the Aesthetic Education of Man* [translated by Reginald Snell]. *Originally published in 1795 as Über die Ästhetische Erziehung des Menschen in einer Reihe von Briefen*. New York: Friedrich Unger.

Sessions, George. 1992. Radical Environmentalism in the 90s. *Wild Earth* 2, 3: 64–7.

Smith, Neil. 1990. *Uneven Development: Nature, Capital and the Production of Space*. Oxford: Blackwell.

Soja, Edward. 1989. *Postmodern Geographies: The Resurrection of Space in Critical Social Theory*. London and New York: Verso.

Susskind, Lawrence, and Jeffrey Cruikshank. 1987. Mediated Negotiation in the Public Sector: The Planner as Mediator. *Journal of Planning Education and Research* 4: 5–15.

Sussman, Carl, ed. 1976. *Planning the Fourth Migration: The Neglected Vision of the Regional Planning Association of America*. Cambridge, MA: MIT Press.

Tuason, Julie A. 1993. *Economic/Environmental Conflicts in 19th-Century New York: Central Park, Adirondack State Park, and the Social Construction of Nature*. Unpublished manuscript, Dept. of Geography, Rutgers University.

Turner, Frederick W. 1983. *Beyond Geography: The Western Spirit Against the Wilderness*. New Brunswick, NJ: Rutgers University Press.

Van der Ryn, Sim, and Peter Calthorpe. 1991. *Sustainable Communities: A New Design Synthesis for Cities, Suburbs and Towns*. San Francisco, CA: Sierra Club Books.

Wiggins, Lyna. 1993. *Geographic Information Systems*. Lecture at the Center for Urban Policy Research, Rutgers University, April 5.

Wilson, Alexander. 1992. *The Culture of Nature: North American Landscape from Disney to the Exxon Valdez*. Cambridge, MA and Oxford: Blackwell.

World Bank. 1989. *Striking a Balance: The Environmental Challenge of Development*. Washington, DC.

World Commission on Environment and Development (The Brundtland Commission). 1987. *Our Common Future*. Oxford: Oxford University Press.

12

Disasters, Vulnerability and Resilience of Cities

Brendan Gleeson

Introduction

In the last week of October 2012 the largest Atlantic storm on record cut a swathe through human affairs. Hurricane Sandy devastated large tracts of the heavily urbanized Atlantic coast of the USA. Its awful finale was the destruction visited on New York City on 29 October. The great citadel of the global economy was breached, its urban fabric engulfed by flooding and torn apart by cataclysmic break-downs in basic infrastructure and services. Many lives were lost, paralysed and immeasurably harmed. The most potent and poignant moment perhaps was the panicked two day closure of the global financial hub, the New York Stock Exchange. Despite its name, Wall Street proved defenceless before a natural tempest that seemed to mock the entire human ascendancy. Nature seemed to scorn the long neoliberal hegemony of the past three decades as the basic machinery of global capitalism was sundered and halted. In the weeks following Sandy, rationing was introduced to control the distribution of basic resources. The invisible hand was never more spectral; the strong arm of state authority ruled the days.

The greatest political event of contemporary liberal democracy, and arguably of world affairs, was buffeted and rebilled by the furies of Sandy. The US Presidential election was made to kneel before an enraged Nature. Chief candidates, President Obama and Governor Romney, had their campaign scripts and electoral possibilities rewritten in the storm and its wake. Lomborg (2012) reported that Sandy was 'the most important factor for 15 per cent of US voters in the US

Original publication details: Gleeson, Brendan. 2014. "Disasters, Vulnerability and Resilience of Cities". In *After Sustainable Cities?* Edited by Mike Hodson and Simon Marvin. Abingdon: Routledge, pp. 10–23. Used with permission from Taylor & Francis Group.

Readings in Planning Theory, Fourth Edition. Edited by Susan S. Fainstein and James DeFilippis.
Editorial material and organization © 2016 John Wiley & Sons, Ltd.
Published 2016 by John Wiley & Sons, Ltd.

Presidential Election a week later'. These effects will long be debated, but one influence was clear—Romney's 'small state' leitmotiv was belittled by natural caprice and human anxiety. His opposition to the Federal Emergency Management Agency (FEMA) was exposed and deposed by the evident necessity of state response in the crisis, and by Obama's deft and decisive leadership. In an electoral contest overshadowed, if not defined, by the extreme libertarianism of the Tea Party movement, Nature it seemed had voted the other way, for the state.

Obama secured a second term, and the American left (using the term advisedly) won the election. Post-election analysis pointed to a failure of conservative politics to grasp the electoral significance of cultural shifts, especially the relentless proportional decline of the traditional 'Anglo demographic'. Radical philosopher Žižek (2012) believes Obama's centrism found the cultural centroid: 'The majority who voted for him were put off by the radical changes advocated by the Republican market and religious fundamentalists'. Reflecting this, the necessity and effectiveness of state emergency response in the moment of the election also evidently played a role in this victory. The broader implications for democracy, however, of this demonstration of state imperative are perhaps less clear.

In terms of magnitude, Sandy surpassed Hurricane Katrina that ravaged New Orleans in 2005. The chaotic, destructive aftermath of Katrina illustrated the social depredations of a weak state response to urban disaster. Local and state capacities were quickly overwhelmed. The globe watched aghast as the city's many black and poor residents were seemingly abandoned by the Bush federal administration, whose reactions seemed marked as much by incompetence as malign neglect.

Sandy's brief but terrible reign provided a striking reinstatement of government authority, and certainly the necessity of a well-resourced and empowered FEMA. Whilst this seems to finally condemn – for now – the 'hands off' Bush response, it does not logically or politically restrict the field of alternatives to progressive models that prioritize the values of urban sustainability, namely social justice, ecological integrity and intergenerational equity. Sandy's conjuring of state power could unleash as many demons as angels. It arguably provides equal grounds for authoritarian – not just democratic – forms of disaster response, and more broadly, urban management. Tellingly, prominent enthusiasts for Obama's strong state response to Sandy included a leading conservative politician, New Jersey Governor Chris Christie, and erstwhile Republican Mayor of New York, Michael Bloomberg.

A 'world at risk' (Beck, 2009) seems increasingly fixed on the spectacles of urban disasters, furnished with great regularity in the past decade. These include Katrina's near annihilation of New Orleans in 2005 and the tsunamis that engulfed parts of Japan in 2010 and which threatened a catastrophic escalation by damaging a nuclear facility at Fukushima. Science continues to debate whether the regular series of natural cataclysms is evidence of global ecological collapse, especially climate warming. But what is not at doubt, as Beck points out, is a progressive and rapid erosion of the human invulnerability bequeathed by the scientific and technical accomplishments of industrial modernity.

The dawning of the risk age (Beck, 1992; Giddens, 1991) has thrown new light, interest and urgency on the heretofore largely technical fields of hazard management (e.g. Showalter and Lu, 2009) and connected these endeavours with the idea of resilience (e.g. Bosher, 2008). Natural hazards are now manifestly connected with, and magnified by, human ambition and prowess. A stark example is the exponential inflation of the potential consequences of the Japanese tsunami by the exposure of nuclear facilities. Whilst global collective response to ecological threat remains elusive, illustrated by the failing Kyoto process, there is increasing manifestation of decisive political and institutional interest in hazards and risks at the meso and local scales, especially through the many fields of urban management that fix on the increasingly compelling, if opaque, object, resilience. A meshing of two distinct urban motifs – disasters and sustainability – seems more and more evident. After Sandy, New York Mayor Michael Bloomberg wrote, 'In just 14 months, two hurricanes have forced us to evacuate neighborhoods – something our city government had never done before. If this is a trend, it is simply not sustainable' (Herper, 2012). The turbulent theme of hazard appears to be breaking upon the long becalmed discourse of urban sustainability. In the face of this, commentary and institutional purpose, not surprisingly, strives for safer shores, the ideal of resilience. In the wake of Katrina, Steiner *et al.* (2006) urged that urban policy chart for 'sustainable resilience'. But what landfall does the vague, if compelling, resilience ideal offer?

The first observation to make of this, and echoing the point above, is that resilience, unlike sustainability, is not an essentially progressive concept. Logically, this construct can be mobilized to support a variety of urban imaginaries, including those with potentially defensive, chauvinistic, Promethean and/or authoritarian values. Less obviously, its deployment by progressive causes may unwittingly free the naturalism and scientism that the construct seems deeply freighted with. Sustainability has long been a windy field of intellectual and political disappointment; its promise never seems to have materialized and asserted itself (Davidson, 2010). Things might now be different. In a world now enthralled and appalled by risk, this may be the setting for a mighty contest between antithetical visions, between a progressive cosmopolitanism that seeks a safer human ecology and a defensive, insular liberalism that, like Prometheus, sees natural necessity only as chains on human ambition (cf. Beck and Grande, 2010).

After decades of Sisyphean effort the 'sustainable city' slides off the stage of human priority or possibility. Its vagaries and breezy possibilities seem manifestly wanting in an age when disasters are visited with vicious suddenness on large urban settings that offer many compounding hazardous possibilities. The need for decisive state response is now apparent but the script for resilience remains largely unwritten. One prospect is that an 'age of disasters' will overshadow the 'age of risk' that Beck (2009) and others speak of. The latter arguably maintains scope for progressive social and state anticipations and responses, accepting, *inter alia*, the precautionary principle that lies at the progressive heart of the sustainability construct. The former opens the way to more reactive, indeed reactionary, governance as emergency response to manifest threats. At the worst, authoritarianism lurks in 'disaster governance', but so do milder regressions that elide the progressive content of sustainability, including anticipatory political economic interventions (limits to growth) and inclusive actions that prioritize the value of human solidarity over group (or city) security. A struggle thus opens for progressive thought and action to define safety as more than survival of the essential, the fittest, the worthiest, the nearest. It seems necessary for this work to usher in new urban models or imaginaries that refuse the regressive lures of isolation, survivalism and fatalism.

This chapter will contribute in a modest way to the work of debating and defining resilience. It takes the risk thesis of Beck (esp. 2009) and his many interlocutors as the setting for consideration of resilience and its allied constructs, such as vulnerability. This is not to supply mere conceptual background; the discussion's guiding premise problematizes autarkic notions of urban resilience. Beck's risk society thesis exposes the bad science and miserable politics that lie behind autarkic enclosure of urban possibility: '… its basic principle is that humanly generated, anticipated threats cannot be restricted either spatially or in social terms' (2009: 81). Cities and human settlements cannot be plucked—ideologically or materially— from the larger human and ecological systems that establish their possibilities and which are saturated, as never before in human history, with risk and perturbation. This necessitates opposition to notions of resilience that posit the containment of endangerment through spatially targeted policy or action. This political ontology resounds with what geographer's once termed 'spatial fetishism' – the granting to space of determining causal powers.

The chapter's main contribution is to essay this view and to point other regressive possibilities that arise from the ever widening institutional and scholarly 'take-up' of the resilience ideal. The principal dangers are the lures of naturalism, and the asocial urban imaginaries that might emerge from renewal of these scientific failings. There is the overarching threat that 'resilient urbanism' aligns all too easily with destructive power structures, such as militarism and the darker prospect of post-democratic capitalism.

The chapter is in two main parts. The first sketches the recent emergence of a human urban age from the risk perspective. The second considers the problems and possibilities that accompany the widening adoption of the resilience construct. The chapter concludes with brief reflections on the challenging, not to say distressing, imperatives for urban governance in an age of risk and surely of species transition.

An Urban Age at Risk

We live in a world at risk. Social and ecological endangerment defines our age as no other. Beck remarks that 'Risks are lurking everywhere' (2009: 13). Whilst social science broadly accepts and debates the idea of an age of global risk (Arnoldi,

2009), the idea is refused in many quarters. Climate sceptics are the most visible denialists but hardly alone. The boldness of denial seems to grow with the scale of risk. One feeds the other, as Beck observes: '… the more emphatically world risk society is denied, the more it becomes a reality. The disregard for globalizing risks aggravates the globalization of risk' (2009: 47).

Following the 2011 Japanese earthquake and tsunami, Boris Johnson, Mayor of London, opined that:

> The most important lesson here is that there are no lessons for human behaviour. There is no rhyme or reason to an earthquake, and we should for once abandon our infantile delusion that we are the cause and maker of everything. (Johnson, 2011)

On the face of it, scientific assessment seemed to support his case. The Japanese quake, horrifying in scale and consequence, was scientifically unremarkable; in the register of expectation. This does not however absolve the errors of refusal. Two considerations suggest lessons are indeed to be drawn from the Japanese catastrophe. The first is the entanglement of natural cataclysm and human self-endangerment in the nuclear reactor breakdowns. Humanity's capacity to magnify natural calamity was underlined again. And the second was that our species' occupation and exploitation of the earth is now so vast and so intensive that almost every natural upheaval is of necessity a human tragedy. The quotidian decision making that drives urbanization ('development') is reshaping natural hazards at the planetary scale: 'In this sense, "pure" natural occurrences are also "risks", because decision-making in world risk society ensures that nature and society are enmeshed' (Beck, 2009: 58).

The age of risk also marks the ascendancy of urbanization. A parade of popular new literature ('urbanology') noisily honks the 'urban age' ideal. These new offerings include *The Triumph of the City* by Harvard economist Ed Glaeser (2011) and *Welcome to the Urban Revolution* by the Canadian urban 'practitioner and thinker' Jeb Brugmann (2009). They tend to varnish one side of the epochal coin – the triumphs and 'challenges' of *homo urbanis* – without much acknowledging, as Beck does, the new plateau of endangerment scaled by human determination.

To acknowledge and adapt Beck, we have crafted an urban world at risk. The project of urbanization began in antiquity and was elevated to species aspiration in the late feudal era. *Stadt luft macht frei* was the first injunction of modernity. The city was the escape raft from a life of servitude and grubbing. Modernization has, however, failed miserably on many accounts and in many quarters, historically and presently. The emergence of a world at risk witnesses simultaneously to the triumphs and malfunctions of modernity. Potency gained, to be sure, but at the cost of species security. For Beck and collaborator Grande, globalized modernity hums with urban disenchantment, especially amongst '… those for whom cosmopolitanism is not a lifestyle choice, but the tragic involuntary condition of the refugee or otherwise dispossessed' (2010: 417). The dispossession and endangerment that define the urban age for many are captured in Davis' (2006) memorable depiction of a 'planet of slums'.

These restless settlements speak of a different urban revolutionary potential; as incubators of counter-reaction within the juggernaut of globalization and modernization. As Beck and Grande put it recently, the accumulating 'collateral damage' of globalization heralds '… a historically new, entangled Modernity which threatens its own foundations' (2010: 410). Whilst the urban revolution thesis (Glaeser; Brugmann) tends towards closure – urbanization as destiny (and salvation) – Beck and Grande insist that Modernity's manifest and complex failures mean that '… we are facing the end of the end of history' (2010: 413).

The contradictions of globalization and cosmopolitanism have fractured the path of modernization, and we face a 'multi-path prospect of modernity' (Beck and Grande, 2010: 420). There is no single urban prospect, but a variety of possible (and surely unknowable) human fates in a world dominated by risks that are escalating in scale and complexity.

Homo urbanis thus has no exemplary capital city: our species exists as '… cosmopolitan communities of fate' (Beck and Grande, 2010: 419). Human connection cannot be explained by appeal to an idealized, enclosable urban diorama. There exists no stable commons of species experience and purpose. The human prospect is a restless field of countervailing threats and possibilities. This is in distinction to Brugmann's view of urban complexity; an increasingly unified urban problematic, complex but driven by common ordering forces: 'We are organizing the planet into a City: into a single, complex, connected, and still very unstable urban system' (2009: ix). The new urbanology tends to emphasize: unity not contradiction; connection not disconnection; certainty not contingency. It warms the grounds for naturalism – a law-bound view of human prospect – and thus the deployment of natural metaphors, such as resilience (of which more later).

By contrast, Beck and Grande stress a unity *through contradiction*, an urban simultaneity through the shared endangerment, 'The world is brought together by global risks (climate change, nuclear threats, financial crisis), the more it is also torn apart by global risks' (Beck and Grande, 2010: 419). In this view, the urban revolution signals a 'Global entanglement and interconnectedness' (ibid.) at multiple spatial scales that defies straightforward abstraction and rule identification. The idea of 'the hidden logic of global urban growth' (Brugmann, 2009: 10) is a ruse that refuses to contemplate the multi-scalar forces – the shifting convergences and contradictions – that are producing an ever larger but increasingly variegated urban system. This is to expose and emphasize the manifest illogicality, including the 'organised irresponsibility' (Beck, 2009: 8), of much that is driving urban change.

None of this is to deny or diminish the significance of underlying structures – notably, capital accumulation and 'neo-liberal urbanism' (Hodson and Marvin 2010a: 21–23) – that are driving contemporary urbanization in erratic ways, producing myriad urban forms and experiences. It vouchsafes the view that the urbanization of capital is a defining feature of mature market societies and of the global economic (dis)order (Harvey, 2010).

The scale, speed and complexity of planetary disorder – human and ecological – move Žižek (2010) to speak of a 'terminal crisis' that looms on the near horizon. 'Four horsemen' drive the present crisis of global capitalism towards apocalypse: worldwide ecological bankruptcy; systemic destabilization of the global economy; biogenetic innovation; and widening social inequalities. The city, a powerful beacon of hope and opportunity through modernization, is now indissolubly linked to natural risk and human endangerment. Hodson and Marvin highlight the 'dual and ambivalent role of the city, as both a victim and cause of global ecological change ...' (2010a: 138). A constant flow of natural and human catastrophes in recent years have underlined the vulnerability of cities to sudden endangerment. The sources of urban crisis are both endogenous and exogenous – a tsunami or flood being an instance of the former; a resource system failure (water, power) representing the latter. The 2005 New Orleans hurricane disaster demonstrated how external natural shocks can engender internal social disorder and systemic breakdown. Beck writes: 'A fateful magnetism exists between poverty, social vulnerability, corruption and the accumulation of hazards ...' (2009: 142).

Cities, the new human homelands, will carry our species through the 'terminal crisis' transition and into what Lovelock (2009) already describes as 'The Next World' – an era much less conducive than now to human flourishing. It may indeed mark our exit from the Anthropocene to a world less tolerant of human existence. Lovelock believes the shift will reduce the world's liveable surface to a few 'lifeboat' regions, which are now the cooler extremes of the globe: '... we have a chance of surviving and even living well. But for that to be possible we have to make our lifeboats seaworthy now' (2009: 22).

Herein lays a tension, perhaps a dilemma, for urban thought in an age of painful global transition. On the one hand, critical social science is correct to insist on the structural origin and global play of threats and crises that manifest at the local or regional scales, for example in urban disasters. This is reinforced by recognition that cosmopolitanism – a world community of fate (Beck, 2006) – is the only scale at which to conceive the transformational politics and actions that must avert catastrophic species crisis ('End Times' – Žižek, 2010). This necessitates ontology of urban conception that rejects localization, enclosure, partiality, and the like, as tropes for understanding the origins of global risk (all are useful, however, for explaining its manifestations and treatments). The science of urban endangerment finds its ontology and methodological markers in the concept of cosmopolitanism as described by Beck: 'a unification enforced by threats is a condition, not a choice' (2009: 198). This is not the hymn of the global village but the sharp refrain that simultaneously captures the political and scientific reality of an urban world at risk – bound, *whether we like it or not*, by perilously disturbed systems, habits, ambitions, ecologies, technologies and structures whose safe resolution cannot be comprehended or achieved through isolated, partial or enclosed actions. Systemic, endemic, planetary work is needed to defray the crisis.

On the other hand, the period of great historical perturbation will be visited upon an urbanized humanity not as global change but as localized stresses and disasters. The climate warming that is 'locked in' for this century alone makes all human settlements vulnerable to some degree. Cities will be the frontlines in disastrous times and must be made as robust as possible and, when overcome, remade and renewed with new purpose. Therefore the necessity of the 'lifeboat' actions urged by Lovelock (2009) and me (Gleeson, 2010) cannot be denied. Nor can the political appeal, indeed necessity, of enclosure, localism, refusal, self-sufficiency and disconnection as values for governance structures that must make their human populations as safe as possible.

How to resolve this dilemma – at once, temporal and spatial? The necessity of fastening the individual urban hatches during a storm, balanced against the need to bring the whole human cargo to the safer common shores we once sketch-mapped as 'sustainability'. Does the construct of resilience—both as necessity and ideal—offer an adaptive means to this resolution? Resilience deployed first as survival, then as arrival—a guiding star for a new urban imaginary? Or is it simply a new marker of popular ambition that merely shifts the larger, unresolved struggles over sustainability to fresh ground?

Resilience and its Discontents

The humble, if unlovely, term 'resilience' has soared to prominence in recent years (Evans, 2011). It has progressively displaced sustainability as the leitmotiv of urban discussion, reflecting the mindset of an epoch ever conscious of vulnerability, and the manifest scale of ecological disruption and threat – especially global warming. Scholarly interest in the resilience construct emerged in systems ecology (e.g. Holling, 1973), foregrounding 'non-linear dynamics of change in complex, linked social-ecological systems' (Wilkinson, 2012: 149). In recent years, and certainly the last decade, resilience theory has recast human ecology as complex, dynamic and adaptive, thus undermining or at least questioning assumptions of stasis and equilibrium that lie at the heart of sustainability constructs (Davidson, 2010).

Scientific displacement of sustainability has been accompanied by rising institutional and popular attachment to the resilience construct. In plain speak, it signifies the imperatives of premonition and pre-emptive response to threats and perturbations. In the language of contemporary policy interest, it evokes the ideal of robustness in the face of shocks and crises thrown up by an increasingly disturbed natural order, and by complex disruptions in human systems such as the global economy. At the same time, it highlights the ability of a context – 'a complex adaptive system' – to recover and respond to external dangers and intrusions (Wilkinson, 2012).

The imperative of pre-emption makes for ready and compelling construct translation to the fields of planning and urban policy (Newman *et al.*, 2009; Pickett *et al.*, 2004). In urban policy fields resilience already seems a commonplace, bridging a complex divide, between the science of natural threat and the socio-political possibilities of institutional response. For example, in its latest urban assessment, the Organisation for Economic Co-operation and Development (OECD) urges 'local governments to build resilience to climate change and low carbon performance into urban infrastructure and development patterns' (Kamal-Chaoui and Sanchex-Reaza, 2012: 143). Various currents of environmental and urban advocacy (e.g. Transition Towns, Permaculture) have applied this ecological metaphor to the dilemmas of the contemporary urban age (also ICLEI, 2009). Within academe, new interdisciplinary networks have emerged to focus on the question of urban and regional resilience – notably, The Building Resilient Regions network and The Resilience Alliance (Evans, 2011). Founded in 2007, the Stockholm Resilience Centre is a new research concentration that distils this ambition.[1]

The new enlistment of resilience in urban policy and theory is potentially transformative of thought and practice. As Davoudi (2012a) maintains, emphasis on resilience and related notions of vulnerability and risk tends to recast understanding of environment in planning. This shift '… portrays the environment not so much in terms of assets to be sustained for human benefit, but in terms of threats against which human well-being should be safeguarded' (Davoudi, 2012a: 49). The re-portrayal of contemporary planning's substrate, the environment, invites progressive work on urban metabolic function[2] that improves comprehension of ecological stresses and possibilities (Baccini, 2007; Giradet, 1999; Kennedy *et al.*, 2011) – though this 'improved science' in turn necessitates re-inscription of political ecology (Heynen *et al.*, 2006; Swyngedouw and Heynen, 2003). It also, however, provides new grounds for encounter and possibly joined purpose between urban policy and security policy frames (Coaffee and O'Hare, 2008; Coaffee *et al.*, 2009). The 'common policy cause' lies in the terrifying and terrorizing currents of politico-cultural reaction that have used cities as potent sites to attack Western modernization (Pasman and Kirillov, 2007). The new urban enthusiasm for resilience is matched by security policy and politics that deploy the marker with increasing frequency – for example the UK Conservative Party's 2010 Green Paper, *A Resilient Nation* (Conservative Party, 2010).

Whilst resilience has gained currency across a range of disciplinary and policy areas from international relations to engineering and from global agencies to local government, its broad use belies clarity and specificity. In 2000, Adger ventured that 'its meaning and measurement are contested' (2000: 347), and this assessment arguably still holds. It is far from clear whether the term resilience enjoys a shared understanding within academic disciplines and policy areas and also between them (Davidson, 2010). This increasingly powerful but protean idea could mask any amount of inconsistency and illusion. Its inherent naturalism, and also appeal to security thought and politics, raises concerning prospects for critical social science, whose central precepts are anti-naturalism, and an expansive notion of human flourishing (see Sayer, 2011).

There is an evident need, therefore, to open up these different understandings of resilience both within and between different disciplinary and policy contexts and to understand the resonances and dissonances between them. Unpacking this also requires improved understanding of the urban politics of resilience, the issues that become mobilized as crises or shocks and the forms of knowledge and social interests that constitute such responses (Cote and Nightingale, 2011). It also necessitates recognition of the variability of resilience applications and responses across the diverse phenomenon described by 'urbanisation'. Actually existing urbanization cannot be summarized or ordained by recourse to a unifying model. Contemporary urbanization wears many faces. The phenomenon none-theless faces a set of common threats which beg a unifying, if multivalent, frame of analysis. Vulnerability is apparent, but this is a broad marker for the *unevenly distributed* threats emerging from an increasingly chaotic, feedback ridden 'world system'.

The new social scientific enthusiasm for resilience flags the danger of common-sensical application; viz., the transposition of a scientific concept across disciplinary understandings through the medium of conventional wisdom (especially in policy). Has the rapid take-up of the resilience marker in urban environmental advocacy short circuited the critical adjudicative processes that normally filter the movement of concepts across scientific fields? This question is especially acute considering a conceptual transposition from physical science to social science, where a century of debate has marked out the pitfalls of determinism and empiri-cism that face such a journey. In urban studies, the social ecology of the Chicago School was an early warning of the hazards of biological reductionism and the mechanization of social change. A recent issue of the authoritative *Nature* journal foregrounded urban ecological analysis ('cities under the microscope') 'in which scientists study cities as if they were ecosystems' (Humphries, 2012: 514). Two years previously it had reported work by physicists that sought nothing less than 'A unified theory of urban living' (Bettencourt and West, 2010). One senses in this new scientific ambition the spectre of Chicago School urbanism and its (discred-ited) postulation of a 'natural spatial order' (Jackson and Smith, 1984).

As Simmie and Martin observe (with considerable understatement) 'there are issues about abducting a model from one disciplinary field … to another …' (2010: 42). Historically, such 'abduction' has been the principal means through which naturalism and scientism have made incursions into social science (Sayer, 2009). It is surely necessary and timely to debate the risks of 'model transposition' in the field of urban studies where resilience thinking now has a wide hold, including in areas of policy and advocacy interface. Does the application of resilience, and its kindred constructs (vulnerability, evolution, adaptability), raise the spectre of naturalism and reaction in social science, in particular the cross-disciplinary field of urban studies? Are regressive and exclusionary resiliences possible – for example, the idea of bounded communities where the needs of elites are protected from wider system malfunction?

Hodson and Marvin (2010a) speak of the new 'premium ecological communities' and of 'urban ecological security' as a new paradigm of resilience. The 'Charter Cities' championed by the US economist Paul Romer are redolent with refusal – of wider human solidarity, of equality, of justice. Chakrabortty (2010) scorns the concept for its inherent colonialism, authoritanrianism and social inequity. Romer is attracted to the ideas of the influential physicist, Geoffrey West,[3] whose work on 'superlinear cities' has raised the spectre of naturalism again in urban studies and policy (see Gleeson, 2012). A regressive confluence of authoritarian inequity and scientific positivism seems suggested by these encounters and take-ups. Several fundamental questions emerge for contemporary critical social science. Can the resilience construct meaningfully accommodate and deploy the question of justice? The inequity of exposure, of vulnerability, is doubtless the first human question for resilience. Beck: 'A fateful magnetism exists between poverty, social vulnerability, corruption and the accumulation of hazards' (2009: 142). Can the concept be reconciled to the variegation of human need, identity and aspiration? To the growing asymmetries within and between cities?

Resilience has emancipatory potential if positioned within the guiding idea of human flourishing that Sayer (2011) insists is axiomatic to critical social science. What is it that we wish to protect, make strong and adaptive? To the point, *which* social and ecological relationships are worthy of protection? Shocks and stress have the potential to bring the questions of solidarity and cooperation, surely keystones of flourishing, to the fore, as illustrated in times of war. In such instances they strengthened not eroded collective resolve for improvement in the post-crisis phase, exemplified in the social democratic reform surge that followed the Second World War in the West and in the struggles for liberation from colonialism in the global south. Stretton (2005) argues that a great lesson of modern history is the salience of equity and solidarity as guiding values for institutional and political action in times of threat and perturbation. They do not impart complete immunity – the Parisian Communards bickered and before too long succumbed to superior, overwhelming external forces.

Nonetheless, solidarity and deliberation stand in contrast to the deadening consensus insisted upon by scientism – a society that takes science as its universal moral and political guide. Authoritarianism has a poor record. Tyrants have fallen with their cities. But its appeal may be strengthening in the unsettled mists of the risk society. Beck grimly offers: 'when people are confronted with the alternative "Freedom or security", a large majority of them seem to prefer security, even if that means curtailing or even suppressing liberties' (2009: 61). It is vital that resilience – an ideal of strength – be steered well clear of the shoals of authoritarianism.

This is the warning testimony of history. Its lessons can be taken up in the quest for resilience. The hard work of grounding the concept in the deeper epistemologies and methodologies of critical social science cannot be avoided or shortchanged. The wider risks and fallacies of naturalistic social science have been well rehearsed (Barnes, 2009). They include cloaking ('naturalizing') the human play of power under the cover of science. This has the consequence of depoliticizing social conduct, surrendering it to the inevitability of natural law. None of this is to deny or diminish the profound necessity of translating natural science to human science,[4] but to highlight the danger of transliteration.

In a recent assessment, Evans points out that resilience thinking tends to highlight the 'un-plannability' of cities and cites its wider potential to 'depoliticise urban transition ... by constraining governance within a technocratic mode that remains inured to the tropes of scientific legitimacy' (2011: 232–3). If left to natural interpretation alone, the tropes of evolution and equilibrium suggest a law-bound urban ecology that makes social intervention meaningless or self-defeating. Policy may be confined to maintenance of a naturalized urban order. Naturalism, of course, disavows and therefore misrepresents human agency and social possibility. For Davidson (2010), the inability of resilience discourse and policy to – as yet – account for human agency is its greatest failure and the deepest source of her 'nagging doubts' about its wider human deployment. It seems that the stubborn human capacity for autonomy and refusal – even in the face of natural ordination – is the greatest obstacle to any straightforward or unalloyed application of resilience thinking to collective action. Of course, the danger is that political and policy wisdom will simply ignore this obstacle by erasing the fact of individual and collective agency. Worse, faced with this stubborn reality, it might resort to authoritarianism to reduce or suppress its 'inconveniences'.

It would be wrong, however, to underline only ambiguities, weaknesses and dangers. The progressive potential of resilience and vulnerability should not be discounted. It can be summarized as the ability to disrupt the static, equilibrium-focused accounts of the human order, such as neo-classical economics, that have so demonstrably failed to account for natural ontology, human evolution and, in recent history, the ruinous 'progress' of neoliberalism (Harvey, 2010). The construct relentlessly exposes idealism in theory and practice, including, arguably, hyper-conceptualized planning debates that neglect or avoid the question of human ecology (Davoudi, 2012b). Resilience also insists that the future is accounted and prepared for, not discounted through econocratic reason or trivialized through technocratic hubris. Its dynamic, adaptive view of history sits well with a progressive view that humanity is engaged in a massive project of co-evolution with nature, for which we bear responsibility as contributing authors of planetary fate.

As related earlier, realization of this emancipatory human potential rests at least partly on the work of scientific disclosure and interrogation of the resilience construct. The risks of concept 'abduction' by policy and politics have been essayed. Given the rapid deployment of resilience, it seems urgent that social science addresses the tasks of concept examination and translation before it is sidelined or short circuited in a world imperilled by risk and grasping for new answers.

Conclusion

Watching Sandy's devastation from Sydney, Australia, former New York Mayor, Rudy Giuliani, was concerned but reassuring: this was '… New York City, where resiliency is written in capital letters …' (McKenny, 2012). The world's urban leadership may not be so sanguine. In November 2012, the World Bank released a profoundly disconcerting assessment of climate change, *Turn Down the Heat*, which demonstrated that cities will directly bear the full brunt of inevitable warming through increased heat stress, flood inundation and radically unsettled weather (World Bank, 2012). As always with human prospects, the effects of change will be unevenly distributed, socially and geographically – manifestly through the global urban system:

> Of the impacts projected for 31 developing countries, only ten cities account for two-thirds of the total exposure to extreme floods. Highly vulnerable cities are to be found in Mozambique, Madagascar, Mexico, Venezuela, India, Bangladesh, Indonesia, the Philippines, and Vietnam. (ibid.: 34)

In short, the mega cities of the global south lie perilously in the path of the scourges promised by climate warming.

Given the World Bank's status as neoliberal bastion, it is worth noting the report has two important progressive postulates. First, it attempts to turn us into the storm, urging global action to stop it, not just deflect its consequences. Its sub-title insists that 'A … warmer world must be avoided', thereby demanding major – indeed unprecedented – global action to fundamentally change ('de-carbonize') economy, governance and civil society. This refuses the path to policy retreat to adaptation, and 'hunkered down' resilience. Second, the World Bank instates social justice as a leading trope for climate response. Launching the report, World Bank president, Jim Yong Kim, stated:

> We will never end poverty if we don't tackle climate change. It is one of the single biggest challenges to social justice today. … It is likely that the poor will suffer most and the global community could become more fractured and unequal than today. (Arup, 2012)

Turn Down the Heat deploys and defines resilience in a specific way—speaking exclusively of the danger to eco-system resilience represented by climate change. Resilience is not offered as an overarching policy goal, or as the defining quality of a new urban imaginary. The World Bank, at least in this instance, sides with sustainability and its subsidiary constructs such as equity and inclusion, and norms such as 'green growth' and 'poverty alleviation'. Its public is the 'global community', not urban leaders (see World Bank 2012: ix).

Perhaps global institutions will be the last to use resilience in autarkic ways that refuse cosmopolitanism – the idea of common species fate and purpose. Hand in hand with this premise is recognition of the need for structural transformation to address the sources of global endangerment – including a crisis-prone political economy, uneven development, carbon capitalism, militarism and xenophobia (Harvey, 2010; Žižek, 2010). Finally, perhaps progressive sentiment in global institutional policy discussion gives hope of foreclosing on the 'age of disasters' scenario alluded to in the Introduction. Cosmopolitanism of this kind, as advocated by Beck (2009), sees the new 'human proximities' that characterize our age as affirmation of species interdependence and solidarity. It tends to disavow, if sometimes only by implication, the defensive, authoritative urbanism that 'disaster governance' seems ready to usher on to the stage of urban action. This reactionary prospect threatens a final elision of the already weakened, overdetermined sustainability construct, and its assumed attachment to progressive ideals, such as precautionary action and social solidarity.

Such progressive sentiments, and thus resources, seem absent, however, from much global commentary. Amongst the many experts venturing opinion in the wake of Sandy, was 'sceptical environmentalist' Bjorn Lomborg (2012). Lomborg denied any scientific link between this 'Frankenstorm' and global warming, and he may be right. The sceptic, however, used the moment to prosecute his larger, well-known case that fighting global warming 'just isn't worth it'. Better, apparently, to spend policy effort and fiscal resources on defence and adaptation. In the case of New York, 'Much of the risk could be managed by erecting seawalls, building storm doors for the subway, and simple fixes such as porous footpaths – all at a [bargain?] cost of about $US100 million a year' (ibid.).

Considering the global crisis, well-known progressive urbanist Mike Davis (2010) asks 'who will prepare the ark?'. His answer does not align, to put it mildly, with the econocratic prescriptions of Lomborg. The ark metaphor suggests something that bears human hope, as much as human bodies, through the storms of change about to break across the Earth. Its biblical metaphor is a vessel that preserves everything we can ('two of everything') in the journey to safer, saner shores; that is, not just the things that survive cost–benefit analysis. It accepts that humanity brought this catastrophe down on its own head and must as a species take up the burden of survival.

But what are the shores of human prospect? Where is the new urban imaginary that transcends the survivalism beckoned by resilience thinking? In planning debate, Albrecht (2010) asks for transformative urban action to avert the human crisis. Albrecht recognizes that transformation will not occur without new guiding stars. And yet, he calls to a fractured heaven: the cosmopolitan city (Sandercock, 1998); the just city (Fainstein, 2011); the green city (Low *et al.*, 2004); the rebellious city (Harvey, 2012) – *disjecta membra* of progressive urban thought that float outside the popular consciousness. They are powerful, estimable pages of a new urban testimony. But how to bind them in an imaginary that refuses the doom of a darkening human ecology? To restate Davis and to challenge urban theory, who will build the ark?

Notes

1. www.stockholmresilience.org/
2. Anticipated by Wolman (1965).
3. See Geoffrey West's comments on Romer at: http://blog.ted.com/2011/07/26/ qa-with-geoffrey-west/. Accessed 22 November 2012.
4. And of course vice versa.

References

Adger, N. (2000) 'Social and ecological resilience: are they related?', *Progress in Human Geography*, 24, 347–64.

Albrecht, L. (2010) 'More of the same is not enough! How could strategic spatial planning be instrumental in dealing with the challenges ahead?', *Environment and Planning B*, 37, 1115–27.

Arnoldi, J. (2009) *Risk*, Polity, Cambridge.

Arup, T. (2012) 'Catastrophic warming to hit poor, says World Bank', *Sydney Morning Herald*, 20 November. Available at: http://www.smh.com.au/data-point/catastrophic-warming-to-hit-poor-says-world-bank-20121119-29m9b.html (accessed 1 August 2015).

Baccini, P. (2007) 'A city's metabolism: Towards the sustainable development of urban systems', *Journal of Urban Technology*, 4(2), 27–39.

Barnes, T. (2009) 'Positivism' in Gregory, D., Johnston, R., Pratt, G., Watts, M. and Whatmore, S. (eds) *The Dictionary of Human Geography*, 5th edn, Wiley-Blackwell, Chichester, 557–9.

Beck, U. (1992) *Risk Society: Towards a New Modernity*, Sage, London.

Beck, U. (2006) *Cosmopolitan Vision*, Polity Press, Cambridge.

Beck, U. (2009) *World at Risk*, Polity Press, Cambridge.

Beck, U. and Grande, E. (2010) 'Varieties of second modernity: the cosmopolitan turn in social and political theory and research', *British Journal of Sociology*, 61 (3), 409–43.

Bettencourt, L. and West, G. (2010) 'A unified theory of urban living', *Nature* 467, 912–13.

Bosher, L. (ed.) (2008) *Hazards and the Built Environment: Attaining Built-in Resilience*, Routledge, London.

Brugmann, J. (2009) *Welcome to the Urban Revolution*, University of Queensland Press, St. Lucia (also Bloomsbury Press USA).

Chakrabortty, A. (2010) 'Paul Romer is a brilliant economist – but his idea for charter cities is bad', *The Guardian* (UK), 27 July.

Christopherson, S., Michie, J. and Tyler, P. (2010) 'Regional resilience: theoretical and empirical Perspectives', Cambridge Journal of Regions, *Economy and Society 2010*, 3, 3–10.

Coaffee, J. and O'Hare P. (2008) 'Urban resilience and national security: the role for planners', *Proceeding of the Institute of Civil Engineers: Urban Design and Planning*, 161 (DP4) 171–82.

Coaffee J., O'Hare P. and Hawkesworth M. (2009) 'The visibility of (in)security: The aesthetics of planning urban defences against terrorism', *Security Dialogue*, 40 (4–5) 489–511.

Cote, M. and Nightingale, A. (2011) 'Resilience thinking meets social theory: situating social change in socio-ecological systems (SES) research', *Progress in Human Geography*, 36(4), 475–89.

Davidson, D. (2010) 'The applicability of the concept of resilience to social systems: some sources of optimism and nagging doubts', *Society and Natural Resources*, 23(10), 1135–49.

Davis, M. (2010) 'Who will build the ark?', *New Left Review*, 61, 10–25.

Davis, M. (2006) *Planet of Slums*, Verso, London.

Davoudi, S. (2012) 'Climate risk and security: New meanings of 'the environment' in the English planning system', *European Planning Studies*, 20(1), 49–69.

Evans, J.P. (2011) 'Resilience, ecology and adaptation in the experimental city', *Transactions of the Institute of British Geographers*, 36, 223–37.

Fainstein, S. (2011) *The Just City*, Cornell University Press, Ithaca, NY.

Giddens, A. (1991) *Modernity and Self-Identity. Self and Society in the Late Modern Age*, Polity, Cambridge.

Giradet, H. (1999) *Creating Sustainable Cities*, Green Books, Totnes, Devon UK.

Glaeser, E. (2011) *The Triumph of the City: How Our Greatest Invention Makes Us Richer, Smarter, Greener, Healthier, and Happier*, Penguin, Harmondsworth.

Gleeson, B.J. (2010) *Lifeboat Cities*, UNSW Press, Sydney.

Gleeson, B.J. (2012) 'The Urban Age: paradox and prospect', *Urban Studies*, 49 (5), 1–13.

Harvey, D. (2010) *The Enigma of Capital*, Profile Books, London.

Harvey, D. (2012) *Rebel Cities*, Verso, London.

Herper, M. (2012) 'Michael Bloomberg endorses Barack Obama because of climate change'. Available at: www.forbes.com/sites/matthewherper/2012/11/01/michael-bloomberg-endorses-obama-because-of-climate-change/ (accessed 14 November 2012).

Henynen, N., Kaika, M. and Swyngedouw, E. (eds) (2006) *In the Nature of Cities: Urban Political Ecology and the Politics of Urban Metabolism*, Routledge, London.

Hodson, M. and Marvin, S. (2010) *World Cities and Climate Change: Producing Urban Ecological Security*, McGraw Hill, Open University Press, Maidenhead, UK.

Holling, C.S. (1973) 'Resilience and stability of ecological systems', *Annual Review of Ecology and Systematics*, 4, 1–23.

Humphries, C. (2012) 'Life in the concrete jungle', *Nature*, 491, 514–15.

ICLEI (2009) *Resilient Communities and Cities Initiative*, ICLEI – World Secretariat, Toronto.

Jackson, P. and Smith, S. (1984) *Exploring Social Geography*, George Allen and Unwin, London.

Johnson, B. (2011) 'Japan earthquake: Many are the terrors of the earth, but they're not our fault', *The Telegraph* (UK), 14 March.

Kamal-Chaoui, L. and Sanchex-Reaza, J. (eds) (2012) *Urban Trends and Policies in OECD Countries*, OECD Regional Development Working Papers, 2012/01, OECD Publishing, Paris.

Kennedy, C., Pincetl, S., and Bunje, P. (2011) 'The study of urban metabolism and its applications to urban planning and design', *Environmental Pollution*, 159, 1965–73.

Lomborg, B. (2012) 'Simple solutions to Superstorm Sandy', *The Australian*, 19 November.

Lovelock, J. (2009) *The Vanishing Face of Gaia: A Final Warning*, Allen Lane, London.

Low, N.P., Gleeson, B.J., Radovic, D. and Green, R. (2004) *The Green City*, UNSW Press, Sydney, and Routledge, London.

McKenny, L. (2012) 'New Yorkers write resiliency in capital letters: Giuliani', *The Sydney Morning Herald*, 31 October.

Newman, P., Beatley, T. and Boyer, H. (2009) *Resilient Cities: Responding to Peak Oil and Climate Change*, Island Press, Washington DC.

Pasman, H. and Kirillov, I.A. (eds) (2007) *Resilience of Cities to Terrorist and other Threats. Learning from 9/11 and further Research Issues*, NATO Science for Peace and Security Series, Springer, Dordrecht, The Netherlands.

Pelling, M. (2003) *The Vulnerability of Cities: Natural Disaster and Social Resilience*, Earthscan, London.

Pickett, S.T.A., Cadenasso, M.L. and Grove, J.M. (2004) 'Resilient cities: meaning, models, and metaphor for integrating the ecological, socio-economic, and planning realms', *Landscape and Urban Planning*, 69, 369–84.

Sandercock, L. (1998) *Towards Cosmopolis: Planning for Multicultural Cities*, John Wiley, London.

Sayer, A. (2011) *Why Things Matter to People: Social Science*, Values and Ethical Life, Cambridge University Press, Cambridge.

Showalter, P.S. and Lu, Y. (eds) (2009) *Geospatial Techniques in Urban Hazard and Disaster Analysis*, Springer.

Simmie, J. and Martin, R. (2010) 'The economic resilience of regions: towards an evolutionary approach', *Cambridge Journal of Regions, Economy and Society*, 3, 27–43.

Steiner, F., Faga, B., Sipes, J. and Yaro, R. (2006) 'Mapping for sustainable resilience', in Birch, E. and Wachter, S. (eds) *Rebuilding Urban Places After Disaster: Lessons from Hurricane Katrina*, University of Pennsylvania Press, PA, 66–77.

Stretton, H. (2005) *Australia Fair*, New South Press, Sydney.

Swyngedouw, E. and Heynen, N. (2003) 'Urban political ecology, justice and the politics of scale', *Antipode*, 35, 898–918.

Wilkinson, C. (2011) 'Social-ecological resilience: Insights and issues for planning theory', *Planning Theory*, 11(2), 148–69.

Wolman, A. (1965) 'The metabolism of cities', *Scientific American*, 213(3), 179–90.

World Bank, The (2012) *Turn Down the Heat*, The World Bank, Washington DC.

Žižek, S. (2012) 'Why Obama is more than Bush with a human face', *The Guardian*, 13 November.

Žižek, S. (2010) *Living in the End Times*, Verso, London.

13

Spatial Justice and Planning

Susan S. Fainstein

The traditional argument for spatial planning is that it incorporates the public interest into the development of land by suppressing selfish actions and coordinating multiple activities (Klosterman 2003, p. 93). This justification has long elicited criticism for its vagueness (Lucy 2003), a problem that perhaps afflicts any higher-order norm and which will not be elaborated here.[1] Instead I examine its interpretation in contemporary planning practice. I proceed by first discussing the currently dominant direction in planning theory that stresses public participation and deliberation. Next I compare it to the just city approach and elaborate on the latter, evaluating planning in New York City, London, and Amsterdam. In conclusion, I list criteria of justice by which to formulate and judge planning initiatives at the urban level. It is assumed that social justice is a desired goal, and no argument is presented to justify its precedence. Rather, as in the work of John Rawls (1971, p. 4), my argument is based on "our intuitive conviction of the primacy of justice" and also the dictum that disagreement is over the principles that should define what is just and unjust rather than the precedence of justice itself (ibid. p. 5).

Communicative Planning and the Just City

In order to overcome the bias in favor of powerful social groups, an emphasis on democratic deliberation has become central to discussions within planning theory. In this respect it echoes the enormous interest within political philosophy in forms

Original publication details: Fainstein, Susan S. 2013. "Spatial justice and planning".
In *Justice spatiale et politiques territoriales, collection Espace et Justice*, edited by Frédéric Dufaux and Pascale Philifert. Nanterre: Presses Universitaires de Paris-Ouest, pp. 249–88.

of democracy that transcend mere voting and representative government. This direction has evolved out of disillusion with the authoritarian tendencies of socialism as it had really existed, leading to a focus on just processes rather than egalitarian outcomes. It arose also in response to the rise of democratic movements throughout the world. It is premised on the assumption that in a democracy each person's view and opportunity to persuade others should be equal.

Democratic thought arises fundamentally from egalitarianism. Nevertheless, although nineteenth century critics of democracy feared that democratic procedures would be used to expropriate property owners, the underlying egalitarian impetus rarely results in drastic attacks on property within capitalist democracies. While democratic states can tax and redistribute, they remain always susceptible to the hierarchy of power arising from capitalist control of economic resources. When pressed, advocates of deliberative democracy will admit that it operates poorly in situations of social and economic inequality and contend that background conditions of equal respect and undistorted speech must be created in order for it to function well. Yet, oddly, discussions within political theory and within planning focus on democratic procedures and fail to indicate how these background conditions can be attained under conditions of market capitalism. To put this in other words, the discussion is purely political rather than political-economic. Thus, the tension between an equality of primary goods and political equality arises from practical rather than logical contradiction; while in theory a mobilized demos could produce economic redistribution, in actuality economic inequality constantly produces and reproduces hierarchies of power that preclude genuine deliberation.

Since the 1960s, the legitimacy of insulated technocratic decision making by planning authorities has been challenged, citizen participation in planning has become widely accepted, and concepts of deliberative democracy have been imported into planning theory. J.S. Mill's (1951, p. 108) argument concerning the importance of testing ideas against each other provides the rationale for wide participation in planning deliberations: "He [a human being] is capable of rectifying his mistakes, by discussion and experience. [...] There must be discussion, to show how experience is to be interpreted." Supporters of communicative planning are committed to Mill's emphasis on discursive interaction as the basis for planning practice and as the appropriate means for actualizing the public interest.

By now there is little more to say in relation to the debate between proponents of communicative (or collaborative) planning and their detractors. In a nutshell the advocates of a Habermasian or deliberative approach argue that the role of planners is to listen, especially to listen to subordinated groups. Acting as a mediator, the planner must search for consensus and in doing so accept a plurality of ways of knowing, of self-expression (stories, art, etc.), and of truth (Forester 1999; Healey 1997; Innes 1995; Hoch 2007).[2] Criticism of this outlook is not anti-democratic but rather contends that it is a proceduralist approach which fails to take into account the reality of structural inequality and hierarchies of power (Fainstein 2000a;

Yiftachel 1999; H. Campbell 2006). Furthermore, the exclusive focus on process prevents an evaluation of substance and thus cannot promise just outcomes (Fainstein 2005a).

The crux of the debate rests on the ever-present tension between democracy and justice in an existing historical context. After deliberation people may still make choices that are harmful to themselves or to minorities. As Nussbaum (2000, p. 135) notes, the "informed-desire approach ... [depends on] the idea of a community of equals, unintimidated by power or authority, and unaffected by envy or fear inspired by awareness of their place in a social hierarchy." In other words, genuine democratic deliberation requires background conditions of equality. Marx's concept of false consciousness, in which unequal social relations structure people's perceptions, and Gramsci's description of a hegemonic ideology, come into play even in situations where individuals are free to express their thoughts to each other.[3] The original notion that planners could be above the political fray and make decisions based on an abstract formulation of the public interest arose from a perception that the public would choose policies based on short-range selfish considerations rather than long-range contributions to the general good. While this viewpoint obviously can provide a rationale for authoritarianism and privileging of elite interests, at the same time it cannot be dismissed. Citizens like elites can be self-serving, as the prevalence of NIMBYism within forums of popular participation indicates.

Calls for more democratic governance raise Nussbaum's concern over background conditions for deliberation and Mill's worry over the tyranny of the majority. Demands that justice be the primary consideration for policy makers, however, are countered on the left by Marxist admonitions against revisionism – i.e., the impossibility of genuine reform under capitalism, since capitalism necessarily continuously reproduces inequality. Both prescriptions – of communicative planning (as measured by comparisons to Habermas's ideal speech situation or by openness to collaboration[4]) and of the just city[5] (as measured by equity of outcomes)—provoke accusations of hopeless utopianism. The ideal speech situation assumes a world without systematic distortions of discourse, governed by rationality. As transferred to the schema of collaborative planning, participants are expected to redefine their interests as a consequence of hearing other viewpoints. But, although such flexibility may occur in some contexts, it is highly unlikely in those where substantial sacrifice would result. At the same time, the vision of the just city calls for rectifying injustices in a world where control of investment resources by a small stratum constantly re-creates and reinforces subordination, thus resisting attempts at reform. In sum, advocates of strong democracy consider participation a prerequisite to just outcomes; structuralists regard participants in democratic deliberation as doomed to being either disregarded or co-opted but offer only limited hope that structural power can be overcome.

Nevertheless, utopian goals, despite being unrealizable, have important functions in relation to people's consciousness (Friedmann 2000, Harvey 2000). Right now, in most parts of the world, the dominant ideology involves the superiority of the market as decision maker, growth rather than equity as the mark of achievement, and limits on government (Klein 2007). To the extent that justice can be brought in as intrinsic to policy evaluation, the content of policy can change. If justice is considered to refer not only to outcomes but also to inclusion in discussion, then it incorporates the communicative viewpoint as well. Justice, however, requires more than participation but also encompasses, at least minimally, a deontological reference to norms transcending the particular, as will be discussed below.

For both theories of deliberative democracy and social justice, scale presents an important problem. In terms of democratic participation, any deliberation that excludes people who will be affected by a decision is not fair. Yet, as a matter of practicality inclusion of everyone affected, even with the potential offered by telecommunications and information technology, would make decision making either impossibly tedious or simply untenable. Questions of scale are particularly salient to planning, as the presence of jurisdictional boundaries typically limits planning decisions to relatively small places. A decision by the occupants of a gated community to lobby against construction of recreational facilities by the municipality to which they belong may be perfectly democratic and equitable within the community's boundaries while being undemocratic and unjust within the larger entity. Likewise competitive bidding among cities for industry can fulfill democratic and egalitarian norms within each city but undermine both on the scale of the nation. And, most glaringly, barriers to immigration and subsidies to enterprises by wealthy national governments are exclusionary and unjust in relation to inhabitants of other, poorer countries. Yet, in regard to social justice, the elimination of protective tariffs, subsidies, and restrictions on immigration can result in impoverishing everyone, as a completely unhindered flow of labor and capital exacerbates the race to the bottom already underway. If one turns to the specific production of plans and policies, it must occur within formal institutions with delimited boundaries in a restricted time period.

In summary both the communicative and just city models run counter to the unequal distribution of power and resources within modern, capitalist economies and are hence utopian. Both represent attempts to reframe discussion about spatial planning so that poorly represented groups, especially low-income minorities, will benefit more from the uses to which land and the built environment are put. The dilemmas posed by issues of scale confront the two of them. It is maintained here that the just city model subsumes the communicative approach in that it is concerned with both processes and outcomes but that it also recognizes the potential for contradiction between participation and just outcomes. Although the attainment of social justice must take both into account, it is my contention that just outcomes should trump communicative norms when the two conflict. In the next section three components of a just city – material equality, diversity, and democracy – are presented, as well as the tensions among and within them;[6] these are then used to analyze and prescribe approaches to spatial planning in three cities – New York, London, and Amsterdam.

Planning for the Just City

The modern approach to the question of justice usually starts with John Rawls's argument concerning the distribution of values that people would pick in the original position, wherein, "behind a veil of ignorance," they do not know their ultimate attributes and social standing. Rawls, using a model of rational choice, concludes that individuals would choose a system of equal opportunity, which, he says in his most recent formulation, involves "a framework of political and legal institutions that adjust the long-run trend of economic forces so as to prevent excessive concentrations of property and wealth, especially those likely to lead to political domination" (Rawls 2001, p. 44). The metric for equality of opportunity is share of primary goods, which Rawls defines to include self-respect as well as wealth.

There have been innumerable discussions of the meaning of primary goods and the relationship between equality of opportunity and equality of condition. If Rawls's conception of justice is applied to the city, fair distribution of benefits and mitigating disadvantage should be the aims of public policy. Rawls's use of the phrase "prevent excessive concentrations of property and wealth" implies a realistic utopianism – the expectation is not of eliminating material inequality but rather of lessening it. Thus, the criterion for evaluating policy measures, according to Rawlsian logic, is to insure that they most benefit the least well off. This principle, as indicated earlier, exists in tension with a democratic norm under the circumstances of illiberal majorities.

Feminist and multiculturalist critics of Rawls contend that his definition of primary goods deals insufficiently with "recognition" of difference (Young 2000, Benhabib 2002). Whether or not this concept can be subsumed under what Rawls calls self-respect (see Fraser 1997, p. 33, n. 4), its salience for developing a model of the just city requires attention in an age of identity politics, ethnic conflict, and immigration. Within the vocabulary of urban planning, the term diversity refers to such recognition and is the quality that writers such as Richard Sennett and Jane Jacobs argue should characterize city life. The embodiment of diversity ranges from mixed use to mixed income, racial and ethnic integration to widely accessible public space (Fainstein 2005b). Nancy Fraser points to the tension that exists between equality and diversity, or, as she puts it, redistribution and recognition:

> Recognition claims often take the form of calling attention to, if not performatively creating, the putative specificity of some group and then of affirming its value. Thus, they tend to promote group differentiation. Redistribution claims, in contrast,

often call for abolishing economic arrangements that underpin group specificity. …
Thus, they tend to promote group dedifferentiation. The upshot is that the politics
of recognition and the politics of redistribution often appear to have mutually
contradictory aims. (Fraser 1997, p. 16)

Diversity and deliberation, like democracy and just outcomes, are in tension. If
deliberation works best within a moral community under conditions of trust, then
a heterogeneous public creates obstacles to its realization (Benhabib 1996). To be
sure there are theorists like Chantal Mouffe and Richard Sennett who regard
conflict as salutary, but even they expect that there is an underlying commitment
to peaceful resolution of disputes. In cities the issue is particularly sharp in relation
to formal and informal drawing of boundaries. Does the much-decried division of
US metropolitan areas into numerous separate jurisdictions only do harm or does
it also serve to protect antagonistic groups from each other? In various parts of
the world (Ethiopia/Eritrea, the Czech Republic/Slovakia, Serbia/Croatia, India/
Pakistan, etc.), separation has been regarded as self-determination and perceived
as a democratic solution. Iris Marion Young (2000, p. 216), whose work endorses
a politics of difference, resists the ideal of integration, because it "tends wrongly
to focus on patterns of group clustering while ignoring more central issues of
privilege and disadvantage." She supports porous borders, widely accessible public
spaces, and regional government but she also calls for a differentiated solidarity
that would allow voluntary clustering of cultural groups.

Thus, the three hallmarks of urban justice – material equality, diversity, and
democracy – are not automatically supportive of each other and, in fact, in any
particular situation, may well clash or require trade-offs. Moreover, internal to
each of these norms are further contradictory elements. In addition to the aforementioned, hoary question of whether equality of opportunity can exist without
prior equality of condition, there are the issues of whether equal treatment of
those with differing abilities is fair or whether the disabled should get more, and
conversely whether it is fair to deny rewards to those whose effort or ability make
them seem more deserving (what philosophers refer to as the criterion of "desert").
With reference to urban policies this raises the difficulty, for example, of whether,
in terms of allocating public housing, the homeless should receive preference over
those on waiting lists or whether non-profit housing corporations should be able
to select tenants so as to exclude families likely to be disruptive.

In regard to diversity the issue arises of whether recognition of the other should
extend to acceptance of groups that themselves are intolerant or authoritarian.
Within cities this question has shown itself most intensely when groups impose
their rules or life styles on others who share their spaces – Jews who discourage
driving on the Sabbath, Muslims whose calls to prayer stop traffic and are heard by
everyone in the vicinity, anarchists whose loud music and nighttime activities keep
their neighbors awake.[7] The same problem exists concerning democratic inclusion
of those with undemocratic beliefs.

Evaluations of Examples of Planning in Practice

New York

New York City recently released its first effort at a master plan since the John Lindsay mayoralty of the 1970s (NYC Office of the Mayor 2007).[8] In terms of the three criteria of equality, diversity, and participation the plan does best on diversity, calling for mixed-use and mixed-income development. It does so in the context of combined forces of immigration and gentrification, which over the last several decades have caused more neighborhoods to be mixed by income and ethnicity. The plan, which rezones low-income tracts for high-rise development, will encourage further gentrification, resulting in an unstable situation in parts of the city. At the same time, however, the continued existence of rent regulation and the presence of public housing mean that most areas housing low-income people will continue to retain at least some of that population (Freeman and Branconi 2004). Black–white segregation diminished little in the city between the last two censuses and likely will be affected by the new plan primarily to the extent that formerly homogeneously black areas like Harlem are becoming more racially mixed. Although the city promotes mixed-income housing through incentives and builds affordable housing out of its own capital budget, no requirements exist to insure that income mixing will occur. Still, the continued influx of immigrants means that much of the city will become even more ethnically diverse.

In relation to equality, the plan emphasizes development in all five boroughs of the city, promotes the creation of affordable housing, and calls for additional parks and waterfront access in poor neighborhoods. But, while parts of it reflect sensitivity to the concerns of low-income communities, its major projects[9] utilize huge sums of public money and tax forgiveness for endeavors that radically transform their locations, stir up local opposition, and threaten to sharpen the contrast between the haves and have-nots. The components of the plan are restricted to land use and development; it does not link these initiatives to education, job training and placement, or social services (Marcuse 2008). The overall context in which the plan has been framed is one where tens of thousands of housing units are being withdrawn from the affordable housing stock,[10] the middle class is shrinking, and inequality is increasing, while the city is seeing breathtaking levels of wealth acquired by hedge fund managers and investment bankers.[11]

In terms of citizen participation the plan is extremely uneven, with its major projects insulated from public oversight. New York's charter mandates community boards to advise on redevelopment projects conducted by the city. The government has evaded the requirement for local participation by placing large schemes in the hands of New York State's Empire State Development Corporation, which is not bound by this stipulation and has powers to override city zoning and to exercise eminent domain. Thus, while there may be endless meetings and citizen input into arrangements for a small park, there will be nothing but pro forma hearings for the construction of a stadium or a megaproject in central Brooklyn. But, even when public consultation takes place, it does not necessarily protect those being targeted for removal. Thus, in the conversion of the Bronx Terminal Market from an agglomeration of locally owned, ethnic food wholesalers to a retail shopping mall owned by the city's largest speculative developer and populated by chain stores, the community board approved the action (Fainstein 2007), indicating the way in which deliberation does not necessarily promote equality.[12]

London

In 2004 the Mayor published the London Plan (Mayor of London 2004), which subsequently received parliamentary approval and thus, unlike New York's plan, is binding. As well as guiding growth and requiring the construction of housing to accommodate predicted population increase, it concerns itself with affordable housing and promoting policies for education, health, safety, skills development and community services, and tackling discrimination. Thus, at least in intention, it is directed toward social as well as physical issues.

The principal thrust of the plan is toward accommodating growth. While there are sections related to all areas of the city, the main initiative is the redevelopment of the Thames Gateway, an area encompassing the poorest districts of London but also stretching eastward out to the border of Kent and including a variety of residential, commercial, and industrial sites, as well as brownfields and flood plains. This emphasis can be interpreted in two ways: as an effort to upgrade the most disadvantaged part of the city, providing jobs and housing for its present population as well as making provision for further influxes; or as a means of diverting development from the resistant, well-to-do areas that surround central London, where residents are hostile to higher densities (Edwards 2008).

Generally the plan has a much stronger commitment toward equality than New York's, as befits the product of a Labour government. Under Section 106 of the UK Town and Country Planning Act, local authorities bargain with developers for "planning gain" (LTGDC 2006). Whereas the Thatcher administration had opposed requiring developers to provide community benefits except to mitigate the direct effects of development, the succeeding Labour government strongly encouraged the use of planning gain to force developers to provide amenities and social programs as well as affordable housing. It became central government policy that all new developments in London with more than 15 units of housing had to provide 50 percent affordable units (50% market, 35% social rented, and 15% intermediate housing). Some of these would be achieved through cross-subsidy by market-rate units, but in addition substantial sums were available through the nationally funded Housing Corporation to support construction by housing associations.

On the criterion of equality then, London's spatial planning far surpasses New York's. Confronted by the same issues of gentrification, minority group poverty and unemployment, and soaring housing prices as New York, London shows far greater commitment to overcoming disadvantage.[13] Furthermore, even though it similarly encourages economic development based on expansion of advanced service sectors, it does not do so through the provision of large public subsidies to developers and firms. Nevertheless, its policies are not altogether benign in respect to the beneficiaries of public investment. The primary tool for stimulating business development is transport infrastructure provision, which has positive economic and environmental effects. However, although low-income people do receive accessibility benefits from investment in public transit, they must pay substantially for them. Transport for London relies heavily on user fees, causing travel within Greater London to be very costly.

London like New York has an extremely diverse population with immigrants from everywhere in the world. It has nothing like New York's black–white divide, but South Asians do cluster in a number of its wards. The housing plan for London, by requiring that all new developments contain affordable housing, represents a step toward increasing income diversity and, given the likelihood that the low-income units will be taken by immigrant households, ethnic diversity as well. The plan, however, probably will do little to halt gentrification in boroughs like Islington nor will it have a transformative effect on existing upper class areas, either within central London or the suburbs.

The Mayor's Office claims to have consulted very broadly in developing the plan and expects that its implementation will be carried out by partnerships among local authorities, private business, and community organizations.[14] For many years now the government at both national and local levels has emphasized such partnerships, which have proliferated across London and which unquestionably play a significant role in development. They are, however, heavily reliant on private investment; consequently, developers and business firms can easily override citizens by simply refusing to invest. On the other hand, the private sector takes it for granted that it will have to provide a public benefit in order to obtain planning permission and devotes considerable time and energy to wooing local residents with promises of recreational facilities, training institutions, and job commitments. Community participants may not get their way, but they are not shut out of the planning process as is often the case in New York.

Amsterdam

Of the three cities Amsterdam offers the most equality, diversity, and participation (Fainstein 2000b; Gilderbloom et al. 2009). Between 1945 and 1985 about 90 percent of all new housing in the city was comprised of social rented housing (van de Ven 2004). Now, however, many fear that the commitment to justice is diminishing under the assault of globalization and anti-immigration sentiment (Dias and Beaumont 2007; Uitermark, Rossi, and van Houtum 2005). Nonetheless, although the move toward less government support of social housing is a move away from egalitarianism, a slippage from 90 percent to 50 percent social housing still puts Amsterdam way ahead of both New York and London in terms of commitment to equality.[15]

The Amsterdam government is strongly committed to diversity, meaning that it seeks to have every neighborhood mixed by income and ethnicity. As Uitermark (2003) points out, however, when diversity becomes the aim of public policy, it can suppress the potential for mobilization and facilitate social control mechanisms. Furthermore, as noted above in the discussion of Young's defense of neighborhood coherence, bringing about diversity can cause the breakdown of social ties and be opposed by the people it supposedly benefits.

On the other hand the redevelopment of the Bijlmermeer, an enormous social housing complex on the southern periphery of the city, reflects an effort to leave community intact, while also illustrating how various forms of diversity can cut against each other. The project, developed according to modernist precepts during the 1960s and 1970s, consisted of very large buildings surrounded by green space. The scale of the structures, despite the high quality of the apartments, made them unattractive to the native Dutch working class, who were originally envisioned as the occupants. Their availability at the time of Surinam's independence caused the government to place a large number of Surinamese refugees in them. The complex also houses many Africans and Antilleans. While it never became as homogeneously black as a typical American ghetto, the Bijlmermeer nevertheless was perceived as an undesirable area. In the last decade the Amsterdam government has addressed the problem by tearing down many of the original buildings, modifying others, and constructing new, low-rise residences for owner occupation (Kwekkeboom 2002). The revitalization was predicated on a commitment to multiculturalism and community participation, and involuntary displacement was avoided. This shift has been criticized by some for betraying the socialist origins of the project and for resulting in gentrification. Many residents of the new, more expensive units, however, moved into them from the original buildings, express satisfaction at being able to stay in the area, and praise the opportunity to live in a multicultural environment (Baart 2003). Thus reconstruction has caused the area to retain ethnic diversity and to become more mixed in terms of income by providing suitable accommodation for upwardly mobile residents.

Conclusion

Can we distill from these various experiences a set of norms that could apply broadly? Or does each situation lend itself to a different interpretation of the broad principles of equality, diversity, and participation? My approach conforms to the argument presented by Rainer Forst (2002, p. 238) in *Contexts of Justice*:

> The principle of general justification is context-transcending not in the sense that it violates contexts of individual and collective self-determination but insofar as it designates minimal standards within which self-determination is 'reiterated'.

Forst's assertion echoes Nussbaum's (2000, p. 6) contention that there is a threshold level of capabilities (i.e., the potential to "live as a dignified free human being who shapes his or her own life" [p. 72]) below which justice is sacrificed, and that it is incumbent on government to provide the social basis for its availability although not for its actual realization. It is doubtful, however, whether these two philosophers would go as far as to prescribe particular public policy measures as generally applicable.[16]

My list of criteria is thus probably too specific to be acceptable to rigorous deontological philosophers. Nevertheless, I contend that it offers a set of expectations that ought to form the basis for just urban planning. The contents of this list apply only to planning conducted at the local level; the components of a just national urban policy are more complex and will not be discussed here.[17] The list is as follows:

In furtherance of equality:

All new housing developments should provide units for households with incomes below the median, either on-site or elsewhere, with the goal of providing a decent home and suitable living environment for everyone. (One of the most vexing issues in relation to housing, however, is the extent to which tenant selection should limit access to people likely to be good neighbors. It is one of the areas where the criteria of equality and democracy are at odds with each other, and no general rule can apply.)

No household or business should be involuntarily relocated for the purpose of obtaining economic development or community balance.

Economic development programs should give priority to the interests of employees and small business owners. All new commercial development should provide space for public use and to the extent feasible should facilitate the livelihood of independent and cooperatively owned businesses.

Mega-projects should be subject to heightened scrutiny, be required to provide direct benefits to low-income people in the form of employment provisions, public amenities, and a living wage, and, if public subsidy is involved, should include public participation in the profits.

Transit fares should be kept very low.

Planners should take an active role in deliberative settings in pressing for egalitarian solutions and blocking ones that disproportionately benefit the already well-off.

In furtherance of diversity:

Zoning should not be used to further discriminatory ends.

Boundaries between districts should be porous.

Ample public space should be widely accessible and varied but be designed so that groups with clashing lifestyles do not have to occupy the same location.

To the extent practical and desired by affected populations, uses should be mixed.

In furtherance of democracy:

Plans should be developed in consultation with the target population if the area is already developed. The existing population, however, should not be the sole arbiter of the future of an area. Citywide considerations must also apply.

In planning for as yet uninhabited or sparsely occupied areas, there should be broad consultation that includes representatives of groups currently living outside the affected areas.

Adherence to this set of guidelines does not require that people who cannot get along live next door to each other. Indeed people have the right to protect themselves from others who do not respect their way of life. What is important is that people are not differentiated and excluded according to ascriptive characteristics like gender or ethnicity. But neither should people be required to tolerate disorderly conduct or anti-social behavior in the name of social justice.

In response to a lecture I gave on the just city, James Throgmorton (personal communication, 28 January 2006) wrote:

> My experience as an elected official leads me to think that the planners of any specific city cannot (and should not) simply declare by fiat that their purpose is to create the just city. In the context of representative democracy, they have to be authorized to imagine, articulate, pursue, and actualize the vision of a just city. This means that a mobilized constituency would have to be pressuring for change.

In terms of practical politics Throgmorton is completely correct – without a mobilized constituency and supportive officials, no prescription for justice will be implemented. But regardless of authorization or not, it is a goal to continually press for and to deploy when evaluating planning decisions. It is way too easy to follow the lead of developers and politicians who make economic competitiveness the highest priority and give little or no consideration to questions of justice.

Notes

1. See Fischer (1980) for an argument concerning the different levels of normative judgment in policy analysis.
2. Young (2000) supports deliberative democracy as the appropriate procedural norm, arguing that it will promote justice. She does not, however, regard consensus as a likely or desired outcome from deliberation but instead sees conflict as fruitful and unavoidable.
3. Wolff, Moore, and Marcuse (1969) argue that as a consequence of capitalist hegemony, tolerance – i.e., allowing the free play of ideas – can be repressive.
4. There is a range of views concerning whether rationality, in any strict sense, need govern discourse.
5. See Marcuse et al. (2009).
6. Other attributes could be analyzed as well, especially environmental sustainability and justice, levels and character of social control, and definition of the public sphere.
7. See David Harvey's (2002) description of clashing life styles within and around Tompkins Square Park in New York.
8. The plan represents the Mayor's strategy for the city but is not legally binding.

9. These include new baseball stadiums in the Bronx and Queens, high-rise housing on the Brooklyn and Queens waterfronts, a shopping mall in the Bronx that displaces an ethic wholesale food market, a new Harlem campus for Columbia University, and a vast redevelopment of Manhattan's west side, involving high-rise apartments, extension of the subway system, and the carving out of a new boulevard (see Fainstein 2005c, Wolf-Powers 2005).

10. A 30-year limit (or less) characterizes much of the housing stock built in New York under various subsidy programs. It is estimated that the city lost 260,000 affordable units between 2002 and 2005 (NYC Office of the Public Advocate 2007). The cause was the reversion of housing built under the Mitchell-Lama program, the primary provider of housing for moderate-income residents during the postwar years, to market rate, the lapsing of time limits on various federally sponsored housing developments, and the move of privately owned units out of rent stabilization. Thirty years seems a long time when housing is built, but there is no reason to assume once the time passes that housing need will diminish.

11. The proportion of the population in poverty exceeded a fifth in 2006, a level that had not changed in five years (Roberts 2006).

12. The board justified its decision as contributing to economic growth and convenient retail shopping.

13. The fact that it has access to nationally provided housing funding is key. At the time of this writing, with a new Conservative mayor of London and declining Labour support nationally, it is unclear whether this commitment will persist.

14. The Mayor's plan provides guidance to the local authorities (i.e., the London boroughs), which develop their own plans that fill in the specifics and must conform with the guidance.

15. While this is the ostensible goal for London, it only affects new construction, is restricted to larger projects, and is rarely reached in actuality.

16. Nussbaum (2000, p. 78) does specify certain requisites in her list of capabilities that involve public policy, including adequate shelter, adequate education, and protection against discrimination.

17. Markusen and Fainstein (1993) develop the elements of a national urban policy for the US.

References

Baart, Theo, *Territorium*, Rotterdam: NAi. 2003.

Benhabib, Seyla, *The Claims of Culture*, Princeton, NJ: Princeton University Press, 2002.

Benhabib, Seyla, ed., *Democracy and Difference*, Princeton, NJ: Princeton University Press, 1996.

Campbell, Heather, "Just Planning: The Art of Situated Ethical Judgment", *Journal of Planning Education and Research*, 26: 92–106, 2006.

Dias, Candice, and Justin Beaumont, "Beyond the egalitarian city". Paper presented at the meeting of RC21 (Committee on Urban and Regional Research) of the ISA, Vancouver, Canada, August, 2007.

Edwards, Michael, "Structures for development in Thames Gateway: getting them right", in Phil Cohen and Mike Rustin, eds, *London's Turning: The Prospect of Thames Gateway*. Aldershot, Hampshire, UK: Ashgate, 2008.

Fainstein, Susan S., "Global transformations and the malling the South Bronx", pp. 157–65, in Jerilou Hammett and Kingsley Hammett, eds, *The Suburbanization of New York*. Princeton, NJ: Princeton Architectural Press, 2008.

Fainstein, Susan S., "Planning Theory and the City", *Journal of Planning Education and Research* 25, 1–10, 2005a.

Fainstein, Susan S., "Cities and diversity: Should we want it? Can we plan for it?", *Urban Affairs Review*, 41 (1), September, 3–19, 2005b.

Fainstein, Susan S., "The Return of Urban Renewal: Dan Doctoroff's Great Plans for New York City", *Harvard Design Magazine*, No. 22, Spring/Summer 2005, 1–5, 2005c.

Fainstein, Susan S., "New Directions in Planning Theory", *Urban Affairs Review*, 35 (4) (March), 451–78, 2000a.

Fainstein, Susan S., "The egalitarian city: images of Amsterdam", pp. 93–116 in Leon Deben, Willem Heinemeijer, and Dick van der Vaart, eds, *Understanding Amsterdam*, 2nd edn. Amsterdam: Het Spinhuis, 2000b.

Fischer, Frank, *Politics, Values, and Public Policy: The Problem of Methodology*. Boulder, CO: Westview, 1980.

Forester, John, *The Deliberative Practitioner*, Cambridge, MA: MIT Press, 1999.

Forst, Rainer, *Contexts of Justice*, Berkeley, CA: University of California Press, 2002.

Fraser, Nancy, *Justice Interruptus*, New York: Routledge, 1997.

Freeman, Lance, and Frank Braconi, "Gentrification and displacement: New York City in the 1990s", *Journal of the American Planning Association*, 70 (1), Winter, pp. 39–52, 2004.

Friedmann, John, "The good city: in defense of utopian thinking", *International Journal of Urban and Regional Research*, 24 (2), 460–72, 2000.

Gilderbloom, John, Matt Hanka, and Carrie Beth Lasley, "Amsterdam: Planning and Policy for the Ideal City?", *Local Environment: Journal of Justice and Sustainability*, 14 (6), 473–93, 2009.

Harvey, David, "Social justice, postmodernism, and the city", pp. 386–402 in Susan S. Fainstein and Scott Campbell, eds, *Readings in Urban Theory*. 2nd edn. Oxford: Blackwell, 2002.

Harvey, David, *Spaces of Hope*, Berkeley, CA: University of California Press, 2000.

Healey, Patsy, *Collaborative Planning*, Houndmills, Basingstoke, Hampshire, UK: Macmillan, 1997.

Hoch, Charles, "Pragmatic Communicative Action Theory", *Journal of Planning Education and Research*, 26: 272–83, 2007.

Innes, Judith, "Planning theory's emerging paradigm: communicative action and interactive practice", *Journal of Planning Education and Research*, 14 (3) (Spring), 183–9, 1995.

Klein, Naomi, *Shock Doctrine*, New York: Henry Holt, 2007.

Klosterman, Richard, "Arguments for and against planning", pp. 86–101 in Scott Campbell and Susan S. Fainstein, eds, *Readings in Planning Theory*, 2nd edn, Oxford: Blackwell, 2003.

Kwekkeboom, Willem, "Rebuilding the Bijlmermeer, 1992–2002", pp. 73–113 in Dick Bruijne et al., Amsterdam Southeast: Centre Area Southeast and urban renewal in the Bijlmermeer 1992–2012. Bussum, the Netherlands: Thoth, 2002.

London Thames Gateway Development Corporation (LTGDC), "Planning obligations community benefit strategy", Final Report, December. http://www.ltgdc.org.uk/planning/consultation/final.pdf, 2006.

Lucy, William H., "APA's ethical principles include simplistic planning theories", pp. 413–17 in Scott Campbell and Susan S. Fainstein, eds, *Readings in Planning Theory*, 2nd edn, Oxford: Blackwell, 2003.

Marcuse, Peter, "PlaNYC is not a « Plan » and it is not for « NYC »", *Sustainability Watch Working Papers #7*. September 2008. http://www.gothamgazette.com/sustainability/, 2008.

Marcuse, Peter, et al., eds. *Searching for the Just City*. New York: Routledge. 2009.

Markusen, Ann R., and Susan S. Fainstein, "Urban policy: bridging the social and economic development gap", *University of North Carolina Law Review*, 71 (June), 1463–86, 1993.

Mayor of London, *The London Plan. Spatial Development Strategy for London*. London: Greater London Authority [...], 2004.

Mill, John Stuart, ed. *Utilitarianism, Liberty, and Representative Government*. New York: E.P. Dutton, 1951.

New York City (NYC) Office of the Mayor, *PlaNYC: A Greener, Greater New York* [...], 2007.

New York City (NYC) Office of the Public Advocate, *Twelve for 2030: Responses to plaNYC* [...], 2007.

New York State (NYS) Metropolitan Transit Authority (MTA), *Info.com*. http://www.mta.info/metrocard/mcgtreng.htm#top, 2008.

Nussbaum, Martha, *Women and Human Development: The Capabilities Approach*. Cambridge: Cambridge University Press, 2000.

Rawls, John, *Justice as Fairness: A Restatement*, Edited by Erin Kelly. Cambridge, MA: Harvard University Press, 2001.

Rawls, John, *A Theory of Justice*, Cambridge, MA: Harvard University Press, 1971.

Roberts, Sam, "Census figures show scant improvement in city poverty rate", *New York Times*, August 30, 2006.

Uitermark, Justus, "'Social mixing' and the management of disadvantaged neighbourhoods: the Dutch policy of urban restructuring revisited", *Urban Studies*, 40 (3): 531–49, 2003.

Uitermark, Justus, Ugo Rossi, and Henk van Houtum, "Reinventing multiculturalism: urban citizenship and the negotiation of ethnic diversity in Amsterdam", *International Journal of Urban and Regional Research*, 29 (3): 622–40, 2005.

Van de Ven, Jacques, "It's all in the mix: urban dynamics in a frozen built environment." pp. 176–84 in Léon Deben, Willem Salet, and Marie-Thérèse van Thoor, eds. *Cultural Heritage and the Future of the Historic Inner City of Amsterdam*. Amsterdam: Aksant, 2004.

Wolff, Robert Paul, Barrington Moore, Jr, and Herbert Marcuse, *A Critique of Pure Tolerance*. Boston, MA: Beacon Press, 1969.

Wolf-Powers, Laura, "Up-zoning New York City's mixed-use neighborhoods: Property-led economic development and the anatomy of a planning dilemma", *Journal of Planning Education and Research* 24: 379–93, 2005.

Yiftachel, Oren, "Planning Theory at the Crossroads", *Journal of Planning Education and Research* 18(3): 67–9, 1999.

Young, Iris Marion, *Inclusion and Democracy*, Oxford: Oxford University Press, 2000.

Young, Iris Marion, *Justice and the Politics of Difference*, Princeton, NJ: Princeton University Press, 1990.

Part III

Implications of Practice for Theory

Introduction

Introduction

Planning students often think of their required theory course as too abstract and not relevant to the problems they will face in their daily lives. Often, however, when they have years of practice behind them, they appreciate the ways in which theory makes the issues facing them in their work lives intelligible. One of the purposes of theory is to extricate the meaning of quotidian experience and make possible a deeper understanding of the forces shaping planning alternatives and

Readings in Planning Theory, Fourth Edition. Edited by Susan S. Fainstein and James DeFilippis.
Editorial material and organization © 2016 John Wiley & Sons, Ltd.
Published 2016 by John Wiley & Sons, Ltd.

the likely outcomes of different ways of addressing problems. The five selections in this section all represent efforts to relate the specific to the general and show how varying frameworks of analysis lead to different kinds of insights.

The first selection, by Robert Beauregard (Chapter 14), examines the effects of the locations in which planning occurs. He distinguishes among site, place, and context. His thesis is that the micro-politics of planning are profoundly affected by the character and number of these different locations. He tells the story of an Iowa private firm's efforts to expand waste disposal facilities and the various obstacles it confronted. Site refers to the actual spot under consideration – in this case the land on which a disposal facility would be built and its character, which here was fertile farmland. Place refers both to the settings in which planning occurs and the area for which the planners are responsible. In its broadest sense place is the location of meanings and social relations, as opposed to the abstract concept of space. Context also matters in both narrower and broader senses: whether discussion occurs in a small meeting room with controls over access or in a public auditorium; whether the institutional framework of policy making contains many constraints on or incentives to action. In this instance the institutional context brought into play other places like the Federal Aviation Administration. The distinctions Beauregard makes between place and context are fuzzy – sometimes he regards meeting rooms as places and at other times he classifies them as context. Nevertheless, his overall thesis is clear – the circumstances under which planning transpires, especially when a contentious issue like the siting of undesired land uses is under consideration, affect the outcomes of the process.

Planning involves more than the making of plans; effective planning requires that its aims be implemented. The zoning map constitutes one of the principal instruments of plan implementation. In the United States, where master planning primarily involves the establishment of single-use zones, and building within its mandates is "as of right," zoning is the main method for guiding development. Sonia Hirt's contribution (Chapter 15) presents a history of zoning in the United States and Europe, highlighting the distinctive aspects of the American approach. In the United States zoning promotes the model of the detached single-family home and the exclusively residential neighborhood. In contrast, zoning in European cities usually accommodates attached housing and mixed uses. Hirt shows that, while the justification for the American model lies in public health and safety, its purpose also has been to enforce ethnic and class exclusion and the protection of property values. This embodiment of prejudice in planning documents received a gloss of populism through promotion of home ownership for the middle class masses, even if not for the lower class worker or the racial "other." As will be discussed in Part IV of this volume, planning's role in many parts of the world has too often been to enforce segregation not just of uses but of people and thereby to increase disadvantage for those who already suffered from discrimination and poverty.

At the same time many planners have been committed to using the means at their disposal to improve the lives of disadvantaged groups. In Chapter 16 Laura Wolf-Powers addresses the theories of action underlying attempts to find "effective, morally acceptable policy responses to environmental deterioration and human deprivation ...." She discusses community development efforts in urban neighborhoods and lists three diagnoses of the obstacles to neighborhood improvement: (1) insufficient social capital – i.e., not enough bonds among residents and too little civic engagement; (2) neglect of markets and of connections to the wider metropolitan area; and (3) lack of power.

Each of the three diagnoses leads to a different prescription for action. Restoring social capital is associated with the argument that concentration of poverty causes social disintegration; the solution then becomes deconcentrating poverty, either through bringing in wealthier households or assisting poor people to move out to higher-income areas. It also leads to a program for encouraging home ownership on the grounds that owners have a greater vested interest in their communities. Stimulating the growth of markets means attracting capital investment into poor areas through various kinds of subsidies and investment pools as well as providing workforce training. Increasing political capacity requires mobilization through protest movements. It may be directed at some of the same goals as the first two approaches, but it is based on the view that social capital and financial investment will happen only when an active citizenry is pressing its demands. This third view thus accepts conflict as a necessary concomitant of neighborhood improvement, but in doing so marginalizes its adherents in the world of policy analysts and philanthropic organizations on which they are dependent for financing.

Wolf-Powers differentiates between process and outcome orientations and considers that, while advocates for community power may be more concerned with outcomes than process, they nevertheless rely on participation and negotiation to achieve community mobilization. The next two selections, by Frank Fischer and John Forester, zero in on the contribution of good processes to just outcomes. They reflect the concern with citizen participation that has characterized planning since the 1960s. In Chapter 17, Fischer's discussion of participation and deliberation names a number of reasons to foster citizen involvement in planning. First, participation contributes to self-development, as well as bringing local knowledge to bear. Second, it may lead to more efficient implementation and more equitable outcomes, although Fischer indicates that this is not always the result and depends on the social and economic context. Third, and again problematic, participation has the potential to make the distribution of political power more equitable, but only given the right circumstances. The engineering of these circumstances is crucial to the success of participatory processes and to some extent depends on a new kind of expertise – the ability to develop participatory practices.

Forester's chapter picks up on this latter point. He focuses on the role of the facilitator in bringing about consensus in situations of strongly conflicting interests. He examines the techniques of skilled mediators, using three practice stories that illustrate how creative intermediaries can come up with alternatives agreeable to all sides in a dispute. He contends that only by bringing together people whose views initially seem irreconcilable is it possible to find these alternatives. While Wolf-Powers points to the inevitability of conflict in situations of unequal power and resources, Forester argues that conflict is avoidable and assuming that no reconciliation can occur is a product of cynicism.

14

The Neglected Places of Practice

Robert Beauregard

Planning literature is filled with writings about place. We read of redevelopment sites, neighborhoods threatened by gentrification, wetlands needing protection, politicized public squares, regional shopping malls hollowing out small-town retail centers, office parks proliferating across the suburbs, and on and on. Because planning is mainly about "the interconnection of people and places, activities and territories" (Healey, 2005, p. 5), the prevalence of such stories is unsurprising. Yet, little has been written about the ways in which places enter into planning practice and thereby matter in planning theory.[1] Attention is mainly directed at places that have already been or are being planned. Less often considered are the places where planning practice actually occurs and the influence these places have on how planning decisions are made.

Consider three different stories about the places that one is likely to encounter in the planning literature. The first, by Robert Hrelja, involves a large shopping area called Marieberg on the outskirts of the Swedish town of Orebro (Hrelja, 2011). The story concerns how a principled commitment to sustainable mobility, meaning both less sprawl and decreased automobile traffic, was undermined by short-term and small decisions that traded environmentalism for economic development and competitiveness. In presenting the case, Hrelja mentions town planners, representatives of Orebro's Office of Business Development, Steen & Strom (a shopping center operator), municipal commissioners, and local political parties. The second story is from Susan Fainstein (1997) who argues that Amsterdam can serve as a model of an egalitarian and just city. Affordable housing, inclusive public spaces, widely accessible mass transit, and income-integrated neighborhoods are its essential elements and they emerge from a planning that eschews pro-growth policies and, by extension, subservience to capitalism. The third story is one of John Forester's practice cases. Forester (1996) presents a planning event in

Original publication details: Beauregard, Robert. 2013. "The Neglected Places of Practice". In *Planning Theory and Practice*. 14(1): 8–19. Used with permission from Taylor & Francis Group.

which municipal planners in the USA negotiated with a developer, his architect, and his lawyer regarding the construction of multi-family housing. They met in the planning department's conference room. There, they discussed various aspects of the site: density, parking, open space, and sidewalks. The goal of the meeting was to craft a plan that would serve the developer's interests, provide public benefits, and be acceptable to the planning commission.

Each of these planning stories highlights a particular understanding of place. Hrelja's piece represents probably the most common approach; it focuses solely on the place being planned. In doing so, Hrelja emphasizes the technical qualities of the place: accessibility by car and public transit, the mix of retail and commercial uses, changing property values, and the regional competitiveness of Marieberg's retailing. He describes the place as a site; that is, a place targeted for intervention. Those involved in the planning process are acknowledged, but we have no sense of where planning decisions were being made.[2]

By contrast, Fainstein's story focuses on the context of planning. Context consists of the sociopolitical, cultural and economic conditions – in this instance, the Dutch welfare state – that shape the planning process. That, in fact, is her point; planning can only be just when society's institutions are just. As with Hrelja's story, planners are recognized but the places where they act are not. The only place of interest for Fainstein is Amsterdam, the city that symbolizes the Dutch context.[3] Lastly there is Forester; his story occurs in a planning office. Here is a place of practice with the site represented there by drawings, a model, photographs, and (of course) the developer and his consultants. In his focus on the deliberations, though, he ignores how this practice place – the meeting room – might have mediated them.

These stories represent three different ways in which planning theorists think about places: (1) as sites (i.e. places being planned), (2) as context, and (3) as places of practice. When the focus is on sites and context, planning (for the most part) emanates from nowhere. Planning decisions and actions are described and frequently the planners themselves are identified, but they exist in a shadowy and unspecified realm. Left for the imagination are the places – the developer's office, the zoning board meeting room, the planning department, the local bank – where planning decisions are being made.[4] The actors in these stories are spatially untethered. Planning stories of the third kind are more likely to tell us where planning occurred but then do so only in passing; that is, treating the places of practice as a descriptive fact rather than as a consequential practical or theoretical issue. If one believes that where something happens is important for how it happens and its consequences, and that planning theory should be about planning practice, then theorists need to acknowledge the places of practice. A practice-based theory without actors in place is internally inconsistent; that is, embodying the planning process but not the materiality of its settings.

The purpose of this chapter is to argue for including the places of practice in any theory concerned with the micro-politics of planning. Where planning happens affects what is deliberated, who is involved, and the publicity afforded to the deliberations. To this extent, planning's ability to be democratic depends as much on the array of places across which it is distributed as it does on the range of "voices" that are allowed to be heard. To illustrate these points, I will leave aside these three examples in order to delve more deeply into the places of a single planning event, one involving the Bluestem Solid Waste Agency of Linn County, Iowa, USA.[5]

Siting a Landfill

In the mid 1990s, the board of directors of the Bluestem Solid Waste Agency learned that the county's landfills were about to reach capacity. It directed the staff to investigate alternative technologies for managing the county's solid waste.

This simple description of the first phase of the process points to a number of places important for any understanding of this planning event. First are the existing landfill sites. Second are the places where waste is being generated. Third are the offices at Bluestem where the planners and other analysts tracked solid waste disposal and made a technical determination that these sites would soon be unable to accept additional waste. Fourth are the Bluestem meeting rooms where these calculations were discussed and a decision made to mount a new planning initiative. From its inception, this planning event was spread across multiple places.

The planning team began by contacting citizens with an interest in waste disposal and asking them to join a focus group to consider the development of an integrated solid waste management system. At the conclusion of its deliberations, the focus group would recommend a plan of action to the Bluestem board. A series of meetings were held, and likely occurred in one of Bluestem's conference rooms. During this time, the staff worked in its offices to provide information and analyses.[6] After concluding its assessment, the focus group met with the board and proposed that Bluestem expand its recycling and composting efforts, build a facility to manage household hazardous waste, and open a new landfill. Existing sites for recycling and composting would be upgraded, a hazardous waste disposal facility would be built, and a new site for handling the disposal of non-hazardous and non-recyclable materials would be established. In effect, more places would be added to Bluestem's portfolio, thereby expanding its operations and dispersing them further throughout the county.

The Bluestem staff then turned its attention to developing a strategic plan for the identification of a new landfill site. At this stage, a decision was made to have the planning process be as public as possible; that is, involve all of the stakeholders and aim for, if not consensus, a widespread understanding of the appropriateness of the selected site. The planners rejected a site-and-defend approach in which they, as experts, would select a best site for the landfill, commit to it, and then defend it against any and all opposition in as few public meetings as possible. Such an approach, of course, would have reduced the number of places involved by locating most of the planning process within the agency.

The strategic plan focused on obtaining public input as well as identifying outside experts to consult on technical matters. The public process began by meeting with "affected parties" including government agencies. This was followed by the creation of a citizens' advisory committee of about twenty people. The committee met for five to six months with the early meetings devoted to informing its members of the work of the focus group and the later meetings to developing site-selection criteria. The committee was discouraged from re-visiting decisions about alternative technologies made at the earlier stages of the process and from questioning the need – already documented – for a new landfill.

At this point, the planning deliberations "occupied" four places simultaneously: the room(s) where the advisory committee met, the offices of the Bluestem staff where information was gathered and studies done, the business addresses of the consultancies, and the "hypothetical" sites in the county – haunting the deliberations but not yet identified – where the landfill might be located. The last set of places involved not just multiple possible sites but the relationships between these sites and other places. The committee considered the uses of adjacent sites, proximity to the "weighted center" of waste generation in Linn County, nearness to rivers and streams, and road access. It further addressed various qualities of the sites: existing uses, drainage capacity, soil quality, agricultural potential, depth to bedrock, and (later) willingness of the owners to sell at a reasonable price. During this time, the Bluestem staff also met with the county director of planning and zoning in Cedar Rapids to craft an "exclusive use" zoning ordinance for the new landfill. This added a fifth place to the process.

In the end, and with the assistance of the staff, the advisory committee identified 13 possible sites, all privately owned. The property owners were notified and a public meeting was announced and held. It attracted nearly 400 people to a large auditorium and turned into what one Bluestem participant called "the meeting from hell": "There were tears, grandstanding, cheering, clapping, and many horrible accusations about Bluestem staff" (Berkshire, 2003, p. 172). It was an informational meeting and the planners were not allowed to respond: "We had to just sit there and listen" (Berkshire, 2003, p. 172).

This large public meeting was followed by a series of open houses held in various venues around the county. There, the staff set up information booths that presented the rationales behind the selection of sites and specific information about them. Each booth had a representative from either Bluestem or one of the consultants. The open houses attracted between four and five hundred people apiece.

During this time, the county planning director was working on the zoning ordinance. Much to the chagrin of the Bluestem planners, he incorporated language that prohibited any place from being used as a landfill if the land had a corn suitability rating (CSR) indicating that it was quality farmland. All thirteen sites had land with a high rating. At one of its meetings, the county board of supervisors adopted the ordinance and by so doing seemingly negated the work of Bluestem's advisory committee.

The planners then met with the Bluestem board. The board recommended that they proceed with narrowing the search to two or three sites and postpone addressing the new ordinance (which some considered to be illegal). When the planners went back to the advisory committee it refused to proceed, believing that the county board of supervisors would reject any site with high-quality farmland. The advisory committee suggested instead that new criteria be developed and stated emphatically that it would only deal with "willing sellers". The Bluestem staff subsequently began talking with willing sellers and this drew into the process representatives from real estate offices, law firms, and banks. After a year or so, Bluestem found a property owner willing to sell and detailed negotiations began. The parties could not agree though, and the negotiations stalled. Consequently, Bluestem considered a public taking of the site by compulsory means (that is by eminent domain).[7] However, the property was partially located within the boundaries of the city of Cedar Rapids and the Bluestem planners now had to negotiate with the city planners there and hold additional public meetings with the Cedar Rapids Planning Commission.

At this point, the single site not only became the subject of negotiations around a sale price but also the object of hydrological and environmental studies, thereby mobilizing additional actors and places where elements of the planning process were being assembled. These studies were necessary since the landfill needed an operating permit from the state Department of Natural Resources (DNR). The planners began the application process.

Then, three places far from Linn County, Iowa – Washington, DC, Altoona, Pennsylvania, and New York City – entered into this planning event. Bud Schuster, a Pennsylvania congressman, was successful in having a bill passed in Washington that would stop a new regional landfill in his district from accepting waste from New York City. The law prohibited landfills from being within a certain distance of an airport – this being the case for the proposed regional landfill in Altoona.[8] Bluestem's preferred site also violated the restriction. A delegation was sent to the Federal Aviation Administration (FAA) offices in Washington to discuss the law and to determine whether it applied to the Eastern Iowa Airport near the proposed Bluestem site. The likelihood was that the FAA would prohibit the Linn County landfill.

In response, the Bluestem board suspended its eminent domain efforts. A short time later, the FAA ruled that the Bluestem landfill site would be allowed. But, because other permit work had been suspended, the planners were now, in late summer of 2000, in violation of the Department of Natural Resources' permitting timeline. Moreover, the DNR would not issue a temporary permit to allow purchase of the property even though a settlement had been reached with the property owner. Given the situation, the Bluestem board decided to suspend planning for a new landfill. As Berkshire (2003, p. 180) concluded:

> There were just too many "ifs," way too many things out flapping in the wind, for them [sic] to spend any more money to develop a landfill on the Hennessey property.

Despite having undertaken what Berkshire (2003, p. 180) proclaimed to be "the most extensive solid waste planning process that had ever been conducted in the State of Iowa" the process was terminated before it could achieve its objective.

Place and Practice

Read from the perspective of the micro-politics of planning, this case illustrates two aspects of practice places that deserve our attention. The first is their multiplicity and the second is their influence on what is said, who participates, and whether what happens there becomes public. Both aspects speak directly to current concerns with deliberation, negotiation, and collaboration (Forester, 2009; Innes and Booher, 2004) and to the broader goal of democratic and just planning. The array of places within a planning event has consequences for whose voices are heard and poses strategic considerations regarding how planners might engage diverse publics. To the extent that specific places signal expectations about behavior, the array of places also influences what is said even as their degree of openness affects what becomes known beyond their boundaries.[9]

What should be obvious in the way that I have summarized the case is the number and diversity of places involved in what was a relatively simple planning event. Planning was distributed across a variety of places: the offices of the Bluestem planners, county and city planning departments, the lawyers, state and federal agencies, and consultants; the rooms used for focus group, advisory committee, and public meetings; and the numerous sites being considered, publicly debated, and privately negotiated. These places were located not just in divers places within Linn County but in the state capital, Washington, DC, and Altoona, Pennsylvania. Different types of activities occurred in each of these places, with some more important than others.

Note also how the planning event oscillated between relatively private places to which access was controlled and relatively public places where almost anyone could participate.[10] The process began in the privacy of the Bluestem boardroom and its offices and also outside those offices, in public, as the disposal of solid waste pushed against the geographical boundaries of the county's landfills and the limits of recycling and diversion. With the decision to make planning for the landfill a public event, the deliberations traveled from the offices of Bluestem, its consultants, and various city and county agencies to more open arenas, beginning with the places where the focus group and advisory committee met and the general public was convened. The deliberations subsequently oscillated between private analysis and public engagement, and places appropriate to them. Each successive widening of public involvement returned the planners to a more private place where data could be analyzed, public presentations crafted, experiences discussed, and strategy debated. The planners moved through places of varying transparency in order to enable the process to go forward as well as to assess and reassess their understandings and modify their positions.

All of the places, moreover, were connected. What happened at the landfills might have been obvious to a casual observer, but only became organizationally and politically meaningful when the planners translated their observations into technical calculations and findings. The physical environment and its representations were merged. A decision in the Bluestem boardroom, to offer a second example, required a recommendation from an advisory committee that was being informed by analyses developed in the offices of consultants. The places "bled" into each other – their boundaries porous. In addition, the temporal sequence was hardly linear, moving from the small places of expert and policy deliberation to the large places of public announcement and engagement. In fact, not only was the process spatially and temporally disjointed but the planners had only partial control over it. The planners had to negotiate between and among different stakeholders and various places – sometimes simultaneously, each of which revealed different aspects of the landfill issue.

The second aspect of place critical to planning practice has to do with how places influence what is said, who participates, and whether the goings-on in that place are revealed to the larger public. Places shape actions while the content, meaning, and value of talk depend on where it occurs. Places "provide contexts for communication" (Mitchell, 2005, p. 3). Laboratories and government offices are unlike street corners and athletic clubs. As Meyrowitz (1985, p. 41) reminds us: "By selectively exposing ourselves to events and other people, we control the flow of our actions and emotions," as well as the flow of the talk, actions, and emotions of others.[11]

This connection between place and speech has been acknowledged in the planning literature by both postmodernists and feminists. The postmodernists encouraged attention to both the spaces where the voices of the marginalized and oppressed are squelched and the interstitial spaces where they can speak freely (Bhabha, 1994; Sandercock, 1995). The feminists concurred, noting how, for example, Progressive Era women reformers were kept out of the corporate boardrooms and city council chambers where men made the "big" decisions about the city. Women had to find other places where they could speak, and act (Spain, 2001). The spatial segregation of women has always been a way to control their conversations, limit their access to male spheres, and diminish their status (Spain, 1992). In short, "people behave differently in different social 'situations' depending on *where* one is" (emphasis in the original) (Meyrowitz, 1985, p. viii). Our actions and words might not be determined by the places in which they occur, but they are certainly influenced by them.[12]

In their offices, the Bluestem planners debated alternative approaches to public engagement, commented on the costs and benefits of each, and spoke openly about the implications of public involvement for their control over the process, its outcomes, and the agency's political standing. There they could express themselves freely and hypothetically. Such conversations would have been less appropriate at a large public meeting where citizens expect clarity and certainty from experts. Larger venues are better suited to conveying information, engaging the public in discussions of priorities and consequences, and offering opportunities for dissent. The impersonality of an auditorium engenders a different type of engagement than the privacy and exclusivity of a small conference room.

Different spaces allow for different levels of speculation, different degrees of technical discussion, and different expressions of emotions. Engaged in a dispassionate assessment of public engagement procedures or landfill criteria with colleagues, planners can be blunter in their comments, more adventurous in their thinking, and less committed to positions. Intricate technical discussions are best held with fewer people and in smaller places and avoided in large, public meetings. In the latter, such talk often seems obfuscatory and insensitive to the issues that have mobilized publics both for and against the planning proposal.

In public places, the public mostly wants clear answers to its questions, not speculation; it wants to hear as much about fundamental decisions as details, and it wants to know that the planners, elected officials and policy-makers know what they are doing, even though it will often accuse them otherwise. For the most contentious of issues, these publics also want to vent their emotions either because something important about their world is threatened or because they are simply frustrated with government. They are there to express their concerns, not to deliberate. They are there for acknowledgment and validation, not for (just for) information. They are there to discuss the kinds of places in which they want to live, with whom they want to live, and the changes they are willing to tolerate, not technical arguments.[13]

A planning process must provide a variety of places in which these different needs can be met. Just as it is inappropriate to meet only with organized groups in small venues, it is detrimental to democracy to hold only public meetings. Not all meetings need to be open to everyone, nor should they be. Transparency and privacy have to be balanced. Planners, elected officials, protest organizations, and groups lending support need to meet alone to consider strategies and tactics, deliberate positions, and engage the issues. Transparency that hinders dissent is undemocratic in the same way that a lack of transparency thwarts justice and consolidates power.

The array of places also has to be considered in relation to the degree of publicity appropriate to a democracy. In an ideal world, the public would be fully aware of the information used and the decisions made. This is not always possible or even desirable (Kaza and Hopkins, 2009). Small groups need to meet alone to discuss the planning issue; key individuals need to isolate themselves for reflection. In both instances, making their deliberations and thoughts public would be cumbersome. More importantly, places have to exist where policy-makers, experts, and publics can meet without facing the scrutiny of others. Opposition groups require places where they can debate tactics and argue about values and positions. Policy-makers require places where they can consider the political ramifications of their actions. Experts need to engage in technical debates. All of these places appeared in the Bluestem landfill planning process.[14]

Places and participants then are interconnected, not autonomous factors in the crafting of a planning event. Larger spaces allow more voices to be heard. Smaller spaces are usually more selective. Large spaces are often more accessible and more likely to be viewed as public. To this extent, they often enable the most vociferous and best organized people to dominate the proceedings, even to the point of intimidating others. Because different types of people are included, different kinds of talk occur in one-person offices, conference rooms, legislative chambers, public auditoria, and executive suites. Moreover, the various decisions regarding the places (and people) to be part of the planning process are political decisions and thus dependent on the distribution of power across the groups and organizations involved.[15]

From the beginning, Bluestem committed itself to a countywide public process that would involve as many people as wanted to participate. The objectives were not only to gather knowledge and win support but also to portray the landfill as a public obligation. Public meetings would also enable the residents to imagine themselves as part of a political community. Being inclusive required more effort (and frustration) and extended the process in time, but it also, the planners hoped, would make the final decision more legitimate while educating the public about the difficulties of solid waste disposal. Implicit to the process was the framing of the landfill site as a common concern and thus one element in the moral cohesiveness of the community.

The array of places in which to stage the planning process then has implications for the inclusion and exclusion of publics and thus for the morality of places (Smith, 2007). People are treated equally in the extent to which they are allowed to participate equally. Doing so acknowledges their moral worth as well as the social ties that bind the political community. Meetings craft publics, and it is through publics that democracy unfolds (Dewey, 1927). One of the moral obligations of democratic planners is to strive for inclusion. This means recognizing that not all meetings can sustain full, representative participation and that even meetings designed for full participation are likely to fall well short of their ideal. Consequently, planners must think of a planning process not in terms of individual meetings but in terms of a constellation of places and meeting types that serve different political and social needs and involve a range of participants.

None of this discussion is meant to suggest that the places of this or any planning event are practically and/or theoretically significant or even that they are equally important. Was it necessary for the Bluestem planners to have had focus groups, an advisory committee, consultant meetings, meetings with the city and county planning departments, and information booths? While I suspect that the planners tried to avoid superfluous or trivial meetings, I also suspect that many meetings where it seemed that little was accomplished did serve a social or political purpose. In the midst of such a process, it is seldom obvious which meetings are necessary and which can be eliminated. Even after the fact it is often debatable which meetings were most consequential.

To speculate, a place might be theoretically significant when more publics are involved and more aspects of the issue are open to scrutiny. Here, significance would hinge on the transparency and inclusion of places. These places would help the theorist to assess whether the process was democratic and why planners were successful (or not) in achieving their objectives. Or, consider the significance of places in terms of how issues are framed; that is, in terms of the fundamental decisions that shape, even if elusively and often unconsciously, the resultant public deliberations (Gualini and Majoor, 2007; Schon and Rein, 1994). This line of thought confers greater significance on smaller and more exclusive places than if one focused on transparency and inclusion. There, planners and policy-makers develop the discursive frames of projects. In this landfill case, the decisions to (1) require the advisory committee to accept without question the work of the focus group, (2) make the process as public as possible, and (3) impose a farmland quality restriction on site selection were framing decisions and made in relative privacy. It is not enough, then, to identify the places of planning. The planning theorist also has to assess their significance both theoretically and practically, which in a practice-based theory amounts to the same thing.

Site, Place, Context

I began by distinguishing between site, place, and context. In concluding, I want to return to those three concepts, both to add depth to the interpretation of the case and to extend my theoretical argument about the importance of the places of practice.

Throughout, I have used "place" and "site" to refer to where planning occurs. I implied that they are non-overlapping, conceptual categories that contrast the knowledge and experiences of people in their daily lives and the professional knowledge and activities of planners. In reality, however, the distinction is seldom precise. Sites were once places (and will be again if the planners and developers are successful) and thus are best thought of as a place in transition. Consequently, a site is only temporary, an event. If Bluestem had been successful in opening a new landfill, that site would have quickly been turned into a place when work crews laid out access roads, trucks dumped waste, bulldozer operators arranged the waste, environmental officers measured run-off and toxins, local residents discussed the landfill, and birds flocked to pick through the refuse. Moreover, what might be a potential site to one group (for example, developers) might still be a place to another (for example, those who live there). Because they are socially situated in quite different realms, site and lived place can co-exist.

Critics of planning often accuse practitioners of fixating on sites and failing to acknowledge the importance of place to peoples' lives (Graham and Healey, 1999; Stephenson, 2010). Redevelopment initiatives, highway construction, and pro-gentrification policies are viewed as denying history and a "right to the city" to a place's inhabitants, and doing so to serve moneyed interests and tax-hungry local governments. They also accuse mainstream planning thought of being dominated by an essentialist, Euclidean view of the world that casts place as an absolute location within a passive and empty space. Space becomes a container for objects from buildings to neighborhoods whose improvement will result in better places in which to live, work, and play (Murdoch, 2006, pp. 133–8). In response, these critics propose an alternative understanding which infuses place with attachments and meanings, part of an integrated set of social relations that involve identity, history, memory, and moral attachments (Gieryn, 2000; Smith, 2007, p. 7). From this perspective, place is socially constructed or performed and thus open and fluid. It "gathers things, thoughts, and memories in particular configurations" (Escobar, 2001, p. 143; see also Healey, 2005).

By contrast, a site is a place re-cast in professional terms such as lot size, zoning designation, and market value and done so for the purpose of intervention (Beauregard, 2005). The place is being prepared for development by being sanitized and made legible to those who would act on it. The history of planning, in fact, can be organized around the need to create stable and actionable representations – ichnographic maps, GIS displays – of space and place (Soderstrom, 1996). And although state-supported property boundaries and property tax systems overlay all places in the cities and regions of advanced economies (Scott, 1998), only some of these places become targets of state or private-sector intervention and are turned into sites.[16]

From this perspective, the planning relationship between people and place takes three forms: one, the transformation of places into sites and then into new places; two, the preservation and/or conservation of places; and, three, the defense of places. In the first instance, planners design and implement efforts to rationalize land holdings, provide infrastructure, and eliminate unsafe and unsanitary housing while providing state-approved housing or demolishing a slum for commercial development. This is what Soderstrom (1996, p. 271) terms curative intervention. Planners also appropriate sites for public use, thereby eliminating the previous function as with Bluestem's initiative to replace farming with waste disposal. In the second instance, planners protect places from threats to their history and current social relations. Here we find such policy tools as historic preservation ordinances, anti-gentrification laws, and housing code enforcement. Zoning, of course, one of the most ubiquitous of planning tools, is a way of protecting place and also making it relatively easy for places to be bought and sold, developed or redeveloped, cleared or maintained. The third instance involves people defending their neighborhoods and cities from being turned into a different place, one where their concerns have been over-ridden by a politics from which they are excluded. Here we find opposition.[17] All of these planning events inevitably generate controversy with planners on all sides of such issues.

Places are not just different from sites but also from space. Space is endlessly and essentially ethereal; it is, in Casey's (1997, p. 3) phrase, an "utter void." Despite its elusiveness, though, space gives definition to place. Unlike space, places exist because people and things occupy them, give them shared meanings, and situate them in collective memory. Places are not empty but rather filled. Such representations, however, edge close to the problematic space-as-container metaphor.

One solution to the theoretical problems posed by space as an endless void and a container for places is to approach space relationally. Rather than claiming that space exists prior to places and that places are produced "in space" by filling it with social relations, the argument instead is that space is the product of social encounters. As Massey (2005, p. 10) has written: "space does not exist prior to identities/entities and their relations." Space is open to action and not simply a void that pre-exists it. Although such a formulation borders on the metaphysical, it avoids the Euclidean assumptions of space-as-container. The container metaphor hinders understanding of planning practice by ignoring how the diverse places of practice are connected to each other both spatially and temporally.

Still unaddressed is the third term – context – with which I began this article.[18] Context is another way of differentiating space. The reference is usually to the history, current dynamics, and conditions of the metropolitan region as they impinge on its core city, the nation-state as it influences what happens in its provinces, or the neighborhood as it bounds the prosperity of households (Watson, 2008). In the Bluestem landfill case, multiple contexts were in play: legislation emanating from Washington, DC, state environmental permitting policy, city and county zoning regulations, and the agricultural space-economy.

In the planning literature, two meanings of context are deployed. One has to do with the actual setting in which planning occurs: for example, the conference room in which the planners are negotiating with the developer, the low-income neighborhood where activists are organizing to resist gentrification, the city council chambers where a resident group is calling for historic designation of a neighborhood. Action cannot be understood independently of this context (Flyvbjerg, 2001). One acts in a specific place, at a specific time, and within a specific social setting. Abbott (2001, p. 23) captured this understanding well when he wrote: "the social world is made up of situated actions" that are being "continuously embed[ded] … in constraining structures." This is the proximate context.

A second meaning of context is represented by Fainstein's (1997) reference to the Dutch welfare state's influence on planning in Amsterdam. This is the distant context; it is the deep background to the foreground of the proximate context. It focuses on the institutions, history, macro-politics, and socio-economic conditions that arch over any single place rather than the richness and particularities of the place where planning actually happens. Watson (2008, p. 230) refers to this as the "broader economic and political forces" that encase planning practice. From this perspective, planning is doubly situated. It happens both in a specific place and in a more encompassing realm of constraints and opportunities.

As a concept, context is not without its critics. Becker (1995) points to its sloppy use in many sociological studies, a failing also prevalent in planning stories. He writes that scholars often provide background information "even if we don't specify exactly how it's relevant, even if we don't make what we mention an explicit part of our analysis" (p. 54). Little attention is given to the causal paths that link contextual conditions with actual practices. Becker then argues that "if it belongs in that description [of the social event], it belongs in your analysis" (p. 57). Latour (2005) goes even further. He claims that there is no context beyond the action itself. Context, and by this I believe he means the distant context, is a theoretical artifice. Contextual factors, Latour claims, do not deserve, nor do they have, ontological status. For him, if these forces are operative in a particular social event then they should be treated as such, not relegated to the background.

Site, place, and context; these concepts are ubiquitous in practice stories. Often conflated in different combinations and with little attention to the distinction between the proximate and the distant, they are used to explain and interpret how planners think and what consequences ensue from their efforts. What concerns me as regards practice-based planning theory is the disregard of the array of places where practice occurs. Practice places are fundamental to planning's micro-politics. They influence the deliberations, participation, and publicity that are pivotal for a democratic and just planning, and contribute to planning's effectiveness. A practice-based planning theory that fails to take seriously the places of practice deprives its readers of critical insights. The places of practice include more than the sites of intervention. And while I cannot claim that the Bluestem planners would have been more successful if they had been more mindful of the ways in which such practice places function – and I am not even sure that they did not do so – I do claim that planning theorists who neglect the places of practice are missing much that is important about what planners do.

Notes

1. The exceptions include Graham and Healey (1999), Lapintie (2007), Smith (2007), and Stephenson (2010).
2. Many studies treat place similarly. See, for example, Beauregard (2004) and Gualini and Majoor (2007).

3. Fainstein is also interested in the nation, but treats it more as a space than a place, a distinction I discuss below.

4. In any planning event, decisions are made by both planners and non-planners, and thus in the places where planners work and the places where others work.

5. The following is a summary of a case written by Michael Berkshire (2003) who was the regional solid waste planning coordinator for Bluestem during this time. I selected the case because it refers to a variety of places of practice; in presenting it, I emphasize those places.

6. The staff might have also gathered information outside its offices, but this is not mentioned in the case.

7. At this time, the state legislature in Des Moines was debating changes in the existing condemnation (i.e. taking) law. This added another place to the process and increased the pressure on the Bluestem planners to act quickly.

8. The issue here is not why a landfill should be distant from an airport but how politicians are able to use legislation to block a locally unwanted land use.

9. In considering these two aspects of place, I ignore another dimension of practice's materiality and that is the relation of planners to things (but see Beauregard, 2012).

10. Winkler (2011, pp. 260–1) hints at such differences with her typology of closed spaces, invited spaces, and claimed spaces. Clearly, the public–private distinction is a crude one. I use it simply as a way to enter into the discussion.

11. Gieryn (2006) claims that the credibility of scientific knowledge depends, in part, on the place – the truth-spot – from which it emanates, not just who conveys that knowledge.

12. In discussing the places of policy transfer, McCann (2008, p. 900) writes that "these microspaces frame the ways in which policy actors *imagine* their practice and their policies" (my emphasis). A more poignant example involves the essayist and historian Tony Judt who died of amyotrophic lateral sclerosis (ALS) in August of 2010. Of his last days, his wife, Jennifer Homans (2012, p. 6), wrote that "he had lost his students, his classrooms, his desk, his books; he couldn't travel or take a walk. He had lost, in other words, the *places* that had helped him to think through his ideas" (emphasis in original).

13. For an introduction to the relationship of place to democracy, see Jackson's (2008) history of urban renewal in New Haven (CT) that explicitly recognizes "the ways in which social movements are grounded in particular community spaces" (p. 224).

14. In his well-known article "Ends and means in planning", Edward Banfield (1959, pp. 365–6) wrote that it would be imprudent for an organization to publicize a course of action in advance since doing so would invite opposition and give it an advantage. Staeheli and Mitchell (2008, pp. xx–xxiii) make a related point in relation to the politics of public space. As regards community gardens, they write (p. 108) that "since *difference* was so critical to the function of community, these public spaces were created through acts of exclusion to create safe places in which it was possible to conceive of different kinds of [counterpublics]" (emphasis in original). This point, of course, is related to Goffman's (1973) front and back regions where different kinds of performances occur.

15. Scott (1998, p. 78) notes that legibility and transparency confer political advantages on those "who have the knowledge and access to easily decipher the new state-created format."

16. A parallel process occurs when states turn politically robust citizens into clients or beneficiaries (Krause, 2010).
17. Planning stories about the defense of place often equate place with empowerment (for the inhabitants) and site with their victimization. In most of them, planners are stripped of place, and this (arguably and ironically) empowers them by making them less visible, unreachable, and thus less vulnerable.
18. As a supplement to this site–place–context triad, the reader might consider the divisions of territory, place, scale, and network discussed in Jessop, Brenner and Jones (2008).

References

Abbott, A. (2001). *Time matters: On theory and method*. Chicago, IL: University of Chicago Press.

Banfield, E. (1959). Ends and means in planning. *International Social Science Journal, 11*, 361–8.

Beauregard, R. (2004). Mistakes were made: Rebuilding the World Trade Center, phase 1. *International Planning Studies, 9*, 139–53.

Beauregard, R. (2005). From place to site. In A. Kahn and C. Burns (eds), *Site matters* (pp. 39–58). New York: Routledge.

Beauregard, R. (2012). Planning with things. *Journal of Planning Education and Research, 32*, 182–90.

Becker, H. S. (1995). *Tricks of the trade*. Chicago, IL: University of Chicago Press.

Berkshire, M. (2003). In search of a new landfill site. In B. Eckstein and J. Throgmorton (eds), *Story and sustainability* (pp. 167–82). Cambridge, MA: MIT Press.

Bhabha, H. (1994). *The location of culture*. London: Routledge.

Casey, E. S. (1997). *The fate of place: A philosophical history*. Berkeley, CA: University of California Press.

Dewey, J. (1927). *The public and its problems*. Athens, OH: Swallow Press.

Escobar, A. (2001). Culture sits in places: Reflections on globalization and subaltern strategies of localization. *Political Geography, 20*, 139–74.

Fainstein, S. S. (1997). The egalitarian city: The restructuring of Amsterdam. *International Planning Studies, 2*, 295–314.

Flyvbjerg, B. (2001). *Making social science matter*. Cambridge: Cambridge University Press.

Forester, J. (1996). Argument, power, and passion in planning practice. In S. J. Mandelbaum, L. Mazza and R. W. Burchell (eds), *Explorations in planning theory* (pp. 241–62). New Brunswick, NJ: CUPR Press.

Forester, J. (2009). *Dealing with differences: Dramas of mediating public disputes*. New York: Cornell University Press.

Gieryn, T. F. (2000). A space for place in sociology. *Annual Review of Sociology, 26*, 463–96.

Gieryn, T. F. (2006). City as truth-spot: Laboratories and field-sites in urban studies. *Social Studies of Science, 36*, 5–38.

Goffman, E. (1973). *The presentation of self in everyday life*. Woodstock, NY: Overlook Press.

Graham, S., and Healey, P. (1999). Relational concepts of space and place: Issues for planning theory and practice. *European Planning Studies, 7*, 623–46.

Gualini, E., and Majoor, S. (2007). Innovative practices in large urban development projects: Conflicting frames in the quest for "new urbanity". *Planning Theory and Practice*, 8, 297–318.

Healey, P. (2005). Editorial. *Planning Theory and Practice*, 6, 5–8.

Homans, J. A. (2012). Tony Judt: A final victory. *New York Review of Books*, 54(5), 4–7.

Hrelja, R. (2011). The tyranny of small decisions. Unsustainable cities and local day-to-day transport planning. *Planning Theory and Practice*, 12, 511–24.

Innes, J. E., and Booher, D. E. (2004). Reforming public participation: Strategies for the 21st century. *Planning Theory and Practice*, 5, 419–36.

Jackson, M. I. (2008). *Model cities blues: Urban space and organized resistance in New Haven.* Philadelphia, PA: Temple University Press.

Jessop, B., Brenner, N., and Jones, M. (2008). Theorizing sociospatial relations. *Environment and Planning D*, 26, 389–401.

Kaza, N., and Hopkins, L. (2009). In what circumstances should plans be public? *Journal of Planning Education and Research*, 28, 491–502.

Krause, M. (2010). Accounting for state intervention: The social histories of "beneficiaries". *Qualitative Sociology*, 33, 533–47.

Latour, B. (2005). *Reassembling the social: An introduction to actor-network theory.* Oxford: Oxford University Press.

Lapintie, K. (2007). Modalities of urban space. *Planning Theory*, 6, 36–51.

Massey, D. (2005). *For space.* London: Sage.

McCann, E. (2008). Expertise, truth, and urban policy mobilities. *Environment and Planning A*, 40, 885–904.

Meyrowitz, J. (1985). *No sense of place: The impact of electronic media on social behavior.* New York: Oxford University Press.

Mitchell, W. J. (2005). *Placing words: Symbols, space, and the city.* Cambridge, MA: The MIT Press.

Murdoch, J. (2006). *Post-structural geography: A guide to relational space.* London: Sage.

Sandercock, L. (1995). Voices from the borderlands: A meditation on a metaphor. *Journal of Planning Education and Research*, 14, 77–88.

Schon, D., and Rein, M. (1994). *Frame reflection: Toward a resolution of intractable policy controversies.* New York: Basic Books.

Scott, J. C. (1998). *Seeing like a state.* New Haven, CT: Yale University Press.

Smith, D. (2007). Moral aspects of place. *Planning Theory*, 6, 7–15.

Soderstrom, O. (1996). Paper cities: Visual thinking in urban planning. *Ecumene*, 3, 249–81.

Spain, D. (1992). *Gendered spaces.* Chapel Hill, NC: University of North Carolina Press.

Spain, D. (2001). *How women saved the city.* Minneapolis, MN: University of Minnesota Press.

Staeheli, L. A., and Mitchell, D. (2008). *The people's property? Power, politics and the public.* New York: Routledge.

Stephenson, J. (2010). People and place. *Planning Theory and Practice*, 11, 9–21.

Watson, V. (2008). Down to earth: Linking planning theory and practice in the "metropole" and beyond. *International Planning Studies*, 13, 223–37.

Winkler, T. (2011). Retracking Johannesburg: Spaces for participation and policymaking. *Journal of Planning Education and Research*, 31, 258–71.

15

Home, Sweet Home

American Residential Zoning in Comparative Perspective

Sonia Hirt

It has long been a cliché to call America a "nation of homeowners." This statement is true in the sense that most American households – some 66 percent of them – own their homes. But the phrase also implies something else: that homeownership is the embodiment, the "lynchpin," the "crown jewel" of the "American dream," as politicians and journalists continue to tell us (e.g., Lowenthal and Curzan 2011; Forman 2011). It implies that in its unique dedication to homeownership, America stands out among other nations. This notion, however, is demonstrably false. Although homeownership rates were significantly higher in the United States than in other parts of the "Western world" some hundred years ago,[1] this is no longer the case. In fact, when it comes to homeownership, today's America is a middle-range country, ranked seventeenth out of twenty-six "economically advanced countries" (Pollock 2010).[2]

But compared to other industrialized nations, at least those in Europe, America's housing patterns may be distinct in another way. Americans are not simply homeowners; they are *single-family* home owners. About 69 percent of US housing comprises single-family dwellings. In *detached* single-family homes – homes with private yards – America resolutely beats almost all European nations[3] and Europe as a whole. About 63 percent of American housing is detached single-family homes (US Census Bureau 2011a). The comparable average number for the EU 27 is 34 percent; for the 17 countries comprising the Eurozone, it is only 30 (European Commission, n.d.-a). In the United Kingdom, the percentage of households

Original publication details: Hirt, Sonia. 2013. "Home, Sweet Home: American Residential Zoning in Comparative Perspective". In *Journal of Planning Education and Research*, 33(3) 292–309. Reproduced with permission from SAGE and Sonia Hirt.

Readings in Planning Theory, Fourth Edition. Edited by Susan S. Fainstein and James DeFilippis.
Editorial material and organization © 2016 John Wiley & Sons, Ltd.
Published 2016 by John Wiley & Sons, Ltd.

residing in single-family homes is massive (85 percent), but it dwindles when we separate the detached from the attached homes (less than 25 percent in detached homes and more than 60 percent in attached homes, i.e., row housing). In Germany, a minority (45 percent) live in single-family homes and a smaller minority (29 percent) in detached ones (European Commission, n.d.-a). One can dig into the European numbers a bit deeper and detect a story very different from the US one. Notwithstanding recent trends toward urban de-centralization, detached single-family housing is, on the other side of the North Atlantic, often associated with small towns and villages, with a rural way of life. In contrast, large cities are dominated by multifamily buildings. Seventy-eight percent of the population of Amsterdam lives in such buildings, 82 in Berlin, 94 in Paris, 96 in Rome, and 97 in Madrid[4] (Urban Audit, n.d.). Compare this to American cities. Only New York comes close with 80 percent of its housing stock as multifamily housing (the figure drops, though, to 62 for New York's metropolis as a whole). In Chicago, the numbers are 65 percent (city) and 37 (metropolis), in Seattle 46 (city) and 29 (metropolis), in New Orleans 21 (city/parish) and 31 (metropolis), and in Philadelphia only 25 (city) and 20 (metropolis) (US Census Bureau 2011b). Not surprisingly, densities in US metropolises are, likely, the lowest in the world.[5]

It is fair to say then, that there is something quintessentially American about the detached single-family home, as many scholars have already noted (e.g., Kostof 1987; Kelly 1993; Archer 2005). In 1681, William Penn dreamed of Philadelphia as a town for "country gentlemen," a town in which every house would be placed far apart from its neighbors, "in the middle of its plat, as to the breadthway of it, so that there may be ground on each side for gardens or orchards, or fields" (cited by Skaler and Keels 2008, 44). This dream seems to have been realized throughout the country (even though the gardens, orchards, and fields that Penn envisioned eventually became private yards used for recreational rather than productive purposes).

In this chapter, I propose that America's housing patterns are not only spatially but also *legally exceptional*. Specifically, I suggest that the municipal land-use regulations that pertain to single-family housing areas are distinct from regulations in other "Western" countries, at least those in Europe, where municipal land-use-based zoning originated during the nineteenth century. These regulations support the special status of America's landmark housing form – the detached single-family home. I use the verb "suggest" intentionally: the claim I make requires a study of all European countries, which I cannot offer. However, empirical accounts of how the Europeans practice urban land-use regulation have accumulated for some time. We know definitively that the land-use control system in Europe's largest countries, England, France, and Germany, is quite different from that of the United States today. The differences span a variety of issues, including the different role of the public sector in the production and regulation of urban forms and the different treatment of private property rights. The distinction most pertinent to this paper, however, is that the English, French and Germans do not afford the exceptional legal protection of the surroundings of the single-family home that is characteristic of traditional American zoning ordinances. Specifically, the Europeans do not separate residential and nonresidential uses as rigidly as a "typical" US zoning code, nor do they separate single- from multifamily housing as strictly (Delafons 1969; Cullingworth 1993; Lefcoe 1979; Liebmann 1996; Hall 2007; Hirt 2007a, 2007b). A recent study (Hirt 2012) compared land-use control in five European nations: England, France, Germany, Sweden, and Russia, each of which is the largest member of one of the five European planning schools according to the typology used by Newman and Thornley (1996). The study confirmed at a broader European scale that land-use separation by zoning is stronger in the United States.

Segregation and exclusionary single-family zoning have been assailed by US scholars and practitioners on social, economic, and ecological grounds at least since the 1960s (e.g., Jacobs 1961; Sennett 1970; Davidoff and Davidoff 1971). This critique is so well known that it needs no further repetition. As a result of this critique, planners and lawyers have rethought many of the assumptions behind traditional zoning. To an extent, ordinances around the country have been revised as part of the rising wave of Smart Growth and New Urbanism (e.g., Ohm and Sitkowski 2003; Pendall, Puentes, and Martin 2006). Still, systematic empirical data on the extent to which legally mandated land-use and housing segregation have been overcome is limited. Recent studies of some of America's largest cities found that large tracts of developable urban land, some 30 to 60 percent, are still zoned in ways that permit only residential uses and that single- and multifamily homes continue to be separated by zoning (Hirt 2007a, 2013). This finding supports the claims of scholars such as Levine (2006) and Hall (2007) that zoning reforms have been timid.

It is commonly stated that US zoning was imported from Europe, specifically from Germany, in the early 1900s (Lefcoe 1979; Power 1989; Liebmann 1996).[6] Early twentieth-century zoning ordinances in Germany and America were similar. Yet, as I will show, differences emerged early on, including differences in the very names and definitions of the zoning categories. The English carried on the zoning tradition only until the late 1940s – when traditional zoning was at its height in the United States. After World War II, they abandoned the zoning system altogether.[7]

I discuss two important tools that are likely "made in America." Europe lacked them in the early twentieth century (and still does). These are the strict separation of home and business through zoning and the creation of a residential district that permits *only* detached homes. Both of these granted an exceptional status to detached, single-family housing. Even after all the new tools that US planners have invented over the last fifty years – planned unit development, performance, incentive, inclusionary, form-based zoning, etc. – these hundred-year-old zoning constructs are still very much with us today.

I have attempted to reconstruct aspects of early twentieth-century US history from primary and secondary sources: books, master plans, zoning ordinances, speech transcripts, and publications in professional journals and the media. I greatly benefited from the works of three prominent American lawyers and zoning "fathers": Edward Bassett,[8] Ernst Freund,[9] and Frank Backus Williams.[10] My primary goal is to set the historic record straight: US zoning deviated from its European predecessors early on. My data are admittedly fragmented and limited by the types of archival documents I could find at the libraries of two large US universities. Because primary sources on the foreign countries are especially scarce, I cannot offer a full-fledged comparison between the United States, Germany, and England. Rather, my aspiration is to contextualize the US experience (for which my data are much richer) within that of the other two nations.[11] My hope is that this approach will underscore aspects of the American zoning tradition that may have become habitual yet are exceptional if we use the experiences of other countries as a reference point.

I first review the origins of zoning. Next, I establish the historical record showing that American zoning began to deviate early on from German and English zoning in treating land-use separation and residential separation. Finally, I review some justifications for land-use and housing separation, as early American zoning advocates articulated them, and propose some hypotheses of why the United States developed the zoning categories that it did.

Roots of Zoning

As textbooks tell us, zoning is a municipal law that divides the area under a particular local government's jurisdiction into sub-areas or districts in which it "limits the uses to which land can be put" (Levy 2011, 72–3). Typically, it regulates three aspects of built form: function, shape, and bulk (Kayden 2004). Zoning has many sources, whose lineage I will attempt to briefly sum up below.

The first source comprises historic building, nuisance, and housing laws (Nelson 1977). This is especially true if we distance ourselves from zoning's recent, twentieth-century focus on regulating functions (typically classified as residential, commercial, industrial, etc.) and take it, more broadly, as a public act that regulates private building activities. In this case, we can say that zoning's roots can be traced all the way back to the nearly four-thousand-year-old Code of Hammurabi.[12]

In medieval England, urban building codes date back to the twelfth century, when London's first Mayor, Henry Fitzailwin, issued the *Assize of Buildings* (Manco 2009; Green 2011). The early urban codes were primarily concerned with fire safety and thus focused on the regulation of construction materials and, to a lesser extent, the relationship of buildings to their neighbors and the street. German cities such as Munich had fairly sophisticated codes of this type in the fourteenth century. By the seventeenth century, these codes had become a common feature in

Europe's major cities (Hall 2009; Talen 2012). About that time, the Laws of the Indies began to regulate some aspects of settlement form in colonial America (Talen 2009). Restrictions on the size and, particularly, the height of structures entered building codes sometime in the 1700s: for example, in Paris. Some hundred years later, height regulation became practice in American cities such as New York (1887), Washington (1899), Baltimore (1904), and Los Angeles (1904) (Garvin 1996, 356–94; Barnett 2011). Nuisance laws developed in parallel to building laws over a thousand-year-long period. In twelfth-century London, neighbors could bring nuisance claims against each other under the *Assize of Buildings*. In North America, nuisance laws regulating the noxious trades and sometimes banning them from cities date back to colonial times. Along with the building laws, they served as the major means of land-use control until the emergence of zoning in the early twentieth century (Talen 2012). New Amsterdam (later New York) had building rules as far back as 1625 (Delafons 1969). Boston enacted legislation on fire safety and building materials in 1672, followed by restrictions on the location of slaughterhouses, stills, and tallow manufacturers twenty years later. These were Boston's primary land-use control tools until the city's first zoning code in 1924. By the end of the nineteenth century, all major American cities had building and nuisance laws of this type (Garvin 1996). Cities also developed housing tenement laws, like New York's pioneering one from 1867. Legal efforts to limit nuisances existed not only at the municipal level but also at the state and, in Europe, the national level. In 1692, Massachusetts stipulated that slaughterhouses be built only in certain parts of town. In 1703, New York decreed that industries such as liquor and limestone-making must stay at least half a mile away from city halls (Talen 2012). In the British Isles, Public Health Acts provided relatively strong means of controlling urban form by extending the powers of local authorities to enforce building by-laws.[13] French and German building and nuisance laws became highly codified in the eighteenth and nineteenth century.[14] In 1810, a Napoleonic decree created protected districts in French cities, where the location of injurious uses was banned (Reynard 2002; Morag-Levine 2011). The Prussian and the German Imperial Code followed suit soon thereafter: noxious industries had to obtain licenses from the public authorities, which were subject to conditions related to performance. If they failed to meet these standards, the industries were banned from the protected districts of cities (Williams 1914a, 1922; Logan 1976; Hirt 2007a).

These laws, however, did not create specific rules for specific districts of specific cities. They applied citywide and sometimes (in Europe) to cities generally, state- or nation-wide. The division of a specific city's territory into zones with separate rules for each emerged only in the nineteenth century. The Germans – pioneers in the "scientific administration" of cities – were the first to employ this technique (Mullen 1976; Lefcoe 1979; Power 1989; Ladd 1990; Liebmann 1996). For this invention, they were profusely praised in America.[15] Edward Bassett (1922b) and Frank Backus Williams (1914a, 1914b, 1922) claimed that the word "zone" is of French origin and linked it to the medieval practice of taking down the defense walls around French cities and replacing them with "belts" or "zones" – parks, boulevards, etc. Bassett and Williams deeply admired German cities for their long-standing efforts to protect housing by banning the location of industries in certain locations (e.g., where the prevailing winds would drive smoke towards a town's center). As Williams appreciatively noted, "almost from the beginnings of their history, German cities were governed by regulations which were the same for the entire city" (1914b, 1). Note, however, that just as Williams observed in 1914, the German regulations, including those developed during the height of the Industrial Revolution, "did not create ... either residential or industrial districts, much less classify or grade them" (1914b, 27). The German laws placed restrictions only on *some* industries and never excluded them from housing areas altogether. The notion that entire areas of cities should serve as purely residential enclaves and should be guarded as such by law was not yet invented.

There was another way of guarding residential exclusivity, however, although it was used only for the residences of the rich. The tool was *private* regulation: deed restrictions or restrictive covenants. The history of such private regulations spans centuries. Platt (2004), for example, discusses the regulations used during the building boom on the north and west side of London that followed the city's 1666–1667 planned reconstruction after the Great Fire. What eventually became the fashionable West End district was not subject to public rules under the Act for Rebuilding London. Instead, it was built following private agreements between the land's aristocratic owners and its developers and occupants. During the nineteenth century, the private rules became increasingly widespread in the large cities of Europe and America (e.g., London, Paris, New York, Chicago, St. Louis), as well as in their growing suburbs. They regulated all sorts of matters pertaining to the "nice" residential neighborhoods, from the mundane (e.g., how often to mow the lawn) to the functional (what the proper building types should be); from the aesthetic (what the proper architectural styles should be) to the sinister (e.g., what skin color potential buyers could have) (Atkins 1993; McKenzie 1994; Garvin 1996, 355–94; Le Goix and Callen 2010). Thus, they served their purpose well: they guarded the upper classes from the invasion of the growing multiethnic/multiracial proletarian armies. In America specifically, private covenants were so popular that some reject the notion that zoning was a "German invention" – the classic theory postulated by scholars such as Williams (1922, 210) and Ladd (1990, 187) – and claim that it was a US "home product" (Fischler and Kolnik 2006), "a child of the covenants" (Wiseman 2010, 713). Yet in the early 1900s, from the viewpoint of municipal zoning advocates such as Bassett, the private rules were "far from satisfactory": they were piecemeal, had term limits, and could not "stabilize large land areas, different parts of which can properly be put to different uses" (1922b, 317).[16,17] Nuisance and building laws had the opposite problem: they banned or restricted uses citywide, yet all uses that were economically advantageous *had* to have a place somewhere in the city.[18] Enter zoning: a municipal regulatory system that promised a place for everything and everything in its place.[19]

Separating Home from Work

Doubtlessly, some separation between home and work spans the history of urban civilizations (Kolnick 2008). Well prior to the advent of scientific knowledge about health and sanitation, people sensed that certain production activities such as butchering, brick-burning, etc. should be conducted away from living quarters because they are unpleasant, unsightly, or dangerous. The advent of highly polluting manufacturing during the Industrial Revolution, however, made the separation of dwelling from other activities more pertinent than ever before. Industrial-Age cities were already experiencing market-driven land-use specialization expressed in space. Downtowns were losing residents and were increasingly dominated by high-class retail and offices (since the latter could outbid even the most affluent homeowners in the competition for valuable central space); industries and warehousing were grouping in distinct areas to take advantage of common suppliers and transport facilities; and wealthy residents were withdrawing into suburbs (Knox and McCarthy 2005, 115–37). Although workers' housing continued to mingle with industry, for the upper and middle classes the distance between place of living and place of working became greater than during any preceding historic era. As the historian P. Stearns noted: "The biggest jolt the Industrial Revolution administered to the Western family was the progressive removal of work from the home" (cited by Kotkins 2006). In this sense, the land-use laws that spread during the late nineteenth and early twentieth centuries only strengthened processes that were already well under way (Knox and McCarthy 2005).

Even so, somebody at some point must have come up with the idea that cities could, through legal means, be zoned for discrete purposes. Furthermore, the purposes had to be articulated as modern zoning categories: residential, commercial, industrial, etc. Williams believed he knew the source. While acknowledging the role that Napoleon's 1810 decree (and the subsequent German Imperial laws) played in creating protected urban residential zones, he gave special credit to Reinhard Baumeister, a professor at the University of Karlsruhe and one of Germany's "greatest theoretical planners" (Williams 1914a, 1; 1922, 210).[20] In 1876, Baumeister published a book called *Stadterweiterungen in Technischer, Baupolizeilicher und Wirthschaftlicher Beziehung* (Urban Expansion with Respect to Technology, Building Code and Economy). The book presented one of the most comprehensive analyses of urban problems and solutions at the time. Baumeister discussed myriad ideas. One of the most consequential was his observation that economic activities in the industrial city have a tendency to group together more so than during any earlier historic period. Baumeister's proposal was to reinforce this "natural" process by a municipal legal mechanism – districting or zoning. In his view, it made sense to categorize buildings in three classes and locate them in three zones:

> When we built a vision of the future ... we want to distinguish three sections. The first consists of the large-scale industry and wholesaling ... but also the homes of the workers and even the factory owners; the second includes all trades which require direct contact with the public, and similarly the homes which must be united with the trade premises; the third includes homes whose owners have no trade and have different occupations (landlords, officials, merchants, factory owners, workers). (Translated from Baumeister 1876, 80; see also Incorporated Society of Architects and Engineers of Germany 1907).[21]

Williams also praised Mayor Franz Adickes, under whose leadership Frankfurt became the first city in Germany (and, in all likelihood, the world) to fully divide itself into districts, with separate rules for each, as part of a municipal master plan (Mullen 1976). The idea of dividing a city into zones with rules pertaining to function (as well as bulk and shape) spread quickly in Germany and later in Switzerland, Scandinavia, and England (Williams [1916] 1929, 81). Berlin adopted zoning in 1887, Munich in 1904, Düsseldorf and Cologne in 1912, etc. (Ladd 1990).

But the separation of uses in these German ordinances was different from what became typical in twentieth-century America (Light 1999). The pioneering Frankfurt Zoning Act of 1891 had two broad zones: inner and outer. The inner one, the old city core, already had an intricate mixture of existing uses. No land-use-based zoning was enacted for the built-out center: the land uses could continue to coexist; only a few nuisance types were explicitly prohibited. The outer part of Frankfurt was itself divided into inner, outer, and country. In outer Frankfurt, a land-use-based zonal classification system was adopted with three types of districts: residential, industrial, and mixed. But each zone permitted more than a single land-use class. The mixed districts were exactly as their name suggests. The residential districts, however, were far from purely residential. They allowed industries that complied with the industrial performance norms outlined in the Imperial Code (shall we call this performance zoning?). Code-compliant industries were not banned per se. But locating them in the residential areas was hard because they had to meet stringent bulk rules. Often, they were too big to fit (shall we call this form-based zoning?). The industrial areas, on the other hand, were more restrictive than anything else. Most types of dwellings were unwelcome: only those of the service personnel (factory watchmen, caretakers) were allowed by right (Williams 1914a; Logan 1976; Talen 2012).

Fast-forward to America, a quarter of a century later. As readers undoubtedly know, the first comprehensive zoning ordinance in America was enacted in New York in 1916[22] (e.g., see Haar and Kayden 1989; Bressi 1993; Fischler 1998b). Like

Frankfurt, New York had three types of use districts (in addition to the overlapping height and bulk districts). But that was one of few similarities. Unlike the German city, no part of New York was left without land-use zoning – hence New York's claim to pioneering comprehensiveness – although, of course, existing uses could continue to operate under a nonconforming status.[23] New York's use classifications – residential, business, and unrestricted – resembled Frankfurt's mostly in name. To begin with, they were organized using a hierarchical principle: residential on top, industrial at the bottom. This meant that new residences could locate everywhere in the city, commerce could locate in the business and the unrestricted districts but not in the residential zones, and manufacturing could be located only in areas labeled as unrestricted. The contrasts with Frankfurt are perhaps obvious but nonetheless important to highlight. New York created areas *exclusively* for housing, whereas no such thing existed in Frankfurt.[24] According to Garvin (1996, 364), just under half of the post-1916 New York population resided in areas designated only for housing. True, the existing mix of uses was not immediately rooted out (again, because of the nonconforming clause), but the principle of creating pure housing zones was now on the books in ways it was not in Germany, where industry was not banned from housing areas fully, as an entire use class (Logan 1976; Liebmann 1996; Light 1999; Hirt 2007a).

The separation of housing from industry was only part of the process of erecting a more impermeable border between home and work. Not only was manufacturing banned in the residential districts, but so was business. New York's residential districts permitted houses, apartments, hotels, clubs, schools, churches, a few other cultural and institutional uses, and very small businesses that today we could classify as home occupations (doctors' offices, dressmakers, and artists' studios; City of New York [1916] 1920; also Willis 1993). Since most business was no longer allowed in housing zones, New York needed a new autonomous land-use classification – the business zone, which Frankfurt and other German cities lacked. Yes, new dwellings could be located in New York's business zones, but the opposite was banned. Williams noted this contrast repeatedly. Otherwise an admirer of German municipal governments, he was baffled by their failure to see the necessity for creating purely residential zones and therefore for creating separate business zones. From Williams's viewpoint, the business zone was regrettably unknown to the continental Europeans.

Absence of Business Districts. It should be noticed that the Frankfort ordinance does not establish districts for business, from which manufacturing is excluded, as the zoning ordinances in this country do.... In Berlin there is not a single block where business has driven out residences.... Nor could business and industry in Germany be completely excluded from any district by law. (Williams 1922, 215)

This differentiation in between industrial and residential districts in Frankfort, although far advanced, is not complete. The mixed districts, for instance, contain both residences and factories....[T]he results ... have not been altogether good. ...

> A better solution would be to create separate residential and industrial streets ... Another instance of incomplete differentiation between residential and industrial districts occurs in German cities in the case of chief traffic streets. Here may be seen shops and minor industries and residences also; offices too are found here... In [German] cities, residences in the upper stories of buildings occupied on their lower floors by shops and offices are found not only on chief traffic streets, but wherever shops and offices are to be found. In none of the continental [European] cities is there an actual business district. (Williams 1914b, 28)
>
>   The real trouble with the business district in Germany and all continental [European] cities is that there is none. Business is universally done in the lower stories of buildings, with residences above. This is true even in Berlin, and on Berlin's principal street, Friedrich Strasse. Only here and there, there are business buildings in which no one lives. (Williams 1914a, 5)

Purely residential and purely business streets and buildings may have been rare in central New York in 1914 as they were in Frankfurt. Certain uses were perpetually "invading" others. As Toll (1969, 74–116) eloquently describes, the consecutive "intrusion" of upper-class retail, lower-class retail, and the garment industry along Fifth Avenue was one of the important rationales behind New York's zoning resolution. But this was precisely the difference: American zoning proponents saw the mixing of home and work as a problem that had be fixed; the Germans found it less objectionable.[25] In the emerging American way, the separation of home and work was a key goal to be achieved. Zoning advocacy documents from the 1920s commonly used photographs showing that "problem areas" are those where homes were mixed with nonhomes. Monofunctionality was the "ideal" landscape that zoning could mandate.Not surprisingly then, John Nolen, one of America's greatest early twentieth-century planners, called the separation of home from business America's "principal" contribution to the world's planning tradition (cited by Talen 2005, 154). Upon the tenth anniversary of New York's resolution, Bassett celebrated this idea as evidence of American progress in a speech titled "Stores in Residence Zones":

> Before the zoning resolution was adopted ten years ago the occasional grocer or butcher would jump his shop into some street corner in the heart of a residential district. ... Wagon deliveries, noise, litter and increased fire risk were introduced into a quiet home district. ... The zoning plan seeks to keep stores on business streets and residences on residence streets. ... Stores with families above should be relegated to the dark ages of the past. The play space of small children ought not to be near fruits and vegetables for sale. ... Sanitary streets should be all business and no families. One of the best tendencies of zoning is to make business streets business only and residence streets residences only. (1926, 2)

By the mid-1920s, the separation of homes from all else was becoming the norm. First, several state supreme courts (Massachusetts and California) ruled to exclude stores from housing zones (Department of Commerce 1926b). The verdict in

Euclid v. Ambler, the Supreme Court case that affirmed the constitutionality of zoning (Haar and Kayden 1989; Schultz 1989; Wolf 2008), legally cemented the idea of pure residential zones:

> Some of the grounds for this conclusion are promotion of the health and security from injury of children and others by separating dwelling houses from territory devoted to trade and industry; suppression and prevention of disorder; facilitating the extinguishment of fires, and the enforcement of street traffic regulations and other general welfare ordinances; aiding the health and safety of the community, by excluding from residential areas the confusion and danger of fire, contagion, and disorder, which in greater or less degree attach to the location of stores, shops, and factories. (*Euclid v. Ambler* 1926)

That America was embarking on a trajectory different from the European one was repeatedly noted by another contemporary lawyer and zoning advocate, Ernst Freund. Unlike most of the other "fathers" of zoning, Freund was not only an admirer of German municipal administration, but also German by birth. As a "two-culture man" (Toll 1969), he also found the difference important and tried to intuitively make sense of it. Europeans, he thought, were somehow "naturally" more comfortable with the mixture of people and activities:

> The whole zoning problem in this country [America] is affected by two factors that I should like myself to learn more about than I know. They are in a sense peculiarly American. [There is an] ... extraordinary sensitiveness of [residential] property to its surroundings. I know something about foreign cities. As a boy, I lived in two German cities, and I have travelled somewhat in Europe. Conditions there are very different. People do not mind a little store around the corner a bit. When you go to Vienna, you find that the palace of one of the great aristocratic families has a big glass works display room on the lower floor. The family has a glass business in its Bohemian estates, and thinks nothing of advertising the fact in its residence. We wouldn't have that in this country because it is not comfortable to our ideas. One of the millionaires in Frankfurt built his house right across the way from an amusement establishment where there were concerts given twice a day. We wouldn't do that. (Freund 1926, 78)

Williams and Freund did not write nearly as extensively on zoning in England, which was introduced under the 1909 Town and Country Planning Act, as they did on Germany. But, without giving specific examples, Williams believed that the Americans, while very different from all continental Europeans, were somehow like the English in viewing a home/business mix as undesirable (1922, 215). And he was partially right. English early twentieth-century planners, much like their American colleagues, deeply admired German planning and zoning (Cherry 1994).[26] But English zoning schemes went farther than their German counterparts in including language discouraging not only the mix of homes and industry but also the mix of homes and shops. Still, it seems that the English notion of separating home from business was softer than the American one.

The English adopted zoning in the form of "planning schemes" – regulatory plans covering the undeveloped parts of town (i.e., peripheral areas). The first two English cities to adopt such schemes were Birmingham (Chrisholm 1922, 458) and Ruislip-Northwood[27] (Delafons 1997, 35). In Birmingham, the areas labeled for "dwelling houses" prohibited industry outright, but the authorities were required to justify in writing why they withheld consent for the construction of shops (City of Birmingham 1913). In Ruislip-Northwood, there were separate zones for shops and businesses, but the residential areas could include "professional buildings" and buildings for "the carrying on of handicrafts and the selling of the products thereof" if the products sold and the materials used were not displayed in the windows (National Housing and Town Planning Council 1914). In later schemes, such as Doncaster's, streets of continuous shops were declared "desirable," but while the housing areas banned industry and agriculture, they could include "roads, local playgrounds and open spaces, churches, shops and civic centers" (City of Doncaster 1922). Note that the English at the time zoned for undeveloped areas only: in other words, like in Frankfurt of 1891 but unlike in New York in 1916, the English schemes did *not* include a mandate for land-use separation in the existing, built-out city centers.

Creating the Single-Family District

Like the separation of residential from other uses, the separation of different types of housing (especially single- from multifamily) by zoning proceeded in the context of a sociospatial trend that was already well underway: residential segregation. Of course, social groups in both ancient and medieval cities tended to separate themselves, typically along ethnic and occupational lines (e.g., Vance 1990). And people were long accustomed to perceiving each other as insiders versus outsiders – those living within versus outside the city walls – a tradition that, as both Bassett and Williams believed, informed modern land-use segregation through zoning. But the process had gained speed during the Industrial Revolution, as the upper classes began fleeing to suburbs in England and America (Fishman 1987) forming homogeneous communities protected by private rules.

Still, in America of the late nineteenth and early twentieth century, it was not clear at all whether it was warranted or legal to create *public* regulations that separate housing – and therefore people – by type. What should the types be anyway? US cities had been experimenting with municipal rules for residential segregation at least since the 1880s when San Francisco expelled Chinese laundries from certain areas inhabited mostly by Caucasians (And since the Chinese tended to live in the same structures where they worked, this amounted to segregating their residences from the residences of the Caucasians). Modesto, Los Angeles, and other West Coast cities followed soon thereafter (Toll 1969; Garvin 1996). But the exclusion of the Chinese laundries could be generally justified using reasons similar to those for excluding industry: health and safety.[28] Using the law to classify and separate the residential quarters of all kinds of people required another leap of imagination. It was harder to argue that residents of a certain kind create the same public health risk to residents of another kind as do industry or commerce, as Bassett (1922b) realized. At best, the "other" residents, those living in, say, tenements, could be said to pose a property value risk and some vague danger to light and air in an area dominated by high-class "private residences." This was the usual line taken in zoning advocacy documents and defended with abundant illustrations.

But what should residential separation be based on? Resident characteristics or residence characteristics? Part of the difficulty arose from the fact that the courts deemed unconstitutional the creation of housing zones based explicitly on race – the criterion that may have seemed most "natural" at the time. Baltimore was the first city to enact overtly racial zoning in 1910. But this approach was overturned by the US Supreme Court in 1917 in *Buchanan v. Warley* (this case dealt with the racially divisive law of Louisville; Silver 1997).[29] So another way of division had to be found, perhaps following the example of the private covenants. New York's approach in 1916, however, was fairly cautious. Bassett (1922b) was concerned that creating a housing typology as part of the use rules might be illegal. His solution was to use the area rules to achieve a similar effect: the "E area" districts required detached buildings that occupy no more than 30 percent of a lot. "In New York," he explained, "it is not practical to put up any residential building on 30 per cent of the lot except a one-family private residence" (1922b, 323). He believed this to be more legitimate because area rules could more easily be shown to protect sun and air, and thus health and safety, than use rules based on a housing typology.

Elsewhere in America, however, and earlier than in New York, cities had already drawn up pioneering districting plans that used the classification of detached single-family or "private" residence explicitly. It is unlikely that the inspiration came from Germany. The German ordinances did not clearly distinguish single-, two- and multifamily housing. A row of attached homes could be built in all residential zones, if the homes complied with the pertinent bulk and density rules (Liebmann 1996; Light 1999). Frankfurt's 1891 ordinance created two types of residential districts: the first for "country dwellings" and the second for dwellings generally. There was obvious class intent behind it. The country-dwellings quarter was meant for the affluent: it was located in the more scenic peripheral parts of the city farther from the heavy industries. The second, less desirable residential zone was intended for small workers' homes. But the ordinance relied on its bulk rules to distinguish between the two without setting a firm legal border, by classifying them in different types (sort of like New York). A similar approach was adopted in Berlin, Hamburg, Stuttgart, etc. (Logan 1976), where too the mix of different housing forms remained legal (Liebmann 1996; Talen 2012). In 1907, Essen did define a zone for single houses but the authorities *could* authorize two- and multifamily houses. According to the Heights of Buildings Commission "practically everybody [in Essen] applies for permission to build double houses or groups" (1913, 97).

Williams may have been correct, again, that there was something English in this idea of "private houses" (detached single-family ones). The English zoning schemes from this time period include definitions such as the following: "dwelling houses shall mean houses designed for occupation by not more than one family, together with such outbuildings as are reasonably required to be used or enjoyed therewith" (City of Birmingham 1913, 11). Still, the English schemes did not appear to imply that detached dwellings, dwellings occupied only by one family and surrounded by private open space, had to be placed in one area, whereas buildings comprising rows of attached "dwelling houses" had to necessarily go in another. Instead, the "dwelling houses" were classified by the number of units within a building per acre (e.g., twelve, fifteen, or eighteen per acre). There were also rules such as the following: "no more than eight dwellings shall in any place be built under one continuous roof or without a break in building from the ground upwards" (City of Birmingham 1913, 14). All the way until the end of zoning in England, planning schemes still used broad residential classifications (zones for less than twenty-four vs. zones for more than twenty-four houses per acre; City of Manchester 1945). The English–American contrast was captured succinctly by John Delafons – an esteemed British scholar who wrote in the 1960s. Marveling at several features of US land-use control that differed from the English tradition, Delafons noted: "The British planner would probably say 'Let the whole place be "general residence,"' but the more exclusive zones [in US ordinances] do reflect very marked preferences held by the American homeowner" (1969, 47). Hall (2007) and Hirt (2007a, 2012) much more recently showed that, like the English, today the French and the Germans rely on a "general residential" category instead of the many single- and multifamily housing classifications typical of US zoning ordinances.[30]

The notion for a typology giving a privileged status to the detached single-family home seems to have emerged in America. Utica and Syracuse enacted "residence districts" in 1913. These districts allowed single- *and* two-family homes (Scott 1971, 152).[31] But Berkeley, California came up with a district *only* for detached single-family homes (Scott 1971; Fischler 1998b). Berkeley passed its first ordinance in 1916, the same year as New York. This ordinance defined eight use classes. In Class I districts, "no building or structure shall be erected, constructed or maintained which shall be used for or designed or intended to be used for any purpose other than that of a single family dwelling" (City of Berkeley 1916, 1). Using similar language, the ordinance defined the Class II district for both single- and two-family homes. Class III was for row buildings, along with single- and two-family buildings; Class IV for boarding houses, fraternities, and dormitories as well as the above-listed housing types; Class V for apartments, hotels, and restaurants and the above-listed housing types; Class VI for religious and cultural buildings (no mention of housing here); Class VII for warehousing and some light industry; and

Class VIII for the remaining industries (like VI and VII, Class VIII did not permit housing; City of Berkeley 1916, 1–2). Berkeley's ordinance was highly innovative. Not only did it distinguish single-family homes from other housing types. It also applied the hierarchical principle partially (only in the housing zones). Elsewhere the districts were mutually exclusive; that is, they allowed only a single-use class such as only public or only industrial (Toll 1969, 181). Unlike New York, however, Berkeley was not immediately completely covered by zoning districts. Citizens had to petition the city for their area to be zoned. Here is an excerpt of a petition requesting that a neighborhood be labeled as a Class I district, authored by Duncan McDufee, President of the Civic Art Commission:

> The property owners of Elmwood Park and vicinity ask that their district be classified under the District Ordinances as a District of Class I … in which no buildings shall be erected or maintained other than single-family dwellings with the appurtenant outbuildings. The petitioners make this request on the ground that such classification will afford them a protection against the invasion of their district by flats, apartment houses and stores, with the deterioration of values that is sure to follow. (1916, 12)

Ten years later, *Euclid v. Ambler* made clear that the borders of the single-family category were impermeable. Apartments were in the outside space, along with all else.

> With particular reference to apartment houses, it is pointed out that the development of detached house sections is greatly retarded by the coming of apartment houses, which has sometimes resulted in destroying the entire section for private house purposes; that in such sections very often the apartment house is a mere parasite, constructed in order to take advantage of the open spaces and attractive surroundings created by the residential character of the district. Moreover, the coming of one apartment house is followed by others, interfering by their height and bulk with the free circulation of air and monopolizing the rays of the sun which otherwise would fall upon the smaller homes, and bringing, as their necessary accompaniments, the disturbing noises incident to increased traffic and business, and the occupation, by means of moving and parked automobiles, of larger portions of the streets, thus detracting from their safety and depriving children of the privilege of quiet and open spaces for play, enjoyed by those in more favored localities – until, finally, the residential character of the neighborhood and its desirability as a place of detached residences are utterly destroyed. Under these circumstances, apartment houses, which in a different environment would be not only entirely unobjectionable but highly desirable, come very near to being nuisances. (*Euclid v. Ambler* 1926)

By the early 1930s, zoning for "homogeneous types of dwellings" had become a standard line. Note how the position of federal bodies changed as well. In 1926 the *Standard Zoning Enabling Act* dared to propose one-family zones only in a footnote

(Department of Commerce 1926a, 5). A few short years later, the Presidential Conference on Home Building and Home Ownership fully embraced the idea "That zoning separate residence districts by homogeneous types of dwellings" and that "In residential districts they [zoning codes] should provide for one-family dwelling districts, two-family dwelling districts, multiple dwelling districts" (Gries and Ford 1932, 31–2; 44). By the mid-1900s, "flat" zoning codes – those in which each district allows a single use class – had become more popular than the hierarchical ones, and single-family zones had become a nearly universal feature (Gerckens, n.d.; Elliott 2008). Yet, this was not the case in Germany (Logan 1976) and England (Delafons 1969) (Figures 15.1 and 15.2).

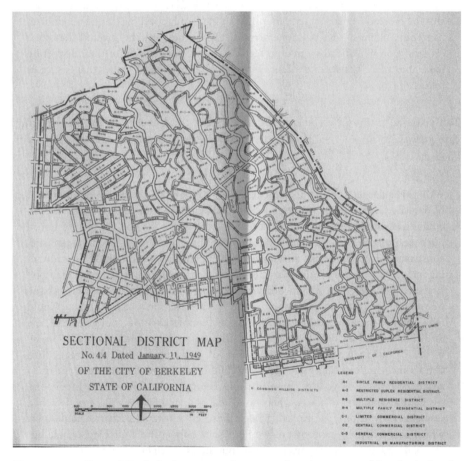

Figure 15.1 Part of Berkeley's 1949 zoning map, showing some of its single-family districts.

Source: City of Berkeley 1949. Reproduced with permission from the City Manager, City of Berkeley.

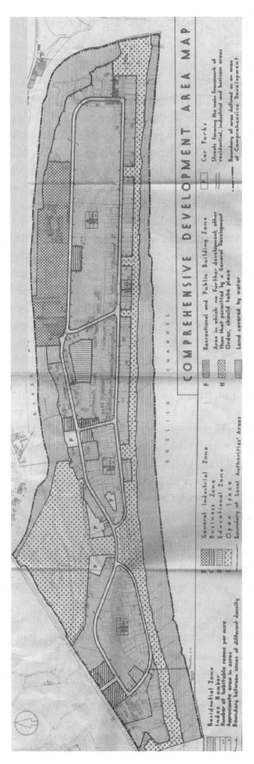

Figure 15.2 An example of an English scheme from the same period. Note the general residence category and the absence of a single-family one.

Source: West Sussex Country Council, 1947. Used with permission from West Sussex County Council.

The American Way: Some Explicit and Implicit Justifications

If the zoning categories commonly used in America were not a ready-made import, if they have a strong original element, on what grounds were they made? The classic and explicit justifications for zoning as formulated, for example, by Bassett in regards to New York's 1916 zoning code, and articulated in his later scholarly and advocacy work (1922b), were for the preservation of public health, safety, morals, and the general welfare. Yet these concepts – and especially the last two, morals and welfare – are general enough to be open to a number of interpretations. Many of the justifications, especially those related to health and safety, should be already apparent to the reader from the citations above. In short, it was strongly believed in the early twentieth century that land-use separation would reduce fire and work-related accidents, will provide citizens with healthier, free-of-pollution living conditions, would improve access to light and air, would reduce traffic jams, etc. On the next few pages, however, I will draw attention to two aspects of the category-building process that did not enter official pro-zoning propaganda to the extent that health and safety did but were very much on the minds (and thus in the writings) of zoning's architects. The first is the extent to which they believed that there is a natural social (especially racial/ethnic) hierarchy, which zoning should seek to enforce in the name of the general welfare (Fischler 1998a). And the second is the extent to which many believed that the detached single-family house is a supreme form of human habitation that is as integral to American civilization as to be declared a public priority. Both had serious implications for property interests. Because land-use and social homogeneity were desirable, it could be argued that property values would be preserved and potentially increased if zoning would reduce land-use and social mix (Mitchel 1916; Grinnalds 1920; Bassett 1922b). This is why big commercial interests such as the Fifth Avenue Association in New York (see Fischler 1998a) and New York's Chamber of Commerce came in support of the zoning idea (New York Chamber of Commerce 1917, 170–1).

The reader probably needs no convincing that racial and ethnic prejudice underpinned much of the zoning process. Some of our predecessors were simply too honest about it. One Berkeley activist explained California's key role in developing the concept of zoning in the United States in the following explicitly racist terms: "We [Californians] are ahead of most states [in adopting zoning] thanks to the persistent proclivity of the 'heathen Chinese' to clean our garments in our midst" (Bither 1915, 175). After *Buchanan v. Warley*, discussions in Baltimore – the city-pioneer of racially divisive ordinances – shifted in the direction of achieving the same goals via different means. Baltimore's Assistant Civil Engineer J. Grinnalds cleverly noted in a newspaper article "the tendency of [a certain kind] of people to live in a certain kind of house." The recommended solution was a "scientific" survey of housing (as a proxy of population) using the following housing types: one-family, two-family, and multifamily. "Some sections of the city will show a preponderance of one-family homes. Some will indicate that there is a considerable grouping into two-family houses. Other neighborhoods will appear to be tenement or apartment districts *almost as if by segregation*" [my italics]. Then, he continued, zoning would legally cement the status quo and eliminate the danger of future crossovers between residential types (and therefore, types of people) (Grinnalds 1921, 2).

But whereas racial and class prejudice have often been used as an explanation for the zoning division of single- from multifamily homes, it is rarely highlighted how the same beliefs partially underwrote the construction of all the other land-use classes. For example, it was well recognized that opening a shop in a stately residential area would bring lower-class outsiders: if not necessarily the shoppers themselves (assuming the store was as high-end as the residences around it), then the sales people and various dubious others. Same applied for opening up a production facility, likely employing lower-class workers. This was plainly said in court cases prior to *Euclid v. Ambler*. In *Civello v. New Orleans*, the Supreme Court of Louisiana justified the legal separation of home and business primarily on the grounds of protection from outsiders:

> A place of business in a residence neighborhood furnishes an excuse for any criminal to go into the neighborhood where, otherwise, a stranger would be under the ban of suspicion. Besides, open shops invite loiterers and idlers to congregate. (1923)

The same logic of class exclusion applied to the separation of business from industry, as in the hallmark case of New York's Fifth Avenue merchants who felt that their businesses would wither if the garment industry workers were allowed to perpetually engulf "the shops, shopkeeper, and the [respectable] shopping public" (cited by Fischler 1998a, 683). It also applied to the business sub-categories that proliferated in zoning codes in the later decades. As Charles Cheney, one of the key advocates of Berkeley's ordinance put it:

> Garages, oil stations, tin shops, plumbing shops, dying and cleaning works and undertakers are not good bedfellows for high class retail stores nor do they attract the same kind of customers; also they are almost always of the lesser rentpaying class ... [and will] seriously deter needed high class retailers from coming in. Hence two kinds of retail business zones need to be established. (Cheney 1929, 33)

These ideas were grounded in the theory that the various races and social classes "naturally" congregate in different parts of town and all would be better off if a public instrument (i.e., zoning) would legally enforce this tendency to the extent possible. This theory went beyond the original Baumeister's idea for natural groupings (since he did not explicitly advocate separating workers' housing from the housing of the wealthy) and appears to have been widely held at the time. In the words of well-known landscape architect S. R. De Boer, who brought zoning to Denver, municipal zoning was the thoughtful extension of "natural zoning." For him, the latter was "the subconscious grouping together of business houses or of residences of a similar nature." He stated: "In residential sections it [zoning] is carried out in the desire of people in one type of house and hating to have another type enter their neighborhood. The type in this case is based mainly on wealth" and "This natural grouping of similar interests ... runs though the life of the whole city" (1937, 12–14).

This "natural" social hierarchy was easy to translate into an imaginary hierarchy of built forms, generally, and housing types specifically. There can be little doubt that one particular type was perceived as sitting on top of the pyramid: the detached single-family home. Part of the explanation was that this type of home was seen as naturally more conducive to homeownership, whereas dwellings in multifamily structures were bound to be rentals. And the rental class was seen – even in New York where it comprised the majority of the population – as a "source of weakness" (Committee on the Regional Plan of New York and Its Environs 1931, 330). Homeownership on the other hand was perceived as bringing in many positive social effects. Bassett (1922a) dedicated a newspaper article on the topic ("Home Owners Make Good Citizens") and the idea was championed at the highest levels of US government, for example, by President Hoover (1931):

> [There is] the high ideal and aspiration that each family may pass their days in the home which they own; that they may nurture it as theirs; that it may be their castle in all that exquisite sentiment which it surrounds with the sweetness of family life. This aspiration penetrates the heart of our national well-being. It makes for happier married life, it makes for better children, it makes for confidence and security, it makes for courage to meet the battle of life, it makes for better citizenship. There can be no fear for a democracy or self-government or for liberty or freedom from homeowners no matter how humble they may be.

But the virtues of the single-family home went farther than its proclivity towards a certain type of tenure. It was the space itself or the peace, the privacy, the serenity that this space gave to the American family that made it an indispensable nation-builder. Certain spaces, our predecessors seem to have believed, taught certain values. The same values could *not* be taught – at least not equally well – in pure environments made of homes with private yards, on one hand, and in apartment buildings in messy urban settings, on the other (even if the apartments were technically owned by their residents). The former were *moral* values, the latter not so much. Here is how in advocating NY's zoning resolution, the Commission on Building Districts and Restrictions explained the impossibility of teaching the right morals in a particular type of space, the dense city, thus making a case for public intervention (zoning) that would lay the path for more private homes in pure residential settings (1917, 20–2, 31):

> The moral influences surrounding the homes are of greatest importance. The sordid atmosphere of the ordinary business street is not a favorable environment in which to rear children. Immediate and continuous proximity to the moving picture show,

the dance hall, pool room, cigar store, saloon, candy store, and other institutions for the creation and satisfaction of appetites and habits is not good for the development of the child. Influences and temptations resulting from the proximity of such business to the homes may affect seriously the morals of the youth of the community. Under such conditions it is difficult to cultivate the ideals of life that are essential to the preservation of our civilization.

Yet preserving the values of civilization is a matter of keen state interest. ... It is important from the standpoint of citizenship as well as from health, safety and comfort that sections be set aside where a man can own a home and have a little open space about it. It makes a man take a keener interest in his neighborhood and city. It has undoubted advantages in the rearing of future citizens.

These "values of civilization" could not be transmitted, ostensibly, in the same way in dense environments dominated by apartment buildings. In fact, in an area of single-family homes, apartment buildings interfered with the "proper social conditions and the development of the proper civic spirit" (Veiller 1914, 11). So detrimental was the mix that "if an area of single homes can keep out apartments, it is better able to retain face-to-face community relationships. The apartment breaks down neighborhood spirit and is not congenial to family life" (Anderson 1925, 159).

It is of course both easy and correct to read class and racial bias in the statements above and, more broadly, in the legal shield around the single-family home that by the 1930s zoning created. Except that zoning's propagandists, while supporting class segregation, also apparently wished to spread the benefits of the single-family home to the wide American masses. Indeed, if such homes were to be a privilege of a small group, how would America's civic spirit go on? Residential zoning, Bassett proudly noted, was having the desired effect: neighborhoods were "rapidly building up with the homes of the best of the citizens who are not wealthy"[32] (1922b). It is this promise of zoning to increase access to the "American dream" of private homes that allowed zoning advocates to adopt a heavy populist tone. If the goal was to give "privacy to private homes" (Bassett 1922b, 419), then by shielding residential purity, zoning could be said to aid the "poor man with a family [who] is as much entitled to live in a home neighborhood restricted from ... undesirable buildings as is the wealthy man" (Cheney 1920, 275–6).

Still, as routine as the single-family home and its district may have by now become, it is worth recalling that despite the early populism, the very idea of having such a district was highly controversial. In Euclid of 1926, the Ambler Realty lawyers, whatever their motivations were, argued mightily against single-family zoning because it would oppress "all the people" who "are not able to maintain a single-family home." Theirs was just one voice in a chorus of early twentieth-century oppositions. Williams was seriously concerned about such zoning. Freund, the "two-culture man," wondered whether the American apartment building should ever be granted the same outsider status in relation to single-family homes as a glue factory (cited by Toll 1969, 266). And is America, the land of no "natural class differences," striving to make them "artificially" (Freund 1926, 79)?

Conclusion

Twenty years ago, Cullingworth (1993) revealed the special features of American land-use planning by placing it in comparative perspective. In this article, I highlighted one of these features. Based on my sources, I believe it can be stated with certainty that far from being a mere European protégé, US zoning quickly developed its own profile. As Babcock (1966) argued decades ago, insulating America's hallmark housing form – the detached single-family home – from intrusion was US zoning's original primary purpose. The class- and race-based underpinnings of such zoning have long been studied and critiqued (Silver 1997). And there has been decades-long pressure from social-equity, good-design and environmental advocates to abolish it. Yet single-family districts remain widespread, reflecting perhaps a strong American ideal of explicitly private living (Perin 1977; Conzen 1996; Archer 2005), or as I term it, an ideal of "discrete domesticity" – domesticity that shields itself from all else through hefty legal and spatial barriers.

Further research using more varied European sources should assess why the Europeans did not adopt US-style land-use categories. I focused on two reasons behind the building of the US categories: race/class prejudice and the belief in the social and spatial supremacy of the single-family home. I suspect that European debates from the same period – the period when European national imperialisms were at their height – were also marked by prejudice. This prejudice did not translate in zoning like it did in the United States; perhaps the Europeans had other means of exclusion. On the other hand, I suspect that the idea that single-family housing is a superior habitat was weaker in Europe. One way or another, compared to Europe, today's America is not a "nation of homeowners," but, if I might end on a semi-serious note, it may well be a "nation of homezoners."[33]

Notes

1. In the late nineteenth century, homeownership rates in the United States were about 48 percent. They fell during the Great Depression but eventually reached the current figure of about 65 percent by 1970 (e.g., Gale, Gruber, and Stephens-Davidowitz 2007). Compare this to England, for example, where until the late 1940s only 10 percent of households owned the dwellings they lived in. The situation was similar in the Netherlands (Hicks and Allen 1999; Munjee, n.d.).

2. Data about homeownership rates in many other countries is widely available. It shows that the United States is not among the world's leaders. The average homeownership rate in the EU's 27 is 73.6 percent; in the Eurozone's 17, it is 72 percent (European Commission, n.d.-b).

3. There are two European countries that have higher numbers of detached single-family housing than the United States. Both are post-communist nations: Slovenia and Hungary. But for various reasons, Eastern Europe has been less urbanized than the

rest of Europe and the United States (Szelenyi 1996). Thus, these numbers can likely be explained by the higher percentage of the population residing in the countryside.

4. Of Europe's largest cities, only London is an exception with its 48 percent, but again we are talking mostly about row housing.

5. According to Bertaud (n.d.).

6. Nobody has proven this with certitude, but many early twentieth-century US planners and lawyers such as John Nolen, Ernst Freund, and Frank Backus Williams have written about the debt they owe to German municipal administrators. Williams (1922, 210) specifically asserts that zoning was a German invention.

7. Zoning in England was eliminated by the Town and Country Planning Act that came into effect in 1948. Since then, no zoning-like regulatory system has guaranteed the rights of private owners to develop their land, as long as they comply with a predetermined set of rules. Development rights are severable from ownership rights. Permissions are granted upon the discretion of authorities who approve or deny proposals after considering precedents and national and local policy documents (Booth 2003; Cullingworth and Nadin 2006).

8. Edward Murray Bassett (1863–1948) is probably familiar to most US planners today. He was an extremely influential lawyer and zoning advocate during the early twentieth century. A graduate of Columbia Law School, he practiced in New York and was the chief author of New York's 1916 zoning resolution (e.g., see Power 1989).

9. Ernst Freund (1864–1932) was born in New York, when his parents were on a brief American visit. He grew up in Frankfurt and Dresden and went back to America as a young man. A graduate of the University of Heidelberg and Columbia University, he became one of the founders of the University of Chicago Law School. He authored several books, including *The Police Power: Public Policy and Constitutional Rights* (Power 1989).

10. Frank Backus Williams (1864–1954) was another very prominent lawyer and zoning advocate in early twentieth-century America. A graduate of Harvard Law School, he practiced law in Connecticut and New York. He is best known for authoring *The Law of City Planning and Zoning* – a comprehensive tractate on planning and zoning in Europe and America (see, e.g., Buttenheim 1955).

11. This is a major limitation of the paper that future research should overcome. Greater access to original English and German documents on the adoption of zoning in these countries would allow a much richer comparison on the *reasons* why the American and the European zoning approaches diverged.

12. For the long international history of urban building codes, see Ben-Joseph (2005) and Marshall (2011).

13. England and Wales passed such laws in 1858; Ireland in 1878; Scotland in 1897 (Manco 2009).

14. For example, the General Law for the Prussian States (*Allgemeines Landrecht für die Preußischen Staaten*) from 1794 and the Building Line Act (*Fluchtliniengesetz*) from 1875 (COMMIN, n.d.).

15. The first few national conferences on city planning held in the United States, and especially the third one, in Philadelphia in 1911, featured long series of speeches praising German municipal planning and zoning. Such speeches were read by figures as authoritative as Frederick Law Olmsted, Lawrence Veiller, Daniel Burnham, Benjamin Marsh, and Ernst Freund.

16. Houston, Texas, the only large American city that does not have municipal zoning today, has solved this problem by using public authority to enforce private deed restrictions (see Lewyn 2004).

17. This critique of private deed restrictions was widespread in early twentieth-century zoning advocacy. Bassett put it succinctly, as did J. Grinnalds (1920), Assistant Engineer to Baltimore's City Plan Committee: "Consider what has been the usual means of protecting residential neighborhoods … [b]y a covenant in the deed when the lot is sold. Usually the purchaser covenants to use the property for residential purposes only for a period of fifteen or twenty years. … Before the covenants have run out the seller has probably disposed of all the remaining lots or retained the corners. … [But] he has probably not covenanted for himself to abstain from using the corners for business. Now if this is the case he can sell the remaining land for whatever purpose would bring the best price. The result of this is merely partial protection for a limited time. The only safe and permanent method is by a zoning ordinance."

18. As Bassett said (1922b, 318), "Uniform building laws do not bring about the orderly condition desired … they apply uniformly over the entire city. … They do not recognize that stores which may be built on car-lined streets should not be built promiscuously among homes. … The usefulness of zoning regulations consists in their being different for different districts." Most famously, Supreme Court Judge George Sutherland expressed this sentiment in *Village of Euclid v. Ambler Realty Co.* (1926). The judge posited that "a nuisance may be merely a right thing in the wrong place, a pig in the parlor instead of the barnyard."

19. This phrase is often used to sum up the nature of zoning as an orderly taxonomy (Perin 1977). Judge Sutherland's opinion, cited in the footnote above, is a case in point. The motto "A place for everything, and everything in its place" was often used to denote the need for household orderliness – the job of women. Disorder was associated with women; "good women" were supposed to overcome it. The zoning primer published under the authority of the then-Secretary of Commerce Herbert Hoover (Department of Commerce 1926b, 1) started with: "Some one has asked: 'Does your city keep its gas range in the parlor and its piano in the kitchen?' That is what many an American city permits its household to do for it. We know what we think of a household in which an undisciplined daughter makes fudge in the parlor. … Yet many American cities do the same sort of thing when they allow stores to crowd in at random among private dwellings."

20. New York's Heights of Buildings Commission (1913, 48, 94–6) made the same acknowledgment.

21. The Heights of Buildings Commission (1913, 67) produced a nearly identical statement 37 years later: "Moreover, advantage of location and the resulting enormous difference in land values tend strongly toward differentiation in the character and intensity of use and this and other social and economic factors tend toward a natural segregation of buildings according to type and use. The city is divided into building districts. We believe that these natural districts must be recognized in any complete and generally effective system of building restriction."

22. By 1915, however, Los Angeles had already covered almost all of its territory by zoning regulations. Like Frankfurt's, LA's zones were called residential, industrial, and mixed (Pollard 1931; Scott 1971).

23. If Frankfurt's approach to leaving parts of its territory un-zoned seems unorthodox, consider that German cities to this very day have continued this tradition: historic, built-out city centers often have no use zoning.

24. Peculiarly, this principle was opposite to Frankfurt's. In New York, the most restrictive zones were the residential ones. In Frankfurt, the most restrictive zones were the industrial ones.

25. German codes, historically, were focused on bulk and density, whereas American ones emphasized land use (Light 1999). According to the City of Philadelphia (1923), the United States had some 120 ordinances regulating use, height, and bulk. About fifty "partial" ordinances had only land-use rules. With few exceptions (e.g., Boston), this was the standard path: landuse-based zoning first, then comprehensive zoning.

26. The classic example is the 1904 book *The example of Germany* by British reformer Thomas Horsfall.

27. At the time, Ruislip-Northwood was a town in West Middlesex. Today it is part of London's metropolis.

28. And the laundries were dangerous because of their heavy use of wood-stove fires and boiling water. The problem is that laundries of Caucasian owners were not similarly excluded, although they too must have been dangerous.

29. This did not stop several southern US cities from using racial zoning for quite some time (Silver 1997).

30. Here I focus on the single- vs. multifamily typology typical of US zoning codes. A related matter is what constitutes a "family." For example, can people unrelated by blood be a family? This is a pertinent debate today, when nuclear families are becoming a minority. However, the legal status of the "family" is complex enough to require its own articles: e.g., see Robertshaw and Curtin (1977) and Pollock (1994).

31. The earliest explicit reference on this I could find in US planning history comes from 1909, when the Chairman of the Congestion Committee Henry Morgenthau proposed to restrict certain zones to one- or two-family houses (cited in Toll 1969, 124).

32. The idea here was that developers were much more willing to construct single-family homes – not just upscale ones but also modest, middle-class ones – in areas which were zoned for residential purposes alone. Banks were also more likely to give loans for homes to be constructed and owned in zoned areas. Thus, single-family zoning was credited with increasing the production of single-family homes and allowing a greater number of people the opportunity to enjoy living in them.

33. I make no reference here to the English "home zones" or the Dutch *"woonerven"*: neighborhoods employing various community-building and traffic-calming techniques. I just mean good old exclusive residential zoning.

References

Anderson, N. 1925. "Zoning and the Mobility of Urban Population." *City Planning 1* (3): 155–9.

Archer, J. 2005. *Architecture and Suburbia: From English Villa to American Dream House, 1690–2000.* Minneapolis, MN: University of Minnesota Press.

Atkins, P. J. 1993. "How the West End Was Won: The Struggle to Remove Street Barriers in Victorian London." *Journal of Historical Geography* 19 (3): 265–77.

Babcock, R. 1966. *The Zoning Game: Municipal Practices and Policies*. Madison, WI: University of Wisconsin Press.

Barnett, J. 2011. "How Codes Shaped Development in the United States, and Why They Should Be Changed." In *Urban Coding and Planning*, edited by S. Marshall. London: Routledge.

Bassett, E. 1922a. "Home Owners Make Better Citizens." *Baltimore Municipal Journal* (March 10).

Bassett, E. 1922b. *Zoning*. New York: National Municipal League.

Bassett, E. 1926. "Stores in Residence Zones." (December 25). Harvard Graduate School of Design Loeb Library VF NAC 1600.

Baumeister, R. 1876. *Stadterweiterungen in Technischer, Baupolizeilicher und Wirthschaftlicher Beziehung*. Berlin: Verlag von Ernst & Horn (in German).

Ben-Joseph, E. 2005. *The Code of the City: Standards and the Hidden Language of Place Making*. Cambridge, MA: MIT Press.

Bertaud, A. n.d. "A Web Page Dedicated to the Study of Urban Spatial Structures." http://alain-bertaud.com/ (accessed June 2, 2012).

Bither, B. 1915. "A Factory Zone Necessary for Industrial Development in Berkeley." *Berkeley Civic Bulletin* III (10).

Booth, P. 2003. *Planning by Consent: The Origins and Nature of British Development Control*. London: Routledge.

Bressi, T. (ed.). 1993. *Planning and Zoning New York City: Yesterday, Today and Tomorrow*. New Brunswick, NJ: Rutgers University Press.

Buttenheim, H. 1955. "Frank Backus Williams." *Journal of the American Institute of Planners* 21 (1): 61.

Cheney, C. 1920. "Removing Social Barriers through Zoning." *The Survey* 44 (11): 275–78.

Cheney, C. 1929. Discussion. In *Planning Problems of Town, City, and Region: Papers and Discussions of the Twenty-First National Conference on City Planning Held at Buffalo and Niagara Falls, New York*. Philadelphia, PA: Fell.

Cherry, G. 1994. *Town Planning in Britain Since 1900: The Rise and Fall of the Planning Ideal*. Oxford: Blackwell.

Chicago Zoning Commission. 1922. *Zoning Chicago*. Chicago, IL: Author.

Chrisholm, H. 1922. Birmingham. *The Encyclopaedia Britannica (Twelfth Edition)*. 30: 457–60.

City of Berkeley. 1916. *Districting Ordinance No. 452-N.S.* Berkeley, CA: Author.

City of Berkeley. 1949. *Zoning Ordinance: Ordinance 3018 No. N.S.* Berkeley, CA: Author.

City of Birmingham. 1913. *Quinton, Harborne and Edgbaston Town Planning Scheme*. Birmingham: Author.

City of Doncaster. 1922. *The Donkaster Regional Planning Scheme: The Report*. Liverpool: University of Liverpool Press.

City of Manchester. 1945. *City of Manchester Plan*. Norwich: Jarrold and Sons.

City of New York. (1916) 1920. *New York City Building Zone Resolution: Restricting the Height and Uses of Buildings and Prescribing the Minimum Sizes of Their Yards and Courts*. New York: Author.

City of Philadelphia. 1921. *Annual Report of the Zoning Commission of the City of Philadelphia*. Philadelphia, PA: Author.

City of Philadelphia. 1923. *Annual Report of the Zoning Commission of the City of Philadelphia*. Philadelphia, PA: Author.

Civello v. New Orleans, City of, 154 La. 271, 97 So. 440 (La. 1923).

COMMIN: The Baltic Spatial Conceptshare. n.d. *National Planning Systems: Germany*. http://commin.org/en/planning-systems/national-planning-systems/germany/1.-planning-system-in-general/ (accessed May 2, 2012).

Commission on Building Districts and Restrictions. 1917. *Final Report*. New York: City Board of Estimate and Apportionment.

Committee on the Regional Plan of New York and Its Environs. 1931. *Regional Plan of New York and Its Environs, Volume VI: Buildings, Their Uses and the Spaces About Them*. New York: Author.

Conzen, M. 1996. "The Moral Tenets of American Urban Form." In *Human Geography in North America: New Perspectives and Trends in Research*, edited by K. Frantz. Innsbruck: Sebstverlag des Insituts für Geographie der Universität Innsbruck.

Cullingworth, B. 1993. *The Political Culture of Planning: American Land Use Planning in Comparative Perspective*. New York: Routledge.

Cullingworth, B., and V. Nadin. 2006. *Town and Country Planning in the UK*. London: Routledge.

Davidoff, P., and L. Davidoff. 1971. "Opening up the Suburbs; Towards Inclusionary Zoning." *Syracuse Law Review* 22: 509–14.

De Boer, S. 1937. *Shopping Districts*. Washington, DC: American Planning and Civic Association.

Delafons, J. 1969. *Land-Use Controls in the United States*. Cambridge, MA: MIT Press.

Delafons, J. 1997. *Politics and Preservation: A Policy History of the Built Heritage, 1882–1996*. London: Routledge.

Department of Commerce. 1926a. *A Standard Zoning Enabling Act under Which Municipalities May Adopt Zoning Regulations*. Washington, DC: Government Printing Office.

Department of Commerce. 1926b. *A Zoning Primer by the Advisory Committee on Zoning Appointed by Secretary Hoover*. Washington, DC: Government Printing Office.

Elliott, D. 2008. *A Better Way to Zone: Ten Principles to Create More Livable Cities*. Washington, DC: Island Press.

European Commission. n.d.-a. *Living Conditions and Social Protection: Housing, Distribution of Population by Dwelling Type, 2009*. http://epp.eurostat.ec.europa.eu/portal/page/portal/statistics/themes (accessed February 15, 2012).

European Commission. n.d.-b. *Living Conditions and Social Protection: Housing, Population by Tenure Status (% of Population)*. http://epp.eurostat.ec.europa.eu/portal/page/portal/statistics/themes (accessed February 15, 2012).

Fischler, R. 1998a. "Health, Safety and Welfare: Markets, Politics, and Social Science in Early Land-Use Regulation and Community Design." *Journal of Urban History* 24: 675–719.

Fischler, R. 1998b. "The Metropolitan Dimension of Early Zoning: Revisiting the 1916 New York City Ordinance." *Journal of the American Planning Association* 64(2): 170–88.

Fischler, R., and K. Kolnik. 2006. "American Zoning: German Import or Home Product?" Paper presented at the Second World Planning Schools Congress, July, Mexico City.

Fishman, R. 1987. *Bourgeois Utopias: The Rise and Fall of Suburbia*. New York: Basic Books.

Forman, S. 2011. "The American Dream: Sick But Not Dead." *The Examiner*, September 16. http://www.examiner.com/politicalbuzz-in-new-york/the-american-dream-sick-but-not-dead (accessed February 17, 2012).

Freund, E. 1926. Discussion. Planning Problems of Town, City, and Region: Papers and Discussions, 18th National Conference on City Planning, St. Petersburg and Palm Beach, Florida.

Gale, W., J. Gruber, and S. Stephens-Davidowitz. 2007. "Encouraging Homeownership through the Tax Code." http://economics.mit.edu/files/6425 (accessed March 27, 2012).

Garvin, A. 1996. *The American City: What Works and What Doesn't.* New York: McGraw-Hill.

Gerckens, L. n.d. *American Zoning and the Physical Isolation of Uses.* www.plannersweb.com/articles/ger065.html (accessed September 19, 2011).

Green, N. 2011. "A Chronicle of Urban Codes in Pre-industrial London's Streets and Squares." In *Urban Coding and Planning,* edited by S. Marshall. London: Routledge.

Gries, J., and J. Ford. 1932. *Home Ownership, Income and Types of Dwellings (President's Conference on Home Building and Home Ownership).* Washington, DC: National Capital Press.

Grinnalds, J. 1920. "Zoning for Real Estate Protection." *Baltimore Municipal Journal: 2* (November 19).

Grinnalds, J. 1921. "The Housing Survey Is Necessary before Zoning." *Baltimore Municipal Journal: 2* (October 21).

Haar, C., and J. Kayden. 1989. *Zoning and the American Dream: Promises Still to Keep.* Chicago, IL: Planners Press.

Hall, E. 2007. "Divide and Sprawl, Decline and Fall: A Comparative Critique of Euclidean Zoning." *University of Pittsburgh Law Review 68:* 915–52.

Hall, T. 2009. *Planning Europe's Capital Cities: Aspects of Nineteenth-Century Urban Development.* London: E&FN Spon.

Heights of Buildings Commission. 1913. *Report of the Heights of Buildings Commission to the Committee on the Height, Size and Arrangement of Buildings of the Board of Estimate and Apportionment of the City of New York.* New York: Board of Estimate and Apportionment.

Hicks, J., and G. Allen. 1999. *A Century of Change: Trends in UK Statistics since 1900.* http://www.parliament.uk/documents/commons/lib/research/rp99/rp99-111.pdf (accessed April 1, 2012).

Hirt, S. 2007a. "The Devil Is in the Definitions: Contrasting American and German Approaches to Zoning." *Journal of the American Planning Association 73* (4): 436–50.

Hirt, S. 2007b. "The Mixed-Use Trend: Planning Attitudes and Practices in Northeast Ohio." *Journal of Architectural and Planning Research 24* (3): 224–44.

Hirt, S. 2012. "Mixed Use by Default: How the Europeans (Don't) Zone." *Journal of Planning Literature 27* (4): 375–93.

Hirt, S. 2013. "Form Follows Function? How America Zones." *Planning Practice and Research 28* (2): 204–30.

Hoover, H. 1931. *Address to the White House Conference on Home Building and Home Ownership.* http://www.presidency.ucsb.edu/ws/index.php?pid=22927&st=home+ownership&st1 (accessed November 23, 2012).

Incorporated Society of Architects and Engineers of Germany. 1907. "Planning Towns and Cities: Principles Advocated by German Authorities for Future Growth, Squares, Class Districts and Buildings." *Municipal Journal and Engineer 22:* 224–7.

Jacobs, J. 1961. *The Death and Life of Great American Cities.* New York: Random House.

Kayden, J. 2004. "Reconsidering Zoning: Expanding an American Land-Use Frontier." *Zoning practice 1* (January): 2–13.

Kelly, B. 1993. *Expanding the American Dream: Building and Rebuilding Levittown*. Albany, NY: State University of New York Press.

Knox, P., and L. McCarthy. 2005. *Urbanization: An Introduction to Urban Geography*. Upper Saddle River, NJ: Pearson-Prentice Hall.

Kolnick, K. 2008. "Order before Zoning: Land Use Regulations in Los Angeles, 1880–1915." Doctoral dissertation, University of Southern California Press, Los Angeles.

Kostof, S. 1987. *America by Design*. New York: Oxford University Press.

Kotkins, J. 2006. *Newsweek* (Special Issue on Petrol Society: Hail to the Suburban Oasis), 85.

Ladd, B. 1990. *Urban Planning and Civic Order in Germany, 1860–1914*. Cambridge, MA: Harvard University Press.

Le Goix, R., and D. Callen. 2010. "Gated Communities: Social Sustainability in Contemporary and Historical Gated Developments." halshs.archives-ouvertes.fr/docs/00/.../legoix_callen_072008_v3.doc (accessed September 29, 2011).

Lefcoe, G. 1979. *Land Development in Crowded Places: Lessons from Abroad*. Washington, DC: The Conservation Foundation.

Levine, J. 2006. *Zoned Out: Regulation, Markets and Choices in Transportation and Metropolitan Land Use*. Washington, DC: Resources for the Future.

Levy, J. 2011. *Contemporary Urban Planning*. Upper Saddle River, NJ: Pearson-Prentice Hall.

Lewyn, M. 2004. "How Overregulation Creates Sprawl (Even in a City without Zoning)." *Wayne Law Review 50*: 1171–208.

Liebmann, G. 1996. "Modernization of Zoning: A Means to Reform." *Regulation 2*: 71–7. http://www.cato.org/pubs/regulation/regv19n2/v19n2-8.pdf (accessed September 21, 2011).

Light, M. 1999. "Different Ideas of the City: Origins of Metropolitan Land-Use Regimes in the United States, Germany, and Switzerland." *The Yale Journal of International Law 24*: 577–612.

Logan, T. 1976. "The Americanization of German Zoning." *Journal of the American Institute of Planners 42* (4): 377–85.

Lowenthal, J., and M. Curzan. 2011. "Dismantling the American Dream." *Politico* (August 24) http://www.politico.com/news/stories/0811/61953.html#ixzz1VwsaPBZI (accessed January 15, 2012).

Manco, J. 2009. "Researching Historic Buildings in the British Isles." http://www.buildinghistory.org/regulations.shtml (accessed May 2, 2012).

Marshall, S. (ed.) 2011. *Urban Coding and Planning*. London: Routledge.

McDuffee, D. 1916. "A Practical Application of the Zone Ordinance." *Berkeley Civic Bulletin* V (1).

McKenzie, E. 1994. *Privatopia: Homeowners Association and the Rise of Residential Private Government*. Binghamton, NY: Yale University Press.

Mitchell, J. 1916. "Speech of Hon. John Purroy Mitchel, Mayor of the City of New York." http://babel.hathitrust.org/cgi/pt?id=njp.32101072359969;seq=22;view=1up;num=14#page/n4/mode/1up (accessed December 1, 2012).

Morag-Levine, N. 2011. "Is Precautionary Regulation a Civil Law Instrument? Lessons from the History of the Alkali Act." *Journal of Environmental Law 23* (1): 1–43.

Mullen, J. 1976. "American Perceptions of German City Planning at the Turn of the Century." http://works.bepress.com/cgi/viewcontent.cgi?article=1029&context=john_mullin (accessed May 3, 2012).

Munjee, N. n.d. "Homeownership Trends Worldwide." http://www.housingfinance.org/uploads/Publicationsmanager/9512_Hom.pdf (accessed April 1, 2012).

National Housing and Town Planning Council. 1914. *Summary and Text of the Ruislip-Northwood Town Planning Scheme, 1914.* London: Author.

Nelson, R. 1977. *Zoning and Property Rights: An Analysis of the American System of Land-Use Regulation.* Cambridge, MA: MIT Press.

Newman, P., and A. Thornley. 1996. *Urban Planning in Europe: International Competition, National Systems and Planning Projects.* London: Routledge.

New York Chamber of Commerce. 1917. *Annual Report of the Corporation of the Chamber of Commerce of the State of New York for the year 1915–1916.* New York: Author.

Ohm, B., and R. Sitkowski. 2003. "The Influence of New Urbanism in Land Use, Planning and Zoning." *Urban Lawyer 35*: 783–943.

Pendall, R., R. Puentes, and J. Martin. 2006. *From Traditional to Reformed: A Review of the Land Use Regulations in the Nation's Largest Metropolitan Areas.* Washington, DC: Brookings Institution.

Perin, C. 1977. *Everything in Its Place: Social Order and Land Use in America.* Princeton, NJ: Princeton University Press.

Platt, R. 2004. *Land Use and Society: Geography, Law and Public Policy.* Washington, DC: Island Press.

Pollard, W. 1931. "An Outline of the Law of Zoning in the United States." *Annals of the American Academy for Political and Social Science 155* (2): 15–33.

Pollock, A. 2010. *Housing Finance in International Perspective.* Washington, DC: American Enterprise Institute.

Pollock, E. 1994. "Rethinking Zoning to Accommodate the Elderly in Single-Family Housing." *Journal of the American Planning Association 60* (4): 521–31.

Power, G. 1989. The advent of zoning. *Planning Perspectives 4*: 1–13.

Reynard, P. 2002. "Public Order and Privilege: Eighteenth-Century French Roots of Environmental Regulation." *Technology and Culture 43* (1): 1–28.

Robertshaw, P., and C. Curtin. 1997. "Legal Definitions of the Family: A Historical and Sociological Exploration." *Sociological Review 25* (1): 289–308.

Schultz, S. 1989. *Constructing Urban Culture; American Cities and City Planning, 1800–1920.* Philadelphia, PA: Temple University Press.

Scott, M. 1971. *American City Planning Since 1890.* Berkeley, CA: University of California Press.

Sennett, R. 1970. *The Uses of Disorder: Personal Identity and City Life.* New York: Knopf.

Silver, C. 1997. "The Racial Origins of Zoning in American Cities." In *Urban Planning and the African American Community: In the Shadows,* edited by J. Thomas, and M. Ritzdorf. Thousand Oaks, CA: Sage.

Skaler, R., and T. Keels. 2008. *Philadelphia's Rittenhouse Square.* Chicago, IL: Arcadia.

Szelenyi, I. 1996. Cities after Socialism – and After. In *Cities after Socialism: Urban and Regional Change and Conflict in Post-socialist Societies,* edited by G. Andrusz, M. Harloe, and I. Szelenyi. Malden, MA: Blackwell.

Talen, E. 2005. *New Urbanism and American Planning: The Conflict of Cultures.* London: Routledge.

Talen, E. 2009. "Design by the Rules: The Historical Underpinnings of Form Based Codes." *Journal of the American Planning Association 75* (2): 1–17.

Talen, E. 2012. *City Rules: How Regulations affect Urban Form*. Washington, DC: Island.

Toll, S. 1969. *Zoned American*. New York: Grossman.

Urban Audit. n.d. "Data Queries." http://www.urbanaudit.org/ (accessed May 1, 2012).

US Census Bureau. 2011. "American Housing Survey 2009." http://www.census.gov/prod/2011pubs/h150-09.pdf (accessed March 5, 2012).

US Census Bureau. 2011. "American Housing Survey: Metropolitan Area Summary Data: 2009." http://www.census.gov/housing/ahs/data/metro.html (accessed March 5, 2012).

Vance, J. 1990. *The Continuing City: Urban Morphology in Western civilization*. Baltimore, MD: John Hopkins University Press.

Veiller, L. 1914. "Protecting Residential Districts." Proceedings of the Sixth National Conference on City Planning. Boston: Boston University Press.

Village of Euclid v. Ambler Realty Co, 272 US 365, 47 S. Ct. 114, 71 L. Ed. 303 (1926).

West Sussex County Council. 1947. *Shoreham and Lancing Beaches Development Plan*. Chichester: Author.

Williams, F. 1914a. *Building Regulation by Districts: The Lesson of Berlin*. New York: National Housing Association.

Williams, F. 1914b. "Housing and City Planning." *Journal of the American Institute of Architects* (January): 27–8.

Williams, F. 1922. *The Law of City Planning and Zoning*. New York: Macmillian.

Williams, F. 1916 [1929]. "Public Control over Private Real Estate." In *City Planning: A Series of Papers Presenting the Essential Elements of a City Plan*, edited by J. Nolen. New York: Appleton.

Willis, C. 1993. "A 3-D CBD: How the 1916 Zoning Law Shaped Manhattan's Central Business District." In *Planning and Zoning New York City*, edited by T. Bressi. New Brunswick, NJ: Rutgers University Press.

Wiseman, H. 2010. "Public Communities, Private Rules." *Georgetown Law Review Journal* 98: 697–768.

Wolf, M. 2008. *The Zoning of America: Euclid vs. Ambler*. Lawrence: University of Kansas.

16

Understanding Community Development in a "Theory of Action" Framework

Norms, Markets, Justice

Laura Wolf-Powers

Introduction

Many theorists have observed that the relationship between knowledge about places and action in them defines the practice of city planning (see Campbell, 2012; Fainstein, 2012; Friedmann, 1987). Among most planning theorists, moreover, it is uncontroversial to assert that knowledge about places is socially constructed and context-dependent. Lake (2013) argues that planning "[constructs] the problems that provide its reason for being," while Lake and Zitcer maintain that the representation of facts on the ground "constitutes the discourse through which the reality can be apprehended" (Lake and Zitcer, 2012, p. 390). The implication of these ideas is not, however, routinely integrated into planning practice and pedagogy.

Campbell (2012) argues that the act of synthesis leading from "is" to "ought," from knowledge to action (in hopes of changing the world for the better) is what defines planning as a profession and as a social enterprise. The actualization of this synthesis, moreover, demands that a "link to normative concerns ... be made from the start" (Campbell, 2012, p. 142). Because action in planning rests on and is delimited by knowledges and meanings that are socially created (see also Marris,

Original publication details: Wolf-Powers, Laura. 2014. "Understanding community development in a 'theory of action' framework: Norms, markets, justice". In *Planning Theory and Practice*, 15(2): 202–19. Used with permission from Taylor & Francis Group.

Readings in Planning Theory, Fourth Edition. Edited by Susan S. Fainstein and James DeFilippis.
Editorial material and organization © 2016 John Wiley & Sons, Ltd.
Published 2016 by John Wiley & Sons, Ltd.

1987), reflective practice requires active examination of these knowledges, and of the spatial practices that emanate from them.

This chapter proposes that three normative theories – theories of action – underlie the practice of neighbourhood regeneration or "community development" planning in the USA. They are based respectively on planners' perceived need for the reinstitution of civil norms, capital markets, and social justice in disinvested areas of cities and regions. Each theory of action links description with prescription, answering both the questions "What's going on in this neighbourhood? (and why?)" and the questions "What to do / what ought to be done to change it?" (see Campbell, 2012, p. 138). I argue that while an outward détente prevails among the "norms," "markets," and "justice" approaches, there are conflicts among them which go to the heart of the struggle to find effective, morally acceptable policy responses to environmental deterioration and human deprivation in urban neighbourhoods. I further argue that these conflicts can be perceived in the reactions of planners in the USA to the mortgage meltdown in the second part of the last decade. In the context of a foreclosure crisis that devastated hundreds of thousands of household economies and that threatened to topple the global banking sector, the practical implications of the distinctions between the three approaches became clearly visible. The paper draws additional parallels between community development policy in the USA during this period and the recent implementation of neighbourhood renewal policy in the UK and Continental Europe, providing some reflections on how European planners and neighbourhood development professionals might usefully interrogate and learn from the state of the profession in the USA.

Community Development as a Field of Inquiry and Practice

Urban neighbourhoods are the creatures of individual residents and the informal social networks in which they are embedded; of land developers and entrepreneurs; of neighbourhood-based and larger-scale non-profit organizations; and of public sector agencies and authorities. Their built and social environments reflect choices and decisions made by, and on behalf of, these disparate actors over many decades. Naturally, political processes on larger scales have significant consequences for neighbourhoods: some are in growing cities and metropolitan regions, while others are components of cities and regions in economic decline. Yet even the wealthiest cities and regions contain deteriorated, disinvested places. In the USA especially, neighbourhoods and their municipalities belong to metropolitan agglomerations in which interjurisdictional competition and Balkanization frustrate and distort the provision of public and private goods, leaving neighbourhoods in tax-disadvantaged municipalities desperately poor.

Community development, practically defined, encompasses diverse efforts to correct these distortions, and to mitigate the consequences of historic patterns of uneven private and public investment. Community development planners typically work in neighbourhoods where the housing is substandard, where crime, property abandonment and low-quality retail and recreational options curtail day-to-day social and economic functions and interactions, where few people have meaningful or well-remunerated work, and where marginalization and lack of recognition limit people's capability to flourish as political subjects. Community developers design and implement place-based interventions that range from top-down public space redesign to guerrilla interventions into public and semi-public realms; from market-rate housing development on vacant lots to the creation of community land trusts on those lots, from the development of indigenous leadership in non-profit organizations to the formation of business improvement districts. At the same time, their interventions are people-based: they help neighbourhood residents obtain housing, childcare and jobs, improve the built and natural environments in which they live, build wealth, get heard in the political sphere, and connect to jobs and housing opportunities. Finally, US-based community organizations help external institutional actors, including market actors, realize goals in neighbourhoods on the assumption that the activation of these institutions and markets will redound to the benefits of neighbourhood residents. A multi-level complex of government, private and non-profit entities supports community development practice and provides a point of reference for people who affiliate with it, such that it can be viewed sociologically as an organizational field (Ferguson and Stoutland, 1999).

Community development is an interdisciplinary arena of social science inquiry as well, combining history, sociology, economics, environmental design and organizational and political theory. But academic planners' perspectives on community development practice vary widely. In the USA, for example, Robert Sampson's ecological approach (Sampson, 1999) and Robert Chaskin's closely related community capacity-building approach (Chaskin, 2001) focus on neighbourhoods as arenas for "realizing common values" (Sampson, 1999, p. 242). These scholars proceed from the premise that it is within the medium of community life that individuals avail themselves of "important public goods, or what many have termed social capital" (Sampson, 1999, p. 242). Sampson and Chaskin are sociologists, but their approach is readily adopted by community planners, particularly those interested in practically applying the concepts of social capital and collective capacity (sometimes known as civic capacity). Neighbourhood efforts based on these ideas feature civic engagement processes designed to strengthen associational bonds among community members. They also feature attempts to inventory, improve and deploy communities' assets (see Kretzmann and McKnight, 1993), and to revive dormant networks of neighbourliness and mutual aid.

Academic discussions of community capacity-building often dovetail with research on the characteristics and performance of community development corporations (CDCs) – organizations founded to fuse civic participation with professional expertise in the redevelopment of disinvested areas (see Gittell and Vidal, 1998; Glickman and Servon, 1998; Rohe, 2009). Such discussions also focus on the role of social networks in reinforcing individual behaviours deemed to be desirable, such as saving money, becoming employed, and valuing education. In this paradigm, a key tool for encouraging desirable individual behaviours is poverty deconcentration: namely, promoting the mobility of low-income households to neighbourhoods with lower poverty rates and/or changing the social character of predominantly poor neighbourhoods by introducing middle-class households. Much research has been undertaken to investigate whether the urban mixed-income neighbourhoods engineered through the HOPE VI housing programme, for example, have engendered the positive social mixing hypothesized to improve network ties between lower- and higher-income residents (Chaskin and Joseph, 2013).

Other academic planners in the USA are sceptical of this approach. To them, the Sampson/Chaskin definition of community development symptomatizes a decades-long shift away from activist models of community engagement and signals the ascendancy of a model in which neighbourhood residents exist as "entrepreneurial subjects" (Lemke, 2001) in a depoliticized environment. In this view, under-resourced neighbourhood organizations increasingly fill gaps in basic service provision left by a retreating state. "Public sector load-shedding" leaves community-based organizations little time to think about broader policy issues, and little political room to question or contest the macro and structural causes of neighbourhood decline (DeFilippis, Fisher, and Shragge, 2006). Particular criticism is levied against the notion that "social capital" (and, by extension, the poverty deconcentration and social mixing initiatives theorized to promote it) is of primary importance in actualizing the potential of poor neighbourhoods (DeFilippis, 2001). These critics hold that while an apolitical version of community development can help people adapt more functionally to the conditions that surround material and social deprivation, it does not provide a platform from which to question these conditions. Thus, "counter-movements" are needed to build institutions that affect the material, political and social circumstances of marginalized people as opposed to simply transforming marginal places and properties (see Marcuse et al., 2009; Fainstein, 2010). As an alternative to conflict-free versions of neighbourhood redevelopment planning, these academic critics urge community development practitioners to map and analyse power relationships, to develop leaders and strategists from within marginalized communities, to have people-oriented as well as place-oriented objectives, to create linkages with organizations and campaigns at scales beyond the local and (most of all) to be prepared for confrontation (see DeFilippis et al., 2006; Marcuse et al., 2009; Saegert, Warren, and Thompson, 2001). These scholars are frequently aligned with "right to the city" and "just city" movements in planning, which will be further discussed below.

A third academic account of community development in the USA proceeds from the premise that other paradigms, whether consensus- or conflict-oriented, have come up short in two ways: first by wrongly casting neighbourhoods as autonomous socio-economic entities (i.e. disconnected from their metropolitan regions), and second, by neglecting the private sector. In a 2004 paper about the "American approach" to neighbourhoods, addressed to colleagues in the UK, Bruce Katz of the Brookings Institution, an influential Washington DC-based think tank, articulates a framework he calls "neighbourhoods of choice and connection" (Katz, 2004) In the neighbourhoods that conform to Katz's "choice and connection" ideal, community development actors have productively abandoned the inward-looking tendencies of the past and begun to "operate in and relate to the metropolitan geography – the true geography of housing markets, of labor markets, of educational opportunity" (p. 22). Additionally, forward-thinking community-based groups and neighbourhood advocates in those places are, in another departure from past practice, "[e]ngaging the private sector in neighbour-hood transformation" (p. 23). In Katz's vision, community-based organizations lead collaborations with the local state to actualize market-led regeneration oppor-tunities while governmental actors, having both withdrawn from social service provision and repudiated the heavy-handed, statist methods of urban renewal, strategically sponsor and subsidize private development initiatives. The purpose of such projects is to address the "isolation and disconnection from mainstream economic activity" that is understood as the main problem afflicting struggling households (Weissbourd and Boudini, 2005, p. 23).[1]

Critics of the market view have objected that weak or non-existent governance mechanisms at the metropolitan level make it difficult for community groups to operate in metropolitan geography (Imbroscio, 2011) and that the portrayal of most neighbourhood-based groups as insular and anti-market is inaccurate. Critics have also charged that market enthusiasts' equation of neighbourhood revitalization with property appreciation appears to disadvantage long-term neighbourhood residents, particularly renters (Logan and Molotch, 1987; Turok, 1992; Wolf-Powers, 2005).[2] Nevertheless, the view that community development is neither metropolitan-focused enough nor market-driven enough is widely shared, particularly among scholars and researchers oriented directly toward policy (see Grogan and Proscio, 2000; Weissbourd and Boudini, 2005). The perspective has become, according to some, "the dominant understanding in community development work in the United States" (DeFilippis, Fisher, and Schragge, 2010, p. 69).

A wider analytical lens enables some parallels to be drawn between recent US community development experience and urban restructuring in Western Europe and the UK. For example, Uitermark (2003) and Kleinhans (2012) argue that under housing reform measures pursued in the Netherlands since 1997, practitioners have put in place initiatives to promote "social cohesion" and "social mixing"; Lees (2008) makes a similar point about the UK. Fallov (2010) notes the prominence of capacity-building concepts in England's and Denmark's efforts to regenerate neighbourhoods and fight social exclusion. These efforts link British and European social policy to US discourse on social capital and civic capacity as well as to US-based strategies of poverty deconcentration in conjunction with physical revitalization in core city neighbourhoods.

The prevalence of market logic is a second parallel. Housing Market Renewal (HMR), a programme promulgated by New Labour in the UK between 1997 and 2010, adhered strongly (as its name suggests) to a markets discourse and perhaps took a cue from Katz in characterizing past urban renewal efforts as inward-looking (Webb, 2010). As Ferrari notes, moreover, it conceived of a subregional housing market as a "new functional and governance territory" not coterminous with pre-defined administrative geography, within which administrators might strive for balance and distributional equity (Ferrari, 2012, p. 271). This theme of Housing Market Renewal resonated strongly with the popular US idea that policy-makers concerned with neighbourhood well-being should operate at the regional geography of the housing market while facilitating and financing development on a project basis in neighbourhoods, using a combination of private, government and "third sector" resources to support market-led regeneration.[3]

A third area of commonality, particularly between the U.S. and the UK, is public sector load-shedding – i.e. the confluence of fiscal austerity measures with the enlistment of community-based organizations as providers of essential services. Policy-makers in both countries explain the decision to externalize or "contract out" social services functions by contrasting the local expertise and place-specific knowledge of community groups with the image of an inflexible welfare state. The casting of local CDC equivalents as conduits for human services (while reducing state funding for such services) began under the UK's Housing Market Renewal Initiative and has accelerated under the "Big Society" and "new localism" initiatives sponsored by the Conservative Government formed in 2010 (Jacobs and Manzi, 2013).[4] Continental European countries are also re-evaluating the role of neighbourhood-based organizations in an age of increased austerity.

Whether in the American or the European context, theoretical and conceptual discussions of neighbourhood regeneration are held more frequently in seminar rooms and scholarly journals than in the field. Among people engaged in the difficult practical work of planning and executing neighbourhood revitalization projects or advocating for local legislation, fine ideological distinctions are of primarily academic concern. This does not mean, however, that practitioners' grounded knowledge, as embodied in their characterizations of neighbourhood assets and problems, is not rooted in theory. In his work, Howell Baum argues that professional planners create structures (both conceptual and procedural) that encourage individuals to identify with communities and enable them to competently undertake the extraordinary work involved in collective solution-seeking (Baum, 1997, 2005). In community development practice there are three interwoven yet ultimately distinct conceptual structures or "theories of action" that echo the academic orientations described above.

Three Theories of Action

As suggested above as well as in Campbell (2012), a theory of action joins a diagnosis or description (which responds to the question "What's going on here?") to an intervention (which responds to the question "What do we do to create change for the better?"). The theory of action which glues them together is inseparable from both. In the diagnostic phase, a theory of action provides a lens through which people perceive and interpret their surroundings. In a second phase, analysis, the theory helps build bridges between knowledge and action by focusing attention on specific sets of interventions that follow from the diagnostics. In a third phase, interventions are chosen and implemented. One might say that a theory of action delineates the possible, furnishing actors with a menu of interventions from which to choose; solution-seekers refract these options though their understanding of baseline conditions, i.e. the "is" identified in the diagnostic phase.

In spite of the lumping together of community development activities under the neutral banner of neighbourhood improvement, the potential for conflict underlies all three phases (diagnosis, analysis, intervention) outlined above. The intellectual origins of the normative structures on which community development rests are worthy of examination, as are their practical ramifications. In community development practice, the three dominant theories of action may be characterized in terms of restoration of norms, restoration of markets and restoration of justice (Table 16.1).

Restoration of norms

One theory of action in community development originates in a conviction that economic and social distress in city neighbourhoods results from the decline of trust, civility, associational ties and (perhaps) individual responsibility and ambition. The "disease" identified during the diagnostic phase is individual and group maladaptation to the social requirements of contemporary city living. Its symptoms are disorder, social dysfunction, intergenerational poverty, and crime.

This theory is an intellectual heir of the ecological model of the Chicago School of Sociology. But while it echoes the Chicago School's focus on adaptation and socialization (along with its preoccupation with crime and disorder), it does not explicitly situate the pathology of disorganization within individuals. As DeFilippis, Fisher and Shragge put it, "nomenclatures of social capital, community capacity, asset building, consensus organizing and so forth, seek to move right-wing discourse away from the deficits and failings of individuals and families to more collective ones at the community level" (DeFilippis, Fisher, and Shragge, 2006, p. 675). Nevertheless, the social critique embedded in the "restoration of norms" theory is a critique not of government retrenchment, nor of structural factors

Table 16.1 Theories underlying community development practice in the USA.

Diagnostic interpretation of neighbourhood distress ("what's going on here?")	Theory of action ("what needs to happen here?")	Tools
Disorganization; lack of social control (inability to control anti-social behaviour) – sometimes interpreted as an outgrowth of cultural deprivation and failure to adapt	Restoration of norms of civility, trust and safety – "the stuff of social capital" – securing of external resources to stabilize neighbourhoods; better coordination among services; comprehensivity	• Saturation of distressed neighbourhoods with services – comprehensive community initiatives • Increasing focus on early childhood intervention • Deconcentration of poverty • Policy to encourage different choices
Lack of functional market institutions Need for market and non-market institutions with the capacity to bring about physical rehabilitation, safer streets, better housing, healthy businesses, good schools and human capital development opportunities	Activation of markets; Activation of participation and ownership by residents Institutional development Coordination among institutions at many levels	• Real estate market-building • Commercial corridor revitalization • Historic preservation • Organizational capacity-building • Public participation in decision-making (espoused to greater and lesser degrees)
Lack of access to levers of power	Intermediaries as key actors bridging government, neighbourhood-level groups and private actors Greater community control and ownership of the agenda	• Protest • Indigenous leadership development
Historic exclusion and exploitation and its current legacies	Redistribution of wealth and opportunity;	• Information/disclosure campaigns • Campaigns to change policy
Environmental injustice; labour injustice	Economic policy geared toward employment fair share of services	• Development of alternative institutions for property control (e.g. community development credit unions, community land trusts)
Demise of welfare state	Environmental justice (relief from environmental degradation)	
Inequity of resources within metropolitan regions		

underlying low wages, high unemployment, limited educational opportunities, and mass incarceration, but of a broken civil society and the decline of virtue. In this, it draws heavily on Robert Putnam and Amitai Etzioni, whose work in the 1990s popularized the application of the term "social capital" to community development efforts (Putnam, 1995; Etzioni, 1997).[5]

It is not far from the "diagnosis" of impaired norms and networks in neighbourhoods to "treatments" designed to restore conditions more conducive to individual and neighbourhood success. First among these are strategies to replace with more salutary residential experiences the documented negative "neighbourhood effects" associated with living in areas in which more than 40% of the population is low-income. In the US, the expansion of the Housing Choice Voucher programme, the replacement of distressed public housing with mixed-income housing in central city neighbourhoods, and the "Moving to Opportunity" experiment (which tracked public housing residents as they moved to less poor neighbourhoods) are examples of this. Interventions based in distressed neighbourhoods themselves include comprehensive service coordination and saturation (such as the "cradle to college to community" model of the Harlem Children's Zone), financial and health education, and civic engagement processes aimed at building place-based trust and mutualism among neighbours. In spite of the rhetorical focus on communities, however, the interventions associated with the "norms restoration" theory of action reduce in many cases to the promotion of changes in individual behaviour. As discussed above, for example, poverty de-concentration proponents predicate their "treatment" partly on the conviction that low-income households will benefit from proximity to middle-class values and virtues as well as to valuable network ties (Chaskin and Joseph, 2013; Lees, 2008).

Restoration of markets

The diagnosis motivating the second theory of action is perhaps self-evident: distressed neighbourhoods lack functioning markets. Homes sell below their replacement value. Retail corridors are riddled with vacancies, and residents must travel long distances to purchase basic goods and services. Despite abundant vacant land and buildings, value propositions are too low to stimulate developer interest, so new housing is not built (or is built only with government subsidy). Labour market participation is low and unemployment high. The solution (the "ought" in Campbell's terms) appears similarly axiomatic: financial and human capital are needed to re-activate dormant markets and create new wealth. Neighbourhood-based organizations serve as workforce intermediaries, supplement the efforts of local schools, and help high school students choose and access post-secondary pathways. They develop real estate, and direct financial capital and infrastructure investment to local businesses. Many are actively partnering with private developers to build and manage housing, under the federal HOPE VI and Choice

Neighbourhoods programmes. They also help deliver financial services to "unbanked" residents and provide counselling to would-be homeowners or, more recently, to people in danger of losing homes to foreclosure. The community development sector, in their view, must play an active role in priming disinvested neighbourhoods for crucial infusions of new private investment and in preparing residents for the opportunities that will result.

In adopting a "market restoration" concept of community development, some policymakers and thought leaders dismiss political organizing as a tool, casting protest as anachronistic and urging that it be mothballed as community developers get down to the more adult business of growing neighbourhood wealth (Lindsay, 2000). Others point out, however, that the financial capital attracted via such efforts often does not lead to wealth creation among incumbent neighbourhood residents:

> Change in the residential real estate market can lead to a stronger, healthier neighbourhood. At the same time, market change can take problematic forms, leading to undesirable outcomes. It can be driven by speculation, triggering little or no improvement in the community's quality of life, or it can disrupt established communities, displacing long-time low- and moderate-income residents. Higher house prices without improvement to neighbourhood vitality and quality of life is neither positive nor sustainable, while change that leads to displacement of an area's lower-income residents is not equitable. (Mallach, 2008, p. 1)

Mallach implies that neighbourhood-level outcomes in the context of market-led revitalization depend crucially upon whether community development and housing policy acknowledge and attend to the multiple levels on which individuals and groups use and value neighbourhood space.

Reversal of injustice

Community development groups espousing the third theory of action are organized around the principle that the condition most troublingly absent from struggling neighbourhoods is a concern with equitable outcomes (as Fainstein puts it in her work on the just city, the question of "who gets what") and a concern with exerting influence on the mechanisms of policy-making that affect these outcomes (Fainstein, 2010, p. 7). Groups like these, out of opportunism and necessity, undertake many projects that are similar to those of organizations in the "norms" and "markets" paradigms. Yet their desire that disadvantaged populations achieve political recognition and power as well as substantive material betterment leads them to situate their work within a broader socio-historical context,[6] to understand it as political, and to be prepared to rely on protest and confrontation as tactics. Many such groups originated in local tenants' rights, "urban homesteading", or anti-redlining movements in the 1960s and 70s (Beitel, 2013; Castells, 1983;

Goetz, 1996; Wolf-Powers, 2008). Squires shows, for example, that the Community Reinvestment Act, a prime element of today's "market restoration" toolkit in the USA, would not have become law in the absence of sustained political activism (Squires, 2003). In addition to building homes, helping people claim public benefits, and assisting with job search, justice-oriented community development groups advocate for city and state policies that shape housing affordability programmes, undertake campaigns to curb exploitative financial services practices such as pay-day loans, and organize to achieve better wages and working conditions for vulnerable and contingent workers (see DeFilippis, Fisher, and Schragge, 2010, chapter 5). Immigrant-led community development organizations are particularly engaged in workers' rights issues, building neighbourhood-level institutions to address the exploitation of day labourers, for example (Theodore and Martin, 2007; Doussard, 2013). To the extent that rent regulation in New York and San Francisco remains in place to preserve dwelling space for non-wealthy tenants, neighbourhood-based tenant advocacy organizations deserve much of the credit (Beitel, 2013; Lawson, 1986). Other such organizations, rather than engaging directly in politics, pursue activities – such as shared equity housing and co-operative enterprises – that embody heterodox approaches to regeneration, approaches arguably more likely to result in the material betterment of historically disadvantaged households and to respond to their aspirations for inclusion and self-actualization (Davis, 2010; Zitcer, 2013).

In the literature that applies conceptualizations of justice to planning and spatial policies, proceduralist (or "deontological") and consequentialist (or "redistribu-tive") approaches frequently rival one another (Fainstein, 2010; Ferrari, 2012; Purcell, 2008). In many respects, organizations applying a justice-oriented theory of action to community development are consequentialist (that is to say, more concerned with outcomes than with process). But there is also an awareness that the achievement of equity and inclusion for marginalized publics relies on the design and administration of differently configured urban and regional institu-tions, which in turn requires a negotiated process that involves participation, delib-eration, organizing and persuasion. Groups identified with the third theory of action thus incorporate into their idea of justice the conviction that social mobili-zation is a central facet of community development.

Like any schematic, the theory of action approach to understanding neighbour-hood revitalization comes with qualifiers. While I have presented the theories sep-arately, most people practising in the field must, for organizational survival, pivot opportunistically among them. As a result, within many community development organizations, activities associated with all three paradigms overlap and coexist with one another. A further point is that any given intervention is plausibly moti-vated by more than one theory of action. Saegert (2006) points to convergence between the consensus-building approach to community capacity and a justice-focused organizing approach. In other contexts, the market paradigm's emphasis on individual choice and behaviour in relationships of exchange relates to the norms paradigm's emphasis on personal (albeit community-mediated) adaptation to the conditions of life as it exists. Most community development organizations identified with a "justice restoration" paradigm nevertheless work to revive private sector demand for land and to support capital access for small businesses, acknowledging that market activation must be a component of neighbourhood revitalization regardless of whether it reflects one's basic theory of community change (see Mallach, 2008). Still, the political logics that support these three theories of action are distinct, and the successes of each in guiding both local strategies and extra-local policy-making have material implications in people's lives.

How Theories of Action Matter: the Case of Recent Housing Policy in the USA

To argue that muted conflict among theories of action produces community development's organizational field and policy landscape, thereby limiting the range of options for significant institutional reform, I now link my proposed typology of local theories of action with the current state of housing policy and finance in the USA. Specifically, I trace the reactions of community development planners to the mortgage meltdown and foreclosure epidemic – phenomena that are the cause of ongoing crises for neighbourhoods and households in the USA and that have had significant repercussions in the global financial system.

While the focus here is to illustrate the way that theories of action have conditioned planners' response to the foreclosure epidemic, some brief background is warranted about the housing policy milieu that prevailed prior to the crisis. From the early 1990s through the mid 2000s, the twin pillars of low-income housing policy in the USA were poverty de-concentration and asset accumulation through home ownership (Saegert, 2013). With respect to poverty de-concentration, a consensus that one key to improving social mobility lay with enabling poor households to exercise greater choice in the housing market – and to live in mixed-income neighbourhoods – led to the expansion of the Housing Choice Voucher programme, and more generally to a reliance on this market-based programme over supply-side programmes involving public construction and maintenance of dwellings. This same consensus supported the redevelopment of inner-city public housing through the HOPE VI programme (Landis and McClure, 2010). Meanwhile, buoyed by research highlighting the individual and social benefits of home ownership (e.g. Rohe and Stegman, 1994), the promotion of ownership, facilitated by low interest rates, became a major focus of government policy. The encouragement of homeownership was in fact the only policy that linked fragmented and ill-coordinated federal housing agencies during the 1990s and 2000s (Levitin and Wachter, 2013).

In this environment, flexible credit standards and the opaque, loosely regulated nature of mortgage-backed securities and associated derivatives enabled lenders to make thousands of mortgages that would soon be unmasked as "toxic". Households who borrowed in the subprime market often did not have the income or wealth to keep the homes they were purchasing, yet became swept up in the fervour around the possibility (and putative moral superiority) of home ownership. In other cases, they were defrauded by predatory lenders.[7] In the 2007–2009 recession, the average American household lost 40% of its net worth, the vast majority of which was in the form of home equity (Levitin and Wachter, 2013, pp. 19–20). While the crisis was much more severe in some states than in others (Martin, 2011), and while its effects were experienced at least as profoundly in suburbs and exurbs as in city cores, a common geographic thread was that of race: long before the bubble burst, researchers presented troubling evidence that subprime and predatory lending activity was being deliberately targeted to neighbourhoods with large non-white, low-income populations, (Ashton and Doyle, 2008; Immergluck and Wiles, 1999; Newman and Wyly, 2004; Squires, 2003). Schafran (2013) further links the ex-urban foreclosure phenomenon with the record number of black, Latino and Asian households who had become homeowners in suburban and exurban municipalities in the previous two decades. Ashton (2011) argues convincingly that the mortgage finance industry, aided by regulators, "mapped high interest rates and onerous loan terms onto earlier forms of racial and class dispossession".

The crisis that exploded in the national media in 2007 and 2008 (once it had begun affecting homeowners with conventional mortgages and destabilizing the nation's banking system) had come to the attention of community development practitioners well ahead of that time. Now, however, the devastating effects of foreclosures on neighbourhoods (Immergluck, 2010; Schuetz, Been, and Ellen, 2008) became a subject of national discussion. During this time, fissures became more noticeable in the détente binding together disparate theories of action in community development.

Restoration of norms

Organizations and actors aligned with a "restoration of norms" theory of action had relied on the empirically supported view that increasing home ownership would revive civic culture, reduce crime and help enforce social norms. As the focus shifted to preventing foreclosure and keeping families in their homes, their work was often motivated by the cognate idea that mortgage delinquency originated with failures of information, financial literacy, and behaviour. Fields, Libman, and Saegert (2010) argue that just as the rapid expansion of homeownership between 1994 and 2005 had been carried forward by a "policy and community development consensus on asset-accumulation ... education and counseling" for financially unsophisticated homebuyers (p. 650), many foreclosure prevention efforts also targeted individual behaviour as the root cause of mortgage-related distress. In relying exclusively or almost exclusively on one-to-one counselling and financial education, government and philanthropic actors implicitly rejected the idea that a broader political and economic context surrounded low-income home-owners' delinquency and default. Further,

> Nonprofit staff tended to characterize mortgage delinquency as being rooted in homeowners' careless, excessive, and irresponsible spending on luxuries that were beyond their means. They argued that low-income homeowners encountered finan-cial problems because "these people have Champagne tastes and they're living on a beer budget." Participants acknowledged the difficulty of spending wisely amidst cultural norms that encourage consumption, but their financial difficulties were rarely a result of simply not prioritizing mortgage payments and other expenses. (Fields, Libman, and Saegert, 2010, p. 666)

The focus on changing individual and community norms and behaviours as the key to controlling the spiralling housing crisis distracted attention from two alternative possibilities. The first possibility was that upstream policy responses – for example, legal deterrents to irresponsibly lax credit standards and usurious lending practices, or efforts to limit the opacity of mortgage securitization – might have done more to prevent the magnitude of the crisis. The second possibility – still actionable today – was the idea that current policy might be more aggressive in its prospective efforts to curtail future abuses. Relatedly, it might expect more significant reparative measures from the corporate entities involved,[8] and more affirmative efforts on the state's part to relieve the pain of affected households. This dilemma is illustrated in the common rhetorical contrast between "investment" in the stability of the finance industry through instruments such as the Temporary Asset Relief Program (TARP) and "spending" on interventions aimed at struggling homeowners and hard-hit neighbourhoods.

Restoration of markets

The "markets" theory of action during the same time period converged at several points with the norms restoration approach. In the run-up to the crisis, academic studies and government white papers, extolling the benefits of expanded home ownership, had fused optimistic predictions about the place-stabilizing, example-setting potential of new homeowners in poor neighbourhoods with the promise of wealth accumulation by poor households. In the market-driven conceptualiza-tion of community development, home ownership had an almost mystical power, initiating a virtuous circle of property appreciation and social stability, gains in financial capital, and gains in social capital at the neighbourhood level. Community development institutions participated in the initiatives that emanated from this theory, funding or facilitating home ownership workshops and (among those engaged in building housing), placing a special emphasis on including units for ownership in the projects they developed.

As prices appreciated steeply in the early 2000s, there persisted a dominant belief that for poor households living in economically marginal or gradually changing neighbourhoods, the accumulation of financial capital and social capital would be mutually reinforcing. In this context, the model asset-accumulating homeowner could be hailed unproblematically as a contributor to neighbourhood well-being. The flaw in this logic, however, was (and remains) that

> many of the homes that low-income households can afford to buy on the open market are located in neighbourhoods where real estate appreciation has been chronically low or nonexistent. When low income households have managed to buy homes in neighbourhoods with a stronger record of appreciation ... they have often done so using adjustable rate mortgages and other forms of creative financing. (Davis, 2010, p. 274)

As noted above, homeowners in low-income, weak-market neighbourhoods were more likely to be targeted for usurious loans than homeowners in other neighbourhoods. As a result, and given that these households were especially vulnerable to the sorts of economic disruptions that predicted delinquency, the grace period of social capital/financial capital fusion was often quite short in poor communities (Fields, Justa, Libman, and Saegert, 2007; Katz, 2009). Unstable low-income neighbourhoods, in Ashton's words, were systematically exposed to "greater downside risk" (2008, p. 760).

Today, as much of the market activity in distressed neighbourhoods has come to consist in large-scale investor purchases of lender-owned properties (Immergluck, 2013a), a new chapter in the market-led path to neighbourhood revitalization is beginning. In spite of the modest achievements of the federal government's Neighbourhood Stabilization Program, a federal government initiative that channels resources to local governments to prevent foreclosures and deal with their neighbourhood-level aftermath, many communities remain filled with vacant homes – some of them owned by investors who have bought them in bulk and have left them vacant for the time being, some of them owned by city governments or non-profits who have not yet been able to dispose of them (Immergluck, 2013b). With the unifying and iconic concept of homeownership-as-solution-to-community-distress tainted by the crisis, there is no clear goal in federal housing policy, nor is there a "clear policy about what to do with the broken housing finance system" (Levitin and Wachter, 2013, p. 5). Mainstream proposals for housing finance reform (fiercely opposed by the industry) primarily contain measures that would improve information about loans bundled for securitization, monitor financial institutions more carefully in order to stem "agency" problems, or work to improve financial literacy at the neighbourhood level. The exploitative practices that dominated in low-income and majority-minority housing markets pre-collapse are widely seen as inappropriate targets for prospective policy-making. Meanwhile, the labour market problems that underlie poverty in areas with distressed housing markets remain as tenacious as ever. Wages are stagnant, well-paying jobs for the non-college-educated are scarce, and municipalities, fiscally impoverished by the housing market meltdown, struggle to offer their residents access to educational opportunities that might provide pathways out of poverty.

Reversal of injustice

Noting that many communities in which neighbourhood-based organizations helped to stabilize the built and social environments in past decades are now filled with vacancies and foreclosed properties, groups identified with the "restoration of justice" theory of action have been active in the post-bubble era. They have spearheaded the creative use of federal Neighbourhood Stabilization Program funding (encouraging the creation of land banks, for example) and continued to advocate for individual households who risk losing their homes and housing wealth. They have pressed for laws, such as California's Homeowner Bill of Rights, aimed at giving distressed borrowers – particularly those who were subject to predatory lending practices – meaningful opportunities to modify their mortgages. Some questionable policies on the part of mortgage servicers (such as "dual-tracking," the practice of initiating or continuing foreclosure proceedings while a borrower is being reviewed for a loan modification) have been curtailed in some states. Diversion programmes in use in some places have helped to mitigate some of the worst neighbourhood consequences of mass foreclosure (Goldstein, Weidig, and Boateng, 2013).

In addition to reacting to the distress wrought by the crisis, community developers have affirmatively pursued practical interventions designed to better position low-income residents and neighbourhoods for housing stability going forward. Prominent in this sphere is the shared equity housing movement, which sponsors and advocates for non-market models that restrict the prices of publicly assisted units across multiple resales in the interest of maintaining long-term affordability (Axel-Lute, 2010; Davis, 2010; Saegert, 2013). Other scholars and practitioners have mobilized around the protection and preservation of existing social housing assets, questioning the prevailing consensus around the demolition of public rental housing and the replacement of project-based subsidy with vouchers (Association of Neighborhood Housing Developers, 2009; DeFilippis and Wyly, 2008; Goetz 2013). In debates about gentrification, voices have emerged that advocate policies which would enable low-income renters and homeowners to remain in once-decaying neighbourhoods that are now becoming places of choice (Mallach, 2008; Godsil, 2014).

To discuss these measures as responses to injustice (or, said differently, to refer to the problems to which they are addressed as structural) tends, however, to marginalize practitioners with respect to mainstream institutions. The argument is made eloquently by Wyly (2013), who casts contemporary housing policy in terms of a struggle between use and exchange value in housing – "a place to live rather than a hamster wheel of economic accumulation" (p. 30) – yet acknowledges that to do this is to forego "a chance of appearing on the required reading lists of policy professionals in New York and Washington" (p. 29). From the perspective of community development practitioners, an important consequence of political marginalization is a perpetual struggle to raise operating funds. Community development planners otherwise oriented toward critique and mobilization have, on the whole, been forced to cast their lot with norms- and market-restorers if they hope to sustain their organizations. The bounds of acceptable community development activity are differently drawn in different places; advocates of community land trusts and resale-restricted housing, for example, have gained political traction and implemented successful projects in some parts of the USA. Yet overall, the impulse to survive drives community development institutions toward largely palliative activities rather than actions aimed at political and institutional change (see Weir, 1999). And it is because of this that critical urbanists in the USA often characterize community development as a timid, reformist endeavour that lacks the capacity for muscular activism (see Stoecker, 2004).

Conclusion

The case described here lends concrete support to Campbell's proposition (Campbell, 2012) that it is crucial in planning practice to consciously and critically connect actions back to the knowledge, interpretations and analyses that underlie and motivate them. During the Great Recession, community development practitioners in the USA strove to prevent and mitigate mortgage foreclosures and to help people cope with their neighbourhood-level impacts. In this, they moved from description and knowledge creation to action: from "is" to "ought". My aim here has been to propose that the theories of action motivating neighbourhood regeneration policy in this milieu were in conflict, and that this conflict constrained practitioners and policy-makers from delivering a greater measure of relief to affected neighbourhoods and households. It is often simplest for practitioners – and for the funders and government agencies that support them – to rationalize away conflict between competing theories of action, preserving community development as a big tent capable of accommodating a variety of actors with distinct motives. In analysing this case, however, I have taken the normative position that the marginalization by government, media and many elements of the philanthropic sector of a theory of action that engaged directly with injustice – a theory, in the words of Iris Marion Young, that took "a moral perspective on structural processes" (Young, 2010, p. 65) – had damaging consequences.

While the neighbourhood-level impact of the mortgage crisis is primarily a US phenomenon, it is important not to overlook the commonalities between the theories of action dominating US community development policy and those that are prevalent in neighbourhood regeneration policy in Western Europe and the UK. The increasing prominence of marketization discourses and practices is evident across contexts, as are the power and persuasiveness of the "civil norms" paradigm, reflected in the emphasis on social cohesion and in the prevalent strategy of engineered "mixing" and deconcentration of ethnically and economically homogeneous groups. The tendency to look to local social sector organizations to respond to service needs created by public sector austerity measures is another parallel. We have seen, across national contexts, a broad marginalization of the position that neighbourhood planners might, firstly, understand place-based deprivation and disinvestment as the product of structural injustice, and secondly, respond by mobilizing around policies (particularly state policies) aimed at reversing that injustice. Planning practitioners in the USA, the UK, and Europe increasingly find themselves (ourselves) both managing and participating in arrangements of "governance-beyond-the-state" by which groups of stakeholders allow the public sector to divest itself of responsibility for vulnerable populations (Swyngedouw, 2005). The argument implied by this analysis – that a theory of action built around the reversal of injustice is entitled to greater attention in neighbourhood regeneration practice – will perhaps help planners focus on building institutions and movements that make it so.

Notes

1. Katz of the Brookings Institution acknowledges the social-historical arrangements that segregate wealth and opportunity within in US metropolitan areas, asserting that "unbalanced growth patterns have been deeply influenced by the politics of racial and ethnic exclusion that are practiced by suburbs throughout the country." His remedy, however, has little to do with political strategies to dismantle these (Katz, 2004, p. 4).
2. Well-known anti-capitalist critiques by David Harvey (1973) and Neil Smith (1986; 2002) go further, identifying neighbourhood regeneration projects with the destructiveness of property market cycles and accusing community development professionals in government and civic organizations of complicity.
3. Webb (2010) argues that "market-led" regeneration in the UK falls more squarely within government's purview than official rhetoric and popular belief suggest.
4. One difference between the USA and its European counterparts is a protest and organizing idiom that is expressly neighbourhood-based. In the USA the dismay of some scholars and practitioners about the state of the community development field arises from a sense that a strategically important historical tradition, one specifically aligned with the neighbourhood scale, is being blunted or absorbed. Contrastingly, counter-hegemonic politics in the UK and Europe has not conventionally been

neighbourhood-centred, and critiques of neo-liberalism in those places have focused more on the weakening of the national welfare state.

5. Putnam's treatment of social capital has led to confusion and imprecision in the use of a concept originally framed as dynamic, individualistic, and interdependent with other forms of capital (Bourdieu, 1986; Coleman, 1988). Putnam and his adherents in the community development sector imply that social capital can accrue to groups and places as well as to individuals; that poor communities "lack" it; and that it is equatable with civic participation, trust and sociability. Many have argued that this represents a distortion of the original formulation (see Skocpol, 1996; DeFilippis, 2001).

6. A critique by Thomas Sugrue of *Great American City*, Robert Sampson's book about Chicago (couched within a generally favourable review), embodies this stance. "In American cities, boundaries have been fundamentally constitutive of racial identities and socioeconomic status," says Sugrue, "But for all his interest in place, Sampson is uninterested in place-making, namely the process by which boundaries are drawn, challenged, reinforced or undermined" (2012).

7. Predatory loans are defined as "high-cost, abusive, and often fraudulent transactions designed to trap homeowners and homebuyers into usurious obligations" (Wyly and Crump, 2008). Predatory lending cannot be conflated with subprime lending in general; nevertheless, many subprime borrowers, because of information asymmetries, fell victim to schemes that overcharged or defrauded them. For example, many borrowers who would have qualified for lower-cost prime loans were put into costly subprime mortgages on which they were likely to default – mortgages whose interest rate terms and fee structures were advantageous only to brokers and servicers.

8. A recent article in the online magazine *Salon* asserts that the indictment and imprisonment of Lorraine O. Brown (formerly the president of the company DocX), on charges of fraud and conspiracy demonstrates the successful targeting of low-level white-collar offenders while larger institutions who participated in mortgage fraud remain undeterred from future misconduct (Dayen, 2013).

References

Ashton, P. (2011). The financial exception and the reconfiguration of credit risk in US mortgage markets. *Environment and Planning A, 43*, 1796–812.

Ashton, P., and Doyle, M. (2008). *Weak market neighbourhoods in Chicago: A baseline analysis. Report prepared for the Department of Housing, City of Chicago*. Chicago, IL: City Design Center, University of Illinois at Chicago.

Association of Neighborhood Housing Developers. (2009). *Permanent affordability: A national conversation*. New York, NY: Author.

Axel-Lute, M. (2010). *Homeownership today and tomorrow: Building assets while preserving affordability*. Montclair, NJ: National Housing Institute.

Baum, H. (1997). *The organization of hope: Communities planning themselves*. Albany, NY: State University of New York Press.

Baum, H. (2005). Interface: How bad structures drive communities – And planners – Crazy. *Planning Theory and Practice, 6*, 536–41.

Beitel, K. (2013). *Local protest, global movements: Capital, community and state in San Francisco*. Philadelphia, PA: Temple University Press.

Bourdieu, P. (1986). The forms of capital. In J. Richardson (ed.), *Handbook of theory and research for the sociology of education* (pp. 241–58). New York: Greenwood.

Campbell, H. (2012). Planning to change the world: Between knowledge and action lies synthesis. *Journal of Planning Education and Research, 32*, 135–46.

Castells, M. (1983). *The city and the grassroots: A cross-cultural theory of urban social movements*. Berkeley, CA: University of California Press.

Chaskin, R. J. (2001). Building community capacity: A definitional framework and case studies from a comprehensive community initiative. *Urban Affairs Review, 36*, 291–323.

Chaskin, R. J., and Joseph, M. L. (2013). 'Positive' gentrification, social control and the 'right to the city' in mixed-income communities: Uses and expectations of space and place. *International Journal of Urban and Regional Research, 37*, 480–502.

Coleman, J. (1988). Social capital in the creation of human capital. *American Journal of Sociology, 94*(Suppl.), S95–S120.

Crump, J., Newman, K., Belsky, E. S., Ashton, P., Kaplan, D. H., Hammel, D. J., and Wyly, E. (2008). Cities destroyed (again) for cash: Forum on the U.S. foreclosure crisis. *Urban Geography, 29*, 745–84.

Davis, J. E. (2010). More than money: What is "shared" in shared equity homeownership? *Journal of Affordable Housing, 19*, 259–77.

Dayen, D. (2013). The recession was her fault: Meet Wall Street's scapegoat, the one person to get jail time for the most massive mortgage fraud in history. *Salon*. Retrieved from http://www.salon.com/2013/02/24/shes_paying_for_wall_streets_sins/

DeFilippis, J. (2001). The myth of social capital in community development. *Housing Policy Debate, 12*, 781–806.

DeFilippis, J., Fisher, R., and Schragge, E. (2010). *Contesting community: The limits and potential of local organizing*. New Brunswick, NJ: Rutgers University Press.

DeFilippis, J., Fisher, R., and Shragge, E. (2006). Neither romance nor regulation: Re-evaluating community. *International Journal of Urban and Regional Research, 30*, 673–89.

DeFilippis, J., and Wyly, E. (2008). Running to stand still: Through the looking glass with federally subsidized housing in New York City. *Urban Affairs Review, 43*, 777–816.

Doussard, M. (2013). *Degraded work: The struggle at the bottom of the labor market*. Minneapolis, MN: University of Minnesota Press.

Etzioni, A. (1997). *The new golden rule: Community and morality in a democratic society*. New York: Basic Books.

Fainstein, S. S. (2010). *The just city*. Ithaca, NY: Cornell University Press.

Fainstein, S. S. (2012). A review of "Insurgencies; Essays in planning theory". *Journal of the American Planning Association, 78*, 490.

Fallov, M. A. (2010). Community capacity building as the route to inclusion in neighbourhood regeneration? *International Journal of Urban and Regional Research, 34*, 789–804.

Ferguson, R., and Stoutland, S. (1999). Reconceiving the community development field. In R. Ferguson and W. Dickens (eds), *Urban problems and community development*. Washington, DC: Brookings Press.

Ferrari, E. (2012). Competing ideas of social justice and space: Locating critiques of housing renewal in theory and in practice. *International Journal of Housing Policy, 12*, 263–80.

Fields, D., Justa, F., Libman, K., and Saegert, S. (2007). American nightmare. *Shelterforce 150*. Retrieved from http://nhi.org/online/issues/150/americannightmare.html

Fields, D., Libman, K., and Saegert, S. (2010). Turning everywhere, getting nowhere: Experiences of seeking help for mortgage delinquency and their implications for foreclosure prevention. *Housing Policy Debate, 20*, 647–86.

Friedmann, J. (1987). *Planning in the public domain*. Princeton, NJ: Princeton University Press.

Gittell, R., and Vidal, A. (1998). *Community organizing: Building social capital as a development strategy*. Thousand Oaks, CA: Sage.

Glickman, N. J., and Servon, L. J. (1998). More than bricks and sticks: Five components of community development corporation capacity. *Housing Policy Debate, 9*, 497–539.

Godsil, R. (2014). *Autonomy, mobility, and affirmatively furthering fair housing in gentrifying neighborhoods*. Washington, DC: Poverty and Race Research Action Council.

Goetz, E.G. (2013). *New Deal Ruins: Race, Economic Justice, and Public Housing Policy*. Ithaca, NY: Cornell University Press.

Goetz, E. (1996). The neighborhood housing movement. In D. Keating, N. Krumholz, and P. Star (eds), *Revitalizing urban neighborhoods*. Lawrence, KY: University Press of Kansas.

Goldstein, I., Weidig, C., and Boateng, C. (2013). The city of Philadelphia's residential mortgage foreclosure diversion program: Addressing the rising tide of foreclosure. *Housing Policy Debate, 23*, 233–58.

Grogan, P., and Proscio, T. (2000). *Comeback cities: A blueprint for urban neighbourhood revival*. New York: Basic Books.

Harvey, D. (1973). *Social justice and the city*. Baltimore, MD: Johns Hopkins University Press.

Imbroscio, D. (2011). *Urban America reconsidered: Alternatives for governance and policy*. Ithaca, NY: Cornell University Press.

Immergluck, D. (2010). The accumulation of lender-owned homes during the US mortgage crisis: Examining metropolitan REO inventories. *Housing Policy Debate, 20*, 619–45.

Immergluck, D. (2013a). *The role of investors in the single-family market in distressed neighborhoods: The case of Atlanta*. Boston, MA: Harvard Joint Center for Housing Studies.

Immergluck, D. (2013b). Too little, too late, and too timid: The federal response to the foreclosure crisis at the five-year mark. *Housing Policy Debate, 23*, 199–232.

Immergluck, D., and Wiles, M. (1999). *Two steps back: The dual mortgage market, predatory lending and the undoing of community development*. Chicago, IL: Woodstock Institute.

Jacobs, K., and Manzi, T. (2013). New localism, old retrenchment: The "Big Society", housing policy and the politics of welfare reform. *Housing, Theory and Society, 30*, 29–45.

Katz, A. (2009). *Our lot: How real estate came to own us*. New York: Bloomsbury.

Katz, B. (2004). *Neighborhoods of choice and connection: The evolution of American neighborhood policy and what it means for the United Kingdom*. Washington, DC: Brookings Institution. [This is a research brief – http://www.brookings.edu/research/reports/2004/07/metropolitanpolicy-katz].

Kleinhans, R. (2012). A glass half empty or half full? On the perceived gap between urban geography research and Dutch urban restructuring policy. *International Journal of Housing Policy, 12*, 299–314.

Kretzmann, J., and McKnight, J. (1993). *Building communities from the inside out: A path toward finding and mobilizing a community's assets*. Evanston, IL: ABCD Institute.

Lake, R. (2013). *Planning desire: Problematization, participation, and, governmentality in constructing the planning subject*. Paper presented at Association of Collegiate Schools of Planning / Association of European Schools of Planning Congress, Dublin Ireland July 15–19.

Lake, R. W., and Zitcer, A. W. (2012). Who says? Authority, voice, and authorship in narratives of planning research. *Journal of Planning Education and Research, 32*, 389–99.

Landis, J. D., and McClure, K. (2010). Rethinking federal housing policy. *Journal of the American Planning Association, 76*, 319–48.

Lawson, R. (1986). *The tenant movement in New York City 1904–84*. New Brunswick, NJ: Rutgers University Press.

Lees, L. (2008). Gentrification and social mixing: Towards an inclusive urban renaissance? *Urban Studies, 45*, 2449–70.

Lemke, T. (2001). "The birth of bio-politics": Michel Foucault's lecture at the Collège de France on neo-liberal governmentality. *Economy and Society, 30*, 190–207.

Levitin, A. J., and Wachter, S. M. (2013). Why housing? *Housing Policy Debate, 23*, 5–27.

Lindsay, L. B. (2000). Community development at a crossroads. *Banking and community perspectives Q3* (pp. 6–8). Dallas, TX: Federal Reserve Bank of Dallas, Retrieved from http://www.fedinprint.org/items/feddpe/y2000iq3p6-8.html

Logan, J., and Molotch, H. (1987). *Urban fortunes: The political economy of place*. Berkeley, CA: University of California Press.

Mallach, A. (2008). *Managing neighborhood change: A framework for sustainable and equitable revitalization*. Montclair, NJ: National Housing Institute.

Marcuse, P., Connolly, J., Novy, J., Olivo, I., Potter, C., and Steil, J. (2009). *Searching for the just city: Debates in urban theory and practice*. Abingdon: Routledge.

Marris, P. (1987). *Meaning and action: Community planning and conceptions of change*. London: Routledge and Kegan Paul.

Martin, R. (2011). The local geographies of the financial crisis: From the housing bubble to economic recession and beyond. *Journal of Economic Geography, 11*, 587–618.

Newman, K., and Wyly, E. K. (2004). Geographies of mortgage market segmentation: The case of Essex County, New Jersey. *Housing Studies, 19*, 53–83.

Purcell, M. (2008). *Recapturing democracy: Neoliberalism and the struggle for alternative urban futures*. New York: Routledge.

Putnam, R. D. (1995). Bowling alone: America's declining social capital. *Journal of Democracy, 6*, 65–78.

Rohe, W. M. (2009). From local to global: One hundred years of neighborhood planning. *Journal of the American Planning Association, 75*, 209–30.

Rohe, W. M., and Stegman, M. A. (1994). The impact of home ownership on the social and political involvement of low-income people. *Urban Affairs Review, 30*, 152–72.

Saegert, S. (2006). Building civic capacity in urban neighborhoods: An empirically grounded anatomy. *Journal of Urban Affairs, 28*, 275–94.

Saegert, S. (2013). *Inequality of forms of capital: Crisis and opportunity in low income housing policy*. Paper presented at RC-43 Conference: Housing and the Built Environment of the International Sociological Association, Amsterdam. July 11.

Saegert, S., Warren, M., and Thompson, P. (2001). *Social capital and poor communities*. New York: Russell Sage.

Sampson, R. (1999). What community supplies. In R. Ferguson and W. Dickens (eds), *Urban problems and community development*. Washington, DC: Brookings Press.

Schafran, A. (2013). Origins of an urban crisis: The restructuring of the San Francisco Bay area and the geography of foreclosure. *International Journal of Urban and Regional Research*, *37*, 663–88.

Schuetz, J., Been, V., and Ellen, I. G. (2008). *Neighboring effects of concentrated mortgage foreclosures*. Working Paper 08-03 New York: Furman Center for Real Estate and Urban Policy.

Skocpol, T. (1996). Unravelling from above. *American Prospect*, *25*, 20–5.

Smith, N. (1986). Gentrification, the frontier, and the restructuring of urban space. In N. Smith and P. Williams (eds), *Gentrification of the city* (pp. 15–39). Boston, MA: Allen & Unwin.

Smith, N. (2002). New globalism, new urbanism: Gentrification as global urban strategy. In N. Brenner and N. Theodore (eds), *Spaces of neoliberalism: Urban restructuring in North America and Western Europe* (pp. 80–103). Malden, MA: Blackwell.

Squires, G. (2003). Introduction: The rough road to reinvestment. In G. Squires (ed.), *Organizing access to capital: Advocacy and the democratization of financial institutions* (pp. 1–26). Philadelphia, PA: Temple University Press.

Stoecker, R. (2004). The myth of the missing social capital and the ghost of social structure: Why community development can't win. In R. M. Silverman (ed.), *Community based organizations: The intersection of social capital and local context in contemporary urban society*. Detroit, MI: Wayne State University Press.

Sugrue, T (2012). *Review of Robert Sampson's Great American city: Chicago and the enduring neighborhood effect*. Retrieved from http://www.publicbooks.org/nonfiction/great-american-city

Swyngedouw, E. (2005). Governance innovation and the citizen: The Janus face of governance-beyond-the-state. *Urban Studies*, *42*, 1991–2006.

Theodore, N., and Martin, N. (2007). Migrant civil society: New voices in the struggle over community development. *Journal of Urban Affairs*, *29*, 269–87.

Turok, I. (1992). Property-led urban regeneration: Panacea or placebo? *Environment and Planning A*, *24*, 361–79.

Uitermark, J. (2003). "Social mixing" and the management of disadvantaged neighbourhoods: The Dutch policy of urban restructuring revisited. *Urban Studies*, *40*, 531–49.

Webb, D. (2010). Rethinking the role of markets in urban renewal: The housing market renewal initiative in England. *Housing, Theory and Society*, *27*, 313–31.

Weir, M. (1999). Power, money, and politics in community development. In R. Ferguson and W. Dickens (eds), *Urban problems and community development* (pp. 139–92). Washington, DC: Brookings Press.

Weissbourd, R., and Boudini, R. (2005). *Market-based community economic development*. A discussion paper prepared for the Brookings Institution Metropolitan Policy Program. Washington, DC: Brookings Institution.

Wolf-Powers, L. (2005). Up-zoning New York City's mixed-use neighborhoods: Property-led economic development and the anatomy of a planning dilemma. *Journal of Planning Education Research*, *24*, 379–93.

Wolf-Powers, L. (2008). Expanding planning's public sphere: Street magazine, activist planning, and community development in Brooklyn, New York, 1971–1975. *Journal of Planning Education and Research, 28,* 180–95.

Wyly, E. K. (2013). Why (not a right to) housing? *Housing Policy Debate, 23,* 29–34.

Wyly, E. K., and Crump, J. (2008). Introduction. Cities destroyed (again) for cash: Forum on the U.S. foreclosure crisis. *Urban Geography, 29,* 745–84.

Young, I. M. (2010). *Responsibility for justice.* New York: Oxford University Press.

Zitcer, A. (2013). *Honest weights and measures: Practicing moral consumption and participatory democracy in urban food co-operatives.* Unpublished Dissertation Manuscript, Rutgers University, New Brunswick, NJ.

17

Participatory Governance

From Theory to Practice

Frank Fischer

Participatory governance is a variant or subset of governance theory that puts emphasis on democratic engagement, in particular through deliberative practices. In academic circles, the concerns of participatory governance have rapidly become important topics in social and policy sciences. Moreover, during the past several decades participatory governance has made its way into the political practices of a significant spectrum of political organizations, both national and international. Generally advanced as a response to a "democratic deficit" characteristic of contemporary political systems, participatory governance has been embraced by major organizations such as the World Bank, the US Agency for International Development, UN Habitat, and the European Union (EU); all have put money and effort into the development of participatory processes. Many of these initiatives have drawn their inspiration from the progressive projects of political parties in India, Brazil, Spain, Mexico, and the UK. To this list one can add civil society organizations, such as Oxfam, Action Aid, and the International Budget project, actively disseminating information and promoting participatory practices.

Both theory and empirical experience with governance demonstrate that there are numerous patterns of participation and non-participation, from non-democratic elitist top-down forms of interaction to radically democratic models from the bottom up. Governance, as such, tends to refer to a new space for decision-making, but does not, in and of itself, indicate the kinds of politics that take place within these spaces. Participatory governance, grounded in the theory of participatory democracy more generally, offers a theory and practices of public engagement through deliberative processes. It focuses, in this regard, on the

Original publication details: Fischer, Frank. 2012. "Participatory Governance: From Theory to Practice". In *Oxford Handbook of Governance*, edited by David Levi-Faur. Oxford: Oxford University Press, pp. 457–71. Reproduced with permission from Oxford University Press.

deliberative empowerment of citizens and aligns itself in varying degrees to work on deliberative democracy in political theory and deliberative experimentation in policy-related fields of contemporary political and social research, as well as political activism on the part of various public organizations and foundations. Participatory governance thus includes, but moves beyond, the citizen's role as voter or watchdog to include practices of direct deliberative engagement with the pressing issues of the time.

Whereas citizen participation in the governmental process has traditionally focused on measures designed to support and facilitate increased public access to information about governmental activities, efforts to extend the rights of the citizens to be consulted on public issues which affect them, and to see that the broad citizenry will be heard through fair and equitable representative political systems, participatory governance seeks to deepen this participation by examining the assumptions and practices of the traditional view that generally hinders the realization of a genuine participatory democracy (Gaventa 2002). It reflects a growing recognition that citizen participation needs to be based on more elaborate and diverse principles institutions and methods. These begin with a more equal distribution of political power, a fairer distribution of resources, the decentralization of decision-making processes, the development of a wide and transparent exchange of knowledge and information, the establishment of collaborative partnerships, an emphasis on inter-institutional dialogue, and greater accountability. All these measures seek to create relationships based as much or more on trust and reciprocity than advocacy, strategic behavior, and deceit. Participatory governance involves as well the provision of means to engage individuals and organizations outside government through political networks and institutional arrangements that facilitate supportive collaborative-based discursive relationships among public and private sectors.

Emerging as a result of a multiplication of existing kinds of participatory arrangements in the 1990s, participatory governance has established new spaces and given rise to different types of civil society actors to inhabit them. In both the developed and developing countries, these have involved a number of important shifts in problem-solving and service delivery, including more equitable forms of support for economic and social development. Along the way it has often meant a transition from professionally dominated to more citizen- or client-based activities, frequently taking place within the new civic society organizations.

The following discussion proceeds in six parts. It first takes up the interrelated questions of citizen competence, empowerment, and capacity-building as they relate to participatory governance, and then turns to its impact on service delivery, social equity, and political representation, including the distribution of power. These implications are seen to depend in significant part on participatory designs. The discussion thus presents the prominent theory of "empowered participatory governance," which offers principles for design. These points are further illustrated by pointing to several experiences with participatory governance, in particular the cases participatory budgeting in Brazil and the people's planning project in Kerala, India. Before concluding, the chapter also raises the question of the relation of citizens and experts in participatory governance and the possibility of new forms of collaborative expertise.

Citizen Competence, Empowerment, and Capacity-Building

Democratic participation is generally considered a political virtue unto itself. But participatory governance claims to offer even more; it is seen to contribute to the development of communicative skills, citizen empowerment, and community capacity-building. First, with regard to citizen competence and empowerment, the practices of participatory governance are put forth as a specific case of the broader view that participation contributes to human development generally, both intellectual and emotional. Empowerment through participation has, as such, been part of the progressive educational curriculum and numerous citizen-based deliberative projects bear out its influence on personal development (Joss 1995; Dryzek 2008).

Many non-governmental organizations (NGOs) engaged with the practices of participatory governance, in particular in the developing world, speak of "people's self-development" and empowerment as primary goals, emphasizing, political rights, social recognition, and economic redistribution in the development of participatory approaches (Rahman 1995). Rather than merely speaking for the poor or marginalized citizens' interests and issues, they have labored to assist people develop their own abilities to negotiate with public policymakers. Beyond institutionalizing new bodies of client or user groups, they have created new opportunities for dialogue and the kinds of citizen education that it can facilitate, especially communicative skills.

The issue is critical for *participatory* governance as it has little or no meaning if citizens are neither capable nor empowered to participate. Studies show that many people in the middle rungs of society can competently deal with policy discussions (Fishkin 2009; Delli Carpini, Lomax Cook, and Jacobs 2004). Research finds, for example, that lay panelists on citizen juries increase their knowledge of the subject under discussion and often gain a new confidence in their ability to deal with complex policy issues generally (Joss 1995). Many participants tend to describe such participatory experiences as having had a stimulating impact on their personal lives, often leading to further involvement in public affairs.

Much more challenging, however, is the situation for marginalized members of society, those who might benefit from participatory governance the most. But here too there are positive signs. The participatory projects in Porto Alegre and Kerala, taken up below, as well as other experiences in developing and underdeveloped countries, show that citizens with less formal education can also, under the right conditions, participate with surprisingly high levels of competence. In the case of Kerala, most of the members of the local deliberative councils would be described as simple farmers. Nonetheless, they impressively participated in planning projects, the likes of which one very seldom finds in the advanced industrial world.

Participation, it also needs to be noted, is more than a matter of competence. Competent people may not perceive an incentive to participate. Thus, getting them to do so is another important issue. Engagement in the public realm is not without its costs, and most people have little interest in participating unless the costs of engagement outweigh the possibility of benefits from it (Osmani 2007). Local people, including competent citizens, may themselves be highly skeptical about the worth of investing their time and energy in participatory activities. In some situations, participation will lack immediate relevance; it may carry more significance for outsiders than it does for those in the relevant communities. Moreover, not everyone within the communities will be able or motivated to participate. Even when there is sufficient interest in participation there may be time barriers. Sometimes decisions have to be taken before deliberative projects can be set up and carried out.

Finally, questions of participation and competence also bear directly on the issue of capacity-building. Capacity-building, as the development of a community's ability to deal collectively with the problems that it confronts, can contribute to a sense of social togetherness. Rather than the relative passive role of the individual associated with traditional conceptions of citizen participation, participatory governance helps to connect and enable competent individuals in local communities build together the kinds of "social capital" needed for joint problem-solving (Putnam 2000). It does this in part by building social trust and the kinds of mutual understanding that it can facilitate.

Basic to the development of building capacity is a devolution of power and resources from central managerial control and toward local democratic institutions and practices, including street-level administrators willing and able to assist community members in taking charge of their own issues. Whereas community members under conventional forms of representative government are more often than not relegated to a vicarious role in politics, under participatory governance they move to a more direct involvement in the political process, as illustrated below by citizen panels but even more importantly participatory budgeting in Brazil.

Service Delivery and Equity

For many, the underlying goal of building capacity for action is to increase the efficiency and effectiveness of the provision and management of public services. For others concerned with participatory governance, as Ron has explained, a primary goal of capacity-building "is to provide citizens with the tools that are needed to reflect on the normative principles that underlie the provision of public services."[1] That is, the goal is to provide citizens with opportunities to critically reflect on the norms and values justifying the equity of the outcomes.

A range of experiences shows that community participation can improve the efficiency of programs (in terms of uses of resources) and effective projects (that achieve their intended outcomes) in the provision of and delivery of services, in both the developed and developing worlds. In fields such as education, health care, environmental protection, forestry, and irrigation, it is seen to lead to quicker responses to emerging issues and problems, more effective development and design of solutions appropriate to local resources, higher levels of commitment and motivation in program implementation, and greater overall satisfaction with policies and programs (Ojha 2006). Furthermore, an emphasis on efficiency typically leads to improved monitoring processes and verification of results.

While there is no shortage of illustrations to suggest the validity of the claim, there is a methodological issue that can make it difficult to establish such outcomes (Osmani 2007). When local participatory governance is found to contribute to efficiency, firmly establishing the cause–effect relationships can be problematic. It is always possible that a positive association between efficiency and participation may only reflect a process of reverse causation – that is, community members had already chosen to participate in those projects which promised to be efficient. To know if participation has in fact contributed to efficient outcomes, investigators have to discern if such extraneous factors are at work. Although this is theoretically possible, it is a difficult technical requirement. Such information is often unavailable or difficult to come by.

Participation also has the potential to combine efficiency with equity. Research shows that decisions made through the participation of community members rather than by traditional elites or unaccountable administrators offers less powerful groups in the community better chances of influencing the distribution of resources (Heller 2001; Fischer 2000). This view is founded on the presumption that through critical reflection in participatory processes disadvantaged citizens have improved chances of expressing their preferences in ways that can make them count.

But this is not always the case. Empirical investigation tends to be mixed on this issue (Papadopoulus and Warin 2007). Many studies suggest that participatory approaches in local arenas can be of assistance to the poor and disadvantaged members of the community, but other research fails to clearly confirm this. Overall, investigation shows that community participation can lead to more equitable outcomes, but it is particularly difficult to achieve such results in inequitable social contexts. Equitable outcomes more commonly occur in combination with other factors, such as those related to the distribution of power, motivation levels of the participants, and the presence of groups that can facilitate the process. One of the difficulties in assessing the impact of such participation is that there is often no reliable information about the distribution of benefits and costs to households, thus making it difficult to render comparative assessments (Osmani 2007).

Some also argue that by diffusing authority and control over management, decentralized participation can also weaken efficiency (Khwaja 2004). But, depending on the design, this need not be the case. And others argue that it can lead to resource allocations that violate the true preferences of community members, as some may withhold or distort information about their preferences and choices. This problem is perhaps most acute in developing countries, in which community participation is related to external donor-funded projects. All too often in these cases, such participation can intentionally advance preferences that are seen to be more in line with the interests of the donors than local interests. The participants simply try to increase their chances of obtaining available resources by telling the donors what they want to hear (Platteau 2007).

In short, while participation can lead to important payoffs, there are no guarantees. It cannot be said without qualifications that decentralized participation leads to greater efficiency and/or equity. What the experiences suggest is that the conditions of success depend on conscientious effort and design, both of which depend heavily on the ability of the participants to effectively present their views. This depends, in turn, on the degree of political representation and the distribution of power that it reflects.

Political Representation and the Distribution of Power

The theory and practice upon which such efforts rest are based on a number of varied sources, including academic theorizing, political activists, social movements, NGOs, and governmental practitioners. On the theoretical front, many of these projects have been influenced by work on deliberative democracy in political theory, an influential orientation designed to revitalize a stronger conception of democracy and the public interest based on citizen participation through public deliberation. It focuses on promoting "debate and discussion aimed at producing reasonable, well-informed opinion in which participants are willing to revise preferences in light of discussion, new information, and claims made by fellow participants" (Chambers 2003: 309). It is grounded in the idea that "deliberate approaches to collective decisions under conditions of conflict produce better decisions than those resulting from alternative means of conducting politics: Coercion, traditional deference, or markets." Thus, "decisions resulting from deliberation are likely to be more legitimate, more reasonable, more informed, more effective and more politically viable" (Warren 2007: 272).[2]

A critical issue is the relationship of such participation to the larger representative structure of society. Because participatory governance is largely introduced to compensate for the failures of representative government to adequately connect citizens to their elected representatives, the ability to bring these two political models together is important (Wampler 2009). Examples of how this can be done are introduced in the next section presenting the experiences from Porto Algre and Kerala.

Closely related to representation is the question of power, or what Osmani (2007) calls the "power gap." A function of the asymmetrical power relations inherent to modern societies, especially those created by the inequalities of rich and poor, this poses a difficult barrier to meaningful participation. When inequalities are embedded in powerful patriarchies such projects are prone to be captured and manipulated by elites, whether they be political leaders and their patronage networks or those providing development assistance from the outside. Again, we can gain insights into this process in the following discussion of Porto Algre and Kerala.

In many ways, participatory governance is a response to this power problem, as it seeks to give a voice to those without power. But one has to be careful in assessing the degree to which it can generate unmanipulated participation. At the current state of development, participatory governance itself often exists as much or more as a strategy for struggling against political imbalances rather than for counterbalancing them outright.

A manifestation of this struggle is the problem of co-optation, which makes it difficult to judge the significance of participation in successful projects. All too often they are in jeopardy of being co-opted (Malena 2009). Experience shows that success is frequently rewarded by governmental institutionalization, at which point they are often manipulated to serve purposes other than those intended. The World Bank, for example, has deftly co-opted various participatory projects and their methods to generate support for their own agendas. Having discovered of the relevance of local involvement and participation from many of its Third World investment failures, the Bank took an interest in the advantages and institutionalized a participatory program designed to facilitate direct local contact with the communities it seeks to assist (World Bank, 1994). Not only have senior bank staff members been directed to get to know a particular region better through personal participation in programs and projects in its villages or slums, the bank has pioneered a technique called participatory poverty assessment designed "to enable the poor people to express their realities themselves" (Chambers, 1997: xvi). It has been adapted from participatory research experiences in more than thirty countries around the world (Norton and Stephens, 1995).

Such instrumentalization of participation can be seen as a "political technology" introduced to control processes and projects, hindering the possibilities of popular engagement. Bourdieu (1977) refers to these as "officializing strategies" that domesticate participation, direction attention to less active forms of political engagement. Given the widespread manipulation of participatory techniques, Cooke and Kothari (2001) are led to describe participation as "the new ideology."

As is the case with service delivery and equity, there is nothing simple or straightforward about either political representation or equitable power arrangements in participatory projects. Indeed, there is no shortage of things that can block effective political participation. It is a question that again raises the issue of participatory design and brings us to a discussion of "empowered participatory governance" which has sought to set out principles for design.

Empowered Participatory Governance

Examining a range of cases designed to promote active political involvement of the citizenry, Fung and Wright (2003) have labored to sort out what works. Acknowledging that complexity makes it difficult for anyone to participate in policy decision-making, they speculate that "the problem may have more to do with the specific design of our institutions than with the task they face." Toward this end, they have examined a range of empirical experiences (including Porto Alegre and Kerala) in the participatory redesign of democratic institutions, innovations that elicit the social energy and political influence of citizens – especially those from the lowest strata of society – in pursuit of solutions to problems that plague them.

Even though these reforms vary in their organizational designs, the policy issues to be deliberated, and scope of activities, they all seek to deepen the abilities of ordinary citizens to effectively participate in the shaping of programs and policies relevant to their own lives. From their common features they isolate a set of characteristics that Fung and Wright define as "empowered participatory governance." The principles they draw from these cases are designed to enable the progressive "colonization of the state" and its agencies. Relying on the participatory capabilities of empowered citizens to engage in reason-based action-oriented decision-making, the strategy and its principles are offered as a radical political step toward a more democratic society.

As a product of this work, they isolate three political principles, their design characteristics, and one primary background condition. The background enabling condition states that there should be rough equality of power among the participants. The political principles refer to (1) need of such experiments to address a particular practical problem; (2) a requirement that deliberation rely upon the empowered involvement of ordinary citizens and the relevant; and (3) that each experiment employs reasoned deliberation in the effort to solve the problems under consideration. The institutional design characteristics specify (1) the devolution of decision-making and the powers of implementation power to local action-oriented units; (2) that these local units be connected to one another and to the appropriate levels of state responsible for supervision, resource allocation, innovation, and problem-solving; and (3) that the experimental projects can "colonize and transform" state institutions in ways that lead to the restructuring of the administrative agencies responsible for dealing with these problems.

While this work is an important step forward, a theory of the design of deliberative empowerment still requires greater attention to the cultural politics of deliberative space (Fischer 2006). Beyond formal principles concerned with structural arrangements, we need as well research on the ways the social valorization of a participatory space influences basic discursive processes such as who speaks, how knowledge is constituted, what can be said, and who decides. From this perspective, decentralized design principles are necessary but insufficient requirements for deliberative participation. We need to examine more carefully how political-cultural and pedagogical strategies can facilitate the deliberative empowerment in participatory governance.

Projects and Practices: Citizens' Panels, Participatory Budgeting, and People's Planning

The theory and practice upon which participatory governance rest are based on a number of varied sources, including academic theorizing, the efforts of political activists, social movements, NGOs, and the works of governmental practitioners. Of particular significance on the practical front have been experimental projects in participatory governance, all designed to bring citizens' reasoned preferences to bear on the policy process (Gastil and Levine 2005). Most of these projects are dedicated to goals closely related to those spelled out by the theory of deliberative democracy, although many do not emerge from it per se. Some scholars, though, have argued that deliberative democratic theory should strive to be a "working theory" for the deliberative experiments of participatory governance (Chambers 2003). There are now some prominent examples of such interaction, in particular on the part of scholars such as Fishkin (2009), Warren and Pearce (2008), and Dryzek (2008). They clearly illustrate constructive "communication between the theorists of deliberative democracy and empirical research on deliberation" (Fischer 2009: 87).

The projects in participatory governance are to be found across the globe, from Europe and the US to the developing and underdeveloped world. In Europe and the US numerous projects have focused on efforts to develop fora through which citizens' views on complex economic and social issues can be brought to bear directly on policy decisions. Some of these have been organized from the bottom, whereas others have emerged from the top down. Such research has ranged from investigations of the traditional citizen survey and public meetings to innovative techniques such as deliberative polling, televoting, focus groups, national issue conventions, and study circles on to more sophisticated citizen juries, scenario workshops, planning cells, consensus conferences, and citizens' assemblies (Gastil and Levine 2005; Fishkin 2009; Joss 1995). These experiences offer important insights as to how to bring citizens into a closer participatory relationship with public decision-makers.

Most important among these efforts have been the citizen jury and the consensus conference. Developed in Northern Europe and the United States before spreading to a range of countries around the world, these two deliberative processes permit a high degree of citizen deliberation on important matters of public policy. They provide citizens with an opportunity to deliberate in considerable detail among themselves before coming to judgment or decision on questions they are charged to answer. During the process, they hear from experts and pose their own questions to them, before deliberating among themselves. But citizens' panels are largely advisory in nature; they supply additional information that can be useful to politicians and the public. Given the limited amount of space available here, the present discussion will focus more specifically on those deliberative arrangements built into the governmental structure itself.

The most progressive projects have developed in the developing world, especially in Brazil and India. These innovations include deliberative processes analogous to citizen juries but have more formally integrated them into the policy processes of established governmental institutions. Of particular importance are the practices of public budgeting in Porto Alegre, Brazil and people's development planning in Kerala, India. These innovations have been influenced by both social movements, NGOs, and left-oriented political parties, both theoretically and practically. Turning first to participatory budgeting in Porto Alegre, by all standards one of the most innovative practices in participatory governance, it has become a model widely emulated around the world.

Under public budgeting in Porto Alegre significant parts of local budgets are determined by citizens through deliberative fora (Baiocchi 2003; Wampler 2009). In a city of 1.3 million inhabitants, long governed by a clientelistic pattern of political patronage, a left coalition led by the Workers' Party took office in 1989 and introduced a publicly accountable, bottom-up system of budgetary deliberations geared to the needs of local residences. Involving a multi-level deliberative system, the city of Porto Alegre has been divided into regions with a Regional Plenary Assembly that meets twice a year to decide budgetary issues. City administrators, representatives of community groups, and any other interested citizens attend these assemblies, jointly coordinated by the municipal government and community delegates. With information about the previous year's budget made available by representatives of the municipal government, delegates are elected to work out the region's spending priorities. These are then discussed and ratified at a second plenary assembly. Representatives then put these forward at a city-wide participatory budgeting assembly which meets to formulate the city-wide budget from these regional agendas. After deliberations, the council submits the budget to the mayor, who can either accept the budget or send it back to the council for revisions. The Council then responds by either amending the budget or overriding the Mayor's veto through a vote of two-thirds of the council representatives.

The second case, that of Kerala, has involved a full-fledged process of people's resource planning (Issac and Heller 2003; Fischer 2000). Located in the southwestern corner of the country, Kerala has gained attention in the development community for its impressive economic and social distributional activities in the 1980s. In the mid-1990s, a coalition of left parties led by the Communist Party of India / Marxist decided to extend these activities to include a state-wide, bottom-up system of participatory planning, the goal of which was to develop the Kerala Five-Year Plan to be delivered to the central government in New Delhi.

Pursuing a devolutionary program of village-level participatory planning as a strategy to both strengthen its electoral base and improve governmental effectiveness, the government decided that approximately 40 percent of the state's budget would be redirected from the administrative line departments and sent to newly established district planning councils, about 900 in number. Each village, supported by the Science for the People social movement and the Center for Earth Sciences, formulated a specific development plan that spelled out local needs, development assessment reports, specific projects to be advanced, financing requirements, procedures for deciding plan beneficiaries, and a system of monitoring the outcomes. These developments were then accepted or rejected by vote in village assemblies. The final plans were send to the State Planning Board and incorporated into the state's Five-Year Plan, sent to New Dehli for inclusion in the overall development plan of the national government.

As a consequence of these activities, from citizen juries to People's Planning, participation has gained a place across the political spectrum in the 1990s as a central feature of "good governance." Promoting decentralization, good governance practices have added an additional layer of local participatory institutions to an increasingly complex institutional landscape that in some cases has given rise to transfers of both resources and decision-making powers.

Returning to the question of political representation, in the case of the citizen jury and the consensus conference, the outcomes are merely advisory. They offer politicians and decision-makers a different kind of knowledge to consider in their deliberations, a form of understanding often more closely akin to the types of thinking they themselves engage in (as opposed to complex technical reports). But in Kerala and Porto Algre, by contrast, deliberation was integrated into the policy decision process. In Kerala, local discussions were hierarchically channeled up to the State Planning Board for inclusion in the official planning document. In Porto Algre they were linked into the official governmental budget-making process; the outcomes of the deliberations determined an important portion of the budget. Success, in both cases, is seen to depend as much on support from political parties at the top as it does from grass-roots movements from below. The top and the bottom of the power structure must work together (Fischer 2009). Given that the dramatic successes of these two experiences are exceptions to the rule, we need much more investigation into this process.

Participatory Expertise: A New Type of Expert?

Of particular significance in these projects is a breed of NGOs working to represent and serve the needs of marginalized or excluded groups. In many of the newly created participatory spaces activists have assisted excluded peoples – such as the poor, women, AIDS victims, and the disabled – in developing a collective presence that has permitted them to speak for themselves. Through such efforts activists and their citizen groups have in many cases succeeded in influencing the policies of mainstream institutions. In some cases, these activities have given rise to a new breed of public servant – frequently schooled in NGOs – devoted to offering assistance to these groups. As government officials or independent consultants to parallel institutions – they have often played an essential role in the development and spread of participatory approaches to governance (Fischer 2009).

The result of these participatory activities has also given rise to a new kind of professional orientation, one that challenges the standard techno-bureaucratic approaches of the modern state (Fischer 2009). These professionals, along with their respective theoreticians, have sought to reconceptualize the role of the public servant as facilitator of public engagement. Feldman and Khademian (2007), for example, have reconceptualized the role of the public manager as that of creating "communities of participation." In their view, the challenge confronting those working in the public sector is to interactively combine knowledge and perspectives from three separate domains of knowing – the technical, political and local/experiential domains. Bringing about more inclusive practices of governance involves inventing participatory contexts in which the representatives of these forms of knowing can discursively share their perspectives in the common pursuit of problem-solving. Beyond merely identifying and disseminating information from these various ways of understanding and analyzing policy problems, such work involves translating ideas in ways that facilitate mutual understanding and deliberation among the participants and discursively promotes a synthesis of perspectives that helps to simulate different ways of knowing relevant to the problem at hand.

In many cases participatory expertise involves the development of citizen/ expert alliances and the use of practices such as community-based participatory research and participatory action research, as was the case in Kerala (Fischer 2000). These methods involve professional experts in the process of helping lay participants conduct their own research on problems of concern to local residents. While there have been important efforts to facilitate deliberation between citizens and experts, there are a number of problems that still need to be dealt with (Fischer 2009). Perhaps most important, professionals are not trained to facilitate participation and many – maybe most – do not believe there is any point in engaging citizens in such issues. The successful efforts, more often than not, are the result of activities engaged in by professionals involved in progressive social movements of one sort or another (Fischer 2009). In addition, they raise difficult but important epistemological questions related to the nature of such knowledge: Does it just involve a division of labor organized around the traditional separation of empirical and normative issues? Or does it require a new hybrid form of knowledge, involving a fusion of the empirical and the normative and perhaps a special role for local lay knowledge? Included in this question is the need to explore the relationship of reason to emotion. Although everybody in politics knows that emotion and passion are basic to the politics of governance, this topic has yet to receive the attention it deserves in the literature on democratic governance and policy.

Concluding Perspective

Many of these participatory activities have offered significant new insights into questions that have long been ignored in traditional political analysis and in democratic theory in particular. Four of these new perspectives stand out especially. The first concerns the need to fill the "institutional void" that the theory of representative government fails to address. The second involves the degree to which citizens are able to participate meaningfully in the complex decision processes that define contemporary policy-oriented politics. The third is the ability to improve service delivery and social equity. And fourth, we have also noted the implications of participatory governance for the nature of professional practices.

Beyond the theoretical realm, however, it should be clear from the foregoing discussion that much of the practical work on governance involves a collection of separate experiments and projects that have common threads but often offer somewhat limited outcomes, projects in Porto Alegre and Kerala being important exceptions. In this regard, it is essential to recognize that the experiences with these efforts have by no means been all positive. It is a story of mixed outcomes, with the experiences ranging across the spectrum from very impressive to disappointing. Indeed, the failures far outnumber the successes. The successful cases, moreover, offer few uniformities.

The task of sorting out the positive and negative elements contributing to the success and failure of such participatory projects thus takes on particular importance. Given that there is no shortage of factors that come into play, such an assessment is challenging. What can be said is that independent of a good deal of the rhetoric associated with discussions about participation, the evidence about new forms of participatory governance illustrates participation to pose difficult issues with no simple solutions. A closer look reveals that while citizens can participate and that participatory governance can improve both democratic decision-making and efficient service delivery, participation has to be carefully organized, facilitated – even cultivated and nurtured.

Given the difficulties involved in designing and managing participatory processes, it comes as no surprise to learn that citizen participation schemes rarely follow smooth pathways. In the absence of serious attention to the quality and viability of citizen participation, it is usually better to forgo such projects. Participatory governance, despite its promise, is a complicated and uncertain business that needs to be carefully thought out in advance (Fischer 2000). This should be the first priority of those engaged in both the theory and methods of the practice.

Notes

1. The observation is drawn from Amit Ron's helpful comments on this chapter.
2. While the theory of deliberative democracy has had the most influence on these projects, the theory of agonistic democracy can also support the theory and practices of participatory governance.

References

Baiocchi, G. 2003. Participation, activism, and politics: The Porto Alegre experiment. In A. Fung and E. O. Wright (eds) *Deepening Democracy*. New York: Verso, 77–102.

Bourdieu, P. 1977. *Outline of a Theory of Practice*. Cambridge: Cambridge University Press.

Chambers, R. 1997. *Who Reality Counts? Putting the First Last*. London: Intermediate Technology Publications.

Chambers, S. 2003. Deliberative democratic theory. *Annual Review of Political Science* 6: 307–26.

Cooke, B. and Kothari, U. 2001. *Participation: The New Tyranny?* London: Zed Books.

Delli Carpini, M. X., Lomax Cook, F., and Jacobs, L. R. 2004. Public deliberation, discursive participation, and citizen engagement: A review of empirical literature. *Annual Review of Political Science* 7: 315–44.

Dryzek, J. 2009. The Australian citizens' parliament: A world first. *Journal of Public Deliberation* 5: 1–9.

Feldman, M. S. and Khademian, A. M. 2007. The role of the public manager in inclusion: Creating communities of participation. *Governance* 20: 305–24.

Fischer, F. 2000. *Citizens, Experts, and the Environment: The Politics of Local Knowledge*. Durham, NC: Duke University Press.

Fischer, F. 2006. Participatory governance as deliberative empowerment: The cultural politics of discursive space. *The American Review of Public Administration* 36: 19–40.

Fischer, F. 2009. *Democracy and Expertise: Reorienting Policy Inquiry*. Oxford: Oxford University Press.

Fishkin, J. S. 2009. *When the People Speak: Deliberative Democracy and Public Consultation*. Oxford: Oxford University Press; New Haven, CT: Yale University Press.

Fung, A. and Wright, E. O. 2003. *Deeping Democracy: Institutional Innovations in Empowered Participatory Governance*. New York: Verso.

Gastil, J. and Levine, P. (eds) 2005. *The Deliberative Democracy Handbook: Strategies for Effective Civic Engagement in the 21st Century*. San Francisco, CA: Jossey-Bass.

Gaventa, J. 2002. Towards participatory governance. *Currents* 29: 29–35.

Heinelt, H. 2010. *Governing Modern Societies: Towards Participatory Governance*. London: Routledge.

Isaac, T. H. and Franke, R. 2000. *Local Democracy and Development: People's Campaign for Decentralized Planning in India*. New Delhi: Left World Press.

Isaac, T. H. and Heller, P. 2003. Democracy and development: Decentralized planning in Kerala. In A. Fung and E. O. Wright (eds) *Deepening Democracy*. New York: Verso, 77–102.

Joss, S. 1995. Evaluating consensus conferences: Necessity or luxury. In S. Joss and J. Durant (eds) *Public Participation in Science: The Role of Consensus Conferences in Europe*. London: Science Museum, 89–108.

Khwaja, A. I. 2004. Is increasing community participation always a good thing? *Journal of European Economic Association* 2: 2–3.

Malena. C. (ed.) 2009. *From Political Won't to Political Will: Building Support for Participatory Governance*. Sterling, VA: Kumarian Press.

Misar, D. 2005. *Participatory Governance Through NGOs*. Jaipur: Aalekh Publishers.

Norton, A. and Stephens, T. 1995. *Participation in Poverty Assessment. Environmental Department Papers Participation Series*, Social Policy and Resettlement Division, World Bank, Washington, June.

Ojha, H. 2006. Techno-bureaucratic doxa and challenges for deliberative governance: The case of community forestry policy and practice in Nepal. *Policy and Society* 25: 11–176.

Ojha, H. N., Timsina, N. P., Chhetri, R. B., and Paudal, K. P. 2008. Knowledge systems and deliberative interface in natural resource governance. In H. N. Ojha, N. P. Timsina, R. B. Chhetri, and K. P. Paudal (eds) *Knowledge Systems and Natural Resources: Management Policy and Institutions in Nepal*. New Delhi: Cambridge University Press, 1–22.

Osmani, S. R. 2007. Participatory governance: An overview of the issues and evidence. In *Participatory Governance and the Millennium Development Goals*. New York: United Nations, 1–48.

Papadopoulus, Y. and Warin, P., 2007. Are innovative, participatory and deliberative procedures in policy making democratic and effective? *European Journal of Political Research* 46: 445–72.

Platteau, J. 2007. Pitfalls of participatory development. In *Participatory Governance and the Millennium Development Goals*. New York: United Nations, 127–62.

Putnam, R. 2000. *Bowling Alone: The Collapse and Revival of the American Community*. New York: Simon and Schuster.

Rahman, M. D. A. 1995. *People's Self-Development*. London: Zed Books.

Rowe, G. and Frewer, L. J. 2004. Evaluating public participation exercises: A research agenda. *Science, Technology and Human Values* 29: 512–57.

Wampler, B. 2009. *Participatory Budgeting in Brazil*. University Park, PA: Penn State.

Warren, M. E. 2007. Institutionalizing deliberative democracy. In S. Rosenberg (ed.) *Deliberation, Participation and Democracy: Can the People Govern?* London and New York: Palgrave Macmillan, 272–88.

Warren, M. E. and Pearce, H. (eds.) 2008. *Designing Deliberative Democracy: The British Columbia Citizens Assembly*. Cambridge: Cambridge University Press.

World Bank 1994. *The World Bank and Participation*. Washington, DC: Operations Policy Department.

18

Cultivating Surprise and the Art of the Possible

The Drama of Mediating Differences

John Forester

What I always tell people is, 'Whenever you get to the table, you still are surprised, because you never can anticipate really fully where people are going to come from.'

Thom (1997)

Challenges of Interdependence

In community settings as well as in workplaces, in the United States and in many other countries too, the contested goals of "inclusion" and "participation" can mean, in part, dealing with differences – differences of culture and class, interest and ideology, values and identities. When we are not all the same and yet have to come to terms with one another – when we are interdependent – we as community members often struggle to learn not only to understand our many cultural, economic, and political differences, but to build bridges so we can work together in and across our multiple subcultures too. So here we will address these challenges in complex disputes that have not only involved bargaining over differing economic interests but required reconciling deeply differing social and cultural identities as well. We shall see, as we explore several disputes involving land use and transportation issues and value conflicts over abortion and sacred sites, that planners and activists,

Original publication details: Forester, John. 2009. *Dealing with Differences: Dramas of Mediating Public Disputes*. Oxford: Oxford University Press, pp. 37–56. Reproduced with permission from Oxford University Press.

Readings in Planning Theory, Fourth Edition. Edited by Susan S. Fainstein and James DeFilippis.
Editorial material and organization © 2016 John Wiley & Sons, Ltd.
Published 2016 by John Wiley & Sons, Ltd.

organizers and managers in many other contexts too have much to learn from experienced intermediaries' skills and insights, stories and strategies.

Cultivating the capacity to mediate such disputes, we shall see, provides no panacea, no technical fix, for the challenges of sustaining plurality and difference within our localities, encouraging not only mutual respect but local community building and practical cooperation as well. When our basic commitments to land or quality of life come into conflict, mediation processes and deliberative practices become not less but more relevant – a potentially important source of practical strategies that can complement legal and legislative action (Susskind and Cruickshank 1987, 2006).

Skepticisms of "just talk?" – and political cynicism

Yet in a world of conflicting interests – to build or not to build, to "protect" or "develop" the land, to invest here or there – many seem skeptical of solutions that depend on the "mere talk" of dialogue or deliberation, of facilitated or mediated processes. The rhetoric and presence of diverse deep differences in our cities or our workplaces challenge both our hope and cynicism: can we imagine in the face of our differences that we can or can't work and live together? For all the rhetoric of multiculturalism and diversity, respect and dialogue, defenders of civil society appear to know much more about "how to talk the talk" than they do about "how to walk the walk" (Fung and Wright 2003, Sandercock 2003a).

We see these challenges in everyday life, for example, as a friend might say about another acquaintance, "There's no use talking to her; nothing's going to be possible" – even when a great deal might really be possible – and the result, we sometimes suspect, is that our friend may just have set him or herself up for failure. Too often, when many of us face differences of values or religion, culture or class, race or gender, a deceptively simple realism seems to blind us by suggesting, "No, we can't really act together with them; they'll never listen; they'll never talk to us about the real issues here."

In community or political settings this familiar skepticism can easily become a seductive cynicism, a practical failure of hope. This threatens not just our friends and acquaintances, but our lives as members of any democratic polity or civil society more generally (Dryzek 2000).

As a matter of everyday life and ethics, our skepticism of others can lead us to miss real opportunities when they're right in front of us: we fail to build informed relationships and suffer the consequences needlessly. As a matter of practical negotiation, we often split differences, settle grudgingly for both-lose outcomes rather than creating substantially better-for-both, mutual gains (Susskind et al. 1999).

As a matter of identity and respect, instead of building mutually respectful relationships, we often presumptively dismiss and feel threatened by differences, even if we know that resentment, of course, is like taking poison and hoping that the other person dies. We are so easily tempted to take "value differences" literally that we miss real practical opportunities – where we might put the stop signs – behind what we take as irreconcilable abstractions ("The natural environment must be protected!").

These problems of everyday politics, ethics, and negotiation of differences have been encouraged, in part, by three widespread presumptions that blind us unnecessarily. First, struck numb if not dumb by cultures celebrating technical expertise and scientific experimentation, we often think about *analysis* and even *rationality* in ways that devalue our emotional sensitivity, expression, and actual responsiveness as merely idiosyncratic, less practically important than our "knowing the right answer" about what might now be done. In the name of being right, doing right suffers.

Second, just as we see consumer preferences changing easily in contrast to apparently more fixed, pious appeals to "bedrock" religious traditions, we often think about "interests" as ever-negotiable but "values" as tied to fixed "identities" somehow immune from transformation in times of conflict and political negotiation.

Third, often being captured by our ideals as much as we espouse them, we often think of "deep value differences" presumptively and automatically as differences we cannot negotiate, practically speaking, at all.[1]

So we need to look carefully at the work of skillful intermediaries to learn how they may have had surprising successes in particular cases as they have faced strong emotions, identity conflicts, or deep value differences, in just those situations in which many of us, community activists and leaders, planners and public managers, for example, might well – left on our own – have thrown in the towel. Looking at such cases, we might really ask, of both these intermediaries and our fellow organizers or public managers as well, "What could they have been thinking?" What were the intermediaries thinking that *helped them* to achieve surprising results – and what thinking might have led the rest of us, though, in exactly the same situations, *to give up too soon*?

Learning from practice when interdependence matters

Why focus here on the practical work of *mediators* of public disputes? Routinely working in between conflicting interests – public and private, communal and religious – mediators can serve us as "canaries in the mine," especially if we want to learn how both to manage tensions in our diverse communities and workplaces and to improve community and public deliberations. So mediators can teach us about handling the inevitable conflicts of interdependence: when parties cannot simply satisfy their interests unilaterally – when neighboring communities can hardly avoid dealing with each other, for example. But more too: mediators know how disputing parties so often can fall into – but also might escape – the traps of producing poor compromises, what we can call lose-lose agreements, as suspicious neighbors or employers or developers are so easily tempted to escalate demands, to exaggerate data, to posture, to hide their interests, and more. Mediators will also, we shall see, help us to think more carefully about settings that involve differences of "values" as well as of interests, differences of identity as well as differences of goals and preferences.

When facilitators and mediators who work with conflicting parties produce surprising results – "We never thought an agreement like this would be possible!" – they can show us possibilities that we, too, will find surprising because we hardly yet understand how those results were achieved at all. When the community leaders or activists or developers in disputes tell us that they themselves have been surprised – the actual parties who know their problems better than anyone presumably! – we, too, as readers may well be surprised ourselves, and we can learn a good deal as a result (Nussbaum 1990, Forester 1999a, 2006a). Iris Murdoch put a part of this beautifully once, when she said of learning from good practice, "Where virtue [good practice] is concerned, we often apprehend more than we clearly understand, and we *grow by looking*" (Murdoch 1970: 31).

So if we look closely at facilitators and mediators – we, too, will *see* that they can teach us that our bodies reach where our intellects often do not: that actual practice can and has led theory, that our good intentions can get us so righteously stuck, that our "analytic understanding" in all its realistic and well-informed glory can persuade us that nothing's possible when trying, sketching, playing, even taking walks and sharing meals can really show us that a great deal's possible after all.

When we listen to experienced mediators, we find that they speak again and again of finding possible outcomes that none of the parties first thought possible. We might recall that T. S. Eliot wrote of poetry as a "raid upon the inarticulate," and so we may come to see that mediators work every day in the face of conflict to "raid the impossible," to bring back working agreements across boundaries of suspicion and distrust, culture and commitment, differences of race and class and gender – agreements that no one first thought possible (Susskind et al. 1999). This daily and practical drama of intermediaries' work can teach us about outcomes (and practices) that we never thought possible, and the surprises we discover can teach us not just about new possibilities but about our old expectations, our old ways of thinking that won't pay off, old ways of looking that have blinded us to what we really can do (Schön 1983, Lewicki, Gray, and Elliot 2003).

We can explore these questions – assessing in particular, what the mediators were thinking – in two parts by working with excerpts from their "practice stories," excerpts we can take not as histories of cases but as windows onto the world of their practice.[2] In the first part we consider the insights of two practitioners who find mediated and facilitated multistakeholder processes always closely intertwined with issues of power and emotion in public disputes.

In the second part we consider three short stories. Mediator and consultant Frank Blechman recalls facing officials' fears of explosive comprehensive planning meetings in three counties (Blechman 2005). Mediator Stephen Thom, recently deputy director of the US Department of Justice's Community Relations Service, reflects on a case involving identity conflict in a California land use dispute. Then we return to another provocative account of Blechman's that involves deep value differences between abortion rights opponents and advocates.

Finally, the conclusion suggests lessons we can learn from these intermediaries' practical and anticipatory (and so theoretical) thinking too. We will ask what these practitioners can teach us about recognizing and even cultivating possible working agreements that others might so easily see as impossible.

Listening to the Mediators

Let us begin with two practitioners who summarize the promise of mediated participation in a world of power and emotion. The first suggests why traditional zero-sum hardball might not work anymore – and why he came, and we might come, to take mediation and practical consensus-building processes seriously.

Frank Blechman, political consultant and planning consultant, worked for many years at the Conflict Clinic at George Mason University. He tells us,

> I've spent most of my career as a conflict generator…
>
> Conflict generating is fundamentally the process of raising an issue to visibility and forcing public polarization so that fifty percent plus one will land on your side: It's essentially the opposite of consensus building processes, although it uses all the same fundamental skills: Understanding where people are coming from, how far they're willing to move, getting people to feel comfortable so that they're willing to reveal information that they initially withhold, all of those…
>
> Sam Rayburn is alleged to have said, "Any bill that passes by more than ten votes wasn't strong enough." Now that's the ultimate statement of the virtue of non-consensus: That if in fact you only need fifty percent plus one to make policy, then in fact getting more votes than that means you gave up more than you had to.
>
> But in many of the public issues that we face today – because we have empowered, over the last generation, so many people to obstruct so effectively – fifty percent plus one is not enough, sixty percent plus one is not enough, seventy percent plus one is not enough, so that indeed you need to get closer to ninety percent plus one in order to actually carry out policy.
>
> And at that point, the skills required to get fifty percent plus one have to be re-tuned toward a different objective – and it may be a hundred percent minus one or it may just be ninety percent plus one depending on the scale.
>
> But most of the work that I now do falls more into the ninety percent plus one to the hundred percent minus one than the fifty percent plus one range.

Now, this is an almost confessional statement of a practitioner's own evolution from being an adversarial, win-lose conflict generator to a more collaborative consensus builder, and his transformation has nothing to do with idealism, but everything to do with pragmatism and power. Fifty percent plus one is no longer enough, he argues: in many situations of ongoing interdependence, it doesn't work; the society and polity has changed, and implementation – getting anything done – becomes the hostage of many parties' abilities to be obstructionist. Still, he suggests that many of the skills, "understanding where people are coming from and how far they're willing to move," remain very much the same for the consensus builder as for the conflict generator!

So far we have a direct account of self-interest: if you want to get something done, pay attention to those who can block or delay or obstruct you. But many situations are not so straightforward and unambiguous. The second story suggests that there's no talking about mediated participation without also talking about suspicion and anger, humor and irony. So listen to a facilitator who thought she'd lost it in a contentious meeting in a small town's land use case. Michelle Robinson Greig – now a planning consultant with Greenplan, Inc., recounts what she did, and so, perhaps, what we might sometimes have the presence of mind to do:

> There were a couple moments in the meeting when things became hot. There was one I remember really well – when a woman in the front of the room became really enraged about attorneys, and she said,
>
> "Well, you know, the problem is that the town just tries to do something, and then somebody tries to stop it, and then it all goes to these attorneys, and they just keep fighting each other and everybody just keeps spending money on these attorneys."
>
> As she was speaking she rhymed off all the major issues in the community like the shopping mall and the franchises ..., and she touched every button in the room. ... I could see every person in the room rising up behind her, you know, filling with rage.
>
> And I thought, "Ohhh no," I felt I was going to lose control of the meeting.
>
> But when she stopped speaking, I just ... sort of lightly made a joke, and I said, "What should we do then? Should we shoot all the lawyers?"
>
> And everybody just burst out laughing, and the moment was kind of salvaged.
>
> But I think ... it's necessary to have a sense of humor about it, and to be mindful of everybody in the room and respectful of everybody in the room, and whenever somebody put something negatively, I would just try to find a positive idea there. I'd try to turn it around to a positive suggestion.
>
> So someone would rant and rave about something, or somebody became angry about ... houses being built in cornfields – they really didn't want to see that – and I said, "Well then, what do you suggest?" and since they had said something about a land trust in the course of talking, I picked out that idea and I said, "So, are you saying it would be good if we had a local land trust that could try to protect some of this land?"
>
> And they said, "Yes" – you see?
>
> So it was really a question – whenever anybody spoke negatively – of trying to turn it around into a positive suggestion, or just coming back with, "Well, what would you like to see happen?"

You know? "What would you like to see happen?" And that set the tone for the meeting, and really had set the tone for our organization as a whole about what we're trying to do, which is find positive solutions. (Greig 1997)

Here we see a wonderfully rich but precarious, contested, and critical moment in which we find a public discussion of land use possibilities confronted by legacies of anger, not just one person's but widely shared anger too; we see a group about to turn on an easy target, a common enemy (lawyers!); we hear an experienced practitioner worry and wonder if the discussion was heading irretrievably south; and we then see more than her handling the anger rippling through an audience too.

We see part of the promise of skillful mediation here, not in comedy but in the quickly linked recognition of anger and the proactive request for proposals. Greig responds sensitively, not dismissively, in a pragmatic and empowering way: her sense of humor and irony acknowledges and then reaches beyond anger and frustration to ask practical questions of what might now be possible. So her humor and recognition are both serious and freeing; they evoke in a gentle yet persistent way a sense of next steps, a sense of hope. "Okay," Greig says, in effect, "we don't want to spend all our money on lawyers, so now what? What do you propose? What can we do?" This moving toward proposals, she suggests to us, is what mediation's all about: searching for practical strategies generated *not by the mediators or facilitators* but by the contentiously divided and diversely interested community members themselves.[3]

From Practical Cases, Practical Lessons

So consider now three short accounts of disputes involving bitter transportation arguments, housing and tribal values, and myriad abortion-related issues. We come to see more clearly both the political and ethical challenges of mediation as well as real practical lessons for the rest of us who work or live all the time with public or community conflict, ethic and cultural differences, or differences of deep value commitments.

Antipathy, distrust, and the baggage of the past: County comprehensive planning in a contested corridor

Frank Blechman tells us of his practice as a mediator working with county governments in a busy East Coast transportation corridor:

We were asked by one of the counties to help them consider how they ought to do comprehensive land use planning … in their part of the … corridor.

Part of their concern was that this is an area which is somewhat more blue collar, a little bit tougher – a little less civil – than you have in other parts of the county: there was a lot of bitterness that the other parts of the county had been getting better service, and there was a feeling that there was no way to open up traditional citizen participation without getting completely out of hand and getting explosive.

And so they asked us: could we propose a process, do process design work, give them advice on how they might proceed with comprehensive planning?

Here's a planning process that had been stymied by fear and evasion, by the threatening difficulties of "traditional citizen participation" and a sense of incompetence in the face of meetings getting "completely out of hand," "explosive." Here's an allusion to missing "social capital" in the form of missing trust, norms, and networks: trust that others at the meeting won't explode, norms that they needed a process design to suggest, networks that the convened parties could begin to form (Briggs 2008).

So what happened? Blechman continues, "We said, 'Would you be interested in considering a process which integrated what you're doing with what's going on with the adjacent jurisdictions in the corridor?' And they said, 'You are out of your mind.'"

Now this might quite reasonably be a point at which many community leaders, public administrators, or planners would pack their bags and look for more promising problems to address. Planners, for example, have been trained to see the impacts that the counties have on one another, but they're often not trained to know how to proceed when they've made a proposal and the key officials respond by saying, "You're out of your mind."

So let's follow Blechman's story:

We said, "Well, let's take a look." We then went out and interviewed about a hundred and thirty people, roughly one-third business, one-third citizen-activist and political types, and one-third governmental officials.

We then constructed four focus groups representing slightly different geographical areas, but each mixed in terms of those three sectors. And we then constructed, out of those focus groups and out of the interviews, a team of fourteen people who represented all of the jurisdictions and all of the sectors – who then formed a negotiating group to discuss a process for integrated planning.

He goes on: "That group, through us, then presented the proposal for a pretty dramatically different kind of process to the planning agencies in two of the counties and to the county council in the third – and it eventually won approval for that new process, which is now beginning." Now this was so far "just" the beginning, and Blechman recognized the enormous amount of hard work remaining to be done, but he also usefully reminded us of what had been accomplished too. He tells us:

Now, this was a consensus building process in the sense that county officials believed initially they could not sit in the same room with each other – but ultimately they sat down and came to an agreement about how the process ought to work. It included the county official who said, "I don't think I can sit in the same room as those people."

Obviously, this is not the same as building a consensus on comprehensive planning, land use, transportation, environmental management, growth and so on in the corridor, but it's clearly the first step.

Now, we will go beyond that first step in a moment, but we should not lose what we can already learn from this beginning. What might planners and other community leaders see happening here?

First, those hoping to convene the interested parties – those facing the contentious situation, facing deeply entrenched and passionately divided interests – were not stopped cold by the officials' visceral skepticism: "I don't think I can sit in the same room as those people." This wasn't a coolly reflective, intellectual skepticism they heard that said, "Pretty dubious." This was, "You're crazy to think about getting all these people together, getting us together with 'those people.'"

Second, we see that from the point of officials' initial worries about cooperation, the process built upon careful representation and "a negotiating group" that discussed, recommended, and then gained official approval and mandate for a process that few people thought possible, that had been dismissed as "crazy."

Third, we see here a deceptively simple – but politically complex – process of learning via interviews. Blechman later suggested how much more than information such crucial "interviews" can produce. He tells us,

> While I love doing surveys ... I know that for purposes of conflict resolution surveying absolutely is no substitute for personal contact. Interviewing is partially information gathering, but it's sixty percent relationship building. You are introducing yourself and inviting people to trust you.
>
> It's a negotiation in itself. And if they trust you, to share information with you, and you treat that information with the respect that you promise, it's then not a very large leap to say, "Now, will you trust me to put together a meeting where you won't get beaten up?"

So interviewing and asking questions, he suggests, can reach far beyond information gathering – and here we see not just qualities of sharing information, manifesting respect, earning trust, building relationships, but all of this then in the service of convening conversations, "a meeting," in which parties' fears of aggression, antipathy, distrust, and disrespect can be overcome in the pursuit of practical learning, real productive negotiations and actual, not idealized, civic deliberation (Reich 1988, Dryzek 2000, Forester 2006b, Yanow et al. 2006).

We need not make too much of this first story – but we can take as simply worth exploring further this achievement of cooperative and officially mandated results in the face of its earlier dismissal, a dismissal not by cranks but by the officials and well-organized participants with local knowledge, those most centrally involved!

But let us turn now to cases involving conflicts over identity and deeper value issues.

Challenges of identity in land use planning

In Southern California a developer wanted to build 100 or more new homes. Local Native Americans opposed the project because the land in question held an ancestral burial ground. Political officials were worried about still other constituents – as we hear from our next practitioner – neither Anglo nor Native American, but Asian American (Thom 1997). Stephen Thom of the federal Community Relations Service begins,

> When the Mayor and county supervisor found out that somebody neutral with the experience that I've had working with Native American issues was available, the mayor immediately asked me to come into a private meeting with him. In his mind there were multiple parties, and he couldn't figure out what their position was, and he wanted to know, could we assist? He was more than willing to sit down and work with the parties, and he wanted to … begin to get a representative body that could enter some constructive forms of negotiations.
>
> So that's when we entered into a series of public meetings. Our role initially was to talk to many of the tribal members in the area. In those meetings, what I attempted to do was to go over … what the developer was proposing, and what the city was permitting the developer to do – acknowledging that there was a sacred burial ground, and acknowledging that the developer would be flexible and try to be respectful to the Native American interests – but the Native American interest needed to begin to grapple with what they felt they wanted to accomplish – what they felt was sacred and religious and respectful.

Here we have a mayor interested in a negotiated solution, not just in pushing through the formal permitting process. But the mayor, we hear, unsure both about the real issues and about the parties, turned to a mediator experienced with tribal issues for help. Thom continues:

> The tribal members wanted to try to keep the ground from getting excavated. They wanted to try to set that land aside so there wouldn't be development on it, and they also had an interest of seeing that whatever was built around complemented the intent of the tribe's use, historically, and demonstrated a respect for what their burial ground would be. … So the picture started clearing up.

At this point, the picture may be clearing up, but we could easily enough worry about impasse, legal suits, and traditional political power. Negotiated outcomes don't appear all that promising when one party says, "Let's get the shovels," and another says, "Don't touch the land – it's sacred."

We seem to have all the signs here of what might easily be an intractable conflict involving identity issues.[4]

So what happened? Our mediator, Stephen Thom goes on:

> Meanwhile the veterans' administration was looking for land, and there were veterans pushing the city to get some kind of a veterans' home, and they were a third party coming into the picture. The city was very interested, and the county was very interested, in having a veterans' home because there was a military base in that area – a large constituency so that the home made political sense to the supervisor and to the city to support.

Now the picture's getting more complicated, and he goes on:

> The developer owned the land. The developer was asking and trying to get permission and permits approved to do the building.
>
> The city and the county were leveraging, "We'd like a veterans' home," and the Native Americans were leveraging, "You're on a sacred burial ground."
>
> So you really had three agendas.

So far, our assessment of the conflict, viewed from the outside, might be as follows: a new housing development versus a veterans' home versus a sacred burial ground; it still doesn't look very promising. But Thom tells us that at their actual meetings they discovered more:

> Now – what was really interesting was that the Native Americans loved the idea of having a veterans' home there, because what that did for them was that it gave the land respect for the elders…
>
> They liked the concept of having a living place for elderly people that would be respectful to their property, and they felt that the veterans would accomplish that. So the veterans and the Native Americans began to talk, and they began to agree – that they supported each others' agendas.

How did that happen? Had representatives of the parties not met face to face, they might never have discovered this much. Thom explains,

> A (Native American) leader had evolved who basically tossed out a couple of concepts that he felt were important. One was setting aside five acres, and a second was building a Native American memorial on that site which would complement a veterans' home and would give some tribute to those Native Americans that participated in America's wars. That became the hook: the Native Americans gravitated to this concept because it was so reverent, respectful of Native Americans, and it so well complemented the veterans home, and it gave tribute, like no other tribute to Native Americans in this nation.

From there, he continues, the negotiation started to take shape:

> The developer had to consider whether to get a permit. He had no objections to building a veterans' home and giving twenty-two acres of land for that purpose. He had no objections to giving some land … to the Native Americans, if that be what they wanted – he was flexible on that – so long as he got to build on the balance of the thirty something acres and build, I think, a hundred twenty homes.
>
> What happened was that the city and the county had very clearly stated that a veterans' home was going to be a clear criterion for allowing the permission for the development. One of the commissioners on the State veterans' review board – who was, I think, of Native American ancestry – had indicated clearly that if the town hoped to gain State approval and hoped the State would come and bring money and build the veterans' home, it was going to have to come in unified with the Native Americans as well as with the veterans. So the leverage was all set for reaching some accord.

So here, a dispute that we could easily have seen initially as irreconcilable – as a dispute to excavate or not, to leave the land untouched or build new housing on it – no longer seems hopeless. We began with images of marketed land versus sacred land, the clash of one group's interests, or perhaps even ways of life, against another's, and now we sense possibilities that might satisfy the interests (and perhaps the ways of life as well) of each of the apparent adversaries (cf. Fuller 2005).

But even more important, we see our own earlier expectations of irreconcilability refuted, and so we find ourselves surprised to see new possibilities we had not imagined. We might find ourselves less cynical, more curious now, and needing to understand better how our earlier practical assessments of likely impasse could have been mistaken. We need to ask seriously, "What were we thinking? Why might *we*, ourselves, so easily have *missed* encouraging and achieving such mutually beneficial outcomes? Why might we so easily – and simplistically – be ready to presume irreconcilability?"

We see here again a "drama of mediation" – and, of course, of negotiation more generally: we start with conflict and apparently irreconcilable interests that have little to do with each other, and we wonder how in the world these parties will ever stop living at cross-purposes, and then skillful negotiators and mediators, organizers and managers can sometimes come up with results that no one expected. We need to explore how these dramas can work: how at times our own comfortable "realism" about struggles of power, interests, and identity can keep us presumptuous or blind (or both), keep us from finding options and possibilities that really do work for the people involved (Forester 2008b, Heifetz and Linsky 2002, Kolb and Williams 2003). So we need to explore, once more, how skillful mediators might snatch possibilities from the apparently impossible, and how community leaders, public managers, and planners working in the face of multiple and conflicting parties might do just the same. If we can learn how our initial presumptions hold us hostage, how our initial socially constructed assessments preempt our learning about real possibilities, we can learn to approach future cases more critically, not less, with more curiosity and less presumption, as skillful practitioners here show us how to do.

Making progress when little negotiation seems possible

Let us turn now to a third story, a third drama of negotiation provided by Frank Blechman (2005). We might come to see, in the wonderful words of Russell Norwood Hanson, that "there's more to seeing than meets the eyeball," that there can well be more going on in a case than we expect, and that when our expectations too quickly narrow our vision, we need to learn to see more, we need actually to learn to learn, to know that we don't know what we need to know, even though we are now confident in what we think we do know (Hanson 1961: 7).

As we'll see, Blechman's account first appears to be full of apparent contradictions: he seems to disavow the promise of "agreement," but he tells us of agreements reached nevertheless. He speaks of nonnegotiable issues, but then points toward evidence of real and productive negotiated agreements. Let's listen closely to appreciate what he really says:

> The program I work with does not start from negotiation theory. Indeed it starts from the premises that: the conflicts that go the longest and cause the most damage are rooted in non-negotiable issues, in race, class, gender, religion, nationality, deeply held values, and that those deep rooted issues, therefore, will not be resolved by negotiation, and that the end product of a resolutionary process is not, therefore, an agreement.
>
> That creates a somewhat different framework for what we do.
>
> So the end product, often, is an understanding. Parties come together, parties who are deeply divided; they join in an analytical process, and they go away not having agreed about a damn thing but having come to understand their own situation and the other people's situation better.

So far, we have an appeal not to any negotiated outcome but to improved understanding, and of course we should want to know what any such "understanding" might be good for: if some parties gain control and resources while others gain "understanding," we might worry about just what they're understanding![5]

Still, understanding our own situations and those of others with whom we must interact might certainly be goods in themselves, but of course there's more to it. Blechman continues:

> With that understanding they act unilaterally in the future in ways that are less conflictual, more constructive for each, and in fact they may find that while they can not get within a shred of agreement on issue X, they in fact have dozens of issues A, B, C, to J on which they *can* cooperate – many of which are essentially negotiable.

How can this work? Listen a bit more, as he goes on:

> I'll give you a classic example. A few years ago, the pro choice and pro life forces in this state, which is heavily Catholic, had really gone to war with each other, and the state police were proposing to go to the legislature seeking new authority to interpose themselves to prevent violence.
>
> There was a meeting arranged between leaders of the pro choice and the pro life forces who immediately agreed that it would be very undesirable if such legislation was passed and that they should jointly oppose it on a variety of free speech grounds.

Now here we have an agreement prompted by what both parties take perhaps for different reasons to be an external threat: increased intervention by the state police. But their discussions produced more, Blechman tells us:

> As the discussions went forward they discovered, not entirely to their amazement, that they also shared strong common interest in increasing health care for at risk teenagers and pregnant teenagers – and they also wound up forming a coalition which voluntarily proposed a set of rules for how they would picket each other to sort of lower the risk of violence, thereby forestalling the state police proposal.
>
> Simultaneously they formed a coalition in the legislature to increase state funding and support for prenatal health care. That coalition, despite all the wars and despite all the interventions of groups like Operation Rescue from outside the State coming in, has held up and for many years since it has succeeded in increasing state funding for health care even at times of budget cuts. And that has, at some level, improved the civility of debate.
>
> Now, on the fundamental issue of abortion, needless to say, the two sides did not convince each other and did not agree, and if the purpose of bringing them together was to seek common ground on that issue, they might never have come together, and my guess is that it would have failed. But, bringing them together in a different context made it possible for them to identify very constructive things that they could do.

We have a great deal to learn here, for Blechman alerts us to distinctly different practical outcomes and to how we might achieve them. First, he tells us, two adversaries that have been involved in deeply and fundamentally value-defined, bitter, and at times violent, conflict have somehow found ways to agree practically:

a   On steps to resist legislative support for increased police power;
b   On steps to develop rules for picketing to lower the risks of violence at demonstrations;
c   On steps to improve healthcare for at-risk teens;
d   On steps to form a coalition to lobby the legislature for prenatal care funding; and
e   On ways to improve the level of adversarial debate, of "civility," at a time when anti-abortion protests were increasingly characterized by the intimidation of

women at clinics and an escalating rhetoric tantamount at times to the incitement to violence.

But these substantial outcomes are still not what's most important here, as surprising and counterintuitive as these agreements between archenemies might be. The far more important lesson for community leaders and organizers, planners and mediators alike follows: "if the purpose of bringing them together was to seek common ground on that issue, they might never have come together. ... But, bringing them together in a different context made it possible for them to identify very constructive things that they could do." Here, Blechman suggests, looking for agreement on the core issue would have led to failure. That's the easy and obvious – but seductively self-fulfilling – conclusion drawn by the political realists who say, "Of course, they'll never agree!"

But Blechman teaches us a still more important and practical lesson. If we failed to bring the parties together at all – because they so obviously and realistically could not agree on the core issue – *that narrow realism, too, would have been a source of failure* and missed opportunity. Again, "bringing them together in a different context made it possible for them to identify very constructive things that they could do."

Now here we started with nonnegotiated "unilateral actions": what parties do on their own, uncoordinated with others, and we have the suggestion that their "understanding," far short of any agreements, might lead these unilateral actions to be less adversarial and more constructive for each party. In such a case, again without any explicit and reciprocal agreements, parties might produce nonnegotiated but mutually fruitful "joint gains" (Axelrod 1985, Winship 2006).

But what follows these nonnegotiated, more mutually constructive actions in Blechman's account is even more interesting: honoring the assumption that on certain issues no agreement – not a shred – will be possible on a central, defining, "focal" issue, still, he suggests that "they may find," they may discover – clearly having not approached one another with this understanding or this expectation – that there may be "dozens of issues on which they *can* cooperate."

But here, of course, we're back to the possibilities of actual negotiation freshly discovered in a bitter setting in which no negotiation at all seemed possible on an overarchingly dominant issue. So what we can come to treat – so realistically, it seems – as a dominant and defining issue, we now see, can paradoxically be a blinding one. We think we see the central issue, it looks nonnegotiable, and we draw the implications for action: Let's get out of here; let's not waste our time and resources trying to do the impossible. But Blechman suggests that this apparently reasonable rationale, "Nothing's possible," hides the real possibilities we have. We risk confusing our obvious disagreement on a central issue with the potentially negotiated agreements we might reach, the outcomes we might yet achieve on many other important issues.

So Blechman shows us that thinking about "agreement" too early on can not only be hopeless, but worse: focusing on the impossibilities of "core issue" agreements can actively disempower us. We don't just set ourselves up for a fall, but we keep ourselves ignorant, narrow-minded, and uninquisitive: we ignore opportunities right in front of us.

So Blechman, like Thom and Greig (Forester 2005), teaches us a striking lesson about our presumptions of others who seem to cherish deep and "fundamentally" different values from our own. The realists – our friends who say, "It's no use talking; they fundamentally disagree" – are being earnest yet far too literal and, so, unfortunately, too superficial as well. As a result, these so-called realists are likely to miss many real opportunities that grow from conversations that are indeed possible – even when a "deeper" central negotiated agreement on a core issue like abortion is certainly not possible.

So we have at least one punch line from this third story: "agreement" can at times be a deceptively simple, inappropriate early goal of dispute resolution or participatory processes, and our perception of "no possible agreement" on a central issue, our own negotiation realism, can lead us to miss real opportunities. So this is all a story about realism that can become a blinding cynicism despite the best of intentions. We're thinking about deep differences on a key issue; we really do think no agreement's possible, and we're both right, narrowly, and wrong, more practically. We might be happy to learn eventually that we've been wrong, but we'd be even happier to recognize and act on our real opportunities in the first place!

Conclusion

These accounts suggest that skillful and wise intermediaries – and planners, organizers, and managers like them – can surprisingly at times snatch real possibilities from the jaws of impossibility. How, we should continue to ask, do they raid the impossible when others think the game is up? What lessons do they suggest that community leaders, planners, and others need to learn in situations of complex public and private disputes?

Experienced mediators seem to know that in contentious disputes there's always more going on than meets the eye, that parties always care about even more, sometimes much more, than they say or announce or defend as a matter of public posture. So, they suggest, as community leaders, public officials, planners, or citizens we should be very careful about tying our own hands with the political rhetoric of those who seem to be adversaries. To put this more bluntly: in a globalizing world of increasing cultural diversity, we need to listen more carefully both to – and, every bit as important, *beyond* – "the words"! In socially, economically, and politically diverse settings, of course, engaging with and far beyond the spoken word enacts recognition and respect, listening and learning too. Listening merely to "the words" is hardly listening at all, of course, so we need to be less gullible, and less self-satisfied in our political realism about what can't be, so that we can be more curious, more critical, and more creative as we find opportunities that others have presumed not even to exist (Forester 1999b, Menkel-Meadow 2001).

These mediators have their presumptions too, though. So they expect that in times of conflict, stereotypes and fears will often focus parties' attention in limiting ways, so that parties will need to and can in fact learn new things. As parties facing differences in complex disputes, for example, we often come to realize that there's more that we need to find out, so we can come to learn, first, and act as best we can to achieve our ends, second. In a globalizing environment, our increasing need to negotiate cultural, social, linguistic, and religious differences means practically that we have to presume less and learn more – in real time, no matter how well we are "prepared." Being prepared will mean, in part, being able to pay attention and learn.

These skillful mediators assume that parties can surprise one another with new information, gestures, offers, disclosures of self, and more that can enable them – enable us all – singly and together to act in new ways as they and we learn from and respond to one another. So after initial assessment comes convening. After and through convening comes learning. After and through learning, negotiation that takes advantage of mediation assistance then becomes possible.

So these mediators presume that in the first place, initially and practically, conversation matters more than *and must precede* any agreement, as we saw in all three cases. In many settings in which participation or inclusion matter, then, this means we must resist the urge to bargain too quickly, to look for fast and simple deals, simply to trade and exchange rather than allowing ourselves to talk and to listen and probe, to inquire and to find new ways to avoid the stereotyping that ends up making us blind, self-righteous, and less informed, rather than perceptive and more insightful.

Furthermore, these astute mediators know, too, that when disputes take win-lose or zero-sum complexions, then complications – additional interests to negotiate! – can actually help. We look stuck, but more information and more concerns, new relationships and news of environmental change can get us unstuck, as the role of the veterans played in the second case. Additional complexity – additional facts that matter, additionally relevant details or stakes – can save us from our own "rush to interpretation," our own preemptive, presumptuous "realism" that blinds us to possibilities we really have (Coles 1989). This can sound easy, but it makes personal demands that are not always simple: we need to tolerate ambiguity and complexity, to take seriously beliefs unlike our own, to respect ways of organizing the social and cosmological world that are unlike what we know. Community leaders and organizers, public managers and planners who can appreciate difference in these forms will help cultivate diversity – and cooperation – in communities and workplaces rather than run from it or suppress it.

The mediators whose work we have explored assume that dispute resolution involves not only knowledge and broad value claims and commitments – not only differences over epistemological and ethical claims – not only words but small offers, reciprocal gestures, the sharing of information, and the building of trust that we saw in the richness of interviewing practices. Here reassurance and respect take shape not so much in words but in tone and body language, in eye contact and posture, in the minute ritual performances of the ways we break bread and share meals, not in verbal promises or flattery.

More precisely, these mediators' practice tells us to focus less on contradictory words, less on conflicting arguments, less on general and abstract knowledge and value claims, and more on the specific tone, style, and conditions of conversation and dialogue – the practical, expressive character of others' and our own ways of speaking and listening. So in environments of diversity and plurality, citizens and planners alike must not only think differently but act differently: we must not dismiss but really take advantage of a cup of tea here, a walk on the site there, the diverse conventions and rituals of meeting and listening, talking and eating, walking and working together through which we can usefully learn about one another. The work of inclusion and participation happens not only in words but in deeds together as well.

Finally, these mediators presume in the face of conflict that when parties typically and inevitably care about much more than they say, those parties will also have to manage multiple, conflicting, and ambiguous goals, responsibilities, and obligations – and that, as practical people, many of these parties can and will improvise, innovate, and cooperate practically to serve their own interests, to solve shared problems, and to build new strategic working relationships (as the abortion opponents and advocates did) in unforeseen and unimagined ways. So, too, as they face increasingly diverse and interdependent relationships, community members and activists, public managers and planners alike will come to appreciate that our many differences are not just issue defined but are far more complex and ambiguous – and that very complexity and ambiguity can provide us with real opportunities, as well as with obstacles, in our work together.

So this analysis makes few claims for mediation as any general technical fix. Instead, drawing from thoughtful mediators, we can learn about the ways our own presumptions can often hold us captive, learn about our own gullibility and cynicism, our failures to inquire critically and to act on good judgment, our own failures of imagination and hope. In situations that can look to the facile realist's eye quite irreconcilable, these mediators teach us, we can at times, surprisingly, discover cooperative, consensual outcomes in the shadow of looming impossibility. All this we can explore, even as we face contentious and seemingly irreconcilable value differences.

Notes

1. Cf. here Susan Collin Marks's surprising and eye-opening book about mediators' important work under conditions that many would think impossible (Marks 2000). She writes at one point, "'Monitors' became a catchall word for most peace workers,

especially on marches, at demonstrations, or in crises. When we were called out to monitor a mass demonstration and ended up mediating, when our presence was enough to prevent violence, whether we were called mediators, observers, or monitors did not matter. We were too busy doing it to think about what we should call ourselves" (Marks 2000: 67).

2. The mediators' "practice stories" we consider here form part of a longer term research project to explore the micropolitics of planners' and mediators' practices in a range of politically contested settings (Forester 1999a, Forester, Peters, and Hittleman 2005). Our oral history interviews focus on accounts of the challenges and opportunities presented by cases and projects; we do not focus upon life histories. Instead, we work to gather the accounts of insider-actors, not outside-spectators. We ask distinctive questions to focus on practice rather than attitude, belief, or espoused theory: we ask not, "What do you *think* about X issue?" but instead, "How in this case did you *handle* X issue?" As a result, we document not full case histories or opinions about issues but rather the practiced sense of engaged intervention of practicing planners and mediators, and we try to examine their accounts not as last words about cases, but as accounts needing triangulation and corroboration as any interpretive evidence does (Forester 2006a).

3. Other students of urban conflict and difference similarly recognize passion, humor, and emotion as central to the story of practical rationality in the face of conflict (Forester 2004b, Sclavi 2006a,b; Sandercock 2003a).

4. On identity conflicts, see Rothman (1997), and on intractable conflicts, for example, see Lewicki, Grey, and Elliott (2003).

5. The classic statement here, no less apt than when first published, is Sherry Arnstein's clear-eyed discussion of the dangers of "we participate, they profit" in her "A Ladder of Citizen Participation" (Arnstein 1969). Bent Flyvbjerg (1998) and Oren Yiftachel (1998) extend Arnstein's warnings by arguing that in settings of political conflict, we can expect the power of rationalization to trump rationality and that much "planning" serves not broader aspirations of diverse publics but hegemonic agendas of spatial control.

References

Axelrod, Robert. 1985. *The Evolution of Cooperation*. New York: Basic Books.

Blechman, Frank. 2005. "From Conflict Generation through Consensus-Building Using Many of the Same Skills: A Profile of Frank Blechman." In *Mediation in Practice*, ed. J. Forester, 1–17. Ithaca, NY: Cornell University, Department of City and Regional Planning. (Edited from original interview, January 21, 1993.)

Briggs, Xavier de Sousa. 2008. *Democracy as Problem Solving*. Cambridge: MIT Press.

Coles, Robert. 1989. *The Call of Stories*. Boston: MA Houghton Mifflin

Forester, John. 1999a. *The Deliberative Practitioner*. Cambridge, MA: MIT Press.

Forester, John. 1999b. "Dealing with Deep Value Differences: How Can Consensus Building Make a Difference?" In *The Consensus Building Handbook: A Comprehensive Guide to Reaching Agreement*, ed. Lawrence Susskind, S. McKearnan, and J. Thomas Larmer, 463–494. Thousand Oaks CA: Sage.

Forester, John. 2005. *Mediation in Practice: Profiles of Facilitators, Mediators, Coalition- and Consensus-Builders.* Ithaca, NY: Cornell University, Department of City and Regional Planning. (Typescript.)

Forester, John. 2006a. "Exploring Urban Practice in a Democratizing Society: Opportunities, Techniques, and Challenges." *Development South Africa 23, no 5* (December): 569–86.

Forester, John. 2006b. "Policy Analysis as Critical Listening." In *Oxford Handbook of Public Policy*, ed. M. Moran, M. Rein, and R. Goodin, 124–51. New York: Oxford University Press.

Forester, John. 2008. "Are Collaboration and Participation More Trouble than They're Worth?" Editorial for *Planning Theory and Practice 9*, no. 3 (December): 299–304.

Fuller, Boyd. 2005. "Trading Zones: Cooperating for Water Resource and Ecosystem Management When Stakeholders Have Apparently Irreconcilable Differences." PhD diss., MIT Department of Urban Studies and Planning.

Fung, Archon, and Erik Olin Wright. 2003. *Deepening Democracy: Institutional Innovations in Empowered Participatory Governance.* London: Verso.

Greig, Michelle Robinson. 1997. *Interview by Kristen Grace.* Profiles of Practitioners Project. Cornell University, Department of City and Regional Planning, Ithaca, NY.

Hanson, Norwood Russell. 1961. *Patterns of Discovery.* Cambridge: Cambridge University Press.

Heifetz, Ronald, and Martin Linsky. 2002. *Leadership on the Line.* Boston: Harvard Business School Press.

Kolb, Deborah, and Judith Williams. 2003. *Everyday Negotiation: Navigating the Hidden Agendas of Bargaining.* San Francisco: CA: Jossey-Bass.

Menkel-Meadow, Carrie. 2001. "Aha? Is Creativity Possible in Legal Problem Solving and Teachable in Legal Education?" *Harvard Negotiation Law Review 6*: 97–144.

Murdoch, Iris. 1970. *The Sovereignty of Good.* London: Ark.

Nussbaum, Martha. 1990. *Love's Knowledge.* New York: Oxford.

Reich, Robert. 1988. "Policymaking in a Democracy." In *The Power of Public Ideas*, ed. R. Reich. Cambridge, MA: Ballinger.

Sandercock, Leonie. 2003. "Dreaming the Sustainable City: Organizing Hope, Negotiating Fear, Mediating Memory." In *Stories and Sustainability*, ed. Barbara Eckstein and Jim Throgmorton, 142–64. Cambridge, MA: MIT Press.

Schön, Donald. 1983. *The Reflective Practitioner: How Professionals Think in Action.* New York: Basic Books.

Susskind, Lawrence, and J. Cruikshank. 1987. *Breaking the Impasse.* New York: Basic Books.

Susskind, Lawrence, and J. Cruikshank. 2006. *Breaking Roberts Rules.* New York: Oxford University Press.

Susskind, Lawrence, S. McKearnan, and J. Thomas-Larmer, eds. 1999. *The Consensus Building Handbook: A Comprehensive Guide to Reaching Agreement.* Thousand Oaks, CA: Sage.

Thom, Stephen. 1997. Interview by Kristen Grace. *Profiles of Practitioners Project.* Ithaca, NY: Cornell University, Department of City and Regional Planning.

Winship, Christopher. 2006. "Policy Analysis as Puzzle Solving." In *Oxford Handbook of Public Policy*, eds Michael Moran, Robert E. Goodin, and Martin Rein, 109–23. New York: Oxford University Press.

Yanow, Dvora and Peregrine Schwartz-Shea, ed. 2006. *Interpretation and Method: Empirical Research Methods and the Interpretive Turn.* Armonk, NY: M.E. Sharpe.

Part IV

Wicked Problems in Planning
Identity, Difference, Ethics, and Conflict

Introduction

The planning theorist Melvin Webber deployed the term "wicked problems" to characterize planning issues that yield no satisfactory solution for all parties involved. He argued that aspirations of planners to use scientific methods to determine correct strategies founder because there are no right answers to social questions. Social divisions caused by class, caste, religion, gender, etc. mean that

Readings in Planning Theory, Fourth Edition. Edited by Susan S. Fainstein and James DeFilippis.
Editorial material and organization © 2016 John Wiley & Sons, Ltd.
Published 2016 by John Wiley & Sons, Ltd.

any choice will leave some groups unhappy. The selections in this section all conceive of planning as political and not yielding easy solutions. They differ regarding the role that professionals can play in overcoming difference and the extent to which acceptable outcomes can be achieved that do not disadvantage the already disadvantaged. In Part III of this volume the contribution by John Forester (Chapter 18) expressed a faith in the reconciliation of difference. The readings here root conflict in racial/ethnic difference and economic structure not readily accommodated by negotiation. Some also, however, present paths to accommodation of difference, not just through mediation but also through advocacy.

The section begins with a chapter excerpted from Iris Marion Young's 2000 book *Inclusion and Democracy*. This selection builds upon her seminal 1990 book, *Justice and the Politics of Difference*, in which she argues that society should be viewed as made up of groups not atomized individuals. Her vision of urban life is one in which social relations affirm group differences rather than fusing them into a single identity. City life becomes "the being together of strangers," and supports "unassimilated otherness" (echoing Jane Jacobs's ideal of city streets and their ability to handle strangers).

In the text reproduced here, Young, who was the rare political philosopher who concerned herself with cities, extends the idea of "the politics of difference" and outlines a set of conceptual distinctions regarding structural vs. cultural group differences. She argues that critics have wrongly reduced the politics of difference to "identity politics" (i.e., the expression of cultural meaning). Although she recognizes the appeal of assertions of identity, she sees identity politics as potentially counterproductive. She does not, however, regard cultural conflict as the defining issue of group relations. Rather, her primary focus is on the structural foundations of the politics of difference. The assertion of group identity is not usually a stand-alone cultural goal, but instead is usually linked to group demands for substantive, structural outcomes: access to better education, housing, work opportunities, social services, etc. Finally, Young challenges the common perception that society has only two choices in the face of social differences: either devolution to a competition among private interests or the complete sublimation of difference in the name of social cohesion. This is, for Young, a false dichotomy. The expression of group identity need not invariably cause social fragmentation and a loss of the collective public good. She instead argues for a third path, where civility does not require the suppression of difference and where a shared public space can be shaped beyond parochial interests. Young argues against a forced consensus of political debate and provides an alternative perspective that envisions civic spaces as fostering diversity while facilitating a shared civic political culture. (Hers is a contemporary variation of Paul Davidoff's influential 1960s criticism of a false unitary "public interest"; Chapter 21, this volume.)

Leonie Sandercock (Chapter 20) echoes Young's normative goals in justifying the need for interaction among diverse cultures. She then explores practical ways in which this can be achieved through "quite banal" activities. Arguing that shared place is insufficient for the formation of community bonds, she calls for a politics of difference that embraces new, hybrid identities and recognizes the inevitability of conflict. In doing so, she is espousing an approach that rejects assimilationism but also does not define people by their ancestry. She prefers the term "interculturalism" to multiculturalism, as it avoids embracing cultural essentialism while at the same time recognizing that everyone requires a sense of rootedness. In other words, identities persist but are not fixed and evolve as a consequence of interaction. She considers a micro-place, the Collingwood Neighbourhood House, as producing the sort of banal interaction she desires to take hold more broadly. The lesson of her essay for planners lies in its overcoming the easy assumption, often held by designers, that simply the physical proximity of others who are different suffices to bring about mutual understanding. She admits that the success of the Neighbourhood House depends on its being lodged in a larger, national (Canadian) political culture committed to ideals of bridging the differences among cultures. At the micro-scale, however, the creation of cosmopolitan spaces depends on local leadership that is itself diverse and which develops programs that systematically reach out to marginalized groups. For planners this means going beyond spatial strategies to program planning.

Both Forester and Sandercock focus on differences in values and do not address the structural issues raised by Young. Paul Davidoff, in a classic and still definitive 1965 article, "Advocacy and Pluralism in Planning," argues that unitary planning perpetuates a monopoly over planning power (Chapter 21, this volume). In his scenario planners are not mediators but instead must advocate for the interests of the disfranchised, since it is their interests that are overlooked under normal circumstances. Traditional planning creates at least two barriers to effective pluralism. First, planning commissions in the United States and bureaucratic planning agencies elsewhere are undemocratic and poorly suited to represent the competing interests of a pluralist society. Second, traditional city planning too narrowly addresses issues of physical planning, separating the physical from the social and thereby neglecting social conflict and inequality in the city. In this light, Davidoff's call for a move from land use to social-economic planning reflects a more general effort to shift the identity of the planner from the objective technocrat of the conservative 1950s to the engaged, social advocate of the contentious 1960s. It also incorporates the move away from physical design to social analysis that increasingly characterizes the planning discipline if not the actual practice of planners.

June Manning Thomas (Chapter 22) worries that planners are typically members of the dominant social grouping – i.e., the white middle class. In "The Minority-Race Planner in the Quest for a Just City," she examines the promises and shortcomings of recruiting more underrepresented minorities to the ranks of planners in the larger pursuit of social justice. Through her interviews with minority planners, Thomas explores the complex roles and conflicted challenges faced by these professionals. Their voices add a rich detail and nuance to her analysis.

Thomas concludes that increasing minority participation in the profession is not a guarantee of greater urban equality: the evidence that the composition of planning staffs makes a substantive difference is often inconclusive, particularly so with influencing outcomes. That said, Thomas finds evidence that minority-race planners do make a difference with process. These planners often play a bridge role between city government and the minority community, increasing lines of communication and advocating for marginalized communities. But this exceptional role has a potentially debilitating downside: the bridge position can place the minority planner in an awkward, difficult role, overworked and marginalized by (often white) co-workers. Thus, stronger minority presence on planning staffs alone may not be sufficient to overcome the entrenched, institutionalized inequality in many communities. In these situations, the culture of "deep differences" also requires more structural, systemic reforms to achieve the just city.

Martin Wachs (Chapter 23, this volume) approaches the effect of planners' value systems from a different angle. His inquiry into the ethics of planning differentiates between the ethical behavior of planners in the narrow, procedural sense of honesty and in the substantive issue of the moral content of plans. In other words planners without being corrupt can nevertheless produce plans that lack legitimacy or are unjust. He asserts that the efficiency criterion constitutes the usual measure of planning efficacy but that morality requires the inclusion of other values. He returns to the topic raised by many of the readings – the relationship between process and outcome – commenting that recognition of improper professional behavior is easier than identifying the moral content of plans. Rather than examining the interaction of stakeholders in the making of decisions, as is done by Healey (Chapter 7) and Forester (Chapter 18), he looks at the kind of information that participants receive. Wachs particularly points to the ethical issues embedded within forecasting. In numerous studies that he cites, forecasts have underestimated project costs and overestimated benefits. Various explanations exist for this "optimism bias," but the frequent ability of forecasters to profit from further work if the project goes ahead provides one significant incentive. Political pressure to justify desired projects also contributes to overly sanguine predictions. In discussing planners' codes of ethics and their implementation, Wachs finds the occasional indictment of planners for dishonesty but does not discover instances where they have been sanctioned for biased predictions.

The lineaments of conflict assume different forms in post-colonial settings, in those parts of the world now encompassed by the label "the global south." Although many of the areas demarcated by this term are actually located north of the equator, it has replaced "third world" as the shorthand way to refer to relatively poor countries. In her contribution (Chapter 24) Faranak Mifaftab shows skepticism regarding the outcomes of citizen participation, arguing that neoliberalism has co-opted it to serve the interests of economic elites. In her view neoliberalism has replaced the direct rule of colonialism with the more indirect depredations of capitalism. She builds on the concept of hegemony, originally developed by

Antonio Gramsci, to describe how citizens in the global south have accepted new forms of domination. According to Gramsci, people adhere to ideology contrary to their own interests because of the ability of powerful social groups to control their consciousness. She argues that insurgent planning, a descendant of Davidoff's advocacy planning, provides an instrument for countering domination. While advocacy planning depends on planning professionals to frame alternatives, under insurgent planning communities take planning into their own hands. Miraftab asserts that only through the resulting transformation of subaltern consciousness can city residents resist the imposition of the model of the modern Western city and promote the strengths of informal urban development.

Miraftab's vision is essentially conflictual. It establishes a normative model in which oppressed people assert themselves and work outside official processes for inclusion. She uses examples from South African cities to illustrate how insurgency operates to gain material benefits for vulnerable people. In her view insurgent groups make use of official institutions like planning commissions and courts, but they also express their demands through street protests and informal construction. Hers is a depiction of urban societies with deep-seated structural divisions, rooted in a history of colonialism and economic exploitation. She considers that the achievement of just outcomes requires radical dissent rather than officially approved participation.

References

Young, Iris Marion. 1990. *Justice and the Politics of Difference*. Princeton, NJ: Princeton University Press.
Young, Iris Marion. 2000. *Inclusion and Democracy*. Oxford: Oxford University Press.

19

Inclusion and Democracy

Iris Marion Young

[…]

Social Difference Is Not Identity

Those who reduce group difference to identity implicitly use a logic of substance to conceptualize groups. Under this logic a group is defined by a set of essential attributes that constitute its identity as a group. Individuals are said to belong to the group in so far as they have the requisite attributes. On this sort of account, the project of organizing in relation to group-based affiliation and experience requires identifying one or more personal or social attributes which make the group what it is, shared by members of the group, and which clearly exclude others. Identifying the group of Latinos, for example, means finding the essential attributes of being Latino, such as biological connection, language, national origin, or celebration of specific holidays. Saying that gay people are a group, to take another example, means identifying the essential attributes that members of the group share that make the group a group. In their efforts to discover the specificities of their group-based social positions and forge relations of solidarity among those similarly located, group-based social movements themselves have sometimes exhibited

Original publication details: Young, Iris Marion. 2000. *Inclusion and Democracy*. Oxford: Oxford University Press, pp. 87–99, 102–11; based on chapter 3 in *Deliberative Democracy: Essays on Reason and Politics*, edited by James Bohman and William Rehg. Cambridge, MA: The MIT Press. © 1997 Massachusetts Institute of Technology. Used with permission from Oxford University Press and The MIT Press.

these essentializing tendencies. We did not need to wait for neo-republican or socialist critics of "identity politics" to point out the problems with such identity claims. Group-differentiated political movements themselves, along with their theoreticians, have developed sophisticated critiques of such tendencies.[1]

Whether imposed by outsiders or constructed by insiders to the group, attempts to define the essential attributes of persons belonging to social groups fall prey to the problem that there always seem to be persons without the required attributes whom experience tends to include in the group or who identify with the group. The essentialist approach to defining social groups freezes the experienced fluidity of social relations by setting up rigid inside–outside distinctions among groups. If a politics of difference requires such internal unity coupled with clear borders to the social group, then its critics are right to claim that such politics divides and fragments people, encouraging conflict and parochialism.

A politics that seeks to organize people on the basis of a group identity all members share, moreover, must confront the fact that many people deny that group positioning is significant for their identity. Some women, for example, deny reflective awareness of womanly identity as constitutive of their identity, and they deny any particular identification with other women. Many French people deny the existence of a French identity and claim that being French is nothing particularly important to their personal identities; indeed, many of these would be likely to say that the search for French identity that constitutes the personal identities of individual French men and women is a dangerous form of nationalism. Even when people affirm group affinity as important to their identities, they often chafe at the tendency to enforce norms of behaviour or identity that essentialist definitions of the groups entail.

Thirdly, the tendency to conceive group difference as the basis of a common identity which can assert itself in politics implies for many that group members all have the same interests and agree on the values, strategies, and policies that will promote those interests. In fact, however, there is usually wide disagreement among people in a given social group on political ideology. Though members of a group oppressed by gender or racial stereotypes may share interests in the elimination of discrimination and dehumanizing imagery, such a concern is too abstract to constitute a strategic goal. At a more concrete level members of such groups usually express divergent and even contradictory interests.[2]

The most important criticism of the idea of an essential group identity that members share, however, concerns its apparent denial of differentiation within and across groups. Everyone relates to a plurality of social groups; every social group has other social groups cutting across it. The group "men" is differentiated by class, race, religion, age, and so on; the group "Muslim" differentiated by gender, nationality, and so on. If group identity constitutes individual identity and if individuals can identify with one another by means of group identity, then how do we deal theoretically and practically with the fact of multiple group positioning? Is my individual identity somehow an aggregate of my gender identity, race identity, class identity, like a string of beads, to use Elizabeth Spelman's metaphor. In addition, this ontological problem has a political dimension: as Spelman, Lugones, and others argue, the attempt to define a common group identity tends to normalize the experience and perspective of some of the group members while marginalizing or silencing that of others.[3]

Those who reduce a politics of difference to "identity politics", and then criticize that politics, implicitly use a logic of substance, or a logic of identity, to conceptualize groups. In this logic an entity is what it is by virtue of the attributes that inhere in it, some of which are essential attributes. We saw above that attempts to conceptualize any social group – whether a cultural group like Jews, or structural groups like workers or women – become confused when they treat groups as substantially distinct entities whose members all share some specific attributes or interests that do not overlap with any outsiders. Such a rigid conceptualization of group differentiation both denies the similarities that many group members have with those not considered in the group, and denies the many shadings and differentiations within the group.

By conceiving social group differentiation in relational rather than substantial terms, we can retain a description of social group differentiation, but without fixing or reifying groups. Any group consists in a collective of individuals who stand in determinate relations with one another because of the actions and interactions of both those associated with the group and those outside or at the margins of the group.[4] There is no collective entity, the group, apart from the individuals who compose it. A group is much more than an aggregate, however. An aggregate is a more or less arbitrary collection of individuals according to one or more attributes; aggregation, when it occurs, is from the point of view of outsiders, and does not express a subjective social experience. Insurance companies may aggregate smokers for the purposes of actuarial tables, and the Cancer Society may aggregate persons known to have contributed to health insurance advocacy groups. When constituted as aggregates, individuals stand in no determinate relations to one another. The members of groups, however, stand in determinate relations both to one another and to non-members. The group, therefore, consists in both the individuals and their relationships.

Associations are one kind of group. An association is a group that individuals purposefully constitute to accomplish specific objectives. These may be as minor and transient as forming a neighbourhood welcoming committee or as grand and long-lasting as a constitutional state. Certainly associations are constituted relationally. Their members or affiliates stand in certain relations with one another around particular objectives, and those relations are often defined by explicit rules and roles, although many of the relationships in associations will also be informal and tacit. The argument of this chapter requires conceptualizing *social* groups, however, as distinct from associations.[5]

Considered relationally, a social group is a collective of persons differentiated from others by cultural forms, practices, special needs or capacities, structures of power or privilege. Unlike associations, social groups are not explicitly constituted. They emerge from the way people interact. The attributes by which some individuals are classed together in the "same" group appear as similar enough to do so only by the emergent comparison with others who appear more different in that respect. Relational encounter produces perception of both similarity and difference. Before the British began to conquer the islands now called New Zealand, for example, there was no group anyone thought of as Maori. The people who lived on those islands saw themselves as belonging to dozens or hundreds of groups with different lineage and relation to natural resources. Encounter with the English, however, gradually changed their perceptions of their differences; the English saw them as similar to each other in comparison to the English, and they found the English more different from them than they felt from one another.

In a relational conceptualization, what makes a group a group is less some set of attributes its members share than the relations in which they stand to others. On this view, social difference may be stronger or weaker, it may be more or less salient, depending on the point of view of comparison. A relational conception of group difference does not need to force all persons associated with the group under the same attributes. Group members may differ in many ways, including how strongly they bear affinity with others of the group. A relational approach, moreover, does not designate clear conceptual and practical borders that distinguish all members of one group decisively from members of others. Conceiving group differentiation as a function of relation, comparison, and interaction, then, allows for overlap, interspersal, and interdependence among groups and their members.[6]

Groups differentiated by historic connection to territories and by culture have received the most attention both in recent political theory and practical politics, for example in nationalist politics, on the one hand, and in efforts to institute multicultural policies, on the other. Cultural groups are differentiated by perceived similarity and dissimilarity in language, everyday practices, conventions of spirituality, sociability, production, and the aesthetics and objects associated with food, music, buildings, the organization of residential and public space, visual images, and so on. For those within it or who practice it, culture is an environment and means of expression and communication largely unnoticed in itself. As such, culture provides people with important background for their personal expression and contexts for their actions and options. Culture enables interaction and communication among those who share it. For those unfamiliar with its meanings and practices, culture is strange and opaque. Cultural difference emerges from internal and external relations. People discover themselves with cultural affinities that solidify them into groups by virtue of their encounter with those who are culturally different in some or many respects. In discovering themselves as distinct, cultural groups usually solidify a mutual affinity and self-consciousness of themselves as groups.

Political conflict between cultural groups is common, of course. Outsiders condemn or denigrate a group's practices or meanings, and/or assert the superiority of their own, sometimes attempting to suppress the denigrated group's practices and meanings, and impose its own on them. It is important to remember, however, that much of the ground for conflict between culturally differentiated groups is not cultural, but a competition over territory, resources, or jobs. The last chapter of this book [original text] focuses on some issues of cultural difference by examining contemporary arguments about liberal nationalism and self-determination. Later in this chapter I will discuss the politics of multiculturalism as a kind of "identity politics".

More important for the central argument of this chapter, however, is the concept of *structural*, as distinct from cultural, group. While they are often built upon and intersect with cultural differences, the social relations constituting gender, race, class, sexuality, and ability are best understood as structural.[7] The social movements motivated by such group-based experiences are largely attempts to politicize and protest structural inequalities that they perceive unfairly privilege some social segments and oppress others. Analysing structural difference and structural inequality, then, helps to show why these movements are not properly interpreted as "identity politics". I turn, then, to an account of structural differentiation.

Structural Difference and Inequality

Appeal to a structural level of social life, as distinct from a level of individual experience and action, is common among social critics.[8] Appeal to structure invokes the institutionalized background which conditions much individual action and expression, but over which individuals by themselves have little control. Yet the concept of structure is notoriously difficult to pin down. I will define social structure, and more specifically structural inequality, by rebuilding elements from different accounts.

Marilyn Frye likens oppression to a birdcage. The cage makes the bird entirely unfree to fly. If one studies the causes of this imprisonment by looking at one wire at a time, however, it appears puzzling. How does a wire only a couple of centimetres wide prevent a bird's flight? One wire at a time, we can neither describe nor explain the inhibition of the bird's flight. Only a large number of wires arranged in a specific way and connected to one another to enclose the bird and reinforce one another's rigidity can explain why the bird is unable to fly freely.[9]

At a first level of intuition, this is what I mean by social structures that inhibit the capacities of some people. An account of someone's life circumstances contains many strands of difficulty or difference from others that, taken one by one, can appear to be the result of decision, preferences, or accidents. When considered together, however, and when compared with the life story of others, they reveal a net of restricting and reinforcing relationships. Let me illustrate.

Susan Okin gives an account of women's oppression as grounded in a gender division of labour in the family. She argues that gender roles and expectations structure men's and women's lives in thoroughgoing ways that result in disadvantage and vulnerability for many women and their children. Institutionally, the entire society continues to be organized around the expectation that children and other dependent people ought to be cared for primarily by family members without formal compensation. Good jobs, on the other hand, assume that workers are available at least forty hours per week year round. Women are usually the primary caretakers of children and other dependent persons, due to a combination of factors: their socialization disposes them to choose to do it, and/or their job options pay worse than those available to their male partners, or her male partner's work allows him little time for care work. As a consequence the attachment of many women to the world of employment outside the home is more episodic, less prestigious, and less well paid than men's. This fact in turn often makes women dependent on male earnings for primary support of themselves and their children. Women's economic dependence gives many men unequal power in the family. If the couple separates, moreover, prior dependence on male earnings coupled with the assumptions of the judicial system makes women and their children vulnerable to poverty. Schools', media, and employers' assumptions all mirror the expectation that domestic work is done primarily by women, which assumptions in turn help reproduce those unequal structures.[10]

This is an account of gender difference as structural difference. The account shows gender difference as structured by a set of relationships and interactions that act together to produce specific possibilities and preclude others, and which operate in a reinforcing circle. One can quarrel with the content or completeness of the account. To it I would add, for example, the structures that organize the social dominance of norms of heterosexual desire, and the consequences of this heterosexual matrix for people of both sexes and multiple desires. The example can show at an intuitive level the meaning of structural social group difference. Social groups defined by race or class are also positioned in structures; shortly I will elaborate these examples. Now I will systematize the notion of structure by building up definitions from several social theorists.

Peter Blau offers the following definition. "A social structure can be defined as a multidimensional space of differentiated social positions among which a population is distributed. The social associations of people provide both the criterion for distinguishing social positions and the connections among them that make them elements of a single social structure."[11] Blau exploits the spatial metaphor implied by the concept of structure. Individual people occupy varying *positions* in the social space, and their positions stand in determinate relation to other positions. The structure consists in the connections among the positions and their relationships, and the way the attributes of positions internally constitute one another through those relationships.

Basic social structures consist in determinate social positions that people occupy which condition their opportunities and life chances. These life chances are constituted by the ways the positions are related to one another to create systematic constraints or opportunities that reinforce one another, like wires in a cage. Structural social groups are constituted through the social organization of labour and production, the organization of desire and sexuality, the institutionalized rules of authority and subordination, and the constitution of prestige. Structural social groups are relationally constituted in the sense that one position in structural relations does not exist apart from a differentiated relation to other positions. Priests, for example, have a particular social function and status in a particular society by virtue of their structured and interdependent relations with others who believe they need specialists in spiritual service and are willing to support that specialization materially. The prestige associated with a caste, to take another example, is bought only through reproduced relations of denigration with lower castes. The castes exist by virtue of their interactive relations with one another, enacted and re-enacted through rituals of deference and superiority enforced through distributions, material dependencies, and threats of force.

More generally, a person's social location in structures differentiated by class, gender, age, ability, race, or caste often implies predictable status in law, educational possibility, occupation, access to resources, political power, and prestige. Not only do each of these factors enable or constrain self-determination and self-development, they also tend to reinforce the others. One reason to call these structural is that they are relatively permanent. Though the specific content and detail of the positions and relationships are frequently reinterpreted, evolving, and even contested, the basic social locations and their relations to one another tend to be reproduced.

It is certainly misleading, however, to reify the metaphor of structure, that is, to think of social structures as entities independent of social actors, lying passively around them, easing or inhibiting their movement. On the contrary, social structures exist only in the action and interaction of persons; they exist not as states, but as processes. Thus Anthony Giddens defines social structures in terms of "rules and resources, recursively implicated in the reproduction of social systems".[12] In the idea of the duality of structure, Giddens theorizes how people act on the basis of their knowledge of pre-existing structures and in so acting reproduce those structures. We do so because we act according to rules and expectations and because our relationally constituted positions make or do not make certain resources available to us.

Economic class is the paradigm of structural relations in this sense. Understood as a form of structural differentiation, class analysis begins with an account of positions in the functioning of systems of ownership, finance, investment, production, and service provision. Even when they have shares of stock or participate in pension funds, those who are not in a position to live independently and control the movement of capital must depend on employment by others in order to gain a livelihood. These positions of capitalist and worker are themselves highly differentiated by income and occupation, but their basic structural relation is an interdependency; most people depend on employment by private enterprises for their livelihoods, and the owners and managers depend on the competence and co-operation of their employees for revenues. Important recent scholarship has argued that a bipolar understanding of economic class in contemporary societies is too simple, and we must also analyse the structural differences of professional and non-professional employees, as well as self-employed, and those more or less permanently excluded from employment.[13]

People are born into a particular class position, and this accident of birth has enormous consequences for the opportunities and privileges they have for the rest of their lives. Without a doubt, some born to wealth-owner families die paupers, and others born poor die rich. Nevertheless, a massive empirical literature shows that the most consistent predictor of adult income level, educational attainment, occupation, and ownership of assets is the class situation of one's parents. While class position is defined first in terms of relations of production, class privilege also produces and is supported by an array of assets such as residence, social networks, access to high-quality education and cultural supplements, and so on. All of these operate to reinforce the structural differentiations of class.

Defining structures in terms of the rules and resources brought to actions and interactions, however, makes the reproduction of structures sound too much like the product of individual and intentional action. The concept of social structure must also include conditions under which actors act, which are often a *collective* outcome of action impressed onto the physical environment. Jean-Paul Sartre calls this aspect of social structural the *practico-inert*.[14] Most of the conditions under which people act are socio-historical: they are the products of previous actions, usually products of many co-ordinated and unco-ordinated but mutually influenced actions over them. Those collective actions have produced determinate effects on the physical and cultural environment which condition future action in specific ways. As I understand the term, social structures include this practico-inert physical organization of buildings, but also modes of transport and communication, trees, rivers, and rocks, and their relation to human action.

Processes that produce and reproduce residential racial segregation illustrate how structural relations become inscribed in the physicality of the environment, often without anyone intending this outcome, thereby conditioning future action and interaction. A plurality of expectations and actions and their effects operate to limit the options of many inner-city dwellers in the United States. Racially discrim-inatory behaviour and policies limit the housing options of people of colour, con-fining many of them to neighbourhoods from which many of those whites who are able to leave do. Property-owners fail to keep up their buildings, and new investment is hard to attract because the value of property appears to decline. Because of more concentrated poverty and lay-off policies that disadvantage

Blacks or Latinos, the effects of an economic downturn in minority neighbourhoods are often felt more severely, and more businesses fail or leave. Politicians often are more responsive to the neighbourhoods where more affluent and white people live; thus schools, fire protection, policing, snow removal, garbage pick-up, are poor in the ghetto neighbourhoods. The spatial concentration of poorly maintained buildings and infrastructure that results reinforces the isolation and disadvantage of those there because people are reluctant to invest in them. Economic restructuring independent of these racialized processes contributes to the closing of major employers near the segregated neighbourhoods and the opening of employers in faraway suburbs. As a result of the confluence of all these actions and processes, many Black and Latino children are poorly educated, live around a higher concentration of demoralized people in dilapidated and dangerous circumstances, and have few prospects for employment.[15]

Reference to the physical aspects of social structures helps to lead us to a final aspect of the concept. The actions and interactions which take place among persons differently situated in social structures using rules and resources do not only take place on the basis of past actions whose collective effects mark the physical conditions of action. They also often have future effects beyond the immediate purposes and intentions of the actors. Structured social action and interaction often have collective results that no one intends, and which may even be counter to the best intentions of the actors.[16] Even though no one intends them, they become given circumstances that help structure future actions. Presumably no one intends the vulnerability of many children to poverty that Okin argues the normal gender division of labour produces.

In summary, a structural social group is a collection of persons who are similarly positioned in interactive and institutional relations that condition their opportunities and life prospects. This conditioning occurs because of the way that actions and interactions conditioning that position in one situation reinforce the rules and resources available for other actions and interactions involving people in the structural positions. The unintended consequences of the confluence of many actions often produce and reinforce such opportunities and constraints, and these often make their mark on the physical conditions of future actions, as well as on the habits and expectations of actors. This mutually reinforcing process means that the positional relations and the way they condition individual lives are difficult to change.

Structural groups sometimes build on or overlap with cultural groups, as in most structures of racialized differentiation or ethnic-based privilege. Thus cultural groups and structural groups cannot be considered mutually exclusive or opposing concepts. Later I will elaborate on the interaction of cultural groups with structures, in the context of evaluating what should and should not be called identity politics. Not all ethnic or cultural group difference, however, generates structural group difference. Some structural difference, moreover, is built not on differences of cultural practice and perception, but instead on bodily differences like sex or physical ability. Some structures position bodies with particular attributes in relations that have consequences for how people are treated, the assumptions made about them, and their opportunities to realize their plans. In so far as it makes sense to say that people with disabilities are a social group, for example, despite their vast bodily differences, this is in virtue of social structures that normalize certain functions in the tools, built environment, and expectations of many people.[17]

People differently positioned in social structures have differing experiences and understandings of social relationships and the operations of the society because of their structural situation. Often such differences derive from the structural inequalities that privilege some people in certain respects and relatively disadvantage others. Structural *inequality* consists in the relative constraints some people encounter in their freedom and material well-being as the cumulative effect of the possibilities of their social positions, as compared with others who in their social positions have more options or easier access to benefits. These constraints or possibilities by no means determine outcomes for individuals in their ability to enact their plans or gain access to benefits. Some of those in more constrained situations are particularly lucky or unusually hardworking and clever, while some of those with an open road have bad luck or squander their opportunities by being lazy or stupid. Those who successfully overcome obstacles, however, cannot be judged as equal to those who have faced fewer structural obstacles, even if at a given time they have roughly equivalent incomes, authority, or prestige.

[...]

What Is and Is Not Identity Politics

Some critics of a politics of difference wrongly reduce them to "identity politics". They reduce political movements that arise from specificities of social group difference to assertions of group identity or mere self-regarding interest. Often group-conscious social movements claim that social difference should be taken into account rather than bracketed as a condition of political inclusion for furthering social justice. Yet the label "identity politics" is not entirely misplaced as a characterization of some claims and self-conceptions of these movements. Now I want to sort out those concerns and public activities plausibly called identity politics from those that are not.

Historically excluded or dominated groups all have organized discourses and cultural expressions aimed at reversing the stereotypes and deprecations with which they claim dominant society has described them. Politically conscious social movements of indigenous people, for example, promote a positive understanding of indigenous governance forms, technology, and art, as a response to colonialist definitions of "civilized" institutions and practices. Many African Americans in the

United States historically and today cultivate pride in the ingenuity of African American resistance institutions and cultural expression as a response to the invisibility and distortion of their lives and experience they have seen in dominant discourses. Where dominant understandings of femininity equate it with relative weakness and selfless nurturing, some feminists have reinterpreted typically womanly activities and relationships as expressions of intelligence and strength. Interpretations and reinterpretations of typical experiences and activities of group members in response to deprecating stereotypes can rightly be called "identity politics". They are often expressed in cultural products such as novels, songs, plays, or paintings. Often they are explicit projects that individual persons take up as an affirmation of their own personal identities in relation to group meaning and affinity with others identified with the group. Their function is partly to encourage solidarity among those with a group affinity, and a sense of political agency in making justice claims to the wider society.

Any movements or organizations mobilizing politically in response to deprecating judgements, marginalization, or inequality in the wider society, I suggest, need to engage in "identity politics" in this sense. Working-class and poor people's movements have asserted positive group definition in this sense as much as gender, racialized, or colonized groups. Such solidarity-producing cultural politics does consist in the assertion of specificity and difference towards a wider public, from whom the movement expects respect and recognition of its agency and virtues. The public political claims of such groups, however, rarely consist simply in the assertion of one identity as against others, or a simple claim that a group be recognized in its distinctiveness. Instead, claims for recognition usually function as part of or means to claims against discrimination, unequal opportunity, political marginalization, or unfair burdens.

Another kind of movement activity often brought under the label "identity politics", however, I find more ambiguous. The project of revaluation and reclaiming identity often involves individual and collective exploration of the meaning of a cultural group's histories, practices, and meanings. Many people devote significant energy to documenting these meanings and adding to their creative expression in music, visual images, and written and visual narratives. The exploration of positioned experience and cultural meaning is an important source of the self for most people. For this reason exploring the expressive and documentary possibilities especially of cultural meaning is an intrinsically valuable human enterprise, and one that contributes to the reproduction of social groups. In themselves and apart from conflict and problems of political and economic privilege or civil freedom, however, these are not *political* enterprises. To the extent that social movements have mistaken these activities for politics, or to the extent that they have displaced political struggles in relation to structural inequalities, critics of identity politics may have some grounds for their complaints.

Projects of the exploration of cultural meaning easily become political, however, under at least the following circumstances. (1) Sometimes people find their

liberty to engage in specific cultural practices curtailed, or they face impediments
in forming associations to express and preserve their cultural identity. (2) Even
where there is social and cultural tolerance, sometimes political conflict erupts
over educational practices and curricular context because different groups believe
they are entitled to have their children learn their cultural practices and meanings
in public schools. (3) Even when they have a formal liberty to explore their affinity
group meanings, engage in minority practices, and form associations, sometimes
groups find that they cannot get access to media, institutions, and resources they
need to further their projects of exploring and creating cultural meaning. These
are all familiar and much discussed conflicts often brought under the rubric of
"multicultural" politics. I do not wish to minimize the difficulty and importance of
working through such issues. The point here is that most group-based political
claims cannot be reduced to such conflicts concerning the expression and preservation of cultural meaning.

Charles Taylor's theory of the politics of recognition is a very influential interpretation of a politics of difference. Taylor argues that cultural group affinity, as
well as respect for and preservation of their culture, is deeply important to many
people because they provide sources of their selves. A person lacks equal dignity if
a group with which he or she is associated does not receive public recognition as
having equal status with others. Some political movements thus seek recognition
in that sense, as a claim of justice.[18] While I agree that claims for recognition and
respect for cultural groups judged different are often made and are claims of
justice, I disagree with Taylor and those who have taken up his account that mis-
recognition is usually a political problem independent of other forms of inequality
or oppression. On his account, groups seek recognition for its own sake, to have a
sense of pride in their cultural group and preserve its meanings, and not for the
sake of or in the process of seeking other goods. But I do not believe this describes
most situations in which groups demand recognition. Where there are problems
of lack of recognition of national, cultural, religious, or linguistic groups, these are
usually tied to questions of control over resources, exclusion from benefits of
political influence or economic participation, strategic power, or segregation from
opportunities. A politics of recognition, that is, usually is part of or a means to
claims for political and social inclusion or an end to structural inequalities that
disadvantage them.

Political movements of African Americans today have been interpreted by many
as "identity politics". An examination of some of the central claims made by
African American activists, however, puts such a label into question. Many African
Americans call for stronger measures to prevent race-motivated hate crimes and to
pursue and punish those who commit them. Agitation continues in many cities to
make police more accountable to citizens, in an effort to prevent and punish abuse
and arbitrary treatment which African Americans experience more than others.
African American politicians and activists continue to argue that institutional racism persists in the American educational, labour market, and housing allocation

system, and that more active measures should be taken to enforce anti-discrimination and redistribute resources and positions for the sake of the development of disadvantaged African American individuals and neighbourhoods. Making many of these claims involves asserting that African Americans as a group are positioned differently from other people in American society, and sometimes activists also assert a pride in African American cultural forms and solidarity. The primary claims of justice, however, refer to experiences of structural inequality more than cultural difference.

What of movements of indigenous people? Indigenous politics certainly does entail a claim to recognition of the cultural distinctness of these groups. Indigenous peoples everywhere have suffered colonialist attempts to wipe out their distinct identities as peoples. They have been removed, dispersed, killed, their languages, religious practices, and artistic expression suppressed. They demand of the societies that continue to dominate them recognition and support for their distinct cultures and the freedom to express and rejuvenate those cultures. Colonialist oppression of indigenous people has involved not only cultural imperialism, however, but at the same time and often in the same actions deprivation of the land and resources from which they derived a living, and suppression of their governing institutions. As a result of conquest and subsequent domination and economic marginalization, indigenous people today are often the poorest people in the societies to which they are connected. Primary indigenous demands everywhere, then, are for self-determination over governance institutions and administration of services, and restoration of control over land and resources for the sake of the economic development of the people. Self-determination also involves cultural autonomy.

The "identity" assertions of cultural groups, I suggest, usually appear in the context of structural relations of privilege and disadvantage. Many Muslims in Europe or North America, for example, assert their right to wear traditional dress in public places, and make claims of religious freedom.[19] Many Middle Eastern, North African, and South Asian migrants claim that Germany, the Netherlands, or France ought to accept them with their difference as full members of the society in which they have lived for decades, where their children were born and now live marginal youthful lives. Many of them experience housing, education, and employment discrimination, are targets of xenophobic acts of violence or harassment, and are excluded from or marginalized in political participation. In this sort of context claims for cultural recognition are rarely asserted for their own sake. They are part of demands for political inclusion and equal economic opportunity, where the claimants deny that such equality should entail shedding or privatizing their cultural difference.

Let me review one final example of political claims of justice critics often deride as divisive identity politics: political claims of gay men and lesbians. Especially after internal movement criticisms of efforts to "identify" what it means to "be" gay, more people whose desires and actions transgress heterosexual norms, and who find affinities with gay and lesbian institutions, would deny that they have or express a "gay identity" they share with others. They do claim that they ought to be free to express their desires and to cultivate institutions without hiding, and without fear of harassment, violence, loss of employment, or housing. Many claim, further, that same-sex partners should have access to the same material benefits in tax law, property relations, and access to partner's employment benefits as heterosexual couples can have through marriage. For the most part, these claims of justice are not "identity" claims. Nor are they simple claims to "recognition". They are claims that they should be free to be openly different from the majority without suffering social and economic disadvantage on account of that difference.

To summarize, I have argued in this section that some group-based political discourses and demands can properly be labelled "identity politics". Sometimes groups seek to cultivate mutual identification among those similarly situated, and in doing so they may indeed express conflict and confrontation with others who are differently situated, against whom they make claims that they wrongfully suffer domination or oppression. Such solidarity-forming "identity politics" is as typical of obviously structurally differentiated groups such as economic classes, however, as of marginalized cultural groups. Multicultural politics concerning freedom of expression, the content of curricula, official languages, access to media, and the like, moreover, can properly be called "identity politics". Most group-conscious political claims, however, are not claims to the recognition of identity as such, but rather claims for fairness, equal opportunity, and political inclusion.

Critics of the politics of difference worry about the divisiveness of such claims. There is no question that such claims often provoke disagreement and conflict. When diverse groups make claims of justice, however, we cannot reject them simply on the grounds that others' disagreement with or hostility to them produces conflict. Norms of inclusive communicative democracy require that claims directed at a public with the aim of persuading members of that public that injustices occur must be given a hearing, and require criticism of those who refuse to listen. Appeals to a common good that exhort people to put aside their experienced differences will not promote justice when structural inequality or deep disagreement exist. I shall now argue that such group-based conflict or disagreement is more likely to be avoided or overcome when a public includes differently situated voices that speak across their difference and are accountable to one another.

Communication across Difference in Public Judgement

We can now return to arguments such as Elshtain's that a politics of difference endangers democracy because it encourages self-regarding parochialism and destroys a genuine public life. Elshtain conceptualizes genuine democratic process as one in which other. Either politics is nothing but competition among private interests, in which case there is no public spirit; or politics is a commitment to equal respect for other citizens in a civil public discussion that puts aside private affiliation and interest to seek a common good. I believe that this is a false dichotomy.

Difference, civility, and political co-operation

When confronted so starkly with an opposition between difference and civility, most must opt for civility. But a conception of deliberative politics which insists on putting aside or transcending partial and particularist differences forgets or denies the lesson that the politics of difference claims to teach. If group-based positional differences give to some people greater power, material and cultural resources, and authoritative voice, then social norms and discourses which appear impartial are often biased. Under circumstances of structural social and economic inequality, the relative power of some groups often allows them to dominate the definition of the common good in ways compatible with their experience, perspective, and priorities. A common consequence of social privilege is the ability of a group to convert its perspective on some issues into authoritative knowledge without being challenged by those who have reason to see things differently. Such a dynamic is a major way that political inequality helps reproduce social and economic inequality even in formally democratic processes.

It is especially ironic that some critics on the left, such as Gitlin and Harvey, reject a politics of difference, and argue that class offers a vision of commonality as opposed to the partiality of gender or race. For those aiming to speak from the perspective of the working class have long argued that the economic and social power of the capitalist class allows that class perspective to dominate political and cultural institutions as well, and to pass for a universal perspective. The capitalist class is able to control deliberative modes and policy decisions for the sake of its interests and at the same time to represent those interests as common or universal interests. On this account, the only way to expose that such claims to the common good serve certain particular interests or reflect the experience and perspective of particular social segments primarily is publicly to assert the interests not served by the allegedly common policies, and publicly to articulate the specificity of the experiences and perspectives they exclude. Claims by feminists that the formulation and priorities of issues often assume masculine experience as normative, or by racialized or ethnic minorities that the political agenda presumes the privilege and experience of majorities, are extensions of this sort of analysis. To the degree that a society is in fact differentiated by structural relations of privilege and disadvantage, claims that everyone in the society has some common interests or a common good must be subject to deep scrutiny, and can only be validated by critical discussion that specifically attends to the differentiated social positions.

At least while circumstances of structural privilege and disadvantage persist, a politics that aims to promote justice through public discussion and decision-making must theorize and aim to practise a third way, alternative to either private interest competition or difference-bracketing public discussion of the common good. This third way consists in a process of public discussion and decision-making which includes and affirms the particular social group positions relevant to issues. It does so in order to draw on the situated knowledge of the people located in different group positions as resources for enlarging the understanding of everyone and moving them beyond their own parochial interests.[20]

It is simply not true that, when political actors articulate particularist interests and experiences and claim that public policy ought to attend to social difference, they are necessarily asserting self-regarding interests against those of others. Undoubtedly groups sometimes merely assert their own interests or preferences, but sometimes they make claims of injustice and justice. Sometimes those speaking to a wider public on behalf of labour, or women, or Muslims, or indigenous peoples make critical and normative appeals, and they are prepared to justify their criticisms and demands. When they make such appeals with such an attitude, they are not behaving in a separatist and inward-looking way, even though their focus is on their own particular situation. By criticizing the existing institutions and policies, or criticizing other groups' claims and proposals, they appeal to a wider public for inclusion, recognition, and equity. Such public expression implies that they acknowledge and affirm a political engagement with those they criticize, with whom they struggle.

Critics who emphasize appeals to a common good are surely right to claim that workable democratic politics requires of citizens some sense of being together with one another in order to sustain the commitment that seeking solutions to conflict under circumstances of difference and inequality requires. It is far too strong, however, to claim that this sense of being together requires mutual identification. Nor should such togetherness be conceived as a search for shared interests or common good beyond the goal of solving conflicts and problems in democratically acceptable ways. Trying to solve problems justly may sometimes mean that some people's perceived interests are not served, especially when issues involve structural relations of privilege. Even when the most just solutions to political problems do not entail promoting some interests more than others, fairness usually involves co-ordinating diverse goods and interests rather than achieving a common good.

Political co-operation requires a less substantial unity than shared understandings or a common good, [...]. It requires first that people whose lives and actions affect one another in a web of institutions, interactions, and unintended consequences acknowledge that they are together in such space of mutual effect. Their conflicts and problems are produced by such togetherness. The unity required by political co-operation also entails that the people who are together in this way are committed to trying to work out their conflicts and to solve the problems generated by their collective action through means of peaceful and rule-bound decision-making. Political co-operation requires, finally, that those who are together in this way understand themselves as members of a single polity. That means only that they conduct their problem-solving discussions and decision-making under agreed-upon and publicly acknowledged procedures.

These unity conditions for democratic decision-making are certainly rare enough in the world, difficult both to produce and maintain. Common good theorists no doubt fear that attending to group differences in public discussion endangers commitment to co-operative decision-making. Perhaps sometimes it does. More often, however, I suggest, groups or factions refuse co-operation because, at least from their point of view, their experience, needs, and interests have been excluded or marginalized from the political agenda, or are suppressed in discussions and decision-making. Only explicit and differentiated forms of inclusion can diminish the occurrence of such refusals, especially when members of some groups are more privileged in some or many respects.

Notes

1. For some examples of critiques of essentialism and a politics of identity from within theories and movements that support a politics of difference, see Elizabeth V Spelman, *Inessential Woman* (Boston: Beacon Press, 1988); Anna Yeatman, "Minorities and the Politics of Difference", in *Postmodern Revisions of the Political* (New York: Routledge, 1994); Michael Dyson, "Essentialism and the Complexities of Racial Identity", in David Theo Goldberg (ed.), *Multiculturalism* (Cambridge, MA: Blackwell, 1994); Steven Seidman, "Identity and Politics in a 'Postmodern' Gay Culture", in *Difference Troubles; Queering Social Theory and Sexual Politics* (Cambridge: Cambridge University Press, 1997).
2. Compare Anne Phillips, *The Politics of Presence* (Oxford: Oxford University Press, 1995), ch. 6.
3. Spelman, *Inessential Woman*; Maria Lugones, "Purity, Impurity and Separation", *Signs. A Journal of Women in Cultural and Society*, 19/2 (Winter 1994), 458–79.
4. For an account of groups as constituted relations, see Larry May, *The Morality of Groups* (Chicago, IL: University of Chicago Press, 1988); and *Sharing Responsibility* (Chicago, IL: University of Chicago Press, 1993).
5. In earlier work I have distinguished these three terms, aggregates, associations, and social groups, and I rely on these conceptualizations here. See *Justice and the Politics of Difference* (Princeton, NJ: Princeton University Press, 1990), ch. 2.
6. Martha Minow proposes a relational understanding of group difference; see *Making All the Difference* (Ithaca, NY: Cornell University Press, 1990), pt. II. I have referred to a relational analysis of group difference in *Justice and the Politics of Difference*, ch. 2; in that earlier formulation, however, I have not distinguished group affiliation from personal identity as strongly as I will later in this chapter. For relational understandings of group difference, see also William Connolly, *Identity/Difference* (Ithaca, NY: Cornell University Press, 1993), and Chantal Mouffe, "Democracy, Power and the 'Political'", in Seyla Benhabib (ed.), *Democracy and Difference* (Princeton, NJ: Princeton University Press, 1996).
7. The following effort to articulate the naming of structural social groups and use that concept to argue against an "identity politics" interpretation of the claims of

difference-based social movements is partly motivated by a desire to think through further some of the issues raised in an exchange I have had with Nancy Fraser See Fraser, "From Redistribution to Recognition? Dilemmas of Justice in a 'Post-Socialist' Age", *New Left Review*, 212 (July–Aug, 1995), 68–99; and Iris Marion Young, "Unruly Categories: A Critique of Nancy Fraser's Dual Systems Theory", *New Left Review*, 222 (Mar–Apr, 1997), 147–60. Fraser's initial paper importantly reminded theorists of justice and multi-culturalism of issues of structural oppression and possible transformation. Fraser herself oversimplifies the meaning of a politics of difference as identity politics, however, and I believe inappropriately dichotomizes issues of culture and structure.

8. See e.g., William Julius Wilson, *When Work Disappears* (New York: Knopf, 1997); see also Jean Hampton, *Political Philosophy* (Boulder, CO: Westview Press, 1997), 189–90.

9. Marilyn Frye, 'Oppression', in *The Politics of Reality* (Trumansburg, NY: Crossing Press, 1983).

10. Susan Okin, *Justice, Gender and the Family* (New York: Basic Books, 1989).

11. Peter Blau, *Inequality and Heterogeneity* (New York: Free Press, 1977), 4.

12. Anthony Giddens, *The Constitution of Society* (Berkeley, CA: University of California Press, 1984).

13. For a clear and thorough account of class in a contemporary Marxist mode, see Eric Olin Wright, *Class Counts* (Cambridge: Cambridge University Press, 1997).

14. Jean-Paul Sartre, *Critique of Dialectical Reason*, trans. Alan Sheridan-Smith (London: New Left Books, 1976), bk. 1, ch. 3.

15. See Douglas Massey and Nancy Denton, *American Apartheid* (Cambridge, MA: Harvard University Press, 1993).

16. Sartre calls such effects counter-finalities; see *Critique of Dialectical Reason*, 277–92.

17. Anita Silvers develops a thorough and persuasive account of why issues of justice regarding people with disabilities should focus on the relation of bodies to physical and social environments, rather than on the needs and capacities of individuals called disabled. See Silvers, "Formal Justice", in Anita Silvers, David Wasserman, and Mary B. Mahowald (eds), *Disability, Difference, Discrimination Perspectives on Justice in Bioethics and Public Policy* (Lanham, MD: Rowman & Littlefield, 1998).

18. Taylor, "Multiculturalism and the Politics of Recognition".

19. See Joseph Carens and Melissa Williams, "Muslim Minorities in Liberal Democracies: Justice and the Limits of Toleration", in J. Carens (ed.), *Culture, Citizenship, and Community: A Contextual Exploration of Justice as Evenhandedness* (Oxford: Oxford University Press, 2000).

20. I find the conception of deliberative democracy elaborated by James Bohman a version of this third way Bohman criticizes communitarian or neo-republican interpretations of publicity and deliberation as requiring too much consensus. He constructs a weaker version of publicity and legitimacy that are explicitly open to social difference and inequality which recognizes that ideals of impartiality and common good are problematic in complex democracies with cultural differences and structural inequalities. See *Public Deliberation* (Cambridge, MA: MIT Press, 1996). In some of his most recent work Jürgen Habermas has shifted from a more unifying view to one which emphasizes more the need to attend to social differences. See "Does Europe Need a Constitution? Reponse to Dieter Grimm", and "Struggles for Recognition in the Democratic Constitutional State", both in *The Inclusion of the Other. Studies in Political Theory* (Cambridge, MA: MIT Press, 1998).

20

Towards a Cosmopolitan Urbanism
From Theory to Practice

Leonie Sandercock

Most cities today are demographically multicultural, and more are likely to become so in the foreseeable future. The central question of this chapter is how to come to terms – theoretically, philosophically, and practically – with this empirical urban reality. What can the practice of the Collingwood Neighbourhood House contribute to our theoretical understanding of the possibilities of peaceful co-existence in the mongrel cities of the 21st century? My argument proceeds in four stages. First, I discuss the challenge to our urban sociological imaginations in thinking about how we might live together in all of our differences. Second, I propose the importance of a deeper political and psychological understanding of difference, and its significance in urban politics. Third, I suggest a way of theorizing an inter-cultural political project for 21st century cities, addressing the shortcomings of 20th century multicultural philosophy. And finally, I link all of these with the actual achievement of the Collingwood Neighbourhood House in the integration of immigrants in Vancouver.

20.1   Introduction

Arriving and departing travelers at Vancouver International Airport are greeted by a huge bronze sculpture of a boatload of strange, mythical creatures. This 7 m long, almost 4 m wide and 4 m high masterpiece, *The Spirit of Haida Gwaii*, is by

Original publication details: Sandercock, Leonie. 2009. "When Strangers Become Neighbours: Managing Cities of Difference". *Planning Theory & Practice*, 1(1): 13–30. Reproduced with permission from Springer Science + Business Media.

Readings in Planning Theory, Fourth Edition. Edited by Susan S. Fainstein and James DeFilippis.
Editorial material and organization © 2016 John Wiley & Sons, Ltd.
Published 2016 by John Wiley & Sons, Ltd.

the late Bill Reid, a member of the Haida Gwaii First Nations from the Pacific Northwest. The canoe has thirteen passengers, spirits or myth creatures from Haida mythology.[1] The bear mother, who is part human, and the bear father sit facing each other at the bow with their two cubs between them. The beaver is paddling menacingly amidships, and behind him is the mysterious intercultural dogfish woman. Shy mouse woman is tucked in the stern. A ferociously playful wolf sinks his fangs into the eagle's wing, and the eagle is attacking the bear's paw. A frog (who symbolizes the ability to cross boundaries between worlds) is partially in, partially out of the canoe.

An ancient reluctant conscript paddles stoically. In the centre, holding a speaker's staff in his right hand, stands the chief, whose identity (according to the sculptor) is deliberately uncertain. The legendary raven (master of tricks, transformations, and multiple identities), steers the motley crew. *The Spirit of Haida Gwaii* is a symbol of the "strange multiplicity" of cultural diversity that existed millennia ago and wants to be again (Tully 1995: 18). Amongst other things, this extraordinary work of art speaks of a spirit of mutual recognition and accommodation; a sense of being at home in the multiplicity yet at the same time playfully estranged by it; and the notion of an unending dialogue that is not always harmonious. For the political philosopher James Tully, the wonderfulness of the piece lies in "the ability to see one's own ways as strange and unfamiliar, to stray from and take up a critical attitude toward them and so open cultures to question, reinterpretation, negotiation, transformation, and non-identity (Tully 1995: 206).

The near extermination of the Haida by European imperial expansion is typical of how Aboriginal peoples have fared wherever Europeans settled. The positioning of the sculpture at Vancouver International Airport, and an identical piece at the Canadian Embassy in Washington, D.C., gives a poignant presence on both coasts of North America to indigenous people who are still struggling today for recognition and restitution.

The Spirit of Haida Gwaii stands as a symbol of their survival, resistance, and resurgence, and also perhaps as a more ecumenical symbol for the mutual recognition and affirmation of all cultures that respect other cultures and the earth.

But this sculpture can also be read as a powerful metaphor of contemporary humanity and of the contemporary urban condition, in which people hitherto unused to living side by side are thrust together in what I have called the "mongrel cities" of the 21st century (Sandercock 2003). Most societies today are demographically multicultural, and more are likely to become so in the foreseeable future. The central question of [this chapter], then, is how to come to terms with this historical predicament: how can we manage our coexistence in the shared spaces of the multicultural cities of the 21st century? What kind of theoretical challenge is this? In the four-stage argument that follows, I suggest that there is first the challenge to our urban sociological imagination of how we might live together in all of our differences.

In order to act within mongrel cities, we must have a theoretical understanding of "difference" and how it becomes significant in urban politics, in spatial conflicts, in claims over rights to the city.

Thus, in the second section, I seek to deepen our psychological and political understanding of the concept of difference and, through this, to explain why a politics of difference is related to basic questions of identity and belonging and therefore cannot be wished away. In the third section, I argue that we need to theorize an intercultural political project for 21st century cities, one that acknowledges and addresses the shortcomings of 20th century multiculturalism and establishes political community rather than ethno-cultural identity as the basis for a sense of belonging in multicultural societies.

And finally, I link all of these with the actual achievement of the Collingwood Neighbourhood House in the integration of immigrants in Vancouver.

20.2   How Might We Live Together? Three Imaginings

20.2.1   Richard Sennett: Togetherness in difference

In *Flesh and Stone* (1994: 358) Sennett laments that the apparent diversity of Greenwich Village in New York is actually only the diversity of the gaze, rather than a scene of discourse and interaction. He worries that the multiple cultures that inhabit the city are not fused into common purposes, and wonders whether "difference inevitably provokes mutual withdrawal". He assumes (and fears) that if the latter is true, then "a multicultural city cannot have a common civic culture" (Sennett 1994: 358). For Sennett, Greenwich Village poses a particular question of how a diverse civic culture might become something people feel in their bones. He deplores the ethnic separatism of old multi-ethnic New York and longs for evidence of citizens' understanding that they share a common destiny. This becomes a hauntingly reiterated question: nothing less than a moral challenge, the challenge of living together not simply in tolerant indifference to each other, but in active engagement.

For Sennett then, there is a normative imperative in the multicultural city to engage in meaningful intercultural interaction. Why does Sennett assume that sharing a common destiny in the city necessitates more than a willingness to live with difference in the manner of respectful distance? Why should it demand active engagement? He doesn't address these questions, nor does he ask what it would take, sociologically and institutionally, to make such intercultural dialogue and exchange possible, or more likely to happen. But other authors, more recently, have begun to ask, and give tentative answers to, these very questions (Parekh 2000; Amin 2002).

In terms of political philosophy, one might answer that in multicultural societies, composed of many different cultures each of which has different values and practices, and not all of which are entirely comprehensible or acceptable to each other, conflicts are inevitable. In the absence of a *practice* of intercultural dialogue, conflicts are insoluble except by the imposition of one culture's views on another. A society of cultural enclaves and de facto separatism is one in which different cultures do not know how to talk to each other, are not interested in each other's wellbeing, and assume that they have nothing to learn and nothing to gain from interaction. This becomes a problem for urban governance and for city planning in cities where contact between different cultures is increasingly part of everyday urban life, in spite of the efforts of some groups to avoid "cultural contamination" or ethnic mixture by fleeing to gated communities or so-called ethnic enclaves.

A pragmatic argument then, is that intercultural contact and interaction are necessary conditions for being able to address the inevitable conflicts that will arise in multicultural societies. Another way of looking at the question of why intercultural encounters might be a good thing would start with the acknowledgement that different cultures represent different systems of meaning and versions of the good life.

But each culture realizes only a limited range of human capacities and emotions and grasps only a part of the totality of human existence: it therefore "needs others to understand itself better, expand its intellectual and moral horizon, stretch its imagination and guard it against the obvious temptation to absolutize itself" (Parekh 2000: 336–7). I'd like to think that this latter argument is what Sennett might have had in mind.

20.2.2   James Donald: An ethical indifference

In *Imagining the Modern City* (1999), James Donald gives more detailed thought to the question of how we might live together. He is critical of the two most popular contemporary urban imaginings: the traditionalism of the New Urbanism (with its ideal of community firmly rooted in the past), and the cosmopolitanism of Richard Rogers, advisor to former Prime Minister Tony Blair and author of a policy document advocating an urban renaissance, a revitalized and re-enchanted city (Urban Task Force 1999). What's missing from Rogers' vision, according to Donald, is "any real sense of the city not only as a space of community or pleasurable encounters or self-creation, but also as the site of aggression, violence, and paranoia" (Donald 1999: 135).

Is it possible, he asks, to imagine change that acknowledges difference without falling into phobic utopianism, communitarian nostalgia, or the disavowal of urban paranoia.

Donald sets up a normative ideal of city life that acknowledges not only the necessary desire for the security of home, but also the inevitability of migration, change and conflict, and thus an "ethical need for an openness to unassimilated otherness" (Donald 1999: 145). He argues that it is not possible to domesticate all traces of alterity and difference. "The problem with community is that usually its advocates are referring to some phantom of the past, projected onto some future utopia at the cost of disavowing the unhomely reality of living in the present" (Donald 1999: 145). If we start from the reality of living in the present with strangers, then we might ask, what kind of commonality might exist or be brought into being? Donald's answer is "broad social participation in the never completed process of making meanings and creating values ... an always emerging, negotiated common culture" (Donald 1999: 151). This process requires time and forbearance, not instant fixes. This is community redefined neither as identity nor as place but as a productive process of social interaction, apparently resolving the long-standing problem of the dark side of community, the drawing of boundaries between those who belong and those who don't.

Donald argues that we don't need to share cultural traditions with our neighbors in order to live alongside them, but we do need to be able to talk to them, while also accepting that they are and may remain strangers (as will we).

This is the pragmatic urbanity that can make the violence of living together manageable. Then, urban politics would mean strangers working out how to live together. This is an appropriately political answer to Sennett's question of how multicultural societies might arrive at some workable notion of a common destiny. But when it comes to a thicker description of this "openness to unassimilable difference", the mundane, pragmatic skills of living in the city and sharing urban turf, neither Donald nor Sennett have much to say. Donald suggests

> reading the signs in the street; adapting to different ways of life right on your doorstep; learning tolerance and responsibility – or at least, as Simmel taught us, indifference – towards others and otherness; showing respect, or self-preservation, in not intruding on other people's space; picking up new rules when you migrate to a foreign city (Donald 1999: 167)

Donald seems to be contradicting himself here in retreating to a position of co-presence and indifference, having earlier advocated something more like an agonistic politics of broad social participation in the *never completed process* of making meanings and an *always emerging* (never congealed), *negotiated common culture*. Surely this participation and negotiation in the interests of peaceful co-existence requires something like daily habits of perhaps quite banal intercultural interaction in order to establish a basis for dialogue, which is difficult, if not impossible, without some pre-existing trust. I will turn to Ash Amin for a discussion of how and where this daily interaction and negotiation of ethnic (and other) differences might be encouraged.

20.2.3   Ash Amin: A politics of local liveability

Ash Amin's report, *Ethnicity and the Multicultural City. Living with Diversity* (2002), was commissioned by the British government's Department of Transport, Local Government and the Regions in the wake of the (so-called) "race riots" in three northern British cities in the summer of 2001. This report is a self-described "think piece" that uses the 2001 riots as a springboard "to discuss what it takes to combat racism, live with difference and encourage mixture in a multicultural and multi-ethnic society" (Amin 2002:2). Amin's paper is in part a critique of a document produced by the British Home Office (*Building Cohesive Communities*, Home Office 2001). It goes deeper and draws on different sources than the Home Office document. The political economy approach of the Home Office analysis of the riots never once mentions globalization, or the colonial past (see Chapter 1 of this book). That is Amin's starting point. The dominant ethnic groups present in Bradford, Burnley and Oldham are Pakistani and Bangladeshi, of both recent and longer-term migrations. What this reflects is the twin and interdependent forces of postcolonialism and globalization.

As several scholars have pointed out (Sassen 1996; Rocco 2000), the contemporary phenomena of immigration and ethnicity are constitutive of globalization and are reconfiguring the spaces of and social relations in cities in new ways. Cultures from all over the world are being de- and re-territorialized in global cities, whose neighborhoods accordingly become "globalized localities" (Albrow 1997: 51). The spaces created by the complex and multidimensional processes of globalization have become strategic sites for the formation of transnational identities and communities, as well as for new hybrid identities and complicated experiences and redefinitions of notions of "home". As Sassen has argued:

> What we still narrate in the language of immigration and ethnicity … is actually a series of processes having to do with the globalization of economic activity, of cultural activity, of identity formation. Too often immigration and ethnicity are constituted as otherness. Understanding them as a set of processes whereby global elements are localized, international labor markets are constituted, and cultures from all over the world are de- and re-territorialized, puts them right there at the center along with the internationalization of capital, as a fundamental aspect of globalization. (Sassen 1996: 218)

This is the context for Amin's interpretative essay on the civil disturbances, which he sees as having both material and symbolic dimensions. He draws on ethnographic research to deepen understanding of both dimensions, as well as to assist in his argument for a focus on the everyday urban, "the daily negotiation of ethnic difference". Ethnographic research in the UK on areas of significant racial antagonism has identified two types of neighbourhood. The first are old white working class areas in which successive waves of non-white immigration have been accompanied by continuing socio-economic deprivation and cultural and/or physical isolation "between white residents lamenting the loss of a golden ethnically undisturbed past, and non-whites claiming a right of place". The second are "white flight" suburbs and estates that have become the refuge of an upwardly mobile working class and a fearful middle class disturbed by what they see as the replacement of a "homely white nation" by foreign cultural contamination. Here, white supremacist values are activated to terrorize the few immigrants who try to settle there. The riots of 2001 displayed the processes at work in the first type of neighborhood, but also the white fear and antagonism typical of the second type (Amin 2002: 2).

What is important to understand is that the cultural dynamics in these two types of neighbourhood are very different from those in other ethnically mixed cities and neighbourhoods where greater social and physical mobility, a local history of compromises, and a supportive local institutional infrastructure have come to support co-habitation.

For example, in the Tooting neighbourhood of South London, Martin Albrow's research inquired about the strength of "locality" and "community" among a wide range of local inhabitants, from those born there to recent arrivals, and among all the most prominent ethnic groups. His analysis reveals that locality has much less salience for individuals and for social relations than older research paradigms invested in community allow. His study reveals a very liquid sense of identity and belonging. His interviewees' stories suggest the possibility that:

> Individuals with very different lifestyles and social networks can live in close proximity without untoward interference with each other. There is an old community for some, for others there is a new site for community which draws its culture from India. For some, Tooting is a setting for peer group leisure activity, for others it provides a place to sleep and access to London. It can be a spectacle for some, for others the anticipation of a better, more multicultural community. (Albrow 1997: 51)

In this middle income locality there is nothing like the traditional concept of community based on a shared local culture. Albrow describes a situation of "minimum levels of tolerable co-existence" and civil inattention and avoidance strategies that prevent friction between people living different lifestyles. The locality is criss-crossed by networks of social relations whose scope and extent range from neighbouring houses and a few weeks' acquaintance to religious and kin relations spanning generations and continents.

This study gives us an important insight into the changing social relations within globalized localities. Where is community here? It may be nowhere, says Albrow, and this new situation therefore needs a new vocabulary.

How meaningful is the newly promoted (by the Home Office) notion of community cohesion, when people's affective ties are not necessarily related to the local place where they live? Where is the deconstruction, and reconstruction, of what "community" might mean in the globalized localities of mongrel cities? "Globalization makes co-present enclaves of diverse origins one possible social configuration characterizing a new Europe" (Albrow 1997: 54).

While Albrow's research seems to support the urban imaginings of James Donald, discussed earlier, in terms of the feasibility of an attitude of tolerant indifference and co-presence, the difference between Tooting and the northern mill towns that are the subject of Amin's reflection is significant. In those one-industry towns, when the mills declined, white and non-white workers alike were unemployed. The largest employers soon became the public services, but discrimination kept most of these jobs for whites. Non-whites pooled resources and opened shops, takeaways, minicab businesses. There was intense competition for lowpaid and precarious work. Economic uncertainty and related social deprivation have been a constant for over twenty years and "a pathology of social rejection … reinforces family and communalist bonds" (Amin 2002:4). Ethnic resentment has bred on this socio-economic deprivation and sense of desperation. It is in such areas that social cohesion and cultural interchange have failed.

What conclusions does Amin draw from this? How can fear and intolerance be challenged, how might residents begin to negotiate and come to terms with difference in the city? Amin's answer is interesting. The contact spaces of housing estates and public places fall short of nurturing inter-ethnic understanding, he argues, "because they are not spaces of interdependence and habitual engage-ment" (Amin 2002: 12).

He goes on to suggest that the sites for coming to terms with ethnic (and surely other) differences are the "micro-publics" where dialogue and prosaic negotiations are compulsory, in sites such as the workplace, schools, colleges, youth centers, sports clubs, community centers, neighbourhood houses, and the micro-publics of "banal transgression", (such as colleges of further education) in which people from different cultural backgrounds are thrown together in new settings which disrupt familiar patterns and create the possibility of initiating new attachments. Other sites of banal transgression include community gardens, child-care facilities, community centers, neighbourhood watch schemes, youth projects, and regener-ation of derelict spaces. I have provided just such an example (Sandercock 2003: Chapter 7), the Community Fire Station in the Handsworth neighbourhood of Birmingham, where white Britons are working alongside Asian and Afro-Caribbean Britons in a variety of projects for neighborhood regeneration and improvement. The Collingwood Neighbourhood House in Vancouver is an even better example of a successful site of intercultural interaction, as I will argue in the final section of this chapter. Part of what happens in such everyday contacts is the overcoming of feelings of strangeness in the simple process of sharing everyday tasks and com-paring ways of doing things. But such initiatives will not automatically become sites of social inclusion. They also need organizational and discursive strategies that are designed to build voice, to foster a sense of common benefit, to develop confidence among disempowered groups, and to arbitrate when disputes arise. The essential point is that "changes in attitude and behavior spring from lived experiences" (Amin 2002: 15).

The practical implication of Amin's work, then, is that the project of living with diversity needs to be worked at "in the city's micro-publics of banal multicultures" (Amin 2002: 13). It is clear from Albrow's work, as well as that of Amin, that in today's globalized localities one cannot assume a shared sense of place and that this is not the best "glue" for understanding and co-existence within multicultural neighbourhoods. Ethnographic research on urban youth cultures referred to by Amin confirms the existence of a strong sense of place among white and nonwhite ethnic groups, but it is a sense of place based on turf claims and defended in exclusionary ways. The distinctive feature of mixed neighbourhoods is that they are "communities without community, each marked by multiple and hybrid affiliations of varying geographical reach" (Amin 2002: 16).

There are clear limits then to how far "community cohesion" can become the basis of living with difference. Amin suggests a different vocabulary of local accommodation to difference – "a vocabulary of rights of presence, bridging difference, getting along" (Amin 2002: 17). To adopt the language of Henri Lefebvre, this could be expressed as the right to difference, and the right to the city. The achievement of these rights depends on a politics of active local citizenship, an agonistic politics (as sketched by Donald) of broad social participation in the never completed process of making meanings, and an always emerging, negotiated common culture. But it also depends on an *intercultural political culture*, that is, one with effective antiracism policies, with strong legal, institutional and informal sanctions against racial and cultural hatred, a public culture that no longer treats immigrants as "guests", and a truly inclusive political system at all levels of governance. This is the subject of the third section of this chapter. In the second section I take up the issue of difference and identity in relation to national belonging and question the adequacy of framing the issues of an intercultural society through the language of race and minority ethnicity. A significant dimension of the civil disturbances in Britain in 2001 was this aspect of identity and belonging, and this spills over into the next section.

20.3   Thinking Through Identity/Difference

We have norms of acceptability and those who come into our home – for that is what it is – should accept those norms (David Blunkett, quoted in Alibhai-Brown 2001).

> … seven years ago I finally decided this place was my place, and that was because I had a daughter whose father was of these islands. This did not make me any less black, Asian or Muslim – those identities are in my blood, thick and forever. But it made me kick more vigorously at those stern, steely gates that keep people of color outside the heart of the nation then blame them for fighting each other in the multicultural wastelands into which the establishment has pushed them. A number of us broke through. The going was (and still is) incredibly hard but we are in now and, bit by bit, the very essence of Britishness is being transformed. (Alibhai-Brown 2001)

The above remarks of David Blunkett were made in December of 2001, after Britain's summer of "race riots". It was a time of questioning of the previous half-century of immigration, the race relations problems that had emerged, and the policy response of multiculturalism. At the heart of this questioning was a pertur-bation over what it meant/means to be British (an agonizing which has only heightened since the terrorist bombings in London in the summer of 2005). Notions of identity were being unsettled. The response of Blunkett, the Home Secretary in the Blair government, was a rather crude reassertion of us-and-them thinking. His words epitomize a long-standing but much-contested view that immigrants are guests in the home of the host nation and must behave the way their hosts want them to behave: adopt the norms of "Britishness", or get out. Implicit in this view is that there is only one correct way to be British and that it is the responsibility of newcomers to learn how to fit in with that way. Yasmin Alibhai-Brown, herself an immigrant of three decades standing, contests this pure and static notion of national identity, counterposing it with a notion of a more inclusive, dynamic and evolving identity which can accommodate the new hybrid realities of a changing culture. She urges "a national conversation about our collective identity" (Alibhai-Brown 2000: 10).

At stake here, and across European (or any of the large number of globalizing) cities today, are contested notions of identity and understandings of difference, and conflicting ways of belonging and feeling at home in the world. The Home Secretary expresses the view that there is a historic Britishness that must be pro-tected from impurity (sections of the Austrian, Danish, French, Italian and Dutch populations have expressed similar antagonisms in recent years). In this view, what it means to be British, to be "at home" in Britain, is being threatened by immi-grants who bring a different cultural baggage with them. Interestingly, the (fragile) notion of identity at the heart of this view is one that is both afraid of and yet dependent on difference. How does this apparent psychological paradox work?

When a person's self-identity is insecure or fragile, doubts about that identity (and how it relates to national identity may be part of the insecurity) are posed and resolved by the constitution of an Other against which that identity may define itself, and assert its superiority. In order to feel "at home" in the nation and in the wider world, this fragile sense of identity seeks to subdue or erase from con-sciousness (or worse) that which is strange, those who are "not like us". Attempts to protect the purity and certainty of a hegemonic identity – Britishness, Danishness, and so on – by defining certain differences as independent sites of evil, or disloyalty, or disorder, have a long history.[2] There are diverse political tactics through which doubts about self-identity are posed and resolved, but the general strategy is the establishing of a *system of identity and difference* which is given legal sanctions, which defines who belongs and who does not. Over long periods of time, these systems of identity and difference become congealed as cultural norms and beliefs, entrenching themselves as the hegemonic status quo. Evil infiltrates the public domain, Connolly (1991) argues, when attempts are made to secure the surety of self- and national identity – and the powers and privileges that accompany it – with spatial and social and economic policies that demand conformity with a previously scripted identity, while defining the outsider as an outsider, (a polluter of pure identities), in perpetuity.

There is a fascinating paradox in the relationship between identity and difference. The quest for a pure and unchanging *identity* (an undiluted Britishness, or Brummie-ness, or Danishness…) is at once framed by and yet seeks to eliminate difference; it seeks the conformity, disappearance, or invisibility of the Other. That is the paradox of identity. But what of *difference* and *its* political strategies? Surely difference, too, is constituted by its Other – as woman is in patriarchal societies, or to be gay and lesbian in heterosexual societies, or to be Black in white societies – and so is constituted by the hegemonic identity which it resists and seeks to change. Difference, defined as that which is outside, in opposition to the congealed norms of any society, is constituted by / against hegemonic identity. Identity and difference then are an intertwined and always historically specific system of dialectical relations, fundamental to which is inclusion (belonging) and its opposite, exclusion (not belonging). Here then is a double paradox. Some notion of identity is, arguably, indispensable to life itself (Connolly 1991), and some sense of culturally based identity would seem to be inescapable, in that all human beings are culturally embedded (Parekh 2000: 336).[3] But while the politics of pure identity seeks to eliminate the Other, the politics of difference seeks recognition and inclusion.

A more robust sense of identity must be able to embrace cultural autonomy and, at the same time, work to strengthen intercultural solidarity. If one dimension of such a cultural pluralism is a concern with reconciling old and new identities by accepting the inevitability of "hybridity", or "mongrelization", then another is the commitment to actively contest what is to be valued across diverse cultures. Thus Alibhai-Brown feels "under no obligation to bring my daughter and son up to drink themselves to death in a pub for a laugh", nor does she want to see young Asian and Muslim women imprisoned in "high-pressure ghettoes … in the name of *culture*", a culture that forces obedience to patriarchal authority and arranged marriages (Alibhai-Brown 2001). Negotiating new identities, then, becomes central to daily social and spatial practices, as newcomers assert their rights to the city, to make a home for themselves, to occupy and transform space.[4]

What now seems insidious in terms of debates about belonging in relation to the nation is the way in which the identities of minorities have been essentialised on the grounds of culture and ethnicity. The ethnicization and racialization of the identities of non-white or non-Anglo people in western liberal democracies, even the most officially multicultural among them (Canada and Australia), has had the effect of bracketing them as minorities, as people whose claims can only ever be minor within a national culture and frame of national belonging defined by others and their majority histories, usually read as histories of white belonging and white supremacy (Amin 2002: 21; Hage 1998). But the claims of the Asian youths in Britain's northern mill towns, just as those of Black Britons or "Lebanese Australians" or "Chinese Canadians", are claims for more than minority recognition and minority rights. Theirs is a claim for the mainstream (or perhaps it is a claim for "the end of mainstream" (Dang 2002)), for a metaphorical shift from the margins to the centre, both in terms of the right to visibility and the right to reshape that mainstream. It is nothing less than a claim to full citizenship and a public naming of what has hitherto prevented that full citizenship – the assumption that to be British, Canadian, Danish, Dutch, and so on, is to be white, and part of white culture. As long as that assumption remains intact, the status of minority ethnic groups in all the western democracies will remain of a different order to that of whites, always under question, always at the mercy of the "tolerance" of the dominant culture, a tolerance built on an unequal power relationship (Hage 1998).

The crucial implication of this discussion is that in order to enable all citizens, regardless of "race" or ethnicity or any other cultural criteria, to become equal members of the nation and contribute to an *evolving national identity,* "the ethnic moorings of national belonging need to be exposed and replaced by criteria that have nothing to do with whiteness" (Amin 2002: 22). Or as Gilroy (2000: 328) puts it, "the racial ontology of sovereign territory" needs to be recognized and contested. This requires an imagination of the nation as something other than a racial or ethnic territorial space, perhaps an imagination that conceives the nation as a space of traveling cultures and peoples with varying degrees and geographies of attachment. Such a move must insist that race and ethnicity are taken out of the definition of national identity and national belonging "and replaced by ideals of citizenship, democracy and political community" (Amin 2002: 23). This brings me to the necessity of rethinking 20th century notions of multiculturalism (based on ethno-cultural recognition), and that is the subject of the third section of this chapter.

20.4 Reconsidering Multiculturalism

As a *fact*, multiculturalism describes the increasing cultural diversity of societies in late modernity. Empirically, many societies and many cities could be described today as multicultural. But very few countries have embraced and institutionalised an *ideology* of multiculturalism. Australia and Canada have done so since the late 1960s, as have Singapore and Malaysia, although the latter pair of countries have a different interpretation of multiculturalism than do the former pair. During the same period, the USA has lived through its "multicultural wars", still uneasy with the whole notion, preferring the traditional "melting pot" metaphor and its associated politics of assimilation. France has been most adamant that there is no place for any kind of political recognition of difference in their republic. The Dutch and the Danish, once most open to multicultural policy claims, have each begun to pull up the drawbridges since 2002. Each country has a different definition of multiculturalism, different sets of public policies to deal with/respond to cultural difference, and correspondingly different definitions of citizenship.

As an *ideology*, then, multiculturalism has a multiplicity of meanings. What is common in the sociological content of the term in the West – but never spoken of – is that it was formulated as a framework, a set of policies, for the national accommodation of non-white immigration. It was a liberal response that skirted the reality of the already racialized constitution of these societies and masked the existence of institutionalised racism.[55] The histories of multicultural philosophies are in fact much more complex and contested than this, and genealogical justice cannot be done without a much more contextualised discussion of each country, which is not my purpose here. So instead, drawing on the distinguished British cultural studies scholar Stuart Hall, I will simply summarise the *range* of meanings that have been given to multiculturalism as ideology, and some of the dangers embedded in it.

Hall (2000) theorizes the multicultural question as both a global and local terrain of political contestation with crucial implications for the West. It is contested by the conservative Right, in defense of the purity and cultural integrity of the nation. It is contested by liberals, who claim that the "cult of ethnicity", the notion of "group rights", and the pursuit of "difference" threaten the universalism and neutrality of the liberal state. Multiculturalism is also contested by "modernizers of various political persuasions". For them, the triumph of the (alleged) universalism of western civilization over the particularisms of ethnic, religious, and racial belonging established in the Enlightenment marked an entirely worthy transition from tradition to modernity that is, and should be, irreversible. Some postmodern versions of *cosmopolitanism* oppose multiculturalism as imposing a too narrow, or closed, sense of identity. Some radicals argue that multiculturalism divides along ethnic lines what should be a united front of race and class against injustice and exploitation. Others point to commercialised, boutique, or consumerist multiculturalism as celebrating difference without making a difference (Hall 2000: 211).

Clearly, multiculturalism is not a single doctrine and does not represent an already achieved state of affairs. It describes a variety of political strategies and processes that are everywhere incomplete. Just as there are different multicultural societies, so there are different multiculturalisms.

Conservative multiculturalism insists on the assimilation of difference into the traditions and customs of the majority. Liberal multiculturalism seeks to integrate the different cultural groups as fast as possible into the "mainstream" provided by a universal individual citizenship ... Pluralist multiculturalism formally enfranchises the differences between groups along cultural lines and accords different group rights to different communities within a more ... communitarian political order. Commercial multiculturalism assumes that if the diversity of individuals from different communities is recognized in the marketplace, then the problems of cultural difference will be dissolved through private consumption, without any need for a redistribution of power and resources. Corporate multiculturalism (public or private) seeks to "manage" minority cultural differences in the interests of the center. Critical or "revolutionary" multiculturalism foregrounds power, privilege, the hierarchy of oppressions and the movements of resistance … And so on (Hall 2000: 210).

Can a concept that has so many valences and such diverse and contradictory enemies possibly have any further use value? Alternatively, is its contested status precisely its value, an indication that a radical pluralist ethos is alive and well?

Given that we live in an age of migration (Castles and Miller 1998), we are inevitably implicated in the politics of multiculturalism. This in turn demands a rethinking of traditional notions of citizenship as well as a lot of new thinking about the social integration of immigrants. Given this 21st century urban reality, we need to find a way to publicly manifest the significance of cultural diversity, and to debate the value of various identities/differences; that is, to ask which differences exist, but should not, and which do not exist, but should.[6] Far from banishing the concept to political purgatory, we need to give it as rich a substance as possible, a substance that expands political possibilities and identities rather than purifying or closing them down. This leads me to re-theorise multiculturalism, *which I prefer to re-name as interculturalism,* as a political and philosophical basis for thinking about how to deal with the challenge of difference in the mongrel cities of the 21st century.

My intercultural theory is composed of the following premises:

The cultural embeddedness of humans is inescapable. We grow up in a culturally structured world, are deeply shaped by it, and necessarily view the world from within a specific culture. We are also capable of critically evaluating our own culture's beliefs and practices, and of understanding and appreciating as well as criticizing those of other cultures. But some form of cultural identity and belonging seems unavoidable.

"Culture" cannot be understood as static, eternally given, essentialist. It is always evolving, dynamic and hybrid of necessity. All cultures, even allegedly conservative or traditional ones, contain multiple differences within themselves that are continually being re-negotiated.

Cultural diversity is a positive thing, and intercultural dialogue is a necessary element of culturally diverse societies. No culture is perfect or can be perfected, but all cultures have something to learn from and contribute to others. Cultures grow through the everyday practices of social interaction.

The political contestation of interculturalism is inevitable, as diverse publics debate the merits of multiple identity/difference claims for rights.

At the core of interculturalism as a daily political practice are two rights: the right to difference and the right to the city. The right to difference means recognizing the legitimacy and specific needs of minority or subaltern cultures. The right to the city is the right to presence, to occupy public space, and to participate as an equal in public affairs.

The "right to difference" at the heart of interculturalism must be perpetually contested against other rights (for example, human rights) and redefined according to new formulations and considerations.

The notion of the perpetual contestation of interculturalism implies an agonistic democratic politics that demands active citizenship and daily negotiations of difference in all of the banal sites of intercultural interaction.

A sense of belonging in an intercultural society cannot be based on race, religion, or ethnicity but needs to be based on a shared commitment to political community. Such a commitment requires an empowered citizenry.

Reducing fear and intolerance can only be achieved by addressing the material as well as cultural dimensions of "recognition". This means addressing the prevailing inequalities of political and economic power as well as developing new stories about and symbols of national and local identity and belonging.

There are (at least) two public goods embedded in a version of interculturalism based on these understandings. One is the critical freedom to question in thought, and challenge in practice, one's inherited cultural ways. The other is the recognition of the widely shared aspiration to belong to a culture and a place, and so to be at home in the world (Tully 1995). This sense of belonging would be lost if one's culture were excluded, or if it was imposed on everyone. But there can also be a sense of belonging that comes from being associated with other cultures, gaining in strength and compassion from accommodation among and interrelations with others, and it is important to recognize and nurture those spaces of accommodation and intermingling.

This understanding of interculturalism accepts the indispensability of group identity to human life (and therefore to politics), precisely because it is inseparable from belonging. But this acceptance needs to be complicated by an insistence, a vigorous struggle against the idea that one's own group identity has a claim to intrinsic truth. If we can acknowledge a drive within ourselves, and within all of our particular cultures, to naturalise the identities given to us, we can simultaneously be vigilant about the danger implicit in this drive, which is the almost irresistible desire to impose one's identity, one's way of life, one's very definition of normality and of goodness, on others. Thus we arrive at a lived conception of identity/difference that recognizes itself as *historically contingent and inherently relational*; and a cultivation of a care for difference through strategies of critical detachment from the identities that constitute us (Connolly 1991; Tully 1995). In this intercultural imagination, the twin goods of belonging and of freedom can be made to support rather than oppose each other.

From an intercultural perspective, the good society does not commit itself to a particular vision of the good life and then ask how much diversity it can tolerate within the limits set by this vision. To do so would be to foreclose future societal development. Rather, an intercultural perspective advocates accepting the reality and desirability of cultural diversity and then structuring political life accordingly. At the very least, this political life must be dialogically and agonistically constituted. But the dialogue requires certain *institutional preconditions*, such as freedom of speech, participatory public spaces, empowered citizens, agreed procedures and basic ethical norms, and the active policing of discriminatory practices. It also calls for

> such essential political virtues as mutual respect and concern, tolerance, self-restraint, willingness to enter into unfamiliar worlds of thought, love of diversity, a mind open to new ideas and a heart open to others' needs, and the ability to persuade and live with unresolved differences. (Parekh 2000: 340)

A notion of the common good is vital to any political community. From an intercultural perspective, this common good must be generated not by transcending or ignoring cultural and other differences (the liberal position), but through their interplay in a dialogical, agonistic political life. Finally, a sense of belonging, which is important in any society, cannot in multicultural societies be based on ethnicity or on shared cultural, ethnic or other characteristics. An intercultural society is too diverse for that. A sense of belonging must ultimately be political, based on a shared commitment to a political community (Parekh 2000: 341; Amin 2002: 23).

Since commitment, or belonging, must be reciprocal, citizens will not feel these things unless their political community is also committed to them and makes them feel that they belong. And here is the challenge. An intercultural political community

> cannot expect its members to develop a sense of belonging to it unless it equally values and cherishes them in all their diversity, and reflects this in its structure, policies, conduct of public affairs, self-understanding and self-definition. (Parekh 2000: 342)

It would be safe to say that no existing (self-described) multicultural society can yet claim to have achieved this state of affairs, for reasons that have already been elaborated: political and economic inequalities accompanied by an unresolved postcolonial condition that we may as well name as racism. But in recent years these issues have been identified, increasingly documented, and are becoming the focus of political activity in many countries.

20.5   Conclusions: The Marriage of Theory and Practice

This chapter has outlined three main elements of a cosmopolitan urbanism, or intercultural political philosophy. What has emerged from the descriptions and analysis of the Collingwood Neighbourhood House in previous chapters is that this local institution is a catalyst for and a working example of living together and bridging vast cultural differences. With many different ethnocultural groups living in this one territorially defined neighbourhood, it is neither the existence of a common culture (ethnically defined) nor a shared sense of attachment to place that makes this neighbourhood a community. Rather, what has happened in the period of twenty years of rapid demographic change from a predominantly Anglo-European to a much more ethnically mixed population is exactly what James Donald theorized, "a broad social participation in the never completed process of making meanings and creating values, an always emerging, negotiated common culture".

But that "common culture" is not ethno-culturally grounded, nor is it the result of one dominant culture imposing its lifeways on all the rest. Rather, it is a negotiated sharing of values, established through broad social participation. This is community redefined neither as identity nor as place, but as a productive process of social interaction. The CNH is indeed a physical place: many folks even refer to it as a blessed place (as the DVD shows), one that has helped to create a sense of belonging. But, perhaps paradoxically, that belonging is only partially to do with the actual physical place, and more profoundly to do with the lived experience of building relationships. As James Donald proposed in his normative ideal, we don't need to share cultural traditions with our neighbours in order to live alongside them, but we do need to be able to talk to them. CNH has created that space for intercultural dialogue, for exchange across cultural difference, which is the precondition for relationship building.

The secret of this remarkable achievement is in the CNH mission, which embodies Ash Amin's normative ideal of a politics of local liveability, nurtured through daily habits of "quite banal intercultural interaction in order to establish a basis for dialogue". At CNH, these daily habits of banal interaction occur around childcare, around the learning of English as a second language, around preparing and/or sharing meals together, and sharing a multitude of other training and learning and recreational opportunities. In these "micro-public spaces", these sites of everyday encounter and prosaic negotiation of difference, people from different cultural backgrounds come together, initially in quite practical ways, but in these moments of coming together there is always the possibility of dialogue, of initiating new attachments. And that is what happens at and through CNH. Part of what happens through such everyday contact is the gradual overcoming of feelings of strangeness in the simple process of sharing everyday tasks and/or challenges and comparing ways of doing things.

But such initiatives do not automatically become sites of social inclusion. They need organizational and discursive strategies that are designed to build voice, to foster a sense of common benefit, to develop confidence among disempowered groups, and to arbitrate when disputes arise. And that is precisely, and systematically, what the CNH Board and leadership have done through two decades of social and demographic change. They have consciously diversified as a Board, and in the selection of staff and nurturing of volunteers. They have consciously chosen not to provide any programs or services on an ethno-culturally specific basis. They have systematically conducted outreach to marginalized groups such as First

Nations and youth. They have systematically organized anti-racism and diversity training for staff and volunteers, and empowered youth to run their own anti-bullying, anti-racism and drug counseling programs. And they have proactively developed programs for homeless people. All of which reflects the values of social justice and social inclusion embedded in the mission of CNH.

CNH's vocabulary of accommodation to difference is a vocabulary of "rights of presence, bridging difference, getting along", just as proposed in Amin's normative ideal. And an important part of this pragmatic vocabulary is the recognition of conflict as inevitable, and a commitment to work through such conflict, acknowledging whatever fears and anxieties have been triggered, and devoting time to listening, talking through and arriving at new accommodations that work for residents. But these local, neighbourhood-based organizational and discursive strategies cannot endure, let alone thrive, in the absence of a broader intercultural political culture: that is, one with effective anti-racism policies, with strong legal, institutional and informal sanctions against racial and cultural hatred and a public culture that no longer treats immigrants as "guests".

One very important aspect of Canada's evolving political culture at federal government level, especially in the past decade, through the Department of Canadian Heritage, has been the effort to create a sense of national identity and national belonging that is grounded in ideals of active citizenship, democracy and political community, rather than in notions of "Canadianness" grounded in race or ethnicity (the latter being the case in most European countries). This very important shift is also a shift in the meaning of multiculturalism, from its earlier incarnation emphasizing recognition and support of all immigrant cultures and the celebration of ethno-cultural differences, to an intercultural position emphasising the building of bridges between cultures. And this has been reflected in actual funding shifts, away from the support of ethno-culturally specific organizations or facilities (such as a Chinese Cultural Centre or a Vietnamese Seniors Centre) to organizations with explicit intercultural mandates, like CNH. In the process, the essential political virtues of a cosmopolitan urbanism (or an intercultural society) are being nurtured: the virtues of mutual respect and concern, tolerance, self-restraint, love of diversity, minds open to new ideas and hearts open to the needs of others. In embodying these virtues, nurturing them, and pursuing them through relationship building in everyday life, the Collingwood Neighbourhood House is a microcosm of all that Canada aspires to be (but is not, yet). It is a marriage of the theory and practice of cosmopolitan urbanism.

Notes

1. The following description is taken from James Tully's account of the sculpture (Tully 1995: 17–18).
2. For much of my interpretation in this section I am indebted to the work of William Connolly (1991, 1995) and Julia Kristeva (1991).

3. "Culturally embedded" in the sense that we grow up and live within a culturally struc-
    tured world, organise our lives and social relations within its system of meaning and
    significance, and place some value on our cultural identity (Parekh 200: 336).
4. Or as previously dominated groups such as gays and lesbians, women, people with
    disabilities, decide to engage in a politics of identity/difference, a politics of place-
    claiming and place-making (Kenney 2001).
5. See Hage (1998), on Australia; Hesse (2000) and Hall (2000), on the UK; Bannerji (1995,
    2000), on Canada.
6. See Chantal Mouffe's discussion of this dilemma in her case for an agonistic democratic
    politics in *The Democratic Paradox* (2000).

References

Albrow M (1997) Travelling beyond local cultures: Socioscapes in a global city. In:
    Eade J (ed.) Living the global city. Globalization as a local process. Routledge,
    London.

Alibhai-Brown Y (2000) Diversity versus multiculturalism, The Daily Telegraph, 23 May.

Alibhai-Brown Y (2001) Mr. Blunkett has insulted all of us, The Independent, 10 December.

Amin A (2002) Ethnicity and the multicultural city. Living with diversity. Report for the
    Department of Transport, Local Government and the Regions. University of Durham,
    Durham.

Bannerji H (1995) Thinking through. Women's Press, Toronto.

Bannerji H (2000). The dark side of the nation: Essays on multiculturalism, nationalism
    and gender. Canadian Scholars' Press Inc., Toronto.

Castles S and M Miller (1998) The age of migration, 2nd edn. The Guilford Press:
    New York.

Connolly W (1991) Identity\difference. Cornell University Press, Ithaca.

Connolly W (1995) The ethos of pluralization. University of Minnesota Press,
    Minneapolis.

Dang S (2002) Creating cosmopolis: The end of mainstream. Unpublished Masters Thesis,
    School of Community and Regional Planning, University of British Columbia.

Donald J (1999) Imagining the modern city. The Athlone Press, London.

Gilroy P (2000) Between camps. Penguin, London.

Hage G (1998) White nation: Fantasies of white supremacy in a multicultural society. Pluto
    Press, Sydney.

Hall S (2000) Conclusion: The multi-cultural question. In: Hesse B (ed.) Un/settled
    multiculturalisms. Zed Books, London.

Hesse B (2000) Introduction: Un/settled multiculturalisms. In: Hesse B (ed.) Un/settled
    multiculturalisms. Zed Books, London.

Home Office (2001) Building cohesive communities: A report of the ministerial group on
    public order and community cohesion. Home Office/Her Majesty's Government,
    London.

Kenney M (2001) Mapping gay L.A. The intersection of place and politics. Temple
    University Press, Philadelphia.

Kristeva J (1991) Strangers to ourselves. Columbia University Press, New York. Translated
    by Leon S. Roudiez.

Mouffe C (2000) The democratic paradox. Verso, London.

Parekh B (2000) Rethinking multiculturalism. Macmillan, London.

Rocco R (2000) Associational rights-claims, civil society and place. In: Isin E (ed.) Democracy, citizenship and the global city. Routledge, London.

Sandercock L (2003) Cosmopolis 2: Mongrel cities of the 21st century. Continuum, London.

Sassen S (1996) Whose city is it? Globalization and the formation of new Public Culture, 8: pp. 205–223.

Sennett R (1994) Flesh and stone. The body and the city in Western civilization. Norton, New York.

Tully J (1995) Strange multiplicity. Constitutionalism in an age of diversity. Cambridge University Press, Cambridge.

Urban Task Force (1999) Towards an urban renaissance. E & FN Spon, London.

Young I (1990) Justice and the politics of difference. Princeton University Press, Princeton, NJ.

21

Advocacy and Pluralism in Planning

Paul Davidoff

The present can become an epoch in which the dreams of the past for an enlightened and just democracy are turned into a reality. The massing of voices protesting racial discrimination have roused this nation to the need to rectify racial and other social injustices. The adoption by Congress of a host of welfare measures and the Supreme Court's specification of the meaning of equal protection by law both reveal the response to protest and open the way for the vast changes still required.

The just demand for political and social equality on the part of the African-American and the impoverished requires the public to establish the bases for a society affording equal opportunity to all citizens. The compelling need for intelligent planning, for specification of new social goals and the means for achieving them, is manifest. The society of the future will be an urban one, and city planners will help to give it shape and content.

The prospect for future planning is that of a practice openly inviting political and social values to be examined and debated. Acceptance of this position means rejection of prescriptions for planning that would have the planner act solely as a technician. It has been argued that technical studies to enlarge the information available to decision makers must take precedence over statements of goals and ideals:

> We have suggested that, at least in part, the city planner is better advised to start from research into the functional aspects of cities than from his own estimation of the values which he is attempting to maximize. This suggestion springs from a conviction that at this juncture the implications of many planning decisions are poorly understood, and that no certain means are at hand by which values can be measured, ranked, and translated into the design of a metropolitan system.[1]

Original publication details: Davidoff, Paul. 1965. "Advocacy and Pluralism in Planning". In *Journal of the American Planning Association*, 31 (4): 544–55. Used with permission from Taylor & Francis Group.

Readings in Planning Theory, Fourth Edition. Edited by Susan S. Fainstein and James DeFilippis.

While acknowledging the need for humility and openness in the adoption of social goals, this statement amounts to an attempt to eliminate, or sharply reduce, the unique contribution planning can make: understanding the functional aspects of the city and recommending appropriate future action to improve the urban condition.

Another argument that attempts to reduce the importance of attitudes and values in planning and other policy sciences is that the major public questions are themselves matters of choice between technical methods of solution. Dahl and Lindblom put forth this position at the beginning of their important textbook, *Politics, Economics, and Welfare.*[2]

> In economic organization and reform, the "great issues" are no longer the great issues, if they ever were. It has become increasingly difficult for thoughtful men to find meaningful alternatives posed in the traditional choices between socialism and capitalism, planning and the free market, regulation and laissez-faire, for they find their actual choices neither so simple nor so grand. Not so simple, because economic organization poses knotty problems that can only be solved by painstaking attention to technical details – how else, for example, can inflation be controlled? Nor so grand, because, at least in the Western world, most people neither can nor wish to experiment with the whole pattern of socio-economic organization to attain goals more easily won. If for example, taxation will serve the purpose, why "abolish the wages system" to ameliorate income inequality?

These words were written in the early 1950s and express the spirit of that decade more than that of the 1960s. They suggest that the major battles have been fought. But the "great issues" in economic organization, those revolving around the central issue of the nature of distributive justice, have yet to be settled. The world is still in turmoil over the way in which the resources of nations are to be distributed. The justice of the present social allocation of wealth, knowledge, skill, and other social goods is clearly in debate. Solutions to questions about the share of wealth and other social commodities that should go to different classes cannot be technically derived; they must arise from social attitudes.

Appropriate planning action cannot be prescribed from a position of value neutrality, for prescriptions are based on desired objectives. One conclusion drawn from this assertion is that "values are inescapable elements of any rational decision-making process"[3] and that values held by the planner should be made clear. The implications of that conclusion for planning have been described elsewhere and will not be considered in this chapter.[4] Here I will say that the planner should do more than explicate the values underlying his prescriptions for courses of action; he should affirm them; he should be an advocate for what he deems proper.

Determinations of what serves the public interest, in a society containing many diverse interest groups, are almost always of a highly contentious nature. In performing its role of prescribing courses of action leading to future desired states, the planning profession must engage itself thoroughly and openly in the contention surrounding political determination. Moreover, planners should be able to engage in the political process as advocates of the interests both of government and of such other groups, organizations, or individuals who are concerned with proposing policies for the future development of the community.

The recommendation that city planners represent and plead the plans of many interest groups is founded upon the need to establish an effective urban democracy, one in which citizens may be able to play an active role in the process of deciding public policy. Appropriate policy in a democracy is determined through a process of political debate. The right course of action is always a matter of choice, never of fact. In a bureaucratic age great care must be taken that choices remain in the area of public view and participation.

Urban politics, in an era of increasing government activity in planning and welfare, must balance the demands for ever-increasing central bureaucratic control against the demands for increased concern for the unique requirements of local, specialized interests. The welfare of all and the welfare of minorities are both deserving of support: Planning must be so structured and so practiced as to account for this unavoidable bifurcation of the public interest.

The idealized political process in a democracy serves the search for truth in much the same manner as due process in law. Fair notice and hearings, production of supporting evidence, cross-examination, reasoned decision are all means employed to arrive at relative truth: a just decision. Due process and two (or more) party political contention both rely heavily upon strong advocacy by a professional. The advocate represents an individual, group, or organization. He affirms their position in language understandable to his client and to the decision makers he seeks to convince.

If the planning process is to encourage democratic urban government, then it must operate so as to include rather than exclude citizens from participating in the process. "Inclusion" means not only permitting citizens to be heard. It also means allowing them to become well informed about the underlying reasons for planning proposals, and to respond to these in the technical language of professional planners.

A practice that has discouraged full participation by citizens in plan making in the past has been based on what might be called the "unitary plan." This is the idea that only one agency in a community should prepare a comprehensive plan; that agency is the city planning commission or department. Why is it that no other organization within a community prepares a plan? Why is only one agency concerned with establishing both general and specific goals for community development, and with proposing the strategies and costs required to effect the goals? Why are there not plural plans?

If the social, economic, and political ramifications of a plan are politically contentious, then why is it that those in opposition to the agency plan do not prepare one of their own? It is interesting to observe that "rational" theories of planning have called for consideration of alternative courses of action by planning agencies.

As a matter of rationality, it has been argued that all of the alternative choices open as means to the ends ought be examined.[5] But those, including myself, who have recommended agency consideration of alternatives have placed upon the agency planner the burden of inventing "a few representative alternatives."[6] The agency planner has been given the duty of constructing a model of the political spectrum and charged with sorting out what he conceives to be worthy alternatives. This duty has placed too great a burden on the agency planner and has failed to provide for the formulation of alternatives by the interest groups who will eventually be affected by the completed plans.

Whereas in a large part of our national and local political practice contention is viewed as healthy, in city planning, where a large proportion of the professionals are public employees, contentious criticism has not always been viewed as legitimate. Further, where only government prepares plans and no minority plans are developed, pressure is often applied to bring all professionals to work for the ends espoused by a public agency. For example, last year a federal official complained to a meeting of planning professors that the academic planners were not giving enough support to federal programs. He assumed that every planner should be on the side of the federal renewal program. Of course government administrators will seek to gain the support of professionals outside government, but such support should not be expected as a matter of loyalty. In a democratic system opposition to a public agency should be just as normal and appropriate as support. The agency, despite the fact that it is concerned with planning, may be serving undesired ends.

In presenting a plea for plural planning I do not mean to minimize the importance of the obligation of the public planning agency. It must decide upon appropriate future courses of action for the community. But being isolated as the only plan maker in the community, public agencies as well as the public itself may have suffered from incomplete and shallow analysis of potential directions. Lively political dispute aided by plural plans could do much to improve the level of rationality in the process of preparing the public plan.

The advocacy of alternative plans by interest groups outside government would stimulate city planning in a number of ways. First, it would serve as a means of better informing the public of the alternative choices open, *alternatives strongly supported by their proponents*. In current practice those few agencies that have portrayed alternatives have not been equally enthusiastic about each.[7] A standard reaction to rationalists' prescription for consideration of alternative courses of action has been, "It can't be done; how can you expect planners to present alternatives of which they don't approve?" The appropriate answer to that question has been that planners, like lawyers, may have a professional obligation to defend positions they oppose. However, in a system of plural planning, the public agency would be relieved of at least some of the burden of presenting alternatives. In plural planning the alternatives would be presented by interest groups differing with the public agency's plan. Such alternatives would represent the deep-seated convictions of their proponents and not just the mental exercises of rational planners seeking to portray the range of choice.

A second way in which advocacy and plural planning would improve planning practice would be in forcing the public agency to compete with other planning groups to win political support. In the absence of opposition or alternative plans presented by interest groups, the public agencies have had little incentive to improve the quality of their work or the rate of production of plans. The political consumer has been offered a yes/no ballot in regard to the comprehensive plan; either the public agency's plan was to be adopted, or no plan would be adopted.

A third improvement in planning practice that might follow from plural planning would be to force those who have been critical of "establishment" plans to produce superior plans, rather than only to carry out the very essential obligation of criticizing plans deemed improper.

The Planner as Advocate

Where plural planning is practiced, advocacy becomes the means of professional support for competing claims about how the community should develop. Pluralism in support of political contention describes the process; advocacy describes the role performed by the professional in the process. Where unitary planning prevails, advocacy is not of paramount importance, for there is little or no competition for the plan prepared by the public agency. The concept of advocacy as taken from legal practice implies the opposition of at least two contending viewpoints in an adversary proceeding.

The legal advocate must plead for his own and his client's sense of legal propriety or justice. The planner as advocate would plead for his own and his client's view of the good society. The advocate planner would be more than a provider of information, an analyst of current trends, a simulator of future conditions, and a detailer of means. In addition to carrying out these necessary parts of planning, he would be a *proponent* of specific substantive solutions.

The advocate planner would be responsible to his client and would seek to express his client's views. This does not mean that the planner could not seek to persuade his client. In some situations persuasion might not be necessary, for the planner would have sought out an employer with whom he shared common views about desired social conditions and the means toward them. In fact one of the benefits of advocate planning is the possibility it creates for a planner to find employment with agencies holding values close to his own. Today the agency planner may be dismayed by the positions affirmed by his agency, but there may be no alternative employer.

The advocate planner would be above all a planner, responsible to his or her client for preparing plans and for all of the other elements comprising the planning process. Whether working for the public agency or for some private organization, the planner would have to prepare plans that take account of the arguments made in other plans. Thus, the advocate's plan might have some of the characteristics of a legal brief. It would be a document presenting the facts and reasons for supporting one set of proposals, and facts and reasons indicating the inferiority of counter proposals. The adversary nature of plural planning might, then, have the beneficial effect of upsetting the tradition of writing plan proposals in terminology that makes them appear self-evident.

A troublesome issue in contemporary planning is that of finding techniques for evaluating alternative plans. Technical devices such as cost–benefit analyses by themselves are of little assistance without the use of means for appraising the values underlying plans. Advocate planning, by making the values underlying plans more apparent, and definitions of social costs and benefits more explicit, should greatly assist the process of plan evaluation. Further, it would become clear (as it is not at present) that there are no neutral grounds for evaluating a plan; there are as many evaluative systems as there are value systems.

The adversary nature of plural planning might also have a good effect on the uses of information and research in planning. One of the tasks of the advocate planner in discussing the plans prepared in opposition would be to point out the nature of the bias underlying information presented in other plans. In this way, as critic of opposition plans, the planner would be performing a task similar to the legal technique of cross-examination. While painful to the planner whose bias is exposed (and no planner can be entirely free of bias) the net effect of confrontation between advocates of alternative plans would be more careful and precise research.

Not all the work of an advocate planner would be of an adversary nature. Much of it would be educational. The advocate would have the job of informing other groups, including public agencies, of the conditions, problems, and outlook of the group he or she represented. Another major educational job would be that of informing clients of their rights under planning and renewal laws, about the general operations of city government, and of particular programs likely to affect them.

The advocate planner would devote much attention to helping the client organization to clarify its ideas and to give expression to them. In order to make clients more powerful politically the advocate might also become engaged in expanding the size and scope of his or her client organization. But the advocate's most important function would be to carry out the planning process for the organization and to argue persuasively in favor of its planning proposals.

Advocacy in planning has already begun to emerge as planning and renewal affect the lives of more and more people. The critics of urban renewal[8] have forced response from the renewal agencies, and the ongoing debate[9] has stimulated needed self-evaluation by public agencies. Much work along the lines of advocate planning has already taken place, but little of it by professional planners. More often the work has been conducted by trained community organizers or by student groups. In at least one instance, however, a planner's professional aid led to the development of an alternative renewal approach, one that will result in the dislocation of far fewer families than originally contemplated.[10]

Pluralism and advocacy are means for stimulating consideration of future conditions by all groups in society. But there is one social group that at present is particularly in need of the assistance of planners. This group includes organizations representing low-income families. At a time when concern for the condition of the poor finds institutionalization in community action programs it would be appropriate for planners concerned with such groups to find means to plan with them. The plans prepared for these groups would seek to combat poverty and would propose programs affording new and better opportunities to the members of the organization and to families similarly situated.[11]

The difficulty in providing adequate planning assistance to organizations representing low-income families may in part be overcome by funds allocated to local antipoverty councils. But these councils are not the only representatives of the poor; other organizations exist and seek help. How can this type of assistance be financed? This question will be examined below, when attention is turned to the means for institutionalizing plural planning.

The Structure of Planning

Planning by special interest groups

The local planning process typically includes one or more "citizens" organizations concerned with the nature of planning in the community. The Workable Program requirement for "citizen participation"[12] has enforced this tradition and brought it to most large communities. The difficulty with current citizen participation programs is that citizens are more often *reacting* to agency programs than *proposing* their concepts of appropriate goals and future action.

The fact that citizens' organizations have not played a positive role in formulating plans is to some extent a result of both the enlarged role in society played by government bureaucracies and the historic weakness of municipal party politics. There is something very shameful to our society in the necessity to have organized "citizen participation." Such participation should be the norm in an enlightened democracy. The formalization of citizen participation as a required practice in localities is similar in many respects to totalitarian shows of loyalty to the state by citizen parades.

Will a private group interested in preparing a recommendation for community development be required to carry out its own survey and analysis of the community? The answer would depend upon the quality of the work prepared by the public agency, work that should be public information. In some instances the public agency may not have surveyed or analyzed aspects the private group thinks important; or the public agency's work may reveal strong biases unacceptable to the private group. In any event, the production of a useful plan proposal will require much information concerning the present and predicted conditions in the community. There will be some costs associated with gathering that information, even if it is taken from the public agency. The major cost involved in the preparation of a plan by a private agency would probably be the employment of one or more professional planners.

What organizations might be expected to engage in the plural planning process? The first type that comes to mind are the political parties; but this is clearly an aspirational thought. There is very little evidence that local political organizations have the interest, ability, or concern to establish well-developed programs for their communities. Not all the fault, though, should be placed upon the professional politicians, for the registered members of political parties have not demanded very much, if anything, from them as agents.

Despite the unreality of the wish, the desirability for active participation in the process of planning by the political parties is strong. In an ideal situation local parties would establish political platforms, which would contain master plans for community growth, and both the majority and minority parties in the legislative branch of government would use such plans as one basis for appraising individual legislative proposals. Further, the local administration would use its planning agency to carry out the plans it proposed to the electorate. This dream will not turn to reality for a long time. In the interim other interest groups must be sought to fill the gap caused by the present inability of political organizations.

The second set of organizations that might be interested in preparing plans for community development are those that represent special interest groups having established views in regard to proper public policy. Such organizations as chambers of commerce, real estate boards, labor organizations, pro- and anti-civil rights groups, and anti-poverty councils come to mind. Groups of this nature have often played parts in the development of community plans, but only in a very few instances have they proposed their own plans.

It must be recognized that there is strong reason operating against commitment to a plan by these organizations. In fact it is the same reason that in part limits both the interests of politicians and the potential for planning in our society. The expressed commitment to a particular plan may make it difficult for groups to find means for accommodating their various interests. In other terms, it may be simpler for professionals, politicians, or lobbyists to make deals if they have not laid their cards on the table.

There is a third set of organizations that might be looked to as proponents of plans and to whom the foregoing comments might not apply. These are the ad hoc protest associations that may form in opposition to some proposed policy. An example of such a group is a neighborhood association formed to combat a renewal plan, a zoning change, or the proposed location of a public facility. Such organizations may seek to develop alternative plans, plans that would, if effected, better serve their interests.

From the point of view of effective and rational planning, it might be desirable to commence plural planning at the level of citywide organizations, but a more realistic view is that it will start at the neighborhood level. Certain advantages of this outcome should be noted. Mention was made earlier of tension in government between centralizing and decentralizing forces. The contention aroused by conflict between the central planning agency and the neighborhood organization may indeed be healthy, leading to clearer definition of welfare policies and their relation to the rights of individuals or minority groups.

Who will pay for plural planning? Some organizations have the resources to sponsor the development of a plan. Many groups lack the means. The plight of the relatively indigent association seeking to propose a plan might be analogous to that of the indigent client in search of legal aid. If the idea of plural planning makes sense, then support may be found from foundations or from government. In the beginning it is more likely that some foundation might be willing to experiment with plural planning as a means of making city planning more effective and more democratic. Or the federal government might see plural planning, if carried out by local anti-poverty councils, as a strong means of generating local interest in community affairs.

Federal sponsorship of plural planning might be seen as a more effective tool for stimulating involvement of citizens in the future of their community than are the present types of citizen participation programs. Federal support could be expected only if plural planning were seen not as a means of combating renewal plans but as an incentive to local renewal agencies to prepare better plans.

The public planning agency

A major drawback to effective democratic planning practice is the continuation of that nonresponsible vestigial institution, the planning commission. If it is agreed that the establishment of both general policies and implementation policies are questions affecting the public interest and that public interest questions should be decided in accord with established democratic practices for decision making, then it is indeed difficult to find convincing reasons for continuing to permit independent commissions to make planning decisions. At an earlier stage in planning, the strong arguments of John T. Howard[13] and others in support of commissions may have been persuasive. But it is now more than a decade since Howard made his defense against Robert Walker's position favoring planning as a staff function under the mayor. With the increasing effect planning decisions have upon the lives of citizens, the Walker proposal assumes great urgency.[14]

Aside from important questions regarding the propriety of allowing independent agencies far removed from public control to determine public policy, the failure to place planning decision choices in the hands of elected officials has weakened the ability of professional planners to have their proposals effected. Separating planning from local politics has made it difficult for independent commissions to garner influential political support. The commissions are not responsible directly to the electorate, and the electorate in turn is at best often indifferent to the planning commission.

During the last decade, in many cities power to alter community development has slipped out of the hands of city planning commissions, assuming they ever held it, and has been transferred to development coordinators. This has weakened the professional planner. Perhaps planners unknowingly contributed to this by their refusal to take concerted action in opposition to the perpetuation of commissions.

Planning commissions are products of the conservative reform movement of the early part of this century. The movement was essentially anti-populist and pro-aristocracy. Politics was viewed as dirty business. The commissions are relics of a not-too-distant past when it was believed that if men of goodwill discussed a problem thoroughly, certainly the right solution would be forthcoming. We know today, and perhaps it was always known, that there are no right solutions. Proper policy is that which the decision-making unit declares to be proper.

Planning commissions are responsible to no constituency. The members of the commissions, except for their chairperson, are seldom known to the public. In general the individual members fail to expose their personal views about policy and prefer to immerse them in group decision. If the members wrote concurring and dissenting opinions, then at least the commissions might stimulate thought about planning issues. It is difficult to comprehend why this aristocratic and undemocratic form of decision making should be continued. The public planning function should be carried out in the executive or legislative office and perhaps in both. There has been some question about which of these branches of government would provide the best home, but there is much reason to believe that both branches would be made more cognizant of planning issues if they were each informed by their own planning staffs. To carry this division further, it would probably be advisable to establish minority and majority planning staffs in the legislative branch.

At the root of my last suggestion is the belief that there is or should be a Republican and Democratic way of viewing city development; that there should be conservative and liberal plans, plans to support the private market and plans to support greater government control. There are many possible roads for a community to travel, and many plans should show them. Explication is required of many alternative futures presented by those sympathetic to the construction of each such future. As indicated earlier, such alternatives are not presented to the public now. Those few reports that do include alternative futures do not speak in terms of interest to the average citizen. They are filled with professional jargon and present sham alternatives. These plans have expressed technical land-use alternatives rather than social, economic, or political value alternatives. Both the traditional unitary plans and the new ones that present technical alternatives have limited the public's exposure to the future states that might be achieved. Instead of arousing healthy political contention as diverse comprehensive plans might, these plans have deflated interest.

The independent planning commission and unitary plan practice certainly should not coexist. Separately, they dull the possibility for enlightened political debate; in combination they have made it yet more difficult. But when still another hoary concept of city planning is added to them, such debate becomes practically impossible. This third of a trinity of worn-out notions is that city planning should focus only upon the physical aspects of city development.

An Inclusive Definition of the Scope of Planning

The view that equates physical planning with city planning is myopic. It may have had some historical justification, but it is clearly out of place at a time when it is necessary to integrate knowledge and techniques in order to wrestle effectively with the myriad of problems afflicting urban populations.

The city planning profession's historical concern with the physical environment has warped its ability to see physical structures and land as servants to those who use them.[15] Physical relations and conditions have no meaning or quality apart from the way they serve their users. But this is forgotten every time a physical condition is described as good or bad without relation to a specified group of users. High density, low density, green belts, mixed uses, cluster developments, centralized or decentralized business centers are per se neither good nor bad. They describe physical relations or conditions but take on value only when seen in terms of their social, economic, psychological, physiological, or aesthetic effects upon different users.

The profession's experience with renewal over the past decade has shown the high costs of exclusive concern with physical conditions. It has been found that the allocation of funds for removal of physical blight may not necessarily improve the overall physical condition of a community and may engender such harsh social repercussions as to severely damage both social and economic institutions. Another example of the deficiencies of the physical bias is the assumption of city planners that they could deal with the capital budget as if the physical attributes of a facility could be understood apart from the philosophy and practice of the service conducted within the physical structure. This assumption is open to question. The size, shape, and location of a facility greatly interact with the purpose of the activity the facility houses. Clear examples of this can be seen in public education and in the provision of low-cost housing. The racial and other socioeconomic consequences of "physical decisions" such as location of schools and housing projects have been immense, but city planners, while acknowledging the existence of such consequences, have not sought or trained themselves to understand socioeconomic problems, their causes or solutions.

The city planning profession's limited scope has tended to bias strongly many of its recommendations toward perpetuation of existing social and economic practices. Here I am not opposing the outcomes, but the way in which they are developed. Relative ignorance of social and economic methods of analysis has caused planners to propose solutions in the absence of sufficient knowledge of the costs and benefits of proposals upon different sections of the population.

Large expenditures have been made on planning studies of regional transportation needs, for example, but these studies have been conducted in a manner suggesting that different social and economic classes of the population did not have different needs and different abilities to meet them. In the field of housing, to take another example, planners have been hesitant to question the consequences of locating public housing in slum areas. In the field of industrial development, planners have seldom examined the types of jobs the community needed; it has been assumed that one job was about as useful as another. But this may not be the case when a significant sector of the population finds it difficult to get employment.

"Who gets what, when, where, why, and how" are the basic political questions that need to be raised about every allocation of public resources. The questions cannot be answered adequately if land-use criteria are the sole or major standards for judgment.

The need to see an element of city development, land use, in broad perspective applies equally well to every other element, such as health, welfare, and recreation. The governing of a city requires an adequate plan for its future. Such a plan loses guiding force and rational basis to the degree that it deals with less than the whole that is of concern to the public.

The implications of the foregoing comments for the practice of city planning are these. First, state planning enabling legislation should be amended to permit planning departments to study and to prepare plans related to any area of public concern. Second, planning education must be redirected so as to provide channels of specialization in different parts of public planning and a core focused upon the planning process. Third, the professional planning association should enlarge its scope so as not to exclude city planners not specializing in physical planning.

A year ago at the American Institute of Planners (AIP) convention it was suggested that the AIP constitution be amended to permit city planning to enlarge its scope to all matters of public concern.[16] Members of the Institute in agreement with this proposal should seek to develop support for it at both the chapter and national level. The constitution at present states that the institute's "particular sphere of activity shall be the planning of the unified development of urban communities and their environs and of states, regions and the nation *as expressed through determination of the comprehensive arrangement of land and land occupancy and regulation thereof*."[17]

It is time that the AIP delete the words in my italics from its constitution. The planner limited to such concerns is not a city planner, but a land planner or a physical planner. A city is its people; their practices; and their political, social, cultural, and economic institutions as well as other things. The city planner must comprehend and deal with all these factors.

The new city planners will be concerned with physical planning, economic planning, and social planning. The scope of their work will be no wider than that presently demanded of a mayor or a city council member. Thus, we cannot argue against an enlarged planning function on the grounds that it is too large to handle. The mayor needs assistance, in particular the assistance of a planner, trained to examine needs and aspirations in terms of both short- and long-term perspectives. In observing the early stages of development of Community Action Programs, it is apparent that our cities are in desperate need of the type of assistance trained planners could offer. Our cities require for their social and economic programs the type of long-range thought and information that have been brought forward in the realm of physical planning. Potential resources must be examined and priorities set.

What I have just proposed does not imply the termination of physical planning, but it does mean that physical planning be seen as part of city planning. Uninhibited by limitations on their work, city planners will be able to add their expertise to the task of coordinating the operating and capital budgets and to the job of relating effects of each city program upon the others and upon the social, political, and economic resources of the community.

An expanded scope reaching all matters of public concern will not only make planning a more effective administrative tool of local government, it will also bring planning practice closer to the issues of real concern to the citizens. A system of plural city planning probably has a much greater chance of operational success where the focus is on live social and economic questions instead of rather esoteric issues relating to physical norms.

The Education of Planners

Widening the scope of planning to include all areas of concern to government would suggest that city planners must possess a broader knowledge of the structure and forces affecting urban development. In general this would be true. But at present many city planners are specialists in only one or more of the functions of city government. Broadening the scope of planning would require some additional planners who specialize in one or more of the services entailed by the new focus.

A prime purpose of city planning is the coordination of many separate functions. This coordination calls for planners with general knowledge of the many elements comprising the urban community. Educating a planner to perform the coordinator's role is a difficult job, one not well satisfied by the present tradition of two years of graduate study. Training urban planners with the skills called for in this article may require both longer graduate study and development of a liberal arts under-graduate program affording an opportunity for holistic understanding of both urban conditions and techniques for analyzing and solving urban problems.

The practice of plural planning requires educating planners who would be able to engage as professional advocates in the contentious work of forming social policy. The person able to do this would be one deeply committed both to the process of planning and to particular substantive ideas. Recognizing that ideological commitments will separate planners, there is tremendous need to train professionals who are competent to express their social objectives.

The great advances in analytic skills, for example in techniques of simulating urban growth processes, portend a time when planners and the public will be better able to predict the consequences of proposed courses of action. But these advances will be of little social advantage if the proposals themselves do not have substance. The contemporary thoughts of planners about the nature of individuals in society are often mundane, unexciting, or gimmicky. When asked to point out to students the planners who have a developed sense of history and philosophy concerning the place of individuals in the urban world, one is hard put to come up with a name. Sometimes Goodman or Mumford might be mentioned. But planners seldom go deeper than acknowledging the goodness of green space and the soundness of proximity of linked activities. We cope with the problems of the alienated citizen with a recommendation for reducing the time of the journey to work.

Conclusion

The urban community is a system composed of interrelated elements, but little is known about how the elements do, will, or should interrelate. The type of knowledge required by the new comprehensive city planner demands that the planning profession comprise groups of people well versed in contemporary philosophy, social work, law, the social sciences, and civic design. Not every planner must be knowledgeable in all these areas, but each planner must have a deep understanding of one or more of these areas and must be able to give persuasive expression to this understanding.

As members of a profession charged with making urban life more beautiful, exciting, creative, and just, we have had little to say. Our task is to train a future generation of planners to go well beyond us in its ability to prescribe the future urban life.

Notes

1.   Britton Harris, "Plan or Projection," *Journal of the American Institute of Planners*, 26 (November 1960) 265–72.
2.   Robert Dahl and Charles Lindblom, *Politics, Economics, and Welfare* (New York: Harper and Brothers, 1953) p. 3.

3. Paul Davidoff and Thomas Reiner, "A Choice Theory of Planning," *Journal of the American Institute of Planners*, 28 (May 1962) 103–15.

4. Ibid.

5. See, for example, Martin Meyerson and Edward Banfield, *Politics, Planning and the Public Interest* (Glencoe: The Free Press 1955) pp. 314 ff. The authors state: "By a *rational* decision, we mean one made in the following manner: 1. the decision-maker considers all of the alternatives (courses of action) open to him; ... 2. he identifies and evaluates all of the consequences which would follow from the adoption of each alternative; ... 3. he selects that alternative the probable consequences of which would be preferable in terms of his most valued ends."

6. Davidoff and Reiner, op. cit.

7. National Capital Planning Commission. *The Nation's Capital: a Policies Plan for the Year 2000* (Washington DC: The Commission, 1961).

8. The most important critical studies are Jane Jacobs, *The Life and Death of Great American Cities* (New York: Random House, 1961); Martin Anderson, *The Federal Bulldozer* (Cambridge: MIT Press, 1964); Herbert J. Gans, "The Human Implications of Current Redevelopment and Relocation Planning," *Journal of the American Institute of Planners*, 25 (February 1959) 15–26.

9. A recent example of heated debate appears in the following set of articles: Herbert J. Gans, "The Failure of Urban Renewal," *Commentary* 39 (April 1965) p. 29; George Raymond, "Controversy," *Commentary* 40 (July 1965) p. 72; and Herbert J. Gans, "Controversy," *Commentary* 40 (July 1965) p. 77.

10. Walter Thabit, *An Alternate Plan for Cooper Square* (New York: Walter Thabit, July 1961).

11. The first conscious effort to employ the advocacy method was carried out by a graduate student of city planning as an independent research project. The author acted as both a participant and an observer of a local housing organization. See Linda Davidoff, "The Bluffs: Advocate Planning," *Comment*, Dept. of City Planning, University of Pennsylvania (Spring 1965) p. 59.

12. See Section 101(c) of the United States Housing Act of 1949, as amended.

13. John T. Howard, "In Defense of Planning Commissions," *Journal of the American Institute of Planners*, 17(2) (Spring 1951) 89–95.

14. Robert Walker, *The Planning Function in Urban Government*, second edition (Chicago: University of Chicago Press, 1950). Walker drew the following conclusions from his examination of planning and planning commissions. "Another conclusion to be drawn from the existing composition of city planning boards is that they are not representative of the population as a whole" (p. 153). "In summary the writer is of the opinion that the claim that planning commissions are more objective than elected officials must be rejected" (p. 155). "From his observations the writer feels justified in saying that very seldom does a majority of any commission have any well-rounded understanding of the purposes and ramifications of planning" (p. 157). "In summary, then, it was found that the average commission member does not comprehend planning nor is he particularly interested even in the range of customary physical planning" (p. 158). "Looking at the planning commission at the present time, however, one is forced to conclude that despite some examples of successful operations, the unpaid board is not proving satisfactory as a planning agency" (p. 165). " ... (it) is believed that the most fruitful line of development for the future would be

replacement of these commissions by a department or bureau attached to the office of mayor or city manager. This department might be headed by a board or by a single director, but the members or the director would in any case hold office at the pleasure of the executive on the same basis as other department heads" (p. 177).

15. An excellent and complete study of the bias resulting from reliance upon physical or land-use criteria appears in David Farbman, "A Description, Analysis and Critique of the Master Plan," an unpublished mimeographed study prepared for the Univ. of Pennsylvania's Institute for Urban Studies, 1959–1960. After studying more than one hundred master plans Farbman wrote:

> As a result of the predominantly physical orientation of the planning profession many planners have fallen victims to a malaise which I suggest calling the "Physical Bias." This bias is not the physical orientation of the planner itself but is the result of it …
>
> The physical bias is an attitude on the part of the planner which leads him to conceive of the principles and techniques of *his profession* as the key factors in determining the particular recommendations to be embodied in his plans …
>
> The physically biased planner plans on the assumption (conviction) that the physical problems of a city can be solved within the framework of physical desiderata: in other words, that physical problems can be adequately stated, solved and remedied according to physical criteria and expertise. The physical bias produces both an inability and an unwillingness on the part of the planner to "get behind" the physical recommendations of the plan, to isolate, examine or to discuss more basic criteria …
>
> … There is room, then, in plan thinking for physical principles, i.e., theories of structural inter-relationships of the physical city; but this is only part of the story, for the structural impacts of the plan are only a part of the total impact. This total impact must be conceived as a web of physical, economic and social causes and effects. (pp. 22–6).

16. Paul Davidoff, "The Role of the City Planner in Social Planning," *Proceedings of the 1964 Annual Conference*, American Institute of Planners (Washington DC: The Institute, 1964) 125–31.

17. Constitution of AIP, Article II "Purposes," in *AIP Handbook and Roster – 1965*, p. 8.

22

The Minority-Race Planner in the Quest for a Just City

June Manning Thomas

Ann Markusen once suggested that the urban planning profession is losing the battle with economics for the shaping of urban space in part because planners value equity as a normative criterion, whereas economics values market efficiency. Efficiency has won out in whatever war of values might have taken place (Markusen, 2000). While it may be true that planners value equity, any such commitment may run counter to political and social conditions. Furthermore, either widely accepted tools are not available to create such equity, or political conditions in fact support inequitable, purposeful oppression. These situations have emerged in several very different contexts around the world (Bollens, 1999, 2004; Fainstein, 2005; Flyvbjerg, 2002; Forester, 2000; Yiftachel, 2006; Yiftachel and Ghanem, 2004).

One modest but tangible way to help bring about equity in the urban context may be to ensure that the ranks of professional planners include diversity in race and ethnicity, particularly in urban societies where severe inequities by race and ethnicity exist. Diversity in the urban planning profession and the connection between diversity and the "just city" are not topics that have recently received a great deal of attention in the scholarly planning literature, but professional diversity would seem to be one visible, tangible, and basic measure of the profession's commitment to social equity. If the urban planning profession cannot itself reflect commitment to social equity in the form of its own demographics, it could seem contradictory for professional planners to argue for social equity in society at large.

Original publication details: Manning Thomas, June 2008. "The Minority-Race Planner in the Quest for a Just City". In *Planning Theory*, 7 (3): pp. 227–47.

Readings in Planning Theory, Fourth Edition. Edited by Susan S. Fainstein and James DeFilippis.
Editorial material and organization © 2016 John Wiley & Sons, Ltd.
Published 2016 by John Wiley & Sons, Ltd.

This article will explore possible reasons for focusing on the diversity – in this article, we will largely address racial diversity, particularly in the United States – of the profession as we continue to dialogue about the just city, and we will discuss some of the subtleties of circumstance that may make the diversity of the profession difficult to maintain. Racial diversity could conceivably bring tangible benefits to the workplace and to the community, especially in those social contexts characterized by racial conflict or segregation. If this potential contribution is to unfold, however, we will need to come to terms with the difficult work contexts which may face minority-race planners, and with the possible need to address dysfunction within these contexts before attempting to address dysfunction within the world at large. After offering a few definitions related to race, we will explore these issues by considering the theoretical background of the "just city", as well as initial thoughts concerning the means for reaching such a city. We will reference as well the results of interviews with a few African American US planners, to gain some sense of the challenges that may face minority-race planners in their work environments in at least one country, the US.

Minority-Race People

In this discussion, we reference "minority-race", "race", and "ethnicity" because of a lack of better language. We continue to use these terms only because they have social meaning to many people today, but their scientific meaning is vague, and meaning varies by nation or continent. "Race" is a social construct with little biological justification. Its modern usage arose only a few hundred years ago in order to justify the economic oppression of darker-skinned people under conditions of slavery, colonialism, and industrialization, and it serves particularly poorly as a concept in societies characterized by populations of diverse origins which have intermarried.[1] In the US, the context for much of the discussion of this article, definitions are sometimes fluid but race remains a powerful concept because of a cultural reality: people continue to treat others differently because of perceived race, with particularly strong distinctions between "black" or African American and "white" or Caucasian, even though both of these categories include extensive mixture and variation (Farley et al., 2000; Hirschman, 2004; Moses, 2004). Furthermore, centuries of different treatment, by individuals and by institutions, have left a lasting mark on the urban landscape, with far different circumstances for people perceived to be of minority race or ethnicity in terms of living conditions, residential patterns, and social and economic opportunities, particularly for those of low income (Wilson, 2003).

While in some national contexts "ethnicity" is a good substitute for "race", this is not necessarily true in the US. "Ethnicity" often refers to tribal, national, regional, language grouping or other variations which may be less physically obvious than the popular conception of race (Hirschman, 2004). Yiftachel (2006) has argued that ethnic divisions, more so than racial divisions, are particularly difficult in the Southern and Eastern parts of the world. He suggests that the North and West – meaning North America and Western Europe – benefit from a number of basic liberties and social welfare provisions that make life even for their disadvantaged racial minorities relatively more stable than life for many oppressed ethnic groups in Southern and Eastern places such as Israel, apartheid South Africa, Eastern Europe, and many other countries.

While this is undoubtedly true, the economic, social, and spatial divisions by race and ethnicity in his designated North and West – particularly in US cities – pose continuing, ongoing dilemmas that have yet to be resolved and may not be resolved in the foreseeable future. Planners will probably have much less credibility and efficacy in helping to bring about social equity in situations of racial or ethnic division or conflict if their membership is composed largely of the dominant race or ethnicity, or if their planning work environments do not support the effective functioning of members of minority races or ethnic groups as planning professionals. These are two variants of the phenomenon wherein planners in conflict-laden societies have found it necessary to negotiate difficult shoals of allegiance and reform, or in fact have become tools of the state used to create and legitimize situations of spatial control of oppressed racial, ethnic, or religious groups (Bollens, 1999, 2000; Yiftachel, 2000).

The postmodern era celebrates non-exclusion, and so it is unfortunate that it is necessary to raise yet again this topic of racial diversity in the profession. The main reason is not to hold on to modernist or structuralist notions of binary reality that Soja (1997) referred to as outmoded – that is, to view everything in exclusionary terms of black or white, worker or capitalist, immigrant or native, male or female – but rather to ground dialogue in the reality of the fragmented metropolis and to understand that the "politics of difference" (Merrifield, 1997) is a messy affair, requiring focused attention and effort. In the US, it is not surprising that professional organizations such as the American Planning Association (APA) (2005a, 2005b, 2006a, 2006b) and the American Institute of Certified Planners (AICP) (2005b) have witnessed or participated in continued dialogue about racial diversity in the profession.

The Ends

In this discussion of the just city, it is important to consider both means and ends. By ends we refer to the goal that planners are trying to achieve in today's cities and urban regions, and means refers to the process by which this goal is attained. Ends and means may be interrelated, contingent upon one another and dynamic according to situation (Healey, 2003).

Concerning the goal of a just city, first we must note that values such as equity or justice may not be so much universal as individualized, necessitating that we take great care in analyzing the context under consideration (Watson, 2006). Furthermore, definitions are not simple matters. The definition of justice, for example, varies according to conditions of knowledge and power, or context (Healey, 2003; Young, 1990), with not a little confusion caused by successively varying historical understandings of the meaning of the concept of justice, dating from Aristotle to Marx to Rawls and beyond (Fleischacker, 2004; Merrifield and Swyngedouw, 1997; Stein and Harper, 2005). Some Marxists or political economists may eschew "justice" as a vague moralism, while some liberal scholars may champion the concept but strip their discussion of urban context or means of implementation (Katznelson, 1997). Nevertheless, it is still possible to argue that planners should strive for the "just city" as a main end or goal of planning action (Fainstein, 2000, 2005; Krumholz and Forester, 1990; Harvey, 2003; Krumholz and Clavel, 1994). Fainstein argues that planning theory should take "an explicitly normative position concerning the distribution of social benefits" (Fainstein, 2000: 467). She presents a definition of the "just city" that is twofold, looking at both process and product: "A theory of the just city values participation in decision making by relatively powerless groups and equity of outcomes" (Fainstein, 2000: 468).[2] It is this dualistic definition that we use in this article.

Focusing on results or "equity of outcomes" – as opposed to process – is an important component of this definition, even though the power of planning to shape outcomes is and always has been limited (Fainstein, 2005). Outcomes often stem from processes during which powerful economic interests dominate decisionmaking, a fact which has taught us to beware of actions touted as being in the "public interest" which nevertheless have led to grossly inequitable results for vulnerable populations. Scholars such as Paul Davidoff and Norman Krumholz have called for advocacy and equity planning, approaches which focus on process but also on equity of results in the field, particularly for the disadvantaged (Davidoff, 1965; Krumholz and Forester, 1990). Their work helps keep us on track, although it is important to note that they have not focused on the social structures that underlie uneven distribution, a situation described by Fainstein in her criticism of "post-structural"[3] thinkers, who have "identified the way in which space embodies power without necessarily locating its source in particular groups of people" (Fainstein, 1997: 26). It is one thing to identify with the disadvantaged, as did Davidoff, but it is another to recognize and analyze which people and organizations are in power, creating the situation that leads to others' disadvantage. The work of political economists such as Harvey remind us that economic considerations, particularly structural manifestations of economic power, influence the outcomes we see in cities (Harvey, 1973, 1992; Watson, 2006).

Watson has explicitly examined the usefulness of normative theories such as the just city for oppressed residents of urban South Africa, warning that solutions supposedly designed for social justice (such as the destruction of substandard housing) may indeed work to the detriment of people seeking autonomy (as in intentional informal settlements; Watson, 2002). She has also argued that current forms of justice as defined and promoted by authors such as Rawls and Habermas assume conditions of liberalism and universality which do not fit non-Western contexts, particularly situations characterized by "deep differences" (Watson, 2006). Building on Bollens's work concerning fractured urban societies (Bollens, 2004), she has seen the situation of "deep difference" – which appears to be growing in part because of the uneven development that accompanies globalization, leading to enhanced fragmentation by race, income, class, and other categories – as particularly problematic because of vastly different value systems that accompany growing social disjuncture around the world. Although she argues that no universal definition of justice exists, she too urges planners to undertake efforts that create just outcomes, and she references several of Harvey's suggestions, such as creation of social organizations and economic systems that minimize the exploitation of labor, and action that recognizes the ecological impact of social projects (Watson, 2006).

Leonie Sandercock has suggested that diversity is part of the goal in urban contexts (Sandercock, 2003). She defines a just city as one in which everyone is treated with respect, no matter their race, ethnicity, nationality, gender, class, or sexual orientation. During some such discussions of diversity, however, race may be submerged under the larger umbrella of multiculturalism.[4] This in itself is a problem because some dilemmas (ethnic oppression in some parts of the world, racial oppression in North America, poverty) are much more deeply ingrained within key social and economic institutions than other forms of inequity (Catlin, 1993; Thomas and Darnton, 2006; Thomas and Ritzdorf, 1997; Yiftachel, 2006). Therefore, a simple call for respect for all kinds of difference may not be enough to address the concerns of those suffering the longest and deepest inequities. This situation, too, reminds us of Fainstein's warning that post-structuralist thought, although rightly concerned about social injustice, may place too much emphasis on diversity as opposed to political action and economic equality (Fainstein, 1997).

The goal of the "just city" appears to be important even if a commonly accepted definition of what this means may not exist. Even without transparency of definition, at least one professional organization in what Yiftachel calls the North-West, the AICP in the US, has adopted a Code of Ethics (2005a) which refers to "social justice" as a legitimate goal for planners. One of several main principles of that code states: "We shall seek social justice by working to expand choice and opportunity for all persons, recognizing a special responsibility to plan for the needs of the disadvantaged and to promote racial and economic integration." If we assume that the just city, characterized by some form of "equity" of outcomes, is indeed an important goal or "end" for urban planning, how are we to reach it?

The Means

The above discussion suggests that the definition of means to reach the "just city" will vary by national or regional (continental or sub-continental) context. For the US, the AICP Code assumes that the means is clear: planners must simply plan for the disadvantaged and promote integration, as well as "urge the alteration of policies, institutions, and decisions that oppose such needs" (AICP, 2005a). This is essentially the approach of "equity planning", as well (Krumholz and Forester, 1990), with an important difference in assumptions. The US professional code does not mention political context, has conceptual roots in the faith in expertise characteristic of the rational process, and implies that the practice of planning can help lead to "social justice" if this is so mandated by the professional organization. The code gives no guidance about what to do when principles of loyalty (to employers and other powers-that-be) and social reform (for the disadvantaged) *compete*, a not-uncommon situation for planners. This code also does not address the simple question of how to ensure that a planner has the motivation or ability to pursue social justice when local contexts argue against this. Krumholz (and his co-authors) clearly knew that the political context was complicated, and these writings attempted to educate planners about the essential nature of social justice and its promotion, but again the issue of motivation was barely addressed (Krumholz and Clavel, 1994; Krumholz and Forester, 1990).

Davidoff's conception of advocacy planning suggested that planners recognize the presence of multiple publics, and provide professional services for disadvantaged populations, but these concepts of advocacy (Davidoff, 1965) arose at a time in the US history when federal programs such as Model Cities provided disadvantaged central-city residents with the resources and autonomy necessary to hire planning services, a situation that seldom exists in modern times (save for developmentally advanced organizations such as certain community development corporations). Theorists of neither equity planning nor advocacy planning addressed the possible danger of planners focusing on social equity as philanthropic act rather than collaborative endeavor among equals.

Communicative (Innes, 1995, 1996) and collaborative (Healey, 2003) planning have emerged as popular vehicles for addressing the concerns of multiple parties in situations characterized by competing values and interests. These paradigms clearly have drawbacks in situations of uneven power, however, a situation that has been explored in the planning theory literature (Flyvbjerg, 2002; Watson, 2002; Yiftachel, 2006). To put the commentary simply, some people are more powerful than others, and the less powerful are usually disadvantaged in any dialogue or collaboration that might take place. Although these authors rely upon a Foucaultian framework and so they surely understand that power is always manifest (Gutting, 2005), the question is whether the innately uneven distribution of power can be suspended at least while deliberations are underway.

Flyvbjerg (2002) has offered possible strategies for overcoming such manifestations of power, such as exploring the abuse of power, and then publicizing and moving to counteract injustice, an approach which he has modeled in Denmark concerning transportation plans for the central business district of the city of Aalborg. Denmark, however, is more homogeneous than several other countries in the North and West, and exhibits relatively few internal differences of the kind Watson describes as "deep differences". Flyvbjerg's ability to publicize his research in the local Danish media, revealing the negative effects of an established pattern of power, in effect illustrates Watson's point that not all contexts offer equivalent opportunities for reform.

For societies characterized by long-standing inequities, reflected in an urban landscape fractured by major differences in social and economic opportunity, with patterns of racial or other segregation that affect all aspects of daily life, the following questions are very important: what might motivate a planner to seek to work for the goal of the just city? How can we find or train planners willing to overcome the strictures of bureaucratic complacency and seek to work at least in part to enhance either the outcome or process of the just city? For it does little good to promote the goal of social justice if means for insuring or encouraging practice which leads to social justice are not at hand.

Here is where, among a collection of strategies, we might place recruitment and retention of members of the minority-race population into the ranks of the planning profession. The desired behavior – which for the sake of shorthand discussion we might term *advocacy*, by which we mean the promotion of the just city as defined by Fainstein in citations above – can be exhibited by any one, of any race, gender, ethnicity, nationality, or any other criterion, and we should expect support for principles of social justice from all planners of good conscience. Inevitably, however, some will be more motivated in this direction than others.

Hypothetically, we might expect that a profession which contained representatives of populations disadvantaged *for that societal context* might very well find its responsiveness towards social justice *in that society* to be enhanced. In modern South Africa, for example, it would seem to be very difficult for the urban planning profession to attend to the needs of social justice in the spatial reorganization of urban society if the former ethnic and racial victims of apartheid did not also become lead politicians or members of the planning profession, or at least become involved in the planning process, and develop the knowledge, will, and motivation needed to help steer decision-making toward the goal of social justice. This is not to suggest that professional inclusion is a sufficient condition – in modern South Africa, for example, economic conditions of inequality and underdevelopment are so entrenched that largely black governmental leadership and increasingly inclusionary planning have generated progress but have not yet been able to bring about equitable cities (Lund and Skinner, 2004; Ozler, 2007; Parnell, 2004) – but rather that it is a necessary one. In apartheid South Africa and in Israel, and in other places characterized by "deep difference" backed by rule of law (Yiftachel and

Ghanem, 2004), it is not clear that the racial and ethnic characteristics of planners would matter at all.

In at least the North American context, however, particularly in metropolitan areas severely fractured by race and poverty lines or their intersections – as is the case in US metropolitan areas, which have many such intersections (Wilson, 2003) – it would seem to make sense to recruit to the profession members of the society's most marginalized racial minorities. Many large metropolitan areas still reflect high levels of racial segregation, with central cities typically containing much larger percentages of minority races than surrounding suburbs, and the level of racial segregation is particularly high in Midwestern and Northeastern metropolitan areas such as Detroit, Chicago, and New York City (Farley et al., 2000). Although subtle barriers such as municipal fragmentation and socio-economic stratification supported by tools such as zoning and inadequate public transportation often reinforce informal barriers, particularly for the poor, gains in civil rights legislation and popular perception have loosened racial constraints supported by law, and blatant racial discrimination in such matters as formal access to housing is not legally defensible. Differences are deep, therefore, but not so deep or so entrenched legally as to be insurmountable.

The Minority-Race Planner

It is of course not so much the race or ethnicity of planners as their orientation and skill sets that are important. Forester (2000) has noted that planners will increasingly need to work with social inequalities, and they will need to be aware of the role of race, gender, and ethnicity. He suggests that planning does not need complacent bureaucrats, but rather people who "speak articulately to the realities of poverty and suffering, deal with race, displacement, and histories of under-served communities in ways that do not leave people's pain at the door" (Forester, 2000: 259). Given this situation, planners of many different racial or ethnic backgrounds could meet these criteria concerning the ability to "deal with race" and to address problems of poverty, displacement, and insufficient service without leaving "people's pain at the door" – a possible reference to advocacy – and all minority-race planners would not necessarily have the ability to do so. However, it would seem conceptually reasonable to assume that some minority-race planners could prove to have particularly useful skills related to these specific tasks, perhaps because of bonds of culture, history, community, or sentiment. If so, agency effectiveness could be diminished if racial minorities were severely underrepresented in the planning profession.

In a remarkable book chapter on urbanization and injustice, Marshall Berman (1997) once wrote about the political value of African American rap, an art form that was perhaps purest in its earliest state, before violent tendencies took over certain "gangsta rap" practitioners. As he described the early characteristics of this phenomenon, rap was once a way for disenfranchised, disadvantaged ghetto youth to address the circumstances of their confinement in ways eloquent and focused. He noted that the humble but sophisticated lyrics written by the first wave of rappers said a lot of what we need to know about power and protest in the contemporary US, and this form soon became popular for a wide range of people around the world who wanted to speak from the street. If black youth raised in the ghetto have special skills or insights which enable them to represent the truth of disadvantage in creative ways, might not planners living as racial minorities in a severely fragmented metropolis have comparable effects in the milieu of urban planning and decision-making?

And yet underrepresentation by both race and gender has been a problem in the past. In Canada and the US, diversity by gender has grown over the last few years, although not as rapidly as might be expected given the increasing presence of women in planning student populations (Rahder and Altilia, 2004). The presence of racial minorities, however, is low relative to total population figures. In the US, the body of professional planners, APA, probably includes fewer than 10 percent racial minorities, compared with over 30 percent of the general population. In 2004, APA estimated that 2.7 percent of its members were black or African American, 2.9 percent Asian, and 2.2 percent Hispanic (APA, 2005a). This situation has led the professional planning organization in the US to initiate a series of strategies designed to increase recruitment and retention of racial minorities in the planning profession (APA, 2005a).

Does the presence of racial minorities in the urban planning profession better lead to the "end" of the just city? To this simple question it would be hard to reply "yes". The conceptual difficulties of claiming this would be several, but the main problem is the required indication that planners who are racial minorities somehow help produce better outcomes leading to a just city than planners who are not. Berman (1997), Merrifield (1997) and Soja (1997) among others have warned against the tendency to claim exclusion of reform sensibility or binary thinking characteristic of modernism, that is to claim that "just us" (of a certain race or of certain disadvantages) can bring about positive social change, a position which can cause serious problems of isolation and exclusion. To be sure, a few planning narratives have suggested that the race of the planner can have a positive effect on planning results. Two primary US examples are Catlin (1993), who argued that his African American heritage was of decided advantage in the quest for just solutions to the planning problems of Gary, Indiana, and Thomas (1997), who offered narrative accounts of black planners who saw themselves as the best representatives of the black community during the battles in Detroit over urban renewal during the 1950s and 1960s, and who logged limited successes in changing the outcomes of specific urban renewal projects to the benefit of predominantly African American communities. Other supportive commentary for such a concept is difficult to find, however.

Another problem with answering such a question in the affirmative is that it implies that a planner's efforts can change conditions of injustice in the urban context, *and* that the race or ethnicity of the planner affects this effort. Although efforts to correct injustice do exist, some would argue that the political economy is in effect rigged to subvert true reform, and some evidence supports this claim (Fainstein, 1997; Logan and Molotch, 2007; Soja, 1997).[5] This would logically be true regardless of the genetic background of the planner, and indeed one might argue that planners who are racial minorities in situations of uneven opportunity may have much less personal power to move the system than planners who are not.

While much of the above commentary concerning the just city and minority-race planners stems from conceptualization, it is possible to envision empirical research designed to explore these thoughts. In some allied disciplines, researchers have found that the race of the professional does appear to lead to more just outcomes for minority-race communities; this is not exactly the same as a just city, but it comes closer than several alternatives. The most prominent of such examples of research would be in public administration. In one branch of public administration scholars have pursued a concept known as "representative bureaucracy", referring to the relative presence of various classes, educational levels, etc. in government service (Brudney et al., 2000; Lim, 2006; Meier, 1975; Murray et al., 1994; Sowa and Selden, 2003). One subset of research studies looks at racial diversity within government as being of particular benefit for racial-minority communities, for several tangible reasons. Often based on a number of large-scale survey questionnaires, this research suggests that minority communities may gain greater access and better service results when served by a public sector which includes representatives of their racial group (Brudney et al., 2000; Sowa and Selden, 2003).

One potential step between conceptualization and extensive empirical work comparable to that in public administration would be to carry out qualitative research designed to explore the processes at work from the perspective of a few individuals belonging to some subset, such as, here, minority-race planners. Creswell (1994) describes this approach particularly well. As he noted, such a qualitative approach could start with theory – as, in this case, the possibility that minority-race planners make unique contributions but face unique challenges – but not *test* the theory so much as explore possibilities for further inquiry. The examples he cites often reflect interviews with or intense study of a very few individuals or cases (Creswell, 1994). In such studies, the aim is not to generalize to any population or to proclaim "findings" but rather to further clarify the issues at play (beyond, in this case, the author's own thoughts).

The author identified a few African American planners to interview in the fall of 2006, based on questions informed by the representative bureaucracy literature and the need to explore this concept of the "just city". The attempt was not to represent all black American planners, but rather to anchor theory in reality by seeing how a few such planners reacted to in-depth questions concerning the interconnections of race and the planning profession, an area not well explored, and to identify issues needing further research (APA, 2005a; Hoch, 1994). These six were "representative" of only their subset: graduates from one urban planning program in Michigan, representing perhaps a fourth of the group who had graduated from that program between 1990 and 2001 and who could be traced, and about one-half of this university's black graduates in that cohort who were working for in-state public agencies.[6] We chose these planners not because of any outstanding professional accomplishments or expressions of content or discontent, but rather because of their accessibility to the author, their work experience in a US state where at least moderate if not "deep" difference – racial segregation and greatly unequal life circumstances – are known to exist (Darden et al., 2007; Farley et al., 2000; Orfield and Luce, 2003), their employment by public sector agencies, and the fact that they had been in the field (since at least 2001) long enough to be at least tentatively "established". The six were located throughout the state, but all had at least some experience working as a planner in metropolitan Detroit, an area characterized by extensive historical and contemporary racial segregation, inequality, and antagonism (Farley et al., 2000; Sugrue, 1996; Thomas, 1997).

When asked directly if their work benefited the needs of African American or other minority communities, these Michigan planners were able to offer very few specific examples of such benefit. One transportation planner mentioned his ability to facilitate a project involving an Indian tribe more quickly than had been the case before, and he directly credited this to his personal experience with disadvantage as a minority, but his explanation focused more on process than on product. "Being black in this country, you are able to understand how to sympathize with people when they are put out. When they are being worked against for the wrong reasons ... I could be seen as more sensitive to their needs." Another planner referred to her work with HOPE VI, again citing her ability to advocate for the needs of the local residents and help complete the project. Such examples, however, do sound more process-oriented than product-oriented, since they apparently focus on communication and access rather than on altered results.

For the second category of concern, process or means, we have suggested that the presence of minority-race urban planners may offer distinct advantages for certain kinds of work. The workplace diversity literature notes tangible benefits of a diverse work staff for the internal workings of organizations and for their work in society at large. Although much is yet to be learned and documented about this process, specific benefits internal to the workplace seem to include improvement in functionality and creativity. For example, the presence of a diverse workforce may bring ideas and strategies to the organization that would not otherwise be present. Wise and Tschirhart (2000) review this burgeoning "diversity in the workplace" literature and summarize these arguments. Other, related sources suggest that diverse workers create more effectiveness in the field for some professions. Social work scholars have explicitly determined that effective practitioners need to understand oppression and value diversity, in part by developing "cultural competency", and they have developed models of classroom training which help future practitioners develop necessary skills and sensibilities (Marsh, 2004; Min, 2005; Schmitz et al., 2001). Such efforts could conceivably benefit from the presence in social work of professionals who already have, because of their personal background, facility with the culture experiencing oppression.

When we asked these black Michigan planners how their work benefited minority communities, their process-oriented answers suggested that they saw themselves as playing an important role in improving processes. These planners became extremely animated and detailed when describing their contributions to the process of inclusion for minority-race or low-income communities. One of the questions that seemed to elicit the most response was: "What are the particular advantages or disadvantages associated with being a black planner in your work-place, or in the areas you serve?"

The commentary that erupted is too detailed to explain fully here, but two main categories of response related to these planners' ability: (1) to defend the interests of the minority or disadvantaged community within the agency, and (2) to serve as a bridge, that is to link communication between urban communities and planning agencies. Concerning the defense of community function, several of these planners were very assertive in their stated belief that they were able "watch out for" the interests of low-income minority communities. A typical account would relate to a specific project, such as a transportation project involving a community with a high proportion of minorities, where the planner found himself or herself explaining to his or her colleagues that public meetings would have to be held at times convenient to the working-class residents, and the planner attributed this greater sensitivity to the planner's minority race. One planning agency staffer discussed the reactions of her majority-race colleagues to the presence of representatives of the minority-race central city on a multi-jurisdictional board, and suggested that the central-city residents were treated by majority-race planners as "retards, but they are city offi-cials, experts, planners, engineers and they have a background in doing quality work for decades now". This planner claimed that without her presence this casual dismissal of the minority-race representatives' opinion would go unchallenged.

Concerning the "bridge" function, the second major category, several of these planners indicated that they communicated with underrepresented populations better than their colleagues. One said "you figure that you can work better with your kind". Another noted: "I feel like when I do go to Detroit or smaller commu-nities that feel like they don't have a voice, it is easier for me to build a relationship with those communities. And it doesn't necessarily have to be a black community, it could be the Latino community, it could be a poorer community." She felt that her "sincerity" was stronger than that of most planners. "I can't say it is for all blacks in the planning profession, 'cause there might be some sincere other folks as well." Speaking of her colleagues in one former job, located in a predominantly black city, and apparently linking race and motivation, she commented: "they were all black planners and [therefore] they all felt compelled to really do something for the greater good."

One noted that his white colleagues saw him as a bridge:

> In the field, sometimes as an African American you are always expected to be able to deal with urban environment issues and you are kind of a guide. You may get tagged to do certain things because some of your white counterparts might not feel comfortable working in these areas.

This planner saw a distinct disadvantage to being one of a few blacks in the workplace; colleagues relied upon him to serve as a bridge, oblivious to his other work commitments. Other black planners offered specific examples of community residents, rather than themselves or their colleagues, offering the opinion that black planners served as a bridge. One planner noted that, when her white colleagues went to a particular public meeting with a large number of low-income racial minorities, the planners came back to the office and reported that no one seemed to have anything to say about the issue the planners were trying to discuss. When the black planner went to meet with the same population, however, she heard a flood of opinions, which apparently had been saved until she – perceived either as a part of the community or as a more sensitive ear – arrived.

These few accounts suggest that it is important to explore whether indeed a special role exists for minority-race planners to assist with the process of inclusion, by facilitating enhanced participation by disadvantaged minorities, helping to fulfill one half of Fainstein's definition of what a theory of a just city "values" (2000: 468). But the interviewed planners, and the literature, suggest that a steep price may be paid for these apparent benefits.

Researchers in other professional fields have noted the possible problems. In the medical field, a recently published study of African American internal medicine physicians in six states outlined the substantial experience of race-related challenges for interviewed physicians. Among the implications of race was the emergence of what the researchers called "racial fatigue", born of persistent experiences of racial discrimination and distrust, and leading to several negative consequences for their personal and professional lives (Nunez-Smith et al., 2007).

Public administration researchers have found that those racial minorities working in the public sector (and offering better service to racial minority communities) may pay a price. One of the first public administration scholars to describe that price was Adam Herbert (1974), whose work laid the groundwork for more recent research (Murray et al., 1994). According to what is known as the "Herbert thesis", minority public administrators can find themselves facing at least six key dilemmas. The first (1) is that their workplace may expect them to comply with official policies, but those policies could be in conflict with the goals of the minority community. Two other concerns were: (2) they are likely to be assigned to marginal job categories which deal with minority issues but true resolution of those issues could be very difficult to achieve; and (3) they may experience pressure from their colleagues to support the organization and its goals rather than to support the minority community's interests. Finally, three other concerns were: (4) the minority community expects them to be accountable to that community, in spite of their work situation demanding accountability to the organization; (5) they may indeed feel a strong personal commitment to carry out policies that promote the interests of that community; but (6) they may also feel pressure to ignore the interests of the community in order to advance in their personal careers (Murray et al., 1994). Such professionals must decide how to respond when competing goals confront them in their work, and their work may indeed suffer because of the effort involved.

In terms of the Herbert thesis, our interview questions asked about only three dimensions of the six listed above – concerning system demands (the first problem listed above), community accountability (the fourth listed), and personal commitment (the fifth) – but respondents offered comments, on their own, about other dimensions as well, particularly concerning colleague pressure.

It appeared that the pressures described by the Herbert thesis did apply to these black planners in Michigan. To a series of questions about system demands, accountability, and personal commitment, several respondents noted that they were indeed feeling pressure and conflicting demands at their work-places, serious enough to cause at least two of the six to consider leaving the field.

System demands largely related to the expectation that the planner conform to the policies of the agency, even if he or she perceived those policies to be harmful, or not helpful, to the black community. For example, one planner noted that his organization was supposed to look at impacts on the community of its actions, and that it gave lip service to this goal, but that the agency appeared to have a blind side when it came to certain decisions related to a project that could pose great difficulties for a nearby minority or low-income community. Another planner recalled the reaction when she specifically asked to study an issue that related to the health of a project's nearby low-income community, populated in large part by Hispanics; she was told that such concerns were "a lot of crap". Asked to rate their organizations' "dedication to seeking minority community input and participation", on a 10-point scale, the six gave responses ranging from 1 to 10, with an average of 5.5. Efforts to change the culture of the organizations seemed futile, however: one person noted, "it's difficult to move an organization of this size".

Concerning community accountability, these planners saw themselves as accountable to the "minority community", which in the case of one respondent actually made up the majority of her community or area of jurisdiction. They rated their role as "actively advocating on behalf of and providing leadership to increase minority or disadvantaged community participation and input" from 8 to 10, with an average for the six of 9.1. However their perception was that either they had to persuade their majority-race colleagues and supervisors to include the minority community in meaningful ways, or the reaction of their fellow planners blocked their efforts to engage, or at least respect, representatives of that community who attempted to participate in decision-making. One example is the previously referenced situation of a planner's constant need to remind his colleagues that daytime "participation" meetings were of no use to working-class people.

As far as "personal commitment" was concerned, these planners saw themselves as highly motivated and committed to advocating within their agency for the needs of minority or economically disadvantaged groups, and several gave personal accounts of such commitments. When asked whether they would suggest the profession as an option for students choosing a career, these planners' responses indicated a high level of personal commitment and dedication to their profession, at least before they encountered such difficulties. Concerning recruitment, five of the six indicated that they would recommend planning as a career for young students, and the sixth said he would not but only because "there are better ways to effect change". One made comments arguing for representatives of several races and age groups, such as: "We need more color represented and I would say that for every race ... and we have a poor planning system because it is underrepresented by the population that we have." He went on to argue: "You need a champion for you to say, I'm a black person, I understand your problems and that goes a long way ...". Another commented that:

> I think having blacks in planning that are committed to civic pride and service and who can really stand firm whatever their belief would definitely help the future of communities ... it's really important to keep that diversity in there because you're not dealing with monotone populations, you know. You're dealing with diverse populations these days.

In addition to such accounts, several respondents offered personal stories of their attraction to the profession speaking to the issue of motivation: they indicated that they entered planning because they were responding directly to the conditions of poverty and disinvestment which affected their own minority-race neighborhoods.

Yet these respondents felt insecure in their efforts. One interviewee mentioned, several times in his interview, the danger of being "pigeon-holed" if he pressed too hard on behalf of minority or disadvantaged communities. Another interviewee frankly felt harassed because of his efforts to support low-income disadvantaged minority populations, and at least one of his colleagues – also interviewed for this study – agreed that she perceived the colleague as being regularly harassed because he was an outspoken black male. Several told stories of what they perceived as flagrant mistreatment by their colleagues or supervisors, such as the planner who commented that:

> there are a lot of white men in planning and they really don't trust or feel that blacks are capable of making higher-level decisions that most planners have to. I think that sometimes black planners are very honest in their assessment of what's really going on and people don't like that.

Some interviewees questioned how long they would be able to work at their agency under these conditions.

Diversifying the Profession

These planners indeed found the workplace itself challenging, and felt that system demands and other pressures unique to minority-race planners stymied their efforts to promote the cause of social justice. The theme that emerged most often was that they felt that they offered a unique perspective concerning the special needs of minority communities, as well as low-income communities of any race. They saw themselves as serving the agency in special ways, and serving particularly minority communities in special ways. They claimed that they were highly motivated to enter the profession because of the perception of severe inequalities in their own communities. But they did not feel supported, by the planning agency or by their colleagues, in their work for social equity.

At least in Michigan, and by implication perhaps in the US, and possibly beyond, the planning profession may need minority-race (or minority-ethnic, etc.) planners in order to help create local conditions of access in those processes necessary for a just city. Yet the effective presence of such racial minorities in the profession may face major barriers, not a few of which exist on the job. Little justification exists for any claim that only minority-race planners can bring about just results, the "ends" we discussed earlier. Neither can it be argued that only minority-race planners can work in minority-race contexts or create better access for minority-race communities; the necessity of fighting for social justice should rest with all planners. As a practical matter, however, in deeply conflicted contexts, communities disadvantaged in some way may very well look at the diversity of local urban planners as a symbol of access or "means" toward the goal of social justice. Minority-race planners may see themselves as having a special role to play in the process of local decision-making, and it is entirely conceivable that the perceptions of local minority-race communities may reinforce that tendency. But if minority-race planners cannot survive in the profession, their potential to assist with the process of social change is stillborn.

As we have noted, these thoughts need further exploration and research. Yet if our conceptualization of the issues is correct, one theory to be tested is that minority-race planners in fragmented metropolitan areas can help improve the planning process for minority-race people in matters such as access and connection. If this is indeed true, then at least one appropriate course of action would appear to be fairly obvious. This would be to enhance efforts in minority-race recruitment, in educational programs as well as professional settings, in the reasonable hope that such acts will give greater voice to those who have little. Another theory to be tested is that such minority-race planners face major institutional barriers to their success and effectiveness comparable to those identified by researchers in other professions (Murray et al., 1994; Nunez-Smith et al., 2007). If this is indeed true, much wider institutional and bureaucratic reform would be necessary, far beyond simply recruiting racial minorities to the profession.

Corrective action would necessitate examining the social and institutional contexts of planning organizations, in order to discern and correct those barriers which minority-race planners face and which threaten retention, recruitment, and job effectiveness.

Notes

1. "Minority" as a sole descriptor, without linkage to race as in "minority-race", is problematic; it collapses together a number of categories of social groups which may have little in common with each other. Some have therefore called for social scientists to abolish use of the term (Wilkinson and Butler, 2002). In the context of the US, the focus of much of this article, minority-race people may be considered to be those of African American, American Indian, Asian, and other specific racial backgrounds as defined by the US Census Bureau (2008). "Race" (or racial background) is also a problematic concept, however. Former thinking that humanity is composed of separate and fairly exclusionary racial categories such as "black", "white", "Asian", etc. has begun to yield to scientific evidence that humanity forms a continuum not easily classified, and to the social reality that many people have ancestral backgrounds from several different "races" (Hirschman, 2004). Hirschman recommends replacing the concept of "race" with "ethnicity", but he recognizes the complexities of this suggestion, particularly for purposes such as national censuses.

2. Although we could further explore the term "equitable", we may for this article infer the concept of "fair" and clarify that this does not mean absolute equality in services or outcomes, which is not possible in a democratic society, and quite possibly not in any society.

3. Fainstein (1997) uses post-structuralism as a term inclusive of several theoretical approaches which tend to focus on cultural criticism rather than a strong political-economy analysis.

4. As is gender; see Rahder and Altilia (2004).

5. Some evidence suggests the contrary, arguing that planners can bring about positive change; see, in particular, Krumholz and Clavel (1994).

6. Michigan does not have a large number of minority-race planners, with minority-race attendance at statewide planning conferences notably lacking, and the state professional planning chapter does not have a major initiative to enhance racial diversity in planning, as does California (Dinwiddie-Moore, 2006). The six people interviewed were in positions of reasonable responsibility (none were in entry-level jobs, and two headed small planning divisions), and were known to work in locations of potential interest: state, regional, or local agencies with mixed-race staff, covering jurisdictions with at least some racial mixture. Three were women, and all graduated from the accredited planning program referenced. Four had an undergraduate degree in urban planning, and the other two had higher degrees in planning. All 60- to 90-minute interviews were taped, transcribed, and analyzed through formation of categories of responses suggesting certain patterns, as described in Creswell (1994). The author has maintained communication with the three women over some period of years, allowing for a more in-depth knowledge of their careers.

References

American Institute of Certified Planners (AICP) (2005a) Code of Ethics. Adopted 19 March 2005, available online at: [http://www.planning.org/ethics/conduct.html], accessed 2007.

American Institute of Certified Planners (AICP) (2005b) 'Introduction' to Educational Testing Service, 'The Technical Report for the Minority Pass Rate Project', March, available online as part of document at: [www.planning.org/certification/pdf/minorityreport.pdf.], accessed 2006.

American Planning Association (2005a) 'APA Diversity Task Force Report', M. Silver and R. Barber, co-chairs, American Planning Association, available online at: [http://www.planning.org/diversity/index/htm], accessed 2006.

American Planning Association (2005b) 'Diversity Summit, APA National Conference PowerPoint', available online at: [http://www.planning.org/diversity/index/htm], accessed 2006.

American Planning Association (2006a) available online at: [http://www.planning.org/diversity/index.htm], accessed 2006.

American Planning Association (2006b) 'Diversity Subcommittee Status Report', 23 April, available online at: [http://www.planning.org/diversity/index/htm], accessed 2006.

Berman, M. (1997) 'Justice/Just Us: Rap and Social Justice in America', in A. Merrifield and E. Swyngedouw (eds) *The Urbanization of Injustice*, pp. 161–79. New York: New York University Press.

Bollens, S. (1999) *Urban Peace-building in Divided Societies: Belfast and Johannesburg*. Boulder, CO: Westview Press.

Bollens, S. (2000) *On Narrow Ground: Urban Policy and Ethnic Conflict in Jerusalem and Belfast*. Albany, NY: State University of New York Press.

Bollens, S. (2004) 'Urban Planning and Intergroup Conflict: Confronting a Fractured Public Interest', in B. Stiftel and V. Watson (eds) *Dialogues in Urban and Regional Planning*, pp. 209–46. London and New York: Routledge.

Brudney, J.L., Hebert, F. and Wright, D. (2000) 'From Organizational Values to Organizational Roles: Examining Representative Bureaucracy in State Administration', *Journal of Public Administration Research and Theory* 10(3): 491–512.

Catlin, R. (1993) *Racial Politics and Urban Planning: Gary Indiana 1980–1989*. Lexington, KY: University Press of Kentucky.

Creswell, J. (1994) *Research Design: Qualitative & Quantitative Approaches*. Thousand Oaks, CA: SAGE.

Darden, J., Thomas, R. and Stokes, C. (eds) (2007) *The State of Black Michigan*. East Lansing, MI: Michigan State University Press.

Davidoff, P. (1965) 'Advocacy and Pluralism in Planning', *Journal of the American Institute of Planners* 31: 331–7.

Dinwiddie-Moore, J. (2006) 'California's Efforts to Encourage Diversity', PowerPoint available online at: [www.planning.org/diversity/resources.htm], accessed 2007.

Fainstein, S. (1997) 'Justice, Politics and the Creation of Urban Space', in A. Merrifield and E. Swynegedouw (eds) *The Urbanization of Injustice*, pp. 18–44. New York: New York University Press.

Fainstein, S. (2000) 'New Directions in Planning Theory', *Urban Affairs Review* 35(4): 451–78.

Fainstein, S. (2005) 'Planning Theory and the City', *Journal of Planning Education and Research* 25(2): 121–30.

Farley, R., Danziger, S. and Holzer, H. (2000) *Detroit Divided*. New York: Russell Sage Foundation.

Fleischacker, S. (2004) *A Short History of Distributive Justice*. Cambridge, MA: Harvard University Press.

Flyvbjerg, B. (2002) 'Bringing Power to Planning Research: One Researcher's Praxis Story', *Journal of Planning Education and Research* 21 (4): 353–66.

Forester, J. (2000) 'Why Planning Theory? Educating Citizens, Recognizing Differences, Mediating Deliberations', in L. Rodwin and B. Sanyal (eds) *The Profession of City Planning: Changes, Images and Challenges: 1950–2000*, pp. 253–60. Rutgers, NJ: Center for Urban Policy Research.

Gutting, G. (2005) *Foucault: A Very Short Introduction*. Oxford: Oxford University Press.

Harvey, D. (1973) *Social Justice and the City*. London: Edward Arnold.

Harvey, D. (1992) 'Social Justice, Postmodernism and the City', *International Journal of Urban and Regional Research* 16(4): 588–601.

Harvey, D. (2003) 'The Right to the City', *International Journal of Urban and Regional Research* 27(4): 939–41.

Healey, P. (2003) 'Collaborative Planning in Perspective', *Planning Theory* 2(2): 101–23.

Herbert, A.W. (1974) 'The Minority Administrator: Problems, Prospects, and Challenges', *Public Administration Review* 34(6): 556–63.

Hirschman, C. (2004) 'The Origins and Demise of the Concept of Race', *Population and Development Review* 30(3): 385–415.

Hoch, C. (1994) *What Planners Do: Power, Politics and Persuasion*. Chicago, IL: Planner's Press.

Innes, J. (1995) 'Planning Theory's Emerging Paradigm: Communicative Action and Interactive Practice', *Journal of Planning Education and Research* 14(4): 183–9.

Innes, J. (1996) 'Planning through Consensus Building: A New View of the Comprehensive Planning Ideal', *Journal of the American Planning Association* 62(4): 460–72.

Katznelson, J. (1997) 'Social Justice, Liberalism, and the City: Considerations on David Harvey, John Rawls, Karl Polanyi', in A. Merrifield and E. Swyngedouw (eds) *The Urbanization of Injustice*, pp. 45–64. New York: New York University Press.

Krumholz, N. and Clavel, P. (1994) *Reinventing Cities: Equity Planners Tell Their Stories*. Philadelphia, PA: Temple University Press.

Krumholz, N. and Forester, J. (1990) *Making Equity Planning Work: Leadership in the Public Sector*. Philadelphia, PA: Temple University Press.

Lim, H. (2006) 'Representative Bureaucracy: Rethinking Substantive Effects and Active Representation', *Public Administration Review* 66(2): 193–204.

Logan, J. and Molotch, H. (2007) *Urban Fortunes: The Political Economy of Place, 20th anniversary edn*. Berkeley, CA: University of California Press.

Lund, F. and Skinner, C. (2004) 'Integrating the Informal Economy in Urban Planning and Governance: A Case Study of the Process of Policy Development in Durban, South Africa', *International Development Planning Review* 26(4): 431–56.

Markusen, A. (2000) 'Planning as Craft and as Philosophy', in L. Rodwin and B. Sanyal (eds) *The Profession of City Planning*, pp. 261–74. Rutgers, NJ: Center for Urban Policy Research.

Marsh, J. (2004) 'Social Work in a Multicultural Society', *Social Work* 49(1): 5–6.

Meier, K. (1975) 'Representative Bureaucracy: An Empirical Analysis', *American Political Science Review* 69(2): 526–42.

Merrifield, A. (1997) 'Social Justice and Communities of Difference: A Snapshot from Liverpool', in A. Merrifield and E. Swyngedouw (eds) *The Urbanization of Injustice*, pp. 200–22. New York: New York University Press.

Merrifield, A. and Swyngedouw, E. (1997) 'Social Justice and the Urban Experience: An Introduction', in A. Merrifield and E. Swyngedouw (eds) *The Urbanization of Injustice*, pp. 1–15. New York: New York University Press.

Min, J. (2005) 'Cultural Competency: A Key to Effective Future Social Work with Racially and Ethnically Diverse Elders', *Families in Society* 86(3): 347–58.

Moses, Y. (2004) 'The Continuing Power of the Concept of "Race"', *Anthropology and Education Quarterly* 35(1): 146–8.

Murray, S., Terry, L., Washington, C. and Keller, L. (1994) 'The Role Demands and Dilemmas of Minority Public Administrators: The Herbert Thesis Revisited', *Public Administration Review* 54(5): 409–17.

Nunez-Smith, M., Curry, C., Bigby, B., Berg, D., Krumholz, H. and Bradley, E. (2007) 'Impact of Race on the Professional Lives of Physicians of African Descent', *Annals of Internal Medicine* 146(1): 45–52.

Orfield, M. and Luce, T. (2003) 'Michigan Metropatterns: A Regional Agenda for Community and Prosperity in Michigan', Michigan Area Research Corporation report, available online at: [http://www.metroresearch.org/maps/region_maps/michigan_1c.pdf], accessed 2007.

Ozler, B. (2007) 'Not Separate, Not Equal: Poverty and Inequality in Post-Apartheid South Africa', *Economic Development and Cultural Change* 55(3): 487–529.

Parnell, S. (2004) 'Building Developmental Local Government to Fight Poverty: Institutional Change in the City of Johannesburg', *International Development Planning Review* 26(4): 377–99.

Rahder, B. and Altilia, C. (2004) 'Where Is Feminism and Planning Going? Appropriation or Transformation?', *Planning Theory* 3(2): 106–16.

Sandercock, L. (2003) *Cosmopolis II: Mongrel Cities*. London: Continuum.

Schmitz, C., Stakeman, C. and Sisneros, J. (2001) 'Educating Professionals for Practice in a Multicultural Society: Understanding Oppression and Valuing Diversity', *Families in Society* 82(6): 612–22.

Soja, E. (1997) 'Margin/alia: Social Justice and the New Cultural Politics', in A. Merrifield and E. Swyngedouw (eds) *The Urbanization of Injustice*, pp. 180–99. New York: New York University Press.

Sowa, J. and Selden, S. (2003) 'Administrative Discretion and Active Representation: An Expansion of the Theory of Representative Bureaucracy', *Public Administration Review* 63(6): 700–10.

Stein, S. and Harper, T. (2005) 'Rawls's "Justice as Fairness": A Moral Basis for Contemporary Planning Theory', *Planning Theory* 4(2): 147–72.

Sugrue, T. (1996) *The Origins of the Urban Crisis: Race and Inequality in Postwar Detroit*. Princeton, NJ: Princeton University Press.

Thomas, J. (1997) *Redevelopment and Race: Planning a Finer City in Postwar Detroit*. Baltimore, MD: Johns Hopkins University Press.

Thomas, J. and Darnton, J. (2006) 'Social Diversity and Economic Development in the Metropolis', *Journal of Planning Literature* 21(2): 1–16.

Thomas, J. and Ritzdorf, M. (eds) (1997) *Urban Planning and the African American Community: In the Shadows*. Thousand Oaks, CA: SAGE.

United States Census Bureau (2008) Definitions of race in glossary online at: [http://factfinder.census.gov/home/en/epss/glossary_r.html], accessed 2008.

Watson, V. (2002) 'The Usefulness of Normative Planning Theories in the Context of Sub-Saharan Africa', *Planning Theory* 1(1): 27–52.

Watson, V. (2006) 'Deep Difference: Diversity, Planning and Ethics', *Planning Theory* 5(1): 31–50.

Wilkinson, D. and Butler, J. (2002) 'The Clinical Irrelevance and Scientific Invalidity of the "Minority" Notion: Deleting It from the Social Science Vocabulary', *Journal of Sociology and Social Welfare* 29(2): 21–34.

Wilson, W.J. (2003) 'Race, Class and Urban Poverty: A Rejoinder', *Ethnic and Racial Studies* 26(6): 1096–114.

Wise, L.R. and Tschirhart, M. (2000) 'Examining Empirical Evidence on Diversity Effects: How Useful Is Diversity Research for Public-sector Managers?', *Public Administration Review* 60(5): 386–94.

Yiftachel, O. (2000) 'Social Control, Urban Planning and Ethno-class Relations: Mizrahi Jews in Israel's "Development Towns"', *International Journal of Urban and Regional Research* 24(2): 418–38.

Yiftachel, O. (2006) 'Re-engaging Planning Theory? Towards "South-Eastern" Perspectives', *Planning Theory* 5(3): 211–22.

Yiftachel, O. and Ghanem, A. (2004) 'Understanding "Ethnocratic" Regimes: The Politics of Seizing Contested Territories', *Political Geography* 23: 647–76.

Young, I. (1990) *Justice and the Politics of Difference*. Princeton, NJ: Princeton University Press.

23

The Past, Present, and Future of Professional Ethics in Planning

Martin Wachs

Planning has historically been about shaping our shared built environment, but over time it has also come to be about forming our collective institutional and social environments. The meaning of plans is in their impacts on communities and in the actions that affect relationships among people within social and physical environments. Every collective or social decision is based in part on explicit or implied moral values, and it is inevitable that every act of planning is to some extent inspired by thought about morality. Programs addressing housing, air quality, mobility, and economic development all have complex technical content but are motivated ultimately by social concerns about achieving the right and the good.

As we look back over fifty years, we can see that analytic techniques have attained primacy in guiding academic curricula and planning practice. Gradually increasing status has been accorded to the professors and practitioners who developed sophisticated analytical tools and a commitment to utilitarian analysis. The field of economics has become increasingly quantitative and increasingly influential, and schools of public policy have emerged in many places, competing with planning programs for resources, the best students, and the most influential faculty members. In a number of universities, schools or departments of planning have been eliminated and replaced by programs in public policy. In other cases, urban planning departments have been moved from schools of architecture to schools of public policy. Even where this has not happened, curricula in planning programs have shifted. Classes in modeling, simulation techniques, and statistical

Original publication details: Wachs, Martin. 2013. "The Past, Present, and Future of Professional Ethics in Planning". In *Policy, Planning, and People: Promoting Justice in Urban Development*, edited by Naomi Carmon and Susan Fainstein. Philadelphia, PA: University of Pennsylvania Press. pp. 101–19. Reproduced with permission from University of Pennsylvania Press.

Readings in Planning Theory, Fourth Edition. Edited by Susan S. Fainstein and James DeFilippis.
Editorial material and organization © 2016 John Wiley & Sons, Ltd.
Published 2016 by John Wiley & Sons, Ltd.

methods have become more central, and design studios and courses dealing with legal structures and decision-making processes less so. This reflects current trends in planning as well; practice justifications for planning decisions are usually framed in terms of data analysis rather than contributions to just outcomes. Thus, both theory and practice reflect a commitment to a particular view of scholarship and action that is basically utilitarian – it gives increasing weight to the calculation of benefits, costs, and predicted consequences of policies rather than the morality or ethical content of the actions taken by those in positions of authority. This says something about current worldviews of ethics and morality.

On the Difficulty of Aligning Social Morality with Planning

In the current environment, the recognition that planning is inherently about social morality does little to help us prepare better plans, become better planners, or even be more ethical people. Planning is a collective or social undertaking and societies have much more difficulty reaching consensus about what is right or good than about which plans to adopt and on how to deploy resources to implement them. People and institutions often are able to reach consensus on a plan or policy precisely because plans can be made and actions affecting the environment can be taken even when those who plan or take action together retain different – even dramatically different – ethical or normative positions. To put it perhaps too simply, the acts of planners and policy-makers are widely recognized as being richly imbued with ethical and moral content whether or not they make the world better, and plans most often fail or succeed not because they promote particular moral imperatives but because they are silent, ambiguous, or accommodating to alternative ethical positions (Lindblom and Cohen 1979).

A second issue complicates the application of ethics to planning. Planning almost always is about shaping the future, and the future is always characterized by uncertainty. For most practical purposes, pervasive uncertainty reduces our ability to assess plans and policies on the basis of fundamental approaches to morality. The extent to which an action will be inherently supportive of worthy principles – or to which the consequences of plans or policies will be on balance beneficial – is almost always at least partly unknown. Plans must by definition be made in advance of the actions they are intended to guide. Moreover, even if we could predict the moral impact of an action in advance of planning it, the society in which the plan is to be adopted most likely would still not be able to agree on the inherent moral value of the projected outcome. Indeed, if society could agree on the material outcomes of a plan or policy and also agree that it places positive moral value on that outcome, planning would be merely a technical or administrative activity. Planning exists as a social function precisely because there is uncertainty about both ends and means, and the moral values associated with each. Those uncertainties are fundamental to our work, yet they also ensure that the ultimate morality of planners' actions is, to a great extent, always unknown (Thatcher 2004; Lempert et al. 2003).

Since the stated goal of this book is to "think social," we might be tempted to be guided by hedonistic philosophies that value the goodness of actions, plans, and policies in terms of their most direct impacts on the well-being of people (Frankena 1973). Yet, with accelerating concern for the long-term well-being of the earth, we could just as well make the case that anthropocentric views of what is right are ultimately shortsighted and incomplete (Beatley 1994). Again, the uncertainty that confronts us is greater than our ability to foresee. We can debate whether there is a moral imperative to protect our planet primarily because doing so eventually benefits people or whether we have a moral imperative to protect the earth even if doing so in the end reduces the well-being of people in relation to other elements of nature (Silva 2008). But, once again, the uncertainty that always confronts us far outweighs our ability to decide. We cannot comprehend all the longer-term implications for the earth of current plans and the impacts of earth-changing actions on the people who inhabit the planet, so our values must guide us even as we know our understanding of the choices is dominated by uncertainty.

Planners are not going to resolve by consensus fundamental disagreements based on differences in values. Planning is fundamentally about taking action to change the nature of the world around us in uncertain situations when value differences dominate public debates. We must, therefore, be prepared to take action and support policies cognizant of their moral dimensions while accepting that the most fundamental moral dimensions of our practice present pervasive contradictions as well as the uncertainties already noted. For example, we try to preserve the individual rights of all people and advance the well-being of the most needy and underrepresented. These values suggest different and often competing actions. Planners can and should focus always on the rightness or goodness of our activities, but we cannot let such concerns immobilize us. As professionals, we must try to arrive at positions that align our personal actions with our values. Yet, we must do so while understanding that the societies in which we work will often be unable to arrive at plans or policies clearly based on moral imperatives.

Professional Ethics, Codes, and Sanctions

Given the broad scope of these persistently unsolvable dilemmas, planners have historically – probably inevitably – separated the moral content of plans and programs from the ethical content of the daily professional practice of planning. Professional ethics are encapsulated in codes that have been adopted by planners in many countries with a degree of institutional formality. Our values, however, are imbued in us less by our profession than by our parents, by our teachers, and by the religious and cultural dimensions of the world. They are not primarily the result of planning education, not fundamentally affected by our professional roles and formal codes of ethics, not deeply affected by technical analysis of alternative courses of action (Wachs 1990).

Professional codes of ethics state ideals of the profession and seek to protect the public and planners themselves from improper actions on the part of individuals who might act improperly in the course of their work (Silva 2008; Kaufman 1990; Lawton 2003). Professional ethics do much less to help us decide whether the content of a plan, design, or program is or ever can be morally right.

In a classic paper that remains timely, even though it was published nearly forty years ago, Peter Marcuse (1976) reminded us that even the very motives for adopting professional codes of ethics themselves can be interpreted as less than morally pure. Knowing that planning was not widely regarded as a "profession," and seeking the self-aggrandizement that comes with professional recognition, planners decided that they needed codes of ethics in part because medicine, law, and accounting were widely recognized as professions and were distinguished by having such codes. In other words, adoption of professional codes was intended to show the world that planners are worthy of special recognition, status, and financial rewards because we are, after all, a "profession." Silva (2008) points out that professional planning codes of ethics have, in most countries, been introduced quite recently. While the Town Planning Institute in the United Kingdom adopted its first code in the 1930s, the organization now known as the American Institute of Certified Planners (AICP) did not adopt a code until 1971, which, perhaps surprisingly, was earlier than organizations in most other countries. Ethical codes have been published with a degree of pomp and enforced with a degree of solemnity. Yet, in many cases, their enforcement is quasi-legal in terms of rules of evidence and procedures.

In the many countries in which professional planners have adopted codes of ethics, these rules are intended to bind us together by having planners accept as a collective responsibility the prosecution of those among us who violate principles encapsulated in the codes. In exchange for professional status and its associated rewards, we agree to regulate and police ourselves to assure ethical behavior. Having made this "bargain," we hopefully benefit society by adhering to codes of professional behavior, but our goal in adopting the codes was not only for the protection of the societies we serve, but also for our own protection. Professional codes protect both planners and the public from a wide variety of inappropriate behaviors on the part of other planners such as lying, cheating, reliance on political influence, harassment and overt discrimination on the basis of personal characteristics, price gouging, and making improper claims when advertising qualifications or competing for commissions to do professional work. Fortunately, it is easier to recognize and regulate improper professional behavior than to recognize the essence of morality in the content of actual plans.

It is important that codes of ethics govern professional practice even as we advance the more philosophical position that great and lasting uncertainties in society limit our ability to know the ultimate moral value of a plan or policy. This is because adoption of a plan or policy inevitably redistributes wealth and other measures of well-being to a greater extent than it improves the world for all. Plans can bestow immediate benefits on some and costs on others, even when their long-term impacts are not fully understood and remain open to further analysis and debate. Populations are relocated, windfall profits accrue to owners of some land, and environmental "externalities" improve the lives of some and harm those of others. If planners have deliberately taken action to benefit some or harm others and their principal motives were to obtain direct financial or status rewards for themselves, their families, or their associates, such actions can do substantial harm, and we must collectively respond by sanctioning those responsible. If we do not act on the basis of relatively clear principles of professional ethics, we risk a loss of respect for planning on the part of society at large. The motivation to act collectively to sanction behavior defined as unethical could originate in a self-motivated concern for the loss of income, privilege, and status that might follow from a diminution of our professional standing. Yet most of us are honestly more concerned that a failure to prosecute ethical violations will diminish the public welfare.

Some planning codes of ethics also tip their hats to the deeper moral questions that are far more abstract and yet are intellectually more important to the definition of our field. For decades and through several revisions of its code, for example, the American Institute of Certified Planners (AICP) has included in its code hortatory language that is significant despite being ambiguous. The code asserts that "our primary obligation is to serve the public interest." The requirement that the public interest be served is addressed through a list of principles, including the following, among others:

a)   We shall always be conscious of the rights of others.
b)   We shall have special concern for the long-range consequences of present actions …
c)   We shall provide timely, adequate, clear, and accurate information on planning issues to all affected persons and to governmental decision makers.
d)   We shall give people the opportunity to have a meaningful impact on the development of plans and programs that may affect them. Participation should be broad enough to include those who lack formal organization or influence.
e)   We shall seek social justice by working to expand choice and opportunity for all persons, recognizing a special responsibility to plan for the needs of the disadvantaged and to promote racial and economic integration …
f)   We shall promote excellence of design and endeavor to conserve and preserve the integrity and heritage of the natural and built environment. (American Institute of Certified Planners 2010)

A small number of planners have been brought up on charges and dismissed at the recommendation of Ethics Committee after formal action of the elected Commission of the AICP. The AICP web site informs us that the number is well under a dozen per year over the last several years, and most of those accused of ethical violations have avoided prosecution by simply letting their memberships lapse and thus avoiding the prospect of being expelled. In some cases, the civil or criminal justice system more formally prosecuted individuals when their actions were considered illegal as well as unethical. There are comparable examples in Britain, Canada, Israel, Sweden, and elsewhere of planners punished for infractions including bribery and fraud. I could not find a single case of a planner who was dismissed from membership because he or she violated the public interest, failed to have special concern for the long-range consequences of planning actions, or failed to protect the integrity of the natural environment.

Part of each professional code of ethics is intended to be the basis for action in cases of clearly recognizable ethical failings by practicing planners. But it is also important that the codes are intended to be hortatory and perhaps inspirational. The goal of such provisions is to elevate the thought processes of practicing planners, urging them to consider the broader philosophical and moral dimensions of their work along with their immediate statutory and technical responsibilities. It is certainly possible for us to elevate our thought processes and clarify the ways personal commitments to policies reflect our values, but doing so is not equivalent to endowing particular policies, plans, or actions in the larger society with explicit ethical content.

Unquestionably, in the past fifty years, practicing planners have become increasingly aware of the existence of codes of ethics (Silva 2008), and concerns for ethical behavior by professional planners have become a more significant theme in the education and professional lives of planners (Barrett 2001). Professional societies require that ethics be addressed in the curricula of university programs, and practitioners in a number of countries are eligible to be "certified" to practice planning only after they have graduated from universities that include such courses and have taken professional entrance or certification examinations that include questions relating to ethical principles. Professional planning societies in a number of countries – most aggressively in the United States – include sessions on ethics in their annual conventions and encourage their constituent bodies or "chapters" in particular cities, states, or provinces to hold periodic "ethics awareness" sessions. They publish ethics columns in newsletters, magazines, and journals, and practicing planners have published a wide variety of books and pamphlets on themes relating to professional ethics (Barrett 2001). The AICP publishes "ethical advisory rulings" that elaborate on the precise language of the code by detailing circumstances in which planners can be accused of sexual harassment, gender discrimination, conflict of interest, and bias in forecasting.

Professional planning ethics awareness programs, training sessions, and publications demonstrate similarities to one another and taken together reveal some important characteristics of ethical considerations in the field of professional planning. Many of these are presented as scenarios or situations in which a planner or organization is confronted with a complex or difficult situation in which someone has made a proposal for a project or an offer to a planner that reveals multiple dimensions of consideration or can be interpreted in different ways. The planner or organization is portrayed as being in a situation taken to be an "ethical dilemma" in which several choices can be made, depending on alternative interpretations of available data, competing demands on loyalties of different sorts, and alternative readings of different ethical principles that comprise relevant professional codes. Readers and participants in workshops are invited to engage in dialogue or debate the alternatives, all to try to reach consensus on what adoption of a particular course of action (in some cases multiple courses of action) would imply about their understanding of the particular ethical dilemma. Many of the books, articles, and workshops feature a "discussion" of the ethical implications of these exemplary situations, while very often leaving conclusions to be drawn by the reader or the workshop participants (Barrett 2001). In other words, the ethical dilemmas to be considered are rarely clearly structured to give rise to a "right answer."

It is not surprising that discussions of practical professional ethics in planning are typified by the presentation of dilemmas that often confront practitioners and are amenable to discussions supportive of different and sometimes competing courses of action. It is easy to see how the principles in the AICP code could suggest alternative and competing actions that would be viewed as appropriate under particular circumstances. One clause requires that a planner be loyal to his or her employer, while another requires responsiveness to the public interest. Planners are expected to pursue protection of the natural environment while paying attention to the needs of diverse and underrepresented groups. One clause suggests that decisions be based upon data and analysis, while another suggests that due consideration be given to the long-run interrelatedness of policies and actions. Thus, while discussions of ethics inform and enrich thought processes of practitioners in hypothetical situations, those actually faced by planners are rarely so clear-cut that ethical implications of alternative actions are obvious or trivial.

Still, we have to hope and very much want to believe that practicing planners benefit from exposure to such dilemmas through their professional training and by reading continuing coverage of the ethical issues in planning in their professional newsletters, magazines, and journals. David Thatcher (2004) writes that this concept – use of analytical case studies and careful review of precedents – is an important way in which professions elucidate collective understandings of ethical principles. Case law is an extremely important element of legal scholarship, and in medicine individual cases are studied and compared in order to deepen professional understanding. In what he calls the "casuistical" approach to planning ethics, Thatcher argues that careful study of cases can also advance planners' understanding of more complex ethical principles. When confronted with genuine ethical dilemmas in their professional practice, we hope that planners mobilize and act somewhat more decisively based on this understanding and that the professional practice of planning is thereby enriched by continuous analysis of complex cases that have actually occurred.

Planners' Perceptions of Their Ethical Roles as Revealed in Research

Some evidence from empirical studies of planners' attitudes toward ethics may shed light on practicing planners' perceptions of ethics. In their landmark study of ethical attitudes and beliefs of a sample of roughly a hundred practicing planners, Elizabeth Howe and Jerome Kaufman found wide variation in the ways in which North American planners conceived of their roles in relation to the public interest (Howe 1994). They asked participants to respond to "scenarios" of the sort discussed above and developed a typology of planners based on their orientation to planning ethics. Practicing planners were considered "politicians" if their responses led to the conclusion that they defined their role as active intervention to promote ends related to their value-driven commitments. These planners wanted to make change and their commitments to change were ethically charged; they were activists who pursued "causes." They wanted, for example, to advance the well-being of the poor or to promote investments in environmental betterment. This group of planners sought to practice what Peter Marcuse (2011: chapter 56) refers to as the "critical social justice" model of planning. Planners were labeled "technicians" if they consistently conceived their role as carrying out analysis and developing plans in pursuit of goals that to a great extent had been identified by others. Technicians thought of themselves as relatively value neutral and of their work as consisting mostly of manipulating data, models, and methods. They developed plans in detail while following through on commitments and goals set for them by more senior policy-makers including elected officials.

A third group of planners, classified in Howe and Kaufman's typology as "hybrids," appear to me the most complex and intellectually interesting of the three groups. Hybrids were professional planners who possessed some of the traits of both of the first two groups. Sometimes they perceived their roles to be the promotion of particular ends that were purposely chosen, and sometimes their judgments were more consistent with the role of the technical expert, in that they were relatively value neutral and data driven, operating within bounds set by more senior planners and elected officials. To some extent hybrids were people who found that planning placed different requirements on practitioners depending upon circumstances.

Howe and Kaufman analyzed and interpreted the patterns of belief revealed by their data. They compared the groups on the basis of personal traits and whether they considered themselves to be primarily deontologist (i.e., rule-oriented), consequentialist, or utilitarian in their orientation. While most planners would support the notion of "serving the public good," they could legitimately differ with respect to what that obligation required of them. This reflected planners' "need to balance the various, sometimes competing, procedural obligations to provide independent professional advice, to be responsive to the public, and to be accountable to decision makers" (Howe 1994: 60). Marcuse (2009) points out that the field of planning has in particular situations seen tension between "subservient" and "activist" perspectives, but in the end the hybrids dominate the field, meaning that the two perspectives for all practical purposes coexist in planning organizations and even within individual professional planners.

Morality in Planning and Policymaking

Thus far, I have dealt with ethics of individual planners as they might encounter challenges when working on particular assignments or devising particular plans or policies. When examining planning ethics in this way, it is not difficult to arrive at the conclusion that our profession remains indecisive and clumsy about the meaning of ethics within its work despite many decades of observation and analysis. We agree that ethical behavior is a critical element helping define our profession and the roles of planners, but we agree only in abstract generalities as to what this requires us to do in particular situations.

Beyond particular issues faced in daily work assignments, any serious review of ethics in planning also must turn to broader challenges that face us collectively as a profession and even as a society. To be ethical and for planning as a profession to have virtue, we must address global environmental sustainability, the alleviation of deep and sustained inequality, and the provision of fundamental human rights to those who are deprived of them. Indeed this is a basic tenet that brings us together as planners: we believe our work involves technical application of tools of analysis, but we apply our analysis and methods in the service of moral and ethical commitments to the well-being of people and their environment. We must consider the ethics *of planning* as well as the ethics of individuals engaged *in planning*. Saying this in another way, consideration of ethics in planning requires us to address the collective morality of our professional work as well as the ethical dimensions of acts carried out by individual planners in particular situations.

But, if we cannot be confident about what constitutes ethical behavior in a narrowly defined situation affecting a particular individual or team, how can we possibly arrive at a consensus as to what makes for an ethical land use policy (Beatley 1994) or a plan for controlling the emission of greenhouse gases that is based on morality? What does it mean to agree that such questions have at their roots even more fundamental questions about the right and the good, while we struggle to understand what they require of us as planners?

The Ethics of Forecasting: An Illustration of Moral Dimensions of Collective Planning Practice

Forecasts are used regularly in the process of planning and designing a variety of public facilities. Plans for housing, economic development, schools, hospitals, power plants, water supply systems, and transportation facilities all begin with forecasts of population, economic activity, and demand for a service or product. Countries and international financial organizations require that the demand for and cost of public programs be forecast in advance and that the anticipated benefits versus the expected costs be shown to justify a particular project. In addition, many private sector organizations depend on such forecasts to evaluate whether to invest private capital in public works projects, including many privately financed bridges, tunnels, ports, and toll roads that are becoming more common as "public-private partnerships" proliferate around the world.

Most planning activities are collectively performed by individuals who work as part of the numerous teams that make up complex organizations and interact with teams in other organizations. A housing plan for a developing country, a comprehensive airport plan for an industrialized country, and an air pollution reduction program for a province or metropolitan area are but three examples showing that plans produced by interactive processes are crucial among complex organizations. Application of professional ethics in such planning processes has proved difficult or impossible. Professional codes of ethics are all written as though they are intended to apply to individual or personal behavior, while such planning processes involve many people and organizations, and in collective social undertakings it is difficult to assign responsibility to any one person or group. In addition, by their nature such plans are intended to guide actions in the future, and it is difficult to identify the ethical consequences of actions that have yet to be taken. When they are eventually taken, it may be decades since the planning has taken place and thus impossible to find the people who exercised critical judgments affecting the moral consequences of the plans.

The ethical dimension of large-scale public works planning has in recent years received increased attention as the result of recurrent, widely publicized dramatic cost overruns in public works projects. The Central Artery Project in Boston, Massachusetts, known popularly as the "Big Dig," cost more than five times the original forecast, and construction took three times as long. The "Chunnel" or rail tunnel under the English Channel also cost many times its original forecast cost and proved to be far less cost-efficient than its planners had asserted (Flyvbjerg et al. 2006). When bids were opened to construct the new structure to replace the earthquake-damaged eastern span of the San Francisco-Oakland Bay Bridge, the lowest bid from a contractor was roughly for five times the budget estimated by consultants only a few years earlier. Why does this happen and what can be done about it? Can societies learn from experience to make better forecasts of costs and benefits when undertaking major public investments? While some scholars believe this is a simple technical matter involving the tools and techniques of cost estimation and patronage forecasting, there is growing evidence that the gaps between forecasts and outcomes are the results of deliberate misrepresentation and thus amount to a collective failure of professional ethics (Flyvbjerg 2005).

Planning firms in many countries specialize in preparing forecasts for policy assessment, based in theory on the understanding that regional plans, large capital investments, and long-term commitments of public resources to operating and maintaining networks of facilities will certainly be controversial. Often, however, firms making the forecasts stand to benefit if a decision is made to proceed with the project. Contracts to perform preliminary engineering and design follow early planning exercises if a decision is made to proceed with implementation of the plan, but such funding opportunities do not eventuate if projects are not approved, so optimistic forecasts can be used to "generate business" (Wachs 1990).

Interest groups including industries that would be served by the projects, community residents, environmentalists, and local chambers of commerce surely pursue different objectives from the policymaking process. Some communities desperately want growth and the expansion of facilities to serve them; others organize in fierce opposition to certain plans for projects or to particular design characteristics that are proposed. If forecasts are honestly prepared, it should be possible to find compromises and decide on options that perform better than others with respect to widely accepted criteria such as cost effectiveness. Demand and cost forecasting is not expected to prevent or resolve political differences or debates. Rather, it is intended to inform and facilitate debate, contribute to rational decision-making, and facilitate compromises, especially in complex and politically charged situations. If this goal is to be served, the professional values of the forecasting community must be based on the principle that forecasts should influence political processes rather than vice versa. Forecasts are always subject to error and uncertainty, but they should be honestly prepared, data should not be falsified, and assumptions should be chosen on defensible and technical grounds, not because they favor certain outcomes over others.

A lively debate has emerged over the past twenty years about the extent to which demand and cost forecasts are objective or influenced by politics. In a well-known and controversial report, Don H. Pickrell (1992) argued that in the United States the majority of a sample of seven rail transit projects he studied were forecast to have ridership levels higher than actually achieved when the projects were built, and the vast majority experienced higher capital and operating costs than forecast at the time funds were committed to their construction. Thus, actual costs per rider turned out to be consistently much higher than the forecasts. Pickrell was judicious in explaining these observed divergences, but his work leaves the reader with the strong impression that they were the result of deliberate misrepresentation. Other authors, including Jonathan Richmond, argue that the outcomes of such forecasts are politically inspired, and that for reasons that can be explained in terms of planning consultants' behavior, forecasts deliberately reach beyond reasonable expectations. To put it very directly, it is widely believed that consultants prepare forecasts of the costs and future use of large public works projects that are falsified in order to justify expenditure of public funds on those projects. In the minds of many analysts, this is a major reason there have been enormous cost overruns in projects like the "Chunnel" and the "Big Dig" (Richmond 2005).

The late Robert Moses, public works czar of New York City, actually boasted that lying was his best strategy for justifying large public investments. Once construction was underway, he said, public officials had no option but to spend the funds to complete the projects. So lying to get big projects started was always an effective political strategy (Caro 1975: 218).

A group of European scholars led by Professor Bent Flyvbjerg added fuel to the fire that has characterized this debate. His team has studied hundreds of projects in many countries, including roads, highways, and bridges, built over as span of more than fifty years. They found that costs are far more likely to be underestimated than overestimated prior to construction, while actual patronage or facility use is far more likely to be overestimated than underestimated. If estimates were truly unbiased and deviations from actual patronage and cost were the result of honest errors, overestimation and underestimation should be roughly equally likely. Interestingly, this research team argues that the margins by which differences between forecast and actual patronage and cost have occurred have not declined in almost a century. This trend suggests that the performance of forecasting models and cost estimation techniques is not improving despite many efforts by sponsoring agencies to improve the mathematical models and computer algorithms in such forecasts. They also found that such differences were persistent across investment sectors and from country to country (Flyvbjerg et al. 2006).

There are different interpretations of these findings, so they are often the basis for suggesting alternative courses of action. On one hand, perhaps consistent with the technocratic planning tradition, such findings suggest the need for deeper and continuing research to isolate the specific causes of divergence between forecast and actual performance. This is made more difficult by the fact that funds are rarely made available by public bodies in any country to do follow-up analyses of the performance of forecasts after facilities have been built. Others have described the apparent "optimism bias" in forecasts as innocent and unsurprising. There is a sort of "selection bias" clearly at work. Projects are less likely to be built and plans less likely to be implemented, it is said, if their forecasts of cost are high and predictions of expected use are low, so it is not surprising that errors of the opposite sort dominate among projects and investment programs that have actually been built. While this might be true, others respond that optimism bias is hardly the result of innocence, and in some cases researchers have been able to document "strategic misrepresentation" in the form of "adjusted" model coefficients and "refined" parameters from one model run to another. Modelers have told stories of political influence and threats that they would lose their jobs unless they produced forecasts that supported certain outcomes (Wachs 1990). It is, of course, quite likely that some or part of the observed divergence between forecasts and outcomes is not intentional while some is quite deliberate. This illustrates how critical professional ethics can be in cases of collective action in the policy arena, yet I am not aware of a single example of the application of professional codes of ethics to an organization that has prepared an analytical forecast.

It is both necessary and possible to chart a responsible and ethical course even as debates rage in academia and the media as to the causes of this apparent problem. The Department for Transport in Great Britain has issued a "white paper" on procedures to control "optimism bias" in forecasting (Flyvbjerg et al. 2004). Requirements that assumptions be reported and explained by consultants, that critical "outside" peer review be performed of forecasts, and that standards be published for data use and assumptions in forecasting are all helpful. The Federal Transit Administration in the United States has gradually – over more than a decade – been developing a set of guidelines and procedures designed to ensure that "best practices" are routinely employed in forecasting for rail and bus transit project "new starts." These would, at the very least, allow egregious deviations from objectivity and good practice to be recognized and criticized.

The divergence between forecasts and performance of large public works projects is a complex multidimensional problem rich in ethical or moral content. It is likely to be illustrative of issues that arise in every aspect of planning and policy making. While it is possible to state with naive optimism that ethical planning requires that forecasts *should be* as free as possible from deliberate distortion or misrepresentation, it remains difficult to prescribe mechanisms that ensure this outcome. Heightened awareness of the extent of the problems and increased familiarity with the debates and the data do, however, contribute to the inclusion of these concerns in the development of planning and evaluation processes. Inclusion of case studies of these problems in graduate planning curricula also help to alert the next generation of practitioners to ethical challenges they are likely to face in practice. Documentation and dissemination of information about the problem itself can contribute to limiting the most egregious exaggerations. But recognizing the problem does not resolve it; rather, it demonstrates that the planning profession has little to bring to concerns for ethics in one of the most fundamental aspects of planning practice.

Applying Ethical Principles to Collective Actions by Planners

Nearly four decades ago, Brian Barry and Douglas Rae (1975) wrote that planning and policy-making should strive to meet several criteria that can help us understand our view of ethics and morality in planning and policy. They argued that effective policy should be judged in part on its *internal consistency*. By this they mean it is logical to come to a conclusion that a policy is effective or appropriate only if the criteria by which it can be judged are clearly understood and can be hierarchically ranked. In addition, they argued that standards by which policies are judged must be *interpretable* – a standard for judging a policy outcome must be understood by different parties to mean something they have in common. Furthermore, a policy or plan must lead to a *choice even in the face of risk or uncertainty*. Failure to make a decision or choice is to make one by default. This means that it is necessary to *aggregate or combine multiple criteria* to reach a judgment about any policy or plan. It also means that *short-term and long-term consequences must be weighed and balanced* against one another. In addition, while society must make decisions collectively, the decision-making process should make some logical connection between a collective social decision and a conception of *individual or personal welfare.*

Criteria such as these for judging the outcome of planning processes and utility of planned or implemented programs do appeal to our rationality as planners and help justify the growing focus on analytical methods and tools in planning thought. This is a trend I do not necessarily criticize; I have learned through application of more sophisticated methods of analysis that some conclusions I considered reasonably obvious have proved to be quite incorrect.

But it is also true that scholars including Charles W. Anderson (1979) and Alasdair MacIntyre (1977) almost immediately responded to such arguments by asserting that they were incomplete: while valid, they were mechanistic in that they did not include "principles" such as justice, freedom, and community which are critically important if planning is to serve us well in the pursuit of human ideals. To return to words I used earlier when referring to relatively formal codes of ethics in planning, they did not address "the public interest" nearly as well as they described the process of reaching a decision. While the public interest is extremely difficult to define, we must continue to explore the notion that it consists of something more than an aggregation of disparate individual interests.

In order to add moral or ethical content to plans and public policies, three more considerations are needed, not only for those in schools of planning and public policy but also for consideration of judgments about public policy when they are exercised by people whose backgrounds lie in any discipline. Planners should define their scholarship and our practice in terms of the following considerations.

First, plans and policies need to be attentive to the nature, role, and exercise of *authority*. This means that the person, group, or government reaching decisions and implementing them must be legitimate and justifiable. Conclusions and decisions must be arrived at through due process. Decisions that weigh benefits versus costs and emphasize efficiency may be appropriate, but perhaps not when undertaken by a decision-making body or individual who does not have legitimate authority to speak or decide on behalf of those for whom the decision is being made and who must live with the consequences of that decision.

Second, plans and public policies also need to be based on the concept of justice (see Fainstein and Fainstein in this volume). Justice is, of course, a difficult criterion to implement, but it deals ultimately with fairness and especially with regard for those who have less power and recourse to the control of resources than do others. Policies and plans must be attentive to distributive consequences and especially to impacts on those in disadvantaged positions.

Third, and finally, we also have an ethical obligation to attempt to use public resources with *efficiency*. Means and ends must be logically linked to achieve wise use of public resources, whether the resources under consideration are human or composed of land or capital.

The criteria outlined by Barry and Rae and the evolution of planning thought and public policy all seem to fit most easily with the search for efficiency. Modern approaches to planning, the application of tools and techniques of program and project evaluation, innovations in planning curricula described earlier, and distribution of rewards and prestige in the field all tend to reward improvements in efficiency rather than being concerned with the legitimacy of authority and obtaining justice. If, however, planning ethics is to guide the worldview of our scholarly and professional communities over the coming decades, it will be because we have the courage and commitment to assert that issues of authority and justice ought to have at least equal weight with efficiency. It is not clear that this can be achieved. Nevertheless, examination of current planning crises in particular countries as well as a whole set of international issues from sustainability to human rights suggests that this is the core issue facing planners today just as it was fifty years ago.

References

American Institute of Certified Planners. 2009. *Code of Ethics and Professional Conduct.* Adopted March 19, 2005; effective June 1, 2005; revised October 3, 2009. http://www.planning.org/ethics/ethicscode.htm, accessed May 2011.

Anderson, Charles W. 1979. The place of principles in policy analysis. *American Political Science Review* 73: 711–23.

Barrett, Carol D. 2001. *Everyday ethics for practicing planners.* Chicago, IL: American Planning Association.

Barry, Brian, and Douglas W. Rae. 1975. Political evaluation. In *Handbook of political science,* vol. 1, ed. Fred I. Greenstein and Nelson W. Polsby, 337–401. Reading, MA: Addison-Wesley.

Beatley, Timothy. 1994. *Ethical land use: Principles of policy and planning.* Baltimore, MD: Johns Hopkins University Press.

Caro, Robert. 1975. *The power broker: Robert Moses and the fall of New York.* New York: Vintage.

Flyvbjerg, Bent. 2005. Design by deception: The politics of megaproject approval. *Harvard Design Magazine* 22: 50–9.

Flyvbjerg, Bent, Nils Bruzelius, and Werner Rothengotter. 2006. *Megaprojects and risk: An anatomy of ambition.* Cambridge: Cambridge University Press.

Flyvbjerg, Bent, Carsten Glenting, and Anne Kvist Rønnest. 2004. *Procedures for dealing with optimism bias in transport planning: Guidance document*. London: British Department for Transport.

Frankena, William K. 1973. *Ethics*. 2nd ed. Englewood Cliffs, NJ: Prentice-Hall.

Howe, Elizabeth. 1994. *Acting on ethics in city planning*. New Brunswick, NJ: Center for Urban Policy Research, Rutgers University.

Kaufman, Jerome. 1990. American codes of planning ethics: Content, development, and after-effects. *Plan Canada* 30: 29–34.

Lawton, Alan. 2003. Developing and implementing codes of ethics. Presented at conference of European Group of Public Administration, Oeris.

Lempert, Robert J., Steven W. Popper, and Steven C. Bankes. 2003. *Shaping the next one hundred years: New methods for quantitative, long-term policy analysis*. Santa Monica, CA: RAND Pardee Center.

Lindblom, Charles E., and David K. Cohen. 1979. *Usable knowledge: Social science and social problem solving*. New Haven, CT: Yale University Press.

MacIntyre, Alisdair. 1977. Utilitarianism and cost-benefit analysis: An essay on the relevance of moral philosophy to bureaucratic theory. In *Values in the Electric Power Industry*, ed. Kenneth Sayre. South Bend, IN: Notre Dame University Press.

Marcuse, Peter. 1976. Professional ethics and beyond: Values in planning. *Journal of the American Institute of Planners* 42: 264–74.

Marcuse, Peter.. 2009. Social justice and power in planning history and theory. Paper submitted to Planning with People Workshop. http://p-p-workshop.net.technion.ac.il.

Marcuse, Peter. 2011. The three historic currents of city planning. In *The New Blackwell Companion to the City*, ed. Gary Bridge and Sophie Watson, 643–55. Oxford: Wiley-Blackwell.

Pickrell, Don H. 1992. A desire named streetcar: Fantasy and fact in rail transit planning. *Journal of the American Planning Association* 58: 158–76.

Rawls, John. 1971. *A theory of justice*. Cambridge, MA: Harvard University Press.

Richmond, Jonathan. 2005. *Transport of delight: The mythical conception of rail transit in Los Angeles*. Akron, OH: University of Akron Press.

Silva, Carlos Nunes. 2006. Urban planning and ethics. In *Encyclopedia of Public Administration and Public Policy*. 2nd edn, ed. Evan M. Berman. Boca Raton, FL: CRC Press.

Thatcher, David. 2004. The casuistical turn in planning ethics: Lessons learned from law and medicine. *Journal of Planning Education and Research* 23: 269–85.

Wachs, Martin. 1990. Ethics and advocacy in forecasting for public policy. *Business and Professional Ethics Journal* 9: 141–57.

24

Insurgent Planning
Situating Radical Planning in the Global South

Faranak Miraftab

This article revisits the notion of radical planning, which in the last two decades has placed major emphasis on inclusion and participation. The article articulates the notion of insurgent planning as those radical planning practices that respond to neoliberal specifics of dominance through inclusion. It highlights the hegemonic drive of neoliberal capitalism to stabilize state–citizen relations by implicating civil society in governance, and it stresses the importance to radical planning of the contested terrains of inclusion and dominance. Emerging struggles for citizenship in the global South, seasoned by the complexities of state–citizen relations within colonial and post-colonial regimes, offer an historicized view indispensable to counter-hegemonic planning practices. As post-welfare societies shrink the sphere of public responsibility, strengthening inequality and alienating the marginalized populations in the metropole, the insights to be gained from the standpoint of the global South have increasing relevance for radical planning in the era of global neoliberalsim.

The article contributes to two current conversations within planning scholarship. One discussion, addressing the implication of grassroots insurgent citizenship for planning, builds on the concept of insurgent citizenship first articulated by Holston (1995, 2008), and incorporated into planning discourse by Sandercock (1998a, 1998b), Friedmann (2002), and Miraftab (2006; Miraftab and Wills, 2005). The other conversation concerns the colonization of planning theory that tends to universalize the experience of the metropole (see Simone, 2004; Watson, 2002, 2006; Yiftachel, 2006).

Each of the four sections of the article centers on a key question for understanding the notion of insurgency and insurgent planning. Section one, 'Rethinking

Original publication details: Miraftab, Faranak. 2009. "Insurgent Planning: Situating Radical Planning in the Global South". In *Planning Theory*, 8 (1): 32–50. Reproduced with permission from SAGE.

Readings in Planning Theory, Fourth Edition. Edited by Susan S. Fainstein and James DeFilippis.
Editorial material and organization © 2016 John Wiley & Sons, Ltd.
Published 2016 by John Wiley & Sons, Ltd.

participation', interrogates the role of citizen participation in neoliberal governance. Section two, 'South Africa's Western Cape Anti-Eviction Campaign', examines how the insurgent citizenship practices move across both invited and invented spaces of action. Section three, 'Inclusion and citizenship', closely examines the relation between neoliberal inclusion and insurgent citizenship. Section four, 'Implications for radical planning', teases out the concrete implications of grassroots insurgency for radical planning practice and pedagogy in the neoliberal era. The final section of the article, 'Seeing from the South', identifies important insights drawn from the anti-colonial struggles of the South. This section stresses the importance of liberation for radical planning and lays out guiding principles for it. Insurgent planning practices are characterized as counter-hegemonic, transgressive and imaginative. They are counter-hegemonic in that they destabilize the normalized order of things; they transgress time and place by locating historical memory and transnational consciousness at the heart of their practices. They are imaginative in promoting the concept of a different world as being, Walter Rodney says, both possible and necessary.

1. Rethinking Participation

How does citizen participation articulate with neoliberal governance? Critical to a discussion of citizen participation in the neoliberal era is the recognition of how neoliberalism, as a strongly ideological project, relies on legitimation and citizens' perception of inclusion to achieve hegemonic power. As attested by the global trends in state decentralization, a structure of inclusive governance is critical to neoliberal governance. Whenever possible, hegemonic power is pursued through citizens' consent and perceptions of inclusion. Though reserving violence as an option, the neoliberal technology of rule does not rely primarily on coercion and military force, as did the expansionist mercantile capitalism of the colonial era (Rose, 1999). Neoliberalism should be understood as not simply a bundle of economic policies that extract surplus capital, but as a network of policies, ideologies, values and rationalities that work together to achieve capital's hegemonic power (Brown, 2003). For example, the water privatization policies that have spread around the world rest not just on the argument for economic efficiency, but also on a range of value-based discourses to justify the commodification of a basic need – water. A new definition of civic responsibility propounds fee-paying citizens, as the virtuous contrast to 'free-riders'. Freedom of choice, meaning citizens' choice among for-profit providers of basic services, is another value discourse used to legitimize the global spread of water privatization.

In examining the international development agencies' shift toward defining good governance in terms of citizen participation and local government development, a Gramscian reading is enlightening. Understanding hegemony as normalized relations, and counter-hegemonic effort as practices and forces that destabilize such relations illuminates the contested fields of power in neoliberal inclusive governance. Cox (2001) argues that to stabilize state relations with grassroots and informal townships, international development agencies such as the World Bank have since the 1980s employed a hegemonic move from above that adopted development of local states, community participation and participatory development as their institutional mandate. The evidence of this institutional move is the increasing number of state partnerships with CBOs and NGOs over the last two decades (Miraftab et al., 2008). A large body of literature has documented how such routinization of community participation depoliticizes communities' struggles and extends state control within the society. Drawing grassroots movements into NGOs maintains the status quo by stabilizing state–society relations.

Although in low-density democracies neoliberal governance legitimizes its dominance, by creating sanctioned spaces of participation, the process also creates a disjunction that insurgent movements are able to take advantage of. Symbolic inclusion does not necessarily entail material re-distribution. Counter-hegemonic movements may use such contradictory conditions to destabilize the neoliberal hegemonic order.

Cox (2001) likens hegemony to a pillow, which can shift to fit. But dominant power can make itself comfortable on the pillow of hegemony only if there is no firm social and political challenge to hegemony. Consider, for example, the processes of state decentralization. This global trend embodies the state's hegemonic strategy to contain grassroots struggles through local formal channels for citizen participation and claims. Such a hegemonic move, however, creates contradictions that can stimulate grassroots movements building deep democracies from below. Through persistent counter-hegemonic practices, these movements expose and upset the normalized relations of dominance. (In Gramscian terms, they launch a war of positions.)

Examples from Bolivia, Brazil and South Africa are among those that come to mind. Kohl and Farthing (2008), for example, document how in Bolivia the law mandated local participation in decisions through local governments, to stabilize the state's relations with indigenous communities. Inadvertently, however, as Kohl and Farthing document, that process strengthened indigenous rights movements. The result was a shift in the power balance that gave rise to the Eva Morales movement and the election of the country's first indigenous president.

Just as the sites producing power are multiple and shifting, so are the sites for counter-hegemonic movements. Analysis of squatter movements in the global South reveals how informal settlements as embodiment of citizens' insurgency also serve to stabilize the system. By virtue of their illegality, squatter settlements that provide affordable shelter for the majority poor are the state's opportunity for political manipulation in exchange for much needed services. Yet at the same time they breed counter-hegemonic and insurgent movements, mobilizing beyond the state's control and claiming their right to the city.

In his most recent book Holston (2008) conceptualizes Brazil's informal settlements as arenas of insurgent citizenship that both produce stability in state–citizen relations and destabilize them. Squatters' insurgent practices in Brazil use a universal citizenship and a rights-based discourse to destabilize the old formations of differentiated citizenship. Differentiated citizenship, Holston explains, offers equal rights to equal people and, correspondingly, unequal rights to unequal people – only the literate have the right to vote. Insurgent citizenship, on the other hand, uses Brazil's recently mandated universal citizenship – whereby all people have equal rights – to disrupt the normalized relations produced through differentiated citizenship. In informal settlements, which are the material expressions of poor citizens' insurgency, organized residents enacting their universal citizenship mobilize to claim their entitlement to the city and to urban livelihood. Holston emphasizes the entanglement of differentiated and insurgent citizenship. Just as the state and civil society are never clear-cut categories, neither are the relationships between the squatters and the state, or the citizenship debates that justify them.

The following section, on South Africa's Western Cape Anti-Eviction Campaign, grounds the discussion of how grassroots movements use the hegemonic system's political openings to make counter-hegemonic moves, and vice versa. Insurgent movements do not constrain themselves to the spaces for citizen participation sanctioned by the authorities (invited spaces); they invent new spaces or re-appropriate old ones where they can invoke their citizenship rights to further their counter-hegemonic interests. Fluidity characterizes insurgent citizenship practices: through the entanglement of inclusion and resistance they move across the invited and the invented spaces of citizenship.

2. South Africa's Western Cape Anti-Eviction Campaign

What are insurgent citizenship practices, and how do they move across invited and invented spaces of action?

The contradictory nature of globalized neoliberal capitalism is perhaps best exemplified by the experience of post-apartheid South Africa, where political liberation and economic liberalization occurred simultaneously in 1996. As South Africa's new constitution of 1996 extended political citizenship to all South Africans, the macro-economic policies of Growth Employment and Redistribution (GEAR), adopted the same year, stripped citizens of their substantive citizenship rights. The newly constituted South African citizens became also the fee-paying customers of public and private providers of basic services. This process, more latant in neoliberal, post-apartheid South Africa than in many other states, demonstrates how citizens can be excluded materially even though included symbolically in governance and decision-making.

Today, more than a decade after South Africa's new Constitution, the South African poor still endure forced removals from their homes, albeit for different reasons than under apartheid. In Cape Town, the earlier wave of evictions in the late 1990s was invoked for inability to pay for basic services and/or the failure to pay rent by public housing residents or arrears in mortgages to private banks.[1] The more recent wave of forced removals, which has received both greater media attention and collective resistance, has served the eradication/relocations of informal settlements along highway N2 connecting the international airport to the city – a plan that is important in relation to the city image and the 2010 soccer World Cup to be held in Cape Town.

The Western Cape Anti-Eviction Campaign or Western Cape AEC, a movement officially founded in early 2001, serves as an umbrella body for a number of community organizations, crisis committees, and resident groups that emerge in Cape Town's poor townships to resist such evictions and service cutoffs and demand their rights to shelter and basic services. As one Campaign activist put it, they defend their right to the city, to water and roofs over their heads because these are necessities, not privileges. Their struggle is against 'privatization of these basic rights, which leads to dehumanization of the poor and of those who cannot afford them' (Robert Wilcox, interview 2002). The Campaign is an agglomeration of discontented residents, civic organizers, retrenched workers, union activists and shop stewards and ex-members of the ruling tri-partite coalition (ANC, Communist Party, and Cosatu). It does not align itself with any political party and defends its independence from either of the parties, ANC or DA, that currently struggle for power in the Western Cape and Cape Town (for more on AEC practices, see Oldfield and Stokke, 2006).

The AEC groups also insist on their autonomy from NGOs, which they declare often control social movements through the power of their funds and legitimation. NGOs use their power of funding, according to a WCAEC press release, 'to speak for and essentially take over popular struggles in South Africa'. The Campaign seeks to insist on 'democratic horizontally organized networking forums and the right to speak for themselves' (WCAEC, 2007: 1). AEC has coalesced with several other grassroots movements, most closely in recent years with the KwaZulu Natal shack dwellers' movement Abahlali BaseMjondolo.

While some of the AEC strategies, such as rent boycotts and mass protest demonstrations, echo those used in the anti-apartheid struggle, others have emerged from the post-apartheid context and the newly gained universal citizenship. Movement members sit in boardrooms and use both the court and judicial systems and formal politics to pursue the citizenship rights granted by the new 1996 Constitution. But they combine that use of formal, legal strategies with informal survival livelihood practices and with oppositional practices. Their strategies range from informal negotiations with the agents of forced eviction to ignore or postpone its implementation, to capacity building and creating their own data about the plight of evicted or threatened families, to operating weekly soup kitchens to feed children, to defiant collective actions such as reconnection of disconnected services by so-called 'struggle plumbers and electricians' and relocation of evicted families back into their housing units, to mass mobilizations and protests, sit-ins, and land invasions – as well as the use of courts and legal claims. They use their constitutional rights and a rights-based discourse to achieve their just claim to shelter and livelihood, but have no illusions about limiting their struggle to the court procedures of claim-making or to the sanctioned governmental and nongovernmental channels. They use formal spaces when they are advantageous, and defy them when they prove unjust and limiting. When formal channels fail, they innovate alternative channels to assert their citizenship rights and achieve a just city.

A more recent example of Western Cape AEC's struggle against evictions in Delft and Joe Slove reveals the range of formal and informal legal and extra-legal practices they mobilize to wage their struggle for the rights to the city and to shelter.[2] The N2 Gateway Project is a joint endeavor by the national Department of Housing, the provincial government and the city of Cape Town to build some 25,000 units, and has been described by Housing Minister Lindiwe Sisulu as 'the biggest housing project ever undertaken by any Government' (Chance, 2008: 2). It is a project prioritized by the City of Cape Town and other spheres in light of the 2010 World Cup and its high visibility linking Cape Town International Airport with the City.

To make way for the N2 project, some 6,000 shack dwellers must be relocated from Joe Slovo to temporary houses being constructed in Delft, an area 40 km outside of Cape Town. But the shack dwellers living along and close to the highway do not want to be relocated to Delft, and have fiercely resisted relocation, knowing that they will not be able to afford and move back to their neighborhood once the project is completed. In the meantime the swelling numbers of backyard dwellers in over-crowded houses in Delft, some of whom had been on the housing waiting list for 30 years, took advantage of the almost completed temporary houses constructed in Delft for relocation of the Jo Slovo families. On 19 December 2007 Delft families in need of housing moved into these vacant units and claimed them as theirs, spray painting their names on the exterior walls. Hence continuing the N2 project then involved authorities' eviction of about 1,600 people from occupied units in Delft, and the forced removal of about 6,000 Joe Slovo shack dwellers to Delft – a process that at best can be described as 'a bureaucratic madness' (Manjuvu, 2008: 1).

In this process the Campaign has acted to bring together the struggles of both the Delft and the Joe Slovo poor communities against the forced removal processes. They waged a legal and extra-legal struggle against the process of forced removals imposed on the poor from Pretoria. With the help of the Campaign's Legal Coordinating Committee (LCC),[3] concerned residents in both communities filed a court case against the evictions. They claimed their constitutional rights to shelter and basic services (articles 26 and 27 of the 1996

Constitution of the Republic of South Africa), thus making a claim to substantive citizenship and to the city.

The Campaign's use of formal legal procedures, however, was innovative, in that they turned the bureaucratic legal procedure into a spectacle (field notes, Ken Salo 2008). Instead of going one by one to the court to register their claims for housing, the 1,600 Delft residents threatened by eviction and their supporters massed in front of the courthouse. Unable to handle such a large crowd inside the building, the court's clerical staff brought out tables and chairs to the street and conducted the bureaucratic procedure of filing and stamping the paperwork for the long line of plaintiffs on the street. Singing anti-apartheid protest songs on the steps of the courthouse, they made their presence and demand visible and strong. In other words, as they took their housing struggle to the court, they also brought the courts and its inherent limitations out to the street.[4]

Following almost two months of daily demonstrations and public protest, on 5 February 2008 Cape High Court ruled in favor of the evictions and granted an order to the provincial government and Thubelisha homes (the sub-contracted developer) to evict backyarders in Delft. The eviction of 1600 Delft residents was pursued on 19 February 2007 with the help of police, private security and dog units that went door to door with a brutality that wounded more than 20 people including a three-year-old child, gaining much media attention. The evicted residents were then left on the pavement, and their belongings – furniture, bedding, clothes – packed onto trucks by the eviction team and taken to the local police precinct (Chance, 2008).

In the days immediately after the evictions, half of these evicted families relocated to temporary tents offered by the DA politicians (the current ruling party in Cape Town). The other half, affiliates of AEC, protecting their autonomy from political party manipulation, refused the tents and stayed on the pavement across from the N2 temporary houses on the Symphony Road. To date, three months since their eviction, the Symphony Road pavement dwellers have not moved. They have set up shacks on the sidewalk and displayed their solidarity and community building. They have set up a community crèche; they run a 'pavement camp' for children on school holiday, including soccer and netball clinics; they collect children for discussions on life and life-skills; and they have organized a Symphony Way Fashion Show, with the help of a newly created Delft-Symphony Children's Committee (Delft-Symphony Anti-Eviction Campaign, 2008).

Elsewhere (Miraftab, 2006), reflecting on my earlier ethnographic work on the Campaign practices in Cape Town during the 2001–6 period, I conceptualize their actions in terms of *invented* and *invited* spaces of citizenship. 'Invited'[5] spaces are defined as those grassroots actions and their allied non-governmental organizations that are legitimized by donors and government interventions and aim to cope with systems of hardship. 'Invented' spaces are defined as those collective actions by the poor that directly confront the authorities and challenge the status quo. The two sorts of spaces stand in a mutually constituted, interacting relationship, not a binary one. They are not mutually exclusive, nor is either necessarily affiliated with a fixed set of individuals or groups or with a particular kind of civil society.

Insurgent citizenship practices, as observed in the case of the AEC, are fluid, moving across invited and invented spaces of participation. Their activities engage both the formal and informal arenas of politics, and aim to combine the struggles for redistribution and for recognition (echoing Nancy Fraser's theorizations, 1997). While some AEC actions such as 'struggle plumbers' reconnecting services and resistance to evictions directly pursue redistribution, other AEC practices aim for recognition of poor residents' plight, their histories, their struggles and their plea for justice. In the example of their recent struggle recounted above, the insurgent grassroots use, but do not view as sufficient, the legal path to make their citizenship claim to shelter and basic services. They also literally and metaphorically bring to the public eye the inadequacy of the judicial system, by bringing its bureaucratic system to the street. By staying on the pavements they display their continued plight and hence the contradictory and limited nature of their formal citizenship in the post-apartheid era. Most importantly, their sidewalk presence provokes a collective memory of apartheid's ugly legacy and its brutal forced removals. Doing so expresses and produces an historical consciousness of their oppression.

The institutions of hegemonic power – the media, the state, and the international development agencies, however, frame the complex, diverse, and fluid range of grassroots citizenship practices as a binary relation. They celebrate grassroots and their collective actions selectively (World Bank, 1998), applauding those that help the poor cope with inequality, while criminalizing the others. Planning practices that celebrate inclusive planning through citizens' participation, yet remain uncritical of the complexities of inclusion and resistance in the contemporary neoliberal era, are complicit in the binary misconception of civil society and public action. Section four discusses this challenge to planning. First, however, in section three, I offer an overview of the notion of inclusion that was exemplified in detail above, placed in its historicized context.

3. Inclusion and Citizenship

What is the relation between neoliberal inclusion and insurgent citizenship?

Holston and Appadurai (1999) argue that citizenship should be understood as a drama that varies with its conditions. British indirect rule in its colonies through native collaborators is perhaps an early example of domination through inclusion. During the colonial era, selective inclusion of the natives and tribal chiefs is well known to have been a colonial approach to stabilize relations of dominance in the colonies. However, as Mamdani (1996) explains, in the British white settler colonies such inclusion did not necessarily mean citizenship. To the bifurcated state, only the white settlers were citizens; natives were mere subjects. Under French colonialism, however, the drama of citizenship differed from British colonialism in that French colonized subjects could become citizens if they showed the ability to 'civilize' to the status of a Frenchman [*sic*] (Fanon, 1986).

For the authoritarian post-'independence' state, a connoisseur of state-centered modernist planning, development projects shaped the drama of modern citizenship. To stabilize their rule among the newly declared citizens, post-colonial states tried to construct modern citizenship through a combination of development, coercion and corruption. This model of citizenship, however, reveals internal contradictions between form and substance: an entitlement to political and social rights does not necessarily guarantee substantive rights to livelihood. Feminist scholarship has made an important contribution to understanding the fallacy of the liberal drama of citizenship, demonstrating that despite its formalistic assumption that citizens constitute a single, all-rights-bearing entity with equal rights and obligations, the entitlements and obligations in actuality are unequal being differentiated according to gender, race, and ethnicity (Gouws, 2005; Lister, 1997).

Thus the contemporary neoliberal era's universal formal citizenship has brought selective material inclusion. People may gain more access to state institutions through local governments and the possibility of participation, as well as social and political inclusion in institutions of the state, but that does not necessarily mean their substantive inclusion. As people's political rights expand, their access to livelihood resources may simultaneously erode. The disjunction can be seen in the examples of political liberation in post-socialist Eastern Europe and post-apartheid South Africa, where socioeconomic inequalities have intensified as citizens' political and civil rights have expanded.

It is this disjunction between formal and substantive inclusion that motivates the contemporary practices of insurgent citizenship (Sandercock, 1998b). In this neoliberal moment tangible citizenship does not arrive through the state's legislative institutions. It rather grows under the skin of the city, that is as an invisible city, through the insurgent practices of marginalized communities – be it disenfranchised immigrants; ethnicized, racialized and gendered minorities of the industrialized world; or the squatter citizens of the global South.

I argue that in this neoliberal moment the hypocrisy of modern citizenship can be most clearly observed in the global South. In the liberal democracies of the global North, citizens experience the pretense of neoliberal capitalism through the shrinking of the public sphere and some infringement on civil liberties. In the global South, however, for example in Brazil and South Africa, new found universal citizenship rights are starkly contradicted by the material inroads on citizens' lives made by neoliberal capitalism. Their political citizenship and abstract formal rights have expanded, yet simultaneously their economic exploitation and the abdication of public responsibility for basic services continue, and their livelihood erodes. In societies that have emerged from a colonized legacy, 'citizens have gained rights they cannot eat!'

4. Implication for Radical Planning

What does insurgency mean for the practice and pedagogy of radical planning?

Legitimation is central to hegemonic relations of power. So far we have discussed how neoliberalism seeks legitimation through governance that promotes political inclusion, but avoids translating it into redistributive equity. Rather, neoliberalism's structures of inclusion and participation contain citizens' collective action into sanctioned spaces of invited citizenship – for example, formal, decentralized state channels or a legitimated NGO sector that functions to replace social movements. This strategy is often complemented by a bifurcated conceptualization of civil society as authentic versus a criminalized ultra-left.

In such a context, radical planning practices should be insurgent. To promote social transformation, insurgent planning has to disrupt the attempts of neoliberal governance to stabilize oppressive relationships through inclusion. Insurgent planning, then, constitutes radical planning practices that challenge the inequitable specifics of neoliberal governance operating through inclusion. Insurgent planning should read through the bluff of neoliberal governance's promise of inclusive citizenship, just as anti-colonial/anti-apartheid struggles 'saw through the bluff of a "modern" civilization in South Africa' (Ahluwalia and Zegeye, 2001: 463). Overcoming the bifurcated construction of civil society, planners should not confine their practices to only the sanctioned spaces of participation – be it through NGOs and NGO-ized community groups, or through formal structures of local officials. Insurgent planning recognizes, supports and promotes not only the coping mechanisms of the grassroots exercised in invited spaces of citizenship, but also the oppositional practices of the grassroots as they innovate their own terms of engagement.

Skeptics may ask if insurgent planning is not a contradiction in terms. In pursuing the notion, I note that the discussion of insurgent planning is framed in terms of its relevance for 'planning', not for 'the planner'. It refers to a set of practices, not to a specific type of actor (insurgent planner). The focus is on a value-based definition of practices we can recognize as insurgent.

Insurgent planning is not an exclusive subjectivity, just as planning practices in general are not confined to professionally trained planners. Indeed, planning is a contested field of interacting activities by multiple actors. That recognition rests on decades of radical planning scholarship debunking the myth of planning as a prerogative of professionals who act in isolation from other spheres of action (Fainstein, 2000; Friedmann, 1973; Leavitt, 2004; Sandercock, 1998a, 1998b). In the 1960s, advocacy planning arose in opposition to an elitist definition of rational planning as activities undertaken by all-knowing actors best able to decide on their clients' interests (Davidoff, 2000[1965]). From that first step there ensued, in the 1980s and 1990s, strides through equity planning, participatory planning, and communicative planning (Forester, 1989; Healey, 1999; Innes, 2004; Krumholz, 1994). Nevertheless, those critical perspectives remained within the bounds of the conventional wisdom that conceptualized planners as professionals who stand outside the society, though reaching out to citizens for inclusion, perhaps through redistribution but at least communication.

A more recent movement in radical planning scholarship has taken steps to open the category of planning to beyond its professionalized borders. The movement responds not only to the prominence of civil society organizations in developing communities, cities and regions, but also to a new generation of planners who are not necessarily employed in traditional public or private consulting organizations (see contributions to Douglas and Friedmann, 1998). This planning scholarship demonstrates how de facto community and urban developments take place through everyday practices of squatter citizens, determined poor women, illegal immigrants and other disfranchised and marginalized communities (Beard, 2003; Friedmann, 1988; Irazábel, 2008; Miraftab, 2005; Sandercock, 1998b). Through their development of houses and infrastructure such actors also build deep democracies (Appadurai, 2001).

That material reality is widely observable in the global South: more than two-thirds of Third World cities are developed through the spontaneous, unplanned activities that Holston (2008) conceptualizes as insurgent urbanization. Eighty-five percent of Third World urban residents 'occupy property illegally' (Winter, 2003: 471, cited in Davis, 2004: 6). Moreover, in the labor market activities of many Third World economies, formal employment channels have only a minor role. Worldwide, the informal economy has grown as a percentage of non-agricultural employment, by the 1990s reaching 43.4 percent in North Africa, 74.8 percent in sub-Saharan Africa, 56.9 percent in Latin America and 63 percent in Asia (Beneria, 2003). These figures make clear that only a limited share of the spatial and economical development in Third World cities occurs through formal structures and professional planning.

In the contemporary global context, then, planning academics' much discussed anxiety about creating a clear definition and professional border for planning practice seems out of place. The majority of marginalized people take into their own hands the challenges of housing, neighborhood and urban development, establishing shelter and earning livelihoods outside formal decision structures and 'professionalized planning'. The protagonists of urban development have thus shifted from planning agencies to community-based informal processes; from professional planners and formal planning to grass-roots activists and strategies. But this reality, more sharply demonstrated through the deep informality of Third World cities and their uneven development processes, should not be assumed as unique. In the global North, for example in the heartland of the United States, where my other research project takes me, much of the rural towns' development takes place by immigrant newcomers and through local commissions and committees that are not staffed or overseen by professional planning practitioners (Miraftab and McConnell, 2008). It is retired teachers, businessmen and women and elected officials that constitute the committees that make the development planning decisions of these small towns. These realities expand the definition of planning. Insurgent planning builds on an expanded definition of radical planning in the ways just described. But insurgent planning has traveled an important further path by revealing how inclusive planning, with its emphasis on citizen participation and civil society partnership, has often become the accomplice of neoliberal governance. Insurgent planning reveals how the interests of global capitalism and the corporate economy misappropriate collective action to depoliticize progressive planning and transform its actors to 'radicals you can take home to mother'.

That revelation pushes radical planning scholarship to historicize the understanding of inclusion and participation. Given that the central task of radical planning is the 'mediation of theory and practice in social transformation', according to its original definition by Freidmann (1987: 391), what insurgent planning does is to rework radical planning to reflect the selective definition and celebration of civil society and citizen participation and the challenges it poses to socially transformative planning practices in the specific context of neoliberal global capitalism. In 'planning in the time of empire', Roy (2006) problematizes the particularities of this mediation and its doubleness for planning practices 'in the belly of the beast', that is in the US, when empire's global hegemony involves selective material inclusions through renewal, reconstruction and redevelopment. Insurgent planning practices shaped by and responding to the historical struggle between selective inclusion and dominance seek to re-appropriate spaces of collective action for liberation.

The practices of insurgent planning acknowledge what the hegemonic drive of neoliberal capitalism tries to obscure: the potent oppositional and transformative practices that citizens and marginalized populations invent outside global capitalism's definition of inclusion. Insurgent planning practices strip 'democracy' and 'inclusion' of their formalistic elements, recognizing the importance to counter-hegemonic movements of choosing their own ways of constituting their collectivities and their participation (Gills, 2001).

To emphasize those values is not, however, to naively celebrate any and all disrupting and oppositional actions, but rather to be guided by an historicized understanding. Critical planning must rely on contextualizing planning – that is, recognizing the power struggle within which it is practised. To contextualize insurgent planning and informal politics is to recognize a broad arena that cannot be conflated into a single category. For example, informal politics have sometimes been co-opted or corrupted into criminal elements, whether by the state or by despotic elites, and in that form have served the interest of the status quo though clearly outside formal institutions. Hence, grassroots mobilizations and initiatives outside the formal arena of politics ('community activism') should be carefully characterized according to their historical origins, their political and cultural roots, and their agendas. The insurgent movement and oppositional practices described in this article, as historicized, reveal their political and cultural roots to be in political formations that resisted the inequalities produced by colonialism, apartheid – and now, neoliberalism.

The importance of historical consciousness is reflected in the much-cited rhetorical question posed by Marx: 'Are bees architects?' (cited in Mitchell, 2002: 45). For Marx, historical consciousness and the ability to imagine one's creation distinguish architects from bees. For this discussion of insurgent planning, the distinction is drawn not in terms of who acts, but in terms of the actions themselves. A range of actors may participate in insurgent planning practices: community activists, mothers, professional planners, school teachers, city councilors, the unemployed, retired residents, etc. Whoever the actors, what they do is identifiable as insurgent planning if it is purposeful actions that aim to disrupt domineering relationships of oppressors to the oppressed, and to destabilize such a status quo through consciousness of the past and imagination of an alternative future. In conclusion, the following section elaborates on the guiding principles of insurgent planning practices.

5. Seeing from the South: Principles for Insurgent Practices

What insights are gained by seeing radical planning through the anti-colonial struggle of the South? What are the principles of insurgent planning practices?

Earlier in this article I historicized the notion of citizenship and how both the colonial struggle for dominance and the anti-colonial resistance have often been mediated through inclusion. To elaborate here on principles of insurgent planning, I return to the insights gained from the global South and its anticolonial struggles.

The writings of African intellectuals teach us that liberation of the colonies could happen only through 'decolonizing the mind': upsetting the internalized inferiority of the colonized and the superiority of the colonizer (Fanon, 1986 [1967]). The black consciousness movement teaches us that 'the only way to bring about a defeat of black feelings of inferiority was to look anew at the black person to discover what it was that lent him/her so easily to denigrate himself/herself' (Ahluwalia and Zegeye, 2001: 460). Liberation needs a new consciousness, one that is recovered from the colonial moral injury, the profound alienation that believed development of the colony could happen only 'upon condition of rejecting itself' and wholesale importing of non-African scenarios and solutions (Davidson, 1992: 199).

For planning in this era a similar process means decolonizing planners' imagination by questioning the assumption that every plan and policy must insist on modernization. This mental decolonization requires recognizing how the ideal of the Western city has been deployed historically in the colonial era, and is now deployed in the neoliberal era to advance a certain paradigm of development and capital accumulation. A collective of developers, planners, architects and politicians and a powerful industry of marketing and image-making have promoted the Western city as an object of desire (Perera, 1999). As Edward Said (1994) revealed the material power of orientalist imagery in literary text and art to further colonial domination, so insurgent planning scholarship exposes the role of Western urban imaginary in enforcing exclusionary cities and citizenship. In that regard, planning that one might view as analogous to Orientalism honors the Western ideals and imaginations of the city and urban development as its norm, and represents cities of the South that have not fit into that Western model as failures. Often they have been constructed as the 'elsewhere', which is systematically demonized or made 'invisible'. The work by urban scholars like De Boeck and Pilssart (2004), Mbembe (2004), Mbembe and Nuttall (2004), Mobogunje (1990) and Simone (2004), for example, critiques how African cities are presented as cases of extreme chaos, lawlessness, complete incomprehensibility, irrelevance; as cases of failed urbanization – in short, as something that was supposed to be something else.

The persistence of Western planning ideals in our post/neocolonial, neoliberal times suppresses the subaltern conceptualization of cities and of planning. Insurgent planning scholarship aims at decolonizing the planning imagination by taking a fresh look at subaltern cities to understand them by their own rules of the game and values rather than by the planning prescriptions and fantasies of the West. An 'upside-down' look at the world of development allows that perhaps the deep informality of third world cities is not their failure, but as Simone (2004) suggests, a triumphant sign of their success in resisting the Western models of planning and urban development. I assert the need for a new consciousness that liberates planning imaginations, echoing Steve Biko, the father of the black consciousness movement in South Africa, who insisted that the liberation of the colonies could happen only through a new consciousness looking at the colonial subject (1978).

If colonialism and colonial power seek to suppress memory, anti-colonial struggles teach us to locate politicized historical memory at the very heart of liberating practices (Werbner, 1998). Historicizing the notion of inclusion from the vantage point of the ex-colonies allows us to see how the participation of the oppressed in their own conditions of oppression functions to normalize those oppressive relations, in the post-colony as it had in the colony. That helps us to understand the political career of citizen participation, how the inferiority and superiority of oppressed and oppressor may well continue in an 'inclusive' planning process.

Such historicized consciousness is a constitutive principle of insurgent planning. While neoliberal capitalism promotes a collective social amnesia, an important task of counter-hegemonic, insurgent planning is to stimulate historical collective memories and historicize the problems arising from the actions and inactions of authorities – what Sandercock calls insurgent historiographies (1998a). For example, AEC's showcasing of sidewalk dwellers purposefully provokes the memory of apartheid's forced removals. Exposing the historical parallels between current evictions and apartheid removals helps the AEC fight against South Africa's neoliberal policies of displacing less affluent urban citizens for the sake of gentrification projects. Similarly, insurgent planning scholarship values the oral histories of marginalized people as both a significant knowledge form and an emancipatory methodology. Insurgent planning scholarship and practice locates memory at its center.

In *Prospect of Cities* (2002), Freidmann lists the normative principles of insurgent planning that concerns marginalized and oppressed groups: offer critical analysis and understanding of the structural forces that marginalize and oppress people; understand that a problem must be attacked simultaneously at multiple scales; aim for both material and political rights; and engage state and state-like formations. This list concurs with aspects of the guiding principles of insurgent planning practices as discussed in this article and synthesized below: transgression, counter-hegemony and imagination.

Insurgent planning is transgressive in time, place, and action

It transgresses false dichotomies, by public actions spanning formal/informal arenas of politics and invited/invented spaces of citizenship practice. It transgresses national boundaries by building transnational solidarities of marginalized people. It transgresses time bounds by seeking a historicized consciousness and promoting historical memory of present experiences. Being transgressive, insurgent planning is not Eurocentric in its theorization. It rather recognizes how the global core and the peripheries North and South might exist within each other.

Insurgent planning is counter-hegemonic

It destabilizes normalized relations of dominance and insists on citizens' right to dissent, to rebel and to determine their own terms of engagement and participation. Insurgent planning seizes advantage from the contradictory nature of neoliberal capitalism, exposing the rift between inclusion and redistribution. It understands the world of such contradictions contrapuntally, looking not only at how systems of oppression are conceptualized and exerted, but also at how they are contested.

Insurgent planning is imaginative

It recovers idealism for a just society – the imagination that the neoliberal illusion of TINA, There Is No Alternative, has suppressed. Insurgent planning recognizes the symbolic value of insurgent citizenship activities that offer hope from which to work towards alternatives.

Above all, insurgent planning holds stubbornly to its ideal of justice.

Notes

1. One calculation in 2001 carried out by the Municipal Services Project and the Human Science Research Council (HSRC) marked nearly two million people evicted since 1994 (see McDonald, 2002).

2. My knowledge of AEC practices relies on earlier ethnographic field work conducted in Cape Town during the 2001–6 period (2001, 2003, 2004 and 2006). The more recent struggle of 2007–8 around the N2 project draws on information gathered from the WCAEC website and more specifically from the reports by Chance (2008), Delft Symphony Anti-Eviction Campaign (2008), Manjuvu (2008), WCAE (2007); and field notes by Ken Salo as the events unfolded December 2007 to February 2008.

3. In 2001, the Campaign formed a Legal Coordinating Committee (LCC) who undertook legal training to be able to represent families facing eviction or service disconnection in magistrate's court. This, the Campaign declares, is to use the courts to maximize citizens' benefit, be it by overturning and delaying eviction and disconnection orders, by frustrating those processes, or simply by documenting citizens' struggle through the formal system (Oldfield and Stokke, 2006).

4. I am grateful to Ken Salo for his insightful commentaries and discussions with me highlighting this point.

5. I borrow the term 'invited spaces of citizenship' from Andrea Cornwall (2002: 50) to develop the notions of invited and invented spaces of citizenship.

References

Ahluwalia, P. and Zegeye, A. (2001) 'Frantz Fanon and Steve Biko: Towards Liberation', *Social Identities* 7(3): 455–69.

Appadurai, A. (2001) 'Deep Democracy: Urban Governability and the Horizon of Politics', *Environment and Urbanization* 13(2): 23–43.

Beard, V. (2003) 'Learning Radical Planning: The Power of Collective Action', *Planning Theory* 2(1): 13–35.

Beneria, L. (2003) *Gender, Development and Globalization: Economics as if People Mattered*. New York: Routledge.

Biko, S. (1978) *Black Consciousness in South Africa*. New York: Random House.

Brown, W. (2003) 'Neoliberalism and the End of Liberal Democracy', *Theory and Event* 7(1).

Chance, K. (2008) 'Housing and Evictions at the N2 Gateway Project in Delft', a report for Abahlali baseMjondolo, available online at: [http://www.abahlali.org/], accessed 8 May 2008.

Cornwall, A. (2002) 'Locating Citizen Participation', *IDS Bulletin* 33(2): 49–58.

Cox, R. (2001) 'Gramsci, Hegemony and International Relations: An Essay in Method', in B. Gills (ed.) *Globalization and the Politics of Resistance*, pp. 35–47. New York: Palgrave.

Davidoff, P. (2000[1965]) 'Advocacy and Pluralism in Planning', in R.T. Legates and F. Stout (eds) *The City Reader*, pp. 423–33. London: Routledge.

Davidson, B. (1992) *The Black Man's Burden: Africa and the Curse of the Nation-State*. New York: Times Books.

Davis, M. (2004) 'Planet of Slums', *New Left Review* 26, March/April.

De Boeck, F. and Pilssart, M.-F. (2004) *Kinshasa: Tales of the Invisible City*. Ghent: Ludion; Tervuren: Musée Royal de l'Afrique Centrale.

Delft-Symphony Anti-Eviction Campaign (2008) 'Solidarity: Delft-Symphony Pavement Dwellers Building a New World – One Child at a Time', available online at: [http://www.abahlali.org/node/3467], submitted 14 April 2008, accessed 21 May 2008.

Douglas, M. and Friedmann, J. (eds) (1998) *Cities and Citizens*. New York: Wiley.

Fainstein, S. (2000) 'New Directions in Planning Theory', *Urban Affairs Review* 35(4): 451–78.

Fanon, F. (1986) *Black Skin, White Mask*. London: Pluto Press.

Forester, J. (1989) *Planning in the Face of Power*. Berkeley, CA: University of California Press.

Fraser, N. (1997) *Justice Interruptus: Critical Reflections of the Post-Socialist Conditions*. New York: Routledge.

Friedmann, J. (1973) *Retracking America: A Theory of Transactive Planning*. New York: Anchor Press.

Friedmann, J. (1987) *Planning in the Public Domain: From Knowledge to Action*. Princeton, NJ: Princeton University Press.

Freidmann, J. (1988) *Life Space and Economic Space: Essays in Third World Planning*. New Brunswick, NJ: Transaction Books.

Friedmann, J. (2002) *The Prospect of Cities*. Minneapolis/London: University of Minnesota Press.

Gills, B. (2001) 'Introduction: Globalization and the Politics of Resistance', in B. Gills (ed.) *Globalization and the Politics of Resistance*, pp. 3–11. New York: Palgrave.

Gouws, A. (2005) *(Un)Thinking Citizenship: Feminist Debates in Contemporary South Africa*. Burlington, VA: Ashgate.

Healey, P. (1999) 'Institutionalist Analysis, Communicative Planning and Shaping Places', *Journal of Planning Education and Research* 19: 111–21.

Holston, J. (1995) 'Spaces of Insurgent Citizenship', *Planning Theory* 13: 35–52.

Holston, J. (2008) *Insurgent Citizenship: Disjunctions of Democracy and Modernity in Brazil*. Princeton, NJ: Princeton University Press.

Holston, J. and Appadurai, A. (1999) 'Cities and Citizenship', in J. Holston and A. Appadurai (eds) *Cities and Citizenship*, pp. 1–18. Durham, NC: Duke University Press.

Innes, J. (2004) 'Consensus Building: Clarification for the Critics', *Planning Theory* 3(1): 5–20.

Irazábal, C. (2008) *Ordinary Place/Extraordinary Events: Democracy Citizenship, and Public Space in Latin America*. New York: Routledge.

Kohl, B. and Farthing, L. (2008) 'New Spaces, New Contests: Appropriating Decentralization for Political Change in Bolivia', in V. Beard, F. Miraftab and C. Silver (eds) *Planning and Decentralization: Contested Spaces for Public Action in the Global South*, pp. 69–85. New York: Routledge.

Krumholz, N. (1994) 'Dilemmas in Equity Planning: A Personal Memoir', *Planning Theory* 10(11): 45–56.

Leavitt, J. (1994) 'Planning in the Age of Rebellion: Guidelines to Activist Research and Applied Planning', *Planning Theory* 10(11): 111–29.

Lister, R. (1997) 'Citizenship: Towards a Feminist Synthesis', *Feminist Review* 57: 28–48.

Mamdani, M. (1996) *Citizens and Subjects: Contemporary Africa and the Legacy of Late Colonialism*. Princeton, NJ: Princeton University Press.

Manjavu, M. (2008) 'Joe Slovo's Housing Struggle', 11 March, available online at: [http://www.zcommunications.org/blog/view/1457], accessed 21 May 2008.

McDonald, D. (2002) 'The Theory and Practice of Cost Recovery in South Africa', in D. McDonald and J. Pape (eds) *Cost Recovery and the Crisis of Service Delivery in South Africa*. London: Zed Books.

Mbembe, A. (2004) 'Aesthetics of Superfluity', *Public Culture* 16(3): 373–406.

Mbembe, A. and Nuttall, S. (2004) 'Writing the World from an African Metropolis', *Public Culture* 16(3): 347–72.

Miraftab, F. (2005) 'Informalizing the Means of Reproduction: The Case of Waste Collection Services in Cape Town, South Africa', in L. Beneria and N. Kudva (eds) *Rethinking Informalization: Precarious Jobs, Poverty and Social Protection*, pp. 148–62. Ithaca, NY: Cornell University e-Publishing Program.

Miraftab, F. (2006) 'Feminist Praxis, Citizenship and Informal Politics: Reflections on South Africa's Anti-Eviction Campaign', *International Feminist Journal of Politics* 8(2): 194–218.

Miraftab, F. and McConnell, E.D. (2008) 'Multiculturalizing Rural Towns: Insights for Inclusive Planning', *International Planning Studies* 13(4): 343–59.

Miraftab, F. and Wills, S. (2005) 'Insurgency and Spaces of Active Citizenship: The Story of Western Cape Anti-Eviction Campaign in South Africa', *Journal of Planning Education and Research* 25(2): 200–17.

Miraftab, F., Silver, C. and Beard, V.A. (2008) 'Situating Contested Notions of Decentralized Planning in the Global South', in V. Beard, F. Miraftab and C. Silver (eds) *Planning and Decentralization: Contested Spaces for Public Action in the Global South*, pp. 1–18. New York: Routledge.

Mitchell, T. (2002) *Rule of Experts: Egypt, Techno-Politics, Modernity*. Berkeley, CA: University of California Press.

Mobogunje, A. (1990) 'Urban Planning and the Post-Colonial State in Africa: A Research Overview', *African Studies Review* 33(2): 121–203.

Oldfield, S. and Stokke, K. (2006) 'Building Unity in Diversity: Social Movement Activistm in the Western Cape Anti-Eviction Campaign', in A. Habib, I. Valodia and R. Ballard (eds) *Globalisation, Marginalisation and New Social Movements*, pp. 25–49. Durban: University of KwaZulu Natal Press.

Perera, N. (1999) *Decolonizing Ceylon: Colonialism, Nationalism and the Politics of Space in Sri Lanka*. Oxford: Oxford University Press.

Rose, N. (1999) *Power of Freedom: Reframing Political Thought*. Cambridge: Cambridge University Press.

Roy, A. (2006) 'Praxis in the Time of Empire', *Planning Theory* 5(1): 7–29.

Said, E. (1994) *Culture and Imperialism*. New York: First Vantage Books.

Sandercock, L. (1998a) 'Framing Insurgent Historiographies for Planning', in L. Sandercock (ed.) *Making the Invisible Visible: A Multicultural Planning History*, pp. 1–33. Berkeley, CA: University of California Press.

Sandercock, L. (1998b) *Towards Cosmopolis*. New York: Wiley.

Simone, A. (2004) *For the City Yet to Come: Changing African Life in Four Cities*. Durham, NC: Duke University Press.

Watson, V. (2002) 'The Usefulness of Normative Planning Theories in the Context of Sub-Saharan Africa', *Planning Theory* 1(1): 27–52.

Watson, V. (2006) 'Deep Difference: Diversity Planning and Ethics', *Planning Theory* 5(1): 31–50.

WCAEC (2007) 'African Movements Continue their Fights against NGO Authoritarianism', available online at: [http://www.wombles.org.uk/article2007121403.php], accessed January 2008.

Werbner, R. (1998) 'Beyond Oblivion: Confronting Memory Crisis', in R. Werbner (ed.) *Memory and the Postcolony: African Anthropology and the Critique of Power*, pp. 1–17. London: Zed books.

Winter, K. (2003) 'Illegal Settlements and the Impact of Titling Programmes', *Harvard Law Review* 44(2): 471.

World Bank (1998) *Social Capital: The Missing Link?* Washington, DC: The World Bank.

Yiftachel, O. (2006) 'Re-engaging Planning Theory? Towards "South-Eastern" Perspectives', *Planning Theory* 5(3): 211–22.

Part V

Planning in a Globalized World

Introduction

Planning theory barely existed as a scholarly endeavor when John Friedmann first made his mark on the field. His subsequent steady output has proved highly influential in setting the agenda for the subject, and he has consistently scrutinized planning in thought and action as it manifested itself throughout the world rather than restricting his efforts to North America and Europe. One of the controversies within planning theory has centered on whether theories based on Western experience apply to recently urbanizing places with large informal settlements. These, once called "third world" cities, have most recently been labeled cities of the "global south," despite their existing as much to the north of the equator as to the

Readings in Planning Theory, Fourth Edition. Edited by Susan S. Fainstein and James DeFilippis.
Editorial material and organization © 2016 John Wiley & Sons, Ltd.
Published 2016 by John Wiley & Sons, Ltd.

south of it. Regardless of the nomenclature, the concern of the authors in this section is with the large informal settlements of cities in poor countries.

Friedmann's own chapter (Chapter 25) starts out with a critique of typical approaches to transforming rapidly growing metropolises. He sees their leadership as unconcerned with the effects on ordinary people as they engage in competition to attract mobile capital and direct their resources to the construction of megaprojects. As a consequence of this lack of attention to everyday life, cities become formless, non-places. He calls the demolition of meaningful places violence and asks for the re-creation of place, which he defines "as a small, three-dimensional urban space that is cherished by the people who inhabit it." Echoing Miraftab's endorsement of insurgent planning (Chapter 24, this volume), Friedmann sees making places as a collective undertaking of inhabitants able to demand incremental changes that accumulate to neighborhood improvement. In many respects the processes occurring in rapidly growing cities mimic the approaches of Baron Haussmann in nineteenth-century Paris and of urban renewal and highway authorities in twentieth-century America. The difference, perhaps, is in the scale of urban slums. As noted above, one feature of urbanization in the global south is the spread of informality. Although the Western world also experienced squatter settlements, the absolute number of people involved and land affected do not compare to the situation in many parts of the developing world.

In Chapter 26 Ananya Roy considers the different interpretations in the literature of the vast, unplanned areas of cities characterized by lack of legal tenure, unregulated construction practices, poor sanitation, and overcrowding. She notes that two dichotomous views exist: (1) such areas are chaotic, crime-ridden, and dependent; (2) they are entrepreneurial, embody a hidden order, and harbor effective political advocacy. She contends that Western theory dichotomizes society into formal and informal sectors when, in fact, the two are strongly connected, and informality is itself a product of state power. She notes that many different types of domicile and of economic production and a range of income levels exist within the category of the informal. She points to the success of the Right to the City movement in Brazil that resulted in a statute establishing collective rights to land and housing as well as to governance. She contrasts this with the failure to stop the displacement of the urban poor occurring in Indian cities. At the same time, however, social movements rooted in the areas under threat within Indian cities are challenging the move to regularize areas classified as slums.

In her claim that planners are implicated in the production of informality, Roy is calling on planners to appreciate the complexity of social systems and the extent to which unequal distribution of privilege not physical form produces bad living conditions. Planning that is sensitive to the arbitrariness of what is called formal and informal would respond by regularizing informal settlements rather than extirpating them. In facilitating the right to the city for all urban dwellers, planners would be returning increases in land values to residents of poor areas rather than exploiting them.

Writing from the point of view of a South African, Vanessa Watson (Chapter 27, this volume) also takes the position that Western theory leads planners astray.

She portrays the institutionalized planning systems within the global south as inadequate and insufficiently oriented toward the needs of the poor. Despite the vigorous critiques of master planning and single-use zoning that emerged in the West (see, for example, Chapters 3, 4 and 15, in this volume), these modernist frameworks persist in cities of the global south, where they serve the interests of local elites. At the same time informalization is increasing, and the monopoly of the state over regulation is shrinking as various individuals and groups jockey for position, wealth, and authority. Thus, planners cannot assume a structure able to command obedience to its dictates even while they are expected to impose order and efficiency. Furthermore, the spread of neoliberalism has meant the submission of all spheres of action to market rationality. Planners have to operate in a contradictory environment where they must both remove blockages to the workings of the market and somehow assist the urban poor, who become ever more numerous. An emphasis on communication and arriving at consensus evades dealing with serious differences within communities and the structure of inequality that produces them.

In the concluding chapter of this volume, Gavin Shatkin attacks analyses that fail to distinguish among cities in the developing world. Referring to the popularity of the global cities analysis, he criticizes it for overlooking important divergences among very large cities. In particular, he contends that the emphasis within the global cities literature on command and control functions overemphasizes their importance in non-Western megacities. Crucial to Shatkin's analysis and to the potential of planning is the role of human agency in affecting the outcomes of urban change. Like Watson he notes the influence of Western planning models in the global south, but he names the cultural norms and social patterns of national and local actors as key factors in producing variation. On the one hand a commitment to direct state intervention in development (i.e., "the developmental state") remains a powerful force in much of the world. On the other, even as privatization of planning functions has become a universal trend, it leaves open the possibility of government and community-based interventions, and its effects vary markedly from place to place.

Thus, this book of theoretical readings ends up by showing the limits of generalization. Although theorizing requires generalization, paradoxically one overarching concept is that the local matters and that generalization should not imply uniformity. In other words general arguments about processes and outcomes should not mean that similar processes in different contexts will produce the same results. The argument for recognizing variation calls into question the current model of "best practices," with its easy strategy of taking what works in one place and simply transferring it to another. Rather it demands careful dissection of the relationship between process and outcome under disparate conditions, of the connection of global and local at different stages of historical development, and of the effect of planning strategies within diverse constellations of power and institutional structure. It is therefore a plea to avoid determinism and, for planners, a call to seize opportunities for the betterment of places and especially for improvement in the lives of the disadvantaged.

25

Place and Place-Making in Cities
A Global Perspective

John Friedmann

Introduction

For the world as a whole, the twenty-first century will be seen as the concluding chapter of a three-centuries-long saga, the urban transition. Beginning in the final decades of eighteenth century Europe, when urban population stood at less than 10% globally (Bairoch, 1993, p. 143), current projections suggest a rise to 70% urban by 2050, a percentage that will surely increase still further toward the end of this century. The global dimension of the urban, however, can be said to begin only with the post-World War II era, when the urban population in the less developed regions of the world increased by nearly eight times, rising from 310 million in 1950 to 2.4 billion in 2007, or from 18% to 44% globally (United Nations, 2009, table 1). Around the same time, and for the first time in history, the global rural/urban split, marked in purely demographic terms, shifted towards a majority urban.

Although smaller cities account for more than half the urban growth, the vast assemblages of the urban in certain regions, many of them in Asia, are of critical importance. The Population Division of the United Nations estimates that by 2025, the world will have 447 of these so-called mega-cities of ten or more million residents, among them such behemoths as Tokyo, Mumbai, Delhi, Dhaka, São Paulo, Mexico City, and Calcutta, each with more than twenty million residents

Original publication details: Friedmann, John. 2010. "Place and Place-Making in Cities: A Global Perspective". In *Planning Theory & Practice*, 11(2): 149–165. Used with permission from Taylor & Francis Group.

Readings in Planning Theory, Fourth Edition. Edited by Susan S. Fainstein and James DeFilippis. Editorial material and organization © 2016 John Wiley & Sons, Ltd. Published 2016 by John Wiley & Sons, Ltd.

(United Nations, 2009, p. 19, Table 4). All of this is happening, even as national states appear to be losing control over urban policy, having devolved substantial powers for managing urban growth to local governments (Brenner, 2004).

The result has been intense competition among cities in their hunger for global capital for infrastructure, housing, and production. Along with this, the private sphere has expanded at the expense of the public, as governments, eager to capture the attention of potential investors, turn entrepreneurial themselves, hoping their cities will reach world-class status through public–private partnerships essentially geared to profits. Many local governments attempt to "brand" their cities, as if cities were a commodity for sale, promoting extravagant projects to catch the attention of the world such as Dubai's Burj Khalifa super-skyscraper that rises 825 m into the air. In this frenzy of excess, the needs of ordinary people and the neighborhoods they inhabit have been forgotten. It is an old, perhaps universal story; in the current eagerness to build glass-sheathed office towers, airports, opera houses, and spectacular sport facilities for the newly rich, this forgetfulness is shrugged off as the inevitable "cost of progress."

My intention in this paper runs counter to this narrative: it is to recall something that is, in essence, a moral imperative. As will be shown, the recent literature on place and place-making is extensive, as a range of disciplines have engaged the topic. But there are relatively few treatments written for and by planners, and even fewer that look at the sprawling metropolises of Asia where urbanization is rampant.[1] This is the lacuna I hope, at least in part, to fill.

The following is a discursive essay rather than an empirically based article. It is a personal view based on observation, extensive reading, and long reflection. There are two loosely related parts. The first is an attempt to formulate an operational definition of place along with some criteria by which places can be identified. This is followed by a commentary about planners and place-making, with examples taken from Japan, China, and Canada. Amidst widespread fascination with mega-projects and the huge assemblages of the urban, I want to enter a plea for the small spaces of the city and their importance both for the people who inhabit them and for the planners who, in the developing but rapidly urbanizing world, are paying them far too little attention.

A Placeless Scenario

The literature on the city is filled with references to desolate placelessness and a yearning for place, for some solid connection to the earth, to the palpable physicality of cities and the everyday need for social contact. As sprawling suburbs move steadily outwards towards the horizon, the very concept of "city" has become diluted and vague. For those of us who live in the urban, it is a labyrinthine network of power and disempowerment.[2] A few years ago I called the forces of contemporary life that steadily eat away at our sense of being anywhere at all, erasing our sense of place, "entropic" (Friedmann, 2002, p. 13).[3] I argued that, applied to the human habitat, entropy can be read as a measure of disorder. Unless countervailing flows of negentropic energy – human energy, the product of mind and body – can overcome the constant dissipation of energy which is everywhere around us, random events will become increasingly common, life forms will cease to flourish (Schroedinger, 1992 [1945]).

Here is a story by French Nobel Prize winner J.-M. G. Le Clézio (2002). "Ariadne" tells of a brutal gang rape by a motorcycle gang in one of the desolate public housing projects (*banlieues*) that "warehouse" immigrant workers on the edge of Paris and other large French cities, such as Marseille.[4] His opening description of this *quartier* captures the sense of desolation and lack of human connection that give rise to random acts of violence by young men who, surplus to society, prowl the streets and corridors of these projects in search of anything that will at least temporarily release their anger at a system that excludes them.

> On the banks of the dry riverbed stands the high-rise project. It is a city in its own right, with scores of apartment buildings – great gray concrete cliffs standing upright on the level asphalt grounds, surrounded by a sweeping landscape of rubble hills, highways, bridges, the river's dusty shingle bed, and the incinerator plant trailing its acrid heavy cloud over the valley. Here, it's quite a distance to the sea, quite a distance to the town, quite a distance to freedom, quite a distance from simple fresh air on account of the smoke from the incinerator plant, and quite a distance from human contact, for the project looks like an abandoned town. Perhaps there really is no one here – no one in the tall gray buildings with thousands of rectangular windows, no one in the stairwells, in the elevators, and still no one in the great parking lots where the cars are parked. Perhaps all the doors and windows have been bricked up, blinded, and no one can escape from within the walls, the apartments, the basements. And yet aren't the people moving around between the great gray walls – the men, the women, the children, even the dogs occasionally – rather like shadowless ghosts, disembodied, intangible, blank-eyed beings lost in lifeless space? And they can never meet one another. As if they had no names.
>
> From time to time, a shadow slips by, fleeing between the white walls. Sometimes one can get a glimpse of the sky, despite the haze, despite the heavy cloud drifting down from the chimney of the incinerator plant in the west. You see airplanes too, having torn free of the clouds for an instant, drawing long cottony filaments behind their shimmering wings.
>
> But there are no birds here, no flies, no grasshoppers. Now and then one finds a stray ladybug on one of the big cement parking lots. It walks along the ground, then tries to escape, flying heavily over in the direction of the planters filled with parched earth, where a scorched geranium stands. (p. 67)

You will argue that "Ariadne" is an extreme case. There are many working-class suburbs where such outbreaks of random violence are unlikely, where life conforms by and large to the customary rules of civility. Extremes should not be taken as an accurate depiction of urban life as we know it. From a global perspective, however, this story illustrates where we seem to be headed, as in many parts of the world ever larger numbers of young people are, in effect, declared redundant and so are pushed to the margins of society. In rich countries such as France, they are "warehoused" in heavily policed suburban projects. In poor countries, such as in Africa, they disappear into the vast irregular settlements surrounding the small central cores that are the natural habitat of business elites and government. Simone calls them "spectral cities" (Simone, 2004, chapter 3, pp. 92–117 *passim*).[5] As their hopes of finding sustaining work are dwindling, they succumb to the yawning marginality of their lives, seeking by whatever means on offer – drugs, physical violence, criminality, terrorism, genocidal rage – to drown out awareness of their actual conditions of life. It is a growing malaise caused by the ceaseless entropic forces that are at work in many of the world's large cities.

My answer to this problem – and here I speak as a planner – is to reclaim the bits of the human habitat that are given us as residents in the urban, and to reconnect our lives with the lives of others in ways that are inherently meaningful. I began with the horror of placelessness. In the remaining pages I will attempt to show how the recovery of places, specifically the small spaces of the urban, can begin to release constructive energies of negative entropy, taking back what societal forces geared to maximizing profits and narrowly defined efficiencies have taken from us. I believe that we can re-humanize the urban by focusing on and reviving urban neighborhoods.

A First Approach: What Is a Place?

It is difficult to take a word such as place, which is in everyday use and applied in all sorts of ways, and turn it into a concept that has a precise and operational meaning. The academic literature on place (and the related idea of place making) is growing rapidly across a spectrum of the human sciences and the professions, including geography, social anthropology, landscape architecture, architecture, environmental psychology, planning, and philosophy.[6] Much of this literature as well as many items not included in this foreshortened bibliography are critically examined in Cresswell's *Place: A Short Introduction* (2004). Cresswell is a geographer, and his view of places is, so to speak, from the outside in: an outside observer's gaze on places, hierarchically arranged, from single room to planet Earth.

In contradistinction to the multiple scales of the geographer, the scale I propose to adopt here is exclusively the local, and the perspective on place will be from the inside out, that is, as place is experienced and sometimes transformed by those who dwell in the urban. Before venturing a more formal definition, however, I would like to provide a sketch of such an intimate place of social encounter in order to make the idea of place more palpable and real. Here is a word painting of a temple ground on the periphery of Taipei, Taiwan's capital city.

This is a story about Shan-Hsia, a country town located in what some would call the peri-urban area of Greater Taipei where city folk meet country folk. Actually, Shan-Hsia is only about 25 km from the center of the capital city. We could also say, of course, that there is no longer any "peri-urban" in Taiwan, since urban growth sprawls uninterruptedly from north to south along the west coast of this island nation, backed by a chain of mountains some of which rise to over 2,000 m.

I visited Shan-Hsia on a Saturday morning in the Spring of 2006. As we approached, we passed a number of massive apartment complexes which anywhere else would have been an architect's nightmare but here were loudly hawked to customers eager to experience what they imagined to be the heaven of modern living.

Arriving, we parked our car, no small feat in itself in a street choked with vehicles and people. Hundreds of motor scooters, like frenzied mosquitoes, darted in and out of the traffic. You had to be nimble to avoid being knocked over.

It was market day in Shan-Hsia, and as we wended our way to Tsu-Sze Temple, which was our goal, we walked past dozens of market stands crowding the sidewalk, with eager customers jostling each other to buy fresh fish, meats, vegetables, and fruits spread out before them in splendid profusion.

Tsu-Sze Temple is famous throughout the region. Originally constructed in 1769, it was destroyed and rebuilt three times. The latest rebuilding started in 1947 and is still incomplete. The temple is dedicated to Chen Tsao-Yin, a native of Henan Province on the mainland who, together with some of his people, had migrated to a place called Chuan Chu in Fujian Province on the coast. His image was enshrined in the temple, and the local folks in Chuan Chu showed respect for his exploits and regarded him as their patron saint. When the original settlers from the district arrived from the mainland in the eighteenth century, they built the temple in memory of their saint.

Today, it is wedged into a small corner of the town, fronting a broad but shallow river. A small irregularly shaped square containing some shade trees was bustling with people. Children raced each other playing tag, the ubiquitous mosquito scooters had temporarily slowed to participate in the scene, a smell of incense was in the air, and adults in small groups were chatting with each other while a sound truck hovered in a corner of the square, encouraging people to vote for a Mr. Wu, the local candidate for city council.

Looking around me, I thought for a moment I was magically transposed from the twenty-first century into a scene of the famous scroll painting, "Spring on the River" depicting a northern Song Dynasty cityscape alive with people going about their daily affairs. Here life washed in and out of the temple, as worshippers sent their silent prayers to the saints on incense smoke, including a female divinity and her heavenly entourage, pleading for health or money or a husband or a good grade on the next exam, in a fusion of the secular and sacred. People gawked and talked, bowed down and prayed, wandered about (as we did), admiring the intricate, delicate carvings with which every square inch of the temple, including its 122 columns, was adorned.

A pedestrian bridge spanned the river. We ascended by some steps to get a better view. The bridge was lined on both sides with booths, most of which sold some sort of food: freshly fried pancakes prepared under the watchful eyes of waiting customers, a variety of aromatic soups, delicious noodles and dumplings, iced fruit and vegetable juices, and sinful sweets. Nine out of ten stands were cookeries with mostly middle-aged ladies stirring, ladling, cutting, frying, and selling their handiwork for ridiculously low prices to hungry customers. On the far end of the bridge, a stage had been set up, and people were beginning to sit down for a show. Meanwhile, a loudspeaker blared what I took to be a Taiwanese version of hard rock. I decided a rural festival was under way, because a long table had been cordoned off on which dozens of competing trays laden with the pride of local farmers, a large but to me unfamiliar root vegetable used in making soup stock, were on display. Presumably, the winning tray would receive a blue ribbon prize. (Friedmann, 2007, pp. 357–8)

Granted this story is still a view from outside, but it draws attention to a center of neighborhood life whose participants, most but perhaps not all of whom are neighbors, are drawn from a larger area with which this temple ground and its immediate surrounds stands in a close, reciprocal relation, thus constituting a distinctive neighborhood, the heart of a territorial place. Cresswell's observations are apposite here:

> The work of Seamon, Pred, Thrift, deCerteau and others show us how place is constituted through reiterative social practice – place is made and remade on a daily basis. Place provides a template for practice – an unstable stage for performance. Thinking of place as performed and practiced can help us think of place in radically open and non-essentialized ways where place is constantly struggled over and reimagined in practical ways. … Place provides the conditions of possibility for creative social practice. Place in this sense becomes an event rather than a secure ontological place rooted in notions of the authentic. Place as an event is marked by openness and change rather than boundedness and permanence. (Cresswell, 2004, p. 39)

Urban places, according to Cresswell, are embedded in the built environment but come into being through "reiterative social practices" such as the activities recorded in the neighborhood centered on Tsu-Sze Temple in the town of Shan-Hsia, Taiwan. Some of them are daily, such as prayer and worship, others obey an annual calendar of festivities. The temple and its grounds must be maintained – a responsibility of the community of the faithful. The county fair is held in the same place on a seasonal basis. Political elections for local office are held whenever they are due, and candidates vie for votes wherever potential voters are gathered. The nearby farmers' market is held on weekends. All these activities occur in the tight space of a few hundred meters from the temple itself. Indeed, one could say, with Cresswell, that the temple grounds are a sort of "performance stage." It is also an open, inclusive place, so that those who wish to do so can join in the festivities, whether for worship, business, politics, or just being social. And so, to repeat once more with Cresswell, Tsu-Sze Temple could be described as an event whose precise spatial configuration and rhythms are dynamic even though its pattern of social interaction has remained fairly constant over time; recall that since its founding in 1769, the temple was destroyed and rebuilt three times and is currently still under construction.

We are now in position to define place more formally, with reference to places not only on the periphery of Taipei but wherever in the world they may be found. Accordingly, a place can be defined as a small, three-dimensional urban space that is cherished by the people who inhabit it. To the characteristics of urban places identified by Cresswell above – reiterative social practices, inclusiveness, perform-ability, dynamic quality – we can now add three more: the place must be small, inhabited, and come to be cherished or valued by its resident population for all that it represents or means to them.[7]

In this definition, the question of scale is left indeterminate, but my inclination is to argue for a pedestrian scale, which allows people to interact in a variety of mostly unplanned ways, on the street or in business establishments among other spaces of habitual encounter. In this perspective, neighborhoods are defined from the inside out as the area that neighbors acknowledge as their home or, as sociolo-gists would say, as their primary space of social reproduction. This criterion tells us nothing, however, about the intensity of the interaction in question: some forms may be quite superficial, such as being recognized by name on the street or in a store, or simply by a friendly greeting as neighbors go about their daily errands.

The second criterion of inhabiting is obviously a necessary condition of living in a neighborhood, and therefore excludes certain non-places, such as large hotels, department stores, shopping malls, banks, airports, bus terminals, and office build-ings among others that have no soul (Augé, 1995, Kunstler, 1993). By being lived in, the actual physical and social spaces of an urban neighborhood come to be modi-fied and possibly even transformed. This happens naturally through the simple fact of being lived in and the spatial patterns of social interaction that are formed over time, as newcomers arrive, old residents depart. It may also be a result of specific joint actions undertaken by neighbors.[8] External circumstances and forces impinge on the neighborhood as well, contributing to its changing character. In the course of these several actions and changes, the neighborhood acquires particular meanings for its inhabitants, though not all of them may be shared; it thereby becomes a distinctive place and may even acquire a name.

Finally, there is the matter of attachment to place, which is included here as constitutive of place. Attachment is a subjective, invisible attribute – invisible, that is, under normal circumstances. It may occasionally become visible when a neighborhood is threatened with demolition and organizes (or not) to fight for its survival, or when its social composition changes rapidly, and the integration of newcomers becomes stressful and problematic. It is indicated by the way neighbors respond to newcomers, or the manner in which groups of neighbors decide to join up in an effort to improve the physical conditions of neighborhood life. The number and variety of local organizations that depend primarily on local volunteering can perhaps provide an additional, if indirect, measure of place attachment.

The "Centering" of Place: Spaces of Encounter and Gathering

Yet a fourth criterion important to the formation of places is the existence of one or more "centers" or spaces of encounter and/or gathering. This criterion was suggested by the British anthropologist of religion, Stephan Feuchtwang (2004), as a structural imperative for places to come into being. Tsu-Sze Temple is an instance of such a center for a neighborhood whose boundaries are unspecified but clearly have local dimensions. Feuchtwang is somewhat vague about the process of centering. He writes: "Small-scale territorialization is a series of actions and their repetition, centring and thereby making a place" (p. 4). In a case study from China in the same volume, he goes a little further, describing the processes of place-making as involving "gathering, centring and linking" (chapter 9). The entire passage is worth quoting:

> The Chinese strategy of location that I have singled out celebrates the name of a village or a line of descent that is also a set of links and social connections. ... Through it, powerful leaders and donors make their mark by combining their own face with that of a locality in a process of indirection, that is via an ancestor or a temple that is the space where meetings, networks, and gossip are gathered. The leader is respected for a local loyalty. I am suggesting that there is a distinctively Chinese sense of public space as a tacit space of gathering, linking and centring.
>
> By contrast with both, in China and elsewhere, the cosmology of the project of modernity is spatially signified by a line that is the arrow of progress or development, not the centre but the pursuit of the vanishing point of abundance and infinity. As lived, the time and space of modernity remains a space, not a place. In China, it is likened to the ocean. ... Everyone indeed fishes in the ocean of fortune. But it is nevertheless spoken about in China, including of course, by those that live by it, as chaotic. Modernity is the chaos of ordinary life, as out of abstract space and its lines to infinity, places and networks of trust, if not friendship, are made, imposing upon it a more sacred landscape of places, curved eaves, and homes by the three gestures of gathering, centring, and linking. (p. 178)

Feuchtwang's language is allusive here. What he calls the "chaos of ordinary life" is here counterposed to the networks of traditional practices and rituals, the building of ancestral halls, a temple dedicated to a local deity, all of which, in turn, become points of attraction for a village (or urban neighborhood) to talk, gossip, tell stories. Networks so formed are based on familiarity and trust, Feuchtwang claims, and help to bring about a sense of what it means to live in this village, this particular neighborhood. This may ultimately lead to a degree of belonging or attachment, to a sense of place and, ultimately, of one's place in the cosmos. Territorial places in Feuchtwang's sense are centered but not bounded. Or rather, the boundary of centering is a ragged, dynamic, indeterminate edge that shades off into other territories or the unloved spaces of random events that surround us.

We don't have to accept the full implications of Feuchtwang's specifically Chinese version of place-making to accept his criterion of centering – of encounter and gathering – where the former is the weaker term, while the latter suggests a coming together for a purpose. If the whole idea of place is of an environment conducive to sociality or, which is much the same thing, civility (Ho and Douglass, 2008), then communication among people who are known to each other, whether repetitive and patterned or purposeful, is at the nub of this process. Feuchtwang goes on to argue that centering calls into being interiority: "Territorial openness is without walls," he writes.

> But it is not without interiority. It is identified usually by a name and by one or more centres: focal points that may well be buildings with enclosed places. It may contain smaller-scale places or differently defined places of the same name according to different mental or symbolic maps. But so long as it is marked and centred in addition to having extension, the open ground – the market place, the street, the square, part of a park, the neighbourhood, a territorial cult, the streets of a carnival or a village – is also an opening to a greater variety of interactions than more enclosed spaces. (p. 4)

Interiority points to inwardness, the identity of a place, but for most of us this can only be one identity among others, and not necessarily the most important. Sense of place and place identity speak to this; even so, we need to remember that centered places are always open to the world, so that, with the passage of time, they will inevitably change. In the way I use this term here, places undergo their own transformations; they are not forever. But this doesn't mean that they are unimportant.

Randolph Hester is a landscape planner and designer who works with local people to map their own communities. Instead of "centering," he speaks of the sacred spaces, which in the course of redesigning a locality, such as Manteo, a declining fishing village in North Carolina, should be left untouched (Hester, 2006). He ascribes to them an almost metaphysical quality.

> The sacred places in Manteo are buildings, outdoor spaces, and landscapes that exemplify, typify, reinforce, and even extol the everyday life patterns and rituals of community life. They are places so essential to the life of residents through use of symbolism that the community collectively identifies with the places. The places are synonymous with residents' concepts and uses of their town. The loss of such places would reorder or destroy something or some social process essential to the community's collective being. (p. 120)

> Manteo's Sacred Structure, for the most part consisted of humble places ("holes-in-the-wall") that were the settings for the community's daily routines. ... Even to locals, the sacred places were outwardly taken for granted. (p. 122)

> On a practical note, mapping sacred places transforms vague descriptions like "quality of life" that typically fuel emotional disputes into concrete measurable factors. ... In Manteo ... the Sacred Structure map depicted fundamental social

patterns and cultural settings more effectively than any other planning document. ... If I could make only one map of any community to use as a basis of decision making, I would opt for a map of sacred places. That information most enables community. (pp. 125–6)

In relation to place-making, centering and acknowledging that certain sites are endowed with a sense of the sacred are much the same thing. But the local state is typically unaware of sacrilege when it reduces a neighborhood to rubble in order to make way for a profitable real estate venture such as an office building or shopping mall. By whatever name, whether it's slum clearance or gentrification, the results are the same: the erasure of places is a violent act, as established patterns of human relationships are destroyed.

The Invisible Costs of Displacements

The destruction of places, the very opposite of place-making, is one of the more heart-rending stories of city building, resulting in the displacement of millions of people worldwide. It isn't simply that older and often overcrowded parts of the city must inevitably be redeveloped, that no place is forever. This much is true, though erasure is not a natural phenomenon but a consequence of human action. It is actual people who make these decisions, who tell the bulldozers to move in and do their dirty work.

Imagine you are an elderly person living on one of Beijing's alleyways (*hutong*) in the central part of the city. One night you go to sleep, and when you awake in the morning, a huge character sign has been painted on the outside wall of your modest dwelling, with the one-word proclamation, RAZE! This, as it turns out, is your official eviction notice. The invisible planning authorities (Meyer refers to them as The Hand) have condemned your rental unit or property, and have given you two weeks or at most two months to accept a compensation payment (set by the state) and vacate the dwelling where you have lived for decades. Between 1998 and 2001, more than half a million people were officially displaced from their old neighborhoods in the center of Beijing and moved into apartments on the city's periphery beyond the fourth ring road (Meyer, 2009, p. 40). In the run-up to the Summer Olympics, several hundred thousands more followed the first contingent, as entire *hutong* quarters were earmarked for demolition to make way for shopping malls, office buildings, and high-rise luxury condominiums. Expelled from the inner city, erstwhile neighbors suddenly lost their place in the world, the faces they had known for decades, the intimate streets they had walked, the web of meanings they had spun over a lifetime of talk. Displaced, some of them were moved into modern apartments with indoor plumbing and central heating, but the apartments were located in distant, under-equipped, and generally dismal suburbs, where they would suddenly find themselves perhaps on the seventeenth floor of a vast housing complex, disconnected from the earth's energy, with strangers on all sides.⁹ This story of urban displacement is unique only in its specifics. Jane Jacobs' classic, *The Death and Life of Great American Cities* (1962) tells a similar tale, as do books by Peter Marris on re-housing in Lagos, Nigeria (1962), Janice Perlman's *The Myth of Marginality* (1976) and *Favela* (2009), and Mindy T. Fullilove's *Root Shock* (2004), the last of which documents the deep trauma experienced by African Americans when thirty years earlier they were uprooted from inner-city neighborhoods. Now it is the turn of Beijing's *hutong* and their inhabitants.¹⁰

It is of course true that by the turn of the millennium, Beijing's centuries-old *hutong* were vastly over-crowded, and that the physical infrastructure of the housing was, to put it mildly, badly in need of updating and repair. Still, *hutong* alleyways had been part of Beijing's cityscape for over 500 years, and their inhabitants had created a distinctive environment and way of life – an interiority, as Feuchtwang would have it. I don't want to dwell on this process of erasure or place breaking, but if place is something to be valued (though not in terms that can be measured in dollars and cents), and if there is anything to the notion that cherishing a neighborhood in which one has spent a significant part of one's life is a meaningful concept, if sense of place and identity are at issue, then the demolition of places large and small inevitably imposes immense human costs.¹¹

And yet, displacement is one of the most common phenomena in modern city life. We often use other words to talk about it – people removal, squatter eradication, slum clearance, gentrification, rehousing, redevelopment – some terms more benign, others more brutal, but in the end, the results are the same. The world where ordinary people made their home, people without the power to offer more than token or symbolic resistance, is bulldozed down to make way for more profitable buildings, and in a matter of hours the neighborhood is gone.¹² Of course most of those who were displaced survive, even though a few may die of broken hearts or loneliness, and some may even take their own lives. The media hardly notice. They celebrate the new Wal-Mart, the Golden Arches, the 8-lane expressway, the luxury hotel, all of them symbols of a globalizing world without soul.

Some well-known academics appear to have sided with this world. Nigel Thrift, a British geographer, notes the presence of new technology – the Internet, the cell phone and their various off-shoots – in what has become a nano-second world that annihilates communicative space. Technology, he argues, has become embedded in cyborg men and women who walk with a plug in their ear, oblivious to what's around them. In such a world, he asks, what is place?

> The short answer is – compromised: permanently in a state of enunciation, between addresses, always deferred. Places are "stages of intensity". Traces of speed and circulation. One might read this depiction of "almost places" ... in Baudrillardean terms as a world of third-order simulacra, where encroaching pseudo-places have finally advanced to eliminate places altogether. Or one might record places ... as strategic installations, fixed addresses that capture traffic. Or finally, one might read them ... as frames for varying practices of space, time, and speed. (Thrift, 1994, pp. 212–13, cited in Cresswell, 2004, p. 48)

The long answer is the same: Thrift observes a world where the notion of place has become redundant. We now live in a different space–time continuum, unmoored from real places, except for a few that have been saved for posterity (and tourists) as third-order simulacra.

In a more recent book jointly authored with Ash Amin, Thrift continues this celebration of speed, movement, and power. He now refers to this as the "distantiated world," which is neither here nor there but always suspended "in between" structured around "flows of people, images, information and money moving within and across national borders" (Amin and Thrift, 2002, p. 51). So perceived, cities, or rather the urban economy from which any mention of people has been surgically removed, are neither bounded nor punctured entities but "assemblages of more or less distantiated economic relations which will have different intensities at different locations" (p. 52). This distantiated view of the urban and its economic relations – that is, a view beheld at a distance – is to me a class-based perspective of those who, like the authors and indeed like myself, frequently jet-set across the oceans, have more friends and colleagues who live far from home, and who only occasionally come down in their own neighborhoods where they are likely to leave essential shopping and other locally based activities to others. Yes, we who are part of the power elites, tend to see the world "at a distance." It is a spectral world without people.

I have made a number of claims in this essay, beginning with the working-class housing project on the edge of a large city in southern France, with its numbing atmosphere of terror. This project and others like it, whether in Rio de Janeiro or Moscow, in Lagos or Shanghai, is what place-making is not. I then introduced a number of criteria by which we can determine the degree to which neighbor-hoods are places: being small, inhabited, cherished by most of those who live there, and centered as revealed in its sacred spaces, reiterative social practices and rituals. Above all, it is a space where the daily drama of small events is enacted for the benefit of everyone who cares to watch.

But these lived spaces, what Lefebvre calls *espaces vécus*, do not just exist in a moment of time; they have a history, a past as well as a future, and it is this last that from a planner's perspective is the most important. And so we need to ask: how should we as planners proceed to approach the recovery of places?

Making Places Is Everyone's Job

Contrary to command planning, which globally speaking is still the dominant form, I would argue that planners need directly to engage those who reside in neighborhoods, and that this engagement means to establish a moral relation that from the start acknowledges people's "right to the city" which is to say their right to local citizenship (Lefebvre, 1996).[13] From the beginnings of urban history 5,000 years ago, there have been neighborhoods. Some were planned by designers, developers, the government, but most probably were not. They happened in all sorts of physical settings, a result of being lived in by people who came there, stayed, perhaps eventually moved on, and who dealt with each other on a daily basis. Each neighborhood has a unique social profile. Over time, it acquires a character of its own, perhaps also a name, but whereas names are sometimes retained, a neighborhood's character inevitably changes, its name is a legacy to the future. The point is that the very act of inhabiting a neighborhood will shape its character, its daily and seasonal rituals, and the recurrent socio-spatial patterns that imprint themselves on its memory.

In this essay I've been primarily concerned with the neighborhoods of ordinary people, all of them struggling to make ends meet. The corollary of this is that there are always improvements that can be made, beginning with sanitation or playgrounds or making a street corner safe for pedestrians, or simply paving a street that during the rainy season turns into ankle-deep mud. These are small things, but they loom large for the neighbors who may approach the authorities or undertake to do the work themselves. Making neighborhoods is essentially a collective undertaking, and Japan's traditional neighborhood associations are a well-known instance of this (Hashimoto, 2007).[14]

Although never very powerful, when the central government failed, as it did following the devastating Kobe earthquake, it was the well-organized neighborhoods in the demolished areas that recovered most quickly (Ito, 2007). Japan's *machizukuri* – a form of citizen participation in local governance – could be described as an urban movement that spread rapidly during the economic doldrums of the 1990s (Sorensen and Funck, 2007). Describing a diverse range of citizen involvement, it is not a precise term and has multiple and contested meanings. What is beyond dispute is its importance for the ways Japanese cities are being governed today, no longer exclusively at a distance from central ministries, but more frequently through the synergies of local effort. "Thousands of *machizukuri* processes have been established nationwide, in an enormous outpouring of local energy ... in which local citizens play an active role in environmental improvement and management processes" write the editors (p. 1). The traditional planning determinations by the central government are losing legitimacy in Japan, and recent legislation enabling non-profit organizations (NPOs) supports *machizukuri* processes with professional services and expertise.

China is undergoing a similar restructuring of neighborhood governance. During the Maoist period, every urban worker belonged to a *danwei* that designated a work unit of a state-owned enterprise. When fully functioning, *danwei* were in effect miniature cities grouped around a production unit, including housing and a wide range of facilities from health and education to recreation and child care. Following the introduction of a competitive market system in the 1980s, however, surviving *danwei* were no longer able to provide virtually free housing and other birth-to-death services to their remaining workers and retirees. This occasioned

China's unprecedented housing boom, which (among other things) gave rise to the massive displacement of *hutong* residents discussed earlier. Cities outdid each other in the rapidity with which they transformed their central districts even as they pushed built-up areas further and further towards the periphery, overrunning fields and villages. The post-reform call was now for city people to change from being state-dependent *"danwei* persons," living collectively, to "persons of society" relying on self, family, and neighborhood.[15]

The official name for the reconstruction of neighborhood governance was *Shequ* Construction, meaning the promotion and building up neighborhoods. The term *shequ* is a neologism, officially defined as "the social collective body formed by those living within a defined geographic boundary." As conceived, a *shequ* residents' committee was to be a self-governing people's organization providing services to the elderly, the poor, the young, and the disabled; organizing cultural and recreational programs, such as a library and dances; and offering convenience services of the 7/11 variety as a modest source of revenue. Each designated neighborhood (there are now over 80,000 throughout the country) would have a physical facility staffed by a small contingent of "social workers" whose salaries would be paid by the District government. In practice, most social workers are middle-aged women, many of them Party members, who have received an intensive course in *shequ* management. The elected *shequ* committee is entrusted with maintaining social order in the neighborhood, including helping to resolve neighborhood disputes. Despite the official emphasis on self-governance (*zizhi*), most residents understand their *shequ* center to be an extension of the District government. Still, neighborhood autonomy is vouchsafed in China's Constitution.

This scheme, which has been in place for about a decade, is still undergoing an experimental phase, with multiple variants (so-called models) across China's cities. It is even possible to argue that the *shequ* construction policy is a strategy for action more than a rigid formula. For instance, in some cities, it is being used to link non-profit social enterprises to provide essential social services such as to the elderly. In this respect, *shequ* construction is not unlike Japan's *machizukuri*, representing an Asian response to a similar challenge: how to manage and maintain a semblance of civic order in the chaotic urban environments of late capitalism. But unlike Japan, physical planning in China does not as yet reach down to the neighborhood level, nor does it attempt to engage the local citizenry, which remains disengaged from urban planning (Friedmann and Chen, 2009).

I would like to conclude these comments on "making places" with a return to North America and the story of the Collingwood Neighborhood House (CNH) in Vancouver, British Columbia. It is a story of how a particular institution – the neighborhood house – was able to "center" this neighborhood and enable its successful transition from predominantly Anglo to one of Vancouver's most mixed, multi-lingual community areas.

CNH, which started up in 1985, was an offshoot of the settlement house movement, initiated by Jane Addams and Ellen Gates Starr when they co-founded

Hull House on Chicago's south-side nearly a century earlier. It evolved over a lengthy series of meetings between City of Vancouver planners and residents of what was then the Collingwood (later Renfrew-Collingwood) neighborhood. The City was interested in helping to renew the neighborhoods, through which a new mass transit line, the Skytrain, would travel, particularly in the vicinity of local stations, one of which, at Joyce Street, later helped in relocating the fledgling neighborhood house to its present site. An important consideration was that a working-class suburb such as Collingwood, which was rapidly becoming a reception area for immigrants from many countries, needed a "gathering place" that would help newcomers to get settled. Inspired by the Hull House experience, CNH would be an inclusive, non-judgmental, democratically managed, non-profit organization. Most importantly, it would invite people to become involved with its many activities, acting as a hub of information and resources for immigrants, fostering leadership, and building relationships. In short, it would bring people together to take part in building a community (Sandercock and Cavers, 2009, p. 125).

The story is too long to relate here in full; it is the subject of both a book and a DVD (Sandercock and Attili, 2009). Its senior author here summarizes the experience:

> Over the course of twenty years, Collingwood redefined itself as a productive process of social interaction. The CNH is indeed a physical place ... that has helped to create a sense of belonging. But perhaps paradoxically, that belonging has only partially to do with the actual physical place, and more profoundly ... with the lived experience of building relationships ... CNH has created [a] space for intercultural dialogue, for exchange across cultural difference, which is the precondition for relationship building.

But such initiatives do not automatically become sites of social inclusion. They need organizational and discursive strategies that are designed to build voice, to foster a sense of common benefit, to develop confidence among disempowered groups, and to arbitrate when disputes arise. And that is precisely, and systematically, what the CNH Board and leadership have done through two decades of social and demographic change (Sandercock, 2009, pp. 224–6).

Three countries – Japan, China, Canada – three experiments in making places, creating living neighborhoods. In the end, there is no single, best method; each way is culturally attuned and has its own historical trajectory. But what we see in all three cases is what may seem a paradoxical finding: on the one hand, the critical role of government in getting local initiatives underway and, on the other hand, the encouragement (including financial resources) given to what, in principle, are autonomous neighborhood institutions – Japan's traditional (but newly energized) neighborhood associations, China's elected *shequ* residents' committees, and British Columbia's not-for-profit settlement houses. It is in this specific sense that I argue that making places is everyone's job.

Concluding Thoughts

Speaking globally, and fixated as they often are on globalization, planners in the newly industrializing countries but elsewhere as well seem to have forgotten about the small spaces of the city, the self-defined neighborhoods of urban life. These days, everything we dream about is "mega," those functional structures that, geared to profits, lack soul. Except when state and capital need the land on which ordinary people are living, they and their stake in the city are largely forgotten. Without ado, they are displaced, given inadequate compensation, and with luck, rehoused in the outer reaches of the urban. None of this, of course, enters the national income accounts, as though ordinary people and their livelihood are redundant. I have tried to muster arguments against this view and the related ideas of some geographers that place no longer matters, that in the age of nanotechnology, we can earn good money without living anywhere at all, in what some of them call an "in-between" world. According to this perspective, the city is reduced to a functional assembly of interchangeable parts, a kind of hotel, where all of one's needs are provided for at the push of a button.[16]

I have focused on the small and ordinary because small and ordinary are mostly invisible to those who wield power, unless, when stepped upon, they cry out. But genuine places at the neighborhood scale have order, structure, and identity, all of which are created, wittingly or not, by the people living there. The order is civil, the structure is centered, and the identity (Feuchtwang's "interiority") is constantly being made and remade, because neighborhood places are dynamic, and every snapshot is nothing more than a moment in the flow of life. Michael Meyer insists on this point when he writes:

> Outsiders often called the *hutong* neighborhoods slums, but the neighborhood did not cause pathologies or problematic behavior. Our neighbourhood was not a pit of despair; you heard laughter and lively talk and occasionally, tears and arguments, just like everywhere else. People treated each other with something I missed the minute I set foot outside the *hutong*: civility. Residents recognized each other, so there was no cursing or name-calling directed at anonymous faces, without repercussions. Cars could not blare the horn, cut you off, and motor away. In the lanes, belligerence was not a virtue, tolerance was. Strangers knew they were guests, not authorities. (Meyer, 2009, p. 162)

A successful neighborhood is cherished by its inhabitants, even when housing is ill-maintained and the infrastructure inadequate. But housing can be renewed, new infrastructure can be emplaced. The neighborhood is cherished for very different reasons: because it has places of encounter where people reaffirm each other as who they are, or comment on the day's events; because life has a certain rhythm with which all are familiar and to which all expectantly look forward; because there are places that are "sacred" to the people; and because there are special places of gathering where events important to the community transpire. It is this rhythm, these repetitive cadences that are always the same and yet a bit different as well, like a seasonal festival, that is a measure of a neighborhood's vitality.

Ordinary neighborhoods, I would argue, need to be brought back into view, so that planners and local citizens can engage in a joint search for genuine betterment in the physical conditions of neighborhood life. This is a challenge for both parties who, for the most part, are inexperienced in what is, in effect, a moral engagement from which both have something to gain. Official planners represent the state and power, but local people don't speak that language. When confronted with authority, they lower their eyes and fall silent. An engagement with agents of the state must thus be undertaken in good faith. The ground on which both parties stand must be leveled so that an authentic dialogue can ensue.

Notes

1. A notable exception is Douglass and Ho (2008) and Douglass et al. (2008).
2. The "labyrinth of power" acknowledges the impossibility to obtain an unambiguously holistic view of the urban in which the actually existing networks of power are clearly delineated. Our knowledge of the urban is therefore always fragmentary, partial, and inevitably biased. The contrary view is upheld by David Harvey whose neo-Marxist theory lends a certainty to his interpretations of the urban that other scholars do not necessarily profess. See, for example, Nigel Thrift (2006).
3. "Outside its specific application in molecular physics, entropy can be conceived of as a measure of steady deterioration in social organization, the built environment, and natural resource wealth" (Friedmann, 2002, p. 13).
4. For French debates around public policy with respect to these working class suburbs, see Kipfer (2009). A major riot in 2005, and smaller ones since then, have generated a small industry of commentaries by academics and activists.
5. Of Douala, Cameroon, Simone writes: "the challenge is how residents keep each other in some kind of consideration and keep open the possibilities of a common future. In part this occurs through circulation of meanings, styles, vantage points, experiences, and ways of talking – tried and discarded and perhaps tried again. These elements thus come to belong to no one, even though particular groups may make strong claims on them at any given time. This performance of circulation – which produces an incessant sense of incompleteness and haunting in whatever arrangements are momentarily put together by diverse residents trying to figure each other out and live together – is what I refer to here as the spectral" (Simone, 2004, pp. 93–4).
6. Jacobs (1962), Relph (1976), Tuan (1977), Heidegger (1977), Seamon (1979), Norberg-Schulz (1980), Whyte (1980), Pred (1984), de Certeau (1984), Lefebvre (1991), Kunstler (1993), Hayden (1995), Augé (1995), Cooper (1995), Feld and Basso (1996), Beatley and Manning (1997), Gelder and Jacobs (1998), Kenney (2001), Escobar (2001), Aravot (2002), Low and Lawrence-Zúñiga (2003), Feuchtwang (2004), Massey (2005), Hester (2006), Douglass and Ho (2008), Douglass et al. (2008).

7.   In a personal communication, Janice Perlman argues that places can be feared and despised rather than cherished. I find this argument difficult to accept. Neighborhoods that are not only drug centers but also areas ruled by killer gangs are entropic settlements in process of dissolution. I purposely chose to talk about cherished neighborhoods, because their conviviality is a negentropic energy that leads to community rather than fortress mentality and fearful isolation.

8.   An excellent example of joint neighborhood action comes from Penang, Malaysia (Zabielskis, 2008).

9.   "According to the Widow, the best thing about living in a courtyard home is that it keeps one's feet on the ground, which is healthier than living in a high-rise apartment. The concept is called *jie digi* in Chinese, 'to be connected to the earth's energy.' The Widow once demonstrated by gently tapping her foot on our gate's granite step, wooden threshold, and surrounding muddy lane. At every touch, she repeated connected" (Meyer, 2009, p. 7).

10. Michael Meyer, a 36-year-old American who lived for many years in Beijing, could be called a reincarnation of Jane Jacobs. When he writes about his inner-city Beijing neighborhood Dazhalan, he writes with Jacob's love and passion for the place and with anger at the displacement and dispersal of its good people. It is a neighborhood comprising 114 *hutong* alleyways, 1,500 businesses, seven temples, and 3,000 homes. Dazhalan's half square mile contains some 57,000 residents, one of the highest population densities in the world. Today, Dazhalan stands no more; Meyer's book is at once its obituary and memorial (Meyer, 2009, p. 5).

11. Marris (1962) has extensive data on what it means to be moved involuntarily from the center of Lagos to new housing estates on the periphery. Family relations are disrupted, livelihoods are destroyed, sociality is impeded, street trade is diminished, the costs of housing, transport, and food are raised, while the quality of life in the suburban housing estates is diminished. Within a year, 196 households (about 20% of all tenancies) were evicted from their new suburban housing for failure to pay rent (see chapter 8). He concludes with a question: "The fundamental problem raised by the Lagos slum clearance scheme is this: How can a neighborhood be physically destroyed, without destroying at the same time the livelihood and way of life of the people who have settled there? If these are disrupted, the clearance of slums is likely to do more harm than good (p. 129).

12. I stress "ordinary," although I might have used the less familiar "subaltern" to describe the people most affected by dis/placement. The rich and powerful are rarely dis/placed; they live in their own compounds and, as I point out below, are frequently more at home in the hotels of global cities than they are in their own neighborhood enclaves, condominiums, or whatever. See Robinson (2006) as my inspiration for using "ordinary" with this specific meaning.

13. The Right to the City (RttC) is now building a social movement in the USA. See www.righttothecity.org.

14. Their functions were typically limited to contacts with municipal government; presenting petitions from residents; management of a community center; cleaning and beautification of a neighborhood; festivals, athletic meets, travel; cooperation with charities and blood donation drives; installation of street lights and security lights (Hashimoto, 2007, p. 226).

15. This section draws on a doctoral dissertation in process by Leslie Shieh a doctoral candidate in the School of Community and Regional Planning at the University of British Columbia (Vancouver campus).

16. Such a "hotel," 152 storeys high, is under construction in Seoul, Korea. According to Mike Douglass of the University of Hawaii, "Another touted globopolis plan is 'U-Town,' short for Ubiquitous Town. The idea is to create a 'ubiquitous life' by constructing self-contained, autonomous living, work, shopping, entertainment and leisure complexes that will supply residents with 'everything within a single building complex. As described by a director of its project in Daejon, by adding residential units to a shopping and business complex, all of life's needs are met without having to leave the interconnected complex of buildings of U-Town. Apropos to the motives of globopolis, the director of U-Town declares that there are only two goals in making this self-contained mini-city: profit and customers to spend money in its many commercial buildings" (personal communication, 22 July 2009).

References

Amin, A. and Thrift, N. (2002) *Cities: Reimagining the Urban* (Cambridge, Polity Press).

Aravot, I. (2002) Back to phenomenological placemaking, *Journal of Urban Design*, 7(2), pp. 201–12.

Augé, M. (1995) *Non-Places: Introduction to an Anthropology of Supermodernity* (London, Verso).

Bairoch, P. (1993) *Economics and World History: Myths and Paradoxes* (New York, Harvester/Wheatsheaf).

Beatley, T. and Manning, K. (1997) *The Ecology of Place* (Washington, DC, Island Press).

Brenner, N. (2004) *New State Spaces: Urban Governance and the rescaling of Statehood* (Oxford, Oxford University Press).

Cooper, M.C. (1995) *Home as a Mirror of Self: Exploring the Deeper Meaning of Home* (Berkeley, CA, Conari Press).

Cresswell, T. (2004) *Place: A Short Introduction* (Malden, MA, Blackwell).

De Certeau, M. (1984) *The Practice of Everyday Life* (Berkeley, CA, University of California Press).

Douglass, M. and Ho, K.C. (eds) (2008) Place-making and livability in Pacific Asian cities, Special Issue, *International Development Planning Review*, 30(3).

Douglass, M., Ho, K.C. and Ooi, G.L. (2008) *Globalization, the City and Civil Society in Pacific Asia* (London and New York, Routledge).

Escobar, A. (2001) Culture sits in places: reflections on globalism and subaltern strategies of localization, *Political Geography*, 20(2), pp. 139–74.

Feld, S. and Basso, K.H. (1996) *Senses of Place*, pp. 259–62 (Santa Fe, NM, School of American Research Press).

Feuchtwang, S. (2004) Theorizing Place, in: S. Feuchtwang (ed.) *Making Place: State Projects, Globalisation and Local Responses in China*, pp. 3–30 (London, UCL Press).

Friedmann, J. (2002) *The Prospect of Cities* (Minneapolis, MN, University of Minnesota Press).

Friedmann, J. and Chen, F. (2009) Towards sustainable neighborhoods: the role of social planning in China: a case study of Ningbo, Zhejiang Province, *Urban Planning International*, 24(1), pp. 16–24 [in Chinese].

Friedmann, J. (2007) Place and place-making in the cities of China, *International Journal for Urban and Regional Research*, 31(2), pp. 257–79.

Fullilove, M.T. (2004) *Root Shock: How Tearing up City Neighborhoods Hurts America, and What We Can Do about It* (New York, One World/Ballantine Books).

Gelder, K. and Jacobs, J.M. (1998) *Uncanny Australia: Sacredness and Identity in a Post-colonial Nation* (Melbourne, Melbourne University Press).

Hashimoto, S. (2007) Neighbourhood associations and machizukuri processes: strengths and weaknesses, in: A. Sorensen and C. Funck (eds), *Living Cities in Japan*. Nissan Institute/Routledge Japanese Studies Series, ch. 11 (New York, Routledge).

Hayden, D. (1995) *The Power of Place: Urban Landscapes as Public History* (Cambridge, MA, MIT Press).

Heidegger, M. (1977) Building Dwelling Thinking, in: D.F. Krell (ed.) *Martin Heidegger: Basic Writings*, pp. 319–40 (New York, Harper & Row).

Hester, R.T. (2006) *Design for Ecological Democracy* (Cambridge, MA, MIT Press).

Ho, K.C. and Douglass, M. (2008) Place-making and livability in Pacific Asian cities. Special issue, *International Development Planning Review*, 30(3).

Ito, A. (2007) Earthquake reconstruction machizukuri and citizen participation, in: A. Sorensensen and C. Funck (eds) *Living Cities in Japan*, ch. 7 (New York, Routledge).

Jacobs, J. (1962) *The Death and Life of Great American Cities* (New York, Random House).

Kenney, M. (2001) *Mapping Gay L.A.: The Intersection of Place and Politics* (Philadelphia, PA, Temple University Press).

Kunstler, J.H. (1993) *The Geography of Nowhere: The Rise and Decline of America's Man-Made Landscape* (New York, Simon & Schuster).

Le Clézio, J.-M.G. (2002) *Round and Other Cold Facts* (Lincoln, NE, Nebraska University Press).

Lefebvre, H. (1991) *The Production of Space*, D. Nicholson-Smith (Trans.) (Oxford, Blackwell).

Lefebvre, H. (1996) *Writings of Cities*, E. Kofman and E. Lebas (trans., eds) (Oxford, Oxford University Press).

Low, S.M. and Lawrence-Zúñiga, D. (2003) *Space and Place: Locating Culture* (Oxford, Blackwell).

Marris, P. (1962) *Family and Social Change in an African City: A Study of Rehousing in Lagos* (Evanston, IL, Northwestern University Press).

Massey, D. (2005) *For Space* (London, Sage).

Meyer, M.J. (2009) *The Last Days of Old Beijing: Life in the Vanishing Backstreets of a City Transformed* (New York, Walker).

Norberg-Schulz, C. (1980) *Genius Loci* (New York, Rizzoli).

Perlman, J. (1976) *The Myth of Marginality: Urban Poverty and Politics in Rio de Janeiro* (Berkeley, CA, University of California Press).

Perlman, J. (2009) *Favela: Four Decades of Living on the Edge* (New York, Oxford University Press).

Pred, A.R. (1984) Place as historically contingent process: structuration and the time geography of becoming places, *Annals of the Association of American Geographers*, 74(2), pp. 279–97.

Relph, E. (1976) *Place and Placelessness* (London, Pion).

Robinson, J. (2006) *Ordinary Cities: Between Modernity and Development* (London, Routledge).

Sandercock, L. (2009) Towards a cosmopolitan urbanism: from theory to practice, in: L. Sandercock and G. Attili (eds) *Where Strangers Become Neighbours: Integrating Immigrants in Vancouver, Canada* (Berlin, Springer).

Sandercock, L. and Attili, G. (2009) *Where Strangers Become Neighbours: Integrating Immigrants in Vancouver, Canada* (Berlin, Springer).

Sandercock, L. and Cavers, V. (2009) The story of the Collingwood Neighbourhood House: a unique gathering place, in: L. Sandercock and G. Attili (eds) *Where Strangers Become Neighbours: Integrating Immigrants in Vancouver, Canada*, ch.5 (Berlin, Springer).

Schroedinger, E. (1992 [1945]) *What Is Life? With Mind and Matter and Autobiographical Sketches* (Cambridge, Cambridge University Press).

Seamon, D. (1979) *A Geography of the Lifeworld: Movement, Rest and Encounter* (New York, St Martin's Press).

Simone, A. (2004) *For the City Yet to Come: Changing African Life in Four Cities* (Durham, NC, and London, Duke University Press).

Sorensen, A. and Funck, C. (2007) *Living Cities in Japan*. Nissan Institute/Routledge Japanese Studies Series (New York, Routledge).

Thrift, N. (1994) Inhuman geographies: landscapes of speed, light and power, in: P. Cloke (ed.) *Writing the Rural: Five Cultural Geographies*, pp. 191–250 (London, Paul Chapman).

Thrift, N. (2006) David Harvey: a rock in a hard place, in: N. Castree and D. Gregory (eds) *David Harvey: A Critical Reader* (Oxford, Blackwell).

Tuan, Y.-F. (1977) Space and place: humanistic perspective, *Progress in Human Geography*, 6, pp. 211–52.

United Nations (2009) *World Population Monitoring: The Concise Report* (New York, United Nations, Department of Economic and Social Affairs, Population Division).

Whyte, W.H. (1980) *The Social Life of Small Urban Spaces* (Washington, DC, The Conservation Foundation).

Zabielskis, P. (2008) Towards a moral ecology of the city: a new form of place-identity and social action in Penang, Malaysia, *International Development Planning Review*, 30(3), pp. 267–92.

26

Urban Informality

The Production of Space and Practice of Planning

Ananya Roy

The geography of the slum has long haunted urban planning. Designated as the "informal space," the slum represents the "unplanable" city that lies beyond the sphere of regulations, norms, and codes. Such informal spaces are viewed as either dismal concentrations of poverty, a tangible manifestation of economic marginality, or as alternative and autonomous urban orders, patched together through the improvisation and entrepreneurship of the urban poor. In both cases, the informal city is understood as the "other" of the planned and formal city. In this chapter, I examine contemporary understandings of the informal city and situate them in a broader history of ideas. I also put forward a conceptual framework for the study of urban informality, one that runs counter to mainstream conceptualizations of the "unplanable" city. I start with AlSayyad's (2004) provocation that it is the "formal" rather than the "informal" that requires explanation. How and why are certain land uses and settlement patterns designated as formal by the state while others are criminalized and maintained as "informal"? Such a question is particularly urgent since, in many instances, the "formal" may not be in conformity with master plans and legal codes and yet by earning the sanction of the state, it has considerably more spatial value than the "informal." It is in and through such differentiated urban geographies that social hierarchies of class, race, and ethnicity are consolidated, maintained, and negotiated. Elite informalities are rapidly converted into a formal spatial order, while subordinate groups are forced to exist in

Original publication details: Roy, Ananya. 2012. "Urban informality: The Production of Space and Practice of Planning". In *The Oxford Handbook of Urban Planning*, edited by Rachel Weber and Randall Craned. Oxford: Oxford University Press. Chapter 33, pp. 691–706. Reproduced with permission from Oxford University Press.

what, following Yiftachel (2009), can be understood as "blackened spaces" of exclusion or, at best, "gray spaces" of ambiguous legal standing. This production and regulation of space, then, is also the production and regulation of social difference. While such selective stigmatization by the state takes place in many different regional contexts and in many different spheres – for example, in the regulation of labor markets – in this chapter I focus on the ownership and use of property, paying attention to the splintered landscapes of spatial value that mark the metropolitan regions of the Global South.

Two Views of Urban Informality

The widespread urbanization of the twenty-first century has been accompanied by a revived interest in the informal city. However, the rediscovery of informality is marked by sharply contrasting perspectives and paradigms. One of the most prominent is Mike Davis's (2006) apocalyptic account of "a planet of slums." For Davis (2006, 14–15), informal urbanization is a stark manifestation of "overurbanization" or "urbanization without growth," which in turn is "the legacy of a global political conjuncture—the worldwide debt crisis of the late 1970s and the subsequent IMF-led restructuring of Third World economies in the 1980s." Davis thus designates this world system as "a planet of slums," a warehousing of the "surplus humanity" released by de-proletarianization and agricultural deregulation in hazardous and miserable forms of urban settlement. Such also is the rhetoric of the United Nations, which has made "cities without slums" one of its key initiatives. It is thus that Gilbert (2007, 697) has lamented that the "the new millennium has seen the return of the word 'slum' with all of its inglorious associations."

Davis's work is part of a substantial genre of research that traces the formation of a "new urban marginality," not only in the Third World but also in Europe and the Americas. While in the 1970s researchers undermined the "myth of marginality" (Perlman 1977), arguing that the informalized poor were integrated into the labor markets, social life, and political systems of the city, they are now making the case for the "reality of marginality" (Perlman 2004). Wacquant's work (1996, 1999, 2007), for example, documents the emergence of an "advanced marginality" that is linked to the "territorial stigmatization" faced by residents of marginalized spaces: the ghetto, the *banlieue*, the *favela*. Similarly, Auyero (2000) charts the emergence of the "hyper-shantytown." Such research is united in its emphasis on the connections between such "advanced marginality" and the hollowing out of economies and welfare states through neoliberal capitalism. The "hyper-shantytown" is thus produced by "hyper-unemployment" (Auyero 1999), a systematic process of de-proletarianization and labor informalization. While the theorists of "advanced marginality" acknowledge the poverty-targeting efforts of the state (for example, in Brazil, the upgrading of *favelas* through the provision of services), they insist that such programs are minor palliatives in the face of a massive structural crisis. In particular, they argue that the communities of the urban poor are now overwhelmed by violence: the violence of state repression, the symbolic violence of stigma and discrimination, and the material violence of poverty and unemployment (Perlman 2004). In short, yesterday's "slums of hope" are today's "slums of despair" (Eckstein 1990).

It is important to note that Davis's argument is not only about economic marginality but also about a new political configuration – what he calls the "law of chaos" (Davis 2004). With the hollowing out of formal labor markets, the urban poor, he notes, are rarely organized and mobilized in collective fashion. Rather, they are fragmented and atomized by vectors such as religion and ethnicity. Davis's lament rehearses a much older argument presented by dependency theorists. For example, in the seminal text, *The City and Grassroots,* Castells (1983) presents an ambitious theory of urban social movements. Studying both formal political organizations and the mobilizations of informal squatter communities, Castells acknowledges the central role of politics in the transformation of the capitalist city, but also analyzes the limits of such politics. In particular, he designates the populist politics of squatter communities as a symptom of the "dependent city," a "city without citizens." He argues that while squatters mobilize to secure access to land, services, jobs, and at times even tenure, they are simultaneously co-opted into systems of political patronage. Thus, they are clients rather than citizens, disciplined subjects of urban populism rather than active agents of structural change. Similarly, Davis's global slum is a space of violence but not of social transformation. It is worth quoting at length:

> What is clear is that the contemporary megaslum poses unique problems of imperial order and social control that conventional geopolitics has barely begun to register. If the point of the war against terrorism is to pursue the enemy into his sociological and cultural labyrinth, then the poor peripheries of developing cities will be the permanent battlefields of the twenty-first century.... Some templates are obvious. Night after night, hornetlike helicopter gunships stalk enigmatic enemies in the narrow streets of the slum districts, pouring hellfire into shanties or fleeing cars. Every morning the slums reply with suicide bombers and eloquent explosions. If the empire can deploy Orwellian technologies of repression, its outcasts have the gods of chaos on their side. (Davis 2004, 15)

In sharp contrast to this framework is one that celebrates the informal city, viewing it as an embodiment of the entrepreneurial energies of the "people's economy." A key interlocutor is Hernando de Soto. De Soto's arc of work, from *The Other Path* (1989) to *The Mystery of Capital* (2000), presents the informal sector as an "invisible revolution" (the subtitle of *The Other Path*), a grassroots uprising against the bureaucracy of state planning. As Bromley (2004) notes, this "other path" is also meant to be the alternative to the political radicalism of the Shining Path, the guerilla movement that waged a class war in Peru, de Soto's home and the setting for *The Other Path*. In *The Mystery of Capital*, de Soto (2000) extends his arguments about the "people's economy" by arguing that the poor are "heroic entrepreneurs." He insists that the poor already possess considerable assets and he estimates that such assets amount to $9 trillion, far exceeding any transfers of aid and assistance that can be directed to them: twenty times the direct foreign investment in the Third World since the Berlin Wall fell and more than forty-six times as much as the World Bank has lent in the last three decades. The cause of poverty is not the lack of assets but, rather, that the poor are relegated to the informal sector in their ownership and use of such assets, a system that de Soto calls "legal apartheid." Thus, Bromley (2004) rightly notes that de Soto's work most closely hews to the ideas of Friedrich von Hayek and its depiction of the state as a bureaucratic obstacle to economic freedom.

Such ideas are compatible with a broader milieu of populist concepts that present the practices of the poor as an alternative to top-down planning. For example, in his influential vision for the "end of poverty," Sachs (2005) outlines a global Keynesianism that promises to take developing countries up the ladder of modernization through investments in physical and human capital. It is against this vision that William Easterly (2006) presents a provocative counter-vision. Critiquing Sachs as a Planner, Easterly condemns these new modernizations as Big Western Plans – neocolonial forms of utopian social engineering that are bound to fail and that will possibly do more harm than good. Easterly contrasts Planners with Searchers, with the grassroots and self-help activities that are incremental, efficient, effective, and accountable. His idea is pithy: that "the poor help themselves" (Easterly 2006, 27) and that they do so through "economic freedom," which is "one of mankind's most underrated inventions" (72). Perhaps his most powerful argument against planning is this: that "the rich have markets, the poor have bureaucrats" (165). In other words, Easterly calls for the liberation of the poor from the bureaucratic chains of international aid and state planning. He argues that the poor are Searchers and that, left to their own devices, they can craft and run systems of great entrepreneurial energy.

A planet of slums where the poor are warehoused in spaces of violence and an entrepreneurial economic order where the poor are able to help themselves are two fundamentally opposed interpretations of contemporary urbanism. Yet, they are marked by a common theme – that of "urban informality as a way of life." Many of these conceptualizations view this way of life as an alternative urban order, one opposed to the planned and formal city.

Urban Informality as a Way of Life?

In a 2004 essay, AlSayyad presents the idea of "urban informality as a way of life." His title refers to the classic 1938 essay by Wirth, "Urbanism as Way of Life." AlSayyad argues that today urban informality is a generalized urban condition. He thus notes that as Wirth had once studied the sociology of the urban condition, so it is possible today to analyze the "forms of social action and organization" associated with urban informality (AlSayyad 2004, 7). AlSayyad's argument resonates with diverse conceptualizations of urban informality. Davis (2006, 178), for example, states that "informal survivalism" is "the new primary mode of livelihood in a majority of Third World cities." Similarly, Bayat (2007, 579) argues that informality is the "habitus of the dispossessed." While Davis views such a habitus as characterized by anomie or extremism, Bayat argues that informality is best understood as "flexibility, pragmatism, negotiation, as well as constant struggle for survival and self-development." In earlier work, Bayat (2000), working in the context of Middle Eastern cities, outlines the repertoire of tactics through which urban "informals" appropriate and claim space. According to him, this "quiet encroachment of the ordinary" by subaltern groups creates a "street politics" that shapes the city in fundamental ways. Bayat's analysis is similar to Michel de Certeau's (1984) conceptualization of the "practice of everyday life" as a set of tactics that can undo the oppressive grid of power and discipline. While planners and rulers seek to create and enforce the "economy of the proper place" through strategies of rule, everyday and commonplace tactics refuse this discipline. In similar fashion, Simone (2006) presents the African city as "a pirate town," where urban residents develop forms of everyday practice that allow them to operate resourcefully in underresourced cities. This is a context of crisis, where "production possibilities" are severely limited; but this is also a context where "existent materials of all kind are to be appropriated" (Simone 2006, 358). While Simone does not use the term "informality," his analysis suggests that he is describing practices that can be designated as such:

> African cities are characterized by incessantly flexible, mobile, and provisional intersections of residents that operate without clearly delineated notions of how the city is to be inhabited and used.... These conjunctions become an infrastructure – a platform providing for and reproducing life in the city. (Simone 2004, 407–8)

Such conceptualizations of "urban informality as a way of life" pay special attention to how the informal emerges as a response to the lack of "stable articulations" of "infrastructure, territory, and urban resources" and becomes a "generalized practice" of "countering marginalization" (Simone 2006, 359). In doing so, they signal that the informal is an alternative urban order, a different way of organizing space and negotiating citizenship. For example, in his work on South Asian cities, Chatterjee (2004, 38) makes a distinction between "civil" and "political" societies. Civil society is bourgeois society and, in the Indian context, an arena of institutions and practices inhabited by a relatively small section of people able to make claims as fully enfranchised citizens. By contrast, political society is the constellation of claims made by those who are only tenuously and ambiguously rights-bearing citizens. Chatterjee (2004, 41) writes that civil society, "restricted to a small section of culturally equipped citizens, represents in countries like India the high ground of modernity." But, "in actual practice, governmental agencies must descend from that high ground to the terrain of political society in order to renew their legitimacy as providers of well-being." The "paralegal" practices and negotiations of this political society is for Chatterjee the politics of much of the people in most of the world.

Chatterjee's work echoes that of Appadurai (2002), who finds in the political actions of Mumbai's slum dwellers a form of "deep democracy"—the ability of the poor to negotiate access to land, urban infrastructure, and services. While Castells (1983) designated the "dependent city" as a "city without citizens," Appadurai (2002, 26) argues that the urban poor of Mumbai are "citizens without a city": a "vital part of the urban workforce" and yet with few of the amenities and protections of urban living. In particular, Appadurai draws attention to the technologies of auto-planning that are used by federations of the urban poor. These forms of "countergovernmentality," as Appadurai calls this, indicate the appropriation of the planner's toolkit by poor and informal communities. It is also in this sense that Benjamin (2008, 719) has made the case for "occupancy urbanism" and the crisis it poses for global capital: "Poor groups, claiming public services and safeguarding territorial claims, open up political spaces that appropriate institutions and fuel an economy that builds complex alliances … locally embedded institutions subvert high-end infrastructure and mega projects." Thus, "'occupancy urbanism' helps poor groups appropriate real estate surpluses via reconstituted land tenure to fuel small businesses whose commodities jeopardize branded chains. Finally, it poses a political consciousness that refuses to be disciplined by NGOs and well-meaning progressive activists and the rhetoric of 'participatory planning.'"

This is the mega-slum, repositioned as an "occupancy of terrain." More broadly, it is the recognition of what Gibson-Graham (2008, 614) has titled "diverse economies" or "projects of economic autonomy and experimentation." Particularly interested in the "social economy," Gibson-Graham celebrates "squatter, slum-dweller, landless and co-housing movements, the global ecovillage movement, fair trade, economic self-determination, the relocalization movement, community-based resource management, and others" (Gibson-Graham 2008, 617). This is of course much more than "urban informality as a way of life"; this is the assertion of such forms of informality as ingredients of a "postcapitalist" order.

Such assertions are a far cry from Davis's "laws of chaos," but they also demand critical scrutiny, especially in their claims of an autonomous, alternative, informal urban sphere. In an echo of Easterly's division between Planners and Searchers, this framework presents the informal city as a way of life that exists in sharp contrast to, or at least in exclusion from, the planned, formal city. But it is a framework that tells us little about how the very categories of formal and informal are constructed, maintained, and deployed. Thus, AlSayyad (2004, 25) notes that what requires explanation is not so much informality as a way of life as does "formality" as a "new mode" of urbanism – one that "was introduced to organize urban society only in the 19th century." In the following section, I build on this observation to pay closer attention to constructions of the formal and informal.

The Informal State

The term "informal" can be traced to the work of Keith Hart and the International Labor Organization (ILO) in the early 1970s. While modernization theory struggled to explain how a "marginal mass" was not absorbed by industrialization, Hart showed that such forms of marginality and informality were structural features of urban economies. Writing in the context of Accra, Hart (1973, 61, 68) identified a "world of economic activities outside the organised labor force" carried out by an "urban sub-proletariat." Hart designated these activities as "informal." At more or less the same time, the ILO (1972, in Kanbur 2009) defined the "informal sector" as the activities of "petty traders, street hawkers, shoeshine boys and other groups 'underemployed' on the streets of big towns, and includes a range of wage-earners and self-employed persons, male as well as female." Hart's conceptualization of informality has been commonly interpreted as "the relationship of economic activity to intervention or regulation by the state" (Kanbur, 2009, 5). This is an accurate inter-pretation of his work. In a reflection on his 1973 paper, Hart (2006, 25) notes that, following Weber, he had argued "that the ability to stabilise economic activity within a bureaucratic form made returns more calculable and regular for the workers as well as their bosses. That stability was in turn guaranteed by the state's laws, which only extended so far into the depths of Ghana's economy." Informal work lay outside this realm of calculable and stable transactions and was thus erratic, with low returns. In many ways, this argument is a precursor to one later put forward by dependency theorists: that the state maintains the informal economy in unregulated form in order to subsidize a system of global capital accumulation (Portes, Castells, and Benton 1989). Indeed, a whole generation of research, much of it produced in Latin America, was to explode the "myth of marginality" (Perlman 1977) and show how informal work and habitat were integral parts of the capitalist city. But Hart also went further. Unlike later interpretations of the "informal sector," he "did not iden-tify the informal economy with a place or a class or even whole persons" (Hart 2006, 25). Instead, he argued that many of Accra's residents sought to forge a multiplicity of livelihoods and income opportunities – in other words, that informality was a gen-eralized condition, a way of life, if you will. Yet, Hart's analysis presents challenges to both the dependency narrative of informality and more populist celebrations. His cautionary note is as valid today as it was in 1973:

> Socialists may argue that foreign capitalist dominance of these economies deter-mines the scope for informal (and formal) development, and condemns the majority of the urban population to deprivation and exploitation. More optimistic liberals may see in informal activities, as described above, the possibility of a dramatic "bootstrap" operation, lifting the underdeveloped economies through their own indigenous enterprise. Before either view – or a middle course stressing both external constraint and autonomous effort – may be espoused, much more empirical research is required. (Hart 1973, 88–9)

Hart's conceptualization of informality is a useful starting point. At the very least, it shifts attention from the informal as the "unplanable" to the role of the state in regulating the formal and the informal. Here, two issues, both also articulated eloquently by Meagher (1995, 259, 279) are crucial: that it is necessary for a conceptual shift "from informality represented as a marginalized sector to 'informalization' conceived as a wider economic response to crisis," and that such a process of "informalization" does not happen "outside the state" but, rather, is a "socioeconomic restructuring instigated by the state." Thus, in our edited volume, *Urban Informality*, Nezar AlSayyad and I (Roy and AlSayyad 2004) argue that the urban informality is not a distinct and bounded sector of labor or housing but, rather, a "mode" of the production of space and is a practice of planning. Let me explain.

The splintering of urbanism does not take place at the fissure between formality and informality but, rather, in fractal fashion *within* the informalized production of space. A closer look at the metropolitan regions of the Global South indicates that informal urbanization is as much the purview of wealthy urbanites and suburbanites as it is of squatters and slum dwellers. These forms of informality, which are fully capitalized domains of property, are no more legal than are squatter settlements and shantytowns. But they are expressions of class power and can thus command infrastructure, services, and legitimacy in a way that marks them as substantially different from the landscape of slums. Most important, they come to be designated as "formal" by the state, regularized and regulated, while other forms of informality remain unregularized and unregulated. My research in Calcutta (Roy and AlSayyad 2004) shows that the differential value attached to what is "formal" and what is "informal" creates an uneven geography of spatial value, a patchwork of valorized and devalorized spaces that is, in turn, the frontier of expansion and development. Informalized spaces are reclaimed through urban renewal while formalized spaces accrue value through their legitimacy. It is in this sense that the informal city is wholly planned and that informality is a practice of planning. For example, in Indian cities, informality is inscribed in the ever-shifting relationship between what is legal and illegal, legitimate and illegitimate, authorized and unauthorized. This relationship is both arbitrary and fickle and yet is the site of considerable state power and violence. Thus, Ghertner (2008) notes that almost all of Delhi violates some planning or building law, such that much of the construction in the city can be viewed as "unauthorized." He poses the vital question of why some of these areas are now being designated as illegal and worthy of demolition while others are protected and formalized. How and why is it that the law has come to designate slums as a "nuisance" and the residents of slums as a "secondary category of citizens," those that are distinguished from "normal," private-property-owning citizens? Ghertner (2008, 66) notes that "developments that have the "world-class" look, despite violating zoning or building bylaws, are granted amnesty and heralded as monuments of modernity." Such differentiation, between the informal and the informal (rather than between the legal and the paralegal), is a fundamental axis of inequality in urban India today.

While elite "farmhouses" on the edges of Delhi are allowed to function legally as appendages of the agrarian land laws, squatter settlements throughout the city are criminalized and violently demolished. Indeed, against Davis it may be argued that the urban catastrophe of the twenty-first century is the sprawling farmhouse and condominium suburbs of the Global South – resource-greedy landscapes of wealth that have been legalized and protected by the state.

Similarly, Holston (2007, 228) notes that Brazilian cities are marked by an "unstable relationship between the legal and illegal." While it may seem obvious and apparent that the urban poor are engaged in an informal and illegal occupation of land, much of the city itself is occupied through the "misrule of law": "Thus in both the wealthiest and the poorest of Brazilian families we find legal landholdings that are at base legalized usurpations" (Holston 2007, 207). What is the relationship between planning and this sanctified "misrule of law"? Who, then, is authorized to (mis)use the law in such ways as to declare property ownership, zones of exception, and enclaves of value? The democratization of urban space in Brazil, Holston (2007, 204) argues, is a process by which the urban poor have learned to use the law and legitimize their own land claims – "they perpetuate the misrule of law but for their own purposes."

A powerful conceptualization of this idea of urban informality comes in the work of Yiftachel (2009, 88–9). Writing in the context of Israel–Palestine, Yiftachel presents the concept of "gray spaces," "those positioned between the 'whiteness' of legality/approval/safety, and the 'blackness' of eviction/destruction/death." He notes that these spaces are tolerated and managed, but "while being encaged within discourses of 'contamination,' 'criminality' and 'public danger' to the desired 'order of things.'" Yiftachel is particularly interested, as I am, in analyzing the manner in which the state formalizes and criminalizes different spatial configurations:

> The understanding of gray space as stretching over the entire spectrum, from powerful developers to landless and homeless "invaders," helps us conceptualize two associated dynamics we may term here "whitening" and "blackening." The former alludes to the tendency of the system to "launder" gray spaces created "from above" by powerful or favorable interests. The latter denotes the process of "solving" the problem of marginalized gray space by destruction, expulsion or elimination. The state's violent power is put into action, turning gray into black. (Yiftachel 2009, 92)

Such processes are evident not only in the Global South but equally in the Global North. The seminal work of Peter Ward (1999) demonstrates how, in the *colonias* of Texas, the working poor come to be housed in the liminal space of "extra-territorial jurisdictions." These *colonias* are privately developed and sold – and thereby tolerated by the state – and yet criminalized and excluded from utilities, services, and legal protection by virtue of their fragile construction. Similarly, Klein (2007b) argues that, in the United States, the deregulation of political economies is tied to the deregulation of space. She shows how, in the last decade, there has been the emergence of a parallel, privatized disaster infrastructure that caters exclusively to the wealthy and the "chosen." This is a world, as Klein notes (2007a, 420), where the wealthy can opt out of the collective system, where the idea of the public interest loses all meaning, and where the city becomes a "world of suburban Green Zones ... as for those outside the secured perimeter, they will have to make do with the remains of the national system."

I am interested in an additional dimension of informality: how the informalization of space is also the informalization of the state. While it has been often assumed that the modern state governs its subjects through technologies of visibility, counting, mapping, and enumerating, in *City Requiem, Calcutta,* I argue that regimes of rule also operate through an "unmapping" of cities (Roy 2003). This is particularly evident on the peri-urban fringes of Calcutta where forms of deregulation and unmapping have allowed the state considerable territorialized flexibility to alter land use, deploy eminent domain, and acquire land. In particular, it has been possible for the state to undertake various forms of urban and industrial development – for example, through the conversion of land to urban use, often in violation of its own bans against such Conversion. In other words, the state is not only an arbiter of value but also an informalized entity that actively utilizes informality as an instrument of both accumulation and authority. Such planning regimes function through ambiguity rather than through rigidity. However, such ambiguity is a sign of a strong, even authoritative state, rather than one that is weak or unsure of its power. An example of these types of state power is provided by Ong (2006) in her analysis of neoliberal forms of government. She shows that sovereign rule often uses zoning technologies to create zones of exception. Such invocations of exception produce a "pattern of noncontiguous, differently administered spaces of graduated or variegated sovereignty" (Ong 2006, 7). It is this uneven geography of spatial value, the fractal geometry of regulated and deregulated space, that is the landscape of urban informality.

The Politics of the Informal City

Much of the urban growth of the twenty-first century will take place in the cities of the Global South. It is therefore tempting to make the case for a "Southern urbanism," one characterized by "urban informality as a way of life," the "habitus of the dispossessed." But as I have already argued, urban informality is not the ecology of the mega-slum; rather, it is a mode of the production of space and a practice of planning. Not surprisingly, the dynamics of urban informality vary greatly from context to context. Thus, in this concluding section, I sketch two contrasting pathways of the informal city, in Brazil and India. Each can be understood to stand in for a broader trajectory – Latin American cities and South/Southeast

Asian cities. However, the issue at hand is less the generalizibility of these specific cases and more the insights they provide for an analysis of the heterogeneity of "Southern urbanism."

Brazil has become famous as the home of the "right to the city" movement. While the Brazilian constitution of 1988 set the stage for a unique brand of participatory democracy, it is only through a long social struggle that the "right to the city" was institutionalized in the City Statute of 2001. The statue constructs a new legal-political paradigm for urbanism, which involves the democratization of access to land and housing in Brazilian cities, as well as the democratization of the process of urban management. It establishes a set of collective rights, including the right to urban planning, the right to capture surplus value, and the right to regularize informal settlements. In particular, it intervenes in the uneven geography of spatial value by seeking to change the ways in which space produces value and functions both as a commodity and as a public good. It is thus that the City Statute conceptualizes a "social function" of property, making it possible for municipal governments to share in the surplus value generated by real estate development (Caldeira and Holston 2005). Opponents of the City Statute have sought to characterize these instruments as a confiscation of private property rights or as "just another tax." But the Instituto Polis (n.d., 30–1), based in Sao Paulo, boldly provides a counter-argument: "What really occurs in our cities ... is the private appropriation (and in the hands of the few) of real estate appreciation that is the result of public and collective investments, paid by everyone's taxes. This private appropriation of public wealth drives a powerful machine of territorial exclusion, a monster that transforms urban development into a real estate product, denying most citizens the right to benefit from the essential elements of urban infrastructure." This is, as Fernandes (2007, 207) notes, an ambitious new "project of the city," translating into spatial terms the "social project" proposed by Henri Lefebvre.

While it remains to be seen how the City Statute is actually implemented, what is important is that it forces a new set of urban meanings on the informal city. It can be argued such meanings have roots in a distinctive urban politics – what Holston (2007, 4) has called "insurgent citizenship," a citizenship that "asserts right-claims addressing urban practices as its substance." Holston (2007, 4) argues that this politics emerges from the auto-constructed peripheries of the urban working poor, where since the 1970s members of this social class "became new citizens not primarily through the struggles of labor but through those of the city." Such rights-based struggles are not necessarily radical; indeed, they often produce and reinforce propertied paradigms of citizenship. Nevertheless, Brazil's City Statute represents a distinctive configuration of city, state, and regulation.

In sharp contrast to such rights-based politics is the case of Indian cities. Here, the turn of the twenty-first century has been marked by the violent expansion of the frontier of urbanization, a making way and making space for the new Indian urban middle class through the smashing of the homes and livelihoods of the rural-urban poor in Delhi, Mumbai, Bangalore, and Calcutta. These new forms of urbanism seek to remake Indian cities as "world class" cities – those that are globally competitive with other Asian successes, such as Shanghai, Singapore, and Dubai. With this in mind, in Calcutta, the government has sought to displace peasants and sharecroppers from agricultural land in order to accommodate special economic zones, foreign investment, and gated suburban developments. In Delhi, "slum clearance" has been carried out through a set of judicial rulings that seek to assert a "public interest" (Bhan 2009). In Mumbai, evictions were starkly evident in the winter of 2004–5. Acting on a bold report by the global consulting firm McKinsey & Company, the city put into motion "Vision Mumbai." A cornerstone of this vision is a world-class, slum-free city, promoted by an elite nongovernmental organization (NGO), Bombay First. In a matter of weeks, government authorities had demolished several slums, rendering 300,000 people homeless. The demolitions came to be known as the "Indian tsunami." The urban poor of Mumbai were quite literally being erased from the face of the world-class city. Vijay Patil, the municipality officer who led the demolitions, stated that it was time to turn Mumbai into the "next Shanghai," and to do so "we want to put the fear of the consequences of migration into these people. We have to restrain them from coming to Mumbai" (BBC News, February 3, 2005). "How can you ask people to stop coming to Mumbai? This is a democracy," noted urban analyst Kalpana Sharma (BBC News, February 3, 2005). Particularly striking about the Vision Mumbai demolitions is that they carried neither the promise nor the pretense of resettlement and rehabilitation. Indeed, the United Nations Special Rapporteur on adequate housing, Miloon Kothari, sharply criticized Mumbai at the UN Commission on Human Rights, noting that the city had effectively criminalized poverty and violated all expectations of humane resettlement (Khan 2005).

Advocacy groups have argued that the "slum" is vital to the functioning of Indian urbanism – that, for example, Dharavi, Asia's, largest slum at the heart of Mumbai, is "a million-dollar economic miracle providing food to Mumbai and exporting crafts and manufactured goods to places as far away as Sweden" (Echanove and Srivastava 2009). But such devalorized spaces are now being rapidly reclaimed in India. Dharavi is also a particularly important urban "asset" (Tutton 2009), at the intersection of the city's infrastructural connections. Mukesh Mehta, the architect who is leading the redevelopment plan, argues that Dharavi could be India's "Canary Wharf" (Tutton 2009). Today, nineteen consortiums from around the world are vying to claim and redevelop the "only vast tract of land left that can be made available for fresh construction activities" at the heart of the city (Singh 2007). Such forms of urban renewal are bolstered, in Indian cities, by the emergence of the forms and structures of middle-class rule. Framed as good governance, these self-organized initiatives seek to reform government, improve service delivery, and assert the rights and needs of middle-class neighborhoods. Many of them are "protection of place" associations that thereby initiate and mobilize the evictions and demolitions of slums and squatter settlements. Baviskar (2003), in the context of Delhi, has rightly labeled these forms of urban governance a "bourgeois environmentalism," one that asserts the rights of "consumer-citizens" to "leisure, safety, aesthetics, and health" and devalues the citizenship of those who are poor and propertyless.

But a new urban politics is now afoot in Indian cities. It seeks to challenge, even blockade, the ferocious redevelopment that has been under way. In the Calcutta metropolitan region, squatters, sharecroppers, and peasants have mobilized to block development projects that displace the rural-urban poor, making it impossible for the state to deploy its power of eminent domain. In Mumbai, the brutal vision of a world-class city is contested by the National Alliance of Peoples Movements (NAPM). Since the Vision Mumbai plan had sought to remake Mumbai in the image of Shanghai, the NAPM has framed the "Shanghaification of Mumbai" as primarily an issue of rights: whether the urban-rural poor have a "right over urban space" (Patkar and Athialy 2005): "In Mumbai, 60 per cent live in the slums. Shouldn't they have a right over 60 per cent of the land in Mumbai?"

The social movements in India signal a heterodox reconstruction of the informal city and its practices of planning. They seek to assert the social function of property and to insist upon a right to the city. A similar confrontation, albeit put forward on very different terms, also marks the case of the Brazilian City Statute. In important ways, such politics reveals the logic of urban informality: the making and unmaking of spatial value. Various state practices and technologies are implicated in this differentiated production of spatial value. Some are more visible than others, such as the demolition of slums and squatter settlements. But there are many others: tools of enumeration and mapping; the zoning of land uses; the provision of infrastructure; the use of eminent domain to confiscate property for a public purpose. Applied in flexible and selective fashion, they ensure the planned production of urban informality.

References

AlSayyad, N. 2004. "Urban Informality as a Way of Life." In *Urban Informality: Transnational Perspectives from the Middle East, Latin America, and South Asia*, edited by A. Roy and N. AlSayyad, 7–30. Lanham, MD: Lexington Books.

Appadurai, A. 2002. "Deep Democracy: Urban Governmentality and the Horizon of Politics." *Public Culture* 14(1): 21–47.

Auyero, J. 1999. "'This Is a Lot Like The Bronx, Isn't It?': Lived Experiences of Marginality in an Argentine Slum." *International Journal of Urban and Regional Research* 23:45–69.

Auyero, J. 2000. "The Hyper-Shantytown: Neoliberal Violence(S) in the Argentine Slum." *Ethnography* 1:93–116.

Baviskar, A. 2003. "Between Violence and Desire: Space, Power, and Identity in the Making of Metropolitan Delhi." *International Social Science Journal* 55(175): 89–98.

Bayat, A. 2000. "From 'Dangerous Classes' to 'Quiet Rebels': The Politics of the Urban Subaltern in the Global South." *International Sociology* 15(3): 533–57.

Bayat, A. 2007. "Radical Religion and the Habitus of the Dispossessed: Does Islamic Militancy Have an Urban Ecology?" *International Journal of Urban and Regional Research* 31(3): 579–90.

Benjamin, S. 2008. "Occupancy Urbanism: Radicalizing Politics and Economy Beyond Policy and Programs." *International Journal of Urban and Regional Research* 32(3): 719–29.

Bhan, G. 2009. "'This Is No Longer The City I Once Knew': Evictions, The Urban Poor and the Right to the City in Millennial Delhi." *Environment and Urbanization* 21(1): 127–42.

Bromley, R. 2004. "Power, Property, and Poverty: Why De Soto's 'Mystery of Capital' Cannot Be Solved." In *Urban Informality: Transnational Perspectives from the Middle East, Latin America, and South Asia*, edited by A. Roy and N. AlSayyad, 271–88. Lanham, MD: Lexington Books.

Caldeira, T., and J. Holston. 2005. "State and Urban Space in Brazil: From Modernist Planning to Democratic Interventions." *Global Assemblages: Technology, Ethics, and Politics as Anthropological Problems*, edited by A. Ong and S. Collier, 393–416. Cambridge, UK: John Wiley and Blackwell.

Castells, M. 1983. *The City and the Grassroots*. Berkeley, CA: University of California Press.

Chatterjee, P. 2004. *The Politics of the Governed: Reflections on Popular Politics in Most of the World*. New York: Columbia University Press.

Davis, M. 2004. "Urbanization of Empire: Mega Cities and the Laws of Chaos." *Social Text* 22(4): 9–15.

Davis, M. 2006. *Planet of Slums*. New York: Verso.

De Certeau, M. 1984. *The Practice of Everyday Life*, translated by S. Rendall. Berkeley, CA: University of California Press.

de Soto, H. 1989. *The Other Path: The Invisible Revolution in the Third World*. London: I.B. Taurus.

De Soto, H. 2000. *The Mystery of Capital: Why Capitalism Triumphs in the West and Fails Everywhere Else*. New York: Basic Books.

Easterly, W. 2006. *The White Man's Burden: Why the West's Efforts to Aid the Rest Have Done So Much Ill and So Little Good*. New York: Penguin Press.

Echanove, M., and R. Srivastava. 2009. "Taking the Slum out of 'Slumdog.'" *New York Times*, February 21. Available at: http://www.nytimes.c0m/2009/02/21/opinion/2isrivastava.html.

Eckstein, S. 1990. "Urbanization Revisited. Inner-City Slum of Hope and Squatter Settlement of Despair." *World Development* 18:165–81.

Fernandes, E. 2007. "Constructing the 'Right to the City' In Brazil." *Social and Legal Studies* 16(2): 201–19.

Ghertner, A. 2008. "Analysis Of New Legal Discourse Behind Delhi's Slum Demolitions." *Economic and Political Weekly* May 17, 57–66.

Gibson-Graham, J. K. 2008. "Diverse Economies: Performative Practices for 'Other Worlds.'" *Progress in Human Geography* 32(5): 613–32.

Gilbert, A. 2007. "The Return of the Slum: Does Language Matter?" *International Journal of Urban and Regional Research* 31(4): 697–713.

Hart, K. 1973. "Informal Income Opportunities and Urban Employment in Ghana." *Journal of Modern African Studies* 11(1): 61–89.

Hart, K. 2006. "Bureaucratic Form and the Informal Economy." In *Linking the Formal and Informal Economy: Concepts and Policies*, edited by B. Guha-Khasnobis, R. Kanbur, and E. Ostrom, 21–35. New York: Oxford University Press.

Holston, J. 2007. *Insurgent Citizenship: Disjunctions of Democracy and Modernity in Brazil.* Princeton, NJ: Princeton University Press.

International Labor Organization. 1972. *Incomes, Employment and Equality in Kenya.* Geneva: ILO.

Instituto Polis. n.d. *The Statute of the City: New Tools for Assuring the Right to the City in Brazil.* Available at: http://www.polis.org.br/obras/arquivo_163.pdf.

Kanbur, R. 2009. "Conceptualising Informality: Regulation and Enforcement." Working paper 2009–11, Department of Economics and Applied Management, Cornell University, Ithaca, NY.

Khan E. 2005. "UN Flays India for Slum Demolition." Radiff News. Available at: http://in.rediff.com/news/2005/mar/30un.htm; accessed January 20, 2008.

Klein, N. 2007a. *The Shock Doctrine: The Rise of Disaster Capitalism.* New York: Metropolitan Books.

Klein, N. 2007b. "Rapture Rescue 911: Disaster Response for the Chosen." *The Nation,* November 19. Available at: http://www.thenation.com/artide/rapture-rescue-911-disaster-response-chosen.

Meagher, K., 1995. "Crisis, Informalization and the Urban Informal Sector in Sub-Saharan Africa." *Development and Change* 26(2): 259–84.

Ong, A. 2006. *Neoliberalism as Exception: Mutations in Citizenship and Sovereignty.* Durham, NC: Duke University Press.

Patkar, M., and J. Athialy. 2005. "The Shanghaification of Mumbai." Countercurrents. org. Available at: http://www.countercurrents.org/hr-athialy110805.htm.

Perlman, J. 1977. *The Myth of Marginality.* Berkeley, CA: University of California Press.

Perlman, J. 2004. "Marginality: From Myth to Reality in the Favelas of Rio de Janeiro." In *Urban Informality: Transnational Perspectives from the MiddleEast, Latin America, and South Asia,* edited by A. Roy and N. AlSayyad, 105–46. Lanham, MD: Lexington Books.

Portes, A., M. Castells, and L. Benton. 1989. *The Informal Economy.* Baltimore: Johns Hopkins University Press.

Roy, A. 2003. *City Requiem, Calcutta: Gender and the Politics of Poverty.* Minneapolis: University of Minnesota Press.

Roy, A., and N. AlSayyad, eds. 2004. *Urban Informality: Transnational Perspectives from the Middle East, Latin America, and South Asia.* Lanham, MD: Lexington Books.Sachs, J. 2005. *The End of Poverty: Economic Possibilities for our Time.* New York: Penguin.

Simone, A. 2004. "People as Infrastructure: Intersecting Fragments in Johannesburg." *Public Culture* 16(3): 407–29.

Simone, A. 2006. "Pirate Towns: Reworking Social and Symbolic Infrastructures in Johannesburg and Douala." *Urban Studies* 43(): 357–70.

Singh, S. 2007 "Dharavi Displacement Project." Civil Society. Available at: www.civilsocietyonline.com.

Tutton, M. 2009. "Real Life 'Slumdog' Slum to be Demolished." CNN travel news. Available at: http://edition.cnn.com/2009/TRAVEL/02/23/dharavi.mumbai.slums/index.html.

Wacquant, L. 1996. "The Rise of Advanced Marginality: Notes on Its Nature and Implications." *Acta Sociologica* 39:121–39.

Wacquant, L. 1999. "Urban Marginality in the Coming Millennium." *Urban Studies* 36: 1639–47.

Wacquant, L. 2007.*Urban Outcasts: A Comparative Sociology of Advanced Marginality.* Cambridge, UK: Polity Press.

Ward, P. 1999. *Colonias and Publicy in Texas: Urbanization by Stealth.* Austin: University of Texas Press.

Wirth, L. 1938. "Urbanism as a Way of Life." *American Journal of Sociology* 44(1): 1–24.

Yiftachel, O. 2009. "Theoretical Notes on 'Gray Cities': The Coming of Urban Apartheid?" *Planning Theory* 8(1): 88–100.

27

Seeing from the South

Refocusing Urban Planning on the Globe's Central Urban Issues

Vanessa Watson

Introduction

The joint meeting of the World Planners Congress and the UN Habitat World Urban Forum, in Vancouver in June 2006, signified a major shift in global thinking about the future of cities. There were two important aspects to this shift. The first was a recognition that, by 2008, for the first time in history, the majority of the world's population would live in cities and, in future years, most of all new global population growth will be in cities in the 'developing' world. The second important insight was that the rate and scale of this growth, coupled with impending issues such as climate change and resource depletion, posed massively serious problems in the cities of the global South and required specific intervention. In effect, UN Habitat was recognising that the profession of urban planning needed to be fundamentally reviewed to see if it was able to play a role in addressing issues in rapidly growing and poor cities. UN Habitat Executive Director Anna Tibaijuka (2006) called on planning practitioners to develop a different approach that is pro-poor and inclusive, and that places the creation of livelihoods at the centre of planning efforts.

The reasons why systems of urban planning have been less than adequate in addressing issues in the cities of the global South are complex and cannot always

Original publication details: Watson, Vanessa. 2009. "Seeing from the South: Refocusing Urban Planning on the Globe's Central Urban Issues". In *Urban Studies*, 46(11): 2259–75. Reproduced with permission from SAGE and Vanessa Watson.

Readings in Planning Theory, Fourth Edition. Edited by Susan S. Fainstein and James DeFilippis.
Editorial material and organization © 2016 John Wiley & Sons, Ltd.
Published 2016 by John Wiley & Sons, Ltd.

be blamed on planning itself. Yet the fact remains that in most of these regions the planning systems in place have been either inherited from previous colonial governments or have been adopted from Northern contexts to suit particular local political and ideological ends. The need for planning systems to be pro-poor and inclusive has therefore not been given much consideration. In many cases, these inherited planning systems and approaches have remained unchanged over a long period of time, even though the context in which they operate has changed significantly.

This article argues that additional and alternative theoretical resources must be brought to bear to allow planners a better understanding of the now-dominant urban conditions and to provide a framework for thinking about planning actions. However, the intentions of this article are to do no more than identify some potentially useful strands of theoretical thinking which will contribute to this shift and to organise these conceptually in relation to the notion of 'conflicting rationalities' (Watson, 2003, 2006). The position taken here is that a significant gap has opened up between increasingly technomanagerial and marketised systems of government administration, service provision and planning (including, frequently, older forms of planning) and the every-day lives of a marginalised and impoverished urban population surviving largely under conditions of informality. The gap between entrenched (and sometimes static) planning systems and new forms of urban poverty is of course not the only one of relevance. Urban space is also increasingly shaped by the workings of the market and the property industry in cities, which may align with urban modernist visions of city governments, but which do little to benefit or include the poor. I suggest here that the conflict of rationalities between state and market (which can also find themselves in conflict) and survival efforts of the poor and marginalised makes the task of meeting the demands of UN Habitat particularly difficult, and thus demands a fundamental rethink of the role of planning.

This article views planning as a central tool through which government manages spatially defined territories and populations: the issue of power is therefore inextricably linked to an understanding of planning systems. The particular position on power adopted here (with writers such as Rose, Scott and Corbridge) holds that these 'problems' in the planning field have not emerged simply because states are ignorant or tardy (although this can happen): rather, there may be a range of reasons (arising within the state and beyond it) for the continuation and manipulation of established planning land rights and institutions, and sometimes strong resistance to changing them. Also with these authors, however, this does not imply that such power is one-directional or totalising, or always negative or repressive. The space for resistance and struggle, and hence other outcomes, is usually present and this article offers a framework for understanding these.

The article begins by briefly contextualising the argument that planning systems in many parts of the global South are increasingly seen as inadequate and often inappropriate. It then moves to make the argument that conditions of urban life in cities (particularly but not only in the global South) are subject to new forces and are displaying new characteristics which any shifts in urban planning would need to take into account. While not attempting here to define precisely what these shifts would be, the article then suggests a way of thinking about this issue which recognises the nature of the 'interface' between two important imperatives: that of survival and that of governing. The argument put forward here is that a starting-point for thinking about the possibilities of planning lies in understanding the potentials which emerge from the highly varied nature of interactions across this interface.

The intention is, quite specifically, not to suggest a dual or multiple set of planning perspectives (one for the global North, one for the South, etc.), particularly given what appears to be a growing convergence of urban issues in a globalising world. Rather, the intention is to call for a widening of the scope of planning thought while grounding it specifically in the highly differentiated contexts within which planners work. Hence, I suggest that a 'view' of planning from outside the global heartland where it has its origins – i.e. a view from the global South – provides a useful and necessary unsettling of taken-for-granted assumptions in planning, essential for a conceptual shift in the discipline.

The Problem with Urban Planning

UN Habitat (2009) and other such agencies may well have grounds for asking planning practitioners to reconsider their role in the rapidly urbanising and impoverished cities of the South. Remarkably, much of the global South, as well as parts of the North, still use variations of an approach to urban planning which emerged in Europe and the US in the early part of the 20th century, adapted to forms of government and urban conditions which have changed significantly.

This early 20th-century approach to urban land management usually comprises a detailed land use plan depicting the desired future of an urban area some 20 years hence and it is underpinned by a regulatory system (zoning) which assigns use rights in land, and manages any alteration of these, in conformance with what is called a 'master plan'.[1] Master planning has, almost everywhere, carried with it a particular vision of the 'good city' which reflects the thinking of early urban modernists such as the French architect Le Corbusier.[2] Urban form is shaped by a concern with aesthetics (order, harmony, formality and symmetry); efficiency (functional specialisation of areas and movement, and the free flow of traffic); and modernisation (slum removal, vertical or tower buildings, connectivity, plentiful open green space). In the early 20th century, master planning and zoning, as tools to promote urban modernist ideals, were enthusiastically adopted by middle and commercial classes who were able to use them as a way of maintaining property prices and preventing the invasion of less desirable lower-income residents, ethnic minorities and traders. At the time, it was noted that the supposed 'public good' objective of planning had been turned into a tool by the wealthy to protect their property values and to exclude the poor (Hall, 1988).

In some parts of the global North, this approach to planning was severely criticised during the mid 20th century. This was largely because its assumptions about the nature and dynamics of cities, and the ability of planning to control market forces, had not held, particularly with the retreat from Keynesianism. New approaches to 'forward planning', such as the more flexible 'structure' and 'strategic' plans, emerged, but the underlying concept of zoning has generally persisted. In countries of the global South, there has been a long history in planning of the transfer of models, processes, policies and regulatory measures from the imperial heartland of the UK, Europe and the US to other parts of the world (see Nasr and Volait, 2003; Ward, 2002). In these contexts, planning was used in part to create acceptable urban environments for foreign settlers and also to extend administrative control and sanitary conditions to the growing numbers of indigenous urban poor.[3] In some respects the imperial territories (particularly those under French control) were used as laboratories for testing out ideas about planning and administration, for later use at 'home'. Processes of diffusion were never smooth or simple: the ideas themselves were often varied and contested, and they articulated in different ways with the contexts to which they were imported.

In much of the global South, master planning, zoning and visions of urban modernism are still the norm.[4] For example, many African countries still have planning legislation based on British or European planning laws from the 1930s or 1940s, but revised only marginally. Post-colonial governments tended to reinforce and entrench colonial spatial plans and land management tools, sometimes in even more rigid form than colonial governments (Njoh, 2003). Similarly in India, master planning and zoning ordinances introduced under British rule still persist. Ansari (2004) notes that some 2000 Indian cities now have master plans, all displaying the problems which caused countries such as the UK to shift away from this approach, and yet the main task of municipal planning departments is to produce more such plans. In other parts of the global South, particularly in Latin America, there has been some experimentation with new forms of master planning and strategic planning, but this is the exception rather than the rule.

In a study of nine cities in Africa, Asia and Latin America, Devas (2001) found that most had planning and building standards which were unsuited to the poor. Fernandes (2003) makes the point that in effect people have to step outside the law in order to secure land and shelter due to the élitist nature of urban land laws. It could be argued, therefore, that city governments themselves are producing social and spatial exclusion as a result of the inappropriate laws and regulations which they adopt. Other authors have suggested that this mismatch between planning requirements and the ability of poorer urban-dwellers to meet them is not innocent. Yiftachel and Yakobi (2003) suggest that in ethnocratic states, and elsewhere, urban informality can be condoned or facilitated by governments as it allows them to present themselves as open and democratic while at the same time using this as a planning strategy to deny particular groups access to rights and services.

Older forms of planning are thus often confronted with a contradiction: on the one hand, top–down, bureaucratic forms of land use control and rigid plans are cast as outdated and inappropriate in the context of 21st-century governance policies and rapidly changing urban environments and, in many ways, this is correct; on the other hand, these same plans offer protection to entrenched and exclusive urban land rights, promote modernist views of urban form which property developers can support and offer a regulatory system which can be used in opportunistic ways by those with political and economic power. Traditional forms of planning may thus appear to be somewhat of a dinosaur in 21st-century cities, but their persistence is not accidental and will not be easily changed.

The New Context for Planning

Cities in all parts of the world have changed significantly over the past several decades. Cities and towns undergoing rapid urbanisation in weak economies have long parted company (other than in élite enclaves) with the visions of orderly development and urban modernism of earlier days. As rates of urbanisation and the number of people living in urban 'slums' rapidly increase (UN Habitat, 2003),[5] there is a widening gap between the norms and objectives informing planning and the harsh realities of everyday life in cities of the global South.

In 2008, for the first time in history, the majority of the world's population lived in cities and, in the years to come, 90 per cent of all new global population growth will be in cities. Significantly, however, the bulk of this growth will be taking place in the global South. A rapidly growing proportion of this population will be urban: in 1950, less than 20 per cent of the population of poor countries lived in cities and towns, but by 2030 this will have risen to 60 per cent (National Research Council, 2003). The implication of these figures is that, globally, cities will increasingly become concentrations of poverty and inequality and hence important sites for intervention, but will at the same time present urban management and planning with issues which have not been faced before.

Compounding all of these problems, this rapid urban growth is taking place in those parts of the world least able to cope: in terms of the ability of governments to provide urban infrastructure, in terms of the ability of urban residents to pay for such services and in terms of coping with natural disasters. The inevitable result has been the rapid growth of urban 'slums', referring to physically and environmentally unacceptable living conditions in informal settlements and in older inner-city and residential areas. The 2003 UN Habitat Report claims that 32 per cent of the world's urban population (924 million people in 2001) lives in slums on extremely low incomes and is directly affected by both environmental disasters and social crises. New forms of planning will have to find ways of responding to rapid and unpredictable growth, in contexts where land and service delivery rely to a far greater extent on community and informal providers, rather than the state.

Within these rapidly growing and changing urban environments, the nature of economy and society is also changing. Globalisation of the economy and the liberalisation of trade over the past several decades have brought economic benefits to some parts of the global South, and to some groups, but have also succeeded in widening gaps between geographical regions and within them. Countries which report economic growth are also reporting growing numbers of unemployed and households in poverty, together with a burgeoning informal 'sector' which increasingly includes households previously categorised as the middle class (National Research Council, 2003). Al-Sayyad and Roy (2003) argue that these recent economic trends have given rise to an exploding informality in cities of the South which is taking on rather different forms than it has in the past. There appear to be new processes of polarisation within the informal economy, with informal entrepreneurs moving into sectors abandoned by the public and formal private sectors, but many as well swelling the ranks of 'survivalist' activities. In effect, informality (in terms of forms of income generation, forms of settlement and housing and forms of negotiating life in the city) has become the dominant mode of behaviour – in many urban centres it is now the norm and no longer the exception (Roy, 2005; Al-Sayyad and Roy, 2003; Yiftachel and Yacobi, 2003).

Economic liberalisation and growing income inequalities have had obvious implications in terms of high levels of poverty and insecurity, but they have implications for other aspects of social and political life as well. In a context of shrinking formal economies, competition between people and households becomes intensified, promoting both the need to draw on a wide range of networks (familial, religious, ethnic, etc.) and continually to manoeuvre, negotiate and protect the spaces of opportunity which have been created (Simone, 2000, 2004). Intensified competition, Simone argues, means that economic and political processes of all kinds become open for negotiation and informalisation. Networks with the state become particularly valuable, both in negotiating preferential access to resources and in avoiding control and regulation, with the result that, increasingly

> public institutions are seen not as public but the domain of specific interest-groups, and indeed they become sites for private accumulation and advantage. (Simone, 2000, p. 7)

The relationship between state and citizens, and between formal and informal actors, thus becomes undercodified and under-regulated, dependent on complex processes of alliance-making and deal-breaking, and particularly resistant to reconfiguring through policy and planning instruments, and external interventions.

As a result, assumptions of a relatively stable, cohesive and law-abiding civil society, on which the enforcement of regulatory planning and support for the urban modernist vision depend, must also be brought into question. In cities in both the global North and South, societal divisions have been increasing, partly as a result of international migration streams and the growth of ethnic minority groups in cities and partly because of growing income and employment inequalities which have intersected with ethnicity and identity in various ways. Thus, assumptions in the 1960s that cultural minorities would eventually assimilate gave way in the 1990s to the acceptance (in the planning literature at least) of persistent multiculturalism (Sandercock, 1998) in cities and ideas about ways in which planners could engage with cultural difference. This is giving way again, in the post 9/11 era, to growing concerns about how planning can engage with civil society in a context of deepening difference (Watson, 2006).

Yet it is vital for planning to recognise that civil society takes on very different forms in different parts of the world. In parts of Africa, de Boeck (1996, p. 93) suggests, understood dichotomies such as state/society or legal/illegal no longer capture reality. In an 'increasingly "exotic", complex and chaotic world that seems to announce the end of social life and the societal fabric as most of us know it', the state is but one (often weaker) locus of authority along with traditional chiefs, warlords and mafias. Definitions of legal and illegal constantly shift depending on which groups are exerting power at the time. Even in contexts that are less 'chaotic' than these, researchers point to the extent to which urban crime and violence, often supported by drug and arms syndicates, have brought about a decline in social cohesion and an increase in conflict and insecurity (National Research Council, 2003). Participatory planning approaches which are based on the assumption that civil society is definable, relatively organised, homogeneous and actively consensus-seeking, have frequently underestimated the societal complexity and conflict in such parts of the world (Cooke and Kothari, 2001).

Of particular importance for planning, is that urban growth and socioeconomic change has impacted on socio-spatial change in cities in dramatic ways, but with global forces mediated by local context. In essence, however, planners and urban managers have found themselves confronted with new spatial forms and processes, the drivers of which often lie outside the control of local government.

Socio-spatial change seems to have taken place primarily in the direction of the fragmentation, separation and specialisation of functions and uses in cities, with labour market polarisation (and hence income inequality) reflected in major differences between wealthier and poorer areas. Marcuse (2006) contrasts up-market gentrified and suburban areas with tenement zones, ethnic enclaves and ghettos; and areas built for the advanced service and production sector, and for luxury retail and entertainment, with older areas of declining industry, sweatshops and informal businesses. While much of this represents the playing out of 'market forces' in cities, and the logic of real estate and land speculation, it is also a response to local policies which have attempted to position cities globally and attract new investment. 'Competitive city' approaches to urban policy aim to attract global investment, tourists and a residential élite through up-market property developments, waterfronts, convention centres and the commodification of culture and heritage (Kipfer and Keil, 2002). However, such policies have also had to suppress and contain the fall-out from profit-driven development through surveillance of public spaces, policing and crime-prevention efforts, immigration control and dealing with problems of social and spatial exclusion.

In many poorer cities, spatial forms are largely driven by the efforts of low-income households to secure land that is affordable and in a reasonable location. This process is leading to entirely new urban ('ruralopolitan') forms as the countryside itself begins to urbanise, as in vast stretches of rural India, Bangladesh, Pakistan, China, Indonesia, Egypt, Rwanda and many other poorer countries (see Qadeer, 2004). As well, large cities spread out and incorporate nearby towns leading to continuous belts of settlement (such as the shanty-town corridor from Abidjan to Ibadan, containing 70 million people and making up the urban agglomeration of Lagos; see Davis, 2004), and as the poor seek a foothold in the urban areas primarily on the urban edge. It is these sprawling urban peripheries, almost entirely unserviced and unregulated, that make up the bulk of what is termed slum settlement and it is in these areas that most urban growth is taking place. These kinds of areas are impossibly costly to plan and service in the conventional way, given the form of settlement, and even if that capacity did exist, few could afford to pay for such services. In fact, the attractiveness of these kinds of locations for poor households is that they can avoid the costs associated with formal and regulated systems of urban land and service delivery.

The context of government and administration also shows important changes (as well as continuities) which are of relevance for planning. Planning and urban modernism originally emerged in contexts in the global North characterised by relatively strong and stable liberal democratic governments, often with comprehensive welfare policies, and in which rates of urban growth and change were relatively slow, predictable and amenable to regulatory control. Within the past three or so decades, and closely linked to processes of globalisation, there have been significant transformations in government in many parts of the world, making them very different settings from those within which planning was originally conceived.

The most commonly recognised change has been the expansion of the urban political system from 'government' to 'governance', which in the global North represents a response to the growing complexity of governing in a globalising and multiscalar context as well as the involvement of a range of non-state actors in the process of governing. In the global South, understanding 'the state' implies comprehending the discourse of the neo-liberal reform agenda which has been promoted through the major aid and development agencies and which has moved through the three phases described as 'structural adjustment', 'good governance' and most recently 'social capital' (Slater, 2004). These 'changing modalities of neo-liberal thought', Slater argues, have not replaced each other, but rather represent an extension of the discursive terrain [so that] by the beginning of the twenty-first century, the economy, the state and civil society have been represented and situated as part of an evolving regime of truth. (Slater, 2004, p. 98)

The implications of all three of these phases for state–society relations have been profound, extending well beyond technical reforms of state and economy to encompass the (continued) inculcation of Western values as well.

At the same time, continuities with past, and sometimes regionally distinct, governance regimes are important. There is no doubt that the processes of colonisation and imperialism fundamentally changed relations between parts of the world, articulating with pre-existing social and governing structures in colonised territories in multiple and complex ways. Such histories continue to express themselves through patterns of inequality affecting economy and society and, importantly, respect for knowledge and expertise (Connell, 2007). Authoritative sources for thinking about urban development and planning, as well as what constitutes a desirable modern city, also reflect these inequalities and partly explain the dominance of particular ideas in this field. As new imperial powers emerge and begin to make themselves felt (for example, China in Africa), it is likely that regional regimes of government and economy will shift again, setting up new relations both to a new metropole and to local citizenry.

Within the post-development literature, the emergence of the neo-liberalised state in parts of the global South has been used to explain the repeated failure of development projects, the widening of inequalities and the depoliticisation of the development effort (Escobar, 2004; Nederveen Pieterse, 2000; Nustad, 2001; Schuurman, 2000). Neo-liberalism, these authors argue, appears to introduce a new, or perhaps newly framed, set of values to the conduct of political, social and economic life and to seek actively to hegemonise them. At one level, these values direct institutional change: minimising the role of the state; encouraging non-state mechanisms of regulation; privatising public services; creating policy rather than delivering services; introducing forms of performance management, etc. Yet at another level they seek to penetrate further. Brown (2003) argues for the recognition of a new neo-liberal political rationality which is a mode of governance not limited to the state but also produces subjects, forms of citizenship and behaviour, and a new organisation of the social. The essence of these values is the submission of all spheres of life (including the political and the personal) to an economic or market rationality, such that all actions become rational entrepreneurial action, seen in terms of the logic of supply and demand.

There are, of course, significant parts of the world where the model of the neo-liberalised state does not hold. While certain regions of China are beginning to show these characteristics, it has been argued that the dominant 'political rationality' in this country remains one in which an independent civil society is difficult to define, given that the family is seen as an integral part of, and a direct extension of, the state (Leaf, 2005). Theocratic regimes (such as Iran) also operate within a rather different political rationality and conception of civil society, as do ethnocratic regimes (Yiftachel, 2006a).

These shifts have had profound implications for urban planning, which has often been cast as a relic of the old welfare state model and as an obstacle to economic development and market freedom. In a context in which the power of governments to direct urban development has diminished with the retreat of Keynsian economics, planning has found itself to be unpopular and marginalised. It has also found itself at the heart of contradictory pressures on local government to promote urban economic competitiveness on the one hand, while on the other dealing with the fall-out from globalisation in the form of growing social exclusion, poverty, unemployment and rapid population growth, often in a context of unfunded mandates and severe local government capacity constraints (Beall, 2002).

Conceptualising 'Conflicting Rationalities'

The purpose of this article is to consider what strands of thinking can be brought to bear to understand what is perceived as an inability of current planning practices to deal with issues confronting particularly cities in the global South, but increasingly cities in many parts of the globe. I suggest that this exploration requires an understanding of a 'conflict of rationalities' arising at the interface between, on the one hand, current techno-managerial and marketised systems of government administration and service provision (in those parts of the world where these apply) and, on the other, marginalised and impoverished urban populations surviving largely under conditions of informality. While an understanding of planning as part of the rationality of government (governmentality) is not new in the planning literature (see Huxley, 2006, 2007), the idea here is that this confronts a different rationality – shaped by efforts of survival – which in turn operates with its own logics and imperatives.

Bridge (2005) develops a concept of rationality which he traces to the Chicago School, to Dewey and to Habermas, who proposed a split between the instrumental rationality of the system (economic rationality and bureaucratic rationality) and the communicative rationality of the life-world. Bridge argues for a somewhat different view of communicative rationality, that moves away from Habermas' dichotomy; that 'involves bodies and gestures, as well as speech and thought' (Bridge, 2005, p. 6); that understands these communicative actions as qualities of a particular situation and context rather than universal qualities; that accepts dissensus as being as much a part of a communicative situation as consensus; and that (drawing on recent work by feminist pragmatists) sees communicative action as implicated in systems of dispersal of power (in a Foucauldian sense) as well as being in resistance to power. Relating these ideas to an understanding of the city and space, Bridge argues that rationality is not necessarily confined to 'a community' as members operate in diverse communities which overlap and collide in various ways. Similarly sharp distinctions between structure and agency dissolve through a focus on power working through social/technical networks and in the constitution of the self.

This perspective on rationality is useful for framing a way of thinking about conflicting rationalities in the environments in which planning operates. It also helps to make the case that, for analytical purposes, planning theory should start from the assumption of a conflict model of society, rather than the prevailing consensus model. Work in planning theory that argues for an 'agonistic' view of society – the 'permanence of conflict, non-reciprocity and domination' (Hillier, 2003, p. 37) – has begun to move in this direction. For normative purposes as well, there are arguments that the goal of consensus in planning processes needs to be treated with caution. While planning would certainly not seek deliberately to create conflict (although sometimes this is inevitable), there may be circumstances in which consensus-driven processes serve to marginalise rather than to include. Hillier (2003, p. 51) draws on Lacan to argue that conflict should be recognised and not eliminated through the 'establishment of an authoritarian consensus'. Porter has argued, in the context of Australia, that a process which assumes that all stakeholders, including an indigenous traditional landowner group, have equal voice

> fails to appreciate their unique status as original owners of a country that was wrested from them by the modern, colonial state. (Porter, 2006, p. 389)

The argument then, is that planners (particularly, but not only, in cities of the global South) are located within a fundamental tension – a conflict of rationalities – between the logic of governing[6] and the logic of survival (both highly diverse and overlapping), in which governing has to do with control *and* development and in which development is generally driven by notions of modernisation and the creation of 'proper' communities living and working in 'proper' urban environments (Watson, 2003). Pile *et al.* (1999) graphically refer to attempts by functionaries of government to extend the grid of formalised and regulated development over what is often termed the 'informal' or sometimes 'unruly' (or unrule-able?) city, where what is generally referred to as the 'informal' represents the survival efforts of those excluded from, or only partially or temporarily included in, regular and secure forms of income generation (or the 'formal' economy). With a restructuring of labour markets occurring in many cities, this informality is reaching new scales and new forms in urban areas in all parts of the world. In effect, informality (in terms of forms of income generation, forms of settlement and housing and forms of negotiating life in the city) has become the dominant mode of behaviour – in many urban centres it is now the norm and no longer the exception (Roy, 2005; Al-Sayyad and Roy, 2003; Yiftachel and Yacobi, 2003). Finding a way in which planning can work with informality, supporting survival efforts of the urban poor rather than hindering them through regulation or displacing them with modernist megaprojects, is essential if it is to play a role at all in these new urban conditions.

By contrast, technical and managerial systems of governing which now operate in many Southern urban areas have embedded within them rationalities which, in many cases, have been inherited from other (often Northern) contexts and are strongly shaped by neo-liberalism. The marketisation and privatisation of services and infrastructure, the on-going promotion of urban modernist forms, the insistence on freehold tenure and the recasting of urban citizens as urban consumers, are all part of this shift. Significantly, however, planning as 'a spatial technology of liberal government' (Huxley, 2007, p. 134) continues to be bound up with these interventions. Here, a 'governmentality' perspective is useful in understanding the sometimes contradictory workings of power, which can be directed at both the ordering and control of space as well as at its development and improvement – usually shaped by some or other utopian urban vision (Huxley, 2007; Dean, 1999, in Huxley, 2007). Traditional and control-oriented forms of planning therefore find their place in modern governments, where they can serve both progressive and retrogressive ends.

To date, mainstream planning theory has provided little guidance to planners working within such tensions, and few informants for the reconceptualising of urban planning systems (Harrison, 2006; Roy, 2005; Watson, 2002a; Yiftachel, 2006b). Thus a central task for planning and urban theorists is to explore the analytical, evaluative and interventive concepts which could help planners faced with such conflicting rationalities, paying attention to what may be termed the 'interface' between the rationality of governing and the rationality of survival. However, it is important that this notion of interface does not set up a questionable binary: between a 'will to order' and something that escapes it (Osborne and Rose, 2004). While techno-managerial and marketised systems of administration, planning and service provision often appear to be entirely sound in their own terms, and may follow 'international best practice', problems arise at the point at which they interface with a highly differentiated and 'situated' urban citizenry. Responses to these interventions are always varied: people in their everyday lives engage with the systems in diverse and unpredictable forms – making use of them, rejecting them or hybridising them in a myriad of ways. It is where linkages occur across the interface that some of the most interesting possibilities for understanding, and learning, arise.

This raises a number of questions. How do we understand and conceptualise this interface between conflicting rationalities, and how do we understand the relationships which it generates? How do we also begin to be able to identify where there is an articulation of interests or benefits across the interface and hence where interventive processes and outcomes can be evaluated as beneficial or destructive? Further, what conceptual strands and theoretical resources might be pulled together into an 'organisation of perspectives', to understand what goes on, and what could go on, at the interface?

Some potentially useful sources for these theoretical perspectives are to be found within existing planning theory, but this source is insufficient. The historical divide between planning theory, which has largely originated in and is addressed to, the global North, and development (and post-development) theory, often also originating in the global North but addressed primarily to the problems of cities and regions in the global South, is an impoverishing one. This intellectual divide has parallels in the one identified by Robinson (2006) between the field of urban studies, which draws on particularly the global cities of 'the West' to explore and celebrate urban modernity, and the urban development literature concerned with policies to improve life in cities, especially for the poorest, and usually in the cities of the South. If planning theory is to secure its relevance in what is rapidly becoming the globally dominant urban condition, then it too needs to overcome this divide and engage with theories which seek to understand and address the socio-spatial and environmental problems which confront what is now the majority of the world's urban population.

The next section of the article identifies some theoretical strands which could be drawn together to understand the nature of this clash of rationalities, between the will to survive and the will to govern.

The Interface: A Zone of Encounter and Contestation

This article suggests that a central concern for planning is how to locate itself relative to conflicting rationalities – between, on the one hand, organisations, institutions and individuals shaped by the rationality of governing (and, in market economies, modernisation, marketisation and liberalisation), within a global context shaped by historical inequalities and power relations (such as colonialism and imperialism) and, on the other hand, organisations, institutions and individuals shaped by (the rationality of) the need and desire to survive and thrive (broadly the 'poors' and the 'informals'). I am not suggesting that these are the only rationalities at play or in conflict in cities (Bridge, 2005), but I am suggesting that they are key ones for planning. It is also undoubtedly the case that individuals are not fixed in positions on either side of some imaginary divide. Bridge's (2005) point that individuals occupy diverse communities is relevant here. For example, it is not unknown for functionaries in government to live in an informal settlement or slum, or conduct informal income-generating activities during or after formal work hours.

The interface is a zone of encounter and contestation between these rationalities and is shaped by the exercise of power. For the poors and the informals, it is a zone of resistance, of evasion or of appropriation. It is the point at which state efforts at urban development and modernisation (provision of formal services, housing, tenure systems), urban administration or political control (tax and service fee collection, land use management, regulation of population health and education, etc.) and market regulation and penetration, are met, or confronted, by their 'target populations' in various and complex ways, and these responses in turn shape the nature of interventions. The nature of interactions at the interface can vary greatly: some products or policy interventions can be of direct benefit and improve the lives of poor households without imposing unnecessary burdens (the incredible spread of cell-phones to even the poorest households suggests that this technology articulates closely with felt needs); some interventions (informal settlement upgrade or 'urban renewal') may benefit some households but may result in the forced removal of others and often the imposition of costs that many cannot afford, and this may be met with resistance; some interventions may be appropriated and hybridised so that they are useful in ways which had never been anticipated or intended.

An illustration of how interventions can be appropriated and hybridised is evident in the way in which formal and informal land markets are beginning to work together in Enugu, Nigeria (Ikejiofor, 2008; Nwanunobi *et al.*, 2004). Finding ways to deliver urban land is a critical issue in rapidly urbanising cities, as formal planning mechanisms are unable to keep up with demand for land supply (it meets only 15 per cent of demand in Enugu) and usually impose costs which most households cannot meet. Further, the individualisation of property rights which occurs through formal land delivery transforms social and economic relations in sometimes problematic ways. Much urban land is therefore delivered through informal mechanisms, but this can lead to conflicts and land use patterns that are difficult to service. Also, informal landholdings preclude recourse to courts of law to resolve conflicts – an option which is available when tenure is formal.

In Enugu, actors in the informal (customary) sector have begun to develop practices that interrelate more closely with the formal land market system. Community leaders are ensuring orderly lay-outs, forms of land transfer registration and tenure security. Further, intricate relationships between government structures, formal land institutions and indigenous landowning groups are emerging. Obtaining formal title to land acquired through customary sources is now possible through the Ministry of Lands, Survey and Town Planning, which will consult the land-owning community and the register which most communities keep. If there are no community objections, then the Ministry will issue a title deed if the land is within an approved lay-out, or a Certificate of Occupancy if it is not. Indigenous communities in Enugu have thus begun to 'borrow' from formal rules and imported land development practices to solve internal problems. It should be possible to learn from these adaptive practices at the 'interface' between different systems, to develop urban development approaches which are more appropriate to the conditions of rapidly urbanising and poor cities.

Theoretical perspectives which have tried to understand the nature of this interface, incorporating an acknowledgement of power, are useful here. Arce and Long (2000) develop an anthropological perspective on the encounter between Western visions of modernity and the *modi operandi* of other cultural repertoires. They explore how ideas and practices of modernity are themselves appropriated and re-embedded in locally situated practices, thus accelerating the fragmentation and dispersal of modernity into constantly proliferating modernities. (Arce and Long, 2000, p. 1)

Thus people do not experience the arrival of 'modernity' as something which can simply replace their 'old' or pre-existing world. Rather, they juxtapose and interrelate different materialities and types of agency and embrace aspects of modernity and tradition together – it could be added, often foregrounding elements that offer opportunities for the exercise of power.

From the field of critical development studies, Corbridge *et al.* (2005) undertake detailed ethnographic work in India to analyse the nature of state–poor encounters and to ask how poorer citizens 'see the state'. They examine the new 'human technologies of rule' in India (associated with a good governance agenda and development) to find where new spaces of citizenship are being created or alternatively remain closed. This involves work on both sides of the interface, to look at 'government in practice' and to see how the state matters to poor people, or where it is something to be avoided or feared. They focus specifically on the everyday-ness of how people inhabit and encounter the state – for example, how an *adivasi* woman negotiates for an appointment with a *sakar*, how she may have to use a local broker to do so, and how she is treated in a formal encounter.

Embedded in the work of both Scott and Rose (who follow a decentred and dispersed concept of power) as well as in the work of a variant of the post-development school (including Corbridge *et al.*, 2005; Williams, 2004, and others) is the belief that power can never be totalising. Therefore there is always the possibility of resistance and struggle ('weapons of the weak' for Scott; 'quiet encroachment' for Bayat) and hence the opening of space for other outcomes. Corbridge *et al.* (2005) argue that the 'good governance' agenda in parts of India, for example, has opened possibilities for improvement in the lives of the poor. In other parts of India it has not and hence the need for grounded research on the 'practices of government' and responses to them (how ordinary people see and regard the state) to determine what makes this difference. Osborne and Rose (1999) – Corbridge *et al.* draw significantly on Rose[7] – make a related point: advanced liberal strategies of government, following the logic of the market, conceive of citizens as active in their own government incurring both rights and obligations in which 'rights to the city are as much about duties as they are about entitlements' (Osborne and Rose, 1999, p. 752). These strategies of governing are inherently ambiguous, as what they demand of citizens may be 'refused, or reversed or redirected', and may 'connect up' and 'destabilise larger circuits of power'.

Of course, the question of state–society interaction around planned interventions has been a major preoccupation of planning theory in the form of 'communicative planning theory' or 'collaborative planning', associated particularly with the work of Forester (1999), Innes (2004), Healey (1997) and others. Within development theory as well, the concept of public participation in development projects has been a central concern (see especially the work of Robert Chambers, 1997) and, in some parts of the South, participation has become an accepted part of government and international agency discourse. However, while the two areas of theorising (in planning and in development) have been grappling with the same issues, there has been very little connection between them.

Both, and particularly planning theory, reflect a turn in normative theorising of the processes of intervention and how such processes might involve planners and development workers, along with citizens or stakeholders, as a way of working towards acceptable plans and projects. The recognition that there are 'different voices' within civil society which represent what may be valid and valuable points of view is vitally important in the South where planning and development interventions in the past have often been top–down or impositionary. There is now a significant body of critique in both literatures, however, which points to the limitations of these processes: the difficulties of reaching meaningful consensus, especially in contexts of 'deep difference' (Watson, 2003, 2006); the varied forms of civil society and different approaches to organised resistance (Bayat, 2004); the need to recognise power (Flyvbjerg, 1998; Yiftachel, 1998); the problem with placing undue faith in processes at the expense of outcomes; and the need to consider broader sustainability and equity issues which may escape local processes (Fraser, 2005). The shift in planning theory away from an assumed consensus model of society, and towards one which instead assumes conflict and 'agonism', has been referred to earlier.

Development theorists have accused participatory exercises of being a form of depoliticisation and a covert mechanism for furthering the aims of liberalisation (for example, Cooke and Kothari, 2001). Williams (2004) provides a useful summary of these arguments in development theory but argues, following a Foucauldian concept of power, that the space for unintended consequences of participation, positive or negative, is always present. He argues for a process of examining ways in which the practices of participatory development play out in concrete situations and a search for opportunities for their repoliticisation. The idea of the interface as a zone of contestation reflecting various and unpredictable forms of encounter across it is compatible with this thinking.

Understanding what goes on at the interface and how planning interventions impact positively, negatively or are hybridised to suit particular local contexts, requires research of the kind carried out by Corbridge *et al.* (2005) and others: in-depth, grounded and qualitative case study research on state–society interactions and the 'dispersed practices of government'.[8] It requires those in the planning field to draw on this wider Southern literature and to consider how understandings such as these can assist in the reshaping of planning thought and action.

Conclusion

This article represents an early attempt to stake out the terrain for a shift in planning theory and practice which acknowledges: first, that approaches to planning which have originated in the global North are frequently based on assumptions regarding urban contexts which do not hold elsewhere in the world (and often no longer hold in the North as well); secondly, that the global demographic transition, whereby Southern cities and their growth dynamics are now the dominant urban reality, requires that planning turns its attention to these kinds of issues; thirdly, that the sharp divide in these cities between an increasingly informalised and marginalised population and techno-managerial and marketised systems of government (within which older and persistent forms of planning occupy a sometimes contradictory position) gives rise to a 'conflict of rationalities'. This conflict between the rationalities of governing and administration, and rationalities of survival (of those who are poor and marginalised), offers one way of understanding why, so often, sophisticated and 'best practice' planning and policy interventions have unintended outcomes (which is not to deny that other less explicit intentions may be driving these interventions).

A further central argument of this article is that expanding theorising in planning to incorporate issues of the global South requires tapping into other literatures. Here, the development (and post-development) studies literature, which has tended to focus on issues of the global South, offers important opportunities. Turning the concept of conflicting rationalities into a useful analytical and normative tool for planning requires an understanding of what goes on at the interface between these imperatives and ways in which such interaction can take positive, negative or hybridised forms. Strands of development literature can make an important contribution to this understanding. The suggestion here is that understanding these interactions (the spaces of citizenship, the successes of encroachment, the cracks, spaces and moments of alternative practice, or the positive hybridities) can provide an important basis from which to develop new and normative insights for planning. The step beyond this will be to explore how we balance these possibly small initiatives with the wider imperatives of resource depletion, environmental crisis and growing global income inequalities.

Notes

1. The concept of land use zoning, a basic element of master planning, originated in Germany and was adopted with great enthusiasm across the US, Britain and Europe in the early part of the 20th century. It subsequently took different forms in different parts of the world. See Booth (2007) for an explanation of why British planning law developed in a different way from European planning law.

2. The Charter of Athens (initiated in 1928) and later strongly influenced by Le Corbusier, was an important document (by 1944) in terms of establishing modernist urban principles.
3. See Huxley (2006) on the 'sanitary' role of planning.
4. Although master planning has given way to various forms of strategic planning in Australia, South Africa and parts of Latin America. Starting in 1986, the UN Urban Management Programme also made efforts, in various parts of the world, to introduce more flexible and integrated forward planning. Success has been partial (UN Habitat, 2005).
5. As well as new impending threats from climate change and natural resource depletion.
6. It can be argued that the logic of governing takes different forms in countries with different socio-political systems and in some parts of the world may be only weakly exercised, but that it is always present to some degree.
7. Rose works within a Foucauldian framework (see Rose, 1999).
8. Also, see Watson (2002b) for the use of case study research in planning.

References

Al-Sayyad, N. and Roy, A. (eds) (2003) *Urban Informality: Transnational Perspectives from the Middle East, Latin America and South Asia*. Boulder, CO: Lexington Books.

Ansari, J. (2004) Time for a new approach in India, *Habitat Debate*, 10, p. 15.

Arce, A. and Long, N. (eds) (2000) *Anthropology, Development and Modernities*. London: Routledge.

Bayat, A. (2004) Globalization and the politics of the informals in the global South, in: N. Al-Sayyad and A. Roy (eds) *Urban Informality: Transnational Perspectives from the Middle East, Latin America and South Asia*, pp. 79–102. Boulder, CO: Lexington Books.

Beall, J. (2002) Globalization and social exclusion in cities: framing the debate with lessons from Africa and Asia, *Environment and Urbanization*, 14, pp. 41–51.

Boeck, F. de (1996) Postcolonialism, power and identity: local and global perspectives from Zaire, in: R. Werbner and T. Ranger (eds) *Postcolonial Identities in Africa*, pp. 75–106. London: Zed Books.

Booth, P. (2007) The control of discretion: planning and the common-law tradition, *Planning Theory*, 6, pp. 127–45.

Bridge, G. (2005) *Reason in the City of Difference: Pragmatism, Communicative Action and Contemporary Urbanism*. London: Routledge.

Brown, W. (2003) Neo-liberalism and the end of liberal democracy, *Theory and Event*, 7, pp. 1–19 (http://muse.jhu.edu.proxy2.library.uiuc.edu/journals/theory_and_event/v007/7.1brown.html).

Chambers, R. (1997) *Whose Reality Counts? Putting the First Last*. London: Intermediate Technology Publications.

Connell, R. (2007) *Southern Theory: The Global Dynamics of Knowledge in Social Science*. Crows Nest, Australia: Allen and Unwin.

Cooke, B. and Kothari, U. (eds) (2001) *Participation: The New Tyranny?* London: Zed Books.

Corbridge, S., Williams, G., Srivastava, M. and Veron, R. (2005) *Seeing the State: Governance and Governmentality in India*. Cambridge: Cambridge University Press.

Davis, M. (2004) Planet of slums, *New Left Review*, 26(March/April), pp. 1–23.

Dean, M. (1999) *Governmentality: Power and Rule in Modern Society*. London: Sage.

Devas, N. (2001) Does city governance matter for the urban poor?, *International Planning Studies*, 6, pp. 393–408.

Escobar, A. (2004) Beyond the Third World: imperial globality, global coloniality and anti-globalisation social movements, *Third World Quarterly*, 25, pp. 207–30.

Fernandes, E. (2003) Illegal housing: law, property rights and urban space, in: P. Harrison, M. Huchzermeyer and M. Mayekiso (eds) *Confronting Fragmentation: Housing and Urban Development in a Democratising Society*, pp. 228–43. Cape Town: University of Cape Town Press.

Flyvbjerg, B. (1998) *Rationality and Power: Democracy in Practice*. Chicago, IL: University of Chicago Press.

Forester, J. (1999) *The Deliberative Practitioner: Encouraging Participatory Planning Processes*. Cambridge, MA: MIT Press.

Fraser, N. (2005) Reframing justice in a globalizing world, *New Left Review*, 36, pp. 69–88.

Hall, P. (1988) *Cities of Tomorrow*. Oxford: Blackwell.

Harrison, P. (2006) On the edge of reason: planning and urban futures in Africa, *Urban Studies*, 43, pp. 319–35.

Healey, P. (1997) *Collaborative Planning: Shaping Places in Fragmented Societies*. Basingstoke: Macmillan Press.

Hillier, J. (2003) Agonizing over consensus: why Habermasian ideals cannot be 'real', *Planning Theory*, 2, pp. 37–59.

Huxley, M. (2006) Spatial rationalities: order, environment, evolution and government, *Social and Cultural Geography*, 7, pp. 771–87.

Huxley, M. (2007) Planning, space and government, in: K. Cox, M. Low and J. Robinson (eds) *Handbook of Political Geography*, pp. 123–40. London: Sage.

Ikejiofor, U. (2008) *Planning within a context of informality: issues and trends in land delivery in Enugu, Nigeria. Case study prepared for Revisiting Urban Planning: Global Report on Human Settlements 2009*, UN Habitat, Nairobi (http://unhabitat.org/grhs/2009).

Innes, J. (2004) Consensus building: clarification for the critics, *Planning Theory*, 3, pp. 5–20.

Kipfer, S. and Keil, R. (2002) Toronto Inc? *Planning the competitive city in the new Toronto, Antipode*, 34, pp. 227–64.

Leaf, M. (2005) Modernity confronts tradition: the professional planner and local corporatism in the rebuilding of China's cities, in: B. Sanyal (ed.) *Comparative Planning Cultures*, pp. 91–112. New York: Routledge.

Marcuse, P. (2006) Space in the globalizing city, in: N. Brenner and R. Keil (eds) *The Global Cities Reader*, ch. 44. London: Routledge.

Nasr, J. and Volait, M. (eds) (2003) *Urbanism: Imported or Exported?* Chichester: Wiley-Academy.

National Research Council (2003) *Cities Transformed: Demographic Change and Its Implications in the Developing World*. Washington, DC: The National Academies Press.

Nederveen Pieterse, J. (2000) After post-development, *Third World Quarterly*, 21, pp. 175–91.

Njoh, A. (2003) *Planning in Contemporary Africa: The State, Town Planning and Society in Cameroon*. Aldershot: Ashgate.

Nustad, K. (2001) Development: the devil we know?, *Third World Quarterly*, 22, pp. 479–89.

Nwanunobi, C., Ikejiofor, C. and Nwogu K. (2004) *Informal land delivery processes and access to land for the poor in Enugu, Nigeria*. Working Paper No. 2, International Development Department, School of Public Policy, University of Birmingham.

Osborne, T. and Rose, N. (1999) Governing cities: notes on the spatialisation of virtue, *Environment and Planning D*, 17, pp. 737–60.

Osborne, T. and Rose, N. (2004) Spatial phenomenotechnics: making space with Charles Booth and Patrick Geddes, *Environment and Planning D*, 22, pp. 209–28.

Pile, S., Brook, C. and Mooney, G. (1999) *Unruly Cities? Order/Disorder*. London: Routledge.

Porter, L. (2006) Planning in (post) colonial settings: challenges for theory and practice, *Planning Theory and Practice*, 7(4), pp. 383–96.

Qadeer, M. (2004) Guest editorial: urbanization by implosion, *Habitat International*, 28, pp. 1–12.

Robinson, J. (2006) *Ordinary Cities: Between Modernity and Development*. London: Routledge.

Rose, N. (1999) *Powers of Freedom: Reframing Political Thought*. Cambridge: Cambridge University Press.

Roy, A. (2005) Urban informality: towards an epistemology of planning, *Journal of the American Planning Association*, 71, pp. 147–58.

Sandercock, L. (1998) *Towards Cosmopolis: Planning for Multicultural Cities*. Chichester: John Wiley.

Schuurman, F. J. (2000) Paradigms lost, paradigms regained? Development studies in the twenty-first century, *Third World Quarterly*, 21, pp. 7–20.

Scott, J. C. (1998) *Seeing Like a State*. New Haven, CT: Yale University Press.

Simone, A. (2000) *On informality and considerations for policy*. Dark Roast Occasional Paper Series, Isandla Institute, Cape Town.

Simone, A. (2004) *For the City Yet to Come: Changing African Life in Four Cities*. Durham, NC: Duke University Press.

Slater, D. (2004) *Geopolitics and the Post-colonial: Rethinking North–South Relations*. Oxford: Blackwell.

Tibaijuka, A. (2006) *The importance of urban planning in urban poverty reduction and sustainable development*. Paper presented at *World Planners Congress*, Vancouver.

UN Habitat (2003) *The Challenge of the Slums: Global Report on Human Settlements*. London: Earthscan.

UN Habitat (2005) The legacy of the urban management programme, *Habitat Debate*, 11(4).

UN Habitat (2009) *Planning Sustainable Cities: Global Report on Human Settlements*. London: Earthscan.

Ward, S. (2002) *Planning the Twentieth-century City: The Advanced Capitalist World*. Chichester: John Wiley.

Watson, V. (2002a) The usefulness of normative planning theories in the context of sub-Saharan Africa, *Planning Theory*, 1, pp. 27–52.

Watson, V. (2002b) Do we learn from planning practice? The contribution of the practice movement to planning theory, *Journal of Planning Education and Research*, 22, pp. 178–87.

Watson, V. (2003) Conflicting rationalities: implications for planning theory and ethics, *Planning Theory and Practice*, 4, pp. 395–408.

Watson, V. (2006) Deep difference: diversity, planning and ethics, *Planning Theory*, 5, pp. 31–50.

Williams, G. (2004) Evaluating participatory development: tyranny, power and (re) politicisation, *Third World Quarterly, 25*, pp. 557–78.

Yiftachel, O. (1998) Planning and social control: exploring the dark side, *Journal of Planning Literature, 12*, pp. 396–406.

Yiftachel, O. (2006a) *Ethnocracy: Land and Identity Politics in Israel/Palestine*. Philadelphia, PA: University of Pennsylvania Press.

Yiftachel, O. (2006b) Re-engaging planning theory? *Towards south-eastern perspectives, Planning Theory, 5*, pp. 211–22.

Yiftachel, O. and Yakobi, H. (2003) Control, resistance and informality: urban ethnocracy in Beer-Sheva, Israel, in: N. Al-Sayyad and A. Roy (eds) *Urban Informality: Transnational Perspectives from the Middle East, Latin America and South Asia*, pp. 111–33. Boulder, CO: Lexington Books.

28

Global Cities of the South
Emerging Perspectives on Growth and Inequality

Gavin Shatkin

Introduction

The literature on global and world cities asserts that the spatial, social, and political development of certain cities is profoundly shaped by their function as 'command and control' centers in the global economy. Very large cities in developing countries have increasingly been analyzed under this rubric, and some have argued that we are seeing a convergence of global/world cities around a model of urbanization that originates in the West, and particularly in the United States (Cohen, 1996; Dick and Rimmer, 1998; Cowherd and Heikkila, 2002; Leichencko and Solecki, 2005). This assertion has proven controversial, however, and a growing chorus has argued that the global/world city concept overstates the power of actors and institutions operating at a global level, and underestimates local agency and contingency (Robinson, 2002; Flusty, 2004; Hill, 2004; Roy, 2005). The question at the center of this debate is: How do we understand change in global cities, and how do we account for local contingency and agency in our analysis? Given the pace of urbanization in developing countries, the unprecedented scale of emerging urban regions, and their economic and political importance for their countries, addressing this question would appear to be a central task of contemporary urban theory.

In this paper, I add to critiques of the idea of convergence, and, through a review of recent studies, identify alternative models for analyzing global city development in developing countries that I believe better account for local agency and variation in outcomes.[1] The problem with prevailing perspectives on convergence, I argue,

Original publication details: Shatkin, Gavin. 2007. "Global cities of the South: Emerging perspectives on growth and inequality". In *Cities*, 24(1): 1–15. Reproduced with permission from Elsevier.

is that they are too quick to zoom in on observed similarities in urban trends, and gloss over important sources of difference rooted in cultural, geography, and institutional dynamics. In other words, many studies begin with outcomes in a few paradigmatic cases such as New York, London, and Los Angeles, and then look to see whether this global city 'shoe' fits in places like Shanghai, Mexico City, or Buenos Aires. In the first section of the paper, I provide a brief review of critiques of the perspective of convergence, and then identify three emerging trends in theorizing global cities that hold the key to analysis that better accounts for local agency: a growing focus on the diversity of cities' experience with globalization; recognition of the inherently negotiated nature of global impacts on urban outcomes; and a focus on actor-centered perspectives in urban analysis. The combined influence of these ideas amounts to a shift from a focus on global/world city 'models' to a more grounded examination of the interaction between global and local actors and institutions in a particular setting. This is an important development for theory as it allows for a much more precise understanding of urban development, and also for policy and planning, because it more accurately identifies the actors who shape and legitimize urban change, and strategies they employ in doing so.

In the final section, the paper draws on these alternative perspectives to reassess one of the central hypotheses of the global cities literature – that certain social inequalities are inherent to the process of global city development. Three specific manifestations of inequality have been a focus of attention:

- The first is *social inequality*, which emerges as social classes in the global city become polarized between a wealthy professional class and an impoverished low-wage service sector class (Mollenkopf and Castells, 1991; Friedmann, 1995; Sassen, 1998).
- The second is *uneven development*, which occurs as social polarization becomes embedded in the spatial form of the city in the form of socioeconomic segregation and unequal access to livable space. This is manifest in the American context in the suburbanization of the wealthy, the phenomenon of gated communities, and the formation of central city 'ghettoes' of the poor (Marcuse, 1997; Marcuse and van Kempen, 2000a).
- Finally, *political inequality* refers to the process by which urban politics comes to be dominated by interest groups who favor growth-oriented policies over the interests of neighborhoods (Logan and Molotch, 1987).

Several recent studies have argued that these outcomes are also apparent in cities like Jakarta, Shanghai, Istanbul, and Mexico City. While certain similarities do indeed exist, I argue that focusing on these similarities distracts us from an examination of important differences, and also from asking questions about what is causing change. Drawing on the literature review presented in the first half of the paper, I endeavor to reframe the global city-inequality hypothesis by employing an actor-centered, historically informed, and contextually grounded approach.

I propose alternative conceptualizations of spatial, political and socioeconomic inequality in global cities that avoid the assumption that such cities in developing countries will inevitably follow the trajectory of the global cities of the advanced economies.

Refocusing the Global/World Cities Lens

Robinson (2002, p. 531) has argued that one of the central contradictions in contemporary urban theory is that cities throughout the world are consistently analyzed with reference to 'the (usually unstated) experiences of a relatively small group of (mostly western) cities.' This observation is particularly relevant to the literature on 'global' and 'world' cities, which has brought attention to the emerging function of certain cities as command points in the world economy and as locations for specialized business firms (Sassen, 2001). A number of empirical studies, notably those of the Globalization and World Cities group (GAWC), have categorized many large developing country cities as global/world cities based on their economic function and the presence of global headquarters and producer service firms. One oft-cited study found that 18 of the 25 largest cities outside of Europe, the United States and Japan ranked somewhere on the roster of world cities (Beaverstock et al., 1999 – see Table 28.1 for a detailed breakdown). These cities tend to achieve global/world city status due to their role in coordinating the integration of their national economies into the global economy, and often lie at the center of large 'global city-regions' (Scott et al., 2001). For example, Metro Manila, Bangkok and Jakarta have emerged as 'gamma' world cities as they have become the center for national headquarters of transnational corporations and producer service firms that coordinate manufacturing production, and increasingly export-oriented services, in their extended metropolitan regions.

Focus on these cities' role as 'command and control' sites has led to questions about the implications of this function for their development. A growing set of studies has attempted to apply frameworks developed primarily in the United States, examining social polarization, the development of urban regimes, and emergent consumer landscapes in a wide range of contexts (Dick and Rimmer, 1998; Firman, 1998; Pirez, 2002; Graizborg et al., 2003; Chiu and Lui, 2004; Firman, 2004; Salcedo and Torres, 2004; Wu and Webber, 2004; Keyder, 2005; Leichencko and Solecki, 2005). Many of these studies have argued for a convergence of urban form and politics, although there is considerable variation in the degree to which the causes of convergence are theorized and potential sources of difference are explored.

While the methodology of quantitative studies measuring global/world city functions undertaken by the GAWC and others can and should be questioned, this paper does not deny that cities play such command and control functions, and that

Table 28.1 The world city status of the 25 largest cities in developing countries according to Beaverstock et al.'s 'Roster of World Cities.'

City	Population (thousands)	Beaverstock et al. ranking[a]
Mexico City, Mexico	19,013	Beta
Mumbai (Bombay), India	18,336	Evidence
Sao Paulo, Brazil	18,333	Beta
Delhi, India	15,334	Evidence
Calcutta, India	14,299	N/A
Buenos Aires, Argentina	13,349	Gamma
Jakarta, Indonesia	13,194	Gamma
Shanghai, China	12,665	Gamma
Dhaka, Bangladesh	12,560	N/A
Rio de Janeiro, Brazil	11,469	Evidence
Cairo, Egypt	11,146	Evidence
Lagos, Nigeria	11,135	N/A
Beijing, China	10,849	Gamma
Metro Manila, Philippines	10,677	Gamma
Karachi, Pakistan	10,032	N/A
Istanbul, Turkey	9,760	Gamma
Seoul, South Korea	9,592	Beta
Tianjin, China	9,346	N/A
Lima, Peru	8,180	Evidence
Bogota, Colombia	7,594	Evidence
Tehran, Iran	7,352	Evidence
Hong Kong, China	7,182	Alpha
Chennai (Madras), India	6,915	N/A
Bangkok, Thailand	6,604	Gamma
Bangalore, India	6,532	N/A

Source: Derived from Beaverstock et al. (1999) and UN Habitat (2005).

[a] 'Alpha' city status means that a city is a 'prime' center for producer service firms, while 'beta' and 'gamma' refer, respectively, to 'major' and 'minor' centers for such firms. 'Evidence' means that there is evidence of world city formation. These rankings are based on an empirical evaluation of the office locations of multinational accounting, advertising, banking and law firms.

this has a profound impact on their spatial, social and political development. Rather, it argues that many studies have privileged similarity with the experience of cities in the West, notably New York and London, and their analysis is consequently skewed. I hypothesize that global/world cities in fact have quite diverse experiences with global integration and may be diverging along some parameters in their functions in the global economy, and in their development. This study is not the first to argue that the search for a specific and universal set of outcomes may be fruitless. In a seminal comparative study, for example, Marcuse and van Kempen (2000a) propose abandoning the term 'global city' altogether, instead adopting the more general term 'globalizing cities'. Inasmuch as all cities in today's world could be said to be 'globalizing' in some way or another, however, this alternative concedes important observations about the role of certain cities as points of coordination of global production and in the process of production. I argue for keeping the terms global and world city, but thinking more carefully about the implications of these roles for a city's development.

The strength and appeal of the global/world cities literature are that it provides a coherent and theoretically grounded account of the dramatic processes of change that many cities have undergone in the past half century. In this account, the restructuring of the global economy has created a need for new types of cities that coordinate decentralized forms of production by playing host to highly centralized coordinating functions such as corporate headquarters, legal and financial services, and research and development (Friedmann, 1995; Sassen, 2001). The modification of cities to these new roles has a profound effect on social and cultural change, leading specifically to the emergence of a new class of highly skilled professionals, and the marginalization of the old industrial working class and immigrants, who are relegated to low-wage jobs in the service economy (Mollenkopf and Castells, 1991; Friedmann, 1995; Sassen, 1998). These economic functions also create an impetus for the retrofitting of the built environment of cities, as developers create new types of office, residential and commercial space to meet the demands of business and the new elite (Marcuse, 1997; Marcuse and van Kempen, 2000a). Simultaneously, the politics of redevelopment require a new type of governance, one that is able to identify the shifting demands of capital in an unstable and rapidly changing economic climate and bring capital to the table in pushing a redevelopment agenda (Logan and Molotch, 1987; Fainstein, 1995). The result is increasingly 'entrepreneurial' local governments.

This narrative has largely been formulated with reference to a select number of cities in advanced industrial economies. Yet it is arguably a rather blunt instrument for understanding change, as it tends to gloss over obvious sources of diversity rooted in history, culture, institutions, and geography (Abu-Lughod, 1999). Three specific critiques of the application of the global city model are notable. The first questions the narrowness of the focus on 'certain stylish sectors of the global economy,' notably producer and business services and high technology industries, as the dominant sectors shaping contemporary urban development (Robinson, 2002, p. 532). It questions the dualistic portrayal in the urban studies literature between places that are being transformed by these sectors and others which are presumed to be shaped by exclusion and marginalization. The implicit critique is that, given the varied ways in which cities articulate with global flows of money, goods, people, and ideas, the meaning of globalization is not adequately captured by a focus on the location decision of a small number of multinational producer service firms.

The second critique argues that the global cities literature as a whole is tinged with ethnocentrism as it assumes that all such cities will follow the trajectory of New York and London, when in fact these cities are uniquely shaped by a liberal economic ideology, a consumerist culture, and a polarized social structure (White, 1998; Hill and Kim, 2000; Hill, 2004). In societies where the state is more inclined to intervene in social issues, the hypothesized outcomes for socioeconomic, political, and spatial polarization in cities are not nearly as pronounced – Paris, Tokyo, and Seoul have been used as examples to illustrate this. As White (1998, p. 464) puts it, 'states can allow or disallow a city to globalize and dualize.'

A third critique argues that much of the global city literature is ahistorical. Davis (2005a) points to a long tradition of studying cities in developing countries in ways that link urban change to integration into the world economy, most notably dependency theory. She questions the recent rediscovery of such links during the current era of market triumphalism, and argues that the global cities literature has started down the slippery slope of past theories of development, and particularly modernization theory, which view the advanced economies as an end state that developing countries are inexorably advancing towards.

At the core of each of these critiques is the contention that the global city models have failed to explain social change, or to prescribe appropriate paths towards desired change, because they have failed to understand both the contingency of local change on dynamics rooted in history and culture, and the shifting nature of the world economy (Davis, 2005a). In response, proponents have defended the global/world cities concept by arguing that 'the gains [of generalizing about global/world cities] have far outweighed the losses' (Taylor et al., 2002, p. 231). While this may be true, there is certainly scope for a more fine-grained analysis. As Yeoh (1999, p. 613) argues, even as we might accept the core premises of the global cities concept:

> ... the need exists for theorizations of the global city which weave together historical, economic, cultural, sociopolitical and discursive dimensions. This is an urgent task, if both the 'global' and the 'urban' are not simply to be reduced to articles of faith. The fact that the term 'global city' is increasingly accepted as common currency does not necessarily imply theoretical rigour; instead, the metaphorical hubris, with which the term is often invested, signals the need to knuckle down to making real sense of what has been frequently called the 'new sensibility' informing urban futures.

One important step in this direction is an effort to find ways to generalize about the experience of global cities that do not depend on myopia with respect to difference and contingency. The next section reviews some of the growing number of studies that have undertaken this task. It identifies three central themes that emerge from these studies: recognition of the diversity of cities' experience with global economic integration; adoption of a perspective that views urban change as a negotiated rather than a top-down process; and a focus on actors in analyzing the global–urban interface.

Recognizing diversity in forms of integration into the global economy

Robinson's (2002, p. 535) important critique of the global city model argues that the exclusive focus on command and control functions of cities results in a perspective in which 'millions of people and hundreds of cities are dropped off the map ... to service one particular and very restricted view of the significance or (ir) relevance to certain sections of the global economy.' There are three main reasons that the focus on finance and producer services is inadequate to explain the diversity of outcomes for cities in developing countries. First, because they function as 'command and control centers' of a much lower order than New York or London, multinational corporate headquarters and producer service firms shape their development to a far lesser degree. Roberts (2005), for example, finds that producer services aimed at organizing production for global markets simply do not constitute as significant a factor in the urban economies of Latin American cities as is predicted by the global cities literature. Second, as Chakravorty (2000) argues, globalization has accompanied the industrialization of many cities in developing countries, and they are consequently unlikely to exhibit the same spatial and social characteristics of 'post-Fordist' cities, such as the decay of old central city industrial districts. Finally, while the global cities literature focuses on cities' role in coordinating manufacturing production for the global market, cities in fact export an increasingly diverse array of products and services, each of which has its own spatial logic. Some examples are listed below:

- Labor has become an increasingly important export commodity 'produced' by global/world cities, and remittances to developing countries from overseas workers totaled an estimated $125 billion in 2004 (Maimbo and Ratha, 2005). In many countries this has far outstripped other sources of foreign investment – in the Philippines, for example, remittances amounted to seven times the amount of foreign direct investment in recent years (Maimbo and Ratha, 2005). Popular perceptions aside, in many countries migrants are disproportionately urban and educated, and the labor export industry is often highly concentrated in large cities (Tyner, 2000). Researchers have only recently begun to examine the implications of this phenomenon for urban development, but in Metro Manila, for example, 'overseas contract workers' and their families have supported a boom in residential and commercial real estate at a time when economic growth in other areas has stagnated (Burgess and Haksar, 2005).
- Tourism is the second largest export sector in the world, and the construction of tourism enclaves is often an important impetus for urban redevelopment (Fainstein and Judd, 1999). This is certainly true in most large Asian cities, which have experienced dramatic increases in tourist arrivals, and which tend to view the promotion of urban tourism as part of a larger agenda of place-marketing. In their efforts to construct a positive image and foster tourist consumption, public and private sector actors may create enclaves that

exacerbate socio-economic segregation. However, urban tourism also provides broad-based economic opportunity as the tourism economy may support a large number of small enterprises such as guest houses, shops, restaurants and craft production (Mullins, 1999).

- The growth of business process outsourcing (BPO) is having a profound impact on urban development and real estate markets in a growing number of cities, with some of the more notable examples being Bangalore, Guadalajara, and the planned high-tech city of Cyberjaya outside of Kuala Lumpur (Bunnell, 2002; Audirac, 2003). This form of development has significant implications for urban development, as it fosters the creation of a new class of highly educated worker, and also creates a powerful imperative for new forms of real estate development and infrastructure.

The development of cities may be shaped by other global forces, including integration into markets for natural resource extraction, through the global criminal economy, through foreign aid, and through international institutions and non-governmental organizations (Simon, 1995; Shatkin, 1998; Robinson, 2002; Taylor, 2005).

The recognition of this diversity has several implications for our understanding of equity issues in global cities. While the distribution of the costs and benefits of these different forms of integration varies, each has created economic opportunity for a large segment of urban populations. Nonetheless, these various forms of integration all carry with them the instability and intense competition for investment that characterize economic development in a globalizing world, and each subsequently brings with it the potential for new forms of economic insecurity. Hence the equity implications of these new economic activities are not immediately apparent, and are contingent on the economic activity in question, and the context of the society.

Historicizing analysis and understanding urban change as a negotiated process

Studies rooted in a variety of disciplinary backgrounds have called for a grounding of global and world city studies in an understanding of local history, and a view of urban change not as imposed from above but rather as an inherently negotiated process (Abu-Lughod, 1999; AlSayyad, 2001a; Kusno, 2000; Nasr and Volait, 2003b; Hill, 2004). They have employed a range of theoretical frameworks to do so, including: one that examines structures of global political and economic power as a 'nested hierarchy' in which 'parts and wholes are not subordinated to one another,' and cities therefore 'both facilitate the globalization process and follow their own relatively autonomous trajectories' (Hill, 2004, p. 374); examination of the role of 'planning culture' in shaping planning outcomes (Sanyaled, 2005); and an examination of cultural hybridity and the development of a 'third space' between the local and the global as people in localities reshape cities according to local social, cultural and political imperatives (Kusno, 2000; AlSayyad, 2001a). The common thread in these frameworks is an effort to restore agency to urban analysis, and refute perspectives that depict local residents as 'impotent, passive and guileless ... spectators observing physical and spatial [as well as social and political] changes that they neither control nor understand' (Nasr and Volait, 2003b).

This emphasis on negotiation between the local and the global has been applied most prominently to studies of the built environment (AlSayyad, 2001a; Nasr and Volait, 2003a; King, 2004). In one recent example, Kusno (2000) demonstrates how the Suharto regime in Indonesia sought to rearticulate both local and colonial/global references in architecture and urban design in Jakarta to create a national memory that suited its own agenda of export-oriented growth and authoritarian politics. In the realm of urban politics, studies have contested the tendency to deny local agency both in critical studies, and in a prescriptive literature emerging from the World Bank and other organizations, which argues that the demands of globalization merit the empowerment of private sector interests and a modest and deferential role for local government (World Bank, 2000). In Asia specifically, studies have argued that 'developmental' states are capable of creating growth and moderating socioeconomic inequity where there is political accountability, and that such accountability emerges where there exist widely held cultural norms concerning state–society relations and close ties between the state and civil society (Douglass, 1994; Douglass, 1995; Hill and Kim, 2000). Two notable examples are Hong Kong and Singapore, which Castells et al. (1990, p. 331) argue have managed to achieve steady economic growth in part by building social cohesion through interventions in the realm of collective consumption, most importantly through the development of public housing. They attribute their ability to do so to historical conditions that led to the emergence of strong states in these two city-states.

Two observations emerge from these perspectives. First, it is apparent that 'models' of urban form and politics that are transmitted by actors operating at a global level inevitably go through a process of adaptation and reinterpretation, and sometimes rejection, as they meet local cultures, institutional dynamics, and social formations. Second, these models may go through a process of transformation over time as local actors gradually reshape them to their own needs. History provides many examples of such transformation. For example, Clarence Perry's neighborhood unit concept has profoundly influenced urban planning in many parts of the world, including India. Yet, in the Indian context, extra-legal modifications of neighborhood layouts over time have led to such a dramatic physical transformation that the influence of this model is no longer apparent in most cities today (Vidyarthi, 2005).[2] Similarly, although political institutions in many postcolonial societies are often modeled on those of the metropole, and have been influenced in many contexts by the diffusion of international 'models', outcomes for the distribution of power in society can vary quite dramatically. It is necessary therefore to avoid premature conclusions about the convergence of urban form or politics, and shift our focus to these processes of adaptation, if we are to understand the impacts of globalization.

Grounding our understanding of globalization in actors and actions

Closely related to the emerging perspective of hybridity is the employment of actor-centered frameworks of urban analysis, which, it has been argued, provide a more concrete understanding of how global forces shape and are shaped by local forces, and how local contingency and agency play a role in urban development (Yeoh, 1999; Olds, 2001; Markusen, 2004). An actor-centered perspective focuses on the social power actors employ and the interests and ideologies they pursue. It views local actors as active participants both responding to pressures in their external environment and trying to shape them to their own ends. This is therefore a view in which '(s)tructure and agency are not contrasted, but complexified and integrated' (Nasr and Volait, 2003b). It is also one that stresses a need for deep historical analysis as a basis for understanding the interests of actors and their basis of power in institutions, social networks, and cultural beliefs.

In general, attention has focused on how actors operating at a global level have shaped urban development, including corporate actors (Beaverstock et al., 1999; Grant and Nijman, 2002), principals at international architectural firms (Olds, 2001; Marshall, 2003; Sklair, 2005), and representatives of international aid and lending organizations (Burgess et al., 1997). However, local actors, or actors whose interests straddle geographic scales, play a key role in shaping outcomes as well. These include local developers and realtors (Dick and Rimmer, 1998; Haila, 2000; Sajor, 2003; Sajor, 2005), and an emerging consumer classes (Davis, 2000). Perhaps most importantly, local and national governments play a key role in providing the legal, policy and regulatory framework in which development occurs (Firman, 1997; Kelly, 2001). There is also a growing realization that the interests and preferences of these actors cannot be understood with reference to the transmission of ideas from the West alone, but rather reflect deep rooted cultural norms and social patterns. Yet local actors also confront incentives and imperatives in the context of global economic and political change. It is through the interaction of these actors and interests that contemporary 'hybridity' is constituted.

Towards a more flexible framework

What emerges from these perspectives is a view of global city development that rejects a uniform model of change and instead focuses on the unique nature of the interaction between global and local actors and institutions in a particular setting. Actors in cities throughout the world are presented with certain opportunities and threats with globalization – opportunities to realize material enrichment and new forms of cultural and political expression through new forms of production and consumption, and threats to existing economic arrangements, political institutions, and ways of life from both external and internal actors who have an interest in global change. The preferences of actors in shaping urban development are informed by their attraction to or repulsion from these new ideas, images, and institutions. The power that they bring to the table in influencing urban development is shaped by historically formed social relationships, institutional frameworks, cultural paradigms, and spatial patterns. The nature of the opportunities and threats posed by globalization also shift with changes in the global economy (for example the recent shift towards the offshoring of services), and these shifts are reflected in changes in urban development.

Table 28.2 brings this discussion back to the question of the link between global city development and inequity by sketching out the implications of these three emerging perspectives for the three central hypotheses of global city-social inequality theory discussed earlier. It is worth noting that the framework that emerges from this table is fruitful for examining variation in the experience of global cities in both developed and developing countries. Hence, while the specific focus of this paper is to question the common view of convergence of developing countries with the Western experience, this paper also finds common ground with those who question more generally the usefulness of broad generalizations about the equity outcomes of global city development. In the next section, I will build on critiques of the idea of convergence and the alternative frameworks presented above by attempting to reframe the link between global city development and inequality in global cities of developing countries.

Understanding Change and Inequality in the Global Cities of Developing Countries

In some respects, cross-national similarities in patterns of urban development are quite apparent. Public and private sector actors seek to build the tallest building, the sleekest rail system, or the most impressive airport, in an effort to draw attention to their global linkages. Wealthy elites in many non-Western countries seek housing that is explicitly modeled on what are perceived as European and American styles. Cities throughout the world have experienced trends towards political and fiscal decentralization that have given them new powers. Such surface similarities, however, mask important differences. This section attempts to reframe discussions of the link between global city development and inequality in a manner that recognizes urban change as a negotiated process, allows for the possibility of divergence in urban outcomes, and explores the role of both global and local actors in shaping equity outcomes. I argue that there is a need to move beyond

Table 28.2 Reinterpreting the global/world city–social inequality link.

	Socioeconomic inequality	Political inequality	Uneven development
Diversity in the global city experience	Labor relations and economic opportunity vary by the degree of global economic integration a city is experiencing and the types of products it produces. Yet global economic integration creates common pressures to develop flexible and competitive labor regimes, creating an inherent tension between growth and equity.	While governments in market economies face a common context of incentives to engage new actors in city-building, who these actors are and the political strategies they pursue are in part a function of the mode of insertion into the global economy (e.g. through manufacturing, business services, tourism, or other export products).	Different modes of incorporation into the global economy have different spatial implications, e.g. different degree of centralization and decentralization, and different impacts on real estate markets.
Historical perspective and hybridity	Efforts to make cities competitive in the global economy play out in the forging of capital–labor relations and local and national state interventions in these relations that reflect historically specific state–society relations.	The political forms that emerge – the form of public–private partnership and the relative strength of the public and private actors involved – is shaped by the historical state-community relations and cultural norms.	Spatial development also reflects the preferences of urban residents, which are shaped in part by global influences, but also importantly by historical spatial patterns, household relations, ethnic, class and other differences, and other social and cultural variables.
Actor-centered perspective	The relative inclusion and exclusion of actors from the benefits of globalization's economic impacts is in part a function of social group relations based on caste, race, ethnicity, property ownership, and other variables.	Fundamental to understanding urban politics is an understanding of who the actors involved in global city-building are and what their basis of social power is.	Spatial change in part reflects demands for new types of space by both firms and households, which in turn reflects changes in social relations in society at large. On the supply side, it also reflects new powers and imperatives to foster 'global city' development among developers and government.

frameworks developed with reference to the West – specifically, the hypothesized trends towards political inequality / growth regime politics, socioeconomic inequality / polarization, and uneven development / segregation and spatial mismatch – to adopt frameworks that are more adaptable to diverse circumstances. Based on a review of recent studies, I propose three alternative ways of conceptualizing political, spatial and social development that are intended as a first step towards a broadly comparative framework for explaining inequity in global cities. These are: the formation of public–private partnerships in urban politics and planning; the spatial implications of the privatization of planning; and the flexiblization of labor.

The formation of public–private partnerships in urban politics and planning

One process of change that is perhaps universal to the experience of global cities is the increasing role of for-profit private sector actors in urban politics, and the growing tendency for local governments to seek partnership with these actors in pursuing development goals. This is evident in the formation of public–private partnerships in urban infrastructure provision, the growing role of the private sector in building and managing urban environments, and increased participation by the private sector in urban policy and planning decisions. This section will explore the applicability of concepts in vogue in the United States and Europe that attempt to explain this phenomenon, notably regime theory and growth regime politics, to cities of developing countries. It argues that these frameworks hold a great deal of promise, but that profound variation in the relationship between the state, the for-profit private sector, and civil society belies any simplistic depiction of the convergence of urban politics.

Fainstein (1995, p. 35) argues that the question of the influence of social power and the 'issue of whether urban politics can affect distributional outcomes' lies at the core of any discussion of urban planning and policy. The literature on planning in developing countries, however, retains a strong focus on the planning process, largely disregarding the role of politics and power. A large prescriptive literature on urban politics, such as that coming out of the World Bank, assumes a pluralist conception which posits that all social groups have sources of power that they can use to achieve their ends. The predominant paradigm is the 'enablement model,' which posits that a decentralized, democratic, and market-oriented form of governance will not only provide for economic efficiency and global competitiveness, but will also provide venues for popular influence on government through nongovernmental and community organizations (World Bank, 2000). Critical studies of global / world cities in developing countries also often assume little agency for local government in the face of economic and political pressures from global economic actors, local elites, and national governments bent on growth.

Recently, however, a handful of studies have endeavored to apply regime theory, the dominant framework for analyzing urban politics in the United States, to a variety of developing country contexts (Zhang, 2002; Xu and Yeh, 2005). Regime theory starts with the assumption that, in cities marked by competition to capture footloose capital, 'leaders must develop policies in concert with those who have access to that capital' (Fainstein, 1995). An urban regime has been defined by Stone (1989, p. 6) as 'the informal arrangements by which public bodies and private interests function together in order to be able to make and carry out governing decisions.' Yet regime theory avoids economic determinism by emphasizing that government does enjoy some autonomy from corporate interests through the space created by democratic politics, and that urban politics is therefore defined by:

> ... the creation of preferences and the translation of those choices into policy. There is a sophisticated recognition that policy is not simply the imposition of preferences by an economic elite but rather the shaping of public opinion by upper class groups. Thus, ideology or public values become crucial to an understanding of what government of the third sector can or should do. (Fainstein, 1995, p. 36)

Regime theory thus disavows a view of urban planners and policy-makers as disinterested technocrats, instead seeing them as political actors who can either promote or contest the dominance of capital by shaping the discourses that surround the implementation growth-oriented politics.

Is regime theory applicable to the context of global cities in developing countries? Stone (1993, p. 2) argues that there are two conditions that regime theory takes as given:

> One is a set of government institutions controlled to an important degree by popularly elected officials chosen in open and competitive contests and operating within a larger context of the free expression of competing ideas and claims. Second, the economy of a liberal order is guided mainly but not exclusively, by privately controlled investment decisions. A regime, whether national or local, is a set of arrangements by which this division of labor is bridged.

These conditions exist to some degree in the context of most developing countries, where the vestiges of authoritarian regimes are gradually being cast off in favor of electoral political systems and market-oriented political orders. The emergence of the export-oriented industrialization model of development has coincided with the development in many parts of the world of decentralized, democratic governance frameworks. In Asia, for example, Jakarta, Taipei, Bangkok, Seoul, Kuala Lumpur, and Metro Manila all have elected local leaders, are engaged in intense competition for global investment, have varying degrees of freedom of the press, and have increasingly embraced the orthodoxy of the public–private partnership. Each has a contingent of non-governmental organizations representing diverse interests. Many cities have experienced recent reforms for decentralization that are premised at least in part on a belief that local government will be able to bring a broader set of resources and interests into the urban development process, thus encouraging growth (Burki et al., 1999).

Yet regimes elsewhere will not necessarily look anything like the quintessential American urban regime. Regime theory as it has developed in the United States reflects a distinct context of racial politics, post-Fordist urban development, liberalism, and localism. Countries also vary in the degree to which electoral contests actually matter. Severe restrictions on political mobilization outside of the ruling party exist in some contexts (such as Singapore, Malaysia, and China), while vote-buying and patronage politics influences outcomes in others (such as Thailand and the Philippines). There is also variation in the degree of freedom of expression in the press and other forums. Nonetheless, the time seems ripe in many cities to raise the questions that are central to the regime theory framework, while remaining alert to contextual differences (Zhang, 2002).

Two particularly important differences warrant special attention. The first is the historical and contemporary relationship between the central and local state. In many countries this relationship has been a significant source of tension, as colonial and post-colonial states have attempted to extend their control over peripheral regions in efforts at nation-building. Centralization further intensified in many countries during the cold war as a consequence of anti-insurgency efforts. Contemporary trends towards decentralization have reflected intense struggle over local power by a variety of actors, including entrenched national bureaucracies, local elites, social movements, and others. The outcomes of these struggles, and the extent of control gained by these actors, have varied widely between different countries and cities. The second source of variation is the relative power and legitimacy of government, which has also been profoundly shaped both by post-colonial experiences with nation-building and central rule, and experiences with global economic integration.

Understanding these two sources of variation is necessary to interpret change in a particular setting. For example, analysts have attributed the fragmented nature of urban governance in Metro Manila, and the consequent capture of local government by economic interests, to the power of local elites and weakness of central government, both of which have deep roots in the Philippines' colonial and postcolonial history (Kelly, 2000). In China, by way of contrast, national governments have exerted a great deal of influence in providing incentives and autonomy to appointed local officials to encourage them to pursue globalization-oriented urban redevelopment (Xu and Yeh, 2005). Here, the lack of accountability of local governments both to capital and communities paradoxically leads to the potential for overinvestment and economic instability.

Analyses of this sort requires an understanding of historical and social context that is taken for granted in studies of urban regimes in the United States. If modified to account for local context – differences in state power and legitimacy, central-local relations, social relations based on gender, ethnicity, caste, landownership, and other variables – regime analysis captures better than any other conceptualization the ways that local governments seek to form partnerships for political change, and the constraints and opportunities they confront in doing so. It may therefore help to explain the roots of contemporary political inequities both in history and in contemporary forms of integration into the global economy, and reveal the ideological constructs that perpetuate these inequalities. At the same time, regime analysis retains a focus on the power of the state, and its potential as an agent for more redistributive policy and planning outcomes. It therefore enables us to ask policy and planning-relevant questions about socioeconomic and political change in the global era: What political and economic interests do urban development outcomes represent? What alternative sources of power exist? And, how might planners employ these to foster more equitable outcomes?

The spatial implications of the privatization of planning

In globalizing cities, urban space is shaped by the interaction between global networks and local actors and institutions. Inasmuch as local cultures and political economies differ, spatial outcomes will differ as well. Yet recent literature has focused on the idea of global convergence of urban form. Inherent in many such analyses are two assumptions: that 'Western' urban form is directly imposed on developing countries through the hegemony of Western planning ideas, and that the desires of emergent elites in developing countries with respect to spatial development simply mimic those of the Western middle class. I argue, however, that cultural differences and local political and institutional dynamics render these assumptions untenable. A more powerful mode of analysis focuses on the shared interests of local and national governments, and both local and multinational investors, to maximize the profitability and global economic competitiveness of urban spaces. This convergence of interests has resulted in some contexts in what I refer to as the privatization of planning, a process that results in different spatial outcomes in different contexts.

The idea of the privatization of planning goes beyond the simple assertion that the private sector influences urban development. Friedmann has defined planning as purposeful social action in the shaping of place, and privatization has been defined as an increase in private sector ownership of or power over activities or assets that had previously been in government hands (Friedmann, 1987; Savas, 2000). Hence I define the privatization of planning as the transfer of responsibility for and power over the visioning of urban futures and the exercise of social action for urban change from public to private sector actors. This shift has been predicated on a view that the for-profit private sector is more qualified and better equipped to restructure urban space in order to realize the goal of economic advancement through global economic integration. This stems in part from a perception that the public sector has failed to achieve these goals due to its proclivity for corruption, inefficiency and authoritarianism, and in part from a belief that the corporate sector is better attuned to the imperatives of economic growth and the desires of multinational corporations and an emerging consumer classes.

The privatization of planning is a function of several common constraints and incentives that governments face in the global era:

- The development of an export-oriented economy has given rise to powerful new political actors, most notably foreign and domestic corporate interests and a consumer class, who demand new types of consumer, residential, office and industrial space that are more economically efficient and consumer-oriented. In Asia in particular, the devaluation of the Japanese Yen following the Plaza Accords resulted in a wave of Japanese offshoring from the mid-1980s on that set in motion fundamental changes in the political economy of urban development (Bello, 2004).
- At the same time, governments in many parts of the world find themselves hemmed in by pressures for fiscal austerity and therefore incapable of responding to imperative to retrofit cities to the needs of capital and consumers. Governments in many parts of the world also face crises of legitimacy stemming from legacies of authoritarianism.
- In this context, privatization has become part of new models of governance advocated by international aid and lending organizations, which emphasize scaled back government, local control and public–private partnership (Burgess et al., 1997; Miraftab, 2004a).
- These changes have accompanied the emergence of a number of multinational architectural and planning consulting firms, and growth in domestic real estate development industries. The latter has been most notable in Asia. In Southeast Asia in particular, developers, often of Chinese heritage, have tapped into abundant sources of equity from international capital markets and networks of overseas Chinese (Haila, 2000; Olds, 2001; Sajor, 2003). It is also evident, however, in cities in Latin America and elsewhere (Pirez, 2002).

In Asia, this process of privatization has been manifest most clearly in the development in many cities of private sector built integrated megaprojects including residential, commercial and industrial space. Notable examples include Lippo Karawaci near Jakarta, Muang Thong Thani near Bangkok, and Fort Bonifacio Global City in Metro Manila, which when initiated had projected populations upon completion of between 250,000 and one million (Dick and Rimmer, 1998; Hogan and Houston, 2002; Marshall, 2003).[3] These megaprojects are linked up by premium transportation infrastructure, including light rail lines and toll roads, that is also usually developed by the private sector, and sometimes by the developers of the megaprojects themselves (World Bank, 2004). Facilitated by government assistance in land acquisition, subsidies for transportation infrastructure, and political support, these projects represent efforts to transfer responsibility for the visioning of urban futures and the definition of social goals to the private sector. In some cities a few large developers have begun to develop 'portfolios' of geographically diversified megaprojects that are reshaping urban landscapes.

A perspective of the privatization of planning helps to explain some cross-national similarities in changes to urban form while revealing the limitations of comparisons with the racially polarized landscapes of many American cities, defined as they are by blighted inner cities surrounded by anti-urban sprawl. It is apparent that, even as urban regions are being reshaped by new types of residential development and spatial expansion, the rejection of urbanity itself that character-izes urban development in many American cities has yet to fully take hold in most other parts of the world, and may never do so. In many megacities, central city housing markets continue to be strong, and integrated megaprojects are often quite dense and urban in character. Indeed, some have argued that the reliance of the wealthy in many societies on services provided by a relatively immobile urban poor precludes the type of spatial polarization seen in the United States (Chakravorty, 2000). One study in Chile finds that the development of gated com-munities has actually decreased spatial separation of the wealthy and the poor as it allowed the wealthy to live close to poor communities while still feeling secure, and that this proximity has had a positive impact on interclass relations (Salcedo and Torres, 2004). Regardless of whether this dynamic can be found elsewhere, the point to be made is that local context and agency are critical to an understanding of spatial change.

Importantly, the perspective of the privatization of planning shifts the focus from a supposedly uniform process of adoption of 'Western' cultural and social mores to policy-relevant questions about how the goals of urban development should be defined, who should define them, and the potential roles of public and private sector interests in bringing about desired change. Why has the transfer of responsibility for city-building been shifted to the private sector, and what is the public rationale for doing so? What roles do public and private actors play in rede-velopment and infrastructure projects? What levers of influence does the public sector continue to employ, and to what ends does it use this influence? Whose interests are reflected in resulting changes to urban form, whose are disregarded, and why?

These questions point to the important observation that any process of privat-ization must involve active government facilitation through the restructuring of urban bureaucracies and relaxation of public influence over urban development. The potential remains for the public sector to influence the direction of change even as the private sector plays a growing role by: playing a role in defining the objectives of privately developed plans; mandating desired outcomes like the development of affordable housing or public participation; and shaping the public discourse around private development projects. Government can also exercise control over regional development through land use regulation and other forms of intervention in land markets, and through transportation planning. There is considerable variation in the degree to which they do so.

In sum, the idea of the privatization of planning departs from a focus on convergence in that it leaves the door open to government and community-based agency. It leads to practical and important questions about the exercise of urban governance for equity objectives.

The flexiblization of labor

Finally, this paper suggests the concept of the flexiblization of labor as an alternative to the perspectives of socioeconomic dualization and polarization. There are at least two reasons that the perspective on dualization and social polarization does not adequately capture the social outcomes of globalization in all contexts. First, as Chakravorty (2000) notes, the deindustrialization that has bred the decline of the middle class in the United States and other post-Fordist societies implies its opposite in developing countries, many of which have seen a growth in manufacturing production. The benefits of this deconcentration of industrial production have spread unevenly, with Latin America and Africa experiencing severe economic dislocation and less benefit than Asia, but a simple focus on polarization denies the significant amount of economic opportunity that this process has afforded. Second, the idea of polarization, if defined based on material living conditions alone, does not capture the complex relationship between economic well-being and social status that has emerged with the globalization of many urban economies. It is apparent that the rhetoric surrounding global city development has shaped popular perceptions of social class in important ways (Machimura, 1998; Kelly, 2000). An excellent example of this is Auyero's (1999) poignant description of the paradoxical situation of residents of one Argentine slum, who have experienced gradual improvement in material living conditions even as their employment prospects have become increasingly tenuous and they have experienced intense discrimination due to public perceptions of their community as economically redundant and socially dysfunctional.

The concept of the flexiblization of labor attempts to capture the coexistence of opportunity and insecurity that characterizes labor markets in the globalizing cities of developing countries. Corporations face increasing competition even as they are able to tap into a global labor pool, and they have reacted by seeking labor that is flexible, trainable, adaptable, and cheap. As labor markets and legal frameworks have responded to this imperative, practices such as outsourcing, employment of home-based workers, and contract work have become commonplace in the corporate sector, and increasingly the public sector as well.

An important outcome of this process has been the employment of a range of formal and informal institutions by local and national governments, and firms, to discipline labor. These include the use by firms of contract and short-term labor, and the placement of age and gender restrictions on employment, and the use by local government of both formal powers and informal social relations to reduce the power of unions and foster the development of a compliant labor force. Research has only begun to examine the development of what Kelly (2001) has referred to as local labor control regimes. One exception is his study of labor market processes in export processing zones in the Philippines, which attempts to overcome simplistic depictions of 'straightforward exploitation of abundant, cheap, and place-bound labor by space-controlling international capital' (Kelly, 2001, p. 2). His analysis reveals the ways in which labor relations are shaped by norms governing local social relations that are deeply rooted in the historical development of the locality. Specifically, it points to the role of gender relations in Philippine households, and to the role of local political bosses in the Philippine political economy, in shaping labor markets and working conditions.

Another aspect of this process of flexiblization is the role of the informal economy. In order to be useful, the concepts of informalization and the informal economy must first be stripped of their ideological overtones. The informal economy represents neither heroic entrepreneurship, as represented in the work of DeSoto and others, nor uniform oppression, as often represented by some on the political left (Roy, 2005). The informal also does not constitute a separate 'sector', cut off from the rest of the economy and mired in backwardness. Rather, the informal economy should be viewed as a set of economic activities that are 'unregulated by the institutions of society, in a legal and social environment in which similar activities are regulated,' and that constitute an increasingly important part of the flexible and adaptable labor markets that drive the global economy (Castells and Portes, 1989: 12). The informal economy has persisted with globalization, and grown in many contexts, reflecting the strategies of economic actors and state institutions as they have sought new modes of economic organization that are conducive to export-oriented production. Castells and Portes (1989) refer to several specific causes of informalization linked to globalization, including: growing anti-union sentiment both among firms and, to a lesser degree, elements of the working class, as a reaction to economic crisis and new opportunities in the global economy; reaction by firms and workers against state regulation of the economy for the same reasons; and the emergence of a particular form of industrialization in many developing countries that relies on less regulated labor markets.

A third aspect of flexiblization is the use of legal and illegal immigrant labor (Douglass, 2001). While this has been discussed extensively in the context of global/world cities in the advanced economies, immigrant labor has come to play a significant role in labor markets in many cities, including Bangkok, Kuala Lumpur, Taipei, and many others.

As is apparent from the preceding discussion, the concept of the flexiblization of labor is useful in analyzing change in most parts of the world, including the developed economies, many of which are witnessing increases in immigration, the rise of contract labor, and informal economic activities. What a focus on the flexiblization of labor allows us to do, however, is to focus on the distinct contexts in which these processes play out rather than an assumed set of socioeconomic outcomes modeled primarily on the American experience. This framework draws attention on the actors involved in urban economic development, including state agencies, firms, and workers, and the social institutions and external pressures that shape their behavior. It also incorporates an understanding of the distributional impacts of changes in labor markets, which may reflect the influence of gender, age, race, ethnicity and other variables on social behavior (Miraftab, 2004b). It reveals specific issues related to labor rights, discrimination based on gender and other forms of difference, and the lack of representation of labor and community interests in local governance, that provide more detail to a political agenda for equity in urban development.

Conclusion

This paper has argued that the growing focus on convergence of political, social and spatial outcomes serves to distract us from a more careful analysis of globalization and urban change in developing countries. It has reviewed a number of emerging perspectives in the global/world cities literature that reveal the highly divergent experiences that cities have had with global economic integration, the ways in which the local interacts with and reshapes global influences, and the importance of understanding actors and interests in an analysis of urban change. Finally, it has made a tentative attempt to reframe the hypothesized link between global city development and social, political and spatial inequality in a way that accounts for difference and local agency.

While the paper has focused specifically on critiquing the strong tendency of studies of global cities in developing countries to assume that their development is following a similar trajectory to those of the West, it has also found common ground with critiques of generalizations about global city development more generally. Indeed the framework developed here might be useful to rethinking global city development in the context of developed country cities as well. It would seem that much of the global cities literature is caught in a rut, repeatedly revisiting the core debates that emerged from the remarkable set of observations regarding the impacts of globalization on a select set of cities made by Sassen and others during the 1980s and early 1990s. The terms of debate appear to have hardened somewhat too early and with reference to too little data. Indeed, it would seem that local responses, and the process of globalization itself, have proven too dynamic and complex to be understood with reference to a small set of 'models' of change (e.g. segregation, polarization, and American-style growth regime politics).

Underlying this discussion has been a concern that a focus on convergence provides a less detailed and precise analysis that causes us to miss critical issues that face global cities. Such cities face a number of pressing challenges – intense economic competition, a global atmosphere of market triumphalism, pressures for fiscal austerity, and calls from international agencies for a scaled back role for government in city-building. A critical task of urban theory is to understand how actors in cities respond to these challenges, and who benefits from the outcomes. How have new economic and political pressures shaped national and local government efforts to bring other actors into policy and planning? And, what are the distributional outcomes of the resulting changes in governance? This paper has argued that the answers to these questions differ significantly in different contexts, and that there is much to be learned from these differences for both theory and for the practice of urban planning and policy. This process of learning, however, requires that we move beyond generalizations based on the experience of global cities in the West and adopt frameworks that embrace complexity and difference, and that contribute to cross-national comparison and learning.

Notes

1. The focus throughout the paper will primarily be on cities in Asia, although examples will be drawn from other regions. This reflects both my own background and the greater prevalence of studies on Asian cities.
2. I am indebted to Sanjeev Vidyarthi for this observation.
3. It should be noted, however, that current populations are much smaller.

References

Abu-Lughod, J. (1999) *New York, Chicago, Los Angeles: America's Global Cities*. University of Minnesota Press, Minneapolis.

AlSayyad, N. (2001a) Hybrid Culture/Hybrid Urbanism: Pandora's Box of the 'Third Place'. In *Hybrid Urbanism*, (ed.) N. AlSayyad. pp. 1–20. Praeger, Westport.

Audirac, I. (2003) Information-age landscapes outside the developed world: Bangalore, India and Guadalajara, Mexico. *Journal of the American Planning Association* 69(1), 16–32.

Auyero, J. (1999) This is a Lot Like the Bronx, isn't it? Lived Experiences of Marginality in an Argentine Slum. *International Journal of Urban and Regional Research* 23(1), 45–69.

Beaverstock, J., Taylor, P., and Smith, R. (1999) A roster of world cities. *Cities* 16(6), 444–58.

Bello, W. (2004) The Anti-Development State: The Political Economy of Permanent Crisis in the Philippines, Department of Sociology. University of the Philippines, Quezon City.

Bunnell, T. (2002) Multimedia utopia? A geographical critique of high-tech development in Malaysia. *Antipode: A Radical Journal of Geography* 34(2), 265–95.

Burgess, R. and Haksar, V. (2005) *Migration and Foreign Remittances in the Philippines*, IMF Working Paper Series Number 05/111.

Burgess, R., Carmona, M., and Kolstee, T. (1997) *The Challenge of Sustainable Cities: Neoliberalism and Urban Strategies in Developing Countries*. Zed Books, London.

Burki, S., Perry, G., and Dillinger, W. (1999) *Beyond the Center: Decentralizing the State*. World Bank, Washington, DC.

Castells, M. and Portes, A. (1989) World underneath: the origins, dynamics, and effects of the informal economy. In *The Informal Economy: Studies in Advanced and Less Developed Countries*, (eds) A. Portes, M. Castells and L. Benton. pp. 11–37. Johns Hopkins University Press, Baltimore.

Castells, M., Goh, L., and Kwok, R. (1990) *The Shek Kip Mei Syndrome: Economic Development and Public Housing in Hong Kong and Singapore*. Pion, London.

Chakravorty, S. (2000) From colonial city to globalizing city?: The far-from-complete spatial transformation of Calcutta. In *Globalizing Cities: A New Spatial Order*, (eds) P. Marcuse and R. van Kempen. pp. 56–77. Blackwell, London.

Chiu, S. and Lui, T. (2004) Testing the global city-social polarisation thesis: Hong Kong since the 1990s. *Urban Studies* 41(10), 1863–88.

Cohen, M. (1996) The hypothesis of urban convergence: Are cities in the north and south becoming more alike in an age of globalization? In *Preparing for the Urban Future: Global Pressures and Local Forces*, (eds) M. Cohen, B. Ruble, J. Tulchin and A. Garland. pp. 25–38. The Woodrow Wilson Center Press, Washington, DC.

Cowherd, R. and Heikkila, E. (2002) Orange County, Java: Hybridity, social dualism and an imagined west. In *Southern California and the World*, (eds) E. Heikkela and R. Pizarro. Praeger, Westport.

Davis, D. (2005) Cites in global context: A brief intellectual history. *International Journal of Urban and Regional Research* 29(1), 92–109.

Davis, D. (ed.) (2000) *The Consumer Revolution in Urban China*. University of California Press, Berkeley.

Dick, H. and Rimmer, P. (1998) Beyond the third world city: The new urban geography of south-east Asia. *Urban Studies* 35(12), 2303–21.

Douglass, M. (2001) Intercity competition and the question of economic resilience: Globalization and crisis in Asia. In *Global City-Regions: Trends, Theory, Policy*, (ed.) A. Scott. pp. 236–62. Oxford University Press, Oxford.

Douglass, M. (1995) Bringing culture in: Locality and global capitalism in East Asia. *Third World Planning Review* 17(3), iii–ix.

Douglass, M. (1994) The 'developmental state' and the newly industrialised economies of Asia. *Environment and Planning A* 26(4), 543–66.

Fainstein, S. (1995) Politics, economics, and planning: why urban regimes matter. *Planning Theory* 14, 34–41.

Fainstein, S. and Judd, D. (eds) (1999) *The Tourist City*. Yale University Press, New Haven.

Firman, T. (2004) New town development in Jakarta metropolitan region: A perspective of spatial segregation. *Habitat International* 28(3), 349–68.

Firman, T. (1998) The restructuring of Jakarta metropolitan area: A 'global city' in Asia. *Cities* 15(4), 229–43.

Firman, T. (1997) Land conversion and urban development in the northern region of West Java, Indonesia. *Urban Studies* 34(7), 1027–46.

Flusty, S. (2004) *De-Coca-Colonization: Making the Globe from the Inside Out.* Routledge, London.

Friedmann, J. (1995) Where we stand? A decade of world city research. In *World Cities in a World System*, (eds) P. Knox and P. Taylor. pp. 21–47. Cambridge University Press, Cambridge.

Friedmann, J. (1987) *Planning in the Public Domain: From Knowledge to Action.* Princeton University Press, Princeton.

Graizborg, B., Rowland, A., and Aguilar, A. (2003) Mexico City as a peripheral global player: The two sides of the coin. *The Annals of Regional Science* 37, 501–8.

Grant, R. and Nijman, J. (2002) Globalization and the corporate geography of cities in the less developed world. *Annals of the Association of American Geographers* 92(2), 320–40.

Haila, A. (2000) Real estate in global cities: Singapore and Hong Kong as property states. *Urban Studies* 37(12), 2241–56.

Hill, R. (2004) Cities and nested hierarchies. *International Social Science Journal* 56(181), 373–84.

Hill, R. and Kim, J. (2000) Global cities and developmental states: New York, Tokyo and Seoul. *Urban Studies* 12(37), 2241–56.

Hogan, T. and Houston, T. (2002) Corporate Cities: Urban Gateways of Gated Communities Against the City: The Case of Lippo, Jakarta. In *Critical Reflections on Cities in Southeast Asia*, (eds) T. Bunnell, L. Drummond, and K. Ho. pp. 43–264. Times Academic Press, Singapore.

Kelly, P. (2001) The political economy of local labor control in the Philippines. *Economic Geography* 77(1), 1–22.

Kelly, P. (2000) *Landscapes of Globalization: Human Geographies of Economic Change in the Philippines.* Routledge, London.

Keyder, C. (2005) Globalization and social exclusion in Istanbul. *International Journal of Urban and Regional Research* 29(1), 124–34.

King, A. (2004). *Spaces of Global Cultures: Architecture, Urbanism, Identity.* Routledge, London.

Kusno, A. (2000) *Behind the Postcolonial.* Routledge, London.

Leichencko, R. and Solecki, W. (2005) Exporting the American dream: the globalization of suburban consumption landscapes. *Regional Studies* 39(2), 241–53.

Logan, J. and Molotch, H. (1987) *Urban Fortunes: The Political Economy of Place.* University of California Press, Berkeley.

Machimura, T. (1998) Symbolic uses of globalization in urban politics in Tokyo. *International Journal of Urban and Regional Research* 22(2), 183–94.

Maimbo, S. and Ratha, D. (eds) (2005) *Remittances: Development Impacts and Future Prospects.* The World Bank, Washington, DC.

Marcuse, P. (1997) The enclave, the citadel, and the ghetto: What has changed in the post-Fordist US city. *Urban Affairs Review* 33(2), 228–64.

Marcuse, P. and van Kempen, R. (2000a) Conclusion: A new spatial order. In *Globalizing Cities: A New Spatial Order*, (eds) P. Marcuse and R. van Kempen. pp. 249–75. Blackwell, London.

Markusen, A. (2004) The work of forgetting and remembering places. *Urban Studies* 41(12), 2303–14.

Marshall, R. (2003) *Emerging Urbanity: Global Urban Projects in the Asia Pacific Rim.* Spon Press, London.

Miraftab, F. (2004a) Public–private partnerships: Trojan horse of neoliberal development? *Journal of Planning Education and Research* 24(1), 89–101.

Miraftab, F. (2004b) Neoliberalism and casualization of public sector services: The case of waste collection services in Cape Town, South Africa. *International Journal of Urban and Regional Research* 28(4), 874.

Mollenkopf, J. and Castells, M. (eds) (1991) *Dual City: Restructuring New York*. Russell Sage Foundation, New York.

Mullins, P. (1999) International tourism and the cities of Southeast Asia. In *The Tourist City*, (eds) S. Fainstein and D. Judd. pp. 245–60. Yale University Press, New Haven.

Nasr, J. and Volait, M. (2003a) *Urbanism Imported or Exported?: Native Aspirations and Foreign Plans*. Academy Editions, London.

Nasr, J. and Volait, M. (2003b) Introduction: transporting planning. In *Urbanism Imported or Exported?: Native Aspirations and Foreign Plans*, (eds) J. Nasr and M. Volait. Academy Editions, London.

Olds, K. (2001) *Globalization and Urban Change: Capital, Culture, and Pacific Rim Megaprojects*. Oxford University Press, Oxford.

Pirez, P. (2002) Buenos Aires: Fragmentation and privatization of the metropolitan city. *Environment and Urbanization* 14(1), 145–58.

Roberts, B. (2005) Globalization and Latin American cities. *International Journal of Urban and Regional Research* 29(1), 110–23.

Robinson, J. (2002) Global and world cities: A view from off the map. *International Journal of Urban and Regional Research* 26(3), 531–54.

Roy, A. (2005) Urban informality: Toward an epistemology of planning. *Journal of the American Planning Association* 71(2), 147–58.

Sajor, E. (2005) Professionalisation or hybridisation? Real estate brokers in Metro Cebu, the Philippines, during the boom of the 1990s. *Urban Studies* 42(8), 1321–43.

Sajor, E. (2003) Globalization and the urban property boom in Metro Cebu, Philippines. *Development and Change* 34(4), 713–41.

Salcedo, R. and Torres, A. (2004) Gated communities in Santiago: Wall or frontier? *International Journal of Urban and Regional Research* 28(1), 27–44.

Sanyal, B. (ed.) (2005) *Comparative Planning Culture*. Routledge, New York.

Sassen, S. (1998) *Globalization and its Discontents*. The New Press, New York.

Sassen, S. (2001) Global cities and developmentalist states: How to derail what could be an interesting debate? A response to Hill and Kim. *Urban Studies* 38(13), 2537–40.

Savas, E. (2000) *Privatization and Public–Private Partnerships*. Chatham House, New York.

Scott, A., Agnew, J., Soja, E., and Storper, M. (2001) Global city-regions. In *Global City-Regions: Trends, Theory, Policy*, (ed.) A. Scott. Oxford University Press, Oxford.

Shatkin, G. (1998) 'Fourth World' cities in the global economy: The case of Phnom Penh, Cambodia. *International Journal of Urban and Regional Research* 22(3), 378.

Simon, D. (1995) The world city hypothesis: Reflections from the periphery. In *World Cities in a World System*, (eds) P. Knox and P. Taylor. pp. 132–55. Cambridge University Press, Cambridge.

Sklair, L. (2005) The transnational capitalist class and contemporary architecture in globalizing cities. *International Journal of Urban and Regional Research* 29(3), 485.

Stone, C. (1993) Urban regimes and the capacity to govern: A political economy approach. *Journal of Urban Affairs* 15(1), 1–28.

Stone, C. (1989) *Regime Politics: Governing Atlanta, 1946–1988.* University Press of Kansas, Kansas.

Taylor, P. (2005) Leading world cities: Empirical evaluations of urban nodes in multiple networks. *Urban Studies* 42(9), 1593–608.

Taylor, P., Walker, D., Catalano, G. and Hoyler, M. (2002) Diversity and power in the world city network. *Cities* 19(4), 231–41.

Tyner, J. (2000) Global cities and circuits of global labor: The case of Manila, Philippines. *Professional Geographer* 52(1), 61–74.

UN Habitat (2005) *Financing Urban Shelter: Global Report on Human Settlements 2005.* Earthscan, London.

Vidyarthi, S. (2005) Informalizing the formal and localizing the global: a theoretical framework to understand acts of appropriation. Paper presented at the *Association of Collegiate Schools of Planning Annual Meeting,* Kansas City, October 27–30.

White, J. (1998) Old wine, cracked bottle? Tokyo, Paris, and the global Cities hypothesis. *Urban Affairs Review* 33(4), 451–77.

World Bank (2004) *A Tale of Three Cities: Urban Rail Concessions in Bangkok, Kuala Lumpur, and Manila.* Report prepared by the Halcrow Group Limited, December 2.

World Bank (2000) *Cities in Transition.* World Bank, Washington, DC.

Wu, F. and Webber, K. (2004) The rise of 'foreign gated communities' in Beijing: Between economic globalization and local institutions. *Cities* 21(3), 203–13.

Xu, J. and Yeh, A. (2005) City repositioning and competitiveness building in regional development: New development strategies in Guangzhou, China. *International Journal of Urban and Regional Research* 29(2), 283–308.

Yeoh, B. (1999) Global/globalizing cities. *Progress in Human Geography* 23(4), 607–16.

Zhang, T. (2002) Urban development and a socialist pro-growth coalition in China. *Urban Affairs Review* 37(4), 475–99.

Index

The letters *b*, *f*, *t*, and *n* after page numbers refer respectively to Boxes, Figures, Tables, and Notes.

Readings in Planning Theory, Fourth Edition. Edited by Susan S. Fainstein and James DeFilippis.
Editorial material and organization © 2016 John Wiley & Sons, Ltd.
Published 2016 by John Wiley & Sons, Ltd.